DEVONSHIRE

A COLLECTION OF

ANNOTATED TESTAMENTARY ABSTRACTS,

TOGETHER WITH

THE FAMILY HISTORY AND GENEALOGY OF MANY
OF THE MOST ANCIENT GENTLE HOUSES
OF THE WEST OF ENGLAND.

BY

CHARLES WORTHY, ESQ.,

*Formerly of H.M. 82nd Regt., and sometime Principal Assistant to the late
Somerset Herald in Ordinary.
Author of " Devonshire Parishes," " Practical Heraldry," etc.*

"ABROAD BY ARMES, AT HOME IN STUDIOUS KYNDE,
WHO SEEKES, WITH PAINFULL TOYLE, SHALL HONOUR SONEST FYNDE."
D. & C., Exon., MS. 3532.

1896.

I DEDICATE THESE PAGES

TO THE MEMORY OF MY DEAR YOUNGER BROTHER,

Edward Athelstan Worthy,

FORMERLY OF WINCHESTER, AND AFTERWARD OF NEW COLLEGE, OXFORD,
BACHELOR OF ARTS,

WHO, AFTER TWENTY-EIGHT YEARS' ABSENCE FROM HIS NATIVE LAND,
DURING WHICH HIS DISTINGUISHED TALENTS WERE CONTINUOUSLY
DEVOTED TO THE INSTRUCTION OF YOUTH, AT
CHRIST CHURCH, NEW ZEALAND,
RETURNED TO ENGLAND, FOR WELL EARNED REST, IN THE SPRING
OF 1894, AND, DURING A SUBSEQUENT TOUR ON THE CONTINENT,
WAS ACCIDENTALLY DROWNED, OFF THE SOUTH COAST OF FRANCE,
ON THE FOLLOWING 31ST OCTOBER,
IN THE FIFTY-FIRST YEAR OF HIS AGE.

———

"AND MAY THERE BE NO SADNESS OF FAREWELL,
WHEN I EMBARK!"

PREFACE.

THE following pages are but the very partial outcome of the researches, and extensive genealogical correspondence, of well nigh a quarter of a century, and of my personal labours at the several public depositories of the records I have herein abstracted, or cited; and although the present work may be regarded, in some sort, as a continuation of my previous volumes on the parochial and family history of Devonshire, culled from the same original sources, and with which it is uniform, and although, in the midst of other literary work, I have now contributed some seventeen hundred closely printed pages, exclusive of pamphlets and periodical articles, to this single subject, I must freely admit that the history of Devonshire, as a whole, yet remains to be written, and that it would most certainly entail the entire devotion of considerably more than an ordinary lifetime to properly accomplish the task.

Therefore, it must be distinctly understood that I am now simply offering my friends and supporters a further instalment of a work, to the extension of which I can only trust I may be eventually able to devote the whole of my time and attention, not with the most distant hope, or, shall I say, wish, of being spared to complete it, but in order to add to those materials which will some day conduce, and I trust considerably so, to a complete record of a county which has hitherto received but scant justice at the hands of its pseudo "historians," who seem chiefly to have relied upon the palpably inadequate information, and, manifestly, in numberless instances, careless, investigations of the *father* of them, Sir William Pole, when they have not repeated tradition as matter of fact. Thus the works of Westcote and Risdon, and, in later times those of Polwhele and Prince, are also full of inaccuracies, and the same may be said, in but a slightly lesser degree, of the Devonshire volumes of the *Magna Britannia*, for, although Samuel Lysons was "Keeper of His Majesty's Records," there is evidence in nearly every page of the joint production of himself and his brother, that those records were not rendered available to any considerable extent, and that when adduced they are frequently misquoted or misinterpreted.

Whatever may be my own shortcomings, I feel that I can fairly claim to have avoided the slightest suspicion of plagiarism, and I offer these pages to the public, not as the "sequence of a perusal of printed accounts and documents, strengthened by much help from friends who have made the archives their study," a course, thus admittedly, adopted by the late Professor Freeman in connection with his *History of Exeter*, but "after studying the said archives," according to his own suggestion, "as they must be studied in manuscript," and that study (in connection with the county which produced Drake, Ralegh, and Grenville, with which Queen Elizabeth, of famous memory, was proud to claim family connection, which gave birth to that great General who procured for us the blessing of a restored monarchy ; and with which historic Shire the early days of our own beloved Sovereign were closely identified), as anticipated by the late Regius Professor of Modern History, has truly "called for the offering of no small part of a life."

I will only add that my present notices of *Gentle Houses* may be looked upon as somewhat scanty and partial, but it must be remembered that the limits of this volume have had to be considered, and that many of the most illustrious families of Devonshire, such as the Redvers and Courtenays, the De Brions, the Drakes, the Russells, the Grenvilles, the Yardes, the Mohuns, the Arundells, and many others, have been commemorated in my previous works, whilst an exhaustive "digression" on the Earldom of Devon will be found in my *Suburbs of Exeter*. In conclusion, I am always glad to welcome correspondence in connection with the family history of my native county.

CHARLES WORTHY.

Heavitree, Exeter,
March, 1896.

TABLE OF CONTENTS.

PART I.

WILLS AND ADMINISTRATIONS.

	PAGE
ARCHDEACONRY COURT OF EXETER	1- 52
,, ,, BARNSTAPLE	53- 80
,, ,, TOTNES	81-101
BISHOP OF EXETER, CONSISTORIAL COURT	102-117
,, ,, PRINCIPAL REGISTRY	118-145
PREROGATIVE COURT OF CANTERBURY	146-156
DEAN AND CHAPTER OF EXETER	157-168
VICAR'S CHORAL ,, ,,	169-170

PART II.

ARCHDEACONRY COURT OF EXETER	171-249
,, ,, ,, BARNSTAPLE	250-268
,, ,, ,, TOTNES	269 291
BISHOP OF EXETER, CONSISTORIAL COURT	292-299
,, ,, PRINCIPAL REGISTRY	300-309

PART III.

GENTLE HOUSES OF THE WEST.

INTRODUCTORY	310-316
ACLAND, OF KILLERTON, ETC.	468-474
BAMPFYLDE, OF POLTIMORE	474-484
BASTARD, OF KITLEY	491-499

TABLE OF CONTENTS.

	PAGE
Bremridge, of Bremridge	411-417
Brito, House of	351-363
Britton, of Bitton	370-374
Bruton, of Langley	363-368
Bruton, of Alwington	368-370
Chafy, of Chafecombe	317-331
Cheverstone, of Wray	386-390
Fortescue, House of	456-468
Fulford, of Great Fulford	417-430
Gibbs, of Fenton and Clist St. George	485-491
Gidley, of Gidley	394-399
Hamlyn, of Widecombe-in-the-Moor	399-403
Horniman, *alias* Herniman, of Bradworthy, etc.	331-335
Kelly, of Kelly	408-410
Northcote, of Pynes	441-447
Northmore, of Cleve	335-340
Nott, of Bydown	348-351
Pyke, of Widworthy	344-348
Venn, of Peyhembury	404-408
Walrond, of Bradfield	447-453
Walrond, of Dulford	453-455
Weekes, of Honeychurch	383-386
Wise, of Sydenham	340-343
Worth, House of	431-441
Worth, of Worth	438-441
Worthe, *alias* Worthy, of Marldon and Exeter	437-438
Wrey, of Tawstock	390-394
Wykes, of Northwyke	374-383
Pedigrees " Disclaimed " in 1620	500-502
Index	503-516

LIST OF SUBSCRIBERS.

Aldenham, Lord, Aldenham House, near Elstree, Herts.
Asher & Co., Messrs., 13, Bedford Street, Covent Garden, London.
Athill, Chas. H., Esq., F.S.A. (Richmond Herald,, Herald's College, London.
Batten, J., Esq., F.S.A., Aldon, Yeovil.
Bartlett, Wm., Esq., Highfield House, Knotty Ash, Liverpool.
Bartlett, J. A., jun., Esq., B.A., Christ Church, Oxford.
Bartlett, J. A., Esq., Lynson, Mossley Hill Road, near Liverpool.
Bartlett, T., Esq., 12, Pembroke Place, Liverpool.
Bastard, Baldwin, J.P., Esq., Buckland Court, Ashburton.
Bethell, W., Esq., Rise Park, Hull.
Bridgman, H. H., Esq., 42, Poultry, London.
Birmingham, Mr. W., Plymouth. (Two copies.)
Britton, P. W. P., Esq., F.S.A., Bitton House, Enfield.
Boase, Rev. C. W. (the late), Exeter College, Oxford.
Bonython, J. L., Esq., J.P., Adelaide, South Australia.
Broadmead, W. B., Esq., Enmore Castle, Bridgwater.
Bulwer, Col. L., Quebec House, E Dereham, Norfolk.
Brushfield, T. N., Esq., M.D., The Cliff, Budleigh-Salterton, Devon.
Bruton, D. Yeo, Esq., Stone House, Heathfield, Sussex. (Two copies.)
Burnard, Robert, Esq., 3, Hillsborough, Plymouth.
Chafy, Rev. W. K. W. C., D.D., Rous Lench Court, Evesham.
Carkeet, W., Esq., 64, Watling Street, London.
Caunter, W. A., Esq., 15, Bedford Circus, Exeter.
Clark, Geo. T., Esq., Taly-Garn, Pontyclown, Glamorgan.
Clements, H. J. B., Esq., Killadoon, Celbridge, Co. Kildare.
Colby, Rev. F. T., D.D., 12, Hillsborough Terrace, Ilfracombe.
Cole, C. F., Esq., Flintfield, Warlingham, Surrey.
Cokayne, G. E., Esq. (Clarenceux), College of Arms, London.
Churchward, F., Esq., Clarendon House, Granville Park, Blackheath, London;
    and Hill House, Stoke Gabriel, Devon.
Commin, Mr. James G., 230, High Street, Exeter.
Cust, Lady E., 13, Eccleston Square, London.
Drake, A. J., Esq., Stratford, Essex.
Drake, H., Esq., 23, Upper Phillimore Gardens, London.
Drake, Sir Wm., 12, Prince's Gardens, London.
Drake, W. H., Esq., Maison du Coin, St. Bulades, Jersey.
Dredge, J. I., Esq., Buckland Brewer, Bideford.
Downing, W., Esq., Alton, near Birmingham. (Two copies.)

LIST OF SUBSCRIBERS.

Eland, Mr. Henry S., Exeter. (Two copies.)
Finch, Rev. W., The Monks, Chaddesley Corbett, Kidderminster. (Two copies.)
Fisher, E., Esq., F.S.A. (Scot.), Abbotsbury, Newton Abbot.
Fry, E. A., Esq., 172, Edmund Street, Birmingham.
Gatty, A. S., Esq. (York Herald), College of Arms, London.
Granville, Rev. R., The Rectory, Bideford.
Gray, Mr. H., 47, Leicester Square, London. (Two copies.)
George's Sons, Messrs. Wm., Bristol.
Gibbs, A., Esq., Tyntesfield, near Bristol.
Gibbs, H. M., Esq., Barrom Court, Flax Bourton, R.S.O., Somerset.
Gibbs, Rev. K. F., Aldenham Vicarage, near Elstree, Herts.
Gilbert, W. K., Esq., 6, Dowgate Hill, London.
Gidley, G., Esq., 17, Saltash Street, Plymouth.
Godwin, J. G., Esq., 83, Eccleston Square, Pimlico, London.
Gould, Rev. S. B., Lew Trenchard, N. Devon.
Hawkesbury, Lord, 2, Carlton House Terrace, London.
Hamlyn, J., Esq., Toll Marsh, Buckfastleigh.
Hamlyn, W., Esq., Buckfastleigh.
Hayne, Rt. Hon. Col. C. S., M.P., 6, Upper Belgrave Street, London.
Hems, H., Esq., Fair Park, Exeter.
Holcombe, W., Esq., 30, Orchard Street, Portman Square, London.
Horniman, F. J., Esq., M.P., Surrey Mount, Forest Hill, London.
Hovenden, R., Esq., F.S.A., Heathcote Park Hill Road, Croydon.
Hughes, H. R., Esq., Kinmel Park, Abergele.
Hurrell, J. S., Esq., The Manor House, Kingsbridge.
Lindsay, W. A., Esq. (Windsor Herald), College of Arms, London.
Liverpool Athenæum, Liverpool.
London, Right Rev. the Lord Bishop of, Fulham Palace, London. (Two copies.)
Mallock, R., Esq., Cockington Court, near Torquay.
Masland, W., Esq., 31, Fore Street, Tiverton.
McDowall, S. S., Esq., 54, St. James Street, London.
Mowbray, Rt. Hon. Sir John R., Bart., M.P., Warrennes Wood, Mortimer, Berks.
New England Historic Genealogical Society, Boston, U.S.A.
Nettleship, Mrs. K., 5, Wimpole Street, London.
Nicholls, G. J., Esq., Barrister-at-Law, Bengal Civil Service, Teekenning, Cornwall.
Nicholls, H. Millett, Esq., Culverlands, Shedfield, Botley, Hants.
North Devon Athenæum, Barnstaple.
Northmore, John, Esq. (of Cleve).
Oliver, V. L., Esq., Whitmore Lodge, Suminghill.
Penzance Library, Penzance, Cornwall.
Periam, H. W., Esq., Blossomfield, Solihull, near Birmingham.
Peek, C. E., Esq., Rousdon, Lyme Regis.
Rattenbury, B., Esq., Charlottetown, P.E.I., Canada.
Rawle, E. J., Esq., 10, Colville Terrace, Bayswater, London.
Roddy, John Jordan, 10, Rahere Street, London.
Rowe, J. B., Esq., F.S.A., Castle Barbican, Plympton, S. Devon.
Spalding, Dr. J. A., 627, Congress Street, Portland, Maine.

LIST OF SUBSCRIBERS.

Sillifant, A. O., Esq., Coombe, Copplestone, N. Devon.
Stevens, Mr. B. F., 4, Trafalgar Square, London.
Scribner's Sons, Messrs. C., St. Dunstan's House, Fetter Lane, London.
Smith, Tom C., Esq., F.R.H.S., Longridge, near Preston.
Tremayne, Hon. Mrs., Heligan, St. Austell, Cornwall.
Troup, Mrs. J. R., Rockbeare House, near Exeter.
Venn, Dr. J., Caius College, Cambridge.
Waldron, C., Esq., Llandaff, S. Wales.
Wreford, G., Esq., Prestonbury, Clapham Park, London.
Wrey, Miss F., Tawstock Court, Barnstaple.
Wise, Major L. A. (of Clayton), Watts House, Bishop's Lydeard, Taunton.
White, T. J., Esq., 59, Bryanston Street, London.
Woods, Sir Albert W. (Garter), College of Arms London.

AUTHOR'S LIST.

Britton, A. H., Esq. (Somerset House).
Cutcliff, G., Esq.
Fox, Miss Rita.
Pyke-Nott, J. N., Esq. (of Bydown).

DEVONSHIRE WILLS.

ARCHDEACONRY OF EXETER.

WILLS PROVED, AND ADMINISTRATIONS GRANTED, IN THE COURT OF THE ARCHDEACONRY OF EXETER.

1546. Abstract of the Last Will of Elys Venman, of Sampford Peverell. Mentions wife Katherine and daughter Agnes. Appoints John Venman and Richard Sawnder Overseers. Wife Executor.
Dated 10th Dec., 1546. Proved, 1546.

1546. Thomas Hill, of "twyvordton" (Tiverton), 15th Oct., 1546, desires to be buried in St. Peter's Church Yard there, and gives to "my ghostly father, Sir Edmund Tuckheye," a small bequest.
Thomas Cole, mentioned as Town Clerk.
Proved, 18th Oct., 1546.

NOTE.—" Hill " of Tiverton.
At the commencement of the Parliamentary rebellion, one William Hill, of Tiverton, heard that the soldiers were demolishing what Queen Elizabeth's "visitors" had left of the stately burial chapel of the Earls of Devon, in the Parish Church. William considered that he might as well have a share of the plunder, but found that everything had been pretty well cleared away before his arrival, with the exception of the "Sanctus bell," underneath which he placed a ladder in order to "annex" it. But the bell slipped through his fingers and cut off his toes on both feet, on account of which he was obliged to sell his small property (a tenement and garden) in order to pay for his cure. But he remained a cripple, and was ultimately found dead in a ditch in the parish of East Anstey.

of golde, wherwythe I have sealyd this my last wyll. I geve also to Master Peter Browne my daggar trymed w^h sylv^r, and unto hys wyfe, a rynge of goolde w^h a whyte hedde sett theron called a came stone; and a cussynge w^h the armes of mine Auncestres wrowght w^h corell and sylke. I geve also to Master Thomas Poules wyfe, my other cussynge w^t armes wrowght y^n lyke wyse w^t corell and sylke. I allso geve to Master Thomas Waller a rynge of golde w^t a blewe saver sett theron. The rest of all my goods I geve to Mastris Johan Marwood my mother whome I ordayne and make my executryx, she therewt^h to content and pay my debtys as far as theye shall extende, and yf my sayde goods shall not suffyce to paye my sayde debtys, I wyll that my next heyre, to whome my lands shall dessende, shall cotent and paye the rest of all my debts. Fynally, I shall most hertelye desyre all such as I have offendyd charytablelye to forgive me my offencys, and wrongs comyttyd agenst them; and frelye I forgeve them and all other, endyng my lyfe y^n pf^t faythe, constant hope, and godlye charyte. Thus I comyt agayne my sowle y^n to the hands of Allmyghtye God, to whom be all honor, glory and impery world w^t out end Amen. In wytnesse thys to be my last wyll I have wrote hyt w^t my hand, w^t out entirlynynge, blottynge, or rasynge thereof, subscrybed my name and sett to my seale, the day and yere above wryten

p me Henery Marwood.

Administration granted 13th Sept., 1547.

NOTE.—The above interesting Will is an exact copy of the document, as collated, in an old book of the Archdeaconry, page 45. The original, in testator's "own hand" has disappeared. It is the more important, as it is not referred to in the account of the Marwood family, "Genealogist," N.S. Vols. I. II.— which deals chiefly with Dr. Thomas Marwood, Physician to Queen Elizabeth, and his descendants, one of whom, his grandson, Thomas Marwood, attended James I. in his last illness, of which he left a MS. account, in Latin, and which has been recently printed. Testator appears to have been a great uncle of Dr. Thomas Marwood the elder, who died 1617, aged 105 years. Testator's mother, "Johan," was the daughter of Humphry Courtenay of Bickley, by his wife Elizabeth Pomeroy of Berry.

Arms of Marwood. *Gu.* a chevron *Arg.* between three goats' heads erased Ermine.

1547. The Last Will of Edmond Sherlond.

He bequeaths his soul to God, and his body to be buried within the yle of our Ladye in "my parish of Wasshefylde" (Washfield) paying for the same 6s. 8d. Alsoe to Mr. Parson Worthe "pro decimis" xxd. Item to my ghostly father Wm. Williams to pray for me xiid. To Thomas Scholond the Clerke xiid. Executor Son John Sherlond. Witnesses, William Williams, Pryst, Mr. Symon Worthe. Overseers, Mr. Symon Worthe and John Casswyll.

Proved 17th June, 1547.

NOTE.—Symon Worthe of Worth was the Squire of the Parish. "Mr. Parson Worthe" was his brother Richard, who probably died about 1547. His will is dated that year. William Williams "Pryst" may have been the Curate, but John Castlyn was instituted to Washfield Rectory, then "certo modo vacantem" 28*th Aug.* 1554. No institution has been found between Castlyn and Richard Worthe.

1548. The Last Will of Eliza Toker, "Widow Woman of the parish of Bradninch." Her body to be buried in Churchyard of Bradninch. She leaves her goods "moveable and immoveable" to her "natural daughter" Johan Toker, who is Sole Executrix.

Dated 12th May.   Proved 2nd June, 1548.

Sum £10 11s. 6d.

1549. The Last Will of Robert Toker of Awtrie St. Marie.

He commends his body to Holy Grave.

Item to Sister Alys Tawse, "a purse with four tassels."

Item to John Facie -/12, to Elizabeth Seaward -/12.

Residue to John Tawse, "to bestow for the wealth of my Soul, as he thinks most best."

Dated 22nd Nov., 1548.   Proved 17th April, 1549.

Sum £5 13s. 4d.

1549. Administration to the Will of William Drake of Rewe, granted to Margery his wife and Executrix.

12th Oct., 1549.

1577. Henery Hamlyn of St. Thomas, Exeter, 7th Aug., 1567. He leaves John Peter twenty nobles. To God-children /4d. each. To John Jordeyne "my cassock." Half of the residue to Richard Holman and Joan, my daughter, his wife. The other half to wife Alice who is Sole Executrix.

Brother Symon Hamlyn and Cousin John Hamlyn Overseers. Witnesses, Richard Holman and Richard Harte.

Proved 19th May, 1577.

1583. The last Will of Francis Ffugars, of Bampton, Husbandman. 13th April, 1583. To poor of the said parish, a sack of rye, and to each of his three servants /12d. each.

To daughter Christian, 20 marks, to Godsons, /12d. each.

To Brother, James ffugars, Best Cloak. Residue to wife, Michell, who is Sole Executrix. Supervisors, Father-in-law Michael Burston, James Fugars, Harry Hill and Wm. Comer. "Whereas my wife is now with Child, my will is that his name be put in upon my bargain if he be a man child, but if it be a daughter I leave it to discretion of my Executrix. Testator was indebted in the sum of £5 19s. 8d. to his brother, Humfrie ffugars.

Proved 15th May, 1583.

1583. The last Will of Elyen Connaunte of Collenton Rawlighe, in the County of Devon, Widow, 20th Feb., 25th Elizb. To the four Children of Son-in-law John Kinge, "one whether sheep each." To Jane, dau. of said John Kinge, one pewter dish.

To Johan, dau. of John Bocher, "my best kercher."

To Margaret, dau. of James Eliott, one petticoat. To Thomas Hidon the younger -/6.

Residue to dau. Elizabeth, who is sole executrix. Overseers, Robert Ballemont and Thomas Hidon, who witness the will. Amongst the debts, she owes "my Lady Dennys" 16s. 8d., John Connaute 4s. 8d.

Proved 5th April, 1583.

The Conants, now of the United States, are said to have originated in France; they settled in the district around Sidmouth, and produced many scholars and beneficed clergymen. John Conant, born at Bicton, 1608, was Rector of Exeter College, Oxford.

"Lady Dennys" was the wife of Robert Dennis, the owner of Bicton aforesaid, and patron of its church; he died 1592. He married twice—1st, Mary, daughter of Walter, Lord Mount-Joy; 2nd, Margaret, daughter and heiress of Sir Wm. Godolphin; the latter survived him.

1585 Administration to the Effects of Roger Connett late of Whimple deceased, granted to Joan his wife 31st March, 1585.

James Brodbeare joins the bond.

Sum £16 5s. 4d.

1585. The last Will of Joane Conett of Christowe, Widow, 27th May; 1583.

To Son, Robert Lendon, "a panne of fower gallons, a hoggeshead & the biggest eared tubbe." To Margaret, dau. of Robert Lendon, "one tynnen podger."

To Son, John Connett, one brasen crocke, a panne of three gallons and a tynnen platter & a redde peticote.

Residue to Son Richard Lendon who is Sole Exor.

Witnesses, Clirist Townesente, John Synone, and John Taverner.

Proved 17th April, 1585.

Sum £4 17s. 2d.

1585-6. The last Will of Richard Mountstephen of Cadlighe, 23rd Feb., 28th Elizabeth. He makes his four Sisters, Cislie, Joan, Marie, & Margaret universal legatees and Sole Exors.

In presence of Wm. Norcott parson of Cadlighe, and John Geare, with others. Proved 1586.

NOTE —The Mountstephens were originally of Northampton. The Devonshire branch resided chiefly at Collumpton, and at Heavitree, near Exeter, where their names are found in the Parish Registers.

1586. 21st June, 1586. The Will of John Connaute of Gittisham. He desires to be buried in the parish Church. He gives to Nicholas, his son, his Cupboard. To John, his son, his Table-board. To Matthew, his son, a bed. Residue to his wife Mary, who is sole Executrix.

Amongst the "debts owing" there is mention of a debt due from "one that dwelleth at Lynge who married the widowe Venn's daughter, of Larkbeare, whose name the Testator remembered not."

Proved 20th Sept., 1586.

1586. The last Will of Thomas Kyllande of South Tawton, Yeoman, 9th Oct., 28th Elizb. He desires to be buried at South Tawton, and leaves to the poor men's box "one sheepe." To Wife, Margaret, £20. To Son John, 1 heiffer. To Son William, £5. To Son Mark, £5. To "four youngest Children, Francis, Walter, Elmon, & Isett," £5 each at 21. To Walter & Richard, Children of John Canne, "a Sheep apeece."

"My Executor to find meat & drink sufficient for their degree for Margaret my wife & my four youngest Children, for twelve months after my decease."

Residue to Son Gregory, who is Sole Exor. Overseers, John Canne and Wm. Borne.

Proved 9th Nov., 1586.

Sum £46 7s.

NOTE.—Now spelt Kelland. An old yeoman family long identified with the parish of Lapford, and assumed to be of the same stock as "Kellond" of Paynsford, near Totnes.

1588. Admon. to Effects of Robert Mt.Steven of Payhembury. Granted 10th April, 1588, to Alice, his wife.

Sum £13 19s. 4d.

1586. Administration to the effects of John Eveleighe, Esqr., of Clist St. Lawrence, Intestate. Granted to Joan his relict.

George Eveleighe his Son and Robert Connaute of Bovey Tracy join the bond, £40.
Granted 1586.

NOTE.—This family were of Eveleigh, in Broad Clist. Several of them were Fellows of Exeter College, Oxford. Dr. John Eveleigh was Provost of Oriel; born at Totnes; died 1814.

1592. The last Will of Nicholas Tooker of Upton Pyne, 30th Oct., 24th Elizabeth. To the poor 20/- and to those of Newton St. Cyres and Kirton, Shobbrooke and Thorverton, similar bequests. To Brother William £3. To Cousin William, John Tooker's Son £20. Bequest to each of my Cousin Christopher Sergun's Children. To Brother Thomas Tooker 4/- and "my best cloak, hat and doublett." Also bequests to Brother William's wife, to Cousin's Son Walter Halles, and to Sister Caroline's Son, Richard Pooke. Residue to Mother, Joane Tooker, who is Sole Executrix.
Witnesses, Thos. and Wm. Tooker.
Proved 1st Dec., 1592.

1592. The last Will of Christopher Tooker. He desires to be buried in the Parish Churchyard of Throwley, and "although sicke of bodye, yet hole of memory," &c. gives to daughter Eme her mother's best gowne, the sylvern hookes and one measure of tynning vessell. To daughter Johane, the great brazen crocke. To daughter Margaret, a similar bequest. To son James, "my best brazen horne and my best ewere." To servant, George Venycombe, a doublet and grey jerkyn, a pair of leathern drawers, and second best hatte. Residue to wife Anne, who is Sole Executrix.
Dated 6th Aug., 34th Elizb. Proved 4th Oct., 1592.
Sum £16 15s. 4d.

1604. The last Will of Alice Peeter of ye cittie of Exeter, widow, 4th June, 1604. To Son Humfrie Peeter and his heirs an annuity issuing out of a tenement in the Parish of St. Paul,

Exeter, for ever. Legacies, to daughter, Alice Keridge wife of Thomas K. to be paid by Son, George Peeter. To dau. Welthian Tucker, To daughter Joyse Browning. To Son Morice Peeter, to Cousin Bridgett Watts, to said George Peeter's children, To Son Thomas Peeter, To Cozen Samuel Tucker, to Son Valentine Tucker (her Son-in-law) who has also six silver spoons, a pair of great andirons "which be in his fore chamber at ye new Ine."

Exor. Humfrie Peeter. Overseers, Sons-in-law Valentine Tucker and Thomas Keridge.

"Alle Peeter."

"Concordat cum testamento penes Registrarii remanente. Jaeperus Bridgeman registrarius Archidiaconi Exoniensis testatur."

(From Copy at Exeter Guildhall.)

NOTE.—She would seem to have been the widow of William (fourth son of John Peter, Mayor of Exeter, 1557; died 1579), descended from a brother of John Petre of Tor-Newton, ancestor of Lord Petre.

1606. The Last Will of George Gib, of Clyst St. George.

In the Name of God, Emanuel, Amen. I, George Gib, &c.

To Sixe of the poorer sorte of the parishe, iijd. To John Gib, the elder (his son by Welthean (Gwenllian?), his first wife), one table borde in the hall, his greatest brasen crocke, his Brewing Panne, and his Cricking bute, "which things I was willed by my father to leave unto my eldest sonne."

To Catherine, his daughter, £20, one worsted kirtle, a pair of Silver Hooks, and one Silver Pinne.

To Edward, George, and John, the younger, his sons, £8 each. To Andrewe, his son, £10, to be paid to Andrewe Lovering, his brother-in-law, and John Gib, the elder, his son, to be employed for him in some lawful and honest sorte.

To his Godchildren iiijd. apiece, except George Gib, his son's son, to whom he gives "a yeo lamb at weyninge time."

The residue to Marie, his wief (his second wife), whom he makes his Whole and Sole Executrix.

Witnesses, Edward Osborne, Andrewe Loveringe, and John Gib.

Overseers, Edward Osborne, Andrewe Loveringe, and William Gib.

Will dated 24th of February, 1605/6.

Proved 29th August, 1606.

NOTE.—George Gibbe was buried at Clyst St. George, August 25th, 1606.

1606. The last Will of Elizabeth Mortymer of Tedburn St. Mary, widow. Bequests of Clothes, furniture, or sheep, to Son William and his wife Margery, and their "children." To daughter Thomasine, Cousins Elizabeth and "Mock"(?) and to Thomas and Jone French.

To cousin Walter Mortimer, to Jone Connett and to Goddaughter Rose "Temlett" (Tremlett ?). The last has "a Wastcote, a peare of hose, and shoes."

Residue to Son John, who is Sole Exor.

Two Trustees, viz, James Woodley and Jno. French.

Witnesses, Thomas French, Thomasine Wonstone, and Christian Colliholc.

Proved 19th Dec., 1606.

Sum £5 13s. 8d.

NOTE.—JAMES WOODLEY. The Woodleys migrated to Ashburton, and were Lords of the Manor of Buckland-in-the-Moor, 1593.

Present Representative—James Woodley, J.P., of Halshanger, Ashburton.

1609. The last Will of Lawrence Wreaford of Bickleigh, husbandman.

He gives a sheep to Mrs. Twigge and a lamb to John Twigge, and the residue to Argent, his wife, who is Sole Executrix.

Dated 16th April, 1st James. Proved 10th March, 1609.

Sum £17 9s. 4d.

1613. Symon Tucker of Tedburne St. Mary. 20th Oct., 1613. To be buried in Church of St. Mary, Tedburne. Bequests to said Church and poor. To Jone, daughter of Henry Woodley, £3 5s. at 18 or marriage. To Martha, daughter of Henry and Elioner Woodley, and to their Son, Robert Woodley, at 16. Bequest—To Son Thomas " my table horse" (Trestle ?) and the new house after wife's death. Bequest to Symon Endell.
Witnesses, John and Richard Endell.
Proved 19th Nov., 1613.

1613. The Last Will of Elizabeth Mortimer of Bradridge, Widow, Nuncupative.
Bequests to the poor and towards reparation of the Church.
Residue to Henry Hille, her Son, who is Sole Exor.
Dated and Proved July, 1613.

1613. The last Will, Nuncupative, of Elizabeth Mortimer of Bradridge, widow, 8th July, 1613.
Imprimis. To the poor of Bradridge and to the reparacion of the Church 11/6.
To God-children 1/- apiece.
Residue to Henry Hille her Son, who is Sole Exor.
"Money oweynge to John Hille 303/4."
Proved July, 1613.

1618. Administration to the Effects of Henry Mortimer of Rewe. Granted to Wm. Mortimer of Torrington, Yeoman.
12th May, 1618.
Sum £51 1s. 6d.

1617. William Osmond of Kentisbeare. Sept. 24th, 1617. To Son Samuel £50. To dau. Thomasine Palmer £5. To Edward and Nicholas Sons of Samuel Osmond 10/-. To Agnes wife of said Samuel 10/-. To daughter Isot Butstone, 40/-. To Anne and Wilmot Palmer 5/- each. To Anstice

Osmond, dau. of Thomasine Palmer, 10/-. To Agnes wife of Thomas Symons 30/-. To Thomas son of said Thomas Symons 10/-. To Thomasine wife of Richard Osmond -/12. To John Salter the younger -/6. To poor of Kentisbeare 3/4. To Kentisbeare Church -/20.

Robert Osmond, Sole Exor.

Two rulers, viz.: Ralfe Merson and John Salter with 1/- each.

Proved 19th March, 1617.

Sum £19 17s.

1617. Thomas Wreyforde of Exeter "Taillor" makes Gregory Soper, universal Legatee and Sole Executor.

Overseer, George Trente.

Dated March 20th, 1616. Proved 29th April, 1617.

1617. John Osmunde of Kentisbeare. Sept. 21st, 1616. He leaves small bequests to the Church and to the poor, and the residue to Johane his wife, who is Sole Executrix. Two Overseers, "my eldest son, George Osmunde of Uffculme and my youngest son, John Osmunde of Tiverton."

Witnesses, Robert Bishoppe,
    Saml. James,
    Thomas Bussell.

Proved 2nd July, 1617.

1618. Henry Osmond of Sampford Peverell, 18th June, 1618. To brother Roger my wearing apparel "except my cloak which is to be sold to pay my funeral." He leaves his wife his leasehold dwelling house, determinable on the lives of Brother Matthew Osmond and Sister Anstice Rawling. The goods in house to revert to Servant, Elizabeth Osmond.

3 Trustees, "friend" Arthur Hill, and Cousin John Osmond of Shobrooke, and John O. Son of said John.

Witnesses, Arthur Hill, Thos Welland, Henry and Matthew Osmond, Richard Saunders and John Churly.

Proved 14th Aug., 1618.

Sum £23 5s. 4d.

1618. Thomas Hamlyn of St. Thomas, Exeter, Yeoman. 9th Aug., 1618.

To Daughter Mary £50, Son John £50, Daughter Alice £120, Son Roger £120. All legacies at 21.

Residue to wife Judith, who is Sole Executrix.

Mentions "brothers" Jentill Venycombe and Roger Hamlyn.

Proved 18th Sept., 1618.

NOTE.—A branch of the family of Hamlyn of Widecombe-in-the-Moor and Holne.—See *Post.*

1619. Tristram Tucker of Brampford Speke, Husbandman. 2nd Jany., 1619.

To eldest daughter "Hebbot," the bedstead in the parlour.

Residue to wife Dorothy, who is Sole Executrix.

Witnesses William Flaycross, Clerk, Gregory Ponsford.

Proved at Exeter, 12th Jany., 1619.

Extract from Inventory of above:—

"Rente laid out for ground beforehand £4 5s.

Item—2 kine and 1 yereling £7 5s.

„ 1 mare and 2 foles £12.

„ 4 flitches of bacon 10/-.

„ 14 yards new wollen cloth.

„ 4 brass pans, 1 cauldron and 2 skillets.

„ His dunge."

Sum £58 1s. 4d.

NOTE.—Flaycross was not Vicar. Tristram Heycraft was collated to Brampford Speke 1609-10, and died 1628-9.

1619. Administration of the Goods of Richard Gibbs of Clyst St. George granted to Jane his widow. Henry Smyth of Lympston bound with her. Goods priced by John Gibbe and Henry Goldsworthy, May 25.

Proved May 1st, 1619.

NOTE.—She was widow of . . . Symes; married to Richard Gibbe at Clyst St. George, Sept. 23rd, 1601.

1619. Ralph Owsment (Osmond) of Whimple, 29th July, 1619. To Son, Ralph Owsment, my best suit of apparel. "If my wife marry again I give to my two daughters Anne and Thomasine half my household goods."
Residue to said wife Alice, who is Sole Executrix.
No witnesses.
Proved 29th Sept., 1619.
Sum £11 16s.

1619. The last Will of John Tucker of Potcote in the parish of Tiverton. He gives the poor of the parish 20/- "on the day of his burial."
He leaves "each of my children" 3/4 apiece, "one ewe and one sheep.".
Residue to wife Katherine who is Sole Executrix.
Philip Thorbridge and Wm. Hayleighe Rulers, John Fursdon Overseer. These are left 2/- each.
Witnesses John Fursdon, Hugh Veysey, Richard Tucker.
Dated April 20th, 1618. Proved 1st March, 1619.
Sum £77 19s. 6d.

Inventory.

"Dishes, Spoones, Trenchers, and Cupps, 1/-."
"His Otes, barley and Barley mault, Wheeles, butt drayg, harrowes, Corne in ground, £4. Haye, 10/-. 1 bullocke and 1 pigge, 36/-. Duckes, 2/-."
Item one deede of ffarme or purchas £20.

NOTE.—The Wills of Ellis Tucker, Oct., 1610, and William Tucker, July, 1615, both of Tiverton, were duly proved, according to the Calendars, but are now missing.

1619. Thomas Mortimore of Tedburn St. Mary, 26th Nov., 1619.
He leaves to the maintenance of Tedburn Church 5/-. To Sons Thomas and Nathaniel 40/- each, at 21. "Item—I give unto them one brassen panne contayninge by estimation about forteene gallandes after my wife Wilmott's death."

To dau. Elizabeth and Son John 40/- each at 21. Residue to wife Wilmot, who is Sole Executrix.

Two Trustees, viz.: Wm. May of Dunsford and Richard May of Tedbourn.

Proved 17th Dec., 1619.

Sum £33 8s.

1620. Thomas Osmond of Uplowman. To Son William all my apparel "and after the decease of my wyef my little caldron, pott hookes and hangings, and my great crocke." To daughter Joane, "after my wyef's death or marriage," a pan and crocke. Residue to wife Thomasine, who is Sole Executrix.

Proved 20th April, 1620.

No witnesses.

Testator was a weaver.

Sum £4 5s. 2d.

1621. Wilmot Osmon of Tiverton, widow, 15th Dec., 1621. There are small bequests to the children of John Skynner, senr., of Tiverton, viz., Nicholas, John, Matthew, Elizabeth, Mary, Prudence, and Priscilla Skynner. To Kinsman Symion Thorne, 5s. "Item—I give my "Tanye" (tawny?) gown to my kinswoman Elizabeth Cooddeney, of Crocombe, widow."

Executor, Son-in-law, John Skynner.

Witnesses, John Skynner and John Puddington.

Proved 11th Jany., 1621-2.

Sum £79 9s. 4d.

1622. Elizabeth Osmond of Tiverton, widow. There are bequests, chiefly of household goods, to Sons Henry and Thomas Osmond, to Brother John Puddington, to daughter, Mary Perrye, and to Son-in-law, Richard Perrye. To Nephew Robert Perrye, 20s. Residue to said Sons, Thomas and Henry, who are Joint Exors. Two Trustees, Brother-in-law John Puddington and John Duckham. These are the witnesses, and have -/12 each.

Dated 26th Aug. Proved 3rd Oct., 1622.

Sum £38 15s. 8d.

1622. The last Will of Robert Toucker of Tiverton, Husbandman. To wife Rabidge, life interest in all property, with reversion to daughter Johane. Dated Dec. 1st, 1622. Proved 8th Jany., 1622 3. Sum £38 11s. 7d.

1623. The Effects of Joane Toocker of Tiverton were administered by Nicholas Tucker, 6th March, 1623. £3 16s. 10d.

1628. The Effects of Richard Tucker, alias Glover, of Tiverton, administered by John T., *alias* Glover, his Son, who signs "John Tucker." 21st May, 1628.

NOTES.—The Will of John Tucker of Tiverton, proved March, 1634, is missing.
Robert Tucker of Tiverton, by his Nuncupative Will, proved 23rd May, 1638, left small bequests to his "eight children," and made his wife, Thomazine, residuary legatee and sole executrix.

1623. Administration to the Effects, &c., of John Osmond of Shobrook, granted to Andrew, his son, 30th May, 1623. Sum £127 10s. 10d.

1623-4. Thomas Osmond of Halberton, Yeoman. To each of his Sons 5s., and to their children 2s. 6d. Residue to daughter Elizabeth, who is Sole Executrix.
Witnesses, Nicholas and Michael Osmond.
Dated 26th July, 1623. Proved 11th March, 1623-4. Sum £81 4s. 8d.

1624. John Osmond of Chilloman, in the parish of Halberton, 14th Aug., 1624. Desires to be buried in the parish Church of Uplowman, "where I was born." To kinsmen John Osmond and Robert his brother, 20s. each. To kinswoman Mary Esserye, widow, 30s. To the poor of Uplowman, 20s. To Mary, daughter of Zachary Churly, 20s. at 18. To daughter, Agnes Osmond, -/12.

Residue to daughter, Elizabeth Shackle, who is Sole Executrix.
Witnesses, Arthur Hill and Christopher Osmond.
Proved 29th Oct., 1624.
Sum £29 5s.

1624. Nicholas Hamlyn of St. Mary Steps, Exeter, Cordwainer, 18th Sept., 1624. To Son James, best cloak and one platter. To youngest Son, Nicholas, best doublet and breeches, best jerkin, and one platter dish. Wife Joane, Executrix.
Overseers, Augustine Drake and William Bicklye. Proved 22nd Jany., 1624.
Sum £25 16s. 8d.

1624. John Osmonde of Tiverton desires to be buried in Tiverton Church, and leaves to the poor there, and to those of Kentisbeare, small bequests. Bequests also to Humphry, son of Brother George, to Elizabeth, wife of Alexander Hake of Buckland St. Mary, Somerset, to her daughter Anstis Hake, to her son John Hake, to Alexander Hake the younger, to Margaret and Katherine, daughters of the said Alexander Hake. To said Brother George and his three children, to sisters Thomasine, Anthony, and Mary Cave, to Kinsman Stephen Osmond of Tiverton, and to his brothers. To Joan wife of John Minifer, to Wm. Marshall of Tiverton, Currier, Humphry Bildo of the same, Robert Yarde and John Crooke of Tiverton, labourers, Robert Puddington, weaver, Richard Greane, and George Pooke.

"Residue to my master, John 'Mynefee.' Witnesses, Richard Capron, Robert 'Meavyseale.'"

Testator was a Blacksmith.
Dated 2nd March, 1623. Proved 1st April, 1624.
Sum £221 15s. 6d.

1624. 31st March, 1624. Nuncupative Will of Charells Graunger of Kentisbeare, made in the presence of Walter Chollashe and Bartholomew Butsan. Gives all his apparel to Thomas Graunger his son, and the residue to wife Elizabeth and daughter Jane. They are joint Exors.
Proved 9th April, 1624.
Sum £23 3s. 10d.

1630. Administration to the Effects of Thomas Graunger, late of Withecomb Rawleigh, granted 3rd Feby., 1630, to Margaret his wife.
Sum £111 1s.

1626. Abraham Osmond, 19th Sept., 2nd Charles I., desires to be buried in Halberton Church Yard, and gives to the poor there 10s. To son Francis £3. To daughter Sara £3 and to children's children 5s. each. To Eliza Somers a certain coffer, and another to Elizabeth, daughter of Son Abraham. To apprentice John Stubinges, 3s. 4d. Residue to Son Nycholas, who is Sole Exor.
Trustees, Grandson John Haddridge and Son Abraham.
Witness, John Haddridge.
Proved 17th Nov., 1626.
Sum £76 3s.

1626. Robert Osmond of Halberton, 20th Dec., 1622. To the poor there 40/-, to each of Christopher, Nicholas, and James Osmond's Children -/12 each. To Michael, son of brother James Osmond, 20/-. To Elizabeth, daughter of brother Thomas Osmond, 20/-. To John Osmond of Brethembottom, 40/-. To Cousin Nicholas Osmond, 40/-. Residue to Cousin Christopher, Son of brother John, who is Sole Exor.
Witnesses—Henry Breward.
     Mighell Osmond.
Proved 8th Sept., 1626.
Sum £26 15s. 8d.

1627. Administration to the Effects, &c., of James Osmond of Tiverton.
Granted 20th Feby., 1627, to Avice Osmond, widow.

1627. Administration to the Effects, &c., of Edward Osmond of Kentisbeare.
Granted 5th June, 1627, to Richard Osmond his relict.
Sum £38 7s. 11d.

1629. Nuncupative Will of Thomas Gibbs of Clyst St. George, husbandman, 19th August "or thereabouts," in the presence of Robert Gibbe and Elizabeth Crutchard. He leaves £10 each to his daughters Agnes and Joane Gibbs, and leaves the residue to Joane, his wife.
Goods valued at £162.

NOTES.—Proved in the Court of the Vicars Choral, Oct. 6th, 1642. Wife married secondly, William Darke of Coleridge.

1631. The Last Will of William Gibb of St. George's Clyst, near Exeter.

Devises his tenement and Garden, called Claypitt or Peyght, with 23 acres of land, to his nephew and Executor, John Baker, to whom also he leaves his interest held for two lives in the Moiety of Court Place in the same parish. To the poor of the Parish 20/-.
Goods appraised in £438.
Will dated May 10th. Proved July, 1631.
Witnesses, Richard Baker and Henry Hunte.

NOTES.—Buried July 17th, 1631, at Clyst St. George.
On the death of George Gibbs of Clyst St. George, in 1723, his great nephew, George Abraham Gibbs (father of Sir Vicary Gibbs, Chief Justice of the Common Pleas), inherited as his heir-at-law a small estate in that parish, called then, as now, Pytt.
George Gibb of Clyst St. George was rated in 1650 for part of Court Farm.

1637. The last Will of George "Worthy" of the Parish of St. Sidwells, Exeter, 3rd Sept., 1637. He mentions his Son John "Worthy" and his daughter Joane Wandricke.

Residue to Joan his wife, who is Sole Exor.

Signed "George Worth."

Proved Jan. 21st, 1637.

NOTE.—Testator was fourth son of John Worthe of Crediton, whose Will was proved in the Principal Registry, 4th June, 1596. See *Post*. The said John Worthe was fifth in descent from Thomas Worthe of Worth, in Washfield, alive 1460. Testator inherited, and farmed, an out-lying estate in St. Sidwells. His great aunt, Alice Worthie, daughter of Otho Worthe of Compton, in Marldon (long the principal residence of this branch of Worth of Worth), was a Nun of Polsloe Priory, and was buried in St. Sidwell's Church, June 12th, 1586, being then in receipt of a pension from the Augmentation Office. Her mother's sister, Cecelia (Mylleton), Prioress of Polsloe, died 1530.

1637. The last Will of Mary Redway of Exminster. 26th Oct., 1637.

To be buried in Exminster Churchyard.

To Son, Richard Redway, 1s. and 1 "puter" dish.

To his three children 12 pence apeace.

To Geeles Redway "on ponger" dish.

To Roger Redway "1 crock and on pan and on plater dish."

To John Redway the younger "1 pan and 1 plater dish." Elizb. Redway "on great candlestick and a skillet and 1 lam." Eales Redway "my darter" the bed "whereon I now lye performed with bed clothes, all my wearing apparel, 1 chest and a Coffer."

Residue to Son John Redway, who is sole Exor.

Mentions latter's "three children."

Witnesses, Wm. Horne, Ambrose Smith.

Proved 1st Dec., 1637.

Sum £26.

1638. The Last Will of Rabisha (Rabidge) Tocker of Tiverton, Widow. She leaves her daughter Thomzine Marwood 1s.

To her daughter Mary Reade's Children (wife of Thomas Reade) £3 each.

To Grandson, Robert Reade, small bequest.

To Henry, Dorothy, and Anne Southard, children of dau. Dorothy, £10.

Residue to daughter Joan Tocker, who is Sole Executrix. Dated 20th July. Proved 7th Sept., 1638. Sum £88 2s. 3d.

1640. The Account of Peter Hamlyn, Guardian to the children of Nicholas Brimcliffe alias Gaunicliffe, viz, John, Elizabeth, and Mary.

12th Jany., 1640.

1644. Nuncupative Will of John Gibbe of Clyst St. George, husbandman, made 16th April, 1644, in the presence of Robert Gibbe and others.

He leaves money to his daughters, Mary, wife of John Gibbens, and Anstis Gibbe, and the residue to his son and Executor, Richard Gibbe. Value of Personalty, £118 11s. 4d.

NOTE.—Eldest son of George Gibb (Archd. Exon., Aug. 24, 1606), by Mary, his second wife (Principal Registry, 1603.)

1674. Nuncupative Will of Richard Gibbe of Clyst St. George, made July 15th, 1674, leaving property to his sisters, Mary Gibbens and Anstice Torner, and the Residue to his wife. Chattels appraised by Robert Gibbs and Benedict Webber.

Date of Probate, Sept. 10th, 1674.

Witnesses, Robert Gibbe and Mary Webber.

1660. Inventory of Peter Tucker, of Cadbury, taken 17th Jan., 1660.

"Imprimis." In readie money that was taken out of his pocket when he was taken out of the water by Henry Knolls, £3 4s.

Item two olde Bookes, 1 Cup with a silver mouth, 3/-.

Two bonds of desperate debt £31.

Twelve purses and pouches, a paire of gloves, with other small things in the Apple Chamber.

Five Hogsheads of Cyder with the Casks £6. Two flatches of bacon £1 10s.

"This daie beinge spent we continued our further proccedings in this business until the next daye. Humfrey Wilcockes."

Two Hackney Saddles and one Pillion 13/-.
Three Pack Saddles and their girtes.
Two yearlings £4 10s. Two fat Steers £12.
Twenty weathers £12. Twenty Sheep £9.
Two Sows with Pigs £7. Six Geese, Two Jennies, three Ducks and three hens, 15/-.

Five Acres of wheat and Two of Rye £17.

A moiety of a parcell of ground determinable upon the life of Rose Tucker and Wm Tucker £30.

Two oxen, Two Steers and a heiffer that were driven away under the pretence of right by Edward Godfrey of Collompton which as we are informed were worth £22.

NOTE.—The above quaint inventory will serve well to show the price of farm stock, etc., in 1660.

John Hugh, who administered to the effects, subsequently petitioned to be allowed his charges, from which we gather that the funeral expenses of deceased, including the cost of search for and recovery of the body from the river, amounted to £7.

1661. The Last Will of Philip Gibbe, of Shobrooke.

He leaves 10/- to the poor of the parish; his lands and tenements of Ebford, or Ebbord, in Clyst St. George and Woodbury to his eldest son John (then wanting some years of 21) and his heirs; with remainder to his second son Phillip,[*] and his heirs; with remainder to his daughter Mary; and after her, to the right heirs of Phillip. Mary, his wife, to have the profits of the land till John come of age; and to enjoy for 40 years, if she should so long remain unmarried, the tenement at Little ffulford, in Shobrooke, where he was then living; with remainder to his son Phillip.

He makes his brothers George,[†] Abraham,[‡] and Robert[§]

---

[*] Archdeaconry of Exon., March, 1724-5.
[†] Principal Registry, Oct., 1723.
[‡] Abraham Gibbs, P.P.C., Nov., 1668.
[§] Robert Gibbs, Vic. Chor., Aug., 1688.

"rulers in trust" under his will, and his wife, Mary Gibbe, executrix.
Will dated Dec. 8th, 1656. Proved by Mary, the widow, July 27th, 1661.
Witnesses—

1662. Administration of the Goods of Robert Gibbe, of Topsham, to Rose Westlake, widow, his daughter ; Raymond Westlake being bound with her.
Date of Grant, Jan. 24th, 1662.

NOTE.—He was of Clyst St. George when Rose was baptised.

1666. The last Will of John Redway the elder, of Exminster, Yeoman, 20th Feb., 1665. Son, Nicholas Redway, the 4th and 8th parts of Hall's Tenement. To Son William Redway the 4th part of Bond's tenement, "until half a year after his Uncle Richard Redway's decease." To wife Margaret, "the bed whereon I lye."

To Son Nicholas, "that gold ring which was left unto me by his Mother."

Sons Nicholas and William, then married and childless, are Joint Exors.

Overseers, Wm. Collins and John Collins the elder.
Witnesses, John Skynner, Wm. Tothill.
Proved 18th May, 1666. £157.

NOTE.—Will written on parchment. Large circular Seal attached with strip. Device—A Griffin (arms of Collins).

The Redways (pronounced and frequently written Radway) are an ancient Devonshire family, with coat armour of their own—viz., "*Gu*, a chevron between three owls *arg.* crowned *or*," quartered by Cooke of Thorne. Christopher Cooke, in right of his mother of Thorne. She was Jenetta, daughter and heiress of John Hake, by Janet, his wife, daughter and co-heiress of Nicholas Radway.— *Coll. Ar.*, D. 7, &c.

1666. Administration to the effects of Richard Redway, late of Exminster, deceased. Granted 25th Jan., 1666, to Thomasine his relict. George Collins joins the bond.

1667. The Nuncupative Will of Elizabeth Redway of Exminster, 14th March, 1667, relates that there is given her by the will of John Cuttaford, of Exminster, 20/- p. a. for a certain number of years She gives one moiety thereof to her Sister Mary Redway, and the other to her kinsman, Richard Molton. Present at delivery of the will—Thomasine Redway, Gilbert Pearse, and Charles Stoneman.
Proved 16th Oct., 1668.

1667. John Evans of St. Sidwells in the City of Exeter, Husbandman, 1st May 15th Chas. II.
To daughter Elizabeth, wife of Richard Fillmore, weaver, 1/- " starling money."
Residue to wife Johane.
"And I doe make & ordayne my loueinge friend Agnes Tucker of the parish of St. George in the aforesaid City of Exeter widdowe, Sole Executrix for the use & benefit of the said Johane my wife."
Witnesses, Richard Hingston, Thomas Willing, Thomas Ferris, Thomas Jewell, Richard Jewell.
Sum £26 15s.
Administration granted to Johane the widow, Agnes Tucker having renounced, 15th Oct., 1667.
Seal. A heart, with letters " A. T."

NOTE.—Tooker of Maddington, Co. Wilts., sixteenth century. " *Vert*, on a bend, engraved *arg.*, 3 body hearts *gu.*"

1670. John Wreford Gentleman of the Parish of Bickley, 16th July, 1659. Small legacies to Christopher Son of Gawen Richards, Stephen Burrows and Barbara Blackmore.
Residue to present wife Anne, the daughter of Damaris Chapman. She is Sole Exor.
Seal of Arms. A fesse between 3 stags' heads cabossed.
Proved 1st Sept., 1670.
Inventory made by Wm. Wrayford, of Silverton, Gentm.
Total £1,218 18s.

NOTE —The Arms on the Seal are apparently those of Barton of Smithills, Co. Lancaster.

1670. "Memorandum, that on or uppon the 6th day of febuary Anno Dmi. 1670, Elenor Tucker "late of Sidwells" being of a disposing mind & memory delivered her last Will & Testament in manner and form following, first of all she gave unto Catherine Davids, wife of Morgan Davids, her kinswoman all that she should dye possessed offe, if shee did not live soe long to spend it herself.

"Item she gave to Roger ffollette's daughter one paire of stockings, but as for Roger ffollett he should not have a penniworth of her estate. These words were spoken being then of perfect mind and memory not long before her death in the presence of us," etc.

Proved Feby., 1670.

NOTE.—St. Sidwell's, Exeter—in the Index of this Archdeaconry deceased is described as "Elenor Tucker of Tiverton."

1870. The last Will of Thomasin Redway of Exminster, 14th April, 1670. Giles Redway and each of "his children" "my daus." Mary Stoneman, Grace Redway, late Cousin John Cuttiford, Grandson Richard Molton, and Nicholas Molton, are all mentioned.

She gives her interest in a cottage and nine acres of land at Exminster to Son Richard Redway, with remainder, in default of his issue, to daughters Mary and Grace.

Residue to said Richard Redway, who is Sole Executor.

Proved 27th April, 1670.

Sum £75.

1670. Inventory of all the goods & chatels of Thomasin Redway of Exminster who departed this life the sixteenth day of Aprill in the yeare of our Lord God 1670, taken and appraised by us whose names are under subscribed :—

	£	s.	d.
Imprimis for her wearinge apparel	2	10	0
Item, 3 beds performed	2	10	0
2 chests, 3 coffers, 1 little box	2	0	0
For cloth in the house	3	0	0
For 2 coats	0	16	0

	£	s.	d.
For a Bible	0	5	0
For 9 pans, 2 kittles	2	15	0
4 crockes, 1 posnel	1	10	0
13 pewter dishes	1	3	0
1 Prese	0	12	0
2 Bords, 1 forme, 1 chest, 2 coffers	0	18	0
Corne in house	3	0	0
2 milch kine	6	0	0
2 hogs	0	18	0
1 hoxhead of sider	0	14	0
For timber vessels	1	15	0
For victuals in the house	2	0	0
1 hand gunn	0	12	0
5 bags & 1 packsheet	0	12	0
ffor rede	0	8	0
ffor working tools & 1 twine	0	5	0
ffor woode	0	16	0
„ laders and a cheese wring	0	4	0
„ corne in the grounde	10	0	0
„ Irework about the chimney	0	4	0
„ pte in a tenement	30	0	0
„ things forgotten & not praised	0	8	6
The some	£75	15	6

Roger Smith   Exhibited 29th
Nicholas Turner   April 1670 by Richd. Redway.

1671-2. Will of Richard Redway of Exminster, Husbandman, 14th Dec., 1671.

"I give unto my soon all my land wch I doe now enjoy. I give unto Richard Molton £8, to be paide unto him when my Sonn comes in age in cause they toe doe so long life." To Nicholl Molton 20/-. To Robert Redway and Mary "Redwa" 1/- "a peace," and "to Geils Redway thear father my blew coat which I did weare worken dayes." To Grace Redway 5/- and "2 bushels of wheat to be paid at harvest." To wife Sara Redway "half my goods in doors & out."

Said wife is Executrix. "My Sonn" has the other half of the Residue.
Proved 19th Jany., 1671-2.
Sum £26 16s.

1677. The last Will of Johane Wrayford of Bickleigh, widow, 23rd Nov., 1677. To Mr. Samuel Segar £30 and a mourning ring. To Brother John's two Children £5. To poor of Silverton 20s., and the same sum to the poor of Bickleigh. Mentions her tenement called "Richards." To Mother and Sister Damaris she leaves her wearing apparel. To Sister Gill her wedding ring. "To my brothers" 5s. each. To Aunt Agnes, now wife of Ambrose Goodridge, the Residue. She is Sole Executrix.
Proved 11th December, 1677.
Sum £445.

1680. The last Will of Henry Worth of Washfield, dated 19th Jany., 1677.

He desires to be buried "without superfluity of blackes" but decently, and six of the labourers on the estate to "attend his hearse" and to have 6s. each and a "gowne."

" Item—I give £10 towards the purchasinge some father estate as for buyings of Bibles or some other books of divinity to be yearly distributed amongst the poor people of Washfield for ever."

" To my son, Thomas Worth, 4s. for a ring."

" To my son, Alexander Worth, the lyvinge of Wood which I lately purchased in the parish of Uplowman, to him and his heirs for ever, and the sum of £300 to stock it."

To daughter Dorothy, wife of Robert Collins of Autry (Ottery St. Mary) Clearke, £100.

" To my daughter, Elizabeth Oliver, a ring of 20s. value."

" To my daughter, Mary Worth, £700." " To the Servants at Worth at time of my death 40s. each. To my Son John's wife "my best piece of plate." To brother Arthur Worth, Sons-in-law Robert Collins, Benjamin Oliver, Esq., Humphry Shobrooke Merchant, dau.-in-law Anne Worth, Nephew Wm. Pincombe, two brothers-in-law, Francis and

Thomas Bampfylde a ring each of 20s. value. Residue to Son John Worth, who is Sole Exor.

Witnesses, George Abraham, John Besly, and Emlin Clatworthy.

Codicil, dated 12th Jany., 1679-80.

He leaves his brother Arthur Worth £10, and to the children of his daughter-in-law Ann Worth £10 each. He leaves to his Son Alexander, the books, trunks, boxes, and other things in the study over the porch of Worth House.

Witnesses, Benjamin Oliver, Roger Dodge, Saml. Clemens.

Seal of Family Arms. *Arg.*, an Eagle dispd., wings elevated, with two necks *Sa*, Beaks and legs *Gules*, Helmet and Mantling.

Crest. "An Arm erect vested erms. gloved erm. holding an Eagle's leg couped *or.*"

1680. The last Will of Orlando Evans of Exeter, 10th Aug., 1680. "In-holder." To Sons Richard and Orlando, to daughter Ann Strod, and daughter Sarah Tucker, "equally to be divided between them, such worldly goods as I die possessed of." They are joint Exors.

Witnesses, Joseph Marshalle
  Jo. Erlye
  Jo. Battersby.

Proved 21st Jany., 1680

Seal. A Battle Axe below the letters "O. E.," surmounted by a Royal Crown.

Motto. "Le Roy Vive."

1683. Jonah Tucker of Thorverton, Feby. 19th, 1682. To Sons Jonath, John, and Michael, and to dau. Elizabeth £10 each.

His wife Elizabeth is to "hold & enjoy" his "justment" which he rents of Sir John Davey until 20th March, 1684, then brother Edmond is to have it to "end of term."

Residue to said wife who is Sole Executrix.

Overseer, Brother Edmund Tucker.

Proved 8th June, 1683.

Sum £85 10s.

1683. Administration to the effects of Hugh Tucker of Exeter, Granted to Sarah his relict, 13th July, 1683.

From the Inventory of Hugh Tucker late of the Parish of All Hallows, Goldsmith St., Inn-holder, June 8th, 1683.

"Item 1 Silver Tancket, a tumbler, 3 Spoones & a dram dish 4/8 to 4/10 per oz., £7 15s."

Item a second-hand old watch broken and out of order, £1.

Item a dozen of old case knives at 2/8 a dozen.

Item "Desperate Debts," £194 7s. 3½d.

„ Secure Debts, Thomas Tucker, Esq., £1 13s. 8d.

„ Roger Tucker, £70 19s. 4d.

„ Anne Tucker, widow, £15 5s.

Robert Tucker, £3 17s. 5d.

1684. Administration to the effects of Orlando Evans of Ottery St. Mary, deceased, Granted to Elizabeth his widow. Richard Evans, "Tonsorius," joins the bond.

29th Jany., 1684.

1684. Joan Wrayford of Silverton, widow, 16th April, 1679.

She gives her three daughters, Joan Galard, Ann Holmes, and Grace Bryan, and to their respective husbands, one piece of Gold. To "the Minister" for a funeral Sermon, the same bequest. To each of her Grandchildren 5/-. To eldest Son William the Cider pound with its appurtenances. To the poor of Silverton £5, and to those of Bickleigh £3.

Residue to youngest Son Edward Wrayford, who is Sole Exor.

Proved 4th Feby., 1684. Sum £465 13s. 8d.

Armorial Seal. 3 Piles in Point.

NOTE.—"*Or*, 3 Piles in point azure." These are the well known arms of Brian, of Tor Brian, Co. Devon, but have been used, with very doubtful right indeed, by both English and Irish Bryans for many years. Some vary the Tinctures.

1684. The Last Will of Robert Tucker of Thorverton. He bequeaths his soul to God and his body to Christian Burial.
"I give to my daughter Jan, won shilling. To my Son Georg. won shilling. To my Son Roger, won shilling. To Henry my Sonn in law, won shilling. To Mary my daughter won shilling. To Jud., my daughter, won shilling. To my daughter's Sons, won shilling. To my Son Peter, won shilling. To my daughter Grace, won shilling."

"Also I do mak my house to my wif during her life" with remainder to Son Roger, who is to pay half the moytie to my younger children."

Trustees, my wife and John my Brother.

Witnesses, "Wiliom" Tucker, Henry Tucker.

Administration was granted to Dionysia Tucker the wife in minority of her daughter Peternell Tucker, who had the residue and was Sole Executrix under the will. 11th April, 1684.

1684. Administration to the Will of Robert Tucker of Thorverton, deceased, was Granted to Dyonisia his wife in the minority of the Executrix, Petronell Tucker. 11th April, 1684.

Inventory of Robert Tucker of Thorverton, Decd., Fuller. 5th April, 1684.

Item 3 spinning turns and 2 skewers.
„ 1 pair of fullers' shears, 10/-.
„ 1 fullers' press, 10/-.
„ 1 Chettell lease, £12.

"The Sum is £22 7s. 2d.
The Debt is" 10 0s. 0d.

Remains £12 7s. 2d.

1686. Joseph Wreyford of St. Thomas the Apostle, and County or City of Exeter, Schoolmaster. He leaves his household goods to his wife, Elizabeth. Mentions his Sons Samuel, Joseph, and John, and gives them certain houses. Residue to his wife Elizabeth, who is sole Executrix.

Dated 22nd Nov. Proved 19th Jan., 1686.

Sum £335 5s. 6d.

1686. The last Will of Nicholas Tucker, of Bampton. Dated, 26th May, 1686.

He leaves to his wife, Anne, 3 pewter dishes that are marked with the letters "A. H." To Joan, dau. of Wm. Norrish, deceased, "one Ammory now in my dwelling house, and my greatest Kaddarne under the Ammory standing"; also one brewing ffatt " & "the sum of £5 in money to be paid her by Susanna Blackmore, now living with me."

"To Robert my brother my best sutt, viz., one waistcote, one long cote, & a paire of briches."

To Edward Downe my best hate.

"To Cousin James Butford, my leather deske. To my mother 20/-. To brother-in-law, William Presser, my razure."

"I give to Ann my wife the right to dwell in my house as long as she shall remain a widow, & I do give my house & garden to Susanna Blackmore and residue, and make her sole executrix on this condition that she always dwells in it & does not sell it. In default, there is remainder to Joan Norrish. Cousin John Norrish of Cruse Morchard to be ruler in trust with _ bequest of 5/-."

Administration granted to John Norrish in minority of Susannah Blackmore. 29th Jan., 1686.

Sum £13 11s. 6d.

1686. The last will of Dorcas Evans of Exeter, Spinster, 27th Nov., 1685. To Sister, Mary Titherly, "my farrington gowne and scarlet large petticoat, & a greene mohaire petticoat & a red cloath petticoat, a Cabinet & a paire of curtains & vallens, a cupboard cloath, a purse, pincushion & sheath."
"Item to Joseph Evans, my brother, all my linen undisposed of. To said Sister Mary, two gold rings & one piece of broad gold, in the hands of Cozen Bartholomew Shower of London. To Cozen John Anthony's wife, Covering for a chaire & two stooles. To Roger Light & his wife, a brass pott, a skillett & a butter dish, two spoons and a mustard pot. To s^d Cozen, his wife & daughter £3 for rings. To Cozen Elizabeth Hayne & to Cozens Phineas and Susannah Anthony, sums to buy rings. To the poor of the City 10/-. To brother John Evans two thirds of money remg. after debts &c. are paid."

Residue to John Anthony of Exeter, Merchant, who is sole Executor.
Witnesses—Susannah Marshall.
Margaret Bennett.
Armorial Seal.—On a fess, 3 roses ? between 3 fleur de lis, on a chief, 3 lions rampt.
Crest.—A demi-lion ramp. holding a sceptre
Proved June, 1686.

NOTE.—Evans of London and Shropshire, and Evans of Watstay (now Wynnstay), Co. Denbigh, and represented by Sir Watkins Williams Wynn, Bt., gave "*Arg.* a fesse between 3 fleur de lis *Sa.*"

Administration to the effects of John Lewis, alias Evans, of Exeter, granted to Sarah Lewis, alias Evans, of Exeter, his daughter.
John Vigors, Carpenter, of Exeter, joins the Bond.
15th April, 1706.

1687. Inventory of Jane Tucker, widow, of Cleyhanger, 11th April, 1687.

	£	s	d
Item 14 silver spoons and 3 Gold rings	6	0	0
„ all her books	1	0	0
„ 5 cowes and 2 calves	20	0	0
„ 3 heifers	11	10	0
„ 1 heifer yearling	1	10	0
„ 14 ewes and 14 lambs	9	6	8
„ 24 old sheepe	14	8	0
„ 25 hog „	11	5	0
„ 1 horse and 1 mare	6	0	0
„ 1 Sow, 6 young pigs, and 2 other piggs	3	0	0
„ Corne in the grounde	7	10	0
„ all her hay	3	0	0
„ all her poultry	0	5	0

1687. The last will of Jane Tucker of Cleyhanger, widow. She desires her body to be devoutly buried. To the poor of the parish 10/-.
To Jane Rendall, her Grandchild, £50, "and the table borde

in the parlour, and the best chair in the parlour, and the tester bedstead in parlour chamber, the side saddle," and "my wedding ring."

Bequests to other Grand-children—viz., Dorothy, Honour, and Elizb. Rendall.

£6 to be expended on funeral.

Residue to daughter, Jane Rendall, who is sole Executrix.

"To Thomas Richards of Bradford my kinsman," 40/-.

Proved 12th April, 1687.

Sum £305 5s. 8d.

1690. The last will of Richard Evans of the City of Exeter, Inn keeper, 6th Nov., 1690. He leaves to his Cousin Anne, daughter of his brother Orlando Evans, deceased, £20. To his Sister, Sarah Tucker, widow, £5, "Provided that they do not molest or trouble my Executrix hereafter named in the enjoyment of what I shall leave unto her."

Residue to wife Rebecca, who is sole Executrix.

Proved 17th April, 1691.

1693. The last Will of Dorothy Tucker of Exeter, widow, 13th May, 1693.

She leaves to seven poor widows of Exeter 20s. each.

She bequeaths her interest in an estate and term of years in certain houses to her brother, John Sanford of Virginia and her cousin Ann Chilcote, in equal parts. To all "brothers and sisters" of Testatrix 20s. each for mourning rings.

"I also give the silver bason my deceased father gave me to my brother William Sanford, and my will is that after his decease the said bason shall be a legasie successively unto such as shall bear the name of William Sanford."[*]

Residue to Son, James Tucker, who is Sole Exor.

Seal of Arms. Barry wavy of 12.

Crest. A Martlet.

Proved 30th June, 1693.

---

[*] See Editor's "Practical Heraldry," page 168, etc. London : Redway, 1889 ; now Kegan Paul & Trubner, Ludgate Hill.

1694. The last Will of George Osmond of Tiverton, Husbandman, dated 21st Aug., 1694.

Bequests to Sisters Mary Glass and Allis Hill. To "Cosens" John and Thomas Hill. To Peter Osmond and his Sons Robert and William. To Thomas Osmond of Autrey (Ottery St. Mary) and to Thomas his Son. To George Osmond, Alice Daley, Mary Sellack, and to Thomas Daly's son John. Residue to wife Katherine, who is Sole Executrix.

Witnesses, Endymeon Vacinover
    John Thomas, Junr.
    Michael Frankpitt.

6th Dec., 1694.
Sum £122 4s.

1694. The last will of Thomas Tucker of Dunkeswell, dated 9th Sept., 1684. He leaves his wife Elinor £12 a year as long as she remains unmarried, failing this, £10 p. a.

He charges his estate called Winsor in the parish of Luppitt with this annuity.

"I leave also to Elinor my wife, the halle, and all those two rooms on that side the entry in my said house called Winsor during her life, togeather with the upper garden, & I also give to my said wife for her yearly burning 200 well made faggots of wood." He further gives her the best bed, certain specified furniture, "the best lininge table borde cloth, one side saddle & a pillion." For all these goods she is to give a bond to his Exors. for due return at her decease. Residue to Son Thomas, who is Sole Exor.

Proved 30th Jany., 1694.

1694. Inventory of Thomas Tucker of Dunkeswell, made 18th Jany., 1693-4.

Item.				
	His wearing apparel, cash, and plate ...	£30	0	0
,,	A Chattle estate in Luppitt	500	0	0
,,	In wood and fuel	24	0	0
,,	Debts and Credits	60	0	0
,,	Desperate Debts	20	0	0
,,	240 sheep	96	0	0
,.	10 horses and Colts	33	0	0

Item. Crockes, frying pans, spits, and andirons   £2   0   0
  ,,   Eight flitches of bacon and other victualls
         in the hall   11   0   0
  ,,   Brass and pewter   18   0   0

The above are the most interesting items in the Inventory; the total of the personal estate amounted to £1,046 6s. 5d.

1696. The last Will of Grace Tucker of the City of Exeter, Single woman, one of the daughters of James Tucker, Merchant, deceased.

"To my honoured mother Mistress Joane Tucker, all my property, messuages, &c., in St. Mary's Clist or elsewhere, either in the County of Devon, or in the City or County of the City of Exeter. To be held by her, her heirs and assigns for evermore."

Residue to said Mother, who is Sole Executrix.

Proved 19th May, 1696.

Seal of Arms. Barry wavy, on a chevron embattled, betw. 3 sea-horses, 5 gouttes de poix.

(Tucker of Exeter.)

1696. Christopher Granger of Broadhembury. Administration granted 14th May, 1696, to Mary his wife.

Sum £40 16s. 4d.

1697. The last Will of Alexander Osmond of Tiverton, Yeoman, 25th Oct., 1697.

He leaves to John Newte of Tiverton, Rector, and Matthias Jenkin of the same, Merchant, one yearly rent-charge of £14, in trust for Grand-daughter Elizabeth Wheeler. After death of said Elizabeth, he gives an annuity of £7 to Grandson Peter Morse, together with his dwelling house on Barnes' Hill and £100. To Peter, Laurence, and Sarah, children of said Elizabeth Wheeler, £20 each at 21. He leaves certain Messuages to Grandson Wm. Morse, and "one piece of gold called a Guiney" to Frances wife of said Matthias Jenkin. Residue to said Grandson Wm. Morse, who is Sole Executor.

Trustees, Son-in-law Peter Morse of Tiverton, Mercer, and Edward Bury of the same, Mercer, with 20/- each.

He desires his trustees to take on the administration of the estate of the late Wm. Cannington of Tiverton, Serge Maker, and to care for the education of William and John Cannington.

Witness John Corrain.

Proved 9th Dec., 1697.

1697. The last will of John Tucker of Luppitt, Yeoman, 3rd Jan., 1679.

"To Sarah my wife, whom I make my sole Executrix, all my moiety of the estate known as Ruggepath in said parish of Luppitt, being parcel of the manor of Dolditch Shaugh, together with all other land held on lease from John Ashford of Ashford in the Co. of Devon, Esqr., & determinable on the deathe of the said Sarah my wife, John Tucker & Susannah Tucker, Son & daughter of me the said John."

Proved 27th April, 1697.

Sum £369 6s. 2d.

1699. Administration to the Effects of George Wreford of Exeter. Granted 12th June, 1699, to Urith his wife.

Sum £18 2s. 2d.

1700. Thomas Wreaford of Whitstone, in the Co. of Devon, Husbandman.

3rd Jan, 1700. To brother-in-law Thomas Squabble, dwelling house and garden.

To Sister, Abigail Yewman, £8. To Brother-in-law Henry Skinner, £8. To Cousins Elizabeth and Ann, daughters of Thomas Squabble, Elizabeth Yewman, and Elizabeth and Alice, daughters of Henry Skinner, small bequests.

Cousin Simeon Yewman to be Executor. He remarks that he lent William Best of Crediton, £3 10s. forty years ago.

Proved 13th June, 1700.

Sum £27 7s. 4¾d.

1700. William Wrayford of "Sillferton," Gentleman, 29th April, 1700.
To Mrs. Joane Galerd, widow, 18 twenty-shilling pieces of Broad Gold. "To Andrew Adams, alias Holmes, the money that he owes me." To William Bryannd of Exeter, Goldsmith, £40. To Sylvanus Bryannd, his brother, £10. To Richard Bryannd of Exeter, Apothecary, a tenement worth £30 a year at Sandford, with reversion to kinsman William Wrayford of London, Merchant, and Matthew Wrayford of Cornwall, failing issue. He gives his servant Mary Haubsland £50 and her life upon his houses at Silverton called Buckinghams, but the land belonging to the said houses he desires may be "let out" at a yearly rent for the benefit of the poor of Silverton for ever, at the discretion of the "Pastor, Churchwardens and Overseers of the Parish." Mr. Troyte is mentd. as Rector. To Edward "Bryand," his life in a tenement value £12 p. a. at Bridford. To Sister Joane Galerd, and to John Davise and his wife Margaret, daughter of said Sister Joan, £1 1s. and a mourning ring. Mentions Robert Marsh of Exeter, Mrs. Grace Bryand widow, "Mr. Francis Weare of Silverton, Esq.," and Mrs. Grace Weare, Mrs. Grace Weare the younger, "my Goddaughter," John Weare, and Elizabeth Weare " his younger Sister," Mr. John Slade and Mary his wife. To poor of Silverton, £10, Bickleigh £5, and bequest also to poor of "Chitherly." He adds, "the Silver Tankert, Silver Salt, and Silver spoons I intend to distribute with my own hands." To Mrs. Grace Bryand my Sister £52 10s. & my great gold ring and my Sealing ring with my coat of arms cut upon the ring." There is further mention of Mary and Ann Bryand, daus. of said Sister Grace, Mrs. Agnes Evelleigh, John Holmes, Junr., and Ann his Sister. Residue of Estate, lying in Crediton, Sandford, and elsewhere, to said kinsmen William and Matthew Wrayford, they are joint Exors. Proved 15th Nov., 1700.

Armorial Seal—six times repeated—a chevron between 3 leopards' faces *or* (Parker Lord Macclesfield).

NOTE.—The will of Edward Wrayford of Silverton, Proved 19th Sept., 1691, is sealed with the same Seal.
I believe that a Seal of *Chapman*, who bore somewhat similar arms,

came into the hands of Wm. Wrayford when he made the inventory of John Wreford of Bickleigh, in 1670, and that it was altered and adopted for their own arms by the Wrefords or Wrayfords of Silverton, between 1670 and 1690, possibly by their relative " William Br}annd," the Exeter Goldsmith. Richard Bryan became Rector of Silverton 1675, and died 1688. I presume that he was the husband of Grace Wrayford, and the father of the Bryans mentioned by Testator.

A Coat of *Chapman* may be thus blazoned :—" Per chevron *arg.* and *gu.*, a crescent between 3 leopards' heads counterchanged." It will be seen that the substitution of a chevron for the partition lines would obliterate the crescent. See *ante*, page 25, 1670.

1702. Katherine Osmond of Tiverton, widow. To Dorothy, wife of James Crosse of Collompton, Mercer, dwelling house, with appurtenances in Tiverton. £10 to be expended on the funeral. To Nicholas Tucker, a life annuity of 10/-. To Kinswomen Grace and Dorothy Tucker, 20/- a year. To said Grace Tucker " a paire of my finest sheets and of my finest pillytys." To brother John Conebee £5. To brother Robert Banbury £5. To Sister Elizb. Slee, wife of John Slee, £5, and one gold ring, a dozen table napkins and my rideing suite and mantle. To Sister Jane Banbury 20/-. To Kinsman James Crosse of Collompton, mercer, 20/-. To his daughter Dorothy 20/-. To Sister Elizabeth Slee's four children, John, Nicholas, Edwd., and Elizabeth, 20/- each. To brother John Coneby's two children, John and Thomas, 20/- each. To brother Robert Banbury's five children —— To Kinswoman Grace Banbury 50/- and a gold ring. To Kinsman Robert Banbury the younger 20/-. To Kinswoman Mary Banbury 20/-. To Grace Holle and Elizb. Hooper, my kinswomen, 20/- each. Residue to Dorothy Crosse, wife of James Crosse, " my kinswoman," who is Sole Executrix.

Witnesses, Thos. and Wm. Baron.

Dated 5th May, 1696. Proved 23rd Ap., 1702.

1706. Henry Sanger of Poughill, 19th Oct., 1695. To Father, Henry Sanger, 5s. To Mother, Joane Sanger, 5s. Residue to Sisters, Joane and Elizabeth Sanger, who are joint Exors. Proved 28th June, 1706.

Witnesses, Saml. Chappell and Jone Melhuish.

Sum £47 4s. 4d.

1708. The last Will of James Tucker, the elder, of the city of Exeter, Gentleman, 22nd Dec., 1708. He leaves to his five children, James Tucker; Dorothy, wife of Peter Morse of Tiverton, Grocer; Margaret Tucker, Jane, and Sarah Tucker, in equal parts, all his property and houses in the parishes of St. Edmund and St. Mary Arches, both in the City of Exeter, together with "four estates" in the parish of Collumpton.

The houses in St. Mary Arches Parish were then in possession of Jonathan Fox, Yeoman. Testator had other property in the parishes of St. Pancras and St. Kerrian, both in Exeter.

"To said Jane Tucker, my Chest of Drawers, my books, my brother Risdon's picture, and my mourning ring which I wear outside my signet ring."

To said Sarah Tucker, "my flower dressing box inlaid, my book styled 'The Whole Duty of Man.'"

To Thomasine and Bridget Stephens, a guinea piece of gold each.

"To my Son, James Tucker, my Gold ring with a Cornelian stone, and my Coate of Arms sett and engraved thereon to keep and wear in remembrance of me."

"To Katherine wife of Jonathan Fox, yeoman, my Venise glass."

Residue to daus. Jane and Sarah, who are joint Exors.

Proved 7th Jany., 1708.

1709. The last Will of Joane Tucker of the City of Exeter, widow, 18th June, 1709.

To her Cousin Gertrude, wife of Henry Turney, Gentleman, and to her son, Richard Turney, £100. To Barbara, Sister of sd. Gertrude and wife of John Baker, Clerk, £100.

To Cousin, Courtenay Croker, Esq., £50, in trust for use of Cousin Dorothy, wife of Cousin Samuel Axe.

To said Courtenay Croker £100 in trust for Dorothy, dau. of sd. Samuel Axe and wife of Bernard Pennington.

To Cousin Stephen Bryan £150, and further, £50 in trust for Rachel Bryan, his sister, "lately married." To Cousins Joseph, Samuel, and Elizabeth Bryan, and Cousin Joseph, Son of Samuel Axe, £50 each. To Mrs. Eleanor Moore, Schoolmistress in Exeter, £50, with remainder to her dau., Mrs. Susannah Moore. To Brother and Sister Farthinge, 40s. each for mourning rings. To "Servant maid" Martha Powning, £200 and all her clothes. To William Rous of Faringdon, Gentleman, £50. To Florence Sprague of Mary Clist, widow, £20. To Cousin Robert Bryan, Rector of Clist St. Mary, the advowson of said Church, to him and his heirs for ever, and also a meadow at Clist, to pay out of the latter 8s. p. a. for ever towards repairing the poor houses in Bishop Clist Town. To sd. Robert Bryan and Charles Heron of Exeter, Gent^{m}., the fee simple of a house, Garden, and Orchard in Bishops Clist Town, in trust to permit Edward Lang and Margaret his wife, and Martha Powning, widow, to have the same for their lives, and after their deaths the said house to be an Alms house for two ancient poor persons of Clist St. Mary. To the same Trustees she leaves her house in which she resides in St. Mary Arches for the use of the Minister of that parish.

To her Trustees, for their trouble in executing the said Trust, she gives a broad piece of Gold.

Residue to Robert Bryan, Samuel Axe, and Saml. Bryan, who are joint Exors.

Administration granted to Robert Bryan and Samuel Axe, 8th March, 1709-10.

1712. Susanna Osmond of Halberton, widow, dated 9th Feby., 1711. She confirms a deed bearing date 16th Feby., 9th Qn. Anne, between the said Susanna of the 1st part, and James Osmond of Bycott, Halberton, Gentleman, her son, of 2nd part, Jeremiah Hussey of Okehampton of 3rd part, and Anthony Codner of Cullompton of the 4th part. Provisions of this deed not expressed.

She bequeaths to daughter Susanna £100 in excess of £200 given her by said deed.

"My sylver bowle & Damask Napkins, my pair of Virgennalls, my Side Saddle, fyve sylver spoons marked with the letter M. All my old gold and gold rings, except my new signet ring, which I give to my Exor.

To my Grandchildren Thomas, John, and Mary May, and Grace Sanford, 5/- each. To Son-in-law Phineas May, and daughter-in-law Mary Osmond 5/- each. To Servants 1/- each, and to the poor 10/-.

Residue to Son James, who is sole Executor.

Proved 25th Nov., 1712.

1720. Last Will of Mary Lyle of Topsham, widow.

Whereas her late father Nicholas Downe by his will dated Dec. 31, 1713, gave her daughters Sarah and Mary Lyle certain estates in Rockbeare and Ellesbeare (Aylesbeare) between them, on condition that if Mary should take the whole she should pay her sister £500; and that was not enough in value for the moiety, she therefore gives her daughter Sarah £700 payable on Mary's attaining the age of 21 and exercising the option ; but if she did not, the bequest to be equally divided between them.

She leaves a legacy to her cousin John Saunders of Pinhoe and his son John, and to her sisters Martha Waad and Martha Brand, making them Executors in trust.

If her daughters should die under age or unmarried, she leaves Rebecca, wife of John Saunders the elder, £100; to Mrs. Jane Westcott of Farringdon, Devon, widow, £100 ; and to Deborah, wife of John Bishop, of Marsh Green in Rockbeare, £5.

Will dated Jany. 4th, 1717/8.

First probate, Aug. 6th, 1720, to said Executors.

Second probate, April 10th, 1728, to John Chappell, a quaker, who makes affidavit and values the goods.

Third probate, March 12th, 1728-9, to Sarah Lyle, *alias* Gibbs, widow, and Mary Lyle, *alias* Burridge, wife of Samuel Burridge, daughters and co-executrixes of the deceased.

Seal—*Argent*, 10 billets, 4, 3 2, and 1.

1723. The last Will of George Gibbs of Clyst St. George.

He bequeaths all his goods and chattels in Clyst St. George, and devises all his lands in Clyst St. Mary, being part of the Manor of Ashmore, to Francis Pease, Minister of the Parish, excepting certain legacies, namely, 8 sixpenny loaves to the poor labourers of Clyst St. Mary every Christmas, Easter, and

Whitsuntide, and the 1st Sunday in May, for ever ; and 16 like loaves at the same time to the poor of Clyst St. George ; and, every second year, out of the yearly profits of the said lands, 6 hatts for 6 poor boys, and provision for 4 poor children to be kept to reading school, and that they have each a bible at going off; and if a lad shall happen to be sent from this parish to either University, he is to have £4 a year for 4 years ; provided that all these be in communion with ye Church of England, and constant at ye parish Church. He makes his most affectionate friend and Minister Francis Pease his sole Executor, leaving him all his lands, goods, and chattels for his life, making reference to a conveyance executed some time before. He leaves to his sister Brinley a bond for £100 due by her husband ; also he leaves 10/- to be paid for a charity sermon to be preached on the first Sunday in May for ever ; and desires to be buried without pompe or noise.

Will dated July 18th, 1721. Proved by Francis Pease, Octr. 11th, 1723.

Witnesses—Silvester Suxpitch.
  Richard Humphrey.
  Walter Wood.

NOTES.—Testator was buried at Clyst St. George, August 9th, 1723.
His sister was Elizabeth, wife of Benjamin Brinley, and daughter of George Gibbs, of Clyst St. George, 1683.

1724. Last Will of Philip Gibbs of Shobrooke.

Leaves his lands in Upton Helions and Shobrooke to John Primridge of Sanford, and John Frost of Crediton, in trust during the life of his sister-in-law Sarah Rither, for his daughters Mary, wife of Philip Pyle, and Elizabeth, wife of Anthony Harris, Executor.

Will dated May 20th, 1724. Proved March 4th, 1724-5.

Admon de bonis non granted January 7th, 1732, to William Harris or Winter.

Witnesses—

NOTE.—Testator was second son of Philip Gibbe of Shobrooke, 1661.

1725. John Osmond of St. Sidwells, Tallow Chandler. To wife Elizabeth, an annuity of £20 and one room in his house. Household goods to remain with Sons Joseph and Samuel. To daughter Elizabeth £500, to daughter Grace, wife of Nathaniel Cock of Bideford, Clerk, £50. To said Son, Joseph, £100. To said Sons, his leasehold property in St. Sidwells, and a freehold house in St. George's Parish. To the four Presbyterian Ministers, Mr. S. Enty, Mr. Withers, Mr. Lavington, and Mr. Green £1 1s. each. 20/- to his wife Elizabeth in trust for the poor people of St. Sidwells parish. Residue to said Sons Joseph and Samuel; they are Joint Exors.

Witnesses, Esayah Broadmead, Francis Worth, John Broadmead.

Dated 4th Dec., 1723. Proved 14th June, 1725.

Seal of Arms. 3 horses Courant.

NOTE.—These are the Arms of Fry of Yarty, and the ring seal evidently belonged to Francis Worth, the witness, one of the "four children" of Francis Worth of Exeter, and Great Grandson of Elizabeth, dau. of Nicholas Fry of Yarty, and of her husband Henry Worth of Worth in Washfield.

1726. The Last Will of Abraham Gibbs of Topsham, Gentleman.

Leaves £500 to his son George Abraham Gibbs. £300 to his daughter Anna Gibbs. £21 and no more to his wife Sarah Gibbs.

Exors. in trust, John Ewins, John Rous, and the Revd. Mr. Christopher Ewin (Rector of Feniton).

Will dated 16th Sept., 1726. Proved Oct. 24th, 1726. Witnesses

NOTE.—Testator's wife was daughter and coheir of Robert Lyle of Topsham, widow of . . . Ewings.

1727. Administration to the effects of Stephen Worthy of St. Davids, Exeter. Granted 8th Nov., 1727, to Anne his wife.

NOTE.—He was grandson of George Worth, "or Worthy," of 1637, and great-great-grandfather of the Editor of this work. Since his time, the final "e," abandoned in the elder line by Anthony Worth of Worth, 1517, has been also entirely abandoned by us, and our name written as above; in accordance, however, with the old pronunciation.—ED.

1729. Elizabeth Evans of St. David's, Exeter, Widow, dated 20th April, 1729.

She gives all her goods to Nicholas Hamling of Exeter, in Trust for Magdalen, wife of Thomas Saunders.

Administration granted to Nicholas Hamling, 17th Oct., 1724.

1733. Administration to effects of Francis Evans of Exeter, granted to Edward his Son, 18th Dec., 1733.

1730. Mark Swanger of Clehanger, Yeoman. To brother Moses Swanger £20. To John, Son of John Minchin of Clehanger, £4. To Grace, daughter of said John Minchin, £4. The Moiety of "my estate," called Bond house, to Cousin Robert Milford of Norton Fitzwarren, Husbandman, and to Cousin John, Son of brother Thomas Swanger, and their heirs. And the leasehold moiety of the same estate is also bequeathed to them, but charged with annuities of £10 and £5 to brothers Moses and Thomas. To Cousins Elizabeth, Joan, Mary, and Sarah, daughters of Brother Thomas, £5 each. To Cousin Jane, daughter of Brother Moses, £5. To Brother Robert Swanger and Sarah, his daughter, £5 each.

2 Trustees, Moses and Thomas Swanger.

Residue to said Robert Milford and John Swanger, who are Joint Exors.

Witnesses, John Swanger, Mary Isaac, Richd. Loudon, John Minchin, Senr.

Dated 10th Aug., 1728. Proved 30th July, 1730.

1734. The last Will of Elizabeth Worth of St. Sidwells, Exeter, 26th Jany., 1733.

She desires to be buried with her deceased husband in the Chancel of Washfield Church.

She leaves to her five younger Sons, Henry, Bampfyld, Simon, Reginald, and Samuel Worth, £10 each. She mentions her Son, Furse Worth, lately deceased.

She leaves her daughter Dorothy her gold watch, and to her daughter Susannah her pearl necklace.

To her daughter Matilda her "gold medall" and her diamond ring. To her brother-in-law, the Revd. Mr. Canon Worth, and to her Cousin Francis Worth, a mourning ring each. To Mr. John Parsons, Apothecary, Exeter, and to Mr. John Norman, Apothecary, Tiverton, a mourning ring each.

She leaves the residue of her estate to her said Sons, Simon, Reginald, and Samuel, and to her six daughters, Mary, Elizb., Bridget, Dorothy, Susannah, and Matilda, who are Joint Exors.

Witnesses, John Fortescue, "Catherine Dummitt."

Proved 19th Sept., 1734.

Crest Seal, in red wax : an heraldic tiger, supporting between its paws a shield charged with a bend betw. 2 bendlets. Fortescue.

NOTES.—This was evidently Dr. John Fortescue's Seal. He was of Bampton, Co. Oxon, and a Bachelor of Medicine. He died unmarried in 1752, and was the last of the name of Fortescue at Buckland Filleigh.

Mrs. Worth, the Testatrix, was the widow of John Worth of Worth, Grandson of Henry Worth, whose Will, proved 1680, has been given *ante*. She was dau. and heir of John Furse of Morshead, in the parish of Dean Prior.

1737. The last Will of Richard Huyshe of Baliol College, Oxford, 28th March, 1731. He constitutes his father, Francis Huyshe of Clist-Hidon, universal legatee and Sole Exor.

Proved 25th March, 1737.

NOTE.—He was second son of the Revd. Francis "Huyshe," Rector of Clist-Hidon, and, through Wentworth, Spencer, and Clare, had a direct descent from Joan Plantagenet, second dau. of Edward I., a fact referred to on the funeral monument of his four sisters in Sidbury Church. His niece, Ann H., married John Melhuish of Hill, in Cruse Morchard, and was Editor's great-grandmother.

1738. Administration to the Effects of George Vigor of Exeter, granted 6th Feby., 1738, to Ann Phillips, wife of John Ulrich Passavant, his Sister.

1738. The last Will of Dorothy Wrayford of St. Mary Major's, Exeter, 29th June, 1738. She mentions her Sister, Elizb. Prigg, deceased. She recites that she is under "covert baron," and bequeaths the estate set apart for her separate use. To "brother-in-law" Thomas Lavington, the house in St. Thomas, now in possession of Thomas Savory, Haberdasher of hats, in trust for my dear and loving husband, Angel Wrayford, with remainder to "Cousin" Thomas Lavington the younger.

Executor, the first-named Thos. Lavington.
Seal. A Bull passant. Bevill.
Proved 23rd Aug., 1738.

NOTE.—The Lavingtons were Exeter merchants, and resided for some years at Larkbeare. Thomas Lavington may have been a brother of Andrew Lavington of Larkbeare, who became bankrupt in 1737. Dr. George Lavington, Bp. of Exeter 1746-62, is said to have been of this family, and to have been born at Heavitree, near Exeter. It appears, however, that he was really born at Mildenhall, Herts., of which parish his Grandfather was Incumbent.

1744. The last will of Mary Carwithen of the City of Exeter, Spinster, 12th Jany., 1742. To brother William Carwithen, £10. To Sister Sarah Atkin, £10. To Cousin Penelope Saffin, for mourning, £10. To Cousin Robert Atkin, £20. To Cousin Anne Westcote, £5. To Cousin Charles Carwithen, £5. To Cousin George Carwithen, £5. To Cousin John Carwithen, the Minister, £3. To Cousin John, Son of Cousin Elizabeth Maye, a moidore. To Cousins John and Edmund Atkin, £5 each. To John Bassett, Esq., of Heanton Court, £2 2s. for a ring. To Cousin Wm. Atkin, Esq., her best diamond ring, failing his heirs remainder of said ring to his Sisters. To Cousin Mary Atkin, her gold watch, which belonged to her late brother Cudmore, of Templeton. Legacies to Cousin Edmund Carwithen, and to Miss Mary Walrond, daughter of Dr. Walrond, Sister Sarah Atkin, and to her Cousins, the 6 daughters of her sd. Sister, Sarah Atkin, who are Joint Executrixes of her Will.

By Codicil she gives legacies to Cousins Joseph Carwithen, Mary C., dau. of Cousin Carwithen, of Crediton. To Churchwardens and Overseers of Templeton £10, to be placed at interest to keep a child in the parish school "to learn to read the Bible."

£200 to her said Cousin Penelope Saffin.

Proved by Mary Atkin and Anne Westcote, two of the Exors., Feb. 12th, 1744.

The last Will of Mary Carwithen of the Parish of St. Petrock and City of Exeter, Spinster, 7th Sept., 1751.

She directs that her body shall be buried in a vault in the Parish Church of Crediton, in the grave of her late brother, William Carwithen, and bequeaths legacies to her mother, Esther,* and to her niece, Esther, dau. of brother John.

Residue to said brother, John Carwithen, who is Sole Exor. Proved Feb. 13th, 1752.

1752. Administration to the effects of Joan Worth of Worth, in the parish of Washfield, Granted to Henry Worth, her husband.

Simon Worth of Washfield, Gentleman, and John Brayley of Tiverton, join in the bond.

Granted 5th June, 1752.

N.B.—Henry Worth was second son of John Worth of Worth, M.P. for Tiverton, 1710.

1767. The last Will of Mary, wife of Simon Worth of Washfield, Gentleman, 22nd Nov., 1766.

She settles Treneeres, in the parish of "Maddrin" and Co. of Cornwall, which had been secured to her by settlement, upon her mother Lydia, wife of Samuel Harness of Washfield, Clerk, and upon her husband Simon Worth, unless he marries again. She mentions her Uncle Arthur Harris of Lifton, Clerk.

Her Cousin William Oliver and his heirs have reversion of said estate for ever.

By Codicil, 3rd Dec., 1766, she leaves certain bequests, viz., To John Pierce, Esq., of Chancery Lane, London, £100. To Revd. Philip Atherton and his wife Betty £50 each. To

---

* She was dau. of Henry Walrond, Esq., of Bradfield, Co. Devon.

uncles John and Arthur Harris, and to the Hon. Mrs. Harris. To mother, Lydia Harness, "my watch and all my trinkets, except the Seal with the Oliver Arms, my large chased silver waiter, my father's picture and her picture now in the little parlour at Worth," "the picture of Dr. Oliver, my hoop diamond, and best diamond ring." To cousin "Miss Caroline Oliver," "my shagreen tea chest compleat, my silver tea candlesticks, my best stone shoe buckles, my two best suits of lace, my best sack, my little ruby ring set with brilliant sparks." To Mrs. Elizabeth Acland "my smelling bottle in case" and "my Seal with the Oliver Arms." To Beavis Wood, "my silver labels." To cousin Susannah Benson, a mourning ring. To said husband, Simon Worth, four silver table spoons and six common tea spoons. To said mother, the use of my silver-hafted knives and forks, to revert to uncle Arthur Harris. To Revd. Mr. John Cruwys my silver tea kettle and lamp, and a mourning ring.

Proved Oct. 15th, 1767.

NOTES.—Simon Worth of Washfield was the fourth son of John Worth of Worth, M.P. for Tiverton, by his wife, Elizabeth Furse. Testatrix was the dau. of Lydia, second daughter of Christopher Harris of Hayne, in the parish of Lifton, by Jane (Oliver?), his wife. The Revd. Samuel Harness was Rector of Washfield on the presentation, for that turn, of John Harris of Hayne; he died in 1786.

John Harris of Hayne, who was Master of the Household to George II. and George III., died two days before his niece's Will was proved, 13th Oct., 1767.

"The Hon. Mrs. Harris," his second wife, was a dau. of Francis Seymour, Lord Conway; she died in 1774.

The Revd. Arthur Harris was Rector of Lifton, and died in 1770.

1769. Administration of the Goods of Elizabeth Meachin of Clyst St. Mary's, deceased, granted to Elizabeth Gibbs her daughter, wife of John Gibbs of Topsham, mariner. George Abraham Gibbs of Exeter, Joseph Paul of Thornecombe, and David Williams of Exeter, Sureties.

Date of Grant, Septr. 1st, 1769.

NOTE.—Refer to P. C. C., Jan. 31st, 1795, George Abraham Gibbs. Nov. 3rd, 1778, John Gibbs.

1778. A special Admon of the goods of Isaac Gibbs so far as concerned a term of years, sets forth that Indres of Lease and Release dated March 28th, 1689, were made between Benjamin Oliver, Joseph his son, John Mercer of Ottery St. Mary, Thomas Brooking, Anthony Mapowder, and Isaac Gibbs, Margaret Prideaux of Soledon, widow, and Margaret Mercer, spinster, whom Joseph Oliver meant to marry, and did so marry, and did die leaving issue, Elizabeth, wife of William Williams of Exon., M.D.; and that John Mercer, Thomas Brooking, and Anthony Mapowder died, and Isaac Gibbs survived, but died intestate, and that now there was no legal representative of Isaac Gibbs; and that Admon was therefore granted as prayed.

Date of Grant, 20th September, 1778.

1785. The last Will of John Gattey of St. Sidwells, Exeter, Baker.

He leaves his wife his property in said Parish, with remainder to his son Joseph.

He mentions certain furniture in the room in which his son Edward lodges.

He also mentions his daughters, Elizabeth, wife of Richard Hopkins, Susannah, wife of Shirley Woolmer, and Jemima Gattey.

And his two sons, John and William Gattey. His grandchildren, Patience and John, children of the said John. He refers to his property in Paris Street, St. Sidwells.

Dated 27th Dec., 1784.
Proved 31st Jan., 1785.

NOTES.—The Gatteys are believed to have come to Exeter from Cornwall.

The son, Edward Gattey, was a solicitor in Exeter, and was elected Town Clerk 10th Sept., 1814, resigned 1836. His daughter married Wm., only brother of Sir Francis Sykes, Bart., 17th Dec., 1821, at Lympstone. His brother Joseph followed the trade of a builder. John Gattey was of the Cricklepitt Mills, Exeter, and died 5th June, 1825. The Woolmers were long the proprietors of the *Exeter and Plymouth Gazette.* The property in Paris St. is still known as "Gattey's Court."

1786. Administration to the Effects of Elizabeth Mortimore of the City of Exeter, decd., intestate. Granted Feby. 9th, 1786, to Humphry Mortimore her husband. John Evans of the said City, Gentleman, and Robert Lewis, also of Exeter, "Wool Sorter," join the bond.

1798. The last Will of Mary Carwithen of St. Sidwells, Exeter, April 18th, 1788.

She bequeaths, *inter alia*, " Three family pictures in gilt frames" to the Revd. George Carwithen, and there are also legacies to the Chichester family of Hall. Proved July 28th, 1798.

NOTE.—Some years ago, the Editor saw two or three pictures of the Carwithen family, by Sir Peter Lely, at Gidleigh Park, Chagford, and the owner, Mr. Whipham, told him that they had been given him by one of the sons of the late Revd. W. Carwithen, D.D., of Manaton Rectory, &c., &c. The Carwithens purchased the advowson of Manaton Rectory immediately after the Great Rebellion, and the Revd. W. Carwithen is still the Rector, 1892.

1803. Administration to the Effects of Henry Pearce of the Parish of St. Kerrian and City of Exeter, late mercer, deceased. Granted to Benjamin Mardon, principal creditor, his wife Elizabeth having renounced.

He seems to have left a child, also deceased since his death. Granted 23rd May, 1803.

1806. Special Admon of the Goods of Anne Gibbs of Exeter, widow, so far as related to a term of years. It appears that she died intestate, that her husband, George Abraham Gibbs, was Exor. to Will of Lucy Waymouth, widow, dated Oct. 29, 1770, together with John Trehawke, in trust for Mary, Lucy, John, and George Waymouth, her children; that Lucy Waymouth made a codicil, Jan. 4th, 1779, and died 1781 ; that her children had long since attained the age of 21 ; that Timothy Kenrick, Clerk, had married Mary Waymouth, and died in his (G.-G.-G.'s) lifetime; that Thomas Kenrick died 1805, leaving a will dated June 17th, 1801, and that John Trehawke died 1788.

1827. Administration to the Effects of Robert Pierce, late of the City of Exeter, granted 30th Oct., 1827, to Mary his widow. Under £50.

1878. The last Will of John Francis Worth of Worth House, in the Parish of Washfield, dated Nov. 7th, 1871. He leaves certain furniture and china at Worth to his wife, and certain old furniture there to his daughter. He mentions his brother, Francis Worth, as tenant in tail of Wychanger and Luckham, both in Somerset. He leaves these two estates in equal shares to his children, Reginald and Henrica.

Exors., George Porter of Littleton Rectory, Chertsey, Surrey, Isabella my wife, and Henrica my daughter.

Codicil, 15th May, 1872. He refers to the death of his brother Francis. He mentions that he is only tenant for life at Worth, and desires his son Reginald to allow his widow to remain there for three months after his death.

Proved 30th July, 1878. Under £3,000.

NOTES.—The Worth wills included in this volume are all interesting, since they pertain to one of the oldest Devonshire County Families.

From the "Domesday Survey" of 1087, when Ralph of Worth held Worth under Wm. de Pollei, the elder line of Worth have been seated there in an unbroken succession down to the above Testator.

Towards the end of the twelfth century, Sir Hugh Worthe of Worth, married Avis, daughter of his neighbour at Tiverton Castle, Richard de Redvers, third Earl of Devon. The eighth in descent from him married Margerie, daughter and co-heir of Hugh Beauchamp, about 1385. By this marriage they acquired Beauchamp and other property in Washfield, together with the Manor, and the Advowson of Washfield Church, which had belonged to the Abbots of Plympton, Alice Abbot having been grandmother of Margerie Beauchamp. The fourth in descent from Thomas Worth and Margerie Beauchamp was Anthony Worth of Worth, alive 1523. Amerced at Totnes Castle that year, Washfield Manor being held from the honour of Totnes.

The above Testator, Mr. John Francis Worth of Worth, was ninth in direct descent from the said Anthony Worth. Mr. John F. Worth left two children, viz., the Revd. Reginald Worth, heir-in-tail of Washfield, who married, but died without issue 12th March, 1880. His sister Henrica, mentioned in the Will, was the wife of the Revd. Wm. Lloyd Jones, Rector of Washfield, who assumed the name of Worth by Royal license, 1882, and died January 8th, 1884. Worth House and Manor, with other property in Washfield, were advertised for sale in 1887, when a portion was sold and realized £20,000. In the following year, 1888, another advertisement appeared in the local papers, and the residue of the estate, together with Worth House (a fine old mansion rebuilt about the reign of Queen Anne), was knocked down to a Mr. Thomas (who had made a fortune in South Africa), November 13th, 1888, for £35,000. A portion of the old property was reserved by Mrs. Worth, who subsequently resided at "Beauchamp," and died there 1891.

ARCHDEACONRY OF BARNSTAPLE.

1563. Robert Thassell of Bulkeworthy, in Buckland Brewer, Husbandman, Dec. 12th, 1563. He desires to be buried in the Church of Buckland. To daughter Ema "all the unoccupied woll the sheep bore this year," 5/- in money & a canvas sheet.

Residue to daughter Ales Thassall.

Witnesses—Sir Thomas Moorecroughte, John Burnaberie, Thomas King.

Proved 2nd March, 1563-4.

1565. William Tassell of Rose Ash, 11th March, 1564. Desires to be buried in the Parish Church, to which he leaves 3s. 4d. Legacies to William, John, Jane, and Ann Payne.

Halfendale of goods to wife Margaret, and the other moiety to Sons John and Anthony. Wife and two Sons Joint Exors.

Rulers, Alexander Tasle and Henry Vicarie. *Iis testibus.*

Proved 14th Jany., 1565.

1565. Laurence Tossell of Tawstke (Tawstock), 16th Sept., 1564. He desires to be buried in Holy Grave. "To my four daughters twenty marks in money to be divided equally amongst them, that is, to every one of them £3 6s. 8d.," and "to each two dishes performed & a hiefer a-pice."

To Son William, "six sylver spoones, after the death of my wife."

To John Powe /4d, and "to ye pore mens box /12d.

To Philip Cradocke a yeo. Residue to wief Christian, who is Sole Executrix."
Witnesses—John Combe, "Curat," Lewis Cradocke, John Comer, Richard Bond, with others.
Proved 27th July, 1565.

1565. Roger Worthe of Barnstaple, Gentleman, dated 28th Sept., 1564. He desires to be buried in Barum Ch., "in the Isle of the Blessed Lady as near my wyffe Joan Worthe as may be."

To daughter Johane ten "Portugueses which my mother Webber gave m=," also the Tenement, &c., given me by Henry Webber and Margerie, his wife. To Grace Worthe, my daughter, seven butts of Sacke and one of Malmsey, and the best bed standing in Mistress ffynnels chamber. To daughter Elizabeth and to John Smale "which by the grace of God shall marry her," and to their first child, a tenement "I bought of John Branple of Langtre."

To son Pawle Worthe "my best gowne of scarlet furred with 'fewnes,' my gowne of crymsone ingrayne faced with white satten, my doublett of blacke velvett agged with golde, my tippett of velvett," together with sundry "hangings," and my saile of Armes which I doe seal withall, and my blessing if he be good to my tenants."

To son Walter my ring of golde.

Residue to said Walter, who is sole Executor. He gives his father, Roger Worthe, an annuity of 13/4 "for four years next coming." To the "Spythall house of Pylton & to the Alms House of Barum, 53/4, by the Parson of Marwood.

Proved 27th July, 1565.

NOTES.—Testator was nephew of John Worthe of Compton, and first cousin of John Worthe of Crediton, whose Will was proved in the Principal Registry on the 4th June, 1596 (which see). He was M.P. for Barnstaple, 1553, and was ancestor of the Worths of Timberscombe, Co. Someiset.

His mention of his "Mother Webber," and of his father, "Roger Worthe," proves, conclusively, that the Heralds carelessly omitted a generation at the Visitation of 1564 as they make him son, instead of Grandson, of Otho Worthe of Compton. His wife was Joan Drew.

1565. John Toker of North Molton, 24th July, 1565. To be buried in "y⁕ Church earth" of sd. parish. To the Church /12d. "To the poor mens chest" /12d. To the poor of parish 6s. 8d. To son, Edmund "Tooker," six little silver spoons, two oxen, the best "weyne," and a brass "pott," "according to my promise on his marriage." To son Wm. "Tooker," a table board, six silver spoons, &c. To son John, best yearling and three sheep. To son Peter, a sheep. "Item—to Thomas his (Peter's) son, a yearling." To Owen Smith, the great "standerd," and to his daughter, a yerling. To my "servant," a calf. To daughter Alice, the residue of "my" puter vessels. Residue to his "rulers," for the use of daughters Alice and Mary, if they marry with their permission. Exor., son William. Rulers, brothers William and John Tooker. Overseers, John Slader and Wm. Smith.

Witnesses, John Gred, Vicar, and said Overseers.

Proved 12th Sept., 1565.

1566. Thomas Toker of Trentishoe, A.D. 1566. He desires to be buried in "Holy Turf," and makes his brother John Toker of Dene, in the parish of Torrington (Trentishoe?) Universal Legatee and Sole Exor.

Witnesses, Phillipe Miller, John Hancocke, Davye Howill, and Nicholas Thorne.

Proved 3rd Dec., 1566.

NOTE—See 16th Sept., 1573, *Post.*

1567. Walter Toker of "Rowby," in the parish of Parracombe, 28th Nov., 1565. He desires to be buried there, and gives to the Church, 3/4. To daughter Joan, £22, and a kirtell. To daughter Richorde, £6 at her marriage or at the age of 14. To John Spearman, a mare. Residue to son Robert Tokar, who is Sole Exor.

Witnesses, John Toker, Thomas Harris.

Proved 3rd April, 1567.

1566. The last Will of Walter Carew of Great Torrington, dated 9th Nov., 1566. He bequeaths his gown of Black fur to George Furlong, and leaves the residue to his wife Joane, who is Sole Executrix.

Proved 13th Oct., 1566.

NOTE.—This Walter Carew finds no place in any of the printed Carew Pedigrees.

1566. The last Will of David Melhuish, 13th Aug., 1563. He desires to be buried at Knowstone, and leaves small sums to the poor box there, and to that of Cruse Morchard.

"Item to John Comyn my gray Coat." Residue to wife Johan, who is Joint Executrix with Philip Shapcott.

Proved 13th Sept., 1566.

1567. Margaret Tassell, widow of Ayshe Rose (Rose Ash) 26th Dec., 1567.

To "Mary Payne my daughter's daughter one yeo sheepe." The same to Johane, daughter of John Voysie the younger.

Residue to two Sons, John and Anthony Tassell, who are joint Exors.

Rulers, John Voysie the elder, and John Crocker.

Witnesses, John Voysie and John Laneman, "with others."

Proved 3rd Feby., 1567.

1567. Christian Towker commends her body to Holy Grave in the Church yard of Washford, and leaves to the poor men's box there -/12. To Thamesin Tooker of Washford, widow, "my other best petticoat & two kerchiefs." To Annie Pope, "my petticoat & a pair of chamblet." To four poor men to bear my body to Washford -/12 each. Residue to "Sir Edward Croke," who is Sole Executor.

Dated 12th Aug., 1567.

Witnesses, Matthew Pope, Richard Bright.

Proved 7th Jany., 1567.

1567. Johane Towker of Bratton, widow, 26th March, 1565. Gives her body to " Hallowed grave." To poor men's box -/2. To dau., Alice Baker, "best kirtell," 12 sheep, second best red petticoat, and Sylver girdle. To daughter Margaret Towker, " a podger (porringer) and a platter."
Residue to son John Towker and daughter Margaret, who are Joint Exors.
Witnesses, " Sir John Snowe " and John Dallynge.
Proved 27th Feby., 1567.

1568. John Toker of Marwood, Husbandman, 2nd April, 1565. To be buried in Marwood Church. To maintenance of said Church, 1 Sheep. To son John, " after the lord's fyned of his hariotte," all plough stock and plough gere, " with a guylding and Mare." and after the decease of " Eme his mother," a Table bord, 2 Bushels of wheat, and 6 quarters of " Otes." To Margaret, John, and Katherine, children of the said John, " each of them a heffar." To " Charity, their sister, my yeos." To John Roger, a cow, and to Margaret Roger, 6/8. To son Richard £20, " in peny & penyworth." To Johan Reyd, " my servant," " 3 fleeses of woll." To poor man's box -/12. To daughter-in-law Anstie, " a dish performed." To John Whitbere -/14. Residue to wife Eme, who is Sole Executrix.
Witnesses, John Marwood, Esq., Geffry Clipit, Clerke, Roger Nycholl, and John Whitbere.
Proved 22nd July, 1568.

1568. John Tooker, *alias* Orcharde, of " Frethelstoke," 16th April, 1568. To be buried in the Church of " Frethelstocke." To the poor there -/12. To son William £6 13s. 4d. and 2 silver spoons, and one little Cupboard now with son-in-law John Morrish. To son John Tooker the younger £6 13s. 4d. and 2 silver spoons. To son-in-law John Pep £6 13s. 4d. " if the said John Pep as like his bargaine that he now dwelleth in to Johane my daughter nowe his wief or elles any other as good as that holye to herself." Also one little pan, &c. To John Morrish, a folding board.

Residue to John Tooker, *alias* Orchard the elder, who is Sole Exor.
Witnesses, William Williams, Clerk, Curate, and James Nethewaye.
Proved 2nd June, 1568.

1569. Harrie Toker of Cholocombe-raley, Husbandman, 15th Aug., 1562.
To daughter Johan, £20. To daughter Agnes, wife of Wm. Norman, 6/8. To daughter Richorde, wife of Humphry Borrowe, 3/4. To the poor men's box -/12. Residue to wife Margaret, who is Sole Executrix.
Witnesses, Robert and Thomas Smythe, and Hugh Folker.
Proved 14th March, 1569.

1572. Thomas Tocker, *alias* Tanner of Kings Nyton (Kings Nympton), 6th Sept., 1570. To be buried in the parish Church. To daughter Wilmot Sanger, best brazen pot and 1 dish performed. To Thomasine Sanger, 6 "yowes." To John Borde, 6 sheep. To the poor of the parish -/12. To Martha and Jackett, daughters of John Sanger, "one sheep apiece." To servant, Robert Coblye, one sheep. Residue to wife Agnes, who is Sole Executrix.
Trustees, John Tossell and John Snowe.
Witnesses, Richard Lucke, Thomas Gryffen.
Proved 10th April, 1572.

1572. John Torner, *alias* Toker, of Chumleigh, Husbandman, 19th March, 1571.
• To the children of daughters Elizb. Snowe, Cysslye "Davide," Johan Downinge, and Agnis Hoper, one cowe and one yarlinge to be equally divided between them. To son-in-law John "Davye," "my best cote," and to his wyeff a "thrumich coverlett." To Thomas, son of said John Davye, "my best jerkyn & my white hose." Residue to wife Elizabeth Torner, who is Sole Executrix.
Two Trustees, John Snowe and John Hathewell.
Proved 19th May, 1572.

1572. John Toocker of Kentisbury. Bequests to sons, John the elder, John the younger, Edward, Phillip, Thomas, and to daughters Thomasine and Johane. To a second dau. Thomasine, "the elder," he leaves "one cow if she be ordered & ruled by her friends at her marriage."
To George, son of Wm. "Toker," 1 silver spoon.
To the Church, 1 sheep, and to Wm. Hustote, /4d.
Residue to wife Elizabeth, who is Sole Executrix.
Two Trustees, who witness, viz., Wm. Harris and Wm. Crocker.
Dated 13th Feby., 1571.
Proved 17th June, 1572.

1573. John Toker of Dene in the parish of Trentishoe, 14th March, 1572.
To daughter Elin, a brazen pan, and a brazen crocke. To daughter Johane, the same. To son John, /12d. To Son William, /4d. To sons Richard and Walter, all goods moveable and immoveable after their mother's death. Residue to wife Ellin, who is Sole Executrix.
Witnesses, Robert Stephens, Clerk; Philip Knyle, and Robert Toker; the last two are Trustees, and have /4d. each.
Proved 16th Sept., 1573.

1575. John "Towker" of West Downe, 28th Aug., 1575. He leaves to John "Tocker," "my Sonne & Enymy," 4 oxen with all the plough geare, and "all my wrytinges and evydences." To son Peter, a heifer, &c. To daughter Johane, a heifer calf. To daughter Thomasine, 3 yeos.
Residue to wife Agnes, who is Sole Executrix.
Trustee, Wm. Bright, Vicar of West Downe.
Witnesses, Walter Fosse, John Headen, & Thomas Yeard.
Proved 13th Sept., 1575.

NOTE.—Towards the end of the will the word "enymy," as applied to Testator's eldest son, is erased, and the word "hyeare" substituted. Perhaps by the care of the good vicar of West Downe.

1580. The last Will of John Killond of Lapford, Husbandman, dated 23rd May, 22nd Elizabeth. To be buried on the north side of Lapford Church. To poor, 20/- to be distributed by John Rudge, Gent^m, and Richard Killand. " Item, in consideracion that my son Lawrence Killand is of himself indewed with but small witt or knowledge, and not well able to governe himself with any porcion of goods," " My will is that my kinsman Richard Killand shall deliver to John Rudge of Morchard Bishop, Gent^m, and to John Killond of Down St. Mary, Yeoman, the sum of £40," in trust for maintenance of said son Lawrence, unless Richard Killand elects to provide, himself, for him. Legacies to servants, Margery Killand, Nicholas Thorne and "Ann," and to godson Mychell Rudge. Residue to kinsman Richard Killand, who is Sole Exor.

Overseers, John Rudge and John Killand.

Proved, 20th June, 1580.

Sum £180.

1591. Alexander Sanger, of Mariansleigh. To son, John Sanger the younger, "My Table bord, my selyng, and my coboard, after the death of my wife yf neither of us both have not nede to sell it for ye maintenance of ourselves." To son Henry Sanger, six silver spones and my great brazen panne. Residue to wife Joane, who is Sole Executrix.

My sonne Henry Sanger doth owe me £4.

John Sanger the younger doth owe me 40/-.

Thomas Sanger, my son, doth owe me 40/-.

Admin. granted to Joan Sanger, the Executrix, 8th April, 1591.

Sum £32 9s.

1613. The last Will of John Sanger the Elder of King's-Nympton. He desires to be buried in the Parish Church and "with a Sermon to be preached to the poor" for which he leaves 3/.

"To each of my children /6d."

To son John Sanger, "4 new bordes that lye in the Stable."

To son Robert Sanger and to Marye his wife, "One byrding piece, 1 collyver, and one crosse bowe, with their furniture."

To each grandchild /6d. To John Downe, "my daughter's son," 3/4. To John and Elinore Tomb, *alais* Yelmacole, 3/4. To Lewis Tossell, 3/4 and a coffer containing one bushell or thereabouts. To Agnes, daughter of John Sanger the younger, 3/4. Residue to wife Wilmot, who is Sole Executrix.

Overseers, "Brother" John Bulleid, John Sanger, Thos. Richards, and Francis Southerne, with /20d. each, these being Witnesses.

Debts owed. "Item, I owe to my son-in-law Thomas Tassell, £5. John Bulleid, 42/-. To Agnes Tassell, widow, 30/-."

Sum £45 15s. 8d.

Dated 21st April. Proved 10th June, 1613.

1615. The last will of William Hamlyn the elder of Woolsery, 23rd July, 1615.

To Parish Church, 36/4. To godson W^m. Hamlyn, 20/5. To Willmett and Elizabeth Hamlyn 10/- each. To goddaughter Willmott Denis, 20/6; and to "all the rest of Hugh Denis's Children 10/6 each." To sister-in-law Wilmett Hamlyn, 10/6. To Jane, wife of John Stifyn, 10/6d. Residue "To Isutt Hamlyn my darter."

Witness, Robert Hamlyn.

Proved 1st December, 1615.

NOTE.—Ancestor of the Hamlyn-Williams' of Clovelly, Barts. He is described thus: "The inventory of Wm Merswill" (the name of his residence) "alias Hamlyn of Woulfardisworthie, Husbandman, taken by Thomas Prust, Gentleman, Robert Praunce, Wm Hamlyn, & John Stevens, 1st Dec., 1615.

Sum £49 16s. 4d."

1616. Johan Densham of Lapford, widow, 27th Feb., 1616. To eldest son, Richard Densham, all moveables, &c. To son John, six silver spoons. To son Richard's daughters Mary and Richord, and to his son Richard, small bequests. She leaves the Chattell lease of Trendlebury for the maintenance of sister Alice, with reversion to said son Richard and his heirs.

Residue to said son John Densham, who is Sole Executor.

Proved 29th Oct., 1618.

1618. Richard Harton of Barnstaple, 11th May, 1618. Mentions his brother Robert and step-daughter Anne Clotworthy, god-daughter Mary Gill, Apprentice Agnes Symons, friends John Harrett and John Gill, who are witnesses and overseers. He has leasehold land under Humphrey Colman of Tiverton.
Executrix, his wife Thomasine.
Proved 5th August, 1618.

1618. Phillipe Petor of Rackenford, Husbandman. To son Robert, all his wearing apparel, and to his two children 2/- each. To son John, 2/-, and to John, his son, 2/-. To son-in-law George Vicarye, 1 Bushell of Rye. To wife Johane, 2 plator dishes. To Margaret Pettor, all household stuff. Residue to wife Johan, who is Sole Executrix.
Dated 20th April, 1615.
Witness, John Pettor.
Proved 19th May, 1618.
Sum £9 5s.

1625. Administration to the effects of Mary Tossell, late of Tawstocke, granted to Simon, her son, 22nd June, 1625.
Sum £5 1s. 8d.

1627. Johan Tossell of Brendon, Widow. To the poor there, /12d. To son W^m. Locke, /12d. To son Bartholomew Tossell, /12d. To son Henry Tossell, 5/-. To son Andrew Tossell, 5/-. To daughters Christian "Hurfer," 10/-; Johan Bowden, 10/-; Wilmot Richards, 10/. To grandchildren Richard, George, Johan, Agnes, and Thomsine, children of Richard Bowden; Elizabeth, Richard, Andrew, and Mandlyn, children of David Richards; Wilmot and Ellen, children of Thomas Bowden, small bequests. Residue to son-in-law Richard Bowden, who is Sole Executor.
Witnesses, Bart^w. Mayne, Hugh Sheper, Hugh Brooke.
Proved 13th February, 1627.
Sum £40 13s. 8d.

1639. Administration to the effects of John Tossell of King's-Nympton, granted to Christian, his wife, 11th February, 1639.

Extract from Inventory of Effects of Deceased, made 14th January, 1639.

Item, 3 sylver spoones, 1 sylver boule, and 4 candlesticks, 47/4.

One chattle lease for years on the death of Samuel, John, and George Tossell in a Tenement at King's-Nympton, £35.

Another lease on the lives of son John Tossell, Sara and Cicile Tossell, lands in King's-Nympton, £42.

Specialty, Debts, &c., £1291 2s. 4d.

1639. The last Will of William Hamlyn the elder of Woolfardisworthy, Yeoman, 9th February, 1637.

"John Hamlyn my son to have all my estate in Clifford" (in said Parish) "and the lease thereof, demised and granted by Thomas Prust, of the said Parish, Gentleman, for 99 years on lives of son John and daughter Martha."

He leaves wife Grace, Estate of 9 acres called Trew, determinable on lives of said son John and daughters Elizabeth and Mary. To dau. Thomazine Hamlyn, an annuity of 48/-. To dau. Grace and son William, /4d. each. To aforesaid daughter Martha, £20; at 18 she gives /4d. each to daughter Margaret H. Wilmott, wife of Hugh Braund, and Elizabeth, wife of John How. Residue to wife Grace, who is Sole Executrix.

Overseers, "brothers" Anthony Hamlyn of Hartland, and Richard Bishop of Bradworthy.

Proved 5th March, 1639.

1640. Christian Tossell of "King Nympton," Widow, 13th July, 1640. Bequests for repair of Parish Church, 10/-; to poor, 13/4, and to poor of Romansleigh and of Nymet St. George, 3/4. To godchildren of deceased husband, John Tossell, /12d. To daughters Sara and Cecill, £200 each. To son George, a certain Messuage in Nymet St.

George and £250, with remainder to son John. Mentions daughter Sara's grandmother, "Katherine Furse." To cousin John Bryant, 1 Ewe Sheep. To cousin Andrew Richards 20/-. To kinsman John Hager, Sen*r*., /6d., and to each of his children, /12d. To brothers-in-law Richard and Bartholomew Tossell, 5/-, and to sister-in-law Demos Tossell, 20/-. To god-daughter Johan, dau. of said Bartholomew, 5/-. "*To each of my Cousins, Children of my Brother*" George Furse, /12d. each. To cousin Katherine, daughter of late brother John Furse, one ewe sheep. To cousins Christian and George, children of said brother George Furse, 1 ewe sheep each. To cousin Thomas Tossell of Worlington, 10/-; to god-daughter and cousin Christian Luke, one Ewe Sheep. Her husband is stated to have been Exor. of John Hutchings and of Nicholas and Edmund Molland. Residue to said son John Tossell, who is Sole Exor. Trustees, John Pawle of Great Heale, Gentm., and Nicholas Bulleid of Romansleigh, and George Furse her brother with 3/- each.

Witnesses, Nicholas Bulleid.
John ffures.
Proved 30th Sept., 1640.

NOTE.—Refer to 11th February, 1639.

1640. Extract from Inventory of effects of Deceased made 11th Aug., 1640.

"Item 1 hower glass, 1 Bible & other books, 8/-.

Item 3 silver spoones,* 1 Silver boule & 4 candlesticks, 45/-."
Sum of personalty, £1284 11s.

1641. The last Will of Richard Toker of Great Torrington, "Inkeeper." To the poor of the parish £3. To brother Christopher Toker "one spruce chest & my best cloke," one jug "with a sylver — and a sylver cover." To kinswoman Katherine, daughter of said Christopher Toker, "1 Brasse pan," &c. To Mary, daughter of said Christopher and wife

---

* Refer to Inventory of John Tossell, 11th February, 1639.

of Brute Cole, another brass pan. To Amy, daughter of Brute Cole, a sylver spoone. To kinsman Stephen Tooker, a standing bedstead and "one sylver salte gilte." To Richard, daughter of said "Steven, a sylver spoone." To kinsman Hugh Tucker, sen., a standing bedstead. To Richard, his sone, a middle sized brass crocke. To kinswoman Joan Moysey 40/-. To Mary, wife of Richard Shorte, 40/-. To John Toker my kinsman, Glover, 40/-; Lancellot Lange 5/-; Mabley Toker, widow, 5/-; Peter Toker, "Oackhampton, Cordwainer," 10/- ("my kindsman"). To his brother Roger 5/-. To Marke Lange and his brother, 5/- apiece to each of them. To god-son William, son of William Cornish of Little Torrington, "one sylver plate & one sylver spoone." To brother Wm. Toker, a standing bed. To Samuel, son of said William, two sylver spoones. To servant 10/-.

Residue, "the sealing of my house excepted & the spence in the parlour & hall, which I leave to Wm Cornish," to "my wife Johane," who is Sole Executrix.

Trustees, Arthur Dromant and Wm. Tucker.

Witnesses, George Bray and Richard Swade.

Dated 26th July, 1640. Proved 7th April, 1641.

Sum £71 12s. 10d.

NOTE.—The original of this will was in an excessively decayed condition, and only decipherable with a great deal of care and trouble, when I examined it in 1881. I have, therefore, given a very full abstract for the sake of preserving the names mentioned therein.

1644. Administration to the effects of Hugh Toocker of Bratton Fleming, Granted 16th Oct., 1644, to Robert Collins in the minority of Anthony Toocker, son of deceased.

Sum £33 15s. 8d.

Enclosed with the papers is a scrap, with the following memorandum :—

Edward ye son of Hugh Tooker was baptized ye 16th Aprill, 1631.

Anthony „ „ „ „ 22nd Jany, 1632.
Richard „ „ „ „ 19th July, 1640.

1645. Henry Saunders of Chittlehampton, 13th May, 17th Chas. I., 1642.
To daughter Ann Wollacott, 2nd best pan and one pewter dish. To daughter Johane Ley, 2nd best crocke. Similar bequests and trifling sums of money to daughter Agnes Wollacott; to Henry, son of Symon Wollacott; to Arthur, son of Philip Wollacott; to John Saunder; to Ann, daughter of Symone Wollacott. To Mary, daughter of John Ayre, £5, to be put to the best increase during her minority, with remainder, in case of death, to Elizabeth, dau. of Arthur Saunder, and Ann, dau. of Symone Wollacott.
Mentions land in Estacott, which he holds by assignment from son Arthur.
Residue to wife Mary, who is Sole Executrix.
Overseers, Arthur Saunder and Symone Wollacott.
Proved 10th April, 1645.
Sum £31 3s. 6d.

1669. William Tucker of Clannaburrough in ye Co. of Devon, 18th May, 1668.
To wife "Agnis" £10. To son Thomas £60. To son John £10, a great brasse pot and a chafin dish. To daughters, Phillip, wife of Phillip Sharbrooke, £10, and Agnes, wife of William Wreaford, £10. To John, son of Philip Sharbrooke, £10. To Wm., son of Thomas Tucker, £5. To Mary, daughter of William Wreaford, £5. To all children s children now born, 20/-, "to be bestowed in sheep." To William, son of John Tucker, £5. Residue to sons Robert and William Tucker, who are Joint Exors.
Witnesses, Henry Quicke, Ann and Roger Maunder.
Sum £473 4s.
Proved 2nd Oct., 1669.

1677. The last will of Philpott Bowdon of East Ashford, Widow, 2nd Feby., 17th Charles 2nd. To son James Bowdon 40/-. To James and Marie Bowden, his children, 10/-. She

leaves her leasehold house at Ashford to her daughter Mary Bowden, who is residuary legatee and Sole Executrix.
Witnesses, Edwd. Score and Edwd. Score, jun.
Act missing. Proved 1677.

1681. Administration to the effects of Hugh Rattenbury, late of Winkleigh. Granted to Mary Rattenbury of Monck Okehampton, widow, and to Hugh Rattenbury of the same, wool-comber. 7th May, 1681.
Sum £280 8s.

1690. John Tossell, sen., of King's-Nympton, Yeoman, 18th Oct., 1687. To the poor there 10/-. To children John, George, and Katherine Tossell, 5/- each. To John, son of said George Tossell, one heifer; the same to grandchild Elizb. Thorne. To grandchild Elizb. Bulleid 20/-. To kinsman Walter Tossell and Elizabeth his sister 5/-. To Thomas, their brother, one ewe. Residue to daughter Christian, who is Sole Executrix.

Witnesses, John Treble, Henry Thorne, Mary Speare.

Act of Court missing. In Calendar, as proved May 9th, 1690.

Armorial Seal—An Eagle displayed with 2 necks.

NOTE.—These are the Arms of Worthe of Worth, in Washfield, co. Devon.

1691. The last Will of Thomas Gearing of Bideford, Merchant, 17th Nov., 1690.

£6 to the poor, and legacies to 3 servants. To wife Johan Gearing, £50, and his house in Conduit Lane. To his grandchildren Sarah and Hannah, daughters of son Abraham Gearing. £200 each.

He leaves his estates in Bideford and Woolfardisworthy to his said son Abraham and his heirs male, together with the Residue; he is Sole Exor.

Witnesses, Saml. Denard, Robert Halsworthy, Wm. Kelly, and Christopher Prust.

Proved 3rd Oct., 1691.

1694. Mary "Saunders" of Chittlehampton, Widow, 26th Sept. 169—(obliterated). Mentions her daughter Susan Ley, and granddaughter Mary Ley (under age), grandson Edward Ley (under age), daughter-in-law John (Joan?) Saunders, grandchildren John, Edward, and John (Joan?) Saunders. Residue to son Edward S., who is sole Exor.
Proved June 2nd, 1694.

1698. The last Will of Thomas Melhuish of Morchard Cruse, 18th Jany., 1696.

To wife Joan an annuity of £8, and bedstead and bed in middle chamber, and chest in the parler. The said "parler" to be "at her use" together with the little orchard on the west side of the Moor. To daughter, Katherine Dayment, £20. Bequests to "my five children" Thomas, Fferdinando, Joan Roberts, Mary Brooke, and Katherine Dayment—"one guinea of gold each."

Residue to son John, who is Sole Exor. Trustees, sons Thomas and Ferdinando, and son-in-law, Nehemiah Brooke.

Witnesses, Jno. Sowdon, George Bodley.

Proved 9th July, 1698.

1699. The last Will of Thomas Melhuish of Morchard Cruse, Husbandman, 2nd Dec., 1694. To the poor of the parish 10/-. To sister Katherine Ley 10/-. To sister Alice Genney 10/-. Bequests to Benjamin Budgood jun., and to Joan Mugford. Residue to brother Richard, who is Sole Executor.

Witnesses, John Norrish, John Yeoinge, Grace Yoning, his tenants.

Proved 8th Dec., 1699.

1708. John Saunder the elder, of Chittlehampton, Yeoman, 17th March, 1707. To wife Margaret, a feather bed in the parlour chamber, and a house at Blackwall, a bond of £50, part of her marriage portion, and a cupboard in the house at Eastacote. Daughter Margaret £400 at 21.

Son John Saunder, all rents, remainders, services, tenements, and hereditaments in said parish of Chittlehampton, and also in St. Giles' and Yearnscombe, to him and the heirs of his body lawfully begotten for ever ; said son John has residue and is Sole Exor.

Desires friends Robert Amory of South Molton and Joshua Bawden of the same, to assist Exor.

Witnesses, Geo. Remfry, Edmond Saunder, and Grace Cole.

Proved by Exor. 7th May, 1708.

1715. The last Will of Thomas Melhuish of Cruwys Morchard, 22nd May, 1714. To Jane his wife, " The Bedsteed, &c., in the Middle Chamber and the Chest that hath drawers in it in the Hall Chamber."

To sons, Thomas 10/-, Ffardinando £30, Richard £40 ; to daughters Jane and Dorothy Melhuish £40 each.

To said daughter Jane "my gold ring," and to Dorothy 20/- " to buy her one."

To son John right, &c., in Vincent Dally's Estate in parish of Poughill.

To poor of Cruse Morchard, 10/-.

Residue to son John, who is Sole Exor.

Witnesses, Humphrey Knistone.
    Jane   "
    Jno. Cottihole.

Proved 6th June, 1715.

NOTE.—Testator was eldest son and heir of Thomas Melhuish of Hill in Cruse Morchard ; born 1603, Will proved 1698.—See above. He married, 1647, Jane, daughter of Charles Courtenay of Molland, descended from Sir Philip, second son of Sir Philip Courtenay of Powderham ; hence his issue had descent from Edward I. through Bohun. Arms of Melhuish of Hill, *arg.*, on a bend engrailed *sa*, three fleur-de-lis of the field ; a quarter, *erm.*, charged with a martlet in base and in middle chief point a dagger *az.*, hilted *or*. A Melhuish is said to have pulled the dagger from Prince Edward's arm, A.D. 1271, when the Princess, Eleanor of Castile, sucked the poison from her husband's wound.

1722. The last will of Joshua Tucker of Tawstock, Gentleman, 6th January, 1719. He desires to be buried in High Bickington Church near his father's monument, a stone to be placed over his grave with an inscription showing his age and date of death, and with the single other word "Resurgam." "Whereas I did long since receive about £25 on the brief for Newmarket, which by reason of the death of the person who employed me and to whom I was to pay it, and for several other reasons, although I was always willing to have paid it, is yet in my hands," "I order and desire my Executor to pay the sum of £50 by way of restitution to such person or persons as shall have power to receive it, or else to the Chief Magistrate and Minister there as soon as possible after my death." To the poor of High Bickington £40, the interest to be distributed among them every Christmas Day for ever "by the Rector and Church-Wardens, who I hope will see that it is neither lost or embezzelled." To my "deare sister" Mrs. Worth, "a silver cupp with two handles and a cover, on which cupp my coat of arms is engraven," a five pound guinea of King Charles II., and also a diamond ring, the said ring to revert to her eldest living daughter. To her three daughters £21 each to be spent in plate, if they so please, in remembrance of me. To Major John Worth, my long cane with a silver head in which is my cypher, and a large mourning ring, which was for my late brother Worth, enameled with thigh bones and deaths heads, which I desire him to wear in remembrance of me. To servant, George Miles, £2 2s., and all my linen and woollen apparel, excepting my flowered silk morning gown and cap and six shirts to be chosen by my Executor, if he pleaseth. To the rest of my servants £1 1s. each. Residue to nephew Thomas Worth, Clerk, who is Sole Exor.

Proved May, 1722.

Armorial Seal—" Arg. on a bend engr^d, 3 body hearts."

NOTE.—The Rev. Thomas Worth was son of Henry Worth of Worth, by his second wife, Dorothy Bampfylde of Poltimore. He married Margaret Tucker of High Bickington, 28th Dec., 1674 (Mar. Lic.), and died 1711. He was also Rector of Washfield.

1723. Arthur Saunder, the elder, of Chittlehampton, Yeoman, 22nd May, 1722.

To son John Saunder, and to kinsman William Smale of Chittlehampton, a sum in trust for daughter Elizabeth, wife of James Finney. To children of son Anthony Saunder, Mary, Elizb., John, and Arthur, £100 each, issuant out of lands and out of a quarry and estate called Higher Collacott. Son Anthony to have this property subject to said charge, to revert to his son Anthony, with remainder to latter's younger brothers John and Arthur, and then to sisters Mary and Elizabeth, or to right heirs, etc. He leaves Lower Collacott and New Park, saving the right of John Brayly, to said grandsons Arthur and John. He mentions his grandchildren, Catherine, wife of Charles Nation (formerly Finney), and James Finney. He also bequeaths lands in South Molton to grandson John S. and his heirs. Residue to son Anthony, who is Sole Exor.

Proved 19th April, 1723.

1725. Administration to the effects of Arthur Saunder of Chittlehampton, granted 7th May, 1725, to George Saunder. Agnes Saunder and William Early join the Bond.

1725. Administration to the effects of Anthony "Saunders," of Chittlehampton, granted to Elizabeth, his widow, 4th February, 1725. John "Saunders" of Newton, in said parish, gentleman, and Mary "Saunders" of same, spinster, join in Bond.

1725. The Last Will of Margaret Rolle, daughter of Sir John Rolle of Stevenstone, Knight, 24th Oct., 1725.

She gives to her god-daughter Lucia, daughter of John Rolle, Esqr., 16 broad pieces of old gold. To Barnstaple Charity School £5. To niece Florence, daughter of Sir Bourchier Wrey, Bart., fifty broad pieces of gold to "buy a jewel or other remembrance of her." To nephew Henry Rolle, white cornelian seal. Residue to John Rolle of Stevenstone and

Chichester Wrey, Clerk, Rector of Tawstock, in trust for said niece Florence Rolle. If said Florence die in minority without issue, the family pictures, plate, and china belonging to Testatrix are to be reserved, and the residue of the estate sold and the proceeds spent either in erecting a Charity School, or as Trustees may direct. She desires to be buried privately and at night at Tawstock, in the grave of her brother, Charles Rolle, eight old women to be her bearers, who are to have 5/- each.

Proved 26th Nov., 1725.

1729. The last Will of John Densham of Morchard Bishop, 4th April, 1729.

To daughter Jane Pounsford, 10/6. To Thomas Densham "and his now wife," 5/-. To John Densham "my son" and his now wife, 5/-. To son Robert Densham, 5/-. To daughters Mary James and Sarah Godsland, and to all grandchildren, small bequests.

To son William Densham, Right in Stone Park.

Residue to said William Densham, who is Sole Exor.

Proved 3rd January, 1729.

1731. John Saunder of Newton in Chittlehampton. He mentions his brother Anthony's children, Mary, Elizabeth, John, and Arthur, and his brother Arthur's children, Mary, Anne, and Arthur.

"Cousin" George Saunder, "the fee and inheritance of 3rd part of 'Collacot' to be continued with Newton, and to his son John after him." To cousin James Finney £5, "in trust for his mother." To poor of parish and those of Swimbridge, 20/- each.

Residue to wife Cicely, who is Sole Executrix.

Dated 12th February, 1729.

Proved 7th May, 1731.

Edmond Saunder, a witness.

1734. The last Will of William Tucker of North Molton, Gentleman. To poor there, 20/-. To brother Peter Tucker of Swymbridge, all wearing apparel. To brother Richard Tucker of Chittlehampton, £5. To nephew Peter Tucker of South Molton, glazier, £5. To grandson Lewis Southcombe, Jun., £50. To grandsons George Southcombe £50, and Thomas Southcombe, £5. Residue to granddaughter Elizb., wife of Joshua Hole, the younger, of South-Molton, Apothecary. She is Sole Executrix.
Witnesses, Grace Bryatt
 & Wm. Hill.
Dated 12th April, 1733.
Proved Oct. 16th, 1734.
Armorial Seal—A fess between 3 roses.

1736. William Pollard of Northam, Mariner, 24th February, 1722.

Mentions his mother Joane, and wife Katherine; the latter has residue and is Sole Executrix.

Proved June 4th, 1736.
Crest Seal—A Lion pass. gd.

1741. George Tossell of King's Nympton, Yeoman, 11th Nov., 1741.

To daughter Elizabeth Johnston, leasehold dwelling house orchard, and garden. To granddaughter Mary Tossell Johnston £5 at 21. To son John Tossell 1 guinea in gold. To son George Tossell £130. To brother Walter Tossell 5/-. To son Abraham Tossell, Bidgoods, The Broomfield, and the Broad Meadows, with remainder to son George, charged with a payment of 40/- per annum to Thomas Webber of King's Nympton, Gent^m, and to said son John Tossell, in trust for said daughter Elizabeth Johnston.

Residue to son Abraham, who is Sole Exor.

Witnesses, John Lewis, Susie Bendall, Jeffery Harris.

Proved Dec. 4th, 1741.

1742. John Tossell of King's Nympton, Yeoman, 6th May, 1738.

To sister Miriam Hooper 40/- per annum charged on "Reeds" Estate, during the life of brother Edward Tossell.

To "nephew" Frances Tossell an annuity of £6 to be paid "her" during life of said Edward. Her trustee to be John Bawden the younger of South Molton.

A further annuity of £5 out of "Reeds" to be paid to Elizabeth and Sarah Hooper.

To Elizb. Smith, *alias* Southard, 40/- at 21.

Wearing Apparel and 20/- to John Smith, *alias* Southard.

Residue to said brother Edward, who is Sole Exor.

Witnesses, Thomas and John Lane.

Armorial Seal—"A Griffin Segreant."

Proved February 19th, 1742.

Sum, £73 10s. 10d.

1742. George "Vigures" of Ilfordcombe, Yeoman, 15th Aug., 1741. To son Samuel the fee simple of lands in Little Torrington, charged with payment of £20 to grandson Samuel "Vigers," son of said Samuel, at 21. Bequests to daughters, Thomasine and Agnes Vigers, and Ann Norman, and £2 each to her four children, Thomas, George, John, and Sarah Norman.

Residue to said son Samuel "Viguers," who is Sole Exor

Witnesses, Geo. Sommers, Wm. Vickers, and Abraham Boone.

Proved Jan. 14th, 1742.

1742. Francis Pollard of Clovelly, 23rd Aug., 1728. He mentions his sons Francis and Robert, and his daughter Dorothy Way. His grandsons George, Robert, and Francis Pollard. His granddaughters Mary, Grace, Thomasine, and Dorothy Pollard, and his grandchildren William and Dorothy Way. His son-in-law John Way and his daughters-in-law Dorothy and Margaret Pollard. Residue to wife Thomasine, who is Sole Executrix.

Proved 29th March, 1742.

1743. Thomas Pollard of Northam, 5th March, 1742-3. He leaves his son William 20/-. Residue to his wife Mary, who is Sole Executrix.
Proved 4th Aug., 1743

1743. William Pollard of Clovelly, Mariner. Makes his brother John Pollard, Sen., Mariner, Sole Executor.
Proved May 6th, 1743.

1745. John Tucker of South Molton, Surgeon, 30th March, 1743.

He has assigned "certain particular estates" to Dennis Buckingham, Rector of Charles, and Joshua Bawden of South Molton, Mercer, for the payment of his debts. Residue to his wife Catherine, save 1/- to his father and mother and 1/- to each of his sisters.

Administration granted to Catherine, the widow, 5th April, 1745.

Under £25.

1748. Administration to the Effects of Edward Tossell of King's Nympton, deceased. Granted to Thomas Webber and Francis Clark, in minority of Frances Tossell, his only daughter.
January 13th, 1748.

1752. The last Will of Thomas Melhuish of Morchard Cruwys, 5th July, 1751. He gives to wife Elinor the use of certain rooms in his house at Fork, in said parish—his tea-spoons, tea-pots, coffee service, and whatever else belongs to the garnishing of the tea table. Bequests to daughter-in-law Elinor Sloane and to son-in-law Adam Sloane. " To my trusty friends Mr. Thomas Melhuish of Morchard Cruse, and Mr. Humphry Melhuish of Puddington," £300 in trust for use of " my daughter," Sarah Maunder, and £100 for " my daughter Rebecca Anstey." To daughter Mary Commins " the moiety or halfendale of the overland in Columpton, with remainder to her eldest son. To my 3 grandchildren, George and Mary Maunder and Thomas Melhuish Commins £10 each, and to daughter Joan, wife of John Bragg of Berry Castle, in Woolfardisworthy.

Residue to sons-in-law John Bragg and Thos. Commins, who are Exors.

Witnesses—Wm. Maunder, Richard Manley, Wm. Moxey.

Proved 30th July, 1752.

1753. The last Will of Richard Melhuish of Cruse Morchard, 3rd April, 1726.

To Joan "Crook," daughter, and to Robert "Crooke," grandson, £1 each. To daughter Ann Hewish £20. To daughter Elizabeth Smorth £1. To grandson John Smorth £5 at 21 and £5 to grandson Richard Smorth.

Residue to John and Mary Melhuish, his son and daughter, who are sole Exors.

Witnesses, Wm. Maunder, George Callard, Thomzin Maunder.

Proved May 7th, 1753.

1754. Anthony Saunders of Chumleigh, Wool Coinber, 18th Nov., 1751.

Mentions son William and daughter Mary Lawrence, widow.

Residue to wife Mary Saunders, who is Sole Executrix.

Proved April 29th, 1754.

1754. Administration to the effects of George Tossell of Chulmleigh "Chirurgeon," granted to Elizabeth his widow, April 7th, 1754.

Under £150.

1758. John Tossell of King's Nympton, Yeoman, 14th Nov., 1757. To sons George and Humphrey Tossell £20 each. "My great brass pott and panne and ten pewter dishes to be divided equally between my said Sons." To daughters Mary and Elizabeth £10 each.

1759. Thomas Pollard of Barnstaple, Weaver. With the exception of a legacy to Hannah Hogg, he makes his wife Mary universal legatee and Sole Executrix.
Dated 7th Nov. Proved Nov. 13th, 1759.

1767. Agnes, wife of Richard Tucker, late of Georgeham, but now of Braunton, Gentleman, 16th Nov. 1766.

By power of marriage settlement dated 4th Dec., 1760, she having been therein described as Agnes Peploe of Heanton Punchardon, widow. To husband the said Richard Tucker and to his children, Richard, Susanna, and Mary, she leaves £2 2s. each. To her brother, Richard Heddon of Heanton Punchardon, "warming pan" and £20. To sister Eleanor Incledon, widow, £20. To brother George Heddon "my bureau for life," with remainder to "Cousin" George, son of Sister Eleanor Incledon. Bequest to "niece" Eleanor, wife of Wm. Richmond of Heanton Punchardon, of "Brass crock, pewter dishes, and plates, and brass candlesticks, and a pestle and mortar. Residue to said brother George Heddon and said "Cousin" George Incledon, who are joint Exors.

Witnesses, "Parker" Widlake, Robert Ballyman.
Proved 5th Dec., 1766.
Crest—Seal, "A Wolf's head erased."

1767. John Tossel of King's Ash, otherwise Ashreigny, Surgeon, 15th April, 1766.

He desires to be buried "in a private handsome manner," in late wife's grave in King's-Nympton Churchyard, "in a handsome tomb, another such as now placed on my grandfather's grave," William Ford of "Chiltenholt" (Chiltlehamholt) to make his coffin. Bearers are specified, and are to have a blue or grey coat each. To dear wife Susanna Tossel, a house at King's Ash, and such sums as are hers by marriage settlement, and an annuity of £3 to issue out of land in Winkleigh, Dowland, and Iddesleigh. A further annuity of £5 5s., and a similar sum to daughter-in-law Susanna Foss. To the poor of Burrington 10s. per annum, to issue out of Halisbury in said parish for ever.

To Mary Slader "my mourning ring which I had in remembrance of my late wife, and her Bible." To kinswoman Mary Matthews £2 2s. To Ann, daughter of "my partner" Richard Stucley, £10 10s. To John, son of Thomas Tossel, late of King's-Nympton, £1 1s. a year for five years. To brother-in-law Samuel Johnson £10 p. a. for four years "if he deliver to my brother Abraham Tossel a counterpart of lease of Wood tenem¹ which he lately demised him." To nephew Peter Johnson his choice of fifty of "my medical books" "when he shall have lived abroad two years with an able surgeon and apothecary, also my late brother George's house in Chulmleigh. To said brother Abraham "Puson" in Winkleigh in trust for nephew John Tossel Johnson at 28.

Residue to said brother Abraham Tossel, who is Sole Exor.

He directs his said "grandfather's" tomb and his own to be "enclosed with a handsome pale or palisadoes."

4 sheets of paper.

Proved April 4th, 1767.

Refer to Dec. 4th, 1741, and to April 7th, 1754.

N.B.—" Puson," which is contracted in the will, is probably intended to mean the farm at Winkleigh, known as Punchardon.

With reference to the bequest of 10/- per annum to the poor of Burrington, the Charity Commissioners remark : "Although this gift is void under the Mortmain Act, the Rev. John Tossel Johnson, proprietor of Halisbury Farm, regularly pays the annuity which is bestowed according to Testator's directions."

1772. The last Will of John Saunder of Chittlehampton, 13th Jany., 1772.

Eldest son John Saunder and sons Arthur George and Francis, £10 each.

Daughters, Susanna Harris, Joan Skinner, Mary Brailey, and Grace Holland, £10 each.

Granddaughters, Mary Fewins, a cow, and Ann Holland £10.

Daughter, Ann Burgess £10.

Son Paul Saunder £10 10s.

Residue to wife Grace, who is sole Executrix.

Proved March 6th, 1772.

1784. George Saunder of Chittlehampton, 12th Sept., 1784. To son John "Saunders" £80 at 21. To son William £90 at 21. To daughter Grace £80. To daughter Elizabeth, wife of Giles Skinner, £60. To grandson George Skinner £5 at 21. Residue in equal portions to " my wife " and son George, who are joint Exors.
Proved Dec. 3rd, 1784.

1789. The last Will of Grace Saunders of Chittlehampton, dated 4th Feby., 1788.

She mentions her eldest son John, her son Arthur, and his children, John, Elizabeth, Susan, and Grace. Her son George, deceased, and his children George, John, William, Grace, and Elizabeth, wife of Giles Skinner. Her son Edward and his children John, Francis, Edward, and George. Her son Pawle, his wife Ann, and their children Edward, Ann, Grace, John, Mary, and Betty. Her daughters Susannah Harris, Joan Skinner, Margaret Braily, and Ann Burgess.

Residue to son Francis, who is Sole Exor.
Proved 4th Feby., 1789.

1832. The last Will of John Melhuish of Hill, in Cruwys Morchard, Gentleman, 9th Aug., 1830. To daughter Elizabeth Worthy an annuity of £10 charged on land, and to son George £30, charged on same land ; during the joint lives of said George and of " my son " Thomas Abraham Melhuish.

To nephew Thomas Melhuish of Poughill, Gentm., Jonathan Tanner of Roseash, Gentm., and Thos. Comins of Witheridge, Gentm., the estates known as Eastland and East and West Hill, in trust to pay the rents to the said Thomas Abraham Melhuish for life, with remainder to his children male or female, and with reversion in default thereof to his said son George, with remainder to his grandson John, son of the said George for ever. In pursuance of the power given him by his late father Thomas Melhuish, Gentleman, of Poughill, he further leaves to the said George Melhuish, Rowcliffe, Vulscombe, Sullacks, Hettyland and Hittyland, Burridges, Thorn-hayes, and Thorndown, the moiety of the manor of Yedbury, the tything house and a high rent of 4s. 4d. per annum out of Hickeridge's tenement, together with Edbury Mill, all in Cruse Morchard, for ever. To his said grandson John he gives the Silver Jug with initials engraved thereon. To Mary Maunder, his housekeeper, £20 per annum as long as she remains unmarried, charged upon Eastland and East and West Hill. Residue to said Son George, who is Sole Exor.

By Codicil, 17th Nov., 1830, he revokes the bequest to Mary Maunder, since he has now provided for her by deed.

Witnesses to Will and Codicil—
  Thomas Maunder.
  Thomas   ,,   Jun.

Proved by George Hewish Melhuish, the Exor., 16th June, 1832.

NOTE.—After the death of Rev. Thomas Abraham Melhuish, who died unmarried, 1849, George Melhuish and his son John sold the whole property. Testator had an elder son, John, Captain R.N., predeceased him, unmarried, and another daughter, Mary, wife of Wm. Ford. Elizabeth was Editor's Grandmother. Testator was great-grandson of Thomas Melhuish, see page 69.

1840. The last Will of Elizabeth Richards, widow, of Ilfracombe, Devon.

She gives all her furniture and all stores in the house and money that may remain when all expenses are paid, to the children of the late James Richards of Brighton, and her Plate to the Rev. Thomas Miller Richards and William James Richards, whom she makes her Executors.

Witnesses, Thomas Capel and Jane Capel, his wife, 2 Novr., 1839.

A memorandum enclosed gives her gold watch to her niece Mary Gibbs, and her pearl ornaments, earrings, etc., to the said Mary and her sister Frances between them. To her niece Agnes Richards all her cloathes. To Mrs. Samuel Richards "I give my dear husband's picture, box of pearl fish and counters, and diamond ring on blue." To Miss Balderstone my painted work-table. To Mrs. Capel the cups and saucers on the parlour chimney piece. To Mrs. Alder my hoop rings, pearl, &c., by her desire. I give £5 to Ann Dunn if she is living with me at my death.

ARCHDEACONRY OF TOTNES.

1600. Administration to the effects of Johanne Peeter, late of Wembury, intestate. Granted to John Kember and Elizabeth his wife, sister of the said deceased, 13th Sept., 1600. Under £10.
The endorsement gives the names of other brothers and sisters.
"Ita quod daret Simoni Willielmo et Wilielmo suis fratribus, et Blanche et Katherine ejus sororibus."

1602. The last Will of Mary Arundell of Trerise, in the Co. of Cornwall, Gentlewoman, dated 1st Dec., 1602. To sister "Mrs. Grace Dinham 3 smockes, 3 ruffe bands, 2 goundes, 2 waistcoth, 2 petticotes, 1 cloake and hoode of cloathe, 1 saffgard and all things that are heare, and 2 frenche hoodes of vellett performed." To nephew "John Arundell of Trerise, 1 featherbed performed withe pillyows and courtyans and vallans of silke and 1 long cushion of Tynsell, 2 short cushions, and 1 longe cushion of armes of myne workinge." To God-daughter, Ebbot Grenvile, "my best gounde of tuffe taffeta whiche I never wore." To niece Mrs. Mary Dennis an (1) laze of pearle and gould. "To my mann George Sercombe £10, two boxes of books and all other things and bookes remaining in my great truncke at Penheale, 2 wrought cushions excepted." "More to my man George Sercombe £4 of lawful money owed for wages. To the maid servants in Sister Dinhame's house 2/6 each. Residue to niece Julyan Keckwiche who is Sole Executrix."
Witnesses—Nicholas and Grace Dinham, George Seccombe.
"Memorandum that 1 cheane of gold being at Wortham, at

the time of the signing and sealing hereof, 2 days afterwards, Mrs. Mary Arundell did say that the said Mrs. Julyan Kekewiche should have the saide cheane."
Proved 3rd Dec. 1602.
Endorsed—" Nuper de Lifton."
Sum £37 19s. 4d.

1609. The last Will of John Elford of Meavy. Dated 26th March, 1608. Mentions mother Elenor Elford, brother Wm. Elford, sisters Margaret and Thamsin Elford, Richard Elford, and Peter Francklinge.
Residue to Brother John Elford, who is Sole Exor.
Proved 17th Feb., 1609.

1611. John Wreaford the elder, of Hennock, 12th June, 9th James. To poor of Hannock, 2/0. To daughter Elizabeth, wife of Wm. Strange, £4. To son John Wreaford, £6. To daughter Joane W., £16. To son Stephen, £3 10s. To Robert, son of said Stephen, 10s. To Thomsine, dau. of said Stephen, 1 yeo lamb, and to Mary her sister the same. John, son of Wm. Strange, 10s., and to William, Dorothy, and Elizabeth Strange, a sheep each. To servants Eliza Wreaford and Joane Denford, a yeo sheep and lamb.
Residue to son George Wreaford, who is Sole Exor.
Proved 9th July, 1611.
Sum £98 14s. 4d.

1614. The last Will of William Wreyford, 20th Dec., 12th James. Legacies to poor of Hennock and Teigngrace, Newton Bushill and Newton Abbot. To son James, Bradleigh, in the parish of South Bovey, to him and his heirs for ever. He gives a meadow in Bovey to wife Eleanor, and daughters Christian and Rose. Residue to said wife Eleanor, who is Sole Executrix.
Proved 11th Feb., 1614.
Sum £267 3s. 4d.

1617. The Will of Arthur Cundye of Bridgerule and Co. Cornwall, was proved at Okehampton, 24th May, 1611.

1625. John Wreford of Moreton, Weaver, 17th June, 1625. He gives to eldest daughter, Richard Croote, £6 13s. 4d. To Wilmot Savage, second daughter, 23/4. To servant, Alice Croote, bequest.
Residue to son John, who is Sole Exor.
Proved 30th July, 1625.
Sum £67 13s. 8d.

1626. John Wreford of Hennock, yeoman, 24th Dec., 1624. To poor of Hennock ———. To Richard Cornish, 20s. To Joane wife of Wm. Harris, 10s. To George Wreaford, 10s. To Elizabeth Strange, 9s. Small sums to John, William, Dorothy and Elizabeth Strange, John and Wm. Cornish junr., and John Cornish's two daughters. To Stephen Wreaford my best doublett. To John and Michael W. a yeo sheep each. To Elizabeth, daughter of John Wreaford, late deceased, 1 yeo sheep. To John W. best jerkin and second best breeches, and 5s. To Elling, wife of Wm. Kine, 5s. To Joan Kynes, "my servant," 20s.
Residue to son John, who is Sole Exor.
Proved 1st April, 1626.

1626. The last Will of John Sanger of Buckfastleigh. To the poor of "Lower Town," 3s. 4d. To Peter Petsvene, 4 yards of New Cloth and the sum of 10s. To Weltym Tolyard, 10s. at marriage. To wife Nycole "my close of land," with remainder to Maryne Sanger, my daughter.
Residue to said wife and daughter, who are Joint Exors.
Witnesses—Nycholas Wolacot, Andrew Feseye.
Overseers—Thomas Collard and Daniell Fox.
Dated 23rd May.
Proved 8th Dec., 1626.

NOTE—"Tolyard" is equivalent to Tolchard, still a local name. "Feseye" is the same as Vesey.

1626. Inventory of Richard Sangwill made of Plympton St. Mary, deceased 24th Feb. 1626.

Sum £5 10s. 10d.

NOTE—The wrapper of this document is endorsed "John Sangell, late of Holbeton, intestate, granted to Beatrice his wife, 14th Feb., 1627.
It encloses a second Inventory to the amount of £14 12s. 6d.

1634. The last Will of Thomas, son of John Wreyford of Tamerton ffolyett (Foliot) Batchelor. Mentions brother John Wreyford, sister Elizabeth Edwards, and her sons Nicholas and John Edwards; Elizabeth, daughter of Wm. Gaye. Interest in land at Egg Buckland, to brother Wm. Wreyford.

Residue to sister Joane Wreyford, who is Sole Executrix.

Dated 20th July.

Proved 23rd Oct., 1634.

1637. Alice Wreyford of Moreton Hampstead, Widow, 10th March, 1636. Bequests to son Richard, daughters Wilmot, Anne, Alice, wife of Ciperian Wreyford, Jane (daughter of son John Wreyford). To Wm. Ellicomb, son of dau. Wilmot. To Mary Brocke, daughter of daughter Elizabeth. To Judith Brocke, daughter of daughter Anne. To servant Wilmote Wreyford. "To all my children's children 15d. each."

Residue to son John, who is Sole Exor.

Proved 28th April, 1637.

1640. Administration to the effects, &c., of Elizabeth Thuell of South Brent, granted 12th Feb., 1640. To John Thuell of South Brent, Husbandman. Edward Searle of Exeter, Gentleman, joins the Bond.

NOTE—She was daughter of John Gould, Esq., of Coombe, in Staverton, by his wife Alice, daughter of John Trehawkes, and married John Thuell of Brent.

1660. Matthew Tucker of Hardness (Dartmouth), in the Co. of Devon, Marryner. To poor of Hardness, 20s. He bequeathes to William Bragg of Dartmouth, " Marryner," all his clothes excepting his " searge cloake," and he also gives him the north and south parts, and his Tenement in South Town, Dartmouth, after the death of his Executrix. To Johane, wife of said Wm. Bragg, certain furniture, and to the children of said Wm. Bragg, 20s. each.

To Maryan, wife of Nicholas Risdon of Dartmouth, one cupboard, and to each of her children 20s. each.

Residue to "Ambris" his wife, who is Sole Executrix.
Dated 17th July, 1649. Proved 30th Nov., 1660.
See 22nd Aug., 1663. *post*.

1662. George Rowe of Lamerton, Husbandman, 3rd April, 1662. He gives his father, Robert Rowe, his interest in the lease of Widdeslade, in said parish. Brother Nicholas, best cloak, best coat, and best breeches, and to the children of said brother, and of brother Richard, 1 sheep apiece. Bequests to sisters Elizabeth and "Jonas." Mentions his grandfather, John Colling. Brother Francis, 6d. Servant Margaret Cudlipe, 6d.

Residue to wife Mary, who is Sole Executrix.
Proved 4th June, 1662.
Witnesses—John Rowell, Tristram ffarris.

NOTE—See my " Devonshire Parishes," Vol. I., pp. 207-8.

1663. Administration to the effects of John Hamlin of Withecombe. Granted to Maria his widow. John Hamlin of the same, Husbandman, joins the Bond. Granted 12th Dec., 1663.

NOTE—Inventory made by James and Thomas Hamlyn of Lake.

1663. Administration to the effects of Ambrose Tucker, late of Townstall, in the Parish of Dartmouth, widow. To Joanna Atkins, her cousin and next-of-kin. Granted 22nd Aug., 1663.

1663. Administration to the effects of Ambrose Tucker, late of Dartmouth. Granted to Philip Square of South Huish, Clothier, the nephew. Granted 11th Dec., 1663.

1665. Administration to the effects of Noah Wreford of Moreton. Granted to George Wills, in minority of Elizabeth Wreford, daughter and Executrix.
20th Sept., 1665.

1667. Robert Hamlyn of Chittleford, in the Parish of Withecombe, Yeoman, 4th Dec., 1667. To daughter Florence, Tenement called Venton, for 99 years, on life of John, son of brother William. Term to commence *p.m.* of Robert Hamlyn of Venton, and John Jerman. Also "Lower Dunstone" for 99 years, on lives of Peter, son of Walter Hamlyn and Johane, daughter of said Walter—*p.m.* of Richard, son of Edwd. Hamlyn—under the ancient yearly rent of 46s. 8d for Venton, and 30s. for Dunston. To brother's son, Hugh Hamlyn, the quarter part of Higher North Dunstone for life, upon determination of the estate therein of Wm. and Phillip Hamlyn.

To Sidrack Jerman, jun., and his assigns, the moiety of Blackslade, after determination of estate therein of Mary Hodge and Philip Hamlyn.

To said daughter Florence, and to her heirs, his fee simple lands in Chittleford, Scobtor, and Okehampton. To Susan Hamlyn, 40s., and to her brother Edward Hamlyn, 20s.

To the children of brother Wm. Hamlyn, 12d. each, "and to his 3 grandchildren, 12d." To Robert, son of Richard Hamlyn, 2s. To apprentice, Richard Hamlyn, 12d. To wife Johane, certain specified furniture at Chittleford. To poor of Widecombe, 3s. 4d. for bread.

Residue to sd. daughter Florence, who is sole Executrix.
Proved 1st Jany., 1667.
Sum £200 4s. 10d.

1667. Admon. to effects of Richard Tooker of Modbury. Granted 25th April, 1667, to Susanna his widow.
Extract from Inventory of Richard Tooker:—

"60 sheep & 28 lambs	£22 10	0
"8 labour nags & mares	21 6	8
"Item 60 bushels of corne ready thrashed	11 0	0
"Corne in barn & mowe	21 16	0
"·And in ground	55 10	0
"One ffowling piece & one sword	0 15	11
"Total sum ...	£185 7	2"

1668. Cyprian Wreyford of Moreton, Weaver, 6th June, 1649.

Bequests to sons Abraham and Isaack. To daughters Rebecca, Alice, Mary, and to daughter-in-law Elizb. Heaward. Residue to son Noah, who is Sole Executor.

Administration granted to Marke and Elizabeth Manne of Abbot's Kerswell, 3rd April, 1668.

1670. William Wrayford of Bovey Tracy, Yeoman, 12th Nov., 22nd Chas. II. To son James, my tenement called Bradley, in said parish, to him and his heirs for ever, charged with £40 each to son William and daughter Mary Wrayford. "To Peter son of John Gray my brother-in-law 5/-" To Johan, daughter of brother-in-law Wm. Cater, 5s., and to William, son of brother-in-law Philip Solomon, 5s.

Residue to wife Ellen, who is Sole Executrix.
Proved 6th March, 1670.
Sum £54 0s. 2d.

1672. Julyan Gould of Staverton, Widow, 15th March, 1668.

To poor of Staverton, 40s. To son Henry, £40. To Mary wife of Richard Savery of Ollacombe in Rattery, Gentm., £40, "& the halfendale of all my chest of lynnen, and one gold ring with fower gems." To god-daughter Julyan Row, 40s. ; and to her eight brothers and sisters, 20s. each. To her son John Row, 40s., and to his two brothers and one sister 10s. each.

"To my daughter Julyan Abraham's there daughters 20/- each. 20/- each to Katherine Gould & her three sisters & to Edward Gould & John Gould his brother. To Gt. Granddaughter Elizabeth daughter of Julyan Courtill."

Residue to said daughter Julyan Abraham, who is Sole Executrix.

Proved 14th June, 1672.

Sum £150 13s. 4d.

NOTE—She was widow of Edward Gould of Coombe in Staverton, and is mentioned in the Herald's Visitation of 1620, as daughter and co-heir of Zachary Irish of Chudleigh.

1674. Richard Hamlinge of Withecombe in the Moor, Yeoman, 2nd July, 1667.

Legacies to son Richard and to Richard son of said Richard. The latter then under 14. To dau. Ann Gould. To son-in-law Andrew Downinge. To son Walter H.

Residue to Peter, son of Walter Hamlinge, who is Sole Exor.

Proved 8th Oct., 1674.

Sum £94 8s. 4d.

NOTE—Richard Hamlinge made the inventory.

1675. Nuncupative Will of Mary Tucker of Tavistock, Jany. 4th, 1675. She makes her cousin, Richard Tucker, universal Legatee and Sole Executor.

Proved 19th Jany., 1675.

Sum £3 11s. 10d.

1674. Robert Rowe of Lamerton, 27th Feby., 1673.
Small bequests, viz., 1s. to son Nicholas, 5s. to son Richard, 1s. to daughter Jonne Fursman, 1s. to all grandchildren.
Residue to daughter Elizabeth, who is Sole Executrix.
Witnesses—Thomas Burnaford, Julian Burnaford, John ffarris.
Proved 2nd Dec., 1674.
Sum £47 14s. 10d.

NOTE—Nicholas Rowe the Poet was of the Lamerton family, being son of John Rowe, Sergt.-at-law, died, 1692. See my "Devonshire Parishes," Vol. I., pp. 204-207.

1675. Peter Hamling of Withecombe-in-the-Moor, Yeoman, 6th Dec., 1674.
Legacies to brother-in-law John Jerman. To sister Barbary Jerman, and to Walter and John, sons of John Jerman.
To Cousin Francis Hambling, "my fowling-piece and pistol."
Legacies to "Cosins" Mary and Richard Hamling.
Poor of Parish, 20s.
Residue to sisters Mary and Margaret Hamling, who are Joint Exors.
Witnesses—Richard Hamling and others.
Proved 7th May, 1675.

NOTE—Admon. Bond attached to Will, which was proved by Richard Hamlyn (Uncle of the Executrices Mary and Margaret, in their minority), and by Richard Tupper of Widecombe.

1675. The last Will of Samuel Wrayford, the son of Thomas Wrayford of Moreton, Tailor, 29th June, 1675. To brother Jonathan, all interest in a close of land called Furspark in the Parish of Totnes. Charged with an annuity of 20s. to Aunt Elizabeth Torroway. To Aunt Modistis Browne, 20s. per annum. To Jonathan and George, sons of brother Thomas, 5s. each. To sister-in-law Anne Stone, 2s. 6d.
Residue to said father, Thomas Wrayford, who is Sole Exor.
Sum £14.
Proved 28th July, 1675.

1678. Christopher Hamlyn of Withecombe in the Moor, Yeoman. To Nicholas, son of John Mory, £20. To brother James' children, Katherine and Susan, 20s. each. To Isot, dau. of Edward Woodley, 20s To Joane Berry, dau. of brother John Hamlyn, 20s. To Thomas Hamlyn's children, James, Thomas, and Joane, 20s. each. To Christopher, son of Christopher Hamlyn, 20s. To John, son of Richard Hamlyn, 20s. To John Sherwill's children, William, George, Mary, and Agnes, 20s. each. To Thomas, Edward, Mary, Joane, and Agnes, children of Nicholas Furse, 20s. each. To Edward, Richard, John, Joan, Rabbidge, and Honour, children of Elizabeth Arnell, 20s. each. To Mary and Francis, children of Walter Coulton, 10s. each. Out of tenement called Rowbrooke to brother John Hamlyn, an annuity of £3 during the life of wife Agnes, and Mary wife of John Mory. To poor of Holne, 20s. Lower Hannaford to wife Agnes for life, with remainder to Thomas, son of brother Thomas Hamlyn.

Residue to wife Agnes, who is Sole Executrix.

Witnesses—Thomas Hamlyn, with others.

Dated 15th Feby., 1677.

Proved 8th June, 1678.

Sum £178 10s. 9d.

1681. James Hamlyn the elder, of Withecombe-in-the-Moor, Yeoman, 6th Mar., 1679. To poor of the parish, 5s. Certain furniture, to wife Alice. Mentions daughters Katherine Woodley and her children, Isott and Susannah Woodley, daughter Susannah Townsend, and grandchildren James and Richard Townsend.

To brother John Hamlyn, 10s. To God-daughter Rose Hamlyn, 2s.

Residue to daughter Alice Hamlyn, who is sole Executrix.

Witnesses—John Hamlyn, Agnes Hamlyn junr., Susanna Hamlyn.

Proved 25th April, 1681.

Sum £107 17s. 8d.

1682. William Hamlyn of Withecombe in the Moor. To wife Elizabeth, household furniture. To Daughter Joane, £30. To dau. Mary, wife of Peter Mann, £5. To Peter Mann's children Mary, Elizabeth, Sibella, and Silvester, 20s. each. To Elizabeth, daughter of Ellis Thomas, £5. To Elizabeth, daughter of son John Hamlyn, 20s. To daughter Hannah, "one bed performed."

Residue to son Hugh Hamlyn, who is Sole Exor.

Dated 19th May, 1680.

Proved 20th Jany., 1682-3.

1682. Agnes Tucker of Dartington, in the Co. of Devon, Widow. Legacies to sons William and Samuel, and to daughter Mary, wife of Thomas Adams. To grandson, Thomas Edwards, £3. To grandchildren, son and dau. of Wm. Tucker, 5s. each. To Samuel and John, sons of son Saml., 5s. To granddaughter Mary Tucker, 40s.

Residue to son Thomas, who is Sole Exor.

Witnesses—Edwd. Chastor, Hy. Adams, Hy. Netherton.

Proved 7th Feby., 1682.

1685. Administration to the effects of John Row of Lamerton, in the Co. of Devon, granted to Nicholas Row his father, of the said parish of Lamerton, Gentleman, 15th July, 1685.

NOTE—See *ante*, 2nd Dec., 1674, and 4th June, 1662.

1689. The account of Elias Newcomen, Administrator of the goods, &c., of Thomas Trenhale, late of Kingsweare in the County of Devon, deceased. Delivered 12th Dec., 1689.

Signed, "Elias Newcomen."

NOTE—This was the father of the Inventor of the Stationary Steam Engine, and the grandson of the Revd. Elias Newcomen, Rector of Stoke Fleming, 3rd son of Charles, 2nd son of Brian Newcomen of Saltfleetby, Co. Lincoln. One of the oldest families in that county. See my "Devonshire Parishes," vol. I., pp. 372 *et seq.*

1691. Administration to the effects of John Singer of Plymouth. Granted 10th March, 1691, to Elizabeth Holman of the same, Principal Creditor.

Enclosed is the following Affidavit—

"These are to certify that John Singer of Virginia made a nuncupative Will, & gave & bequeathed all his goods & chattels unto his mother-in-law, Elizabeth Holman, upon the consideration of a daylie support he received from her, the truth of which we doe hereby attest & have sett our hands to the same, all belonging to their Majesty's ship Portsmouth now in Plymouth. 15th Dec., 1691.

"Under £50.

"John Jones, Wm. Wilson, Walter Hockin."

1691. The last Will of Thomas Hamlyn of Ash in the parish of Widecombe in the Moor, Yeoman. To wife Elizabeth, £10, and the Great Bible, the Chest in the Hall Chamber, and an annuity of £5, to issue out of Lightor.

To son Thomas Hamlyn, £10, and an annuity of £5 out of Lightor. To grandchildren, sons and daughters of son James, 40s. each. To seven grandchildren, children of Edward Gifford, 40s. each. To the two children of son Thomas, 40s. each. To the four children of John Hamlyn of Lake, husband of daughter Johane, 40s. each.

Residue lands and goods, &c., to son James Hamlyn, who is Sole Exor.

Dated 16th Jany., 1690. Proved 1st July, 1691.

Sum £237 0s. 4d.

1695. Elizabeth Hamline of Withecombe-in-the-Moor, widow. To son James, 1s. To son Thomas, the Great Bible. To daughter Joane Hamline, 1s., and "half my wearing apparel." "The other half" to daughter-in-law Mary Jefford. To Phillip ffole of North Bovey, widow, 10s.

Residue to son Edward Jefford, who is Sole Exor.

Dated 18th Feby., 1692. Proved 25th July, 1695.

Sum £5 5s. 10d.

1696. Administration to the effects of Thomas Mortimore of Slapton, granted to Rebecca Mortimore, his sister, 11th June, 1696.

1699. Walter Blatchford of Highampton, Yeoman, 23rd April, 1694. Grandson Richard Blatchford, £11 10s. at 16. To brother John Blatchford's children, 10s., that is to say, 5s. to Godson Walter B., and 1s. to the other five children.

To son Robt. Blatchford, leasehold tenement called Stendon, for life, with remdr. to grandson John Blatchford, charged with an annuity of £6 to Thomasin, mother of the said John. To wife "Rachwell," two leasehold tenements called Oadham and Whitacre, with remainder to said son Robert ; who is to put in grandson Walter's life on said tenement. To said grandson Walter B., £50.

Residue to said son Robert, who is Sole Exor.
Witnesses—Thomas and Margt. Stafford and Mary Ffleming.
Proved by Exor. at Hatherleigh, 5th March, 1699.
Sum £255 10s.

1702. Administration to the effects of Jacob Singnar, alias Cisard, of Plymouth, of the Royal Ship "Pembroke." Granted 30th May, 1702, to Maria Bandram his cousin.

1706. John Hamlyn of Widecombe, Yeoman. His leasehold house in Ashburton, courtlage and herb garden (determinable upon the lives of John and Elizb. Cane), to daughter Mary Hamlyn.

To daughters Elizabeth and Susan H., £20. To brother Hugh Hamlyn, the lands in Blackslade : and all head rents to him and his heirs for ever.

To Hugh Hamlyn's children, 12d. apiece. To Sibly, daughter of Silvester Mann, 1s.

Residue to " Joane my wife," who is Sole Executrix.
Dated 29th Aug., 1705.
Proved April, 1706.
Sum £117 0s. 2d.

1707. Administration to the effects of Isaac Tucker of Plymouth. Granted to Sara his sister, wife of John Holditch 5th Nov., 1707.

1719. William Hamlyn of Widecombe-in-the-Moor, Yeoman To the poor, 5s. To daughter Elizabeth Hamlyn, £30, at 21. Mentions Richard Hext "my kinsman" of Hannaford.

Residue of estate in Blackdon Pipard in Widecombe to said daughter Elizabeth after death of Robert Hamlyn, my father, and Elizabeth, my wife. To brother-in-law John Saunders, 1s. To sister Katherine Saunders, 20s. To brother-in-law Saml. Eales, 1s. To brother in-law James Luckham, 1s. To sister-in-law Mary Caunter, 1s. Apprentice Humphry Passmore, 10s. To apprentice Sibil Hamlyn, 5s.

Residue to wife Elizabeth, who is Sole Executrix.

Dated 28th Feby., 1718-19.

Proved 8th July, 1719.

1719. Administration to the estate of James Hamlyn of Withecombe, granted to his father, James Hamlyn, and to Robert Mann, in the minority of James and Thomas Hamlyn, children of said deceased.

There is a memo. which shows that a "Caveat against admon." had been lodged by the two administrators who afterwards agreed.

Admon. granted May 23rd, 1719.

1719. Administration to the effects of Robert Tucker, late of Blackawton, deceased. Granted to Agnes his relict. John Tucker of Blackawton joins the bond.

16th Jany., 1719.

1719. John Hamlyn of Lake in the parish of Widecombe in the Moor, Yeoman. To wife Joane Hamlyn, £10. To son Richard H. all right in Higher Ash in said parish. Bequest to Elizabeth, wife of Thomas Hamlyn, and to her four children.

To daughter Mary Hamlyn, £70, and a similar sum to daughter Joane Hamlyn at 21.

To son James Hamlyn at 21, Corndon in said parish, and in the Manor of Spitchwick for ever. With remainder to said son Richard Hamlyn. Mentions Mary, wife of John Leyman of "Bonehill," Mary Puttercombe, Sara and John Stanckombe.

Residue to said son Richard, who is Sole Executor.

Witnesses—Joane Gefford, Jane Hamlyn.

Dated 11th July.

Proved 31st Aug., 1719.

1719. Richard Hamlyn of Lake in the parish of Widecombe, Yeoman, 22nd Dec., 1719. To brother James H., 3 fields in Higher Hannaford. To poor of Widecombe 10/-. To mother Joane Hamlyn £5, with an additional sum of £10, "formerly given by my father John Hamlyn to my mother." To kinsman John Emmett 20/-. To sister Elizabeth, now wife of Thomas Hamlyn of Ash £5. Residue, remainder of term in Higher Ash and tenement in "Hier" Hannaford to three sisters, Mary, Johane, and Dunes Hamlyn.

Witnesses, James Hamlyn.
         Thomas „

Proved 13th Feby., 1719.

Sum £339 6s. 9d.

NOTE.—Refer to Will of John Hamlyn of Lake, 31st Aug., 1719, *ante*.

1725. Joan Hamlyn of Widecombe, widow. To poor there 20/-. To youngest daughter, Dunes Hamlyn, £15. To daughter Elizabeth, wife of Thos. Hamlyn, "my best gowne." To other two daughters, Mary and Joan, 1/- each. To all my seven grandchildren 5/- each.

Residue to son James, who is Sole Executor.

Dated 11th Oct., 1723. Proved 30th June, 1725.

Sum £44 15s. 4d.

1725. James Hamlyn of Widecombe-in-the-Moor, Yeoman. To son Thomas H. 1/-. To daughter Anne, wife of Richard Peny, 1/-. To daughter Mary, late wife of Henry Caunter deceased, 1/-. To Elizabeth, wife of Thomas Grigg, 1/-.
Residue to "my wife," who is Sole Executrix.
The "Act of Court" proves that his wife was called "Mary."
Dated 8th Feby., 1724. Proved 6th Nov., 1725.
Sum £18 3s. 10d.

1727. Administration to the Effects of Maria Tucker of Hatherleigh Granted to William Tucker, her husband. Feby. 19th, 1727. John Tucker joins in the bond.

1729. Hugh Hamlyn of Widecombe, Yeoman. To wife Joane, Scobbator, in said parish, for life, with remainder to son William, and to the latter "all my lands in the Manor of Dunstone for ever."
To son Hugh, "my right in Blackslade, which Anne Brewsey now possesses," with reversion to son Edward H. To son John £12. To three daughters, Hannah, Jane, and Susanna, £7 each. To daughter Joane, wife of Robert Hamlyn, £3 3s. To daughter Elizabeth, wife of John Tarr, £2 2s. To my two grandchildren, daus. of John Tarr, 5/- each.
Residue to wife Joane, who is Sole Executrix.
Dated 20th Feby., 1728. Proved at Newton Abbot, 21st May, 1729.

1736. William Hamlyn of Widecombe-in-the-Moor, Yeoman. To wife Katherine his goods, in trust to provide for all his children.
He recites that his late father, Hugh Hamlyn of Widecombe, bequeathed him all his lands in the Manor of Dunstone, to him and his heirs, and he leaves the said Manor to the child now conceived by his wife if it be a man child, but if not,

then Dunstone is to be divided amongst all his daughters, with reversion to brother Hugh Hamlyn.
Overseers : Peter Hamlyn and Sylvester Mann.
Witnesses: Edward Hamlyn, with others.
Dated 16th Oct. Proved 1st Nov., 1736.

1736. Jane Tooker of Milton Abbot, "*Spinster.*" To her daughter Elizb. Trais 1/-. To daughter Mary Tooker 1/-. Residue to son John Tooker, who is Sole Exor. John Ward Exor. in Trust during minority.
Witnesses : Pierce Edgcumbe, Daniel Ward.
Dated 5th Feby., 1735. Proved 9th Feby., 1736.

1740. Administration to the Effects of Charles Blachford of Totnes, late H.M.S. "Burford." Granted to Elizabeth, wife of Azarias Cundett, sister of deceased.
31st Jany., 1740.

1742. Administration to the effects of John Blachford of Totnes. Granted to Christian Blachford of the same, widow, 4th Dec., 1742. John Clift of the same, cooper, and Richard Coll, carpenter, join the bond.
Sum £83 14s.

1746. Will of Richard Heath of Stoke-Damerell, late H.M.S. "Woolwich." Dated 23rd June, 1739. Probate obtained by Ann Cleverton, formerly Heath, relict of said Testator and now wife of John Cleverton, 12th Feby., 1746.
Monition to remove to P. C., Canterbury, 6th Nov., 1751

1750. Thomas Blatchford of Plymouth, 3rd April, 1750. To friend John Cooban of Plymouth, surgeon, freehold dwelling house in Plymouth in trust for son Wm. Blatchford

at 21. Charged with payment of £20 to son Thomas Blatchford at 21. To wife Thomasine use of said house during minority of the said two children.
Witnesses: Elizb. Murch, John Commin, Richard Sandford.
Proved 14th Feby., 1750.

1751. Administration of the effects of John Hamlyn late of Widecombe-in-the-Moor, deceased. Granted to his brother Richard Hamlyn of Widecombe, and to Thomas Hamlyn of Tor Bryan, Thomas Hamlyn the father of deceased having renounced. Granted 29th June, 1751.

1752. John Tucker of Halwell in the Co. of Devon, Husbandman. "I due heare give to my wife Ellenor all my goods & chattels & the tenement called Horseville for life, & after her death to my granddaughter Mary Penny, who is to take care of her grandmother for the rest of her life & to have the said house for the rem^{dr} of ye lease."

To sister Avice a brass crocke. To granddaughter Mary Paige "my deepe bottomed brasse panne which was my mother's." To granddaughter Ann Paige a pewter dish marked J. J. T. To granddaughter Sarah Paige a "Puter dish marked T. H."

Witnesses: Samuel and Joan Wakeham.
Dated June 29th, 1746. Proved 3rd Feby., 1752.

1754. Walter Mortimer of North Bovey, Yeoman. To wife Joan, the best bed, "and one thing of a sort necessary for a single woman to have the use of, for life."

Bequests to eldest son George, to daughter Agnes, wife of John Boone, and to their children, Joan, Mary, Benjamin, Elizabeth, and Susanna Boone. To daughter Mary Mortimer £10, and to son-in-law Richard Honniwill 2/6.

Residue to sons Walter and Nicholas Mortimoor, who are Joint Exors.

Witnesses: John Willcocke, John Tallamy, George Underhay.
Proved 8th May, 1754.

1763. Administration to the effects of Hugh Hamlyn of Widecombe-in-the-Moor, deceased, intestate. Granted to Mary, his widow, 24th March, 1763.

1771. Thomas Hamlyn of Hannaford, in the parish of Widecombe-in-the-Moor. To daughter Elizabeth Smerdon, £5. To grandson John Bedlake, and to granddaughter, Charity Bedlake, £5. To granddaughter Mary, daughter of Richard Cocke, £5. Residue to grandson, Thomas Hamlyn Sherwill, Sole Exor., son of John Sherwill. Overseers during minority, son-in-law George Sherwill, and grandson Richard Burnell.
Dated 3rd July, 1766. Proved 9th March, 1771.
Sum £74 12s. 6d.

1772. Peter Hamlyn of Widecombe-in-the-Moor, Yeoman. To sons Richard, £3, George, 20/-; and Bequests to sons Thomas and Hugh, and to daughter Mary, wife of Wm. Nosworthy. To daughter Ruth Hamlyn, £10. To grandson Peter, son of son Francis Hamlyn, 10/-.

To each of daughter Joan's children, she being late wife of John White, deceased, 10/-. Residue of real estate, lands, &c., to son Peter Hamlyn, who is Sole Exor.
Dated 14th Feb., 1770. Proved 12th June, 1772.

1772. Francis Hamlyn of Widecombe-in-the-Moor, Yeoman. To loving wife Anne, the South Part of Sercombe for 99 years, with reversion to nephew Peter Hamlyn and his male heirs, he being son of brother Peter H. The other sons of said brother Peter have remainder of said estate, viz., Richard, George, Francis, William, Thomas, and Hugh Hamlyn. In default of heirs of these, Sercombe is settled on brother George Hamlyn of Aveton Gifford and his sons, George, Richard, John, Arthur, and Francis Hamlyn, and in default to right heirs of said nephew, Peter Hamlyn. He bequeaths

in similar terms the other moiety of Sercombe, and all his tenements, &c., in Ashburton and elsewhere.
Residue to wife Anne, who is Sole Executrix.
Dated 29th April, 1749. Proved 9th May, 1772.
No Inventory.
(On four sheets of paper.)

1772. John Hamlyn of Corndon in the parish of Widecombe-in-the-Moor, Yeoman. To mother Mary Hamlyn, £15. To brother James Hamlyn, 20/-. To sisters Mary and Elizabeth Hamlyn, £4 each. To sister Anne, wife of Jno. French, 20/-. To brother James' sons, John and James, 5s. each. Bequests of 1/- each to John French's children, viz., Elizabeth, Ann, Susanna, Mary, and Sarah, John and William French. To William, son of "sister Joane," 1/-.
"My brother Richard Hamlyn to be my Executor."
Dated 7th Oct., 1772.
Witnesses—Richard Hamlyn, with others.
Proved 14th Nov., 1772.
Sum £100 9s.

1784. Thomas Hamlyn of Widecombe-in-the-Moor. "To Cousin Thomas White my sister Joane's son," £3 3s.
Residue to Dorothy, otherwise Dolly Hamlyn, my wife, who is Sole Executrix.
Dated 1st Dec., 1767. Proved 20th April, 1784.

1798. The last Will of Mary Howell of Plymouth Dock, widow, 2nd May, 1789.
She leaves her son, Samuel Blatchford, her sylver quart and six spoons. Mentions her grandson Henry, son of said Samuel; Alice, wife of said Samuel.
The residue of plate to daughter Jane Blatchford.
Mentions brother Henry Heath, sisters Sarah Newson,

Susannah Rowe, and her brothers Robert, Samuel, and Richard Heath, who are to have mourning rings.

Residue to said Samuel and Jane Blatchford, who are Sole Exors.

Proved 18th Sept., 1798.

Under £100.

1806. John Hamlyn of Lake in the parish of Widecombe-in-the-Moor, Yeoman. Dated 7th Feby., 1801.

He leaves his daughter Mary £5; and bequeaths the residue to his wife Grace and son William. The latter is Sole Executor.

Proved 11th March, 1806.

Under £100.

CONSISTORIAL COURT.

1541. The last Will of John Hamlyn of Chudleigh. Dated 5th June, 1541.

"To the store of our Lady of Chagford a shepe." To son John Hamlyn of Chagford, all goods remaining there.

To wife Margery all household stuff. Joint Exors., wife Margery and son John.

Witness—Richard Northcote, Clerk.

To poor of Chudleigh, a wether sheep.

No act of proof.

Collated Will Old Bk., Cons. Ct., Fo. 85.

1547. The last Will of Richard Worth, Clerk, Parson of Washfield and Thurlestone. He desires to be buried in the Chancel of Washfield Church, and leaves to "my Cosen Wenefred" /12d. To godson Arthur Worth, /4d. Also to godson "at harpryge," /4d. Residue to servant Wm. Davye "as seemeth him best." Dated 15th May, 37th Hy. VIII. By Nuncupative Codicil made by Michael Brown, according to instructions received from said Wm. Davye and dated 27th July, same year, Testator confirms his former Will, and gives Henry Morgan, Clerk, Vicar of Alwyngton, his "chamlot gowne" and nominated him Joint Exor. with Wm. Davye, in presence of Richard Halse, Clerk, Vicar of Broadclist. Gregory Basset "Parson of St. Martyn's Exeter" witnesses the instructions for Codicil.

Proved 6th Aug., 1547.

Collated Will—Old Book, Consistory Court, Fo. 197.

NOTES.—Testator was fifth son of Anthony "Worth" of Worth, whose brother Roger was ancestor of the Worthes of Compton, Barnstaple, Crediton, and Exeter.

The Worthes presented to Washfield in right of inheritance from the Beauchamps, through Abbot. Thomas Worth of Worth presented, 1410, and his direct descendant Mrs. Worth, whose husband, the late Rev. W. Jones, assumed her name, similarly presented, 1884.

From Abbot, through Beauchamp, the Worthes also derived the Manor of Washfield. These Beauchamps were a younger branch of the White Lackington family, whose heir, in elder line, brought that estate to Speke, and derived from Milo Beauchamp of Eaton, younger brother of Walter Beauchamp, the ancestor of the Earls of Warwick.

1549. The last Will of Henry Gibbe (or Gybbes as in the Calendar) of Woodbury in the County of Devon.

Leaves money to the "poor man's hope" of the said Parish, and money to the poor of Clyst St. George, bequeathing the residue to Joane his wife who, he was sure, would dispose of it in the best way for the good of his soul. He makes her his Executrix.

Witnesses—William Gybbe, Clerk, and George Gybbe of Clyst St. George.

Date of Will, October 2nd, 1549. A Commission was issued to the said William Gybbe, therein described as Rector of Clyst St. Mary,* to prove the Will.

Probate granted Oct. 20th, 1549.

1569. Grant by John Arundell of Lannherne, Co. Cornwall, Miles, of the advowson of the Rectory of St. Columb for one turn whenever or by whatever means it may be vacant, to nephew Nicholas Bosgrave of London, gentm., 20th April, 1569.

Confirmation by John, son and heir of John Arundell of Lannherne, lately deceased, of the next presentation to Rectory of St. Columb to Nicholas Bosgrave, 18th May, 33rd Elizb.

NOTE.—From a Book of Exhibits, Archives Consistory Court, Exeter.

---

* Instituted Sept. 7th, 1543. He was afterward Rector of Clyst St. George.

1571. The last Will of Willyam Gibbe* (Rector) of Clyst St. George.

After some small charitable bequests he appoints John Gibbe, son of George Gibbe, deceased, of St. George's Clist, his Executor and Residuary Legatee. To the poor of Clyst St. George, 10/-. To the poor of Clyst St. Mary, 6/8. To the poor of Sowton, 5/-. To the maintenance and reparation of Apsham† Cawsey, 10/-. To Charles Rugge, Richard Peat, and John Pears the Younger, £3 6s. 8d. apiece, and to the said John's children, 20/- apiece. To his godchildren, 12/- apiece. To William Rugge, £6 13s. 4d. To Thomas Rugge, if he should remain at Oxford a year after the testator's death, £10; otherwise £3 6s. 8d. of it to the poor. To Joane, daughter of Charles Rugge, £10, and six spoons parcel gilt. To Margaret and Mary, daughters of the said Charles, £6 13s. 4d. each. To Jane Rugge, £10, and a silver salt. He mentions also his servants Agnes and Jone Besse.

Will dated May 6th, and proved June 8th, 1571.

Overseers—William Rugge and John Pears.

Witnesses—George Coade, John Pears, and Wm. Eton.

1582. The last Will of Edward Langley of Chudleigh. Dated 7th Jany., 1582.

He leaves his mansion house and lands to his son George Langley "the younger"; son William to have the "workinge shoppe."

He mentions his son George Langley "the elder."

In a Codicil dated 11th Jany., 1582, he mentions daughters Margaret and Margerie.

Proved 16th Jany., 1582.

Sum £55 16s. 11d.

---

* William Gybbe, instituted to the Rectory of Clyst St. Mary, 1543. Still there in 1549. Buried as Rector of Clyst St. George, May 30th, 1571. Called Gybbes in the Index of Wills.

† Topsham Causeway.

1594. James Peter of Marldon, Yeoman, 17th Sept., 35th Elizabeth.

To sons Harry and William Peter, £10 each. To daughter Emlyn Peter, £20 at 24 or marriage. To Oder and Gilbert, sons of Gilbert Peter "my son," "one yoowe each." To Richard, Alexander, and Andrew, sons of John Dodd, "my son-in-law," "one yeowe lambe each"; the same to son-in-law John Comyn's daughter Margerie. He leaves certain household furniture and the moiety of his iron, ropes, and yokes, and plough stuff between his children and his wife Anne. To son John Peter, 30/-.

Residue to wife Anne, who is Sole Executrix.

Overseers—" Loving cousin " John Peter, and friends Wm. Pascowe and John Grendon.

Proved 13th April, 1594.

Sum £147 15s. 8d.

NOTE.—Gilbert was evidently called after Gilbert of Compton Castle, in this Parish. "Oder" (modern, Otho) was a well-known Gilbert Christian name.

1595. Henry Tucker of King's-Nympton, Husbandman. 3rd June, 37th Elizabeth. To be buried in the Parish Church. To the poor there, /12d. To sons Robert, William, and George, £10 each at 21. To son Roger, "in remembrance of fatherly good will towards him," 10/-, "to be delivered to him immediately upon his coming to his mother to do his duty." To daughters Margaret and Johane, £13 6s. 8d. each on their marriage day. To daughter Wilmot, £6 13s. 4d. on her marriage day. To Agnes, daughter of daughter Thomasine Kingdon, 1 lamb. To godson John Cole, /4d. Residue to wife Wilmot, who is Sole Exor.

Two Trustees—John Cole of King's-Nympton and brother George Tucker.

Witnesses—" Edmonde Squer, Pastor of King's-Nympton and Scipio Squier his sonne the writers thereof."

Proved 30th Aug., 1595.

Sum £71 15s. 8d.

NOTE.—" Scipio Squier." Little Fulford, situated partly in the Parish of Shobrooke, and partly in that of Crediton, was granted, before the reign of Edward II., by Michael L' Ercedekne (Archdeacon) to Roger Le Squier. There are seven generations of the Squiers of Heanton Punchardon recorded in the Heralds' Visitation of Devon, 1564. Agnes, daughter and heir of William Squier, and granddaughter of Thomas Squier, or Squire, the first mentioned in the pedigree, married William Marwood, and her daughter and heir Joane was the mother of Sir Lewis Pollard, Kt., and grandmother of Hugh Pollard. The male line of the Squier family had been continued by Thomas, second son of Thomas Squier of Heanton aforesaid. Edmond Squier, Rector of King's-Nympton, was presumably of this family, since the patronage of his Rectory lay with the Pollards. His son, Scipio Squier, was a great local antiquary, and left some valuable heraldic manuscripts relative to the arms in Devonshire churches, which were amongst the collections of Dr. Jeremiah Milles, Dean of Exeter and President of the Society of Antiquaries, 1765. He appears to have paid a visit to Exeter in 1607, when he recorded several notes of arms in the Guildhall, at Polsloe Priory, and other places in the neighbourhood of the city. He must have lived to a great age, as Elias Ashmole, Windsor Herald, made his acquaintance, as shown by his diary, May 24th, 1659, sixty-four years after he wrote and witnessed the above Will. His father, the Rev. E. Squier, died in 1620, and was succeeded at King's-Nympton by William Blake, 12th August that year. Patron, *hâc vice*, Nicholas Blake of Plymouth, Merchant, by grant of Lewis Pollard, Esq., of King's-Nympton, the true Patron. The last of the family, Hugh Squier, built and endowed a school at South Molton. His Will is dated 1709.

John Veysy, alias Harman, consecrated Bishop of Exeter, 1519, died 1554, was the son of Joan, daughter of Henry Squier of Handsworth, Co. Stafford.

1596. Thomas Tucker of Morchard Bishop. 30th June, 1595. He desires to be buried at Morchard. To eldest daughter Joane Tucker, 20/- and one yeo sheep. To eldest son John Tucker, 20/- and "one crossbowe and the buideres." To son Robert Tucker, 20/-. To son Henry Tucker, 20/- and "on paire of lombes." To daughter Maria, 20/-, and the "best brassen crocke after the decease of wife Agnes." Item to daughter Johane Tucker, jun., 20/- and a yeo lamb. To son Simon Tucker, 20/- and a yeo sheep. To daughter Thomasine, 20/- and a yeo lamb. To son Edward, 20/- and the second best pan. To daughter Agnes, wife of Richard Saunder, one yeo sheep. To godson Thomas Pollarde, 1 yeo lamb. All the legacies to be paid to the beneficiares at 21.

Residue to wife Agnes, who is Sole Executrix.

Two Trustees: Laurence Southwoode and William Venicombe.

Proved 22nd April, 1596.

Sum £308 17s. 4d.

1597. Robert Toker (no date) desires to be buried "in the parish Churchyard of St. Stephen's" (by Saltash, Co. Cornwall?). To the poor there, 10/-. To son Walter, £6 13s. 4d. at ten years old. To son Robert, £6 13s. 4d. at same age, and to daughter Siblie at same age, £6 13s. 4d. To godchild John Toker, /6d. To Mablie, daughter of Henry Tooker, one heiffer. Residue to wife Siblie, who is Sole Executrix, on condition that she maintains his mother Margaret Toker, or allows her £6 a year. To sister's daughter, Alice Garnfit, one yeo lamb. To Walter Vigurs and Christopher Horwell, who are trustees, 3/4 each.

Witnesses—Henry Tucker, Walter Vigurs, and Christopher Horwell, " Rober" Bicklie, Thomas Lowes.

Proved 15th Dec., 1597.

Sum £36 9s. 1d.

1603. The last Will of John "Tucker," Clerk, Rector of Cardingham in the Co. of Cornwall, cum Hellande. 15th Nov., 1602. Desires to be buried in the Chancel of Cardingham Church. 100 marks to daughters Mary, Anne, and Tilvey, to be paid when they attain the age of 18. The same to daughters Temperance and Penelope. To son Zacharie Tucker, best silver salte and tunne and best silver goblet, to remain in custody of Exors. until he is a housekeeper. He leaves property at "Trenie, Penquite, Cathan, St. Neot, and Bodmin, to Nichs. and Wm. Clieve, Gentlm., in trust for Anne, his wife, with remainder to son Zacharie."

Residue to wife Anne, who is Sole Executrix.

Three Overseers, viz., Wm. Parker, Official of Cornwall, Wm. Clieve, jun., and Nichs. Clieve, gntlm.

Witnesses—John Sprey, Samuel Tucker, John Tucker, Humfrie Tamlyn.

" Item, I do give my son Zacharie all my books."

Proved 31st Jany., 1603.

1603. The Inventory of Ellyas Petter, alias Berringe, late deceased in the Sherowes ward, made 8th Aug., 1603.
Will and Admon. missing.
Sum £13 3s. 4d.
Endorsed, "Of Torrebrian."

NOTE.—The Peters of Torbryan were a well-known Devonshire family. The name of this Elias Peter, who evidently died a prisoner for debt, does not occur in the Pedigrees, but he was probably a son of John Petre of Tor-Brian and his wife Joan Ridgeway.
William, second son of this John Petre, was the ancestor of the Petres of Ingarstone, Co. Essex, and of the Lords Petre.

1611. Thomas Peter of the parish of Paynton. 5th May, 43rd Elizabeth.

To the poor of the parish, /12d. To son's daughter Ammye Peter, 20/- at 26, and 2 yeo sheep. To Wilmott, her sister. £4 at 26, and 2 yeo sheep.

Residue to son James Peter, who is Sole Exor.

Overseers—James Churchward and Nicholas Lowman with /12d. each.

Proved 13th May, 1611.

Sum £30 12s. 8d.

1618. The last Will of Thomas Peter, Parson of the Church of St. Mawgan-in-Pyder, Co. Cornwall, Clark. 22nd Oct., 1617. He desires to be buried in Mawgan Chancel. Debts to be paid and the residue to be distributed "amongst my children." Wife, Elizabeth Peter, to have the advowson of Mawgan. She is Sole Executrix.

Overseers—James Killstone, Francis Hearl, Clarke, Leo Loveys, Wm. Poynter, Leonard Browne, Wm. Powell, and Thomas Howe.

Proved 6th Nov., 1618.

28th December, 1643. Inventory of the goods of William Bartlett of Marldon, taken by Thomas Bartlett and William Bartlett.

Sum is eight scoore, £7 11s. 8d.

5th November, 1644. Admon. granted in the Consistorial Court of Exeter to Anne Bartlett his widow, who in the Bond is described as of Marldon in County of Devon, widow, and the sureties are William Bartlett, of the same parish, Yeoman, and David Davis, Clerk, Vicar of Paignton, but there are only two signatures.

Sign., A. Anne Bartlett ; David Davies.

NOTE.—The Bond is not signed by William Bartlett.

1647, 10th Feby. Edward Tooker of Langbrocke, in parish of Milton Abbot, Carpenter. To poor of parish, 40/-. To Nicholas Tooker, Clerk, £10. To Phillippe, dau. of kinsman John Tooker, £5 ; to rest of his children, 10s. each.

To Edmund, son of kinsman Roger Tooker, £5, and to his children, 6/8 each.

To Elizabeth, dau. of said John Tooker, "my best crocke."

Other bequests to godson Danl. Sargent; to kinswoman Joy, dau. of Thomasine Adams, widow; and to rest of her six children. To brother Saml. Tooker, godsons Roger, Richard, and Edmund Sargent.

Residue to kinsman John Tooker of Langbroke, and to Joan Crabb, servant ; they are Sole Exors.

Witnesses—Zachæus Jordan, Hy. Tremure. No Proof.

NOTE.—From an old Book of Exhibits in Archives of Consistory Court, Exeter. No Proof.

See Principal Registry, Dec., 1648.

2nd May (22 Chas.), 1646. Thomas Bartlet of Compton, in the County of Devon, Yeoman, by Will gives to Joane Bartlet his wife, his household goods for life, and after to his four sons. To Thomas Bartlet, his grandchild, his greatest bras pan when he shall enjoy the tenement wherein the testator then dwelt.

Residue of goods to three youngest sons. Recites that Walter, Jane als Bartlet, by Deed dated 20th September, 8th Charles, did sell to William Evens and Jasper Pounce of Marldon, moiety of tenement in Compton, upon trust for testator in fee, who gives it to Samuel Bartlet and Odes Bartlet his sons. Proviso, that Thomas Bartlet his grandchild do pay them £25 apiece within two years after the death of testator and wife, the said Thomas is to have said moiety in fee, but if he should die without heirs of his body the moiety is to go to testator's son Samuel in fee.

Wife Juan, Executrix.
Signed—William Bartlet; William Evens.
Teste.—Gualtero Bartlet.

Inventory taken 8th May, 1646, by William Evens, Walter Bartlet, and Henry Bartlet of Marldon, £73 18s. 10d.

Proved 30th May, 1650, by the Executrix, in the Consistorial Court of the Bishop of Exeter.

1658, Dec. 29. Johan Bartlett of Marldon, Devon, by her Will of this date, gives small legacies to her sons Henry, Samuel, and Thomas, and to her son Samuel's children, viz., William and Susan, and appoints her son Otho Bartlett Executor, who proved the said Will the 30th April, 1661.

1661, Jany. 3rd. Otho Bartlett of Marldon, by his Will of this date, gives legacies to William Bartlett and Susan Bartlett, son and daughter of his brother Saml. Bartlett. To Thomas Bartlett his kinsman, to John Bartlett his kinsman, and to his four god-children (not named), and Edward Ford and the poor of Marldon ; and appoints his brother Henry Bartlett and Thomas Bartlett Executors ; to whom Probate was granted 12th April, 1667.

1666. "Admon. de bonis non," of effects unadministered by Richard Bonithon, father of John Bonithon, Executor of the Will of Gilbert Holcombe, late of Mylor, Co. Cornwall, deceased. Granted to Sir Peter Courtenay of Ladock, Co. Cornwall, 26th Nov., 1666.

Seal of Arms—Quarterly 1st and 4th, *Or*, 3 Torteaux; 2nd and 3rd, *Or*, a Lion Ramp., *Azure* (Courtenay).

NOTE.—Gilbert Holcombe, married Ann, sister of Peter, fourth son of Peter Countenay of Ladock. Dead before 1642.

"1666. In the Name of God, Amen. I Walter Bartlett of Compton in the parish of Marldon do make and ordaine this my last Will and Testament in manner and forme following Imprimis I bequeath my soul to God my Maker and Redeemer by whome I hope to have comfort in the later day, and my body I ordaine to bee buried in the Church of Marldon. Item. I give to William Bartlett my sonne all my land to him and his heirs forever. Item. I give to Alice Bartlett, Westerland living with all the right that I have in it. Item. I doe ordaine and bequeath to Katherine Bartlett my daughter too hundred pounds to be paide unto her by Allice her sister in six years after that shee shall enjoy it. Item. I doe ordaine William Bartlett my sonne to bee my hole and sole Executor. Item. If William Bartlett die and have noe heirs then it shall goe to Allice Bartlett, and if Allice have no heirs then it shall goe to Katherine Bartlett and if shee die without heires then to the heires of Thomas Bartlett of Stocke Gaberiell. And I doe institute and ordaine Master John Prouse of Brent to bee one of my rulers of this my last Will and Testament. Item. I ordaine Mr. Elias Phillipps, James Peter, William Bartlett, William Brendon to be the others of my rullers of this my last Will and Testament. And I give unto them Twenty shillings for their paines, and if my goods will not hold out to pay my debts I doe ordaine that Gildon's Feeld and Burlanch shall bee sold. In witnesse heere of I have heere unto put my hand even the 9th day of January in the year of our Lord God 1666."

Witnesse—Watler Bartlett; James IC Cholwill.

Proved on the 26th day of January, 1666, by the Oath of Juliana Bartlett, widow, during the minority of William Bartlett the son and Sole Executor.

9th January, 1666. Walter Bartlett of Marldon, by his Will of this date, gives to his son William Bartlett all his lands, to him and his heirs for ever, and if he die and have no heirs upon the trusts thereinafter mentioned. To Alice Bartlett, Westerland living. To Katherine Bartlett, £200; and appoints his son William Executor.

Admon. with Will annexed granted on the 26th February 1666, to Juliane Bartlett, widow, during the minority of Executor.

1671. The Account of Julyan Bartlett the Relict and Administrix of the goods and chattels of Walter Bartlett, late of Marldon, Devon. Exhibited 27th April, 1671.

	£	s.	d.
The charge	418	19	8
The discharge	437	0	0
	£18	0	4

1674. William Bartlett, by his Will, without date, makes bequests of small nature to his wife (not named), and to his grand-children Allis Katherine Bartlett and William Bartlett; and appoints the said William Bartlett Executor; to whom Probate was granted on the 24th Sept., 1674.

Inventory £24 5s.

1681. Administration to the effects of Margaret Wreyford of Morchard Bishop. Granted 1st March, 1681, to Elizabeth her daughter. Matthew Wreyford joins the bond.

Sum £6 8s.

1688. Administration to the effects of Elizabeth Wreyford of Morchard Bishop. Granted to Matthew Wreyford her brother, 3rd Oct., 1688. William Wreyford of the same parish joins in bond.

NOTE.—Matthew Wreyford was a Wool-comber ("lanionem"). William a weaver ("textorem"); thus described in the Admon. Bond.

1692-3, March 22nd. Henry Bartlett by his Will of this date gives to his brother Thomas Bartlett his half plase in the Common Field at Compton, for the term of years he had therein, on condition of his paying £15 to Testator's Executor and he also makes small bequests to his kinsman Thomas Bartlett, jun., and to the children of Henry Tozer and to his kinswoman Elizabeth Bartlett, whom he appoints Executrix.

Admon., with the Will annexed, granted on the 20th day of June, 1693, to Thomas Bartlett of Stokegabriel, Devon, Elizabeth Bartlett, the Executrix named in the Will, having renounced the execution thereof.

Inventory £55 5s.

1698, January 11th. Admon. to the effects of Susanna Bartlett, late of Marldon, was granted to her husband William Bartlett.

No Inventory.

1705, August 17th. William Bartlett of Compton within the parish of Marldon, Yeoman, by his Will of this date gives to Edwd. Goodridge of Berry Pomeroy, yeoman, James Peter of Marldon, gentleman, and Thomas Bartlett, sen., of Marldon, yeoman, all his lands, tenements, houses, orchards, meadows and fields and his Comon of pasture with the appurts. belonging thereto and all his goods and chattels whatsoever Upon Trust to sell same real and personal Estate and after paying his debts, etc., to pay the balance equally between his two daughters Susanna and Mary when they attain 20 years of age, and if one died to the survivor wholly; and he appointed the said Trustees to be Executors of his Will, who proved the same on 23rd October, 1705.

Inventory £200 8s.

1712. Administration to the Effects of Katherine Gould of Staverton, Granted 9th Nov., 1712, to Jonathan Laskey, her grandson.

NOTE.—Rebekkah, widow of the Rev. Alexander Laskey, curate of Ashburton, died there, 3rd Nov., 1777, and was buried in the church.

License of marriage between Alexander Laskey of Ilsington, clerk, and Rebekkah Laskey of Yealmpton, spinster. Jan. 23rd, 1740. Mar. Lic., Prin. Regy., Exon.

1713, Nov. 12. Thomas Bartlett of Marldon, Yeoman, by his Will of this date gives his two fields called Coombe Park and Wood Park in Kingscarsewell, and the house and orchard in Marldon unto his kinsman Thomas Bartlett and to his heirs and assigns for ever; and he gives the closes of land called Olda Court, Bottom Hood, Hostawill Park, the three Compton Parkes, and the Broom Parkes, unto his said kinsman Thomas Bartlett, until Thomas Bartlett, jun., son of Thomas Bartlett, Testator's kinsman, should attain 20 years of age, and on the said Thomas Bartlett the younger attaining 20 years of age to him for all Testator's term and interest therein. All other the Testator's messuages, lands, and tenements he gave to his said kinsman Thomas Bartlett the elder and his assigns To hold the same until his son the said Thomas Bartlett attained 20 years of age, and on his attaining that age to the said Thomas Bartlett the son and the heirs of his body lawfully begotten on the body of Elizabeth his then wife, and in default of such issue to the said Thos. Bartlett the elder his heirs and assigns for ever. Unto Rebecca Bartlett, daughter of the said Thos. Bartlett the elder, he gives £250 to be paid her when 21, and the same is charged on his lands, and testator also gives small legacies to his cousin John Hurrell, Thomas Bartlett, to Richard Phillipp's children, to Agnes Collins and her daughter (not named).

Residue to kinsman the said Thomas Bartlett the elder, who is appointed executor, and who proved the said Will on the 24th October, 1714.

Inventory £819 6s.

1735, Oct. 11. Thomas Bartlett late of Marldon, Yeoman, by his Will of this date, gives small legacies to his nephews Jacob Bartlett and Thomas Bartlett, and to Thomas, William, Mary Elizabeth, and Jacob Bartlett, sons and daughters of his said nephew Thomas Bartlett, and to the poor of Marldon, and then gives to his wife Elizabeth Bartlett, her heirs and assigns for ever, all that tenement called the Lower Tenement and three closes of land called the Etherhays and Churchward Hay, a field called the Ridgeways Bridge and two fields called the Winkhorns, and a tenement called Martins, and all other his messuages, lands, tenements, and hereditaments, and appoints his said wife Executrix and Residuary Legatee; to whom probate was granted on the 22nd October, 1736.
Inventory £276 19s. 2d.

1736, May 18th. Admon. to the effects of Joan Bartlett, wife of Jacob Bartlett late of Marldon, deceased, was granted to her husband the said Jacob Bartlett on the date aforesaid.
No inventory exhibited. Bond given for £200.

1742, June 30th. Jacob Bartlett of Marldon, Yeoman, by his Will of this date gives to his wife the use of all his household goods as was hers before marriage, and on her death or re-marriage to daughter Joan Bartlett. He also gave to said daughter £200, and charged same on his real and personal estate, and also the yearly sum of £5 till she attained 21. He gives to his son Jacob Bartlett £100, and to his godson Jacob Collier, to his wife (Joane), and to his brothers William and Thomas, £5; and the residue to his son Jacob Bickford Bartlett; and he appoints his said wife and two brothers, William Bartlett and Thos. Bartlett, Executors.
Proved on the 22nd May, 1742, by Joan Bartlett and Thos. Bartlett, two of the Executors, power being reserved to Wm. Bartlett the other Executor.
No Inventory exhibited.

1742, Nov. 8th. Elizabeth Bartlett late of Marldon, by her Will of this date, gives small legacies to her son Henry Holditch and niece Elizabeth Ford ; and gives the residue of her estate and effects to her two sisters Joan Withiell and Judith Ford, and appoints them Executrixes.

Proved on the fourteenth day of January, 1742, by Judith Ford, one of the Executrixes ; Joan Withiell, the other Executrix, having renounced.

No Inventory.

1748. Thomas Bartlett of Marldon, Clothier, 10th Nov., 1748. To wife Christian, house at Marldon, late Mrs. Adams'. Revert to son Nicholas, charged with £50 to daughter Christian. To said wife £300 in trust for said daughter, and for other children, Christopher, John, and Susanna Bartlett. To son Thomas, messuage in which I reside, called "Waymouthe Tenement." Residue to brother William Bartlett of St. Mary Church, Gent^m., in trust for children Thomas, William, Jacob, Mary, and Elizabeth Bartlett, at 21. Said brother William Sole Exor.

Witnesses : Mary Hander, George Lyde, Robert Furneaux. Proved 30th Dec., 1748.

NOTE.—The house at Marldon known as "Madger Place" is the house of "late Mrs. Adams" referred to. "Wife Christian" was daughter of Nicholas Adams by his wife Agnes Drewe. Madger Place was conveyed by Sir Edwd. Carey to Christopher Adams in 1650.

1777, 4th April. Letters of Administration of the personal estate of Thomas Bartlett late of Marldon, deceased, left unadministered by Elizabeth Bartlett his widow, the Sole Executrix of his Will, who died intestate, were granted to John Leach Brown of Stokeinteignhead, Gentleman, so far as related to certain estates vested in the said Thomas Bartlett as surviving Trustee under certain Indentures of Lease and release of 8th and 9th September, 1718.

The property is described as All those messuages and lands called Moretor and Lovetor in Marldon, containing 46 acres ; a messuage and tenement in North Willborough, containing 20 acres ; and several fields or parcels of land therein mentioned.

1785. Administration to the Effects of Samuel Wreford late of Crediton, intestate. Granted 18th March, 1785, to his brothers John Wreford of Clannaborough, and Silvanus Wreford of Bow; Elizabeth Wreford, mother and next of kin to deceased, having renounced.

NOTE.—Refer to 2nd August, 1595, Principal Registry. The recurrence of the Christian name "Silvanus," and the mention of property in West Sandford, close to Bow, and Morchard Bishop, clearly points to the origin of the North Devon Wrefords.

PRINCIPAL REGISTRY.

"In the name of God Amen, the 12th April, 1537. I Roger Wreyyfford stedfast and perfyct of mynd and rembrans make these my last Will and testament after this manner and forme. fferst I bequeth my sowle unto Almighty God and to all the Celestyall Companye yn Heven and my bodye to holy buryall to be beryd yn the Churchyerth of Saynt Swithine Sampford. ffyrst I geve and bequeth unto our ladye brethered of Credyton xij*d*., also to Seynt Swithine of Sampford a yawe, allso I geve and bequeth unto John Podycomb xij*d*., allso I geve and bequeth unto John Owsborne prysh clarke viij*d*. Allso I geve and bequeth unto John Wreyfford my son my best half dossyn of sylveryn spoons allso I geve and bequeth unto the same John my best brasyn pott allso I geve and bequeth unto the same John a pessenott allso I geve and bequeth unto the same John allff a dossyn of vessells pfformyed and a chaffyn dysch of latyn and a candelstyc also I geve and bequeth unto the same John a fflock bed and a per of blanekeytts allso I geve and bequeth unto Richard Cowyll and to Nicholas Dellff to Every of them iij*s*. iiij*d*. allso I geve and bequeth unto Maryytt my servant iij*s*. iiij*d*. or a petycowytt clothe allso I will that Richard Cowyll and Nicholas Dellff shalbe my overseers and governors to see thys my last wyll and testament performyd according to the desyr of my mynd the goods not geve nor bequeth I geve and bequeth unto Maryerye my wyff whom I have ordaynd and made my Executor trustyn she will dyspose for the welth of my sowll as she may se hyt most best or convenynte: herto be wyttnes John Podycomb (clerke), Nicholas Dellff, Nycolas Wrefford, John Owsborne, and William Ffrost."

1595. Thomas Wrayford of Modbury, 15th June, 1594. To daughter Katherine Pearse, 3 silver spoons. To Mary fface her daughter, and to each of Thomas Pearce's children, 6s. 8d.

To daughter Mary Sweete, 3 silver spoons, and to each of Henry Surete's four children, 6s. 8d. To Johane Face, an annuity of 20/- out of land called "Heale," in West Sanford, after death of wife Johane. "To Silvanus, my son's child," 1 gilt salt.

Residue to son William, who is Sole Exor.

Proved 2nd August, 1595.

Sum £128 4s.

1596. The last Will of John Wourth of Crediton, co. Devon, dated 10th Jany., 1595. He gives his son John £8 in money, "all my best gownes, a goblett of sylver parcel gilt, five silver spoons with name engraved on them," etc.

He makes specific bequests of money and furniture to his sons William, George, and Nicholas, and also to his daughters Christian and Elizabeth.

Residue to wife Joane, who is Sole Exor.

Trustees: John Trowbridge and Lawrence Davie.

Proved 4th June, 1596.

NOTE.—Testator was eldest son of John Worthe of Compton Pole, in Marldon, by Agnes, daughter of John Bodley of Dunscombe, Crediton. His wife "Joane" was daughter of Robert Clark of Crediton.

C. 1600. From a terrier in the Principal Registry of the Bishop.

"A note concerning the Rectory of Cardyngham.

"Imprimis that y*e* Earle of Bath and John Arundell of Lanherne, Esquyer, are Patrons of the said benefice and doe give the same *alternis vicibus*, and that Mrs. Arundell is to present y*e* next turne.

"Item there is about one hundred akers of land belonging to y*e* glebe of y*e* said parsonage the said ground being bounded on the East and south with y*e* patron's lands and on the West side with Mr. John Doorleyne's land, and on ye North side with ye Queene's High waye.

"Item there are no implements belonging] to ye said parsonage house.
John Toker.
Registrar's Office.

C. 1600. Helland, co. Cornwall. A note concerning ye Rectory of Helland. Mr. Thomas Hale of Fleet in Devon is patrone of ye said benefice, who presented John Toker, Clerk, now incumbent there. That their is about xvi akers of land belonging to the said Rectory. Item their is no impliments belonging to the said Rectory.
John Toker.
Registrar's Office.

NOTE.—See Rev. John Toker's Will, Consistorial Court, Jan., 1603.

1616. Joan Wrayford of Christow, 12th Oct., 1615. Legacies to "Sister Richorde"; to brother Stephen Wrayford; to Wm. Cornish the younger; to kinswoman Elline Cornish; and to Susan Cornish. Residue to John Cornish, who is Sole Executor.

Proved 26th July, 1616.

Sum, £4 15s. 6d.

1627. Probate of the Will of Alexander Arundell, Rector of Lapford, granted 9th Nov., 1627, to Mary his Relict and Executrix.

Sum, £1,009 16s. 3d.

(Episcopal Registers.)

NOTE.—The Ecclesiastical Commissioners state in their report that they were unable to find this Will.

Mrs. Arundell soon consoled herself with another husband, as she married her husband's successor at Lapford, on the 21st of the following February.

Rev. George Allen, Instituted to Rectory of Lapford, 6th Feby., 1627-8.

License of Marriage between George Allen, Clerk, Rector of Lapford, and Mary Arundell, widow of the same, 21st Feby., 1627.

Probate of the Will of George Allen, Clerk, Rector of Lapford, granted to Mary his Relict, Jany. 29th, 1637. Sum, £225. (*Ibid.*)

1627. Probate of the Will of Edmund Peter, late of Ottery St. Mary. Granted to Emline, his Relict and Sole Executrix, 11th Aug., 1627.
Sum, £24 12s. 10d.
(Episcopal Registers.)

1627. Administration of the Nuncupative Will of Florence Lenfee *alias* Lenfield, of Marwood. Granted to John Tucker of the same Parish, in trust for the children of deceased. 27th Sept., 1627.
(*Ibid.*)

1628. Administration to the effects of Elizabeth Courtenay, *alias* Gorges, relict of Edward Courtenay, and Admon. to effects unadministered by the said Elizabeth, of William Bligh, Esq, deceased, and also of the said Edward Courtenay. Granted to Sir Wm. Courtenay, Knight, brother of deceased, in the minority of Peter Courtenay, Esq., Edward Courtenay, and Hutton Courtenay, children of said Elizabeth.
Granted 18th March, 1628.
(Extracted from the Registers of Bishops of Exeter.)

NOTE.—Sir Wm. Courtenay of Powderham, born 1553, died 1630. Col. Vivian, in his edition of the "Visitations of Devon," only gives him one sister—Jane, wife of Sir Nicholas Parker; and I find no mention of Elizabeth in any other Courtenay pedigree in my possession.

1629. The Bishop of Exeter, at London, from the house of the Earl of Norwich, in the parish of St. Giles-in-the-Fields, admitted Robert Herrick, Clerk, Master of Arts, to the Vicarage of Dean Prior, vacant by the promotion of Barnabas Potter to the See of Carlisle.
(Episcopal Registers.)

NOTE.—This was Robert Herrick, the Poet, author of the "Hesperides," admitted to this little Devonshire Church upon the presentation of King Charles I. He died in 1674, and was buried at Dean Prior.

"The Earl of Norwich," was Edward Denny, knighted by Queen Elizabeth; created Earl of Norwich, 1626; died without male issue, 20th Dec., 1630. The King then gave the Earldom of Norwich to the late Earl's nephew, the celebrated Lord Goring, in 1644.

1631. "Caveat" against Administration to the effects of Katherine "Carey," Widow, of Clovelly, without notice given to John Arundell of Trerise, Esq., and Henry "Carye" of Clovelly, her son, co-exors. of her last Will and Testament, Jan. 2nd, 1631.
(Epis. Regs. Exon.)

1633. Commission for Administration directed to John Saunders, Clerk, Vicar of Bodmin, and to Master Peter Tucker, Rector of Cardinham, in the case of Susannah, widow of Peter Bolt, late of Bodmin, deceased. 29th July, 1633.
(Epis. Regs., Exon.)

NOTE.—To enable her to Administer without incurring the trouble and expense of a journey to Exeter.

1633. A similar Commission to Gregory Arundell, Rector of Sheviocke, in the case of Wm. Bond. 16th Aug., 1633.
(*Ibid.*)

1635. Probate of the Will of Thomas Arundell of Stowford, gentleman, concerning his goods only within the Diocese of Exeter. Granted to Mary, his widow. 12th Jany., 1635.
(Epis. Reg., Exeter.)

1636. Probate of the Will of Wm. Sheeres, Clerk, deceased, late Rector of St. Stephen's, and of All Hallows, Goldsmith Street, Exeter. Granted to Susanna, his wife. 15th March, 1636.
(Epis. Reg., Exon.)

1637. Commission for Administration to —— In the matter of Mary, relict of Sir Edward Gyles, Kt. 19th Dec., 1637.

Administration to the estate of Sir Edward Gyles, late of Dean Prior, deceased, granted to "Lady Marie Gyles," his

relict. 20th Jany., 1637. Sum, £968 5s. 8d. Inventory exhibited, 24th Jany. (*Ibid.*)
(Epis. Reg., Exon.)

NOTE.—Lady Gyles was Mary, daughter and heir of Edmund Drewe of Hayne. She had no issue. Sir Edward Gyles, Knight, was one of Prince's "Worthies" of Devon. For an account of him, see also the Editor's "Ashburton and its Neighbourhood," p. 134, *et seq.;* also "Devonshire Parishes," by same author, Vol. i., p. 306.

1639. Administration of the estate of Silvester Whiteway of Ashburton, deceased. Granted to Humphrey Tooker of the City of Exeter, Merchant. 2nd Nov., 1639.
(Epis. Regs., Exon.)

1640. Probate of the Will of Hugh Clifford, Esq., of Bremell, in the parish of Ashton. Granted to Marie his relict. 27th March, 1640.
Sum, £374 8s.
(Epis. Regs., Exon.)

1643. Probate of the Will of John Baker of the City of Exeter, Merchant, deceased. Granted to Thomas Baker, Clerk, and Anne Tucker, his children and Co-Exors. "Ejus filiis et co-executoribus." 29th Feb., 1643.
(Epis. Regs., Exon.)

1643. The last Will of Marie Gib[*] of St. George's. She leaves £8 to her son John Gibb,[†] and 1/- each to her son John Gibbes his children. £15 to her son Andrew Gibbe, and 10/- each to his children. She leaves also legacies to Marie, the daughter of George Gibb; William, the son of George Gibb; and George, the son of George Gibb. She gives 6/8 to the poor of Clyst St. George, and 4/- to the

---

[*] Second wife of George Gibb, and sister of Andrew Loveringe. Refer to Archdeaconry of Exon., Aug. 24th, 1606. George Gibb, her husband.
[†] Refer to Archdeaconry of Exon., April, 1644.

poor of Whimple. The residue of her goods she bequeaths to George Gibb,* her son, and Executor of her Will.
Overseers—Richard Parker and Robert Gibb,† the son of John Gibb‡ of Clyst St. George.
Will dated August 10th, 1640.
Proved, 1643.§
Witnesses §—

1643. Administration to the effects of Zachary Hooker, *alias* "Howell" (*not Vowell*), Clerk, Rector of Caryhais, deceased. Granted to Grace, his relict. 28th Jan., 1643.
Sum, £194 10s.
(Epis. Regs.)

NOTE.—He was the fourth son of John Hoker, *alias* Vowell, Chamberlain of Exeter, and author of the celebrated "History of the City," still in MS., by his second wife, Anastasia, daughter of Edward Bridgman of Exeter. "Visit. Devon," 1564.
Rev. Zachary Hooker was succeeded at "Caryhayes" by the Rev. John Archer, upon the presentation of Joan Beauford of Columb Major, widow, by grant from the true Patrons—Bernard Tanner, Esq., and John Coke, Esq. 15th May, 1644.
(Epis. Regs., Exon.)

1644. Probate of the Will of William Lake, late of Ashbury, deceased. Granted to John Lake, his son. 15th April, 1644.
Sum, £417 17s. 4d.
(Epis. Regs., Exon.)

1645. Probate of the Will of Nicholas "Carwithy" of the City of Exeter. Granted to Margaret, his wife. 19th June, 1645.
(Epis. Regs., Exon.)

NOTE.—Nicholas Carwithen of St. Petrock's, Exeter. His grandson, John Carwithen, Town Clerk of Exeter, purchased the advowson

---

* Administration in P.C.C., Nov., 1660.
† Court of Vicars Choral, Feb. 27th, 1701-2.
‡ Eldest son of George Gibb, husband of testatrix, by his first wife.
§ Witnesses and precise date of Probate wanting.

of the Rectory of Manaton for £100 for the term of 1,000 years, from Francis Kirkham in 1720; and in 1723 purchased the fee thereof for £5 5s. His brother Thomas Carwithen had been instituted to this Rectory in 1698, and it has ever since remained with his descendants, the present Rector, 1893, being the Rev. William Henry Carwithen, A.M., many years Vicar of Aylesbeare, and a kinsman, through Melhuish, of Editor's. Since 1698, nine Carwithens have been Rectors of Manaton, but there have been four intermissions—1753, 1766, 1848, 1887.

1644. Probate of the Will of Mark Law, Clerk, Vicar of Ashburton. Granted to Marie, his relict. 23rd Jany., 1644.
Sum, £98 18s. 4d.
(Epis. Regs., Exon.)

NOTE.—He was the son of the Venerable Robert Law, Archdeacon of Barnstaple and Treasurer of Exeter Cathedral, and succeeded his father in the Vicarage of Ashburton, 1629. He married Maria Tidball, daughter of the Rev. Samuel Tidball, Master of Ashburton Grammar School, by whom he was himself succeeded in the Vicarage of Ashburton, which Editor's father, the Rev. Charles Worthy, subsequently held from 1861 to his death in 1879.

1644. Probate of the Will of Robert Carey of Launceston. Granted 17th Feby., 1644, to Alice, his wife.
(Epis. Regs., Exon.)

1645. Administration to the estate of Richard Hill, late Rector of Manaton, to James Hill his grandson. And of William Hill, late Rector of Manaton, to said James his son.
Both dated 26th Nov., 1645.
(Epis. Regs., Exon.)

NOTE.—Rev. Richard Hill was instituted to Manaton, March 21st, 1579, and died in 1612, when he was succeeded by his son William, who died 1645.
James Hill, the above Administrator, was instituted to Manaton, 27th Nov., 1645. On his death in 1661, he was followed by the Rev. James Eastchurch, whose successor was the Rev. Thomas Carwithen, 19th May, 1698. (See previous note, 19th June this year.)

1646. Peter Hole, of North-Tawton, 19th Feby., 21st Charles. He gives to wife Margery his whole estate in a Tenement called Farthinges, in the parish of Zeal Monachorum. He mentions Robert Hole his brother. To daughter Alice Hole, £30. To son John Hole, £30 at 21. To daughter Elinor Hole, £30 at 21. To son Andrew Hole, £30 at 21. To wife Margery, an acre of best rye growing at Higher Nichols-Nymet. Exor. to maintain his son John until he is 21, and to have the "labours" of the said John in exchange. Residue to son William, who is Sole Executor.

Rulers—Mark Cottle, Esq., brother Robert Hole, John Gould, gentm., John Splatt and David Westron.

Proved, 5th July, 1646.

NOTE.—The Chatell lease of Nichols-Nymet is valued in the Inventory at £390.
"Farthinges" at £28.

1648. Affidavit of John Tooker and Joane Crabb, Exors. to the Will of Edmund Tooker, Carpenter, of Milton Abbot, made 1st Dec., 1648.

No Will annexed.

Sum, £143 12s. 5d.

NOTE.—The copy of the Will is in "Consistory Archives at Exeter Cathedral." (See "Consistorial Court," Feby., 1647.)

1665. Administration to the effects of Roger Wreyford. Granted to Wm. Tucker, Emanuel Harvey, and Wm. Wreyford, Overseers named in the Will of said deceased, in minority of Nicholas Wreyford the son. 14th July, 1665.

(Epis. Regs., Exon.)

1665. Administration to the effects of Jane Osmond, late of Tiverton, deceased. Granted to Thomas Hussey and John Gill in the Minority of Alice and Jane Bryant, the Executors. 31st July, 1665.

(Epis. Regs., Exon.)

1666. The Will of Edward Arundell, jun., late of North Molton, Gentleman, was proved by John Arundell, his brother and Executor. 25th July, 1666.
(Epis. Regs., Exon.)

1666. Probate of the Will of Dorothy Cary, late of Exeter. Granted to the Very Rev. George Cary, Dean of Exeter. 7th Sept., 1666.
(Epis. Regs.)

NOTE.—She was third daughter of William Cary of Clovelly, by his second wife, Dorothy, eldest daughter of Sir Edward Gorges. Col. Vivian, "Visitation of Devon," notes that she was "dead before 1674."

Her brother George—Dean of Exeter, 1663—was twice offered the Bishopric of Exeter by Charles II., but declined the dignity. King Charles I. had presented him to the Rectory of Clovelly, 1638, and he was buried there, Feby., 1680-1, æt. 69. His eldest brother, "Sir Robert Cary, Kt.," was Gentleman of the Privy Chamber to Charles II.

1667. "Memorandum: That on the 27th March, 1667, Mr. Gascoigne Canham of Arlington, Clerke, as undoubted Patron of Bratton Fleming, did, by deed, grant to the Master and Fellows of Gonville and Caius College, Cambridge, the perpetual advowson of the said Rectory of Bratton Fleming, to present the eldest fellow of said College."
(Epis. Regs.)

NOTE.—Mr. Canham was 55 years Rector of Arlington, and was buried there in 1667. Bratton Fleming has a tithe rent charge, according to the commutation, of £435 per annum, and there are 256½ acres of Glebe. The population in 1881 was 523.

1670. Probate of the Nuncupative Will of George Arundell of Launceston. Granted to Richard Killiowe, the Executor. 9th Feby., 1670.
(Epis. Regs.)

1671. Probate of the Will of Jonathan Fox, late of Lancells, deceased 31st August, 1671. Granted, Sept. 1671, to Wm. Potter, Executor " during minority."
(Epis. Regs.)

1671. The last Will of Peter Toker of Cardinham, Cornwall, Clerk.

To eldest daughter, Mary Toker, and to eldest son, Matthew Toker, all messuages, lands, &c., in Penstrode and Blissland, to them and their heirs, with reversion in default thereof to daughter Katherine, wife of Christopher Worthevail, gentm., and to her heirs of body. To son Mark Toker, "the bidstead on which he now lyeth."

Residue to daughter Katherine, who is Sole Executrix.
No Act.
Sum of personality, £49 16s. 5d.
(Registrar's Office, Exeter.)

NOTE.—Deceased was Rector of Cardinham. Commission to Administer Oaths, dated 8th January, 1671.

1671. The Nuncupative Will of Jonathan Fox of Lancells, Husbandman, dated 20th June, 1671. He gives to his sister, Grace Fox, one white pigge of one year old. To his wife Julian, a Tenement at Ossington in Lancells, Co. Cornwall, *until* she succeeds to the moiety of the tenement at Whitistone in said County, after the decease of her mother Ulalia Addams. Reversion of Ossington then to his children Ulalia and Jonathan Fox. Ossington is held on lease determinable on the lives of Testator's sisters, Mary, wife of Wm. Potter, and Grace Fox. Residue to Philip Boteler of Pancras Wick, and Wm. Potter of Uffculme in trust for said children ; they are Exors.

Witnesses—Wm. Potter, Lydia Cole, and Mary Potter.

Admon. to Wm. Potter, clothier, of Uffculme. 31st Aug., 1671.

Sum, £52 7s. 6d.

1674. The last Will of Thomas Granger of Liskeard, and Rector of St. Melyan in the County of Cornwall, Clerk. Dated, 4th July, 1673. To the poor of St. Melyan, 20/-. To son Thomas Granger, "all my books" and £50, "advanced to him to be laid out on a mortgage of a tenure in the Duchy Manor of Calstock, the said Thomas being now the tenant." To said son's wife Elizabeth, 20/-. To son-in-law Robert Warren, 20/-, and to daughter Priscilla, wife of said Robert, 20/-, and a further legacy of £20.

Residue to wife Priscilla, who is Sole Executrix.

Proved 9th April, 1674.

Sum, £238 10s. 6d.

NOTE.—It appears, from the Inventory, that the Rector's library was valued in £20.

1677. The last Will of Roger Drake of Stoakstowne in the Co. of Wexford, Gentm. 20th Oct., 1677. To each of his daughters, and to that child his wife "now goeth with," £120. He leaves a life interest in his property to his wife Hannah, with reversion to his "only son" John Drake. To sister Anne Skinner, £20.

Residue to wife Anne, who is Sole Executrix.

Two Trustees.

Witnesses—Dennis Driscoll, Clerk, Barbara Rowles, Mary Driscoll.

Proved, Prin. Regy., Exon., 14th March, 1677, by Hannah Drake the Executrix.

(Registrar's Office, Exeter.)

NOTE.—This Will is especially interesting, as it is not to be found at Exeter Probate Court. I came upon it accidentally in the Office of the Registrar of the Diocese. It was evidently, from the names of two of the witnesses, executed in Ireland, and would, therefore, be scarcely likely to be looked for at Exeter.

1682. Will, with Codicil, of John Peter, Clerk, late Vicar of St. Enodoc, Co. Cornwall. Probate granted, 14th Dec., 1682, to "Renato" Peter, son and Exor.

(Epis. Regs.)

1683. The last Will of George Gibbs* the elder, of Clyst St. George, Yeoman. To the poor of the Parish, 40/-. To George Gibbs, his eldest son, the goods and household stuff in his dwelling-house. To Samuel Gibbs, his son, 20/-, and the land which he had purchased for him in Clyst St. George, to him and his heirs for ever. To Sarah Goulsworthy, his daughter, £20. To Henry Goulsworthy, his grandson, 5s. To Thomas Goulsworthy, his grandson, £5. To Elizabeth Henley,† 20/-, and 3/- to each of her three sons. To his son Abraham,‡ all the residue of his goods.

Will dated March 6th, 1682-3. Proved by Abraham Gibbs, Sole Executor, August 1st, 1683.

Overseers—Willm. Clare, Thomasin Toake, Samuel Truelake.

1683. Administration to the effects, &c., of John Wreyford of Beerferrers, granted to Elizabeth his relict 27th Aug., 1683. Matthew Wreyford of Dunterton, Surgeon, joins the bond.

1685. The last Will of Ann, daughter of Nicholas Borlase of Trelodro, Esqr., deceased. Dated 3rd July, 1685. To nephews, Giles Chichester, £100; John Chichester, £200. To niece, Ursula Chichester, £150, and 5 broad pieces of gold. To niece, Prudence Chichester, similar legacy. Legacies to "kinsfolk," children of William Borlace, viz., John, Joan, Ann, and to the youngest son of Phillipe Lincoln and to Margt. Chichester. Legacy to Mary, dau. of Henry Borlace; godchildren, Nicholas James and John Hawton. Servant, Mary James, an annuity of £6. £200 to be spent on the funeral, at direction of "Sister Chichester." Residue to niece, Katherine Chichester, who is Sole Executrix.

Exors. in trust, during minority of Executrix, Walter Blunt, Sir John Southcote, Edward Cary, Esq., and brother, John Chichester. Proved 17th Oct., 1688.

Crest-Seal—" A Wolf passant."

NOTE.—See Dec. 19th, 1701, *post*.

---

* So signed. He is called Gibbs in the Will. Eldest son of John Gibbs the elder, of Clyst St. George, was buried there, July 18th, 1683.
† Wife of Benjamin Brinley. ‡ Afterwards of Exeter, 1668.

1687. George Pollard of Fremington, Esqr., 29th April, 1687. He desires to be buried near his brother " Slowley " if he happens to die in Fremington. If not, then near his brother, Robert Pollard, at King's-Nympton. He mentions his brother "Sir Ames Pollard Bart." and his sister Dorothy Slowley. His cousin, Margaret Pollard.

Proved 8th March, 1687.

1688. Probate of the will of Sir Edward Seymour of Berry, granted to Dame Anne his wife, 15th Jany., 1688.

Epis. Regs.

1692. Michael Wrayford of Bovey Tracy, 9th May, 1692. To sons John, Michael, and William, and to daughters Elizabeth, Sarah, and Mary 1s. each.

Residue to wife Mary, who is Sole Executrix.

Witnesses—George and Elizb. Wrayford.

Proved 2nd Aug., 1692.

Sum £57.

1693. Administration to the effects of Francis Pollard, granted to her niece Margaret Hartnell, wife of John Hartnell, Sir Ames Pollard, brother of deceased, having renounced.

17th April, 1693.

1698. The last Will of Margaret Prideaux* of Shobrooke, co. Devon, widow, " being ancient." She leaves to the poor of Sandford, South Molton, and Holdworthy £10 each parish ; to the poor of Bradworthy 10s., and of Shobrooke £5. £50 to Mary Trosse, daughter of her cousin Mary Trosse of Exeter ; £50 to Thomas Trosse, son of her cousin Thomas Trosse of Upincott ; and £50 to his sister Margaret Trosse, desiring Mr. James Newton their grandfather to be their guardian. £20

---

* Daughter of . . . Lane and widow of . . . Hunt. (See Pedigree of Prideaux and Brune, p. 34). Married Nicholas, eldest son of Nicholas Prideaux, of Soldon, Co. Devon.

to Simon Hall the elder of Shobrooke, and £10 to John Hall his son. £20 to John Croome of Milton Damerel. The advowson of Plymptree and £200 to her cousin Robert Mercer, son of her cousin John Mercer of Ottery St. Mary, deceased. £100 to William Mercer, son of her cousin William Mercer of Budley. £100 to John Mercer, son of her said cousin John Mercer. To John Mercer, grandson of her said cousin John Mercer, all her lands, &c., in Ipplepen, to him and his heirs. Also to Malachy Mercer, brother to said John, and his heirs the messuage called Ford in the Parish of Cheriton Fitz Payne. Also to Richard, brother of the said John and Malachy, and his heirs, her house in Ottery, a house in Shobrooke and £100. Also to Jael Mercer* their sister £800 "if she be not married before my decease." Her cousins Isaac Gibbs† of Exeter and Joseph Olliver of Exwick to be guardians of the four children last named. To her sister Agnes Mercer‡ her tenement in Sowton called Walcombes for life, and after her death to Nicholas and Henry Ashe, sons of her cousin Henry Ashe of Swoton, on condition that they pay their sisters Elizabeth and Anne Ashe £100 each. Also to Margaret, Joseph, and John Oliver, children of her said cousin Joseph Olliver, all her lands in South Molton, North Molton, Chittlehampton, Bishops Nympton, and Bow, on condition that they pay Benjamin, Mary, and Elizabeth Oliver, their brother and sisters, £50 each. Also to Anne Gibbs, daughter of her said cousin Isaac Gibbs, her house in Northgate Street in Exeter. Various legacies to John Hawkins; John Downe; Joane Baker; Mary Ware; Southcott Luttrell, Esqre., and Joane his wife; John Moore, Esq., and Elizabeth his wife . . Olliver of Cowley, Esqre., and his wife; to her cousin Joseph Olliver; to her cousin Isaac Gibbs and Elizabeth Gibbs§ his mother; to her cousin Mr. Henry Ashe of Sowton and his wife; to William Mercer and Budley his wife; to Sarah Mercer‖ of Ottery, widow of John

---

* Mentioned in the Will of Elizabeth Gandy, of Exeter, 1719.—See next page.
† Isaac Gibbs married first Anne, daughter of John Mercer, of Ottery St. Mary, by Sarah his wife. Admon. May, 1726, C.P.C., and Sep., 1778. Archd. Court, Exeter.
‡ Agnes, wife of William Mercer, and mother of John abovenamed.
§ Elizabeth, daughter of Isaac Mauduit, of Exeter, wife of Abraham Gibbs, of Exeter, whose will in C.P.C. Nov. 6, 1668.
‖ Sarah, daughter of Robert Huntington, of Stanton Harcourt, Co. Oxon., married 1657 to John Mercer of Ottery S. Mary.

Mercer, deceased ; to John Mercer of Ottery and his wife; to Mary Trosse of Exeter, widow ; to Thomas Trosse of Upincott and his wife ; to Symon Hall the elder of Shobrooke ; and to the said John Croom and his wife. To John Gibbs,* son of her said cousin Isaac Gibbs of Exeter all her lands in Shobrooke, Cheriton, and Crediton (not before given) to him and his heirs for ever, or, in default of such issue, to his sister Anne Gibbs, or, in default, to the right heirs of her cousin Isaac Gibbs, and in default of such heirs to John Mercer, grandson of her cousin John Mercer, deceased, and to his heirs.

Residue of Realty and Personalty to the said John Gibbs. Will dated March 9, 1697/8.

Admon with will annexed to Isaac Gibbs during the minority of John Gibbs, Sole Exor., 18th Octr., 1698.

Probate to John Gibbs, August 7th, 1704.

Parties to administration bond, Isaac Gibbs of Exeter, Elizabeth Gibbs of the same, widow, and Elizabeth Gandy of the same, widow.

1701. Admon. de Bonis non to the effects of Ann Borlace, late of Trelodro, in the County of Cornwall, and of Arlington, in the Co. of Devon. Unadministered by John Chichester, one of the exors. Granted to Gyles Chichester, nephew of deceased, 19th Dec., 1701.

"The original will was proved in common form y* 7th Oct., 1685, in which bundle you will find y* original will.

NOTE.—See Oct. 17th, 1638, *ante*.

1701. Renunciation of Richard and Daniell Tucker of Cruse Morchard to the effects of Joan Payn of Caddely, who died 1st March, 1700.

"Their own sister's daughter and next of kin."

They desire that admon. be granted to Richard Smith of Cheriton, the Sole Exor. under the said Joan Payne's nuncupative will.

From Archives Prin. Regy., Exeter Cathedral.

---

* John Gibbs, of Exeter. Will in Principal Registry, Exeter, Nov. 1, 1742.

1704. Probate of the Will of William Arundell, late of Filleigh, clerk, deceased. Granted to Honor his relict. 6th Sept., 1704.
Epis. Regs.

1704. Administration of the estate of the male child of John Arundell and Margaret his wife, deceased before baptism. Granted to John his said father 25th Jany., 17C4-5.
Epis. Regs.

1706. Administration of the effects of Robert Cary of Sidbury, granted to Susanna his relict 14th Feby., 1706.
Sum £102 5s. 4d.
Epis. Regs.

1706. William Hole of North Tawton, 21st Oct., 1704 (Yeoman). To wife Joane £80. To daughter-in-law Mary Moore £4. To Thomas Crispin's children, "that he had by his wife Anne," £9. To kinsman Richard Hole of the parish of Bundley "my interest in Loutton in said parish" and the sum of £10. To kinsman Thomas Hole of Zeal Monachorum 20s. To kinswoman Prudence, wife of James French of North Tawton, 40s. per annum. Mentions his kinsman Peter Ware of North Tawton. Residue to brother Andrew, who is Sole Executor.
Proved 22nd May, 1706.
Inventory £653 8s. 4d.
Value of Chattle estates £450.

1708. Admon. of John Tucker of Morwenstow, granted 15th Dec., 1708, to Narcissus Hatherleigh, Gentm., of Bideford, John Honny of Kilkhampton, Gentm., and Arthur Judd of Bradworthy, Gentm.
Under £500.
From Archives Prin. Regy., Exeter Cath.

1709. Appointment of Trustee for Gilbert Yard of his mother Joan Yard, he being a minor of the age of 12 years, and heir at law to the estate of his late grandmother Elizabeth Yard late of Bradley, in the parish of Highweek, intestate.
Signed Gilbert Yarde.
Witnesses—William Rayner and Francis Pocock.
Seal of Arms—*Arg.* a saltire engrailed *erm.* (Rayner) Impaling, *arg.* on a fess indented betw. 3 delves, each charged with a lion ramp., 3 roundles (Rolle).
Date 16th Nov., 1709.
Registrar's Office, Exeter.

NOTE.—Elizabeth Yard, the grandmother, was widow of Gilbert Yard of Bradley, and daughter of Henry Northleigh of Peamore. Joan Yard, the mother, was widow of Gilbert Yard of Bradley, and dau. and heir of Henry Blackaller of Sharpham. Gilbert Yard, aged 12, 1709, sold Bradley to Mr. Thomas Veale in 1751. He had two sons, Giles and James. Giles Yard purchased Trowbridge in Crediton parish, which is now the property of Mr. John Yard. See my "Devonshire Parishes," Vol. II., p. 294.

1710. Thomas Granger, Clerk and "Minister of God's word at Lammerton," Nov. 14th, 1709. He desires to be buried in the churchyard there near his "dear wife." To the poor there 20s. To son Thomas £100. To Lydia, wife of said Thomas, and to each of his children, £1. To daughter Elizabeth, wife of Joseph Vill, and to each of their children, £1. To sister Priscilla Warren and to her daughter Sarah, £1.
Residue to son Edmund, who is Sole Exor.
Witnesses—John Doidge, Thomas Burnaford, Joanna Doidge.
Proved 2nd Nov., 1710.

NOTE.—Refer to 9th April, 1674 The mention of sister Priscilla proves that deceased was son of Thomas Granger, Rector of St. Melynn.

1711. Administration to the effects of Thomas Pollard of Abbots Bickington, granted 7th Nov., 1711, to Sarah his relict.

1719. The last Will of John Osmond of Exeter, M.D. He desires to be privately interred in the night in "the Chappel where Bishop Oldam lies buried in St. Peter's Church, if the Church of Exeter will permit." £100 to be expended on his funeral. To his "wife" £100, and £50, "which was the bequest of her sister Mrs. Dorothy Champneys," together with £10, "the bequest of Mrs. Catherine Pollard." To sister Elizabeth Pyle £20. To nephew and niece, John and Elizabeth Hare, £50 each at 25. "To my dear wife" Rings, Jewels, Gold Box and the "Broad pieces" "that belong to it," "her gold watch, Pearl necklace, wearing apparel, and Books." Plate to be equally divided between "my wife and my executrix." "To my —— Anne Champneys living with me" £20. To "my wife's brother, Mr. Arthur Champneys, and to his daughter, £10.

Residue to sister "Mrs. Rebeckah Osmond, who is Sole Executrix."

Will dated 4th Jany., 1712. Proved 29th March, 1719.

Witnesses—John Vinicombe.
          Wm. Pitfield.
          Christopher Hunt.

Seal—A fess dancettée charged with 9 *ermine* spots.
Crest—An Eagle displayed.

NOTE.—Dr. Osmond was buried as he desired in St. Saviour's Chapel in Exeter Cathedral. He died 3rd April, 1716, æt. 60. From his epitaph we learn that his wife's name was "Honora." His library was sold at his house in the Cathedral Close 16th July, 1716. The arms of Osmond of Uplowman, Halberton, and Tiverton, four descents, are registered in the V. of 1620. They are S. a fess dancettée, *erm.* in ch., an Eagle displd., *arg.*

1719. John Pollard of Beaworthy in the County of Devon, Clerk. He leaves his son Thomas 10s. Daughter Amy, wife of John Shepperd, £5. Daughter Elizabeth, wife of Robert ffiney, £5. Daughter Susanna, wife of Wm. Harris, £5. Daughter Priscilla, wife of John Herring, £5. To son John £10.

Residue to daughter Jane Pollard, who is Sole Executrix.

Dated 12th Nov., 1719. Proved 13th Feby., 1719-20.

Sum £74 12s. 6d.

1724. Andrew Hole of North Tawton. He leaves to his son Andrew his interest in the Tenement known as Wood in Loosebeare and parish of Zeal Monachorum, charged with the payment of £10 to son William. To son Richard, Tenements called Lower Reave and Church Parks in the parish of Brushford, charged with payment of £200 to daughter Susannah. To son Peter Hole, £150. To son John Hole, £5. To daughter Elizabeth White, 20s. To Jane Newcomb, 5s. Mentions " Mr. Robert Hole and Peter Ware." Testator reserves the Tenement called Nymets Nicholl. Residue to son Richard, who is Sole Exor.

Reversion of Brushford property to son Andrew.

Proved 29th Jany., 1724.

1726. William Burlace of Plymouth, Gentleman. Dated 30th March, 1726. He discharges his nephew John Burlace of " Pendiens," Esqr., of £700 due to him, but to pay the interest thereof. To cousin Mary Pendarvis, formerly Mary Pearse, £100 "due to me in her maiden name, and since confirmed by her husband Henry Pendarvis." To Elizb. Condy of Plymouth, £20. Residue to John Gennys of Plymouth, merchant, and his heirs for ever. He is Sole Exor.

Witnesses—John Elliot, sen. and jun. ; John Wicote.

Proved 10th Oct., 1726.

Seal—Arms of Borlase. *Erm.* on a bend, two hands tearing asunder a horse shoe. A crescent for difference (Borlase). Crest, a wolf passant regardant.

1728. Admon. to the effects of Robert Borlase, late of Newlyn, Co. of Cornwall, deceased. Granted 4th Aug., 1728, to Teresa his sister.

1728. John Tucker of Totnes, Dyer, 24th Jany., 1726. To his mother Susanna Tucker, one suit of mourning. To sister Elizabeth the same. To daughter Susanna Tucker, his house and £100 at 21. He gives all his property to said daughter Susanna after the death of her mother, with reversion, failing

heirs, to his said sister Elizabeth, provided his wife is not with child when he dies, but should she have a son, said son to inherit the lands and pay his sister Susanna £100 more.
Wife Elizabeth Sole Executrix.   Residue undisposed of.
Witnesses—Joseph Fox, Frederick Cross, Wm. Churchward.
Proved 6th Aug., 1728.

1730. License granted to James Sheppard, Esqr., to remove the "corps" of his deceased mother from Chudleigh Church, and to re-inter it with his father Sir James Sheppard deceased, one of His Majesty's Sergts. at Law, in the Church of Honyton, April 21st, 1730.
Epis. Reg., Exon.

1733. The last Will of Tryphœna Gibbs of Topsham, "of considerably advanced age."   Leaves £65 to Edward Rowe* of Exeter and Lawrence Rowe† of Shobrooke, Gentn., and all her wrought plate, to be divided between her three grandchildren‡ George Abraham, Anna, and John, the first and second to have £30 apiece, and John £5.
Will dated Nov. 20th, 1727.   Proved May 17th, 1733.
Executors her daughters Elizabeth Pett and Mary Peters.§
Witnesses—Elizabeth Row and John Conant.

1733. Bond of £10 from David Evans of the city of Exeter, Locksmith, and Francis Bidwell of the same, Serge Weaver, to Walter Husband of Whitestone, Co. Cornwall, Gentm.—the condition being that Richard Tucker and Susanna his wife, alias Call, having received a legacy of £10 under the will of Stephen Call, late of Stratton, from the said Walter Husband, surviving Exor. to said will, the above bounden shall be responsible for the debts of said Stephen Call.
Registrar's Office, Exeter.

---

* Her brother.   † Son of her elder brother William Rowe.
‡ George Abraham Gibbs [P. C. C., 1795] and Anna Gibbs, children of her son Abraham [Dean and Ch. 1726] by his first wife Mary Monke; and John his son by his second wife Sarah Lyle.
§ Wife of Nicholas Peters of Topsham, Surgeon [Will Pr. Reg., 1747], married at Clyst St. George, March 8th, 1719.

1737. Thomas Hole of Beere in North Tawton, Yeoman. 9th April, 1737. To wife Elizabeth, £5. To daughter Elizabeth, £200. To daughter Catherine, £200. To kinswoman Elizb. Dennaford, 40s. To son Thomas and his heirs male and female, "the lands of my inheritance known as Beere & my tenmt. called West Lee, in the parish of Coleridge."

Residue to said son Thomas, who is Sole Exor.

Exors. in Trust, all children being under 21, father-in-law, Roger Durant of Zeal Monachorum; brother-in-law, George Durant of North Tawton; *kinsman, Wm. Skinner* of North Tawton.

Testator is owner of "Lower Nichols-Nymet." Provision of £600 for a boy, £200 for a girl, should his wife be *enciente* at his death.

Proved 15th July, 1737, by Roger and George Durant.

NOTE.—The Skinners were of Ashridge in North Tawton. The daughter and co-heir married Orchard; their daughter, Cornish, the present owner of Ashridge.

1738. Edmund Granger of Cruwys Morchard, Clerk. 20th Aug., 1737. Desires to be buried in the churchyard there near his wife. To the poor, 30s.; and to those of Brampford Speke, 20s. To daughters Elizabeth and Susannah Granger, £100 each. To sons Thomas and Edmund Granger, my Study of Books, "they giving my two daughters such books of divinity and morality as shall be thought most proper and consistent for them."

Residue to said children, the two sons being joint Exors.

Witnesses—Daniel Domett; Peter Pridham; William Hakworthy.

Proved 19th April, 1738.

NOTE.—Refer to Nov. 2nd, 1710. Edmund Granger was instituted to the Vicarage of Brampford Speke 24th Aug., 1708. His successor there, Thomas Johnson, was admitted 30th May, 1738. He was buried at Cruse Morchard, as he desired, 21st January, 1737.

1742. The last Will of John Gibbs of Exeter, Esqre. Desires to be buried by his father* in the Church of St. Mary Arches, Exeter. Leaves his lands in Exeter to pay his debts. Gives £20 each to his kinsman Henry Gandy,† and Jael [Mercer] his wife; and to his sons-in-law Stephen Weston, Dr. Ballyman, and Samuel Pierce of Shobrooke, leaving to these three last in trust, for his daughter Anne Ballyman and her heirs, the manor of Cross in Cheriton Fitzpaine, Poughill, and Morchard Cruwys, and all other manors, except that of Shute and Satchfield in Cheriton Fitzpaine, and certain lands in Shobrooke which were entailed by his aunt Prideaux.‡

Sealed with arms and crest as George Gibbs, 1691.
Executrix—Anne Ballyman.
Witnesses.
Will dated Nov. 2nd, 1741. Proved Nov. 1st, 1742.

1744. Administration to the effects of Charles Granger of Woodbury. Granted to Martha his wife 5th Nov., 1744.
Under £15.

1747. Richard Hole of North Tawton, Clerk, 1st May, 1747. Being seized in fee of the perpetual advowson of the Rectory of North Tawton, and intending that it shall remain in his name and family, he bequeaths it to his nephew Thomas Hole, son of brother Robert Hole, and his heirs male; failing such to Richard, son of said Robert Hole, and his heirs.

Upon trust that one of said Testator's name and family shall always be presented upon any avoidance, with preference to the heir in possession if duly qualified to hold it. His "worthy friend" Wm. Hole, Archdeacon of Barnstaple, to have the said Rectory in commendam after his death under a bond of £4,000,

---

* Isaac Gibbs. Admōn. 1726.
† Son of Simon Gandy and Elizabeth his wife, sister of the said Isaac and daughter of Abraham Gibbs, 1668.
‡ Margaret, wife of . . . Prideaux was the aunt of Anne Mercer, wife of Isaac Gibbs.

to resign it when any of Testator's name and family can take it. Every incumbent to give a bond of £1,000 to reside upon the said living. To said nephew Richard Hole the fee-simple of Larkworthy in North Tawton. Mentions niece Mary Hole, daughter of said brother Robert. To nephew Richard, son of brother Emmanuel Hole, £50. To kinsman Wm. Pidsley of Colebrook, £50. To nephew Richard Hole of Colebrook, son of brother Thomas, £50. Bequests to niece Lucy, wife of George Hert of Highampton; niece Rebecca, wife of Roger Hert of Burrington; and to Gertrude Hert and Mary Hert, "my servant maids." To the first child of niece Martha Hearding, £100.

Exors. in trust, Revd. John Heath of Sampford Courtenay; William Pidsley; Richard Hole of Colebrook; and Richard Hole of Exeter (nephew), for benefit of said nephew Thomas Hole.

Proved 27th June, 1747.

1748. The last Will of Ann Gregson* of Exeter. Leaves her husband William Gregson* the manors of Shute and Satchfield in Cheriton Fitzpayne, and lands in Shobrooke (which she thinks were entailed by her aunt Prideaux's will† on Ann Maria Heath for life) for his life; remainder to Samuel Pierce of Gendacott her brother-in-law, and to Stephen Weston, Esqre., of Exeter, in trust for her daughter Elizabeth Pierce.‡ To the same persons also she devises her manors of Cross, &c., and all other her manors in Devonshire, and the rest of the estates which came to her from her father.§

Executor.

Will dated Feb. 3rd, 1747-8. Proved 1748.
Witnesses.

---

* Daughter of John Gibbs of Exeter, by Mary, daughter of Nicholas Hall; married, firstly, Feb. 11th, 1728, Adam Pierce (who died 1732); secondly, Dr. Ballyman; and thirdly, William Gregson, in 1746-7.
† Oct., 1698. Admōn. August, 1702. Probate in the Principal Registry, Exeter.
‡ Married, 1752, to Thomas Taylor, Esq., of Denberry and Ogwell; died 1777; only child.
§ Principal Registry, Nov., 1742.

1762. "Administration de Bonis non" of the effects of Edward Borlace, late of St. Michael's, Penkevil, and County of Cornwall, deceased. Unadministered by Mary Bolitho, daughter of the said deceased. Granted 6th March, 1762, to Simon Bolitho, late husband of the said Mary.

1764. "Admon. de Bonis non" of goods unadministered by Mary Wreford, deceased, and once the estate of Samuel Wreford of Landkey, in the County of Cornwall. Granted 3rd May, 1764, to William Wreford of Clanaborough, yeoman. Wm. Wreford, jun., of the same parish and County of Devon joins the bond.

The affidavit states that the said William Wreford the elder is the Executor named in the Will of said Mary, who administered to the estate of her deceased husband; Saml. Wreford of Landkey, is believed to have died intestate.

1765. Roger Granger of Woodbury, yeoman, 6th June, 1765. To brothers Thomas and Richard, 1s. each. Residue to wife Ann, who is Sole Executrix.

Witnesses—John Stokes; Mary Penguin.

Proved 19th July, 1765.

1767. "Admon. de Bonis non" of the goods unadministered by Cecily, the relict of John Saunder, late of Chittlehampton. Granted 28th June, 1767, to George Saunder the nephew.

NOTE.—See Barnstaple, *ante*. 7th May, 1731.

1770. Administration to the effects of John Pollard of Mariansleigh. Granted to William Bowdon, of Bishops-Nympton, 23rd November, 1770, Margaret the widow having renounced.

NOTE.—William Bowdon, was the son-in-law of deceased.

1779. Administration to the effects of John Pollard of Gwennap, in the county of Cornwall. Granted 9th July, 1779, to Martha Pollard, his widow.

1772. Thomas Hole of North Tawton, Clerk, 26th May, 1770.
To his mother Martha Hole, of Zeal Monachorum, widow, £21.
He leaves the Advowson of North Tawton to his brother, the Rev. Richard Hole and his heirs. Residue to said brother Richard, who is Sole Exor.
Proved 1772.
Armorial Seal—An Annulet between 3 fusils.

NOTE.—"*As.* an annulet *arg.* between 3 lozenges *or.*" Hole of Ebberly in Great Torrington.

1772. Administration to the Effects of Henry Woodley late of Ashburton, deceased intestate. Granted 27th Feby., 1772, to Catherine, wife of Richard Harris, of Ashburton, his sister, and only next of kin.

1777. Edmund Granger of Sowton, Clerk, 1st April, 1772.
To the poor there, 40s.; and to the poor of Clist Honiton, 40s.
Residue to his wife Ann Granger, who is Sole Executrix.
He desires his brother Thomas Granger, his friend Thomas Binford, and his brother-in-law Thomas Prowse to "advice his wife," he wishes her to dispose of his property amongst "the children."
Witnesses—Wm. Wedcott (Westcott?); Jos. Free.
Proved 26th Sept., 1791.
Seal of Arms.—A fess between two acorns.
Crest.—A hand holding a Portcullis.

NOTE.—Refer to 19th April, 1738. This Edmund Granger had a "portion" of Bampton Vicarage, Diocese Oxon., which he exchanged with Elias Taunton for the Rectory of Sowton, near Exeter, 16th Feb., 1750-1. Mr. Granger died 25th Aug., 1777, æt. 64. His wife Ann was buried with him at Sowton, 9th Sept., 1812, æt. 82.

1789. The last Will of John Wreford of Nymet Rowland, yeoman, 7th Aug., 1787. To wife Judith, £21, and best bed. To son William, the Clevehanger estate, subject to wife's jointure, and charged with an annuity of £25 towards the maintenance of daughters Mary, Anne, Catherine, and Judith during their minority. They are to have £100 each at 21.

Clatworthy, in the parish of Coleridge, to Richard Vickery and Thomas Melhuish Comins in trust, together with Brownsland in Colebrook, for the benefit of sons John, Samuel, and Richard Wreford in equal division at 21.

Residue to said Wm. Wreford, who is Sole Exor.

Witnesses—Ann Comins ; Grace Pedler ; Betty Partridge.

Proved 29th May, 1789.

1794. Thomas Osmond of Silverton, Gentleman. Dated 12th Aug., 1786. He gives certain leasehold closes of land in the parish of Willand to trustees, viz., Charles Leigh, Gentleman, of Uffculme, and John Wyett of the same, for the following uses :—To pay an annuity of £10 to sister Joan Tanner, and to give the rents of a portion of the said property to nephew John, with remainder to his son Thomas Osmond Tanner and his heirs ; failing such to revert to John, second son of said John Tanner and his heirs. To William, son of Thomas Quicke, and Joan his wife, " my late niece," both deceased, he gives the reversion, failing issue of the Tanners of freehold property in Halberton in fee simple ; and he further leaves the sum of £400 in trust for John, James, Henry, and George Quick, the other children of the said Thomas and Joan Quick. Residue to said nephew John Tanner, who is Sole Executor.

Witnesses—John and Ann Head ; John Pudnor, sen.

Five sheets of paper.

Proved 11th March, 1794.

1794. The last Will of John Seaward of the Close, Exeter, 30th March, 1791. Legacies to daughters Martha Jones, and Jane King. He mentions his wife Anne. He refers to his property at Woodbury and St. George's Clist, and to his house in St. Peter's Churchyard, Exeter, now in possession of Mr. Jackson, Postmaster.

Proved 20th Feb., 1794.

Registrar's Office, Exeter.

NOTE.—Testator was doubtless of the family of John Seaward of Clist St. George, whose son, Edward Seaward, a merchant, of Bradninch precinct, Exeter, was mayor of Exeter, 1691, and received the honour of knighthood from William of Orange. He was first Governor of Exeter Hospital. Sir Edward died 1st of May, 1703, and had children —Nicholas, Edward, John, and Hannah, who all pre-deceased him. Hannah was christened at St. Mary Majors, Exeter, May 19th, 1682. Her mother was Hannah, daughter of Nicholas Brooking. Sir Edward's picture is in the chapel of Exeter Workhouse, and he has a fine monument in St. Paul's Church, Exeter. Elizabeth Seaward, of the Clist St. George family, married Peter Chears of Exeter; their great-grandson, Captain H. Bennett, sometime Governor of the Island of Ascension, was the husband of Mary, daughter of Jonathan Worthy, Esq., of Exeter, and their only surviving son, Major-General Henry Worthy Bennett, married, secondly, in 1878, his first cousin, Lucretia, daughter of the late Rev. C. Worthy, Vicar of Ashburton, by whom he has issue.

PREROGATIVE COURT OF CANTERBURY.

1571. The last Will of Roger Mathewe of Clyst St. George, co. Devon.

He leaves to Margaret Gybbe, daughter of John Gybbe,* "a read heaffer." To the said John Gybbe, his best colte, "his herriot being chosen." To Julian, daughter of the said John Gybbe, one ewe shepe and one lambe. To the poor of Clyst St. George, 10/-; to the poor of Stooklonde, 20/-; and to the poor of Upotery, 20/-. To Nicholas, son of Edmund Hutchyn, deceased, £5; and to two other sons of the said Edmund, each a shepe. To William, son of Richard Hutchin, £10. To William Code his son-in-lawe, £20. To his sister Johane Lake, one sparked heifer. To every of the children of Willyam Clode "which he hath by my sister, one shepe." To the children of his brothers Willyam and John Mathewe, each a sheep. To the children of his brother-in-law Thomas Buller the debt which the said Thomas oweth him. John Hutchyn of Upoterie† to have and enjoy "all that my terme of yeares, and interest in the land, meadow and pasture, with the appurtenances, called Huggleshayes in the parish of Upoterie, with common of pasture for threescore shepe thereto belonging." To each of the children of Robert Podyn, a shepe; and a shepe to each of the children of John Lake. To each of the children of Robert Hutchyn, Robert, Roger, Humphrey, Mary, Briget, and Grace, 20/-. To the children of his brother-in-law Thomas Buller, "the debt that he oweth me, to be divided between them." To William Mathew,

---

* Son of George Gybbe of Clyst St. George. Will in Dean and Chapter's Court, Exeter, December, 1593.
† Up Ottery. (*Query*—the same as Mohun's Ottery?)

the son of Robert Mathew, deceased, 40/-. To Elenor and Joyce, daughters of the said Robert, £10 apiece. To each of his godchildren, 2/-. To Mary Mabell, daughter of Hamond Mabell, 5/-. "To my servant Robert Knyght one stere, the price forty shillings and six shillings and eight pence." To each of his servants Thomas Edward, Tristram Haccombe, Christopher Wall, John Bobbyn, and John Scott, 5/-.

Willyam Gybbe, clerk,* Thomas Haydon the younger, and Edmund Were, to be Overseers of his will.

Witnesses—Willyam Gybbe, clerke, Thomas Haydon the younger, gentm., John Gybbe, Thomas Suchespyche, Willyam Eton and others.

Will dated April 20th, 1571. Proved May 11th, 1571, by Christian Mathewe his residuary legatee and Executrix.

1577. The last Will of Christian Mathewe of Clyst St. George, Co. Devon, Widowe.

She desires to be buried at Clyst St. George, by her "last husband Roger Mathewe."

She leaves to her "son in lawe John Gibbe† to the use of his children, twentie pounds." To "my son George Code sixty pounds, on condition that not by any meanes or proceesement he trouble my Executor." Also "sixe silver spoones signed with the Apostles." Also "a white cuppe covered with silver and not gilted." To "Jone his wieff my best russett cassock." "To Cicellie Gibbe my daughter my best silke hatt, my best cassocke, my best two kerchiefs, my best two neckerchiefes with three crosse cloathes." "To Margaret Gibbe my daughter's daughter one cowe." "To John Gibbe's sonne William Gibbe a yew and a lambe, and to Julian Gibbe a yewe lambe."

To the poor of the Parish of "Upawtry,"‡ 20/-. To the poor of Clyst St. George, 10/-, and one dozen wooddis.

---

* Rector of Clyst St. George (and before that of Clyst St. Mary), died 1571. Will in the Consistory Court, Exeter, 1571, June 8th.
† Son of George Gibbe of Clyst St. George. Will in the Archdeacon's Court of Exeter, 20th Dec., 1593.
‡ Up-Ottery, near Honiton.

To Margaret Hutchin, a black kirtell with chamlett bodies. To James Hole, her brother-in-law, £6 13s. 4d. ; and " to his wieff my cassock made of my gownes." To Elizabeth Mais of Clyst Hidon, a yew shepe. To Alice Lake of Loupitte, twentie shillings. To Elizabeth Hunt of Clyst St. George, " my redd kirtell with chamlett bodies." To Morice Payn, 5/-. To her god-children, 12d. each. To her servant Johan Scott, £10, and " my best petticote with taffeto bodies, and my best felt hatt saving one." To Jone Plimpton " a petticote with chamlett bodies." She makes her sonne, William Code, her Executor and Residuary Legatee.

In a Codicil dated March 4th, 1576-7, she leaves to the two daughters of John Gibbe, Margaret and Julian, "two latten pottes standing on the cubborde," and to Margaret one platter and a black cassock. To Margaret Hutchin, a peck of rye and a cheese. To Robert Buckland, person, 10/-. To her manservants, 2/- each. To Johan Edwards, a bushel of malt. " To my mayde Alice Seward," 20/-. " To each of my boyes," 12d. To Dennes Peers, a peck of rye and a bushell of malte. To John Chapman, a peck of rye and a bushell of malte. To Jane Phillip of Apsham,* a peck of rye and 16d. To Johane Scotte, " 10/- more besides that given her on my will." To Grace, daughter of George Code, 20/- ; to Johan, "wieff of George Code my best side sadell." To Agnes Besse, three poundes of lambe towe. To Thomas Suckespiche, half that is due to me.

Will dated Jan. 18th, 1576-7. Proved, with Codicil, April 4th, 1577.

Overseers, William Code and Nicholas Elliott.

Witnesses— Robert Buckland, clerk, parson there, John Gibbe, Edmund Weare, and Nicholas Elliott, with William Eton, writer hereof.

1580. Admon. of the goods of William Gibbes of Fenton, in the Parish of Dartington, in the County of Devon, Esquire. Granted in November, 1580, to John Ayer of

* Instituted 1571.

Penegett, Co. Cornwall, during the minority of William Wotton, son of Silvester Gibbes, *alias* Wootton, daughter of deceased.

NOTE.—William Gibbes was the last of a long line of that name possessors of Fenton (or Venton), which passed at his death to the Wottons, the eldest of his two daughters and co-heirs, Silvestra, having married Walter Wotton, and the youngest, Elizabeth, Edward Wotton, his elder brother, after whose death—sans issue—she married Edmund Drewe of Hayne. See Funeral Certificate at the College of Arms, showing his banner, Gibbes (see under George of Clyst St. George, 1691) impaling Berkeley.

1668. The last Will of Abraham Gibbs[*] of the City of Exeter, and of St. George's, near Exeter.

After divers charitable bequests, he divides his property into three parts: one to his wife Elizabeth[†] absolutely; one to her for life, and afterwards to his children; and one to his children in equal shares.

Executrix, Elizabeth his wife.

Overseers, Isaac Mauditt[‡] and Jasper Mauditt, merchants, his brothers-in-law, and George Gibbs [§] and Robert Gibbs,[§] his brothers.

Witnesses—Samuel Izacke, Phill. fforce.

Will dated 12th Sept., 1668. Proved, 6th Nov., 1668, by Elizabeth Gibbs, Executrix.

1668. The last Will of Abraham Gibbs of the City of Exeter and of St. George's, near Exeter.

After divers charitable bequests, he leaves to his wife Elizabeth (his Executrix) one third of his property, absolutely; and one third for her life with remainder to his children equally; and the other third to his said children, in equal shares.

Overseers—His brothers-in-law, Isaac Mauditt and Jasper

---

[*] Fourth son of John Gibbe the elder, of Clyst St. George, son of George Gibb (Court of Archd., Exon., 29th Aug., 1606). Abraham Gibbs was Steward of Exeter in 1660.
[†] Daughter of Isaac Mauduit of Exeter, J.P. & D.L.
[‡] Steward of Exeter, 1669; Mayor, 1681.
[§] Eldest and third sons of the said John Gibbe. (Principal Registry, 1st Aug., 1683. Court of Vicars Choral, 27th Feb., 1701-2.)

Mauditt, merchants, and George Gibbs and Robert Gibbs, yeomen, his brothers.
Witnesses—Samuell Izacke, Phill. ffurce.
Will dated Sept. 12th, 1668. Proved, Nov. 6th, 1668.
Seal—His merchants mark : the escutcheon, surmounted by an esquire's helmet.

1677-8. The last Will of John Gibbs* of Exeter, Grocer. He bequeaths 40s. to the Rev. Mr. Gillard, a minister of God's word, and rings of 20s. each to Mrs. Prudence Rolston of Exeter, and Mr. John Dyer of Showbrook. He forgives Michael Eastridge £5 of the £10 owing by him, and leaves all the residue of his property to his brother-in-law Benjamin Brinley of Exeter, and his sister Elizabeth,† wife of the said Benjamin, whom he makes his Executors.
Will dated 24th Jan., 1677-8. Proved by Benjamin and Elizabeth Brinley. [13 Reeve.]
Witnesses—Joshua Saunders; Andrew Godfrey; Lewis Bare.

1678. The last Will of John Gibbs of Exeter, Grocer. Leaves 40s. to Mr. Gillard, minister of God's word ; a ring of 20s. each to Mrs. Prudence Rolston of Exeter, and Mr. John Dyer of Showbrook. Forgives Michael Eastridge "Five pound of a debt of £10 which he oweth me ;" gives his Thomasine Voysey 40s. ; and the residue of his property to his brother-in-law Benjamin Brinley, and his sister Elizabeth, wife of the said Benjamin.
Exors.—Benjamin and Elizabeth Brinley.
Witnesses—Joshua Saunders, Andrew Godfrey, Lewes Bare.
Will dated Jan. 24th, 1677-8. Proved Feb. 25th following.
Seal.—A merchant's mark much like that of his uncle Abraham Gibbs, 1668.

---

* Third son of George Gibbe of Clyst St. George. (Principal Registry of the Bishop of Exeter, 3rd Aug., 1683).
† Third daughter of the same.

1678-9. Susanna Bartlett of the City of Exeter, widow, 17th December, 1678. To my daughter Susanna those two houses where Mrs. Hide and Mrs. Carey now live in the parish of St. Petrox, within the city of Exeter, and also the household goods in the house where I now live, save one suit of damask, &c., and my moneys. To Mr. John Bartlett, minister of God's word in Exeter, and to Mr. Thomas Ware, also a minister in the same, £5 each. I give £20 towards the education of my sister Brownsford's children. Residue to my son Tristram Bartlett, and he Exor.

I make Mr. John Starr and Mr. John Horne, both of Exeter, overseers until the expiration of my son's apprenticeship, two years hence.

Witnesses—Yachaire Foswell, James Brownsford.

Proved, February, 1678-9, by Tristram Bartlett, son, and Exor.

1693. The last Will of Jacob Gibbs[*] of the city of London, Citizen and Salter. He leaves all that he has to his brother, the Rev. John Gibbs[*] of Oxford.

Will dated in St. Clement's, Eastcheap, May 23rd, 1693; proved the same day.

Witnesses—Joane Harrison, Sarah Hayes, Stephen Holland.

Sealed with the arms of Holland.

1698-9. Nuncupative Will of John Gibbs,[†] LL.D., Rector of Welwyn, co. Herts., made "on or about 7th Jan., 1698, English style," shortly before his death in January, 1698-9.

He leaves his property to his sister Elizabeth Gandy,[‡] she being a widow and having two children alive. He says that his mother, Elizabeth Gibbs,[§] was old, and well provided for, and that his brother Isaac [||] lacked nothing.

Probate granted to Elizabeth Gandy, 31st March, 1699.

Deponed by three witnesses (same date), William Battell, John Twydell, and Elizabeth Twydell.

---

[*] Sons of Abraham Gibbs of Exeter, 1668.
[†] Second son of Abraham Gibbs of Exeter (P.C.C., 12th Sept., 1668), was of Exeter College, Oxford, and Fellow of All Souls.
[‡] Widow of Simon Gandy (who died 1689). See her Will, P.C C., 1st Sept., 1719.
[§] Daughter of Isaac Mauduit of Exeter.
[||] Eldest son of Abraham Gibbs (C.P.C., 5th May, 1725).

1719. The last Will of Elizabeth Gandy* of Exeter. Mentions her grandson Samuel, son of Abraham Gandy, deceased, to whom she leaves £100 at 21. To her daughter-in-law, Grace Gandy,† £10 for mourning. To her daughter-in-law, Elizabeth Gandy, the same. To her brother, Isaac Gibbs, for his own and her sister's mourning, £10. To her friends, Mrs. Grace Sampson, widow, and Mrs. Jael Mercer,‡ a Jacobus apiece.
Residue to her son Henry Gandy.‡
Will dated Sept. 30th, 1717. Proved Sept. 1st, 1719, by the Executor, Henry Gandy.
Witnesses—George Phillips, Silva. Evans.

1726. Administration of the Goods of Isaac Gibbs,§ late of Exeter, was granted to John Gibbs, Esq.,∥ of the same, son of the deceased; Sarah Gibbs,¶ relict of the said Isaac, renouncing.
Date of Grant, May 5th, 1726.

1732-3. The last Will of Adam Pierce of Yendacott,** Co. Devon, Esquire.
He leaves his coach and four horses, his jewels, wardrobe, etc., to his wife Ann.†† To her, also, and to her father John Gibbs, Esquire,‡‡ and to his brother Samuel Pierce (whom he makes his Executors) he leaves all his freeholds, in trust, to pay his debts, and then to his sons, if any, in tail male;

---

* Daughter of Abraham Gibbs. P.C.C., November, 1668, and widow of Simon Gandy of Ide, Co. Devon.
† Wife of Henry Gandy, daughter of — Sampson. Married, 1705.
‡ Henry Gandy married Jael, daughter of John Mercer, as his second wife, in 1719.
§ Steward of Exeter, 1685; Sheriff, 1692; Receiver, 1693. He was son of Abraham Gibbs (P.C.C., 1668), who was Steward of Exeter, 1660.
∥ Will in Principal Registry of the Bishop of Exeter, 1742.
¶ Sarah, sister of Roger and Phineas Cheeke, and widow of . . . Clutterbrook. Will in C.P.C., 1743-4.
** On the Original is endorsed "Nuper de Yarrenton in parochia de Shobrooke."
†† Daughter of John Gibbs by Mary his wife, daughter of Nicholas Hall, Esq. She married, secondly, Dr. Ballyman; and thirdly, William Gregson; and died, 1748 (leaving one daughter, afterwards married to Thomas Taylor, Esq.) Will in Principal Registry, Exeter.
‡‡ John, son of Isaac Gibbs. Will in Principal Registry, Exeter, Nov. 1st, 1742.

remainder to his daughters as tenants in common; remainder to his brother Samuel Pierce for life, with remainder to his son in tail male; remainder to his brother Thomas Pierce for life, and then to his sons in tail male; remainder to his brother John Pierce for life, and then to his sons in tail male; remainder to his own right heirs for ever.

As to the leaseholds, the same trust, except that failing his own issue male, the remainder of one quarter of the manor and lands at Thorowton to his brother Samuel, absolutely, and the rest of the leaseholds to his own daughters.

The plate to remain as heirlooms in the Pierce family.

Personalty to remain as a fund for the education of his children.

Confirms his Marriage Settlement (February, 1728).

Will dated Dec. 4th, 1732. Proved 27th Feb., 1732-3, by the three Exors.

Witnesses—Francis Blyton, Eliz. Dennis, Nicholas Thomas, jun.

Seal.—1st and 4th, Pierce.[*] 2nd and 3rd,[†] a lion rampant impaling, *argent*, 3 battleaxes *sable* for Gibbs.

1744. The last Will of Sarah Gibbs[‡] of Exeter, widow. She desires to be buried by her husband in the Church of St. Mary Arches. Mentions her brothers Roger and Phineas Cheeke, and makes the latter her Executor; also her sister Susanna Poole and her children, John Poole, Sarah Bellew, and Susanna and Jane Poole. To Anne, daughter of John Pyne, Esquire, of Dartmouth, she leaves a legacy (revoked by a Codicil, Dec. 12th, 1728), and one to Malachy Pyne his son; also one to John Pyne himself; also to her cousin Jane Mayor, wife of John Gill. She leaves money also to the poor of St. Sidwells, and £5 to the poor of St. Mary Arches; but she revokes this last by a Codicil, Oct. 22nd, 1743, having altered her mind as to being buried in that church. Legacies also to the Rev. John Wither,

---

[*] Apparently 3 cross-crosslets on a bend, or bendwise, *Or*, the field *Argent*, but the seal is very small, and I had no magnifying glass.

[†] *Query*—Cossins? E. C. was mother of Adam Pierce.

[‡] Second wife of Isaac Gibbs of Exeter (P.C.C., May, 1726. Archd. Court, Exeter, Sept., 1748), having been before the wife of . . . Clutterbrooke.

and to John Lavington of Exeter; and to Mrs. Enty and Mrs. Green; to John Gibbs, Esquire,* and to his wife Mary† and their two daughters Mary‡ and Anne;§ also to Henry Gandy, Gentleman, and his wife.

Will dated Sept. 30th, 1726. Proved, with two codicils, by Phineas Cheeke, Jan. 17th, 1743-4.

Witnesses—Nosse Clapp; Roger Clapp.

1778. The last Will of John Gibbs|| of Topsham, mariner, Bequeaths all his goods, especially his half share in the Brigantine "Ceres," to his wife Elizabeth,¶ whom he makes his Executrix. George Abraham Gibbs** of the Cathedral Close of St. Peter, Exeter, and Anthony Gibbs†† of St. Mary the More, testify to the handwriting and signature of the deceased, on the 29th of October, 1778.

Will dated June 22nd, 1773. Proved Nov. 3rd, 1778.

1779. The last Will of Elizabeth Gibbs of Topsham, widow.‡‡ She mentions, amongst her other property, the Brigantine "Ceres" and a copyhold close of land in the manor of Royke Regis and Elwell, which by the custom of the manor should go to John Gibbs, her eldest son. She mentions her brother-in-law George Abraham Gibbs,§§ and enumerates her children, William|||| (whom, with John, she makes Trustee for distributing her property), Abraham,¶¶ George,*** Lyle,††† Thomas,‡‡‡ and Elizabeth.§§§

---

* Son of Isaac Gibbs, by his first wife, Anne, daughter of John Mercer. Will in Principal Registry, Nov. 1st, 1742.
† Daughter of Nicholas Hall, Esq., of Exeter, and Elizabeth his wife.
‡ Wife of Stephen Weston, son of the Bishop of Exeter; died July 4th, 1749.
§ Wife of Adam Pierce. P.C.C., Feb., 1732-3.
|| Son of Abraham Gibbs of Topsham, by Sarah [Lyle], his second wife.
¶ Daughter and heir of William Meachin. P.C.C., 1779.
** Son of Abraham Gibbs of Topsham, by Mary [Monk], his first wife. P.C.C., 1795.
†† Son of George Abraham Gibbs by Anne [Vicary], his wife. P.C.C., 1815.
‡‡ Of John Gibbs of Topsham. (P.C.C., 3rd Nov., 1778.)
§§ C.P.C., Jan. 31st, 1795.
|||| Died 1830.
¶¶ He died July, 1816. His only child was grandmother to the present Earl of Pembroke.
*** Died 1793.   ††† Died in Genoa, 1839.   ‡‡‡ C.P.C., 7th Nov., 1796.
§§§ Wife of James Richards.

Will dated 29th Oct., 1778. Proved 28th July, 1779, by her Executors, George Abraham Gibbs and William Gibbs, power being reserved to John Gibbs.

1795. The last Will of George Abraham Gibbs of Exeter, Surgeon. Leaves all his lands in Clyst St. George and Clyst St. Mary, "with any other lands that I am at present or may hereafter be possessed of or entitled to," to his most dearly beloved and excellent wife Anne Gibbs, whom he makes his Sole Executrix and Sole Trustee for his children, leaving her also all monies and other personal property. In a codicil of the same date as the will he begs his brother* John Gibbs, and his friends, William Pitfield, Edward Addicot, and John Mallett, to assist his wife† in her arrangement of his affairs after his death, leaving to each a set of books worth five guineas.

In a codicil dated April 26th, 1775, he leaves Pitfield and Addicot 10 guineas each, and to Pitfield his dearest and best friend whatever set of books he likes. He appoints no Trustees because he is sure that his brother and said three friends will do all that is necessary.

Will dated August 2nd, 1764. Proved Jan. 31st, 1795.

Witnesses—John Stephens, John Stephens, jun., Frances Stephens.

The Will is all in his own hand, whereof John Stoodly and William Cutcliff make oath on the 22nd Jan., 1795.

Seal—Argent, 3 battleaxes, *sable* [Gibbes of Fenton], with the arms of Vicary of Dunkeswell ; *sa.* on a chief, *arg.*, two cinquefoils, *gu.*, on an escutcheon of foretence.

1796. The last Will of Thomas Gibbs,‡ Second Lieutenant of H.M.S. "Minotaur."§ Leaves his nephews William‖ and

---

* Half brother ; son of Abraham Gibbs of Topsham, by Sarah, his second wife.
† Daughter and heir of Anthony Vicary of Exeter.
‡ Sixth son of John Gibbs of Topsham and Elizabeth [Meachin] his wife. P.C.C., June, 1778.
§ Flagship of Admiral McBride.
‖ William Henry Gibbs of Naples and Genoa, merchant, died, unmarried, at Clyst St. George. Principal Registry, London, 1859.

John* Gibbs, sons of his brother William Gibbs† of Topsham, all his share of prize money due for the "Victorieuse" and "Walshingham Packet," and all the proceeds of his kit, which he begs his friend Dr. Remmett‡ to receive and distribute.

Will dated June 20th, 1796.

No Executor named in the Will.

Admon. with Will annexed, granted Nov. 7th, 1796, to William Gibbs, his brother and next of kin.

---

* John Ley Gibbs of Genoa and Manchester. Buried at Blackley, 1837.
† Second son of the said John Gibbs of Topsham.
‡ Of Plymouth; M.D.; husband of Elizabeth, eldest daughter of George Abraham Gibbs. P C.C., 1795.

DEAN AND CHAPTER.

1547. The last Will of Raffe Carsleghe of Buckland-in-the-Moor, dated 22nd June, 1st Edward VI. He leaves his body to holy burial within the churchyard of St. Peter's Church, of Buckland-in-the-Moor. He bequeaths to the "Hed Store" and to the Store of our Lady within the said church 1 yeo sheep to each. To Wm. Brooking, Curate, to pray, &c., xiid. To mother, a steer of 3 years old. To brother's son, Thomas Carsleghe, "my shavyng knives." Residue to wife Wilmot, who is Sole Executrix.

Witnesses—Wm. Brooking, Wm. and Thomas Carsleghe.

Proved 6th Dec., 1547.

Collated Will, Old Book, Peculiar Court, D. and C., Exon.

NOTE.—This Will proves that Buckland Church (united to Ashburton) was dedicated to St. Peter, and not to St. Mary, as hitherto supposed. (See my "Ashburton and its Neighbourhood," p. 54.)

"Bekyngton p. Aysheberton."

1547. The last Will of John Ferris, dated 10th Oct., 1545. He desires to be buried in the churchyard of Seynte Nicholas of Bekenton, and bequeaths to the said Saint, "To our blessed Lady," and to St. Michael, all within the said Church, 4d. each. To Sir Thomas Smardon, 4d. To Robert Kertais, a sheppe. To Roffe Shaptor, a bollocke. Residue to John Shaptor, who is Sole Executor—"He to fynde my wyffe or cause her to be found as long as she lyveth."

Witnesses—Sir Thomas Smardon, Priest; Richard Kirtois (Curtis); Wm. Whytwaye.

Proved 9th Dec., 1547.

Collated Will, Old Book, Peculiar Court, D. and C., Exon.

NOTE.—This Will proves that Bickington Church, separated from Ashburton, 1861, was not dedicated to St. Mary as commonly supposed hitherto. (See my "Ashburton and its Neighbourhood," p. 57.)

1547. The last Will of Richard Wyndeatt of Ashburton, 13th October, 1547. He bequeaths to the "hedd store" within the Church of Ashburton 4d. Residue to wife Joan, who is Sole Executrix.
Witnesses—Nicholas Landeman, Curate.
          John Wyndeatt.
          Thomas Wyndeatt.
          George Wyndeatt.
Proved 18th June, 1548.
Personality, £4 15s. 7d.
Collated Will in Old Book, Peculiar Court, D. and C., Exon.

1548. The last Will of Thomas Toker of Staverton, 2nd Edward VI., A.D. 1548. He desires to be buried in Staverton Church, and bequeaths to the Stoer of St. Peter and Paule there and to the High Cross in the same Church 4d. To the Stoer of SS. Michael and George, 4d. To son Thomas Toker, 40s. To daughter Elizabeth, 40s. Residue to wife Joane, who is Sole Executrix.
Witness—Alexander Shaptor, Curate ; John Prystod.
Sum, £60 12s.
Proved 18th June, 1548.
Collated Will in Old Book, Peculiar Court, D. and C., Exon.

1550. The last Will of Thomas Hamlyn of Staverton, dated "2nd Edwd. VI." Bequeaths his soul to God and body to burial in y° Church earth of Staverton. To wife Luce a third part of all goods. Another third to son John Hamlyn and to daughters Catherine and Ysoth. A third to daughters Eleanor and Bridget, with remainder to son John aforesaid and daughter Emlyn. Residue to said John Hamlyn, who is Sole Exor.
Witnesses—John Ysshel, Thomas Abraham, and John Prystone.
Proved 22nd Sept., 1550.
Sum, £18 14s. 4d.
Collated Will, Old Book, Peculiar Court, D. and C., Exon, fo. 60.

1570. Robert Tocker of Sallcombe, 16th Dec., 1549. To daughter Joan, 40s. To son Nicholas, 20s. To son Thomas, 20s. Residue to wife Isabel, who is Sole Executrix.
Witness—John Upton, "cum aliis."
Proved 2nd Sept., 1570.
Collated Will in Old Book, Peculiar Court, D. and C., Exon.

1580. Wm. Wreford of Ashburton, 20th April, 1579. To each child he leaves a sheep. To son John, half a dole in a tyn work called Wellysfourd, and the twentieth part of a Tynn worke called Allerbrook, and a sixth part of another called Moor Parke Head.
Residue to wife Elizabeth, who is Sole Executrix.
Witnesses—Thomas Taylor, Harry Whiteway.
Rulers—Wm. and Harry Whiteway.
Proved 3rd June, 1580.
Collated Will, Old Book, Peculiar Court, D. and C., Exon.

NOTE.—Allerbrook is a small tributary of the Dart, about five miles from Ashburton, and in the middle of Holne Moor.

1593. The last Will of John Gibbe of Clyst St. George, Yeoman. I, John Gibbe . . . being somewhat sicke in body, but of good and perfect remembrance, thankes be given unto Almightie God, doe make and ordayne . . . &c. I give and bequeathe my soul into the hands of Almightye God, Father, Sonne, and Holie Goste, three persons and one God, trusting that the same my soul shall be received into the fellowshyppe of the ellecte and faythfull persones by the meryt, deathe, and passyon of Jesus Christe the Sonne of God and Seconde Person in Trinitye, by whose means only I hope to be saved and by none other. And I will my Body to be buryed in the parishe Church of Cliste St. George or elswhere, where it shall please God to call me.

He leaves to the poor 20s. To Elizabeth Myddleton, 20s. To Philippe, Stephen, and John Bruton, each one yeo sheepe. To his well-beloved wyffe Cecylie 7 of his best kyne, 40 weathers and five yeowes; also one mare or gelding "which shall not happen to be seased for a heariott by the Lord or his officers;" also the moitye and halfendeale of all his corn and grayne, and (for her life) of all his puter and brasen vessells. He gives her also all Butter, Cheese, Beef, Bacon, and other Provision of House that may be in the House at his death; also one blacke steyre now put to fattynge, and all pultry; also all the haie in the talletts; also all the home-made Clothe in the House; also "the one halfe of all my welle being in my house at the tyme of my death." To his daughter Margarett, £150. To his daughter Christyan, £100, to go, in case of her death under age, to his son William (his Executor), or, if William should die before her, to his daughters Margarett and Jane, and to the survivor of them. To his daughter Jane when she is 21, £80, with the same proviso, the money being divided between Margarett and Christyan in case of William's death. The Residue of everything to go to the said William.

Overseers—William Coade his brother-in-law and George Morris his cousin.

Witnesses—William Keyner of Ottery St. Mary, William Coade, and George Morris.

Will dated Oct. 10th, 1593. Proved Dec. 20th, 1593.

Buried at Clyst St. George, Dec. 14th, 1593.

1619. Administration of the Goods of Robert Gibbs* of Topsham was granted to Katherine Gibbes his widow, William Wotton being bound with her.

1619. The last Will of Laurence Wreyforde of Ayshberton, 29th March, 1619. To daughter Elizabeth Wreyforde, £5. To sister Mawte Norrish, £5. Residue to wife Mary (" nowe wife"), who is Sole Executrix.

Proved 7th May, 1619.

£34 16s. 4d.

---

* This may be the same man as Robert, father of Robert Gibbe of Topsham (and Clyst St. George). See Jan. 24th, 1662, Archdeacon's Court; but, if so, Katherine must have been a second wife, Margaret (Oxenbeare) being the mother of Robert.

1629. John Wreaforde of Ashburton, 19th Jan., 4th Charles. To daughter Peternell, wife of Richard Taprill, a pewter dish. Mentions children of said Peternell, viz., John, Ann, and Peternell.

Residue to wife Barbara, who is Sole Executrix.

Proved 17th April, 1629.

Sum, £21 7s. 5d.

1633. Elizabeth Gould of Ashburton, Widow. Dated   . She gives, amongst other bequests, an annuity of £2 to the poor of Ashburton to issue out of her meadow called Persford.

Proved   , 1633, by James Gould, the Executor named in the Will.

NOTE.—When I saw this Will, 23rd August, 1880, the document was in fragments, and the top and bottom of the paper were both missing. The annuity to the poor of Ashburton has been long discontinued, and I never heard of it during my intimate connection with the parish extending over eighteen years, 1861-1879. Edward Gould, of the same family, was a benefactor to Ashburton by his Will dated 16th March, 1735, and, singularly enough, one of his bequests was a sum of 40/- to the poor of Ashburton and Staverton, 20/- to each parish yearly, charged on land. Can it have been his intention to thus carry out the Will of Elizabeth Gould? He was also a considerable benefactor to Ashburton Grammar School.

1634. William Gould the younger of Staverton, Clothier, 28th October, 10th Charles. To poor of Staverton, 5s. To son Philip, £5 at 15. To daughter Marie, £5 at 16. To daughter Agnes, £5 at 17.

Residue to wife Mary, who is Sole Executrix.

Witness—Leonard Irish.

Proved 18th Nov., 1634.

Sum, £7 9s. 2d.

1666. The last Will of Samuel Tidball of Ashburton, Gentleman. 20th May, 1666. To the poor there, £3. To sister

Martha Tidball he leaves all his fee-simple lands in Ashburton, with remainder to Hugh Stowell, Esq., and his heirs. Residue to said sister Martha, who is Sole Executrix.
Witnesses—Wm. Denet, Dorothy Griffin.
Proved 13th July, 1666.

NOTE.—Testator was son of Rev. Samuel Tidball, who went to Ashburton as Curate to Robert Law, Archdeacon of Barnstaple and Vicar of Ashburton, 1613, and became Master of Ashburton Grammar School, 1616, and succeeded Mark Law, son of the Archdeacon of Barnstaple, as Vicar of Ashburton in 1644; died 1647. The said Mark Law was the husband of testator's other sister, Maria Tidball.

Hugh Stowell was of Herebeare in the parish of Bickington *prope* Ashburton. He was of a younger branch of the Stawels (pronounced Stowel) of Cothelstone, co. Somerset, and his immediate relatives were long resident at Herebeare.

Miss M. Griffin, of the same race as "Dorothy G.," died at Ashburton, May 15th, 1853, aged 105. She had been present at the coronation of George III.

1669. Katherine Osmond of Culmstock, Widow. 11th May, 1669. To brother John Smeath of Burlescomb, 40s. To cousin Anslie Cherriton, best petticoat. Bequests to cousin Charity Smeath and daughter Mary Osmond, "my spinning torne" and £40. To Humphry and Joan, children of John Osmond, 1s. each. Residue to son Humphry Osmond, who is Sole Executor.

Proved 8th Dec., 1669.
Sum, £174 7s. 8d.
Witnesses—Francis Hayzell, James Southwood.

1672. Mary Granger of Clist Honiton, 24th Jan., 1671. There are bequests to daughter Mary Robbins; to sons James and Francis Granger. Residue to son Richard Granger, who is Sole Exor.

Witnesses—John Curell, Mary Robbins.
Proved 27th May, 1672.
Sum, £8 1s. 8d.

1677. Henry Gould of Staverton, Gentleman, 1st Oct., 1675. To daughter Katherine, wife of John Laskey, 40s. To daughter Margaret, wife of John Kingwill, 10s. To daughter Elizabeth Gould, £40.
Residue to wife Katherine, who is Sole Executrix.
Witnesses—John Rowe, Andrew Tarr.
Proved 3rd April, 1677.
Sum, £473.

1677. Walter Palke of the Towne of Ashburton, Yeoman, 5th Nov., 1677. To sister Dionis Townsend, £10, and her life in all lands in Ashburton after decease of wife Agnes. To cousin Margaret, daughter of Dionis Townsend, £10. To cousins John and Joan Townsend, 50s. each. To cousin Walter, son of Thomas Palke, deceased, Reversion of the Ashburton lands after the death of Dionis Townsend and of wife Agnes, charged with an annuity of 20s. to cousin Dionis.
Residue to wife Agnes, who is Sole Executrix.
Witnesses—Thomas Palke, Agnes Hanniford, Wm. and Mary Hanniford.
Proved 19th Dec., 1679.

1679. Inventory of Walter Palke of the Towne of Ashburton, made by George Fabyan and Richard Tapper, 24th Dec., 1679.

" His wearing apparel	£1 0	0
Item one paire of looms, with querling torne and other materials belonging to them ...	0 10	0
10 Pewter dishes	0 16	0 "
Various other articles	63 1	6
	£65 7	6

1680. Administration to the effects of Thomas Palke of Staverton, granted to Susannah his relict; Matthew Palke joins the bond.
Sum, £37 16s. 8d.
Granted 3rd Sept., 1680-1.

1684. Administration to the effects of Frank Granger of Clist Honiton. Granted to Mary his relict.
30th Jan., 1684.
Sum, £18 19s. 2d.

1686. Agnis Granger of Clist Honiton, 10th Dec., 1685. She leaves her leasehold house and orchard in Broadclist to her children, Joan her daughter and Richard her son.
Residue to said Joan Granger, who is Sole Executrix.
Witnesses—John Herne, Wm. Ayre, John Curell.
Proved 13th Aug., 1686.
Sum, £21 3s. 2d.

1693. Mary Granger of Clist Honiton, Widow, 28th March, 1693. Bequests to son Abraham Granger and to daughter Hannah. Residue to daughter Grace Granger, who is Sole Executrix.
Witnesses—Joan Granger, Julyan Pearsse and Thomas Wescott.
Proved 28th April, 1693.
Sum, £37 16s.

1707. The last Will of Walter Palk, sen., of Ashburton, 22nd Feb., 1705. To Walter "Paulk," my eldest son, all my lands after the decease of his mother, charged with the payment of £100 as follows:—£40 to Jonathan, second son; £30 to Thomas, third son; £30 to daughter Grace Palke.
Residue to wife Grace, who is Sole Executrix.
Witnesses—John Smerdon, John Fursman, Robert Jerman.
Proved 27th May, 1707.
£160 10s. 5½d.

NOTE —Testator was the grandfather of Sir Robert Palk, Bart., and therefore the direct ancestor of the present Lord Haldon. Although described as "Cousin" (as was then usual), he was really nephew of Walter Palk, whose will was proved 19th Dec., 1679, to which refer.
His son Jonathan was subsequently Vicar of Ilsington. See my "Devonshire Parishes," vol. ii., p. 325, *et seq.*

1725. The last Will of Abraham Gibß (or Gibbs) of Topsham, Yeoman. Leaves his wife Tryphœna Gibbs* a Rent-charge of £20, and his daughters Elizabeth† and Mary‡ £250 apiece at the age of 21; and all his lands in Crediton and elsewhere to his friends and brothers-in-law, William Rowe§ of Shobrooke, and Benjamin Brindley ‖ of Exeter, and Philip Gibbs his kinsman,¶ in trust for his son Abraham Gibbs,** whom he makes his Executor, the three trustees abovenamed being Overseers.

Will dated July 1st, 1718. Proved Sept. 10th, 1725. Witnesses.

1726. The last Will of Abraham Gibbs†† of Topsham, Gentleman. He leaves £500 to his son George Abraham Gibbs,‡‡ £300 to his daughter Anna Gibbs,§§ and £21 "and no more" to his son John Gibbs.‖‖ The Residue to his wife Sarah Gibbs.¶¶

Executors in trust John Ewins, John Rous, and the Rev. M. Christopher Ewins.

Will dated 16th Sept., 1726. Proved Oct. 24th following.

1733. Abraham Granger of Clist Honiton, Yeoman, 1st March, 1732. To wife Hannah use of all goods for life. To daughter Mary Hayman, eventual moiety of said goods, and £10. To daughter Hannah, the other moiety of his goods, and £10. To son Thomas, £10. To son Roger, £100, and he is to pay all legacies after the death of Testator's wife; he is residuary legatee and Sole Executor.

Witnesses—Thomas Perkins, Richard Granger.

Proved 20th June, 1733.

Sum, £187 2s. 6d.

---

* Will in Principal Registry, 1733.   † Wife of . . . Pett.
‡ Wife of Nicholas Peters of Topsham, Surgeon.
§ Will in Archdeaconry Registry, 1725-6.   ‖ Husband of his sister Elizabeth.
¶ His first cousin (son of his uncle Philip Gibbe). Will, Archdeaconry, 1724 and 1732.
** Will in Archdeaconry Reg., 1726.
†† Son of Abraham Gibbs (Sept. 10th, 1775, same Court).
‡‡ C.P.C., Jan. 31st, 1795.   §§ Afterwards wife of . . . Kemmett of Crediton.
‖‖ C.P.C., 3rd Nov., 1778.
¶¶ Sarah, daughter and coheiress of Robert Lyle of Topsham; married, thirdly, Robert Framingham.

1742. Administration to the effects of Hannah Granger of Clist Honiton. Granted to Thomas Granger her brother, 20th Jan., 1742.
Under £100.

1743. Thomas Granger of Lyons Inn and County of Middlesex, Gentleman. He desires to be buried in the Parish Church of Clist Honiton, Co. Devon. He leaves his Goods, &c., to his granddaughter Lydia Granger at 21, or on her marriage day, with remainder to two nephews, Rev. Thomas Granger and Mr. Edmund Granger, and to niece Mrs. Susan Granger. He appoints his daughter-in-law Margaret, widow of son Thomas deceased, and said two nephews, Joint Exors.
Witnesses—John Roberts and William Bennett.
Dated 12th Feb., 1739. Proved 29th July, 1743.

NOTE.—The testator is shown by a memorandum attached to the Will to have resided at Clist Honiton entirely for the nine months preceding his death.

1743. Hannah Granger of Clist Honiton, Widow, 4th Aug., 1742. To grandson William Hayman, large brass kettle. To granddaughter Mary Hayman, two gold rings. To son-in-law John Hayman, 1s. To son Thomas Granger, £5 5s. To son Roger Granger, 1s. To Rev. Edmond Granger, £1 1s. for preaching a funeral sermon. "Item, I give five bushells of wheat to be baked into bread unto all such poore peopel as usually byes bread of me." Residue to son Richard Granger and to Jane Palmer, who are Joint Exors.
Witnesses—Samuel Drake, Robert Phelp.
Proved 7th Oct., 1743.

1743. Administration to the effects of Elizabeth Granger of Clist Honiton, intestate, granted 14th Oct., 1743, to Thomas Granger her brother.

1763. Martha Granger of Clist Honiton, Widow, 19th Oct, 1761. To son Edward Nott of Tiverton, 1s. To granddaughter Mary Nott, "my house called the Green House at Clist Honiton," with reversion to Sarah and Edward, children of George Nott.
Son George Nott of Clist Honiton, Sole Exor.
Residue undisposed of.
Witnesses—Samuel and William Clarke, George Westcott.
Proved 13th Dec., 1763.
Under £20.

1767, Nov. 7th. William Bartlett of St. Mary Church, Devon, Gentleman, by Will of this date charges his lands devised to his eldest son Jacob Bartlett and his personal estate, with the payment of his Debts, &c. Gives to his son William Bickford Bartlett an orchard at Paignton, which he purchased of William Wallers, and share of Brigantine Vessel called "The Lady," provided he gives a discharge "from one Jacob Bickford his grandfather or any Executor;" also the House in which he (the Testator) lived, and the use of his goods, &c., in case he shall live therein, but if he refuses to live therein £300 instead. Gives to his daughter Mary Hele the £20 which her husband owed him, and £10 to be laid out in mourning. To grand-daughter Susannah Hele, daughter of said Mary, £100 with interest, until she attains 21, and the House and Cellar which Captain Woollcott rents at Torkey, and Household goods in possession of Elizabeth Emling, widow, after her decease. To grand-daughters Agnes Hele, Nancy Hele, Peggy Hele, £10 each on attaining 21. To daughter Grace Jackson, estate called Codners, in Tor Mohun, for life. To his grandson William Bartlett, House, Barn, Orchard, &c., being part of the estate he purchased of William Browse of St. Mary Church and his heirs, and for want of such issue to his grandson James Salter Bartlett and his heirs, and for want of such issue to the right heirs of his own body for ever. To his grand-daughter Elizabeth Bartlett, £100, on attaining 21.

Residue to his son Jacob Bartlett, whom he appoints

Executor, and who proved in the Court of the Dean and Chapter of Exeter, 21st June, 1768.

Witnesses — Wm. Browse, Christopher Waynworth, Ann Henly.

1769. Administration to the effects, &c., of William Granger, late of Clist Honiton. Granted 21st Feb., 1769, to Anne, wife of James Clapp, mother of deceased.

Under £20.

1779. Richard Tucker of Braunton, Yeoman, 15th Dec., 1776. He leaves his household goods, &c., to son Richard Tucker of Georgeham, "and all the things I left at Cryde in Georgeham when I came to Braunton." To daughter Ann, wife of James Burn of Northam, £10. To daughter Mary, wife of Richard Knill of Braunton, Carpenter, and to daughter Susanna Tucker, "the estate wherein I now dwell." Residue to said two daughters, who are Joint Exors.

Witnesses—George Perryman, Thos. Knill, and Robert Dunn.

Proved 12th May, 1729.

NOTE.—Refer to 5th Dec., 1766, Archdeaconry of Barnstaple. It will be noticed that this testator is described in his wife's Will as "Gentleman." He describes himself as "Yeoman," and his daughter, who is a considerable "beneficiare" under the above Will, evidently married a mechanic; this shows that undue stress is sometimes laid upon notes as to social position in Wills and Parish Registers.

1798. Ann Tucker of Braunton, Widow, 4th Nov., 1788. To her daughter Ann Tucker and to her daughter-in-law Prudence Tucker, in trust for three grandchildren, John and Elizabeth Tucker, and Ann, wife of Edmund Barrow, a certain tenement called "The Balls." To son-in-law George Webber 2s. 6d.

Witnesses—John Parker, Robert Dunn.

Proved 11th June, 1798.

COURT OF THE VICARS CHORAL, EXETER.

1642. Administration of the goods of Agnes Gibbs of Woodbury was granted to Joane her mother, wife of William Darke of Coleridge, during the minority of Joane Gibbs, sister of the deceased, her goods being but £10, a legacy of Thomas Gibbs* her father. George Trobridge and Richard Fleming, sureties.
Date of grant, Oct. 6th, 1642.

1671. Administration of the goods of George Gibbs† of Woodbury was granted Aug. 23rd, 1671, to Joane his widow.

1686. Administration of the goods of Samuel Gibbs‡ of Woodbury was granted 23rd Nov., 1686, to Elizabeth his widow, and Robert Gibbs§ of Woodbury, and Abraham Gibbs|| of Clyst St. George.

1701-2. The last Will of Robert Gibbs¶ of Woodbury, Yeoman. He bequeaths certain goods to his loving wife Dorothy** for life, and then to his son Robert Gibbs,†† whom

---

* See Archdeacon's Court (Exon), Aug. 19th, 1629.
† Second son of George Gibbs of Woodbury (P.C.C., Nov., 1660).
‡ Youngest son of George Gibbs of Clyst St. George (Principal Registry, 1st Aug., 1683).
§ Brother of the said George Gibbs and father of Elizabeth, wife of the Testator Samuel Gibbs (Court of Vicars Choral, Feb. 27th, 1701-2).
|| Brother of the Testator (Court of Dean and Chapter, 10th Sept., 1725).
¶ Fourth son of John Gibbe the elder of Clyst St. George.
** Dorothea Crosse.   †† Same Court, 7th Sept., 1721.

he makes his Executor. He mentions his daughter Anstice Pearse,* Dorothy Lyde, and Elizabeth Gibbs,† and his daughters-in-law Joane Kentisbeere‡ and Elizabeth Gibbs.§ To his grandson Robert Gibbs || and to his [own] son Robert¶ he leaves his messuage and tenement at Ebford, between them, "to each such distinct part as in a deed bearing date March 5 in the 3^d year of our Sovereign Lord King James the 2$_d$ that now is on England A.D. 1686, by me made and executed unto my trusty friends Gideon Haydon, Abraham Gibbs, ** and George Gibbs,** yeomen, are particularly set forth and expressed."

Will dated 27th August, 1688. Proved 27th Feb., 1701-2, by Robert Gibbs, jun.

Witnesses—Eleanor Haydon, Sarah Edwards, Henry Ross.

1718. The last Will of George Gibbs†† of Woodbury, Yeoman. He leaves money to his cousins John, Nicholas, Joane, and Mary Leate, sons and daughters of the late John Leate of Clyst St. Mary, and Mary Leate his sister, now of Woodbury, widow, whom he makes his Executrix.

Will dated 20th July, 1717. Proved 3rd Oct., 1718.

Witnesses.

1721. Administration of the goods of Robert Gibbs‡‡ of Woodbury was granted 7th Sept., 1721, to Dorothy Gibbs, spinster, and Elizabeth Duelly *alias* Gibbs his daughters, John Way of Clyst St. George being Surety.

---

* Wife of Roger Pearse.
† Afterwards wife of her cousin Samuel Gibbs (same Court, 23rd Nov., 1686).
‡ John Kensbeere was married at Clyst St. George in 1684 to Joane Gibb, who must have been a second wife of the Testator's son Robert.
§ Wife of his son Robert. || Son of the said Robert.
¶ Same Court, 7th Sept., 1711.
** His nephews, second and fourth sons of his brother George Gibbe of Clyst St. George (Court of the Dean and Chapter, 10th Sept., 1725, and Court of the Archdeacon of Exeter, 11th Oct., 1723).
†† Only son of George Gibbs of Woodbury (same Court, 22nd Aug., 1671).
‡‡ Son of Robert Gibbs of Woodbury (same Court, 27th Feb., 1701-2).

DEVONSHIRE WILLS.

PART II.

ARCHDEACONRY OF EXETER.

1545. Richard Toker of Ottery St. Mary, 10th August, 1545.
Desires to be buried in the churchyard of St. Mary of Ottery, and makes his wife, Margaret, universal legatee and Sole Executrix.
Unindexed. Proved 22nd Sept., 1545.

1567. Nicholas Toker of Holcombe Rogus, 28th Dec., 1566. To daughter Jone, £5. To son Robert, "one steer, and one calfe which is weaned from its dame." To John, son of said Robert, one steer. To god-son Nicholas Wynn, two sheep.
Residue to wife, Chrystin, who is Sole Executrix.
Personal Estate, £21 2s. 8d.
Proved 4th April, 1567.

1617. Administration to the effects of William Tucker of Exeter, granted 13th Sept., 1617, to Anne, his widow.
Theophilus Meddicke and Richard Tremayne join the bond.

1618. Administration to the effects of John Tucker of Exeter, granted 21st May, 1618, to Emelin, his widow. Gregory Wood joins the bond.

1618. The last Will, nuncupative, of Amy Mortimer of Dunsford, Widow, dated 24th June, 1618. She leaves her best gown to son John Mortimer of Bridford ; and the rest of her apparel to her " natural daughter, Jone Hedgeland." Residue to son Thomas Mortimer, who is Sole Exor. Proved 11th July, 1618.

1618. Administration to the effects of John Mortimer, late of Tiverton, deceased, granted 17th Sept., 1618, to Silvester Parkehowse.
Sum £10 5s. 6d.

1618. Agnes Mortimer of Shobbroke, 6th Jany., 1618, Widow, gives certain household goods to Ambrose, John, and Agnes, children of Hugh Gregory of Culmstock.

Said Agnes to have " my best petticoat, and white fustian waistcoat, white linnen apron, partlett & kerchief, at 21 years of age."

To daughter Margaret Wood, " one greate vaute (vat) and best gowne." To Thomasine, daughter of said Margaret, " a skillett and a gridiron." To John, brother of last, " one great brass candlestick and one bran dishe." To latter's brother, Nicholas Wood, another brass candlestick, and to William, another brother, " the least candlestick."

18s. to be expended on her funeral.
Residue to son-in-law, William Wood, who is Sole Exor.
Proved 19th March, 1618.
Sum £4 12s. 6d.

1620. The last Will of John Tooker of Bradninche, and co. of Devon. Bequeaths his body to Christian burial, and small sums to the poor and for the "reparacion" of the parish church.

Daughter Joan, £40, if she marries with her mother's consent.

He leaves said daughter certain household furniture, and a sum of £10, owing to him by John Maudyt of Padbrooke, together with an annuity of £4.

He gives to daughter Dorothy, wife of William Borowe, a close of land, called "Horsepark," in the parish of Cullompton.

Residue to wife, Ellina, who is Sole Executrix.

By Codicil, he leaves all his lands, tenements, and hereditaments in Up-Ottery, to said two daughters, their heirs, etc., etc., in equal portions.

Proved 13th Oct., 1620.

Personalty, £107 19s.

1621. The last Will of William Tucker, of Up-Ottery, and county of Devon, dated 30th May, 1621.

To be buried in parish churchyard.

Leaves his brother John Tucker two pieces of cloth, one being at "Robert Quicke's house."

His "apparel" to John Halsey.

Bequests to sisters Thamsine Jealfrey and Elizabeth Warren, and also to Edward, son of John Goolde.

"Uncle Edmund," residuary legatee and Sole Exor.

Proved 17th Sept., 1621.

1621. The last Will of John Tucker of St. Mary the Great in the city of Exeter, dated "Feast of St. Stephen," 1621.

Bequests to sons John and Hugh, and also to the child his wife expects to bear him.

Residue to wife Ursula, who is residuary legatee and Sole Executrix.

Witnesses—Gregory Soper.
            Dorothy Sparrow.

Proved 16th Jany., 1621.

1622. Administration to the effects of Richard Tucker, late of Southleigh, intestate, granted 15th April, 1622, to William Warren of said parish, in minority of the son, Richard Tucker. Gregory Warren joins the bond.

1622. Inventory of the effects of Andrew Tucker of Cleyhidon, made 20th May, and exhibited 10th Oct., 1622.
Sum £2 4s. 8d.

1622. The last Will of William Tucker of Gideshame dated Dec. 27th, 1622.

Bequeaths "bodye to the grone, & soulle to God who gave it."

To son William, "the beste cubbord & the dishes uppon it."

To son-in-law Thomas Pearse, the "worste cubbord, the old, table-board, the 'sealinge' behind the bench, and the dishes on the cubbord."

Wife to have life interest in said effects.

Residue to said wife, Joan, who is Sole Executrix.

Proved 17th Jany., 1622.

In the inventory "a cowe, an heyffer, and a nagge," are valued together at £6 13s. 4d.

Two "small pigges," 13s. 4d.

"One little mowe of wheate, barley, & oates," 20s.

1622. John Tooker of Halberton "or otherwise Yarnicombe or Varnicombe," by Will dated 17th Sept., 1622, desires his body to be buried in the churchyard of Halberton.

Bequests to Elizabeth Cha (?), George, Philip, and Samuel Parker, and Thamsin Crosse.

Residue to brother "John Tocker," who is Sole Exor.

Proved 8th Jany., 1622-3.

1623. Administration to the effects of Joane Tucker of East Budleigh, granted 15th Aug., 1623, to Gilbert Smythe and Jane Smythe, late Tucker.

1623. The last Will of Jane Mortimer of Poughill, co. Devon, Spinster.
To my mother, Joan Philpe, 40s. To brothers John and Roger Mortimer, 30s. "To the ringers of my knell," 12d. each. Residue to cousin, Robert Gye, who is Sole Exor.
Other bequests to Wm. Dodridge, and to Robert, his son, and to Walter Barton.
Dated 27th Aug., 1622. Proved 19th Sept., 1623.

1624. Administration to the effects of Andrew Tucker of Exminster, granted 17th May, 1624, to Julian Tucker.

1624. The last Will of Joan Tucker of Tedborne St. Mary, Widow, dated 6th Feby., 1618.
To Parish Church 3s. 4d., and to Poor 3s. 4d.
Bequests to son Thomas Tucker, to Johane fford, and to Ursula, daughter of Henry Woodley. To John Endell, the great brass crocke, and to Ellen Endell, 1s.
Residue to Johane, daughter of Henry Woodley. She is Sole Executrix.
Sum £37 2s. 8d.
Proved 21st Jany., 1624.

1624. Inventory of Joan Tucker of Tedburne St. Mary. Extracts—
"Item, one horse xl shillings. Three kine, and a yearling, ix li. (pounds). Nine pigges, 12/-."

1624. Administration to the effects of Nicholas Mortimore of Tiverton, granted 21st Sept., 1624, to John Bastard, his son-in-law.

1625. Administration to the effects of John Mortimer of Upton Hellions, granted 10th June, 1625, to Christopher, father of Christopher Payne, brother-in-law of deceased.

1626. Administration to the effects of Agnes Mortimer, *alias* Payne, of Upton Hellions, granted April 26th, 1626, to Christopher Payne.

1626. The last Will of John Mortimer, *alias* Tanner, of Cadleigh, 13th May, 1625. To be buried in parish church. To sister Elizabeth Sharland, 40s. Bequests to Ralph Tanner, John Berry, Sander Norrish, George Norrish, both of Cheriton, Thomasine Ellat of Poughill, Joan Pathericke, Agnes, Symon, Robert, John and Alice Berrie, of Tiverton, Eleanor and Katherine Passmore, Thomas Beedell, "to the useable workmen of Sir Symon Leache's house," Joan Clokye, Bridget and Mary Norrish, Christian Aisse (Ash), John Langworthy, and John Matthew.

To Richard Aisse of Cadleigh, 2¼ yards of "Meltie Cloth."
Residue to William Matthew, who is Sole Exor.
Proved 19th May, 1626.
Sum £58 10s.

1626. Administration to the effects of William Tucker of Exeter and of the parish of St. Sidwell, granted 23rd June, 1626, to Mary, his relict.

1626. John Mortimer of the "Cytie of Exeter," July —, 1626, leaves his body to Christian burial.

He gives his best cloak to his brother William Mortimer; his "Testament" to "Sister Wilmott." To sister-in-law "Dorothie," "one boke with a broad forrell called the 'Sufferings of Christ.'"

To John Bayle, a book called "The plain Man's Pathway to Heaven."

To cousin William Hellyar, a paire of loomes.

To sister's son, "Richard," "so much of my old cloake as will make him a coat."

"Item, to wife's son Peter, the little loome."
Residue to "my wife," who is Sole Executrix.
Proved 22nd Aug., 1626.

1627. The last Will of Ann Fry, Widow, of Thorncombe, dated 9th April, 1624.

She gives legacies to grandchildren John, Anne, and Mary Fry, children of her deceased son, Gylles (?) Fry, Mentions Alys, wife of John Downe.

She desires to be buried in the churchyard of Thorncombe.
Residue to son William, who is Sole Executor.
Proved at Exeter, 1627.
Inventory made 17th May, 1626.

1627. The last Will of Thomas Fry of Honiton, dated 5th March, 1626. Mentions sons Thomas and William, daughters Johan and Frances.

Son Christopher Fry is Sole Executor.
Inventory made by "William Fry" and others.
Witnesses, Robert Leach.
　　　　　　Walter Abbott.
Proved 28th March, 1627.

1627. Administration to the effects of Alexander Tucker of Stockleigh English, granted May 20th, 1627, to James Tucker.
Richard Tucker joins the bond.

1627. Inventory of Alexander Tucker of Stockleigh English, exhibited 20th May, 1627. Extracts—

"Item, one bond of debt from Henry Tucker, his brother, of £20, for the true payment of £10.

"Item of £6 from Richard Tucker, his brother, for payment of £3."

Sum £23 7s. 8d.

1628. Administration to the effects of Edward Tucker of Broadclist, granted 13th March, 1628, to Grace Tucker, his daughter.

Henry Tucker joins the bond.
Sum £5 7s. 6d.

1628. Inventory of the effects of Richard Tucker, *alias* Glover, of Tiverton, 21st May, 1628. Extracts—
"Item, 17 sylver spoones & household effects, valued at £92 4s. 8d."
Crest Seal—A horse's head issuant from a coronet (Bayly of Hambrook, co. Gloucester).

NOTE.—Refer to year 1628, page 17, *ante*.

1628. The last Will of Mary, Widow of Thomas Fry, dated Columpton, 6th Feby., 1627. Legacies to Henry and Priscilla Howe, and to Sara, wife of Abell Downe.
Daughter Mary to have apparel.
Residue to son Thomas Fry, who is Sole Exor.
Proved 12th March, 1628.

1629. William Tucker of Spreyton desires to be buried at Spreyton, and leaves 1s. to that church and to the poor, and 1s. to the church of Morchard Bishop, with 5s. to the poor there.

To his daughters Katteron and Joane, money bequest at 21, and three silver spoons each, and to each certain "brazen crockes."

To brother Michael's children, sixpence each.

To brother Robert's children, sixpence each, and a like sum to "sister Sibley's" children, and to those of his two brothers-in-law, John Tracey and John Moxhay.

Residue to wife Katteron, who is Sole Executrix.

Dated 30th May, 1629. No proof. Index dated "May, 1629."

1629. Administration to the effects of Jane Tucker of St. Mary the More (*i.e.*, St. Mary the *Great*, commonly called St. Mary Major), in city of Exeter, Widow, granted to Susan Tucker, 6th July, 1629.

NOTE.—Refer to 1621, Part II., *ante*.

1629. The last Will of Mark Fry of Stokeintinhead, dated 1626. Mentions daughters Anstiss and Richord.
A legacy to poor of Stokeintinhead.
Residue to wife Margaret, who is Sole Executrix.
Proved at Exeter, 20th Aug., 1629.

1631. The last Will of Thomas Tucker of Exminster, dated 7th Feby., 1631.
To poor of the parish, 40s., to be distributed on the third Sabbath after his burial.
To daughter Grace, £80, to be paid in two instalments, on the 2nd Feby., 1633, and on the 2nd Feby., 1635; with reversion to Margaret, daughter of Peter Tucker of Kenn, if said Grace should die before she attains the age of four years.
To Grace, daughter of said Peter Tucker, £10 at 21.
To Thomas, son of Edward Tucker of Dawlish, £10 at 21.
To brother Edward Tucker, £5, and like sum to brother Peter Tucker.
Residue to wife Grace Tucker, who is Sole Executrix.
Proved 15th Feby., 1631.

1631. Nuncupative Will of William Tucker of Shobrooke, dated 10th April, 1631. Wife Petronell, universal legatee and Sole Executrix.
Proved April 15th, 1631.
Sum £83 1s. 11d.

1631. Administration to the effects of Tristram Tucker, granted 18th Nov., 1631, to Joan, his widow.

1631. Administration to the effects of John Tucker of Poltimore, deceased, granted 3rd May, 1631, to Mary Tucker, the widow.

1631. Inventory of John Tucker of Poltimore, exhibited 3rd May, 1631, made 29th April.

5 acres and a half of Wheat in the ground	...	£14.
4½ „ of Barley	...	£13.
2 „ of Rye	...	£1.
4½ „ of Pease	...	£3.
6½ „ of Oats	...	£8.
2 Bushels of Wheat	...	£1.

1631-2. Administration to the effects of Alice Tucker, late of Exeter, granted Jany. 24th, 1631-2, to Elizabeth Stabbicke.

1632. Administration to the effects of William Mortimore of Rewe, granted 30th April, 1632, to Christian Mortimore, his widow.

"Dennys Mortimer, widow, was a debtor to the estate of deceased."

1632. The last Will of Thomasine Osmond of Uplowman, Widow, dated 5th Feby., 1631. To son William, 1 Platter dish.

Residue to son-in-law John Darcy, who is Sole Exor.
Witnesses—Bennet Bobishe.
              Phillippe Sheppard.
              Michaell Bobishe.
Proved 25th July, 1632.

1632. Peter Tucker of Upton Pyne, 16th Nov., 1632. Leaves his body to Christian burial. Bequests to William Mogridge and Wilmot, his wife.

To sons John, Peter, and Thomas Tucker, at 16, £10 each.
To brother George and sister Thamsin, 10s. each.
Residue to wife Wilmot, who is Sole Executrix.
Trustees—John Tucker and Robert Pridham.
Proved Dec. 11th, 1632.
Sum £223 12s. 10d.

1633. Administration to the effects of John Tucker of Tiverton, granted March 17th, 1634, to George Parrington, his son-in-law.

1633. Administration to the effects of Thomas Fry, late of Colompton, granted 27th Oct., 1633, to Mary, his widow.

1635. The Will of John Tooker of Brampford Speke, dated 1st April, 1635.

He leaves in trust to Amias and John Warren of Stoke Canon, £80; in trust for son John Tucker.

To said trustees, £90, for son Tristram.

To daughter Ebbot £40 at 24, and to granddaughter Mary Coxx, 20s.

Residue to wife Mary, who is Sole Executrix.

Sum £210 14s.

1636. The last Will of William Mortimer of Bradninch. Gives to "reparacion of parish church, 3s. 4d., and to the poor, 10s."

To his kinswoman Grace, wife of Robert Miller, to Judith Downing's children, to Christopher Taylor's daughter Mary, to John Garnsey's son, and to Thomas Wood,* there are small bequests. To son Thomas Mortimer, the tenement at Bollam in Tiverton.

Residue to wife Johan, who is Sole Executrix.

Dated 31st July, 1635. Proved 3rd March, 1636.

1637. The last Will, nuncupative, of John Mortimer of Bridford, Husbandman.

To the poor of the parish, 2s. To son Edward, and to his children, small bequests; and also to son Gilbert.

Residue to sons John and Symon Mortimer, who are joint Executors.

Proved 28th April, 1637.

Sum £53 12s.

---

* Refer to March, 1618, Will of Agnes Mortimer.

1638. Robert Tocker of Tiverton, by Will nuncupative dated 31st April, 1638, left his eight children sixpence each. Residue to wife Thomazine, who is Sole Executrix.

1638. William Tooker of Broadclist, dated 7th Aug., 1638. By Will nuncupative he then left 20s. each to daughters Richorda, Julian, and Mary Tooker, and mentions his son John.
Residue to wife, Mary, who is Sole Executrix.
Proved 3rd Sept., 1638.

1638. Thomazine "Tacker," late of Tiverton, by Will nuncupative of 20th Sept., 1638, gave her daughter Julian her dwelling-house and all her goods save "one brazen crocke."
Residue to Mary "Tucker," who is Sole Executrix.
Proved Oct. 20th, 1638.

1639. Simon Tucker of St. Mary Steps, Exeter, by Will nuncupative 22nd Sept., "or thereabout."
Bequeaths to poor of the parish 20s. To grandchild Nicholas Coombe, 50s., and an annuity of 1s.
To cousin Emlyn Tucker, £10.
Residue to wife Agnis, who is Sole Executrix.
Proved 15th Oct., 1639.
Sum £108 1s. 8d.
Inventory of above made 14th Oct., 1639.
"Imprimis his purse & girdell & wearing apparell, with his gown, £6 10s."
Item, 2 sylver bowles and a bere bole.
Item, in the Chamber over the Shoppe, one muskett with pair of bandaliers and a sworde, with other articles, £17 6s. 10d.
In the kitchen, 2 Bibles.
Item, for 8 kine, £24.
"for Wheat in the barne £7 16 10
"Hay 3 10 9
"One reeke of woode in the garden, 1s. 6d."

1639. The Nuncupative Will of John Mortimer of Bishop's Cheriton, dated 19th Feby., 1639.

Mentions sons James, John, and Gilbert; daughters Frances, wife of Robert Chapell, and Ann and Joan Mortimer.

Residue to wife Wilmot Mortimer, who is Sole Executrix.

Witnesses—John Woodly.
            Roger Mortimer.

Proved Feby., 1639.

Sum £30 9s. 10d.

1640. The last Will of Richard Tucker of Tiverton. To be buried in parish church or churchyard, and leaves the poor 10s.

To son John Tucker, £30 at 21. To child "wife now goes with," a similar legacy.

If wife marry again to pay £60 to brothers William and Nicholas Tucker, for purpose of said bequest.

Wife Ebbot, Sole Executrix.

Dated "16th year of Charles." Proved July 31st, 1640.

1640. Extracts from Inventory of Richard Tucker, exhibited 31st July, 1640.

Item		
3 score sheepe & lambs	...	£20.
all his hogges	...	£3.
Corn in grounde	...	£46.
Reed, furse, & dunge	...	£1.
1 horse & 1 colt	...	£3 10s.
3 kine & 2 calves	...	£12.
all his poultrye	...	£0 2s. 6d.
Butter, beef, & bacon	...	£1.
Wood, &c.	...	£2.

Total sum of personalty, £123 13s. 10d.

1640. Administration to estate of Elizabeth Tocker of Thorncombe, Widow, granted 12th May, 1640, to William Tocker, her son.

1641. The last Will of Marie Tucker of Brampford Speke, Widow.

She confirms a legacy of her late husband's, "John Toocker," of £90 to their youngest son Tristram, and adds to it £40 and an annuity of 40s., all payable out of a messuage in said parish, and she also gives said son "Tristram" "the occupation of a chamber in her dwelling house." To daughter Mary, wife of Richard Copp, "my best gown." To daughter Ebbot, "my wearing apparell."

Residue to son John Tucker, who is Sole Executor.
Dated Sept. 1st, 1637. Proved 3rd Dec., 1641.
Sum £237 3s. 4d.

1642. Nicholas Tucker of Clayhanger, Husbandman, 9th Sept., 1642, "intreates his surviving friends to bury his corps." Confirms to sister Mary (with remainder to children of late Cilian Cornworthy; aunts Ursula Harte and Christian Webber; and daughter Jane Tucker, with further remainder to sister Joane Tucker), a legacy of £80, thus bequeathed by his father, Nicholas Tucker.

Gives sister "Jaune Tucker" £10, in addition to £10 left her by said father. "To daughter Jane, aforesaid, my Chiste, Bible, and all the rest of my books."

Residue to wife, "Jaune," who is Sole Executrix.

Memorandum—"This is the true intent and meaning of Nicholas Tucker, deceased, but brought unto better form. Edward Gardiner, Clericus."

Witnesses—Hugh Pimme, Denys Mortymore.
Proved 25th Oct., 1642.
Sum £263 10s.

NOTE.—That learned clerk, "Edward Gardiner," was not vicar of the parish, but about this time William Norris was ejected from the living by the Puritans and was afterwards restored.

1643. Thomas Tucker of St. Thomas the Apostle, Blacksmith.

To son George, 5s. To daughter Elizabeth, "the best lattine Candlestick" (*i.e.*, brass candlestick).

To daughters Johane, Mary "the elder," and Mary the younger, furniture and sundry "brasse pannes."

To son Nicholas, freehold house, orchard, and garden, after the expiration of the present lease.

Residue to wife Johan and son Nicholas, who are joint Exors.

Proved 13th Jany., 1643.

Sum £43 8s. 8d.

1643. Administration to the estate of John Mortimer, late of Ashton, granted 19th Feby., 1643, to Elizabeth, his relict.

Sum £21 4s. 2d.

1643. The last Will, nuncupative, of John Mortimoore of Bridford, made in presence of Michaell Dollinge, clearke, and Mary, wife of Gilbert Mortimoore of Bridforde. He leaves the poor of Bridford 4s. To brother Gilbert, 1s.

Residue to two brothers, Edward and Simon, who are Sole Exors.

Proved 29th Dec., 1643.

Sum £23 5s. 4d.

1644. The last Will of Robarte Tucker of Spreyton. He leaves his children William and Mary 20s. each, payable three years after his death, by his widow, Thomasine Tucker, who is residuary legatee and Sole Executrix.

Dated "13th Feby., 19th Charrell."

Proved 26th April, 1644.

Sum £26 17s. 4d.

1644. Roger Tucker of Luppitt, Will, nuncupative, dated 7th June, 1643.

To daughter, wife of Gervase Burroughs, £5; to her two children, Margery and Mary Burroughs, £5 each.

To grandchildren John, Jonathan, Susanna, Mary, and Gertrude, children of son James Tucker, £5 each.

To brother Walter's son, John Tucker, 20s.

Residue to son James, who is Sole Exor.

Proved at Exeter, May, 1644.

NOTE.—This Will is omitted from the Calendars of the Exeter District Registry.

1644. Nuncupative Will of Gilbert Tooker of Kenne, 1st May, 1644.

He gives "one ewe sheep apiece" to each of the children of his sons Edward and Peter, and of his son-in-law, Roger Densham. To son John Tooker, certain furniture, four mattocks, a bill-hook and a hatchet. To son Edward, £10. To Grace, daughter of said son Peter, "one coffer."

Residue to said Peter Tucker, who is Sole Executor.

Proved 31st May, 1644.

1644. The last Will of William Tucker of Cadbury, dated 23rd June, 1643.

To god-daughter Joan, 5s., and to the other children of John Carpenter, 1s. each.

Legacies to sister's children, Henry and Grace Bradford, and to "Cousins" Henry and William Tucker.

Residue to cousin, Peter Tucker.

Two Trustees, of whom "Cousin Henry Bradford" is one.

Proved 22nd Nov., 1644.

Sum £71 9s.

1646. Administration to the effects of Robert Mortimer of Dunsford, granted to his wife, Ursula, 13th May, 1646.

Sum £78 5s. 8d.

1646. The last Will of Mary Tucker, Widow, of Poltimore, dated July 27th, 1646.
Mentions sons Robert, William, and Valentine Tucker, daughter Mary, wife of Roger Druscombe, and her daughter, Mary Druscombe.
Residue to daughter, Elline Tucker, who is Sole Executrix.
Proved 28th Aug., 1646.

1646. Administration to the effects of John Tucker of Tiverton, granted Oct. 21st, 1646, to Agnes, his daughter, and to her husband, John Gill.
Inventory made by "John Tucker" and others.

1647. The last Will of Thomas Tucker of Tedburn St. Mary, 31st Jany., 1646.
3s. 4d. to the poor of the parish, on the day of his funeral.
Legacies to son Robert, and grandchild Bridget, daughter of said son.
Residue to wife, Johan, who is Sole Executrix.
Proved 26th May, 1647.
Sum £61 10s. 4d.

1647. The last Will, dated 3rd Oct., 1646, of John Tucker of Kenne, Yeoman.
Legacies of 15s. to poor of Kenne and Dartington.
To son Henry, all goods, &c., in parish of Dartington.
To daughter Amys Ewen, 20s., and to her children 6s. 8d. each.
Certain furniture in the hall to daughter-in-law Elizb. Nosworthy.
To daughter Mary Tucker, £100 at 22 or at marriage, together with the beds and other furniture in the new chamber, two pieces of plate and a dozen silver spoons, and a dozen best pewter dishes, pots, crocks, and the andirons, brought from Dartington. If said Mary marries without the

consent of her mother, or dies in minority, there is remainder, as follows:—

To son Henry, £40 and a piece of plate, "parsell giltes," to daughter Amys Ewens, £40 and a piece of white plate, and £20 to daughter Elizabeth Nosworthy.

Residue to wife Elizabeth, who is Sole Executrix.

Proved by Executrix, 23rd April, 1647.

NOTE.—Inventory shows that testator's plate consisted of "2 sylver booles, and one dozen syllver spoones," valued at £7.

1648. [*Copy.*] "Margaret Tucker, Tiverton, July 17th, 1646. Imprimis I give unto my two brothers, Allen Tucker and John Tucker, 10s. apiece. Also I give to my sisters, Susan and Elizabeth Tucker, 10 poundes apiece. Item I give unto Jane Browne ffive poundes. Item I have made my lovinge ffather mine Executor.

"Margaret Tucker."

Witnesses—Robert Coad.
Humphry Codner.

1648. Administration to the effects of Margaret Tucker of Tiverton, deceased, granted 2nd Feby., 1648, to Henry Tucker, her father.

1648. The last Will of Thomas Tucker of Tiverton, Apothecary, dated 3rd Sept., 1644.

Leaves to "the minister that preacheth my ffuneral sermon, xx^s."

To Allen, John, Susanna, and Elizabeth, children of brother Henry Tucker, 40s. each.

"I make my Cousin, Margarite Tucker, now my servant, eldest daughter to my brother Henry, residuary legatee and Sole Executrix."

Administration granted to testator's brother, Henry Tucker, 2nd Feby., 1648.

NOTE.—Testator's Will, who evidently died before 17th July, 1646, must have been left unproved by the executrix named therein. See her own will *ante*.

1648. Administration to the effects of William Tucker of Tiverton, granted 14th July, 1648, to Sara Tucker, *alias* Lakey, his relict.
Sum £2 6s.

1649. Administration to the effects of Alexander Toker of Stockley English, granted 12th July, 1649, to Henry "Tooker," his brother.

1649. The last Will of . . . Mortimore (Andrew?) of Upton Helinge, Husbandman, dated 20th Feby., 16th James. He gives his "wife" the residue of a lease of rent-charge upon property in Crediton and Cheriton Fitz-Payne, determinable on the life of Thomas Mortimore; he charges it with an annuity of £5 to son John.

Trustees—William Bremebridge and William Esworthy, with 6s. 8d. each for their trouble.

Name of Exor. omitted; residue undisposed of.

Witnesses—John Passord, Henry Stogdon, John Hayman, Bartholomew Goche.

Administration granted 16th July, 1649, to Christopher Payne, the husband of Agnes, relict and executor, *de jure*, of deceased, called "Andrew" Mortimore, of Upton Hellions, in the Calendars of the district registry, and who had died without proving her father's will.

NOTE.—" William Bremebridge," the trustee, whose family name is otherwise variously written in old documents—Bremelrig, Bremebrig, and now Bremridge, was "aged 21" in 1598, and was son and heir of John Bremridge of Bremridge in Sandford, co. of Devon, who was thirteenth in descent from Robert Bremridge of Bremridge, A D. 1218, great-grandson of Drogo Fitz-Mauger of Bradleigh, and Bremridge its "parcel," sub-tenant of the latter manor in 1087, and also of Bremridge in South Molton. The said Drogo Fitz-Mauger was son of Mauger, Earl of Arquois, son of Richard II., and grandson of Richard I., Dukes of Normandy, by Gunnora, sister of Herfast, the Dane. Bremridge passed, by the marriage of Anna Maria, daughter and ultimate heir of John Bremridge of Bremridge, with Richard Melhuish of Poughill, co. Devon, marriage license 20th Nov., 1775, to her son Thomas Melhuish of Poughill. The Bremridges of Exeter and Winkleigh are a younger branch of this ancient family.

Arms—*Sa.*, a chevron between 3 crosslets, *or*.

1650. The last Will, nuncupative, of Francis Tucker of Exeter, dated 17th Sept., 1650. He gives all the books in his study to his brother Lawrence. "All his ready money, and whatsoever he has in his box to his kinswomen, Mary and Elizabeth Mapowder, daughters of Francis Mapowder of Exeter, merchant.

Admon. granted to said Mary and Elizabeth, 30th Sept., 1650.

1650. The last Will of Edward Mortimore of Bridford, dated 3rd Aug., 1650.

He leaves to the poor of the parish, 3s. 4d. To eldest son, Edward, £40, and like sums to sons Abraham, Nathaniel, and Gilbert, at 21, and to daughter Thomasine.

Lease of "Townsend living" in Dunsford to wife Elizabeth. Trustees, "my good friends Thomas Mortimer of Dunsford and Gilbert Mortimer of St. Thomas."

Residue to said wife, who is Sole Executrix.

Proved 6th Sept., 1650.

Sum £247 12s. 4d.

1651. The last Will of Dorothy Tucker of Thorverton, Widow, dated 19th June, 1649. Bequests to the poor of Thorverton and Shobrooke.

She leaves her daughters Charity Venne of Payhembury, Joan Styling, Agnes Hughes (Tiverton), and Marie Kelland, £10 each.

To John, son of son Henry Tucker of Stoke Canon, and to the latter's other children, Lewis, Elizabeth, and Dorothy, £10 each at 16. Residue to Humphry Thomas of Thorverton, who is Sole Exor.

By the Inventory it appears that Walter Crosse owed testatrix £248 6s. 8d., and also £200; Edmund Browne of Newton St. Cyres, £50.

Proved by Executor named, 30th May, 1651.

Sum £510 10s.

1660. The last Will of Roger Tooker of the city of Exeter, "In holder," dated 13th Oct., 1660. Legacies of £100 to sons Hugh and Roger, at 24.
Residue to wife Amy, who is Sole Executrix.
Proved 18th Dec., 1660.

NOTE.—Indorsed " Roger Curtis Tooker."

1661. Administration to the effects of Henry Tucker of Cadbury, granted to Christian, his widow, 17th Jany., 1661.
He had a chattell lease of a close of land and a house called "King's House," in parish of Tiverton.

1662. Administration to the effects of John Tucker of Whimple, granted 4th Feby., 1662, to Alice Crutchett, next of kin.

1662. The last Will, nuncupative, of Peter Tooker of Kenn, Yeoman, dated 28th July, 1662.
To daughters Margaret Barter, Grace Lamb, and Joan Damarell, £5 apiece. His house to eldest son, Gilbert; a meadow to son Thomas.
Residue to wife Mary, who is Sole Executrix.
Proved 22nd Aug., 1662.
Sum £75 18s. 4d.

1664. The last Will of William Tucker of Tiverton, Husbandman, dated 29th Nov., 1664. To son Humphry and daughter Grace, £50 each.
Residue to son William, who is Sole Exor.
Proved 7th Dec., 1664.
Armorial Seal, in red wax—" an antelope."
Sum, £145 18s. 10d.

1665. Administration to the effects of William Tucker of Axminster, granted to Agnes his wife, 17th May, 1665.
Sum, £13 4s.

1665. Johanna Tucker of Whitstone, granted to Anne Kingwell, her daughter, of Morchard Bishop, 13th June, 1665.

1665. Nicholas Tucker of Plymtree, to Lucy, his relict, 20th Sept, 1665.
Sum, £23 14s. 5d.

1665. The last Will of Elizabeth Tucker of Kenn, Widow. To poor of Kenn, 20s. To daughter Mary, wife of John Wright of Feniton, a silver bowl. To grandchildren Elizabeth, Philip, and Mary Wright, and John, Thomas, and David Nosworthy, 40s. each. To grandchild Honor Nosworthy, "the standing bedstead 'performed' (*i.e.*, perfect), the Spruce Chest, the table board, and the form, all standing in the new chamber, one brass pot and three pewter dishes." Similar bequests of furniture to grandchildren Mary and Elizabeth Nosworthy. Mentions daughter Elizabeth Nosworthy.
Residue to John Nosworthy, the elder, who is Sole Exor.
Proved 20th Oct., 1665.

1666. Administration to the effects of John Tucker of Tiverton, granted 10th May, 1666, to Deborah, the widow.
Sum, £8 10s.

1667. The last Will of Susanna Tucker of Luppit, Widow, dated 20th July, 1657. She gives her leasehold estate called Rugpath, and her best petticoat, to her son John Tucker. She gives son Thomas £90, and his bed, and "my best pot called Thomazine's pot & platter."
To son Joseph, his bed and £90, and the "olde pot." Further bequests to daughters Elizabeth Wiet[*] and Rabbage Flood, and granddaughters Elizabeth Wiet and "five" others, and also Stephen Flood.
Residue to son John, who is Sole Executor.
Proved 10th April, 1667.
Sum, £415 18s. 6d.

---

[*] Elizabeth, wife of Christopher Wiet of Ottery St. Mary.

1667. Administration to the effects of Nicholas Tucker of Bampton, granted 12th Sept., 1667, to Margery, his relict.

1667. Inventory of Nicholas Tucker, made 15th March, 1666.

"Item 6 Steers & 4 Heffers, with 2 yerelings ...	£30	0 0
"36 Sheepe	16	0 0
"4 Pigs	3	0 0
"Corne in barne	9	0 0
"Bacon	3	0 0
"Butter & Cheese	0	10 0
"3 Horses with their takelin*	9	0 0"

Sum, £145.

1667. The last Will of Mary Tucker of Halberton, Widow, dated 16th Oct., 1667.

Tenement in said parish to son Nicholas Tucker; certain furniture, and "the house ladder, hanging over John Hancock's door."

To grandchildren Anne and Rebecca Tucker, "one pewter dish apiece," "which are uppon the cupboard in the parler."

To son-in-law Christopher Burton, "one olde tubbe to keep corn in." Mentions grandchildren Mary and Elizabeth Burton, and Mary Martyn.

Residue to son-in-law, Robert Martyn, who is Sole Exor.
Proved 15th Nov., 1667.

1668. The last Will of Susannah Osmond of Tiverton, Widow, Sept. 26th, 1668.

To kinsman George Osmond, £5. To James Osmond, 40s. Residue to "kinsfolk" Elizb. Ward, and Thomas and Elizb. Osmond, who are joint Exors.

John Osmond a Trustee.
Proved 7th Oct., 1668.
Sum, £185 11s. 8d.

* Harness.

1668. The nuncupative Will of Joseph Tucker of Luppit, 1st Nov., 1667.

To John and Elizabeth, children of John Flood of Broadway, co. Somerset, £12 each at 21. To Susannah, their sister, 40s. To their mother, "Rabetch Flood" (Testator's sister), £14.

To brother Thomas Tucker, to sister Elizabeth, wife of Christopher Wyett, and their children Elizabeth, Christopher, John, Susan, and Samuel Wyett, small bequests at 21.

To brother John Tucker, 10s. at 21.

Residue to said last-named brother, who is Sole Executor. Proved 18th Dec., 1668.

1669. Administration to the effects of Maria Mortimer of Cheriton, granted 6th Oct., 1669, to Thomas Ward, her son. Thomas Ward of Cheriton, husbandman, joins the bond.

1669. Administration to the effects of John Mortimore of Spreyton, granted 19th March, 1669-70, to Alice, his wife.

1669. The last Will of John Osmond of Willand, dated 25th Sept., 1669.

He assigns a legacy "left him by Father" to the maintenance of son James Osmond, to be administered by brothers George and James Osmond as trustees, and he leaves them the residue of his estate in trust for the benefit of wife Mary, with remainder to nephew James, son of said George Osmond, and James, son of brother Thomas Osmond, deceased.

Witnesses, Robert and Elizabeth Dowdney.

Administration granted to testator's said brothers, George and James Osmond, 14th Jany., 1669.

NOTE.—The Dowdneys, otherwise Dewdeneys, were long settled at Doddiscombleigh, and more recently at Stoke Canon.

Arms—*Sable*, a bend *erm.*, cotised *or*.

1669. Administration to the effects of Agnes Tucker of Tiverton, granted 8th Oct., 1669, to Maria Tucker, her daughter.

1670. Admon. to the effects of William Tucker of Halberton, granted 12th Aug., 1670, to Amy, his widow.

1670. "Amy" (or Anne) Tucker of Halberton, Widow, granted 15th Sept., 1670, to Richard Tucker, her brother.

1670. The last Will of Nicholas Tucker of Westmeare in parish of Tiverton, 13th Aug., 1667. Legacies to children John, Elizabeth, Alice, and Margaret Tucker, Mary, wife of Stephen Stone. Special bequest to Margaret, "one coffer, second best paire of Sheets, and one dyaper bord cloth."

Residue to children James and Johan, who are joint Exors.

Kinsman Thomas Tidbolle, trustee.

Proved 9th Sept., 1670.

NOTE.—The Tidboulds, Tidbolles, or Tidballs, are an old Devonshire family, of late years resident at Chulmleigh.

Samuel Tidball, in 1613, accepted the curacy of Ashburton, and was subsequently Head Master of the Grammar School. Upon the death of his son-in-law, Mark Law, who had married his daughter Maria, and had succeeded his father, Archdeacon Law, as Vicar of Ashburton, Mr. Tidball was himself instituted to that preferment in 1644. He died in 1647.

The Will of his son, Samuel Tidball, gentleman, dated 20th May, 1666, was proved in the Court of the Dean and Chapter of Exeter, 13th July, that year.

1670. The last Will of John Tucker of Tiverton, Bachelor, dated 10th Oct., 1670.

To his two sisters Mary Tucker, "the elder," and Mary Tucker, "the younger," £20 each. He settles an estate called "Coomburlleys," in said parish, upon the sons of his brother Philip, and their heirs, with remainder, in default, to his said two sisters. £5 to be spent on his funeral.

Residue to brother William Tucker, who is Sole Exor.

John Hamett, testator's grandfather, and John Burrage, serge maker, are trustees.

Admon. granted to John Burrage and John Chilcott, in minority of Exor., 17th Jany., 1670.

1670. The last Will, nuncupative, of Francis Osmond of Halberton, dated 23rd July, 1670. Mentions sons Robert, Abraham, and John, daughters Jone and Deborah, and grandchild Deborah Lee. Residue to said sons, and to Francis, their brother, and to daughter, Deborah Lee, who are joint Exors.

Proved 5th Aug., 1670.

1670. Administration to the estate of James Osmond, Gentleman, of Halberton, granted 16th August, 1670, to Susannah, his relict.

1671. The last Will of Thomas Mortimore of Harpford, 21st Jany., 1663.

He gives wife Ursula certain furniture, and "that cheare which I brought away from Salterton."

Bequests to Emmet, wife of Robert Harries of Exeter, and to their daughter Mary.

To Richard and Mary, children of late Richard Mortimore, £2 5s. each.

"To the clarke to toll the bell, 1s. 6d."

"To the bedman for his paynes, 1s." To the poor, 1s., and to the poor of Newton Poppleford, 1s.

Residue to John, son of late Richard Mortimore, who is Sole Exor.

20s. to be spent on the funeral.

Witnesses, John Saiward (Seaward), Richard Dagworthy, and Jacob Clarke.

Proved 2nd May, 1671.

1671. The last Will of Thomas Mortymore of Bradninch, 22nd May, 1671. He doubles a bequest of 20s. by father, William Mortymore, in favour of "my two daughters," Elizb., wife of William Maye, and Mary, wife of Thomas Hardinge.

Mentions grandchildren John, Joan, and Richard Hardinge. Grandchild Thomas Venn, "a Bible, five wagges (wedges), and a thort saw" (cross-cut saw). Residue to grandchildren Thomas, Agnes, and Amos Venn, who are joint Exors.

Proved by trustees, Robert Salter and Thomas Hardinge, 7th June, 1671.

1671. Administration to the effects of William Fry, Yeoman, of Upottery, granted 28th April, 1671, to Joan, his relict.

1671. The last Will of Robert Mortimore, of Faringdon, 1st July, 1671.

To son Robert, "my brewing kieve." To daughter Hannah, "a standard, and one pewter dish." To daughter Joan, "a bedstead and bed, with liberty to come and go until she is married or dead." Mentions son Thomas and daughters Alice and Hester. Gives house and garden to son Henry, and makes him residuary legatee and Sole Exor.

Proved 20th Oct., 1671.

1671. Administration to the effects of George Tucker of Shobrooke, granted 3rd Feby., 1671, to Maria Tucker, his daughter.

1672. The last Will of Valentine Tucker of Poltimore, 8th May, 1672. To poor of the parish, 10/-. Gives daughter, Joan Wilcocks, an interest in "Tongington," in parish of Exminster. Mentions "my two sons-in-law," Philip and Amias Wilcocks. Residue to son John, who is Sole Exor.

Proved 7th Jany., 1672.

Sum, £238 17s. 10d.

1673. The last Will of Robert Tucker of Tedburn. To son Robert, £50. To children, Bridget, Elizabeth, Johan, John, Mary, and Peter Tucker, £20 each. To sons Thomas and Mark Tucker, the tenement called Colly-Hay, his residence. Residue to wife Bridget, who is Sole Executrix.

Proved 11th April, 1673.

1673. The last Will of Nicholas Osmond of Halberton, 18th Feby., 1668. To poor of parish, 50/-. Bequests to daughters, Elizb. Osmond and Anne Chamberlyn, and to latter's son, John Chamberlyn. To brother, Francis Osmond; to sister, Sarah Bennett; to Henry Gold the elder; and to his daughter, Maudlyn Gold. Residue to son Abraham Osmond, who is Sole Exor.

Proved 2nd June, 1673.

Sum, £245 13s. 10d.

1673. The last Will nuncupative of Michael Osmond of Halberton, 1st Nov. 1672. He makes his wife Joane, his daughter, Joane Weber, and his son, Christopher Osmond, joint residuary legatees and Exors.

Trustees—Arthur and John Kerslake.

Proved 11th July, 1673.

1674. The last Will of Christian Tuker of Stokeintinhead, Widow, 8th Feby., 1673.

She gives her house and garden to Grace, daughter of brother Abraham Ladimer (Latimer) of the parish of St. Nicholas (Shaldon). Mentions sister, Amy Lang, and gives Sara Lang "one gold ring which was her grandmother's." To Mary Lang, "one drawer of apills." "Cosin" (*i.e.*, nephew) Abraham Ladimer, "George Monk's children," and Joan Poole, are also mentioned. Residue to brother-in-law, Thomas Lang, who is Sole Exor.

Proved 1st May, 1674.

1674. Admon. to the estate of Arthur Tucker, late of St. David's, Exeter, granted 26th June, 1674, to Agnes Blake, otherwise Tucker.

1674. Admon. to the estate of Matthew Mortimore of Christowe, granted 15th Nov., 1674, to Isot, his relict.

1674. The last Will of Simon Mortimer of Dunsford. Gives £20 each to sons Thomas and "Symon," and to daughter Mary Mortimer. Mentions brother Gilbert Mortimer, son-in-law George Mortimer, and sister-in-law Amy Potter. To grandson George Mortimer, £12. Residue to wife Ellinor, who is Sole Executrix.
Proved 24th March, 1674.

1675. The last Will of George Osmond of Broadclist, Yeoman, 1st Dec., 1675. To son James, "my tenement called Goosens" at 21. Residue to wife Margaret, who is Sole Executrix.
Proved 9th Feby., 1675.

1678. The last Will of Agnes Osmond of Halberton, Widow, 8th Sept., 1676. Mentions grandchildren, Agnes Turner, widow, Thomasine Turner, Margt. Turner, Elinor, wife of Edward Weeks, Henry and Abraham, sons of Henry Trent, and Joan, wife of Henry Trent. Daughters Joan, wife of Abraham Turner, and Elizabeth, wife of Edward Hitchcocke. She also mentions "Elizabeth, wife of John Morrish," and Robert Bragg.
Residue to said "grandchild" Joan, wife of Henry Trent, who is Sole Executrix.
Witnesses, Thomas Dowdney and Maudlyn Gold.
Proved 10th June, 1678.

1679. The last Will of Tobias Tucker of Cheriton Fitzpaine, 23rd Dec., 1679. He leaves his "cosens" Gilling, Elizabeth, Mary, and Constance Jones, children of his sister Elizabeth, 40/- each. To Thomasine Easterbrook, 40/-; and to "brother's two children," 40/- each. To Bartholomew Huish, 5/-; to John Huish, senr., 20/- and the "little mare"; to William, son of John Huish, 10/-. To godson, Roger Glanfield, 10/-. Funeral to cost £4. Residue to brother, Richard Tucker, who is Sole Exor.

Proved 6th Jany., 1679.

1679. The last Will of John Tucker of Cleyhidon. To his two daughters Margt., wife of George Pocock, and Elizabeth, wife of Thomas Somerhayes, 5/- each.

£160 to be raised on his estate, and the interest paid to daughter Bridget, wife of John Seyman, with remainder to her sons, John, Edmond, and William Sparke, and Nicholas Seyman. To son-in-law, John Troke, 1/-. He bequeaths a debt of £40, due to him from George Pocock, to his grandchildren, Elizabeth, Joane, Henry, and George Pocock.

And a debt of £10, due to him from Thomas Somerhayes, to grandchild Elizb. Somerhayes. To grandchild Alice Troke, £5 at 21. Residue to son Nicholas Tucker, who is Sole Exor.

Proved 5th May, 1679.

1679. The last Will of Philip Tucker of Tiverton, 15th Dec., 1679. To Mary Pullin and Mary Webber, leasehold house and garden adjoining the Churchyard gate.

Residue of a lease of a house in occupation of William Chilcote, to "cosens" Mary, Agnes, and Susannah Pullen and their issue, for a term of 2,000 years, and also an eighth part of "Way" for similar term.

To brother, William Tucker, 10/-. Residue to said "cosen" Agnes Pullin, who is Sole Executrix.

Proved 21st Feby., 1679.

Admon. granted to Petherick Hopkins, in minority of Agnes Pullin, 21st Feby., 1679.

1679. The last Will of Roger Tucker of St. Thomas, by Exeter, 20th Oct., 1679. To the poor of St. Thomas the Apostle, 30/-.

To nephew Henry, son of late George Tucker of George-Nymet, 40/- *p.a.* The will, which extends over two sheets, is filled with names of his mere acquaintance. To "the children" of his "mother's sister by Thomas Worthen" he gives £9. To Dorothy Godfrey "the remnant of white woollen cloth which was last in her custody, and his Bible." Residue to George, son of said brother, George Tucker, who is Sole Exor.

Proved 26th Feby., 1679.

1680. The last Will of William Tucker of St. Thomas the Apostle, nigh Exeter, 4th Oct., 1680.

Bequests to brother Thomas and his child; to brother Anthony and his wife and child; to brother Samuel and sister Joan.

To "cosen" George, son of George Tucker, £5 at 21. Residue to brother, George Tucker, who is Sole Exor.

Proved 19th Nov., 1680.

1680. Administration to the effects of Stephen Tucker, late of Luppit, granted 21st Oct., 1680, to Anstis his wife.

1680. Administration to the effects of Mary Mortimer of Holcomb Burnell, granted 21st March, 1680, to Mary Braggats Mortimore her daughter.

1680. Administration to the effects of Harry Mortimore of Farringdon, granted 5th Oct., 1680, to Joan his wife.

1680. Admon. to the effects of John Mortimore of Thorverton, granted 12th Jany., 1680-81, to John Norrish, their uncle, for the benefit of Thomas Mortimore and Lewis Melhuish, brothers of deceased.

Dyonisius Melhuish of Thorverton joins the bond.

1681. Admon. to the estate of Gilbert Tucker of St. Nicholas (Shaldon), granted 22nd Oct., 1681, to his daughter Dorothy, wife of Thomas Mudge.

1681. The last Will of Johan Tucker of St. Thomas, by Exeter, Widow, 14th Dec. 1681.

To son Thomas, £5, failing his life, to his wife and to his daughter, Elizabeth Tucker.

To son George, "two rumes of my house, to witt the ground rume, and the chamber over, and halfe of the garden ploot, that is now sett with the saide rumes."

To son Anthony, "the backer chamber, commonly called the chamber over the pentline, and a stable, and the other halfe of saide garden."

To son Samuel, "the other tenement, with a garden ploot, the same size as George and Anthony's, and they to have a piece of ground apiece to build a pig's stye on."

Residue to daughter Johane, who is Sole Executrix.

Proved 10th Jany., 1681.

1681. The last Will of George Osmond of Halberton, June 6th, 1681, Yeoman. To the poor, 10/-.

To son James, £10, and the "silver salt."

To son George, a tenement called "Shilcroft," and certain furniture.

To son Philip, £200, and a "little desk."

To daughter Welthian, £120.

Residue to wife Welthian, who is Sole Executrix.

Proved 20th Sept., 1681.

Sum, £427 2s. 4d.

1681. Admon. to the effects of Andrew Osmond, late of the City of Exeter, granted 14th Oct., 1681, to Edward Bampfield, principal creditor.

1682. The last Will of John Tucker the elder, of the parish of Holy Trinity, and City of Exeter, dated 6th May, 1682. House and Garden, mortgaged to John Tucker, merchant, to son, John Tucker. Mentions "three daughters." Residue to wife Rebecca, and son Morris Tucker, they are joint Exors.
Proved 9th June, 1682.

1682. Induction. Mandate from "Thomas," the Bishop, to the Archdeacon of Exeter (Dr. Edward Lake), to induct Nicholas Tucker, clerk, to the Rectory of Hittesleigh, 10th June, 1682.

NOTE.—"Thomas," Lord Bishop of Exeter, was Dr. Thomas Lamplugh, he became Archbishop of York, Nov., 1688. "Dr. Edward Lake," was the son of an Exeter clergyman; born 1642, at first of Wadham Coll., Oxford, but graduated at Cambridge. He became attached to the household of the Duke of York in 1670, and was chaplain and tutor to the princesses Mary and Anne, afterward Queens of England. He was present at the marriage of the former with her cousin, the Prince of Orange, subsequently William III., and left in his diary a curious account of the ceremony which was solemnized in the bedchamber of the princess at St. James' Palace, at 9 o'clock, on the night of Nov. 4th, 1677, after a formal engagement of fourteen days. Dr. Lake died in London, 1st Feby., 1704, and was buried in the church of St. Katherine, Tower Hill.

1682. The last Will of William Tucker of Cheriton FitzPaine, 11th June, 1678. He leaves £4 to daughter Margaret Sharlen. Residue to son Simon, who is Sole Exor.
Proved 23rd Oct., 1682.

1682. The last Will of Henry Glover of Tiverton, 26th Feby., 1682. He leaves his four children, William, Thomas, Thomazine, and Mary, £4 each. Residue of real estate to wife Thomazine, for benefit of said children. Residue of personality to son Thomas "Glover alias Tucker," who is Sole Exor.
Proved 21st March, 1682.
Sum, £279 7s. 6d.

1683. The last Will of William Mortimore the elder, of Tiverton, 22nd August, 1682. "To William Mortimore's wife my three gold rings." To son, John Mortimore, "one sylver spoone." Residue to sons, William and John Mortimore, who are joint Exors. He desires to be buried in Crediton Churchyard.

Proved 16th May, 1683.

Oval seal in black wax—charged with a fleur-de-lys.

1683. Administration to the effects of John Tucker of Thornecombe, granted 24th April, 1683, to Joan his relict. Inventory of above, made 7th Nov., 1682 :—

"Item 5 cows £15
 „ 3 heifers £7
 „ 2 fatt cows £9 5
 „ 2 yearling heifers £2
 „ One mare and takeling belong to her... £3
 „ 2 Piggs ... ... £2 16."

1683. John Tucker of Newton St. Cyres, July 10th, 1683. He leaves his wife Joan an annuity of 50/-. Residue for the benefit of his children, Joan, Mary, Francis, and John, in trust to brother, Nicholas Tucker, who is Sole Exor.

Proved Sept. 11th, 1683.

1683. Inventory of the effects of John Tucker of Woodleigh, in the parish of Newton St. Cyres, made by Walter Tucker and others, 16th July, 1683.

"Imprimis his purse and apparel £4
 Item one mare with his furniture £3
 „ 2 Bullocks £5 10
 „ One little nursery £1 10
 „ 3 young piggs £1
 „ 1 littel plot of wheat with the cabbage
      plants, carrots & beans £2
 „ All the apples £2 5
 „ 3 brasse crockes, 3 brasse panns, &
      3 brass kettles ... ...£3 19."

1683. The last Will of John Tucker of Brampford Speke. To the poor of the parish and to the "reparashion" of the parish church, 3/4. He leaves certain bedding, with liberty to reside in his house, to beloved wife Thomazine. Small legacies to daughter Mary Sowdon, and to her children Henry and Mary Sowdon. Residue to daughters Alice and Elizabeth Tucker, who are joint Exors.
Proved 28th Nov., 1683.

1684. Richard Tucker of Halberton, bequeaths his "body to the earth from which it was extracted." He devises leasehold property at "Five Bridges" to son Nicholas, and £5 to son Thomas. Mentions "sister, Blackmore," and sister, "Prudence Snow." Residue to wife Rebecca, who is Sole Executrix.
Brother Nicholas Tucker a trustee.
Dated 12th Sept., 1684.
Proved 17th March, 1684-85.

1684. The last Will of Samuel Osmond of Broadclist, Yeoman, dated 1st May, 1684. 20/- to poor for bread, and 2c/- to poor labourers. To wife Thomasine certain furniture; to brother John Osmond, to sister Mary Palmer, and to cousin Jane Osmond, £5 each. To sister Wilmot Walker, and to Samuel Walker, her son, 50/-. Residue to mother, Catherine, who is Sole Executrix.
Proved 10th May, 1684.

1684. The last Will of Abraham Mills of Halberton, otherwise Osmond, 23rd March, 1683. To the poor "twenty dusson of bread." Mentions brother-in-law, George Northcote, "To the parson that preaches my funeral sermon 20/-." Small bequests to Hannah Hookins, Margt. Hill, Thomas Rogers and Thomas Halkwill. To sister Elizabeth, a pair of gloves. Residue to wife Joan, who is Sole Executrix.
Witnesses—John and George Northcote.
Proved 17th April, 1684.

1685. Admon. to the effects of Richard Mortimore, late of Harpford, deceased, granted 9th March, 1685, to his relict Margaret Dagworthy *alias* "Mortymer," now wife of Richard Dagworthy.

NOTE.—The Inventory shows that deceased died 4th Sept., 1658 (twenty-seven years previously), and left personal estate valued at £109 10s. 6d.

1685. Bernard Tucker of Southleigh, Husbandman, 21st May, 1685. Mentions children John, Thomas, and Grace. Residue to wife Mary, who is Sole Executrix.
Proved 23rd Sept., 1685.

1686. The last Will of Thomas Tucker of Southleigh, "old & stricken in years," 21st July, 1682. Leaves certain furniture to wife Judith. Legacies to son Charles and his children Charles and Jane; to son Thomas and his child John Tucker; to daughter Elizb., wife of Wm. French, and to her son, Thomas French; to grandson James, son of James Tucker, deceased. Residue to son and daughter, Richard and Barbara, who are joint Exors.
Witness—Bernard Tucker.
Proved 20th April, 1686.

1686. Humphry Tucker of Pinhoe, nigh Exeter, desires to be buried in the parish yard. To son Humphry (married to "Elizabeth"), leasehold tenement at "Southley alias Sowlee," "known by the name of Holster." Residue to daughter Emline, who is Sole Executrix.
Proved 16th April, 1686.

1686-87. Will, nuncupative, dated 26th Nov., 1686, of Elizabeth Tucker of Brampford Speke, Spinster, £5 to poor, and a like sum to sister Mary Sowdon's four children. To sister Alice Tucker, a field called Cross Park. Residue to mother, Thomazine, who is Sole Executrix.
Proved by Executrix, 4th Feby., 1686-87.

1687. Admon. to the effects of Joanna Tucker of Thornecombe, daughter of John Tucker, deceased. Granted 11th April, 1687, to Joan Tucker, her mother.
Sum, £52 18s. 5¼d.

1687. Gilbert Tucker of Honiton, 9th Nov., 1686, leaves grandchildren Gregory, John, and Elizabeth Oke, 1/- each at 21. Residue to daughter Elizabeth, wife of John Oke, who is Sole Executrix. To be buried in Honiton Churchyard.
Sum, £1 19s. 3d.
Proved 2nd Feby., 1687.

1687. The last Will of George Mortimore of the City and County of the City of Exeter, 16th Feby., 1687. He recites a marriage settlement by which a moiety of "Gibbs," situate at Witnell in County of Somerset, has been granted to daughter Elizb. Bowden, and he bequeaths the other moiety to daughter Deborah Mortimore, together with the sum of £190, a silver tankard, and silver porringer. Bequests to Jonathan, Elizabeth, and Deborah Bowden, children of said daughter Elizb., and to brother Antony Mortimore and his "children." To Elizabeth Blackaller, 10/-.
Residue to said daughters, who are joint Exors.
Proved 15th March, 1687.

1687. The last Will of Symon Mortimer of Dunsford, to nephew Symon, son of Abraham Shilston of said parish, and to Elizabeth, daughter of brother Thomas, 1/- each.
Residue to daughters Ellinor and Dorothy, who are joint Exors.
Remainder to children of brother-in-law, Nicholas Payne, and of Mary, wife of brother-in-law, Wm. Shilston, "my sister."
Witnesses—John Peddericke, Wilmett Hammett, and John Davy.
Proved 11th Nov., 1687.
Armorial Seal—3 Estoiles.

1687. Will, nuncupative, of Thomas Osmond, late of Tiverton, "who died on St. Stephen's day, last past."

To eldest son, Thomas, "best coat & best hatt, best stockings & shoes & 1/-." To second son, George, "close bodyed coat & 1/-." To son Peter, "best breeches & 1/-." Residue to wife Joan, who is Sole Executrix.

Proved 12th April, 1687.

1688. Administration to the effects of Peter Tucker of Cadbury, granted 18th May, 1688, to William his son.

1688. The last Will of Welthyan Osmond of Hearn, in the parish of Halberton, Widow. To son George and his three children, Thomas, Elizabeth, and Joan, £5 each. To son Philip, £5; to daughter Welthyan, £60. To the poor, 20/-. Residue to son James Osmond, who is Sole Exor.

Proved 3rd May, 1688.

1688. The last Will of Nicholas Tucker of St. Thomas the Apostle, nigh Exeter, Schoolmaster. To sister, Mary Bicknell, 5s. To son Thomas, the lease of the schools, and to Mary, Joan, and Agnes Tucker, children of said Thomas, £2 10s. each. Legacies to daughter Mary Rugg, and her children Mary and Thomas.

Residue to wife Agnes, who is Sole Executrix. Dated 17th April, 1688. Latter to have disposal of goods if she remains unmarried, but he wishes his children to have the "benefit of that which he hath carefully gotten."

Proved 3rd Sept., 1688.

1689. The last Will of James Tucker of Tiverton, dated 17th March, 1688-89. His body to be "decently buried, according to the computation of the Church of England." His "wearing cloths" to his brother Roger Tucker.

Residue to wife Ann, and daughter Sarah, who are joint Exors.

Proved 16th April, 1689.

1689. Admon. to the effects of Lewis Tucker of Exeter, granted 9th Sept., 1689, to Dorothy, his widow.

1689. Dorothy Osmond of Uplowman, Widow, 30th Oct., 1689. Legacies to son-in-law James Osmond, and to Agnes his wife, and to Edward and Priscilla, their children.

To Elizabeth, wife of Thomas Osmond, "one suit of apparel which I did usually weare Saboth dayes."

To Mary, wife of Robert Heard, "my best cloth pettycote." To Mrs. Ann Calwoodleigh, 20/-.

Residue to "my friend," Mrs. Thomasine Calwoodleigh, who is Sole Executrix.

Proved 8th Nov., 1689.

NOTE.—"Mrs. Ann Calwoodleigh," baptized at Uplowman, 1662, was daughter of James, and sister of John Calwoodleigh, buried at Uplowman, May, 1663.

The descent of these, doubtful as regards legitimacy, is recorded in the Herald's Visitations of Devonshire, and is traced to John C. of "Calwoodleigh," pronounced and now written Calverleigh, who married a daughter of John Floyer, early in the 15th century. The younger branch removed from Padstow to London.

Arms of Calwoodleigh of Calverleigh—"*As.* two wings, conjoined, *Arg.* surmounted by a fess, *Gu.* thereon 3 bezants."

1690. The last Will of Thomas Tooker of Dunsford, 5th Oct., 1687.

Bequests to sons Robert and Nicholas, daughter Elizabeth, and grandchildren Robert and Margaret Tucker.

Residue to wife Elizabeth, who is Sole Executrix.

Proved 7th March, 1690.

1690. Nicholas Tucker of Halberton, 26th Dec., 1689. Bequests to children Andrew, Nicholas, and Anne. Half of goods to wife Rebecca. Eldest daughter, Rebecca, "to be sole executrix of everything, in doors and out."

Residue undisposed of.

Proved 6th May, 1690.

1690. The last Will of Sarah Osman of Exeter, "single woman." Bequests of 1/- to brother-in-law Abraham Seely, and to his children Abraham, Peter, Elizb., and Joan Seely. £4 to brother John Osman's children. To sister Hannah Seely, "all my cloathes."
Residue to said brother, John Osman, who is Sole Exor.
Dated 28th June, 1689.
Witness—Elizb. Follett.
Proved 27th Sept., 1690.

1690. Admon. to the effects of William Fry of Silverton, granted 15th Aug., 1690, to Dorothy his relict.

1691. The last Will of Johan Tucker of Poltimore, Widow, 20th Dec., 1690. She divides her property amongst her children Amos and Philip Wilcocks, and grandchildren Mary and Johan, Roger and Isaac Wilcocks. Bequests to son-in-law John Tucker, and to kinswoman Ann Harris.
Residue to Philip, son of Philip, and Elizabeth, daughter of Amos Wilcocks, who are joint Exors.
Admon. to Amos and Philip Wilcocks, sons of Testatrix, in minority of Exors.
Granted 29th May, 1691.

1691. Administration to the effects of Richard Tucker of St. Thomas, granted 25th Aug., 1691, to Jane his wife.

1691. The last Will of Jone Osmond of Tiverton, Widow, 16th Jany., 1690. Mentions sons Peter, Thomas, and George Osmond, grandchildren Robert and William Osmond.
Residue to daughter Alice Daley, who is Sole Executrix.
Proved 22nd Dec., 1691.

1692. William Tucker, the elder, of Axminster, Yeoman, Dec. 20th, 1690. To wife Armonell, land in Stockland and Dalwood.

To daughters Joane Callard, Bridget Liddon, and Elinor Newberry, £20 each. To "all his grandchildren," £10 each; William and Richard Newberry only excepted. The latter to have reversion of a cottage and meadow in Dalwood, for residue of a term of 2,000 years.

Cousin Elizb. Haydon, £5; wife's sister's daughter, Joane Davy, £2 2s.

He settles all the land in Stockland and Dalwood upon his son William Tucker and his issue male, with remainder to the children of Matthew Callard and Joane his wife, of Robert Liddon and Bridget his wife, and Richard Newberry and Elinor his wife.

20/- to the poor of the aforesaid three parishes respectively.
To brother and sister's children, 2/6 each.
Residue to son William, who is Sole Exor.
Proved 19th April, 1692.

1692. John Tucker of Southleigh, Husbandman, 24th Sept., 1692.

Bequests to wife Mary, to "cosen" Charles Tucker, to "cosen" Thomas; brother Thomas' son; to cousins John, Thomas, and Grace, children of brother Bernard T., John, son of cousin Thomas Tucker. To Richard, son of said brother Thomas, a tenement called "Mount Drake" in Musbury. Residue to cousin, Margt. Phillips, who is Sole Executrix.

Proved 23rd Jany., 1692.

1692. The last Will of Joseph Fry of Axminster, April, 1692. Mentions late wife Eleanor Howse, and her children Eleanor and Rebecca.

Residue to second wife, Mary, who is Sole Executrix.
Proved 19th April, 1692.

1693. Admon. to the effects of James Osmond of Halberton, granted 23rd Sept., 1693, to George Osmond, his brother.

1693. The last Will of John Tucker of Broadclist, 10th Aug., 1692.

Bequests to daughter Mary West, and to her children, sons and daughters of Matthew West, Mary, John, Elizb., Richard, and Robert West.

Residue to son John Tucker, who is Sole Exor.

Proved 4th May, 1693.

1694. Administration to the effects of William Osmond, late of Silverton, deceased, granted 11th June, 1694, to Mary Nicks, *alias* Osmond, his relict.

1694. The last Will of George Osmond of Tiverton. Bequests to sisters Mary Glass and Allis Hill, to "cosens" John and Thomas Hill. To Peter Osmond and his sons Robert and William. To Thomas Osmond, Autrey (Ottery), and to his son Thomas. To George Osmond, Allis Daley, Mary Sellack, and to Thomas Daley's son, John.

Residue to wife Katherine, who is Sole Executrix.

Proved 6th Dec., 1694.

1694. The last Will of Mary Fry, Widow, of Axminster. She leaves a bequest to "the most ancient poor of the said parish."

Residue to "brother-in-law" John Brewer, "who married my own sister." He is Sole Exor.

Proved 8th Aug., 1694.

1694. Marie Berry of Tiverton. Administration granted 1st June, 1694, to her husband John Berry.

1695. Admon. to the effects of Richard Tucker of St. Thomas, granted 11th March, 1695, to Jane Tucker, his sister-in-law.

1695. The last Will of Jane Tucker of St. Thomas, Widow, 6th July, 1695. To eldest son, Zacharias Tucker, £15. Bequests to son James and daughter Jane. Residue to son Richard Tucker, who is Sole Exor.

1695. Admon. of above, granted 11th March, 1695, to Jane Tucker, daughter-in-law of testatrix; Exor. named therein, brother of Administratrix, having deceased.

1696. Admon. to the effects of Richard Mortimore late of Ailsbeare; granted 29th Dec., 1696, to Mary his wife.

1696. The last Will of Tristram Tucker of Brampford Speke, 17th April, 1696. Mentions his daughter Hannah, her husband John Gale, and their children, John, Samuel, Hannah, and Mary Gale, and leaves the latter a silver spoon each at 21.

Son-in-law John Hooper, 1/-, and sons John and Tucker Hooper, and daughter Grace Hooper.

Son-in-law John Dennis and his children James, Elizabeth, and Mary Dennis, "1 silver spoon apiece."

To ten poor husbandmen, 14d. each, "to be paid on the 23rd June next after my decease."

Residue to daughter Sara Dennis, who is Sole Executrix. Proved 5th March, 1696-97.

NOTE.—This Will is omitted from the calendars. Testator left nine silver spoons, valued at £2 5s. Total sum of personality, £44 12s. 4d.

1696. The last Will of William Tucker of Tiverton, dated 11th March, 1695. Mentions wife Thomazine, son Richard, and his children Richard and Theophilus. Son-in-law Thomas Burton, and his daughter Sidwell Burton, the latter to have "my warming pan."

Son John and his children William, John, Wilmot, Mary, and Richard, 20/- each.

Residue to said son John, who is Sole Exor.

Proved 14th May, 1696.

1697. The last Will of Grace Tucker of Southleigh, Spinster, 29th May, 1696. She divides her household goods between her brothers Thomas and John, and leaves them two small debts due to her from "cousin Thomas Tucker," and "Gideon Phillips, his wife."

"Also I give to Joice Dawley my best white whittle, my best say apron, my searge coate, and one of my best chaires.

"Also to Charity Wislade, my best hatt, and best stiffen waistcoat.

"To sister, Rachel Tucker, my largest red whittle, and to Elizabeth Phillips, who formerly lived with me, my best Bible, & cotton whittle; also to Mary Clarke, my old clothen coat and waistcoat, and my second best hatt."

Residue of her various garments to sister Jane Tucker.

General residue to brother John Tucker, aforesaid, who is Sole Exor.

Proved 27th April, 1697.

1697. Ralph Tucker (no parish mentioned, but refer to Will of John Tucker of Broadclist, proved May, 1693). Mentions Elizb. Newberry, Joan Lane, grandchildren William and Mary West, and wife Joan.

Residue to son Ralph, who is Sole Exor. Dated 5th June, 1697.

Proved 25th June, 1697.

1698. Administration to the effects of John Tucker of Newton St. Cyres, granted 8th March, 1698, to Joan, now wife of William Collins, but formerly of deceased.

NOTE.—Refer to Will of John Tucker of Newton St. Cyres, proved Sept. 11th, 1683, by Exor. Nicholas Tucker in trust for wife and children. The above was, of course, a second Admon.

1698. Admon. to the effects of Sarah Tucker of "Loopitt," granted 11th June, 1698, to Betty and Susanna Lowman, her nieces.

1698. Admon. to the effects of Symon Mortimore of Dunsford, granted 3rd Aug., 1698, to Thomasine his wife.

1699. The last Will of Nicholas Tucker of South Tawton, 9th Sept., 1697.

After the expiration of a life interest by Cressett his wife, and Joan his daughter, he settled the fee simple of a house and garden in Tawton town, upon his son Simon Tucker, with remainder to the "right heir of him, the said Simon, in the name of the Tuckers for evermore."

To sons Christopher and Joseph, £5 each. To "grandson," £5 at 21. To grandchildren Susannah and Joane Tucker, 5/- each ; to Mary Weekes, 5/-.

Residue to said children, Simon and Joan Tucker, who are joint Exors.

Proved 31st March, 1699.

1700. The last Will of Nicholas Tucker of Halberton ; dated 21st June, 1600. To grandchild Mary, daughter of Margaret Tucker by Thomas Elworthy, and to other granddaughters by said Thomas, 40/- each. To grandchildren James Vynecombe, 20/-, and Izaac Salter, 40/-.

To the son and daughter of son William Tucker, 40/-.

Residue to said son William, and daughter Margaret Vynecombe, who are joint Exors.

Two Trustees, viz., Wm. Elworthy and his son Thomas Elworthy.

Proved 1st July, 1700.

1702. Admon. to the effects of Edmond Tucker of Netherex ; granted 26th Feby., 1702, to Elizabeth Tucker, his relict.

1702. Administration to the effects of Nathaniel Mortimore, late of Bridford, granted 3rd Feby., 1702, to Susanna Mortimore, widow. Wm. Mortimore, of Bridford, joins the bond.

1702. Admon. to the effects of John Mortimore of Bridford, granted 3rd Feby., 1702, to Susannah Mortimore his mother. Wm. Mortimore joins the bond.

1702. The last Will of Thomas Osmond of Uplowman, 18th Feby., 1701. He leaves property in Uplowman and in Clisthidon, subject to certain charges in favour of daughter Isot, to wife Mary Osmond.

He divides other property between sons Thomas, Richard, John, Francis, and Robert. Residue to wife Mary, who is Sole Executrix.

Proved 27th Oct., 1702.

1704. The last Will of John Mortimore of Dunsford, 20th April, 1702. His leasehold estate in said parish to wife Johan for life. Legacies to grandchildren, sons and daughters of Robert Harris of Crediton, and Mary his wife, John, Robert, Henry, William, Joseph, and Mary Harris.

Residue to said daughter, Mary Harris, who is Sole Executrix.

Proved 24th May, 1704.

1704. Bridget Tucker of Tedbourn St. Mary, Widow, 27th July, 1703. Small bequests to children Joan, Robert, Peter, and Mark Tucker and Mary Rowe. Residue to son Thomas and daughter Joan, who are joint Exors.

Proved 16th June, 1704, by said Thomas Tucker, his sister Joan having renounced.

1704. Admon. to the effects of Peter Osmond of Tiverton, to Ann his wife, granted 10th Jany., 1704.

1705. The last Will of Christopher Osmond of Exeter, 15th Jany., 1702. Bequests to brother James, and to sisters Gertrude, wife of Walter Purchase, and Elizabeth, wife of Robert Arnold.

Residue to wife Eleanor, who is Sole Executrix.

Proved 28th Aug., 1705.

1705. Admon. to the effects of Matthew Mortimore of Christow, granted 15th March, 1705, to Edward Mortimore his brother.

NOTE.—Deceased died intestate, and his wife Elizabeth renounced her right to administer.

1705. Admon. John Osmond, H.M. Ship *Antelope*, and late of St. Sidwell's, Exeter. Granted to John Osmond, his father, 12th Oct., 1705.

1706. Administration to the effects of Jane Tucker, *alias* Risdon. Granted 1st July, 1706, to James Tucker of the City of Exeter.

"Memorandum.

"This administration was granted to the husband, only for the recovery of a legacy of £100, given to his wife by the will of Jane Risdon, deceased, and contained in the bundle of 1672."

1706. Admon. to the effects of William Tucker of Exeter, granted 7th May, 1706, to Mary Davys, otherwise Tucker, wife of Miles Davys of Colyton, and daughter of deceased.

1706. Admon. of Nicholas Tucker of Axminster, granted to nephew Samuel Tucker, 16th Jany., 1706.

1706. The last Will of Francis Mortimore of Down St. Mary, dated 21st July, 1705.

He leaves his "easter house" to son John, and his "wester house" to his children Roger, Francis, and Elizabeth, after his wife's death.

To children Simon and Hannah, 20/- each.

Residue to wife Elizabeth, who is Sole Executrix. She is to remain a widow or forfeit.

Proved 16th Oct., 1706.

1707. Nicholas Were of Halberton, in the county of Devon, desires his "body to be buried in Christian like manner," 25th June, 1706. Mentions son Nicholas and daughters Elizabeth and Susannah. Residue to wife Susannah, who is Sole Executrix.
Two Trustees, one of them "my beloved friend Robert Manley," Vicar of the Parish.
Proved 30th April, 1707.

1707. "Caveat" against admon. to the Will of Nicholas Were, by John Frankpitt of Uplowman, 14th March, 1707. Subsequently withdrawn.

1707. Inventory of Nicholas Were, otherwise known as Tucker, 1st Feby., 1706-7.
Total £79 2s. 6d.

1707-8. Admon. William Tucker of St. Thomas, nigh Exon., granted to Mary his widow, 26th Feby., 1707.

1707-8. Admon. to the effects of Dorothy Osmond of Silverton, granted 13th Feby., 1707, to Margaret her sister.

1708. The last Will of George Osmond of Halberton, 30th May, 1707.
To son Thomas, certain property in said parish. To daughter Elizabeth Stone, £80.
To daughter Joan Osmond, £120.
To daughter Susannah Osmond, £100.
To grand-daughter Susannah Stone "a piece of plate of 50s. value, with my name ingraven in letters at large in ye said plate."
To daughter Joan aforesaid, "a great chest marked with the letters 'J.O.' in the foreside."
Residue to wife Elizabeth, who is Sole Executrix. Philip Osmond (brother) a trustee.

By codicil, he gives to poor of the parish, 30/-, and to Mr. Robert Manley, minister, a new pulpit cloth.
Thomas Elworthy a witness.

1708-9. Administration to the effects of John Mortimore of Broadclist. Granted 9th Feby., 1708-9, to Agnes his widow. William and Abraham Taylor join the bond.

1709. Admon. to the effects of John Osmond of Broadhambury, deceased, granted 24th March, 1709, to Mary his relict.

1709. Admon. Peter Tucker of Exeter, granted 13th Oct., 1709, to Elizabeth, his relict.

1709. The last Will of Jane Tucker of Exeter, dated 28th Oct., first year of Queen Anne (1702). Legacies to daughters Dorothy, Margaret, Sarah, and Jane Tucker, the latter are residuary legatees and joint Exors.

She leaves her good friend, Mr. George Stoning, £15, for mourning for himself and wife, and to each of them, 20/-, to buy mourning rings.

To "friend" Mrs. Samuel Izacke,[*] 40/-, to buy mourning rings.

Mr. George Stoning and Edward Collings trustees in minority of daughters.

Proved 28th Oct., 1709.

1709-10. Administration to the effects of William Tucker of Colompton, granted 3rd March, 1709-10, to Emeline Andrewes, otherwise Tucker, wife of Jacob Andrewes, and mother of deceased.

---

[*] "Samuel Izacke," her husband, was the son of Richard Izacke, and published a new edition of his father's plagiarism of John Hoker's "MS. History of Exeter," in 1724. He was appointed Chamberlain of Exeter in 1693 and had been previously gratuitously admitted to the freedom of the city. For levying "black mail" upon the common councillors, he was ignominiously disfranchished, 6th October, 1718.

1709. The last Will of Thomas Tucker of Stokeintinhead, dated 18th Jany., 1707. Legacies to brothers John and Richard, sister " Francis," and brother-in-law William —, father-in-law Simon Drew, and Francis his wife.
Residue to wife Ann, who is Sole Executrix.
Proved 10th Jany., 1709.

1711. Admon. to the effects of William Tucker of Downe St. Mary, granted 18th March, 1711, to Joan Tucker, widow. John Tucker of same parish, joins the bond.

1711. Inventory of the effects of William Tucker of Downe St. Mary, made March 6th, 1711.
"Imprimis, all his wearing apparel and money in his purse, £20.
"Item one estate, in reversion, called East Bradford, £110.
"Remainder of our other estate, called Sherlands, £30.
"Item speciality debts, £208.
"Six oxen and steers, £40.
"5 milk cows, £20.
"2 steer yearlings & 3 heiffers, £5 2s. 6d.
"1 horse, 3 mares, & their suckling, £23.
"3 calves, £3.
"20 ewes with their lambs, & 25 hogge sheep, £20.
"All the silver plate, £10."

1712. Admon. to the effects of Elizabeth Tucker of Broadclist, granted 6th Feby., 1712, to Edward her son.

1712. The last Will of Elizabeth Osmond of Halberton, Widow, dated 26th Jany., 1711.
To daughter Jane Osmond, interest in certain leasehold property, a broad piece of gold, a worsted paine, and a ffusting paine (counterpane). To daughter Elizabeth Stone, a broad piece of gold. To daughter Susannah Eastcot, to son Thomas, a broade piece of gold each, the latter to buy his daughter

Grace a silver cup. To cousin Welthyn Osmond, my second suit of apparel. Legacies to grand-daughters Susannah Stone and Elizabeth Eastcot.

Three Trustees, viz., Mr. Robert Manley, minister, cosen Edward Cross, and brother-in-law Philip Osmond.

Residue to said three daughters, who are joint Exors.

Proved 11th March, 1712.

1712. The last Will of Sampson Mortimore of Drewsteignton, dated 15th March, 1711-12. £10 for his funeral. Certain "peculiar goods" to wife Elizabeth.

Legacies to son John, daughters Elizabeth and Ann; Mary, now wife of Mark Cumbe, and to their daughter Sarah; to daughters Sarah and Susannah, and Joan, wife of William Seaward; to grandchildren William Mortimore, and to John, Sampson, James, Edward, and Thomasine, children of said son John.

Residue to son Sampson, who is Sole Executor.

Witnesses, Thomas Amerie, John Symes, and Job Glenvile.

Proved 2nd May, 1712.

Circular Seal.—A stag courant.

1713. The last Will of Nicholas Tucker of the parish of Cleyhidon, dated 2nd May, 1710.

He leaves his house at Hole to wife Mary, and to his daughter Joan £100. To poor of the parish, 20s.

Residue to "son & heir," John Tucker, who is Sole Exor.

Proved 8th May, 1713.

1713. Inventory of effects of Nicholas Tucker of Cleyhidon, made 2nd May, 1713.

Imprimis, wearing apparel	£10 0 0
Item Money in purse and plate	£20 0 0
Item Books	£5 0 0
"Table linen	£1 10 0"
"In the entry chamber, 3 musquetts & other things	£18 0 0"

In the kitchen chamber, a weather glass, 2
brass pistols, four swords, a carbine, and
a clock £11 10 0
His farm stock, worth about £500 0 0
Sum £688 10s.

1713. Admon. to the effects of Isaac Tucker of Downe St. Mary, granted 29th April, 1715, to John Tucker of the said parish, in the minority of William Tucker the son.

1713. Admon. to the effects of John Mortimore of Spreyton, granted 5th June, 1713, in the minority of daughters Catherine, Alice, and Elizabeth, to their uncle, John Hopper.

1716. The last Will of Josias Tucker of Newton St. Cyres, dated 20th Jany., 1704-5. Mentions sister Joan Bowden; kinswoman Susannah Tucker, who is left a house and garden during the life of Mark Oxenham; brother Christopher Tucker.

Residue to brother Simon Tucker, who is Sole Exor.

NOTE.—Exor. and his brother Christopher both declined to administer, and the will was proved 27th Sept., 1716, by Thomas Clarke, of Exeter, a principal creditor.

1716. The last Will of James Mortimer of Uplowman, dated 25th Jany., 1711-12. Legacies to son James and his children, Mary, Susannah, and James; to daughter Susannah and her husband, John Kyte, and their children, Susannah, Mary, Elizabeth, and Agnes; to grandson Richard Mortimer; to Susanna, Mary, and James, children of son John; to grandsons John and Hugh, and granddaughter Jane Mortimer.

Residue to son John, who is Sole Exor.

Trustees, John Chave of Uplowman, and Richard Locke of Sampford Peverel.

Proved 16th April, 1716.

1716. Admon. to the estate of Maria Mortimore of Drewsteignton, granted 20th July, 1716, to John Dicker, her brother.

1663. Edward Younge, D.D., Dean of Exeter, bequeathed a principal sum of £250. The interest to be applied to the Alms House of St. Katherine,* to the Choristers of the Cathedral, and to the Prisoners in the Castle. The income to be distributed by the Dean of Exeter annually on the 29th May, "the day of the blessed restauration of his sacred majesty."
Will dated 6th June, 1663.
Proved 14th Aug. same year.

1718. The last Will of Jane Tucker of Exeter, 30th April, 1717. To Sister Sarah all lands and estates in the city of Exeter and elsewhere. To brother James and sister Margaret a "gold ring of a guinea each." A gold ring to Richard Sandford of Exeter. To servant, Thomazine Stevens, £10. Residue to said sister Sarah, who is Sole Executrix.

Richard and Joseph Sandford, Hugh Mills, and John Hussey to be bearers at funeral, and to each £1 1s. to buy mourning rings, and to each a "mourning hatt band and gloves."

Admon. to Sarah Tucker, 21st Oct., 1718.

NOTE.—Refer to will of Dorothy Tucker, proved 1693, p. 34, *ante*.

1719. Administration to the effects of Jacob Tucker, late of Exeter, granted 31st Dec., 1719, to Alice his relict.

1719. John Mortimer of Exeter, Goldsmith, to "my two daughters 1s. apeece."
Residue to wife Sarah, who is Sole Executrix. Dated Aug. —, 1708.
Proved 23rd July, 1719.

---

* These ancient almshouses—founded by John Stevens, Canon of Exeter (will dated February 3rd, 1457, proved February 27th, 1460)—were, with their chapel, advertised for sale by the trustees in 1893. They were purchased by the "Honble. Lady Hotham" (Jane Sarah, third daughter of second Lord Bridport, and widow of Sir Charles Hotham, R.N., grandson of second Lord Hotham), in December that year, with a view to their restoration and re-application to church purposes.

1720. The last Will of Thomas Tucker of Tedburn St. Mary, dated 4th Sept., 1718. Legacies to brothers Mark, Robert, and Peter Tucker; to kinsman George, son of Peter Tucker; and to kinswoman Ann, daughter of Peter Tucker the elder.
Residue to wife Honor, who is Sole Executrix. Reversion of a moiety of leasehold tenement "Collyhey" in Tedburne to George Tucker, son of brother Peter.
Proved 8th April, 1720.

1720. The last Will of Mark Tucker of Christow, dated 16th May, 1720. Legacies to brothers Robert and Peter, to nephews Mark and Robert, sons of Robert Tucker. "To Mr. Samuel Starkey, one hogshead of cyder or 20s. in lieu thereof." Legacies to Mary, daughter of Peter Tucker "of this parish," and to nieces Mary Browne and Sarah Laskey, daughters of Robert Tucker.
Residue to "kinsman" Peter Tucker "of this parish," who is Sole Exor.
Proved 10th Feb., 1720.

NOTE.—Testator had a moiety of the leasehold estate known as "Collyhey." See preceding will.

1720. Admon. to the effects of William Osmond of Burlescombe, granted 6th May, 1720, to Robert his father.

1720. Admon. to effects of Edmund Osmond of Bradninch, granted 3rd Jan., 1720, to Anne his relict.

1721. Admon. to the effects of Michael Tucker of Bradninch, renounced by Martha his widow, and granted 12th May, 1721, to Nicholas Murch of the same parish, principal creditor.

1721. The last Will of John Tucker of Poltimore, dated 17th Oct., 1719. Legacies at 21 to Sarah, daughter of Roger and Ann Wilcocks. Residue to wife Sarah, who is Sole Executrix.

Admon. granted to said widow 10th Oct., 1721.

1722. The last Will of Welthian Osmond of Halberton, single woman. To brother Philip Osmond and his heirs, two cottages in said parish known as " Lock houses."

Residue to said Philip, who is Sole Exor. Dated 14th Jan., 1719.

Proved 19th April, 1722.

Seal of Arms—A fess dancettée, *ermine*, in chief an eagle displayed.

NOTE.—Refer to page 41, *ante*, and to other wills of Osmond of Halberton.

1722. The last Will of Mary Tucker of St. Leonards (nigh Exeter), Widow.

To son Francis and to grandsons Francis and John Tucker, one guinea each.

To son Arthur and granddaughter Elizabeth Tucker, £6 6s. To sisters-in-law Jane Browning and Sarah Clarke, a mourning ring each.

To brother John Browning, brother-in-law Philip Clarke, and Samuel Pine of Exeter, "Gentleman," certain lands in St. Leonards, Hartland, and Buckland, and in the parish of Holy Trinity, Exeter, in trust for daughter Mary Tucker.

Mentions deceased husband John Tucker. Residue to said Mary Tucker, who is Sole Executrix.

Proved 10th Aug., 1722.

1724. Admon. to effects of Caleb Tucker of Kilmington, granted 6th March, 1724, to son William Tucker of Seaton.

1724. The last will of Peter Tucker of Upton Pyne, dated 10th Dec., 1721.

He leaves his wife "the feather bedd performed" (that is, *perfect*), and to Sarah, daughter of Nicholas Cunniby, of Upton Pyne, £5 at 21.

To two Trustees—John Quick of Brampford Speke and John Butcher, alias Radcliffe, of Thorverton—certain two messuages, in trust for the benefit of wife, Mary, with remainder to the children of John Hooper of Upton Pyne, Francis Gerrard of Exeter, Joseph Hall late of Exeter, tailor, and John Lugg of Torrington, as well as to Sarah, wife of Henry Street of Topsham, and to Richard Moore of Upton Pyne.

Residue to said Trustees on same trusts. Admon. to Mary Tucker the widow, Trustees having renounced.

April 28th, 1724.

1724. Admon. "de bonis non" of John Mortimore, late of Spreyton. Granted 21st Dec., 1724, to Alice Mortimore, of goods unadministered by John Hopper; her sisters, Katherine, wife of John Tregoe of Thorverton, and Elizabeth, wife of Samuel Maine of Colebrook, having renounced.

1725. Eleanor Tucker of Luppitt, Widow, 12th Oct., 1725.

Bequests to Edward, son of Oliver Lee of Exeter, to Hannah Whitlocke, to cousin William Chase of Red Lane. "Parson Lockyer" to preach funeral sermon.

Residue to son-in-law, Thomas Tucker, who is Sole Exor.

Proved 4th Dec., 1725.

1725. Admon. to the estate of Philip Osmond, late of Tiverton, granted 21st May, 1725, to Thomas Osmond of Otterford, during the minority of George Osmond, son of the deceased.

1726. The last will of Robert Osmond of Burlescombe, 19th May, 1725. Legacies to sons Robert and John, and to daughters Agnes, Penelope, Margaret, and Grace.
Residue to "my wife," who is Sole Executrix.
Proved 10th June, 1726.

1727. The last Will of Richard Mortimore of Broadclist, 12th Aug., 1726. Furniture and a legacy of £10 for four years to wife Elizabeth. To brother John Mortimore 1s. To William Evans "my best hatt." Residue to daughter Mary, who is Sole Executrix, with remainder of a tenement at "Burriton" to said wife.
Circular Seal.—A stag courant.

NOTE.—These arms are attached to will of Sampson Mortimore, *ante*, 2nd May, 1712.

Admon. granted 22nd Feb., 1726-27, to Andrew Taylor, principal creditor, the daughter having renounced.

1727. Mark Mortimor of Powderham, Yeoman, 27th Oct., 1727.

In minority of grandson, Mark, son of William Mortimor, a tenement in Powderham to daughter Elizabeth, after decease of wife Mary.

To son William aforesaid, 1s.

Legacies to daughters, Mary, wife of Samuel Ware, "Easter," wife of John Row (Hesther?). To son-in-law, William Davey, "my sarge coat and vest, and blew brichers." To son-in-law "Wm. Row," best great coat.

Residue to said William Row, who is Sole Exor.
Proved 10th Nov., 1727.

1727. Grace Tucker of Cullompton, 7th June, 1720. Bequests to Dorothy, wife of Robert Foss of said parish; to Edward, son of Francis Pratt of Kentisbeare; and to latter's

other children Dorothy, Joan, Agnes, and Elizabeth Pratt. Residue to Dorothy, wife of said Francis Pratt, who is Sole Executrix.
Proved 28th Dec., 1727.

1728. Admon. to the effects of Henry Osmond of Exeter, granted 26th April, 1728, to Elizabeth his wife.
£223 1s. 7d.

1728. Admon. to the effects of Richard Tucker of Upottery, granted 15th May, 1728, to Anne Tucker the widow.
Inventory of said Richard Tucker, 11th April, 1728.

	£	s.	d.
" Item four silver spoons ...	1	0	3
" Books ...	0	0	10
" One hackney saddle, stirrups, and gambadoes "	0	10	6
" One fowling piece	0	5	0
" A clocke and case.			
" A leasehold estate called Harrietwood	140	0	0"

Sum total, £324 6s. 10½d.

1729. Admon. to the effects of Edward Tucker of Tiverton, granted 22nd May, 1729, to Mary Tucker, the widow.
Sum £80 15s. 10d.

1729. The last Will of James Osmond of Sampford Peverell, 27th June, 1729.
To each of his daughters, Mary and Joan Osmond, £450.
Residue to trustees, Robert Blake of Halse, Co. Somerset, Edeth Blake of Sampford Peverell, Gentleman, and Nicholas Harris, Vicar of Culmstock, for benefit of son Thomas Osmond.
Witnesses, Francis Taylor, Thomas Jutsum, and Humphry Marsh Jutsum.
Proved 20th Feb., 1729.
Seal of Arms—A chevron between 3 coots.

NOTE.—*Argent*, a chevron, *sable*, between 3 coots proper.
Attributed to " Cowlin." " John Cowlin " is mentioned in several wills of this neighbourhood and period.
See *post* April, 1733, and Sept., 1736.

1729. Mary Tucker of Brampford Speke, 9th Nov., 1728. Bequests to brothers Francis and Arthur and to Elizabeth Lethbridge ; to Francis Tucker, jun., the great Bible ; to John Tucker, a silver spoon ; to Honour Tucker, gold locket and earrings ; to Mrs. Samuel Rols, one piece of gold ; and to Mrs. Jane Rols, six best table napkins. To Wm. Barwick and Grace his wife, a gold ring each ; and also to Grace, wife of Laurence Harward. 10s. to poor of the parish, and a like sum to the poor of Padstow and of Pilton.

Residue to aunt Sarah, wife of Philip Clarke, who is Sole Executrix.

Proved 25th July, 1729.

NOTE.—Refer to will of Mary Tucker of St. Leonards, Aug., 1722, *ante.*

The bequests to " Mrs. Samuel and Mrs. Jane Rols " are interesting. The latter must have been very aged in 1728 ; she was the wife of Dennis Rolle, brother of Robert Rolle of Heanton Sachville, an ancestor of Lord Clinton. She was the mother of Dennis Rolle, who married Arabella Tucker at Hartland, 14th February, 1697, and also of the said Samuel Rolle of Hudscote, who was buried, at Chittlehampton, 3rd March, 1734-5.

1729. The last Will of John Mortimore of Uplowman, 18th April, 1728.

Legacies to sons James and John, to daughter Mary Finimore and her husband Humphry, each 1s. To Sir Hugh Mortimore remainder of cottage called Crossland ; another tenement called "Cleaks" to daughter Joan.

Residue to said wife, who is Sole Executrix.

Proved 22nd May, 1729.

NOTE.—Refer to will of James Mortimore of Uplowman, April, 1716, *ante.*

1729. The last will of John Tucker of "Church-Tawton, Gentleman."

He divides the lands of which he stands "seized" between Joan, his wife, for life, with remainder to George and William, sons of late Henry Pocock, and Elizabeth, sister of said George ; cousin Clement Waldron, my godson, to Wm. Harford and

William Blackmore, also god-children ; cousins John and Mary Pring. James, son of James Gill and Joan his wife, of Culmstock, Elizabeth Holway and her heirs, Susannah and Mary Holway, and James Holway.

Testator leaves £400 to pay his debts, charged on a tenement which reverts to the aforesaid Gills'. To poor of Cheyhidon and Church-Tawton, 20s.

Residue to Joan his wife, who is Sole Executrix.

Proved 9th Dec., 1729.

NOTE.—The parish in which deceased resided was Church-Stanton, Co. Devon, seven miles from Taunton.

The beneficiare under the above will, "Cousin Clement Waldron," must not be confused with the Walronds of Dulford and Bradfield, although both families are nearly equal in point of antiquity, and may possibly have a common ancestor in the head of the old baronial house of Waleran.

"Clement Waldron's" collateral ancestor, John Waldron, was a merchant at Tiverton of the sixteenth century, and founded the almshouse there still called by his name. He died 18th July, 1579. This John Waldron died issueless, but was succeeded by a nephew of the same name, son of his brother Robert.

Mary Waldron, in 1749, gave land to the poor of the parishes of Hemiock, Church-Stanton, and Cleyhidon. Will dated 11th Oct., that year. Proved by John Southwood, residuary legatee and sole exor. An Irish branch of the Waldrons have long held county rank in Leitrim and Tipperary, etc. They are descended from Sir Richard Waldron, who migrated from the West of England in 1609.

1729. The last Will of Mary Tucker of "Clehidon," 20th Dec., 1729.

Bequests to brother Robert Pring, to cousin Elizabeth Holway, and to Joane, widow of son John Tucker.

Proved 3rd May, 1732.

NOTE.—Refer to 9th Dec., 1729 (John Tucker of Church-Tawton), *ante*.

1730. Samuel Osmond of St. Sidwells, Exeter, Tallow Chandler, 5th Aug., 1729.

Property in said parish to brother Joseph.

To mother, Elizabeth Osmond, £200.

To sisters, Grace Cock and Elizabeth Osmond, £200 each.

To the four Presbyterian ministers, Messrs. Enty, Green, Withers, and Lavington, £1 1s. each.

Residue to brother Joseph Osmond, who is Sole Exor.

Witnesses, Stephen Holditch.
   John Conant.

Proved 2nd May, 1730.

NOTE.—Refer to page 44, *ante*, for the will of the father of above testator.

1731. The last Will of Thomas Osmond of Halberton, 27th Sept., 1727.

Legacies to daughter Mary and to her husband John Pullen. To daughters Agnes, Elizabeth, Grace, and Sarah Osmond.

Leasehold property in said parish and in Sampford Peverell to sons Thomas and Phillip Osmond.

Residue to brothers John and Francis Osmond in trust for wife Elizabeth.

Witnesses, Wm. Lock, Philip Hinimore, Humphry Marsh Jutsum.

Admon. 4th Feb., 1731, to Elizabeth the relict, vice the trustees, who have renounced.

1730. The last Will of Elizabeth Tucker of the city of Exeter, 14th March, 1725.

Bequests to Elizabeth, Anne, and Susannah Dally; to Mistress Leap, widow, their sister, and to Nicholas, Anne, and John, children of Zephaniah Geare of Exeter, notary public.

Residue to George Broughton Hull who is Sole Executor.

Proved 29th Aug., 1730.

NOTE.—The Geares, still well known in Exeter in association with the law, are the descendants of the "Geeres" of Heavitree and Kenn, who registered a pedigree of four descents at the visitation of 1564, and again entered their descent in 1620. Nicholas, Anne, and John are all family names.

Arms—*Gules* on 2 bars *or*, six mascles az., 3 and 3, on a canton of the second, a leopard's face of the third.

Admon. "de bonis non" of Peter Tucker of Exeter, and admon. of estate of Elizabeth Tucker, widow of said Peter, granted 29th Aug., 1730, to George Broughton Hull.

NOTE.—The Hulls were an old Exeter family of some distinction, who resided at Larkbeare, subsequently the property of the Barings, and where the latter effected their rise and progress. John Hull was Recorder of Exeter, 1379. George Hull ultimately sold Larkbeare to Sir Nicholas Smith at the commencement of the seventeenth century. His ancestors had then owned Larkbeare for more than two centuries, and many of them were mayors of Exeter.

Arms of "Henry Hull of Larkbeare."—*Sa.* a chevron between 3 talbots' heads *arg.*—MS. D. and C. Exon., No. 3532.

1730-32. Admon. to the effects of Nicholas Tucker of Halberton, granted 13th Feb., 1730, to Rebecca his widow.

1732-3. Admon. to effects of Nicholas Tucker of Halberton, granted 2nd Jan., 1732-3, to Samuel Tucker his son.

1733. The last Will of James Osmond of Bycott, Halberton, 11th Sept., 1732. He leaves Bycott and his other property, subject to his wife's jointure, to mortgage or sell for a term not exceeding five hundred years, to date from his wife's death, for the benefit of his sister Susannah Osmond for life, with remainder to his nephew Thomas May, his heirs, and assigns. Mentions nephew and niece, John and Mary May, and gives them "hat bands and gloves"; cousins, daughters of John Sanford, and brother-in-law William Sellicke, "Phineas May," "Mr. Thomas Osmond of Hearn," and John Cowlen. "To my said wife, an hood, ring, and gloves."

Residue to said sister Susannah Osmond, who is Sole Executrix.

Seal, A lion rampant.

Witnesses, Nathaniel Marshal, Thomas Osmond, Benjamin Chapman. Proved 28th April, 1733.

NOTE.—Refer to p. 41, *ante*. The "Lion Rampant," being the arms of Marshall, Earl of Pembroke, and the name of one of the witnesses, who very possibly drew the will, being Marshal, is fair evidence that arbitary assumption of armorial bearings, as in this and other instances, is by no means peculiar to the present century, although the contrary is often contended.

This will was subject to a Chancery suit from 19th April, 1737. Thomas May, plaintiff; James and Mary Sandford, John Dally, and Grace his wife, defendants.

1734. The last Will of Elizabeth Osmond of Halberton, Widow, 3rd April, 1732.

She refers to the Executors of her late husband, "Thomas Osmond," having renounced. She states that she has purchased a meadow, which she leaves to her son Thomas Osmond, partly with money left him by Mistress Agnes Chave, and wills him the said meadow. To son Philip £10 owing her by Nicholas Osmond, her tenant.

To son James "the gift of my mother-in-law, Mary Osmond of Uplowman."

"Her Christening Paine" to daughter Grace, or 10s. in lieu thereof.

Mentions daughters Agnes, Elizabeth, and Sarah Osmond, and Mary Pullen.

Residue to brother-in-law John Osmond and son-in-law John Pullen, in trust for sons Philip and James aforesaid.

Proved 25th April, 1734.

NOTE.—Refer to 1731, *ante*, will of Thomas Osmond.

1734. Mary Mortimer of Exeter, Spinster. She leaves to Nicholas Green and Samuel Weymouth of Exeter, tobacconist, £10 in trust, the interest for the use of the minister of the Baptist meeting. 21st March, 1733.

To brother-in-law John Mortimer of Froom, Somerset, £5, and to his brother Joseph £5. Household effects to Sarah, wife of Thomas Wiggington of Exeter, mercer. China, &c., to "Miss Mary Hodges," daughter of "the Lady Hodges." To Mary and Elizabeth Wiggington, a ring each. Teaspoons to Mary Munn. £2 2s. to "Revd. Mr. Stennett." £10 to be spent on funeral.

Residue to nephew and nieces Francis, Susannah, and Jane Taylor, who are joint Exors.
Witness, John Conant.
Mrs. Wiggington being dead, Testatrix leaves by Codicil certain effects to Grace Craddick.
Proved 29th Dec., 1734.

NOTE.—Samuel Waymouth's daughter Hannah married Elias, second son of Thomas Newcoman, of Dartmouth, the inventor of the stationary steam engine. See my "Devonshire Parishes," Vol. I., p. 374.

1735. John Mortimore of Cadbury, 15th June, 1734.
He leaves 5s. each to his wife Susanna and his daughter Elizabeth.
Residue to his mother Joan Mortimore, who is Sole Executrix.
Proved 27th June, 1735.

1736. Admon. to the effects of Richard Mortimore of Broadclist, granted to Ambrose Bussell, husband of the late Mary Bussell, daughter of deceased.
Proved 25th June, 1736.

1736. The last Will of Susannah Osmond of Halberton (refer to 28th April, 1733), dated March 27th, 1733. She states that her mother Susannah Osmond (refer to page 41, *ante*) charged Bycott with £200 for her benefit, which has never been paid, and directs her Exors. to sue for the same.
Legacies to brother-in-law Phineas May; to nephews Thomas and John May; to kinswoman Joan, wife of nephew John May; to cousin Sandford's two daughters Mary and Grace. To John Cowlen and Susannah his wife, "a ring and a silk hood." Ann Wills a hood, and Elizabeth Turpin 10s.
Residue to kinswoman Mary May, who is Sole Executrix.
Witnesses, Wm. Were and Mary Ballamy.
Proved 3rd Sept., 1736.

NOTE.—Armorial Seal, apparently a cross between four coots (?), another device of Cowlin. See, *ante*, Feb., 1729, note.

1737. John Mortimore of Drewsteignton, 30th April, 1734. Bequests to sons William, John, Sampson, James, and Edward, and to daughter Thomasine, in addition to the 20s. each given them by "their grandfather."
To grandson John, son of said John Mortimer, 5s.
Residue to wife Thomazine, who is Sole Executrix.
Proved 11th May, 1737.
By James the son, his brothers and sister having renounced, and their mother having died without proving.
Personality over £200.
NOTE.—Refer to will of Sampson Mortimore, 2nd May, 1712, *ante*.

1738. The last Will of Thomas Tucker of Uplyme. To wife, leasehold property there and at Wootton Fitz-pain, Dorset.
Residue to said wife Ann, who is Sole Executrix.
Proved 22nd May, 1738.

1738. Administration to the effects of Thomas Tucker of Kenn, granted 21st March, 1738, to Goldworthy Tucker, his son.

1738. George Mortimer of Dunsford, 14th April, 1733. Legacies to John and Richard Mortimer, sons, and to George and Elizabeth Mortimer, grandchildren.
Residue to wife Anna, who is Sole Executrix, but must not marry again.
Witnesses, Joseph and Daniel Tucker.
Proved 23rd Oct., 1738.

1740. Joseph Osmond of St. Sidwell's, Exeter, Tallow Chandler. To sister Elizabeth, wife of John Whitehead, Gentleman, of St. Sidwell's, £20 per annum, with reversion of the property on which the legacy is charged to sister Grace Cock. To cousin Mistress Elizabeth Chears, £50. He leaves £100 for dissenting ministers or their widows. Legacies to father-in-law, "Mr. Townsend," and to "each of his children." To

Rev. James Green and Rev. Joseph Hallett, £20 for poor housekeepers of St. Sidwells. Residue to Rev. Nathaniel Cock and Grace his wife, who are joint Exors.
Witnesses, Caleb Youatt, John Conant.
Proved 12th Aug., 1740.

1741. Martha Tucker of Exeter, Widow, 20th May, 1741. To son Nathaniel Tucker of London, Gentleman, one gold ring. To sons Joseph and John Tucker of Exeter, Glaziers (a gold ring to Joseph). To grand-daughter Elizabeth Tucker, "my striped loodstring gowne." Son John has a leasehold house in Matthew's Alley, South Street.
Residue to said John, who is Sole Exor.
Proved 15th June, 1741.

1741. John Tucker of Axminster, 10th Aug., 1741. To wife Elizabeth, his leasehold estates and household goods, charged with an annuity of 30s. to sister Mary Tucker.
Residue to said wife, who is Sole Executrix.
Proved 31st Aug., 1741.

1741. Admon. to the effects of Thomas Osmond of Ottery St. Mary, granted 18th Sept., 1741, to Hannah, wife of Stephen Gill, his great grand-daughter.

1743. The last will of Mary Osmond of Tiverton, Widow, 10th Feb., 1742.

To be buried in "Moores Isle," in Cullompton Church, by the side of her mother.

To kinsman William Bailey the younger, of Tiverton, silver tankard, salver, and punch ladle, the tea cannister, six tea spoons and tongs, and a gold watch. To his wife Mary "a diamond ring with a green stone in it," best white satin gown flowered with gold, and "my linnen gown that I bought in London." To kinswoman Susannah Sellick, "if she be living in the same station at Kensington as I lately saw her," a diamond ring and silver podinger. To kinsman William Sellick, £7 14s. per annum. To kinsman Peter Slape, £50. To kinswoman Ann, wife of Francis Matthews, £100. To Miss Mary Coles, £50, and to her father Thomas Coles and to Susannah Haviland, a mourning ring each. To Mrs. Mary Osmond of Halberton, two pairs of gold buttons, and to Eleanor Floyer, a mourning ring. The arms of her first husband, "Mr. Moore," to be put on her hearse.

Residue to said Wm. Bailey, who is Sole Exor.

Proved 17th Dec., 1743.

Trustees, Saml. Rogers, Rector of Withycombe, Somerset, and Vicar of Halberton; Thomas Balliman, and Thomas Coles.

NOTE.—Testatrix, whose marriage license with "Mr. Moore" is not to be found, and whose maiden name is left blank in the pedigree of Moore of Moorbays, was probably a daughter of William Sellick, who purchased the right of presentation to Cullompton Church, and presented thereto, in 1719.

She was the widow of George Moore of Moorhays, who died 5th Nov., 1711, and by him had an only daughter Mary, the wife of John Blackmore of Sheldon, and the ancestor of the present owner of Moorhays.

1606. The last Will of Catherine Lady "More" of Cullompton, dated 26th April, 1606. Desires to be buried in the parish church, and leaves for the reparation thereof 10s., and to the poor 6s. 3d. To Robert Denys, 10s.

Residue to my servants "Mr. Tryslade and Mrs. Shepherd," who are Sole Exors.

Proved June, 1606.

NOTE.—The personal effects of Testatrix were valued at £21 6s. 1d., inclusive of two horses and a mare, which were valued at £8. She was the widow of Sir John Moore of Moorhays, and the daughter of Sir Thomas Pomeroy of Berry, by Jane, daughter of Sir Piers Edgcombe.

1745. William Tucker of Kenn, 14th May, 1739.

Bequests to poor of Kenn; to Thomas Dewdney of Kenn, and to (his brother) John Dewdney of Stoke Canon; to Elizabeth, wife of William Harris of Kenn; to Grace, wife of Matthias Dyer of Exminster; and to Mary, wife of John Dingle of Exminster. He leaves his messuages, &c., situate at Heavitree, in County of Devon, to Rev. Thomas Ley, Clerk of Kenn, and to John Dingle, and their heirs, in trust for son John Tucker and his issue, male or female, without impeachment of waste, with reversion, failing such, to John Dewdney of Stoke Canon, for life, and then to latter's sons John and Thomas Dewdney, and, failing them, to their sisters Elizabeth and Mary Dewdney, and their right heirs for ever.

Residue to son John Tucker, who is Sole Exor.

Proved 6th Feb., 1745, by nephew, John Dewdney.*

1746. The last Will of Peter Tucker of Kenn, Yeoman, 5th Dec., 1741.

He divides property in the parish, *videlicet*, " Smithny," part of " Whitcombes," " Clapton," part of " Shindlestone," and " Clarke's Meadow," between his sons Peter and Thomas.

To daughters Joan, Elizabeth, and Izost (Tucker), £100 each.

Residue to wife Joan and son Thomas Tucker, who are joint Exors.

Mentions a daughter " Mary Harris."

Proved 13th June, 1746.

29th April, 1746. Laurence Tucker of His Majesty's Ship " Ruby," makes his wife Margaret, of the parish of St. Shadwell's (Sidwell's), Exeter, universal legatee and Sole Executor.

Proved 2nd Sept., 1746.

1748. John Tucker of Exeter, 31st Oct., 1742, leaves Ann his wife two houses in Matthew's Alley, South Street.

Residue to said wife, who is Sole Exor.

Proved 15th Feb., 1748.

---

* The Dewdneys were an old gentle family, long settled in the neighbouring parish of Doddiscombleigh. Arms, *sa.*, a bend, *erm.*, cotised, *or.*

1749. 11th Dec., 1749, William Tucker of Kenn, makes Elizabeth his daughter, wife of John Hutchings of Brenton, Yeoman, universal legatee and Sole Executrix.
Proved 15th Jan., 1749.

1749. Mary Tucker of Exeter, Widow, 19th Aug., 1749.
To son Jonathan Tucker, £510, and certain plate, including a great silver Tankard. To said son's "wife," £10 and plate. To grandson Jonathan Tucker, gold ring and plate.
"Apparel, both linen and woollen, to wife of son-in-law John Tucker and to their daughter Elizb. Soper," save "best gown, quilted coat and cloak," which are bequeathed to granddaughter Sarah, son Jonathan's eldest daughter. To grandson, Richard Evans, silver tankard. Other bequests of plate and money to son-in-law "Mr. Evans," and to Jonathan, son of John Tucker.
Residue to said son Jonathan, who is Sole Exor.
Proved Jan., 1749.

1754. Joan Tucker of "Church Tawton," in the County of Devon, Widow, 14th Oct., 1753.
To cousin Thomas Southwood of Pitminster, Somerset, Gentleman, £10.
To cousin Grace, widow of John Sparrow, and to cousin Jane Barton, £10 each.
Bequests to Samuel, Thomas, and Joan, children of said Thomas Southwood ; to cousin Mary (relict of Clement Waldron, Gentleman), of Wellington, Somerset, to two servants, and to the poor of "Church Tawton and Cleyhidon."
Residue to said Thomas Southwood, who is Sole Exor.
Proved 9th Jan., 1754.

NOTE.—Refer to 1729, Dec. 9th, will of John Tucker of "Church-Tawton."

1754. Samuel Tucker of Cullompton, Yeoman, 24th May, 1754, leaves all his wearing apparel to his brother George

Tucker. Certain property in Halberton to grand-daughters Joan and Mary, daughters of Edward Kerby.

To wife Sarah Tucker, certain messuages called "Tucker's," situate at Ash Thomas, in Halberton, for life, with remainder to Humphry Blackmore, gentleman, and Nehemiah Upcott, serge maker, in trust for grandsons Edward Kirby and Samuel Kirby (in default), in tail male and female.

Mentions daughter Mary, wife of Edward Kerby. Residue to wife Sarah and grand-daughter Agnes Kerby, who are Joint Exors. ; wife to give a bond of £300 to return her share if she marries again, and is directed to leave testator's property, in any case, to such of his children as "shall behave well and kind to her."

Proved 19th July, 1754.

1757. Edward Tucker of Broadclist, 1st Jan., 1755. He leaves daughter Joan "five shillings only and no more," and gives the residue, "in token of many favours received," and "signal benefits," to William Martyn of Broadclist, in trust ; to pay £5 per annum to son Edward Tucker "in weekly payments on Saturdays."

Proved 2nd November, 1757.

1758. Samuel Tucker, late of Cullompton, deceased. Admon. granted to Agnes Ward, formerly Kerby, now wife of Robert Ward, grand-daughter of deceased, 7th April, 1758.

NOTE.—Second admon. Refer to will of Saml. Tucker, 19th July, 1754, *ante*.

1758. Isett Osmond of Uplowman, Spinster, 17th Jan., 1755. She desires to be buried near her father in Uplowman Church, and to have a headstone, and another of the same kind for her father.

Legacies to brothers Thomas, Francis, and Robert Osmond ;

to "cousin" John Stone, son of sister Mary; and sister Alice.

Residue to sister Sedwell Osmond, who is Sole Executrix. Proved 15th Sept., 1758.

NOTE.—Testatrix was daughter of Thomas Osmond of Uplowman (will Oct., 1702, *ante*), and sister of Francis Osmond, " son-in-law of last Testator." See preceding will.
Armorial Seal—A demi-lion rampant, holding a horseshoe.

1758. The last Will of John Osmond of Sampforde Peverel. To son-in-law Francis Osmond certain leasehold property, charged with annuities to daughters Mary and Isett.

There is remainder for Mary's children, Thomas, Joan, and Richard (Osmond).

To John, " son of Francis Osmond," one heifer.

Isett's annuity to be held by her brother-in-law Francis Osmond for her maintenance.

Proved 17th June, 1758.

1762. John Tucker of Tiverton, 13th Feb., 1762. Legacies to daughter Mary, wife of Robert Ferries of Silverton; to her brother John Ferries; and to daughter Grace, wife of Henry Hill of Tiverton.

Residue to wife Grace, who is Sole Executrix.

Seal " J. T.," with an estoile over the letters.

Proved 12th May, 1762.

1764. The last Will of John Mortimer, the elder, of St. Nicholas, Yeoman, 10th Sept., 1763. To son Joseph and heirs of his body, certain land in Kingsteignton called Fostwell and Heathfield, with remainder to other sons John and William. To said son John, two leasehold estates at Preston, in Kingsteignton. To daughter Hannah Drew, £1 1s. To Elizabeth, daughter of said son Joseph, dwelling-house on the Strand at Ringmore. To Elizabeth, daughter of said son William, £5 at 21. To sister Joan Codner, £3 3s. A debt of £40 owing by son Joseph is partly bequeathed to grandsons Joseph and

John, sons of said Joseph, and partly to John, Ann, Mary, and William Mortimer, children of said son John. Residue to said son William Mortimer, who is Sole Exor.
Witnesses, Wm. and Mary Waye and Richard Langdon.
Proved August 22nd, 1764.

NOTE.—Testator was son of John Mortimer of Uplowman, and is mentioned with sister Joan. See the will *ante* A.D. 1729

1766. Admon. to the effects of Susannah Mortimer of Dunsford, granted to John Mortimer her husband, July 15th, 1766.

1767. William Mortimer of Drewsteignton, 18th Sept., 1763. To daughter Mary Frost, widow, small annuity and legacy; the same to daughters Joanna "Houdg" and Thomazine, wife of John Buard; and to grandson Joseph Buard. Residue, with leasehold interest in Knowle estate, to son William Mortimer, who is Sole Exor.
Proved 30th March, 1767.

NOTE.—Testator was son of John Mortimer, 1737 *ante*, and brother of Sampson Mortimer, *post* 1776.

1767. The last Will of Grace Tucker of Tiverton, Widow, 11th April, 1764.

Mentions daughter Mary, wife of Robert Ferries of Silverton; grandsons John and George Ferries; grandchildren John and Mary, son and daughter of Grace, wife of Henry Hill, of Tiverton.

Residue to said daughter Grace Hill, who is Sole Executrix.
Proved 31st March, 1767.

1767. Administration to the effects of Jonathan Tucker the younger, of Exeter, intestate, granted 11th Nov., 1767, to Mary his widow.

1774. Nicholas Tucker of Tiverton. To brothers Roger and Edward, £10 each. To niece Mary Ferris, daughter of late brother John Tucker, £10; to children of brother Roger, John, and Elizabeth, £30 and £60.

To children of brother Edward, viz., Elizabeth Williams and Ann Tucker, £10 and £5.

To niece Grace Hill, daughter of said brother John, 20s. per annum, to issue out of two messuages in Bampton Street, Tiverton. Moiety of tenement called "The Eight Bells," near St. Peter's Church, and the three-eighths part of certain messuages (leasehold 1,000 years) to said nephew John Tucker.

Residue to Nicholas Tucker, son of said brother Roger, who is Sole Exor.

Crest Seal—A mermaid.

Proved 4th Jan., 1774.

1774. Richard Mortimer of Dunsford, 20th Nov., 1768. He gives his son George the Dunsford Mills and the marshes adjoining, "being part of Court," charged with 20s. per annum to " my three daughters."

To Ann, wife of said George, £1 1s.

To daughters Elizabeth and Ann Mortimer, £70 each, and to daughter Mary, wife of John Connett, £20, and one guinea to her husband.

Wife Ann to have life interest both in the mill and messuages. She is residuary legatee and Sole Executrix.

Proved 29th July, 1774.

1775. James Tucker of St. David's and city of Exeter, Innholder, 13th April, 1771.

Mourning rings to David Cox of Ilminster and his wife; to brother Wm. Tucker of Bath and his wife; to wife's mother "Mrs. Bastard;" to Anthony Symons of Broadclist; and to Isaac Sercombe of Exeter, wine cooper.

To wife £100 and a copyhold estate at Stoke Canon, in the

occupation of "Mr. Dewdney." Property to be realised by three trustees, to invest same for son James Tucker.

Residue to said son at 21.

Proved by trustees, Cox, Symons, and Sercombe, aforesaid, 8th May, 1775.

NOTE.—Deceased was the owner and occupant of the "Oxford Inn" in St. David's parish.

1776. Sampson Mortimer of Drewsteignton, 22nd Jan., 1774. To daughter Elizabeth an annuity of 38s. a year out of Knowle, in said parish. He mentions a legacy of £2 given her by her grandfather.

Similar legacy to daughter Thomazine, who is also to have a "family spoon" lettered S. M. Residue to son James, who is Sole Exor.

Proved 5th Jan., 1776.

NOTE.—The legacy to "Elizabeth Mortimer" is not referred to in the will of her grandfather. See *ante*, May, 1737, John Mortimer of Drewsteignton.

1776. Sarah Tucker of Lympstone, Widow, 3rd Sept., 1771.

She leaves her freehold lands in said parish to niece Edith Oats, and legacies to Thomas, Hugh, and Philip Oats, sons of said Edith.

Proved 24th June, 1776.

Seal, Arms, and Crest—The arms are too indistinct for blazon, but the crest is a demi sea-horse.

NOTE.—One of the best known coats of "Tucker" contains three sea-horses, but the crest is a lion's gamb.

1777. Elizabeth Tucker of Exeter, Widow, 17th Jan., 1777. Legacies to son Joseph and to daughters Elizabeth and Mary.

Residue to son William Fryer Tucker, who is Sole Exor.

Proved 27th Feb., 1777.

"William Sanford" a witness.

1778. Admon. George Mortimer of Dunsford, intestate, granted 2nd Feb., 1778, to Ann the widow.

1778. Ann Mortimer of Dunsford, 3rd Feb., 1778. To Elizb., wife of James Connett, £40, and one guinea, instead of a gold ring, six silver teaspoons, and all the "chainea." To daughter Mary, wife of John Connett, £40. To daughter-in-law Ann Mortimer, £1 1s.

To George and Ann Connett she gives, *inter aliis*, " my best looking glass and my new prayer-book, with all the tea dishes, saucers, and basons belonging to makeing of tea, except the spoons." Her son George being dead, she gives the residue of the lease of Dunsford Mills to her daughter-in-law Ann Mortimer, with reversion, for the 99 years, terminable on the death of "brother John Mortimer" to George, John, Elizabeth, and Richard, children of deceased son George.

Proved 3rd July, 1778.

NOTE.—Refer to July 29th, 1774, *ante*.

1779. Philemon Mortimore of Silverton, 13th March, 1772. Legacies to brother Richard Mortimore and to sister Joan, wife of Thomas Heard. Legacies to children of said Richard, William, Thomas, John, Betty, and Ann. Fee simple of houses in Silverton to Mary Furser as long as she remains a widow, with remainder to "nephew Richard Mortimore," charged with an annuity of 20s. to Jenny, daughter of deceased brother Henry Mortimore.

Residue to said Mary Furser, who is Sole Executrix.

Proved 15th Oct., 1779.

1781. John Tucker of Tiverton, Maltster, 17th Nov., 1777. To John Govett, surgeon, and Beavis Wood, gentleman, both of Tiverton, certain property in trust for wife Jane for life, with remainder to son Thomas and Ann his wife, intail upon their son John Tucker.

There are further remainders to daughter Jane Hodge and

her son John Hodge ; to son William Tucker, his heirs and assigns for ever.

Mentions son Richard, his wife Betty, and their children George and John Tucker; granddaughter Sarah, daughter of said son William ; daughter Susannah Vickery. To said son Thomas " the mourning ring presented to me upon the death of the late Lord Chief Justice Ryder."

To said son Richard " my scarlet corporation gown and my mourning ring for late Mr. William Wood."

Residue to said wife Jane, who is Sole Executrix.

Proved 2nd May, 1781.

NOTE.—Sir Dudley Ryder, Kt., Lord Chief Justice of the King's Bench, 1754, died before his elevation to the peerage (the patent for which was signed the day previously), 25th May, 1756 ; his son was created Lord Harrowby twenty years later. The first peer's grandson, Canon Ryder of Lichfield, married secondly, 1841, Eliza Julia, daughter of Lieut.-Col. John Tucker, and by her had issue. The first peer was M.P. for Tiverton.

1782. Mary, wife of John Mortimer of Dunsford, Yeoman, 8th May, 1778.

She bequeaths her separate estate of £180 ; £50 to nephew Edward Ramsey of Exeter, schoolmaster, son of brother Edward Ramsey, deceased. To nephew John Ramsey £50. To Elizabeth, daughter of Richard Mortimer and wife of James Connett, £30.

Residue to husband John Mortimer, who is Sole Executor.

Proved 28th July, 1782.

1787. John Mortimore of Halberton, 30th November, 1786. He leaves John Chave, Esq., of said parish, £30 in trust for daughter Mary, wife of Robert Seaman of Willand.

To daughter Jane, wife of John Templeman, Langford Budvile, Somerset, £20. To daughter Elizabeth, wife of William Webber of " Milocton," Somerset, £20 (Milverton (?), near Langford Budville). To daughters Sarah £20, and Susannah and Ann Mortimore £60 each. Daughter Dinah Mortimore £150, and daughter Joan Mortimore £50.

To said Trustee the estate known as "Burruges," otherwise "Joans," in Bradninch, for use of son John Mortimore at 21. To grandsons John and Thomas Seaman £5 each at 21.

Residue to wife Hannah, who is Sole Executrix.

Proved 9th February, 1787.

1789. Francis Osmond of Lee, in Silverton, 19th September, 1787.

To two trustees Thomas Osmond of Uplowman and Thomas Rowe of Sampford Peverel, an estate called Colebrook, in Cullompton, lately purchased of Richard Hall Clarke for benefit of daughter Joan Osmond for life, charged with an annuity of £5 to daughter Sarah, wife of John Gould. Remainder to granddaughter Mary Gould. Lands in Halberton to similar uses.

Residue to said trustees for benefit of said daughters.

Witnesses—Thomas Floyd, Henry Brutton.

Proved 18th February, 1789.

1789. Richard Mortimore, late of Silverton, intestate, to Susannah Mortimore, widow.

John Reynolds of Pinhoe and William Mortimore join the bond.

9th April, 1789.

1795. Francis Osmond of Halberton, 20th February, 1795. Legacies to son John and to daughter Jenny, wife of Henry Brice. To granddaughter Elizabeth, daughter of Samuel and Betty Norrish, and to grandchildren Samuel, Richard, Mary, and Jenny Norrish.

To son Francis Osmond "Speedland" in Sampford Peverel, charged with payment of a mortgage of £100, and with an annuity of 40s. to son Thomas. John Osmond of Heavitree is a trustee.

Residue to son Robert, who is Sole Executor.

Proved 13th April, 1795.

1797. John Mortimer of Ringmore, in Stokeintinhead. Having already provided for them, he now leaves son-in-law William Langley, daughter Ann Langley, and eldest son John Mortimer, one guinea each.

Mentions daughter Catherine and granddaughter Mary Langley.

Residue to wife Ann, who is Sole Executrix.

Proved July, 1797.

1798. Frances Tucker of Axminster, Spinster, 11th Nov., 1797. £250 each to brother George Tucker; sister Sarah, wife of Rev. John Davey Hodge of Leigh, co. Essex, clerk; Betsy, Uriah, and Mary Ann Dare, children of deceased sister Elizabeth, wife of Uriah Dare; nieces Jane and Mary Ann Andrews, daughters of Thomas Andrews; sisters Ann, Mary, and Amelia Tucker. Smaller legacies to Sarah, wife of Robert Ackland of Tiverton; Mrs. Susannah Tucker the elder, widow, of Axminster; Ann, wife of Thomas Byshop; and Betty Spence of Colyton. To sister Mary aforesaid "gold ring set with pearls." To said sister Amelia " miniature picture and silver castors.'

To godmothers Sarah Tucker and Ann, wife of John Liddon of Axminster, £2 12s. 6d. each for rings. The same to Elizabeth, wife of John Joy of Glastonbury, Esquire. To sister-in-law Elizabeth Tucker "gold ear-rings and drops"; to Sarah, wife of Rev. Mr. Mules, of Ilminster, "red morocco pocket-book bound with silver."

"To Phocion Dare of Lyme Regis, druggist, a mourning ring for his kind attention to me when I was confined at his house at Taunton."

Residue to said brother George, who is Sole Executor.

Proved 6th August, 1798.

1798. Gregory Osmond of Newton St. Cyres, 15th June, 1798. Legacies to daughter Elizabeth, wife of William Ell's, and to daughter Ann, wife of James Moxey. To son Edward £50 in trust for granddaughter Mary Ann Butter.

Residue to said son Edward, who is Sole Exor.

Proved 2nd Nov., 1798.

1805. Admon. of Thomas Osmond of Uplowman, intestate, granted May 27th, 1805, to Thomas his son.

1806. Mary Osmond of Silverton, Widow, 30th May, 1805. Legacies to nephews Charles, Robert, and John, sons of brother Robert Rowe. To nieces Mary Berne, Elizabeth Morgan, and Mary Mortimer, Mary Symes, Emmeline Flood, and Thomasine Drake, £150 each. To nephew John Payne, nephews Richard, Charles, Robert, and James, sons of brother Richard Rowe and their sister Martha Hewitt. Mentions "John and Philip Bastard" of Silverton, " the five children" of former, and John, son of Philip Bastard. £350 for benefit of Mary, daughter of niece Elizabeth Salter, and £50 to Elizabeth, another daughter of said Elizabeth Salter.

Residue for benefit of said niece Elizabeth Salter.
Proved by Trustees as Executors, 24th Oct., 1806.
Witnesses—E. Spry, John Pugh.

1810. James Osmond of Halberton, 7th March, 1804. He leaves his moiety of Neither Mill, in the parish of Halberton, to his son-in-law Henry Radford, with remainder to daughter Sarah Radford for life, to revert to her son James Osmond Radford, in trust, male or female, for ever.

To sister's son John Quant of Bradninch, all wearing apparel.

Proved 26th April, 1810.

1823. Francis Osmond of Halberton, 27th June, 1822.
To son Francis £100 charged on "Speedland" in Sampford Peverel, after decease of brother Thomas Osmond. Legacy to son Richard.

£25 each to daughters Sarah, wife of John Kerslake, Elizabeth, Joan, Mary Ann, and Charlotte Osmond.

Speedwell estate to wife Sarah, who is residuary legatee and Sole Executrix.

Proved 16th January, 1823.

PART II.

ARCHDEACONRY OF BARNSTAPLE.

1563. The last Will of David Melhuish of Knowstone, dated 13th August, 1563. Legacies to the "poor men's box" of his parish, and to that of Cruse Morchard. Bequests to "Richard Melhuish and to John Comyn." Residue to wife Johane and to Philip Shapcote, who are joint Executors.

Proved 13th Sept., 1563.

1565. William Hamlyne of Frithelstock, 12th Dec., 1565. With other bequests, he leaves his son Hugh Hamlyne "a sylver spoone and a sheepe," and there is a similar bequest to son William.

Residue to wife Joan, who is Sole Executrix.

Proved 12th Feby., 1565-66.

1573. The last Will of John Tocker of West Buckland, 25th Feby., 1573.

Mentions son George and daughter Urithe; gives former his sheep, in the parish of Countisbury.

Legacies to Margaret Shaplonde and Davie Holsworthie.

Residue to wife Elizabeth and son John, who are joint Exors.

Witnesses—David Kente, parson of West Buckland; John Waite and George Harris, parishioners; and Oliver Tocker of Chawlegh.

Proved 27th March, 1573.

1593. The last Will of Joane Sanger of Maryansleigh, Widow, 12th March, 1592. Legacies for repair of the church and to the poor.

To godson, son Roger Sanger, 12d.

Legacies to goddaughter Amye Smale and son Thomas Sanger. Residue to John, "my youngest son of that name." He is Sole Exor.

Proved 21st June, 1593.

1597. Elizabeth Hatch of Salterleigh, Spinster, 26th April, 1597. Bequests to poor of Salterleigh; to sister Gertrude's children Marmaduke and Hugh Walsh; to nephews Robert and Lewis, brother Robert's children.

Residue to Rev. Hugh Tooker, Clerk, who is Sole Exor.

Proved July, 1597.

NOTE.—See will of Robert Hatch, October, 1644, *post*.

1597. The last Will of Emmeline Hamlyn, Widow, of Tawstock, 5th March, 1589. Mentions sons Richard and William, and gives them certain household effects.

Residue to son Christopher Hamlyn, who is Sole Exor.

Witnesses—Richard Stribling the elder and Richard Stribling of Exeter, minister.

Proved 1st April, 1597.

1606-7. The last Will of Christopher Wood of Ashridge, in the parish of North Tawton, Esquire, 25th Nov., 1606.

To be buried in south aisle of parish church, and leaves to its "reparacion" 40s.

To the poor 100s. To grandson Christopher, son of John Wood, £40.

Mentions grandson John, another son of said John Wood. Residue to wife Katherine, who is Sole Executrix.

Proved 7th March, 1606-7.

NOTE.—Testator's wife Katherine was the daughter of Sir John "Windham" of Orchard Windham, co. Somerset, and is mentioned in the will of her father, proved 28th April, 1575. Her brother John "Wyndham" was the grandfather of Sir Wm. Wyndham, created a baronet 13th Charles II., 1662. The fourth baronet, by a limitation, succeeded to the Egremont title, on the death of his uncle Algernon, Duke of Somerset. The earldom of Egremont became extinct April, 1845.

1610. Laurence Densham of Lapford. Administration granted 11th March, 1610, to Joane his widow.

1612. Admon. Hugh Hamlyn of Bideford, granted 6th May, 1612, to Thomasine his wife. John Jarman of Bideford joins the bond.

1613. The last Will of Nicholas Mortymer of Winkleigh, 2nd Dec., 1611.

To the poor of the parish 2s. ; to Charethie Mortymer "my beste bande and my best stockins ; to Elizabeth Hatherleigh my second beste dublett and jerkyn, my best wastcoatt, and one canvas shirt ; to Samuel Crocker my second best jerkyn ; to Barnard Reed my greene breeches ; to Johane Joanes my best shoes ; to Johane Bynford my blue stockins ; to Samuel Crocker my new canvas shirt ; to John Hatherleigh my best hatt."

Residue to Master Andrew Beare, who is Sole Exor.
Proved 11th Dec., 1613.

1614. Admon. William Densham of Lapford, granted 28th April, 1614, to Joan his relict.

1615. The last Will of William Mortimore, otherwise Tanner, of Fremington, A.D. 1614 (month omitted). Legacies to the poor and to sons William, Matthew, and James *Tanner*. To daughter Ellynor six silver spoons.

Residue to wife Ellynor, who is Sole Executrix.
Two Trustees, viz., William Farechilde and Robert Hill.
Witnesses—Robert Hill and Thomas Pamer (? Palmer).
Proved 12th Sept., 1615.

1618. Richard Densham of Lapford. Administration granted 29th Oct., 1618, of goods unadministered by Johan his mother, to John Densham his son.

1619. John Hamlyn of Tawstock, 31st May, 1619. To son Marmaduke " my best doublett and jerkyn." Legacies to brothers William, Christopher, and Richard, and to godson Richard Hamlyn.
Residue to wife Sidwell for life, with reversion to said Marmaduke Hamlyn.
Proved 4th May, 1619.

1625. Walter Hammett of Northam. Admon. granted to Dorothy his widow, 6th Oct., 1625.
Sum £13 1s. 4d.

NOTE.—James Hammett, eldest son of Richard H. and Elizabeth Risdon, second son of Richard Hammett of Clovelly, and Thomasine Hamlyn, changed his name to Hamlyn, by Act of Parliament, in 1760. He was created a baronet in 1795.

1628. Richard Hamlyn of Tawstock, 10th Feby., 1624.
Mentions sons Richard, John, William, and Giles, and daughter Mary.
Residue to wife Mary, who is Sole Executrix.
Codicil dated 5th Dec., 1628.
Proved 26th Feby., 1628-29.

1637. The last Will of Elinor Mortimore, otherwise Tanner, of Fremington, Widow. She desires to be buried in the parish churchyard, just by the chancel door, near to the "sepulchre" of husband William Mortimore, *alias* Tanner, and leaves 10s. to the poor of the parish. Mentions sons Matthew and Henry Mortimore, *alias* Tanner, and daughter Elinor

Friend ; also son Tymothy Hatherley and daughter Eylin Hanver.

Residue to said daughter Elinor Friend, who is Sole Executrix.

Witnesses—William Blanchard, minister ; John Barwicke.

Proved 30th Aug., 1637.

NOTE.—Refer to her husband's will, 12th Sept., 1615, *ante*.

1637. Administration to the effects of Lewis Hatch of Salterleigh, granted 14th April, 1637, to Robert his father. John Fisher of Nymet St. George, Clerk, joins the bond (during minority of Lewis and Thomas, younger children of deceased).

1643. Mary Hamlyn of Tawstock, Widow, 1st April, 1643, Mentions sons Richard, John, and William, and daughter Mary, granddaughter Dorothy, child of said Mary.

Sister Dorothy Shorte, and godson " William Shorte."

Residue to son Giles Hamlyn, who is Sole Exor.

Proved 23rd Sept., 1643.

1644 The last Will of Robert Hatch of Salterleigh, Gentleman, 20th April, 1642. Bequests to the poor and parish church. To wife Margery certain furniture at " Hatchington, in the parish of Swimbridge." Mentions daughter-in-law Christian Hatche, widow of son Lewis Hatche deceased, their children Robert (" my grandchild and heir apparent "), Lewis, and Thomas Hatche. He leaves said Lewis Hatche the tenement known as Uphome, in Cheriton, after the death of his said mother Christian. Mentions son-in-law John Mayne and nephews Marmaduke and Hugh Welsh.

Residue to said grandchild Robert Hatch, who is Sole Exor. Overseers, John Fisher, Clerk, Hugh Sparke, and John Paul, Proved 14th Oct., 1644.

NOTE.—There are many discrepancies and inaccuracies both in the pedigrees and historical notices of the family of Hatch.

They derived their name from the manor of Hache, written Hax in

Domesday, which belonged at the Conquest to Baldwin de Brion, and subsequently to Arundel. Upon this estate, in the parish of Loddiswell, "John of Hach," supposed to have been son and heir of "Adam of Hach," resided in 1345-6. Their descendant Jeffry Hatch, described as of "Wolleigh," in the parish of Beaford, was really of South Molton, and gave name to an estate there, hence known as Hatch, which has assisted the confusion I have noted.

This Jeffry Hatch, of South Molton, appears to have had two sons. The elder of these, John Hatch, was the great grandfather of Robert Hatch, who, by his marriage with Wenlyan, daughter and heir of Sir John Murdock, Kt., became possessed of Wolleigh. This Robert died in 1406 (Inq. p. m. 7th Henry IV.), and his branch became extinct in male line about the middle of the sixteenth century, when the Wolleigh property went with the daughter and heir to Mallet; but William and Oliver Hatch, baptised at Kenwyn 1614 and 1616, were cadets of the Wolleigh line, and the former had a grandson, John Hatch, baptised there in 1673.

The second son of Jeffry Hatch of South Molton, Gilbert Hatch, married Claris, daughter and heir of William de Awre of Awre, commonly called Aller, in South Molton. Thomas Hatch of Aller, fifth in descent from Gilbert, was the father of Lewis Hatch of Aller, whose line terminated late in the eighteenth century, upon the death of Thomas Hatch, cousin and heir of Elizabeth (will proved 1747), granddaughter and heir of John Hatch of Aller. Will proved 1731-2.

Thomas Hatch, father of said Lewis, had also a third son, Robert Hatch, who has been entirely overlooked by the heralds, and he was the father of Robert Hatch, the above testator, and also of two daughters, Gertrude and Elizabeth, who are likewise omitted from the visitation pedigrees. The father of the testator, Robert Hatch, married Joan Parker of South Molton, and received by deed of gift from his father, Thomas, the Salterleigh property, by indenture dated 10th Dec., 1553.

The Salterleigh branch of the Hatch family terminated with co-heirs married to Stafford, Drake, and Burdock, upon the death of Robert Hatch of Salterleigh, who was buried there 13th Dec., 1699.

1662. The last Will of Christopher Wood of Ashridge, in the parish of Northtawton, Esquire, 15th Oct., 1661. Legacies to poor; to wife Mary and daughter Mary; daughter-in-law Elizabeth, wife of son and heir Christopher. Residue to wife Mary, who is Sole Executrix.

Proved 22nd June, 1662.

NOTE.—Mary (Fowell) was testator's second wife; she died 1683. Ashridge subsequently belonged to the Skinners, who held it for some descents. The daughters and co-heirs of the last Skinner of Ashridge married Orchard, and Sheriff, and the property now belongs to the late Mrs. Orchard's grandson, Major Charles Orchard Cornish, late 18th, Royal Irish, and 73rd Regiments. See my "Devonshire Parishes," Vol. II., p. 72.

1665. Administration to the effects of Roger Sanger of Mariansleigh, to "Sarah Sanger, Widow."
Henry Sanger joins the bond.
Sum £94 11s.

1669. Sara Sanger of "Marley," Widow, 11th Jan., 1668. Legacies to son John Sanger, to daughter Marian Vicary, and grandson Joseph Vicary and his three brothers, and their sisters Sibil and Francis.

The latter to have my "jump coat and one of my pewter dishes."

To the children of John, James, Henry, and Elias Sanger 2s. each.

Residue to youngest son Elias Sanger, who is Sole Exor.
Proved 14th April, 1669.
Inventory exhibited by Roger and Jonathan Sanger and William Adams.

NOTE.—"Marley" is a corruption of Mary Ansleigh, and about two miles from Meshaw, in the same hundred and deanery. This parish is called in some old documents " Anstey St. Mary."

1669. Administration to the effects of Wilmot Hamlyn, granted 5th Feby., 1669, to William Hamlyn of Hartland, her son.
Sum £41 13s. 6d.

1672. The account of William Hamlyn, son, and administrator of Wilmot Hamlyn of Hartland, dated 7th Dec., 1672.
Sum of personalty £41 13s. 6d.
For funeral expenses £2.
Letters of admon. 12s. 6d.
Drawing and double writing the accompt 10s. 6d.
Balance £38 10s. 6d.

1673-4. The last Will of Lewis "Hacche" of Satterley, "minister of the Gospel," 17th June, 1673. Desires to be buried in the "little window of the chancel of Satterleigh Church." Bequeaths "my books" to nephew Robert Hacche, and other books to "Mrs. Hildersham." Mentions "sister Mrs. Sarah Hacche," cousin Christian Hacche, " Uncle Lavercombe," cousin John Nott, and Thomas Nott his son ; Thomas Wade, his wife and their son Lewis Wade ; John Pincombe of Warkleigh.

Residue to brother " Robert Hacche, Esq.," who is Sole Exor.

Proved 6th Feb., 1673-4.

1674. The last Will of William Mortymer of Great Torrington, dated 17th Feb., 1673.

He leaves directions for a funeral sermon from the text Cor. ii, c. 13, v. 11, " Finally, brethren, farewell." To son Gyles a charge of 18s. per annum out of the house of Anthony Budd during the life of Francis Budd, as per indenture,. &c., of Charles Budd. brother of the aforesaid Anthony and Francis.

To said son " my signet ring," &c.

To daughter Agnes Mortymer £100, i.e., £50 on marriage, and £50 on the birth of "her living child," and there is a like legacy to daughter Dorothy Mortymer. Legacies to poor of Torrington ; to goddaughter Mary, daughter of Anthony Budd ; to Cosen Ann, daughter of Charles Budd ; and to brother George Mortymer's daughters. Mentions " my son " " An " Payne and brother " An " Budd.

Exors., wife Agnes and son Gyles ; brother " An " Budd and George Mortymer to be joint Exors. in trust.

Seal, a heart, with letters " W. M."

Proved 4th July, 1674.

1675. The last Will of William Mortymer of Kentisbury, Yeoman, 13th Aug., 1674. Legacies to poor of said parish, and to the poor of Great Torrington, Berrynarber, Comb Martin, and Parracombe. To daughter-in-law Agnes Mortymer, and to Agnes and Dorothy, daughters of son William Mortymer, deceased. To kinsman Giles Mortymer, to daughter-in-law Philippa Budd, and to her six children. To son-in-law Francis Budd and to his seven children Winifred, Agnes, Giles, Mary, Wilmot, Ellinor, and Francis Budd. To Agnes and Elizabeth, daughters of said Giles Mortymer.

To son Thomas Mortymer certain lands in Berrynarber and others in possession of Amias Serrill. Mentions said son's daughters, Agnes and Dorothy. Dorothy, daughter of son George Mortymer, has £100 and right in "Colley," testator's residence. Mentions Agnes, sister of last mentioned Dorothy, and her mother Wilmott Mortymer.

Residue to son George, who is Sole Exor.

Overseers—Francis and Anthony Budd.

Proved 7th May, 1675.

1679. Admon. to the effects of Grace Hamlyn of Parkham, granted 5th July, 1679, to Margaret, wife of Richard Payne of Stratton, Co. Cornwall.

1684. The last Will of Roger Sanger of Meshaw, *alias* Meshutt, 20th April, 1684. To the poor of Meshaw and "Marleigh" (Mary Ansleigh) 10s. each. He leaves his leasehold estate Prescott, on which he resides, held on the lives of "me Roger Sanger and Agnes my wife," "if Roger, son of brother Jonathan, soe long live," to said Roger his nephew, charged with an annuity of £20 to kinswoman Elizabeth Lithiby. To kinsman Wm. Chardon of Romansleigh, £10. Part of a sum of £12 advanced by said William for William Adams of Marleigh. Legacies to kinsfolk Ann, William, and Joshua Lithiby the younger, and to Daniel, son of Wm. Chardon.

Residue to wife Agnes, who is Sole Executrix.

Proved May (?), 1684.

1685. Agnes Sanger of Meshaw, Widow, 18th June, 1684. Legacies to kinsfolk John, William, and Ann Lithiby, and to John, son of William Addams.

To Alexander Addams; to kinswoman Ann Lithiby the elder.

Residue to kinswoman Elizabeth Lithiby, who is Sole Executrix.

Trustees, Edward Kemp and John Addams.

Witnesses, Edward Kemp and Lewis Deamant (Daymant). Proved Sept. (?), 1685.

1685. Admon. to the effects of John Tossle of Barnstaple, granted 10th April, 1685, to Katherine his widow.

£31 4s. 1d.

1686. The last Will of Jonathan Sanger of Marleigh, *alias* Maryansleigh, 20th Jan., 1682. To the poor of the parish, 2s.

"Having already settled a competent maintenance upon my wife Johana, I give her the lands and tenements settled on her in bar of her dower," together with the use of certain furniture. To son Nicholas, 10s; to son Roger, "my right in Bourne Park"; to son Elias, "my right in Upcote"; to daughters Dorothy and Johane, £50 each.

There are arrangements for the maintenance of son Alexander.

Overseers, kinsmen Richard and Elias Bray.

Witnesses, John Spencer, John Addams, and John Treble.

Sum £804 13s. 4d.

No "act" of proof.

In Calendar, Probate 4th Feb., 1686.

1686. Agnes Mortimer of Great Torrington, Widow, 14th Jan., 1683. Legacies to son Giles Mortimer and his six children; to daughter-in-law Philippis Mortimer; to daughter Anne, wife of Anthony Payne; and to her five children.

Residue to daughter Dorothy, who is Sole Executrix.

Proved Oct. 2nd, 1686.

1687. The last Will of William Hamlyn of Barnstaple, dated 30th Nov., 1687. Bequests to brother James Hamlyn, sisters Martha and Hannah Hamlyn, cousins Mary and Rebecca Lancey.
Residue to wife Mary, who is Sole Executrix.
Proved 13th Feb., 1687.

1692. The last Will of Richard Hamlyn of Tawstock, Yeoman, dated 30th March, 1687. Mentions daughters Mary and Katherine, sons John and James Hamlyn.
Residue to wife Katherine, who is Sole Executrix.
Codicil dated 11th Nov., 1690.
Proved 17th Feb., 1692.

1693. The last Will of John "Hamlin" of Abbotsham, 24th April, 1691.
Mentions sons William and Richard, grandchildren Richard and Grace Ellis.
Residue to daughter Agnes "Hamling," who is Sole Executrix.
Proved 3rd Feb., 1693.

1693. The last Will of John Hamlyn of Barnstaple, dated 22nd Feb., 1692.
Mentions his two daughters Rachel wife of Thomas Wellington of Barnstaple and Mary Hamlyn.
Grandson John Lancey (?), granddaughters Margaret, Dorothy, and Elizabeth Lancey (?).
Residue to daughter Mary Hamlyn, who is Sole Executrix.
Proved 1st September, 1693.

NOTE.—The name of Willington, above written " Wellington," is of great repute and antiquity in the neighbourhood of Barnstaple. Originally seated at Willington, in Derbyshire, Sir Ralph de Willington, living 1252, migrated to Devonshire in consequence of his marriage with Joan, daughter and heir of William Champernowne, of Umberleigh and adjacent parishes, property which had been derived from the Soleignys, by the marriage of Mabel de Suleigny with Jordan Champernowne, the said Mabel having been the granddaughter of Gilbert de

Soleigny, of Stoke Rivers and Umberleigh, by his wife, Lady Avis Redvers, daughter of Baldwin, second Earl of Devon, and aunt of Lady Avis, wife of Sir Hugh Worthe, of Worth, knight.

The son and heir of Sir Ralph Willington and Joan Champernowne was Governor of Exeter Castle in 1253, and Sheriff of Devon four years later. His eldest son, Sir John Willington, was created Lord Willington of Keirkenny, by writ of 11 Edward I., 1283, and was patron of the Church of High Bickington in 1309. This first Lord Keirkenny had a son, who succeeded as second lord, and also seven brothers. The third of the latter, Sir Reginald Willington, was found heir-at-law to his nephew, Lord Keirkenny, in 1348, and also died childless. Another of the brothers was killed at Borough Bridge, another was beheaded in 1322, another was a priest. The heritage ultimately came to Lord Keirkenny's youngest uncle, William Willington, of Huntshaw, who married Margaret, daughter of Sir Alexander Freville, by his wife, a co-heir of Marmion. The last heir male of the elder line, John Willington, of Umberleigh, died S.P. 1397. And all the lands, inclusive of the claim to the then dormant barony of Keirkenny, were divided between his sisters, whilst the peerage honours have since been in abeyance amongst their posterity. The eldest sister and co-heir, Isabel Willington, married William Beaumont, and had the Umberleigh and other property, which ultimately passed to the Bassets. Her younger sister, Margaret Willington, married Sir John Worthe, of Worth, in Washfield, and brought the Worthes considerable estates in Barnstaple and Braunton, which were ultimately entailed upon the second house of Worthe, settled at Compton, in the parish of Marldon, an estate derived from the marriage of Sir John Worthe, father-in-law of Margaret Willington, with Cicelye, daughter and co-heir of Sir John Doddescombe. See notes to Worthe wills, *ante* pp. 21, 44, 52, etc.

The Willingtons of Tamworth, Co. Warwick, and of Killoskehane, and of Castle Willington, County Tipperary, both claim to be cadets of this truly historical family, and their genealogies, as such, are inserted in Burke's "Landed Gentry."

1697. The Inventory of William Rawle, late of Chittlehampton, deceased, Yeoman, exhibited 25th Feb., 1697.

1702. The last Will of William Hamblyn of Hartland, 6th May, 7th William the Third (1695).

Bequests to wardens for repair of the church, 20s. To brothers John and Thomas. To godchildren Henry Snowe; Wilmot, wife of John Alford; William, son of Richard Sherme; Thomas, son of John Barons; and Ishmael, son of Margaret Smale.

Residue to wife Amy Hamlyn, who is Sole Executrix.
Proved 6th March, 1702.
Sum £101 7s. 6d.

1702. Administration to the effects of Joseph Hamlyn of "Clovelleigh," granted 4th July, 1702, to Christiana his wife. William Hamlyn of "Woolsery," yeoman, and William Hamlyn of "Clovelleigh," yeoman, join the bond.

Sum £160 14s. 2d.

1703. George Mortimer of Kentisbury, 10th Oct., 1702. Legacies to poor of said parish, and to those of Comb Martin, Trentisho, and Parracombe. Tenement in Trentisho to son-in-law William Knight, after the death of Julian Gubb. To daughter Dorothy Knight, £10. Legacies to grandchildren William, Elizabeth, Dorothy, and George Knight; granddaughter Agnes Hamond.

Residue to son-in-law William Knight, who is Sole Exor.

Witnesses, John Courtney, William Herding, Robert Troute.

Proved 22nd June, 1703.

1705. Thomas Mortimer of Berrynarber, Yeoman, 21st Aug., 1705. Legacies to daughter Dorothy and her husband William Lerwill; to grandchild Ann, daughter of George Bowden; to daughter Wilmot Mortimer. Mentions "cosen" William Knight, "senr.," of Kentisbury. Said Wilmot to have fee-simple estate in Berrynarber, with remainder to daughter "Thamsin Witheridge's" children. To son-in-law John Witheridge, 5s.

To poor of Berrynarber and Comb Martin, 20s. each. Legacies to "cosen" William Knight of Kentisbury and to his four children William, George, Elizabeth, and Dorothy Knight.

Residue to son-in-law George Bowden, who is Sole Exor.

Proved 5th Oct., 1705.

1706. Admon. to the effects of John Hamlyn of Tawstock, granted 7th March, 17c6, to Gertrude his wife. James Hamlyn, Yeoman, and Richard Limbery join the bond.

1709. The last Will of Catherine Hamlyn of Tawstock, 2nd April, 1708. Bequests to poor, 20s; to son James Hamlyn, his wife Honor, and to their children James and Mary; to daughter Mary Mattack, and daughter-in-law Gartherett Hamlyn; to Judith, wife of Richard Budd, "second best cote of staining cloth."

Residue to daughter Catherine Hamlyn, who is Sole Executrix.

Overseer, brother William Berry.

Proved 6th May, 1709.

Sum £139 12s. 6d.

1709. The last Will of Amy Hamlyn of Hartland, Widow, 8th Feb., 1708-9.

Bequests to parish church; to sister Rebecca Wakely and to James and Richard Wakely; to Agnes Yeo, Richard Sherme, and to latter's sons William, Hugh, and Richard; to sister Mary Vine; to godchildren Matthew Bragg and John Batisholl; to Oliver Simon's wife and her son Charles Budd; to Eme, daughter of William Brown, Susan Bawdon, James Vine, and Thomasine his wife.

She leaves her right in Ponsdowne, in the parish of Pancraswick, to William, son of William Brown. To John Vine, 10s.

Residue to said William Brown the younger, who is Sole Exor.

Proved 4th Nov., 1709.

Armorial Seal—A fesse between three mullets (*argent*, a fesse between three mullets, *sable*, is a well-known coat of "Brown.")

1714. The last Will of James Hamlyn of Tawstock, Yeoman, 17th Aug., 1713.

To son James the tenements known as Bratabeer and Poolly after wife's death.

To daughter Mary, £120 at 21.

To sister Mary Maddicke of Dartmouth, 40s.

To twenty poor people of Tawstock, 20s.
Residue to wife Honour, who is Sole Executrix.
Witnesses, Abigail Berrye, Henry Millford.
Proved 12th Nov., 1714.
Seal of Arms—A lion rampant.

NOTE.—The die evidently bore the name " William Hamlyn." The half of the " W " and the letters " I L L " are only apparent on the impression, which is very indistinct. The ancient arms of the house of Hamlyn were, *gules*, a lion rampant, *ermine*, crowned, *or*, and are hus blazoned for Sir John Hamlyn on the " Boroughbridge Roll," who bore them at that engagement, 16th March, 1322.

1725. The last Will of Joseph Hamlyn of Clovelly, 19th July, 1725.
"To my honoured father, one suit of clothes."
"To my honoured mother, one puter dish."
"To loving brother William Hamlyn, my best hatt."
"To sister Margaret, one of my best nets."
Residue to wife Mary Hamlyn, who is Sole Executrix.
Proved 1st Oct., 1725.
Inventory of effects of above testator :—
"His apparel and purse, £4.
"His part of fishing boat and nets, £10.
"His bed performed, £2 10s."
His Pewter, £1 15s.
Brass crocke, kittell and skillett, 15s.
Table board and four chairs, 4s. 6d.
Chimney stuff, 7s. 6d.
Other lumber not mentioned, 1s. 6d.
Witnesses—Henry Yealland.
　　　　Allce Madge.
　　　　Thomas Yeo.

NOTE.—Refer to admon. of Joseph Hamlyn of "Clovelleigh," July, 1702, *ante*.

1726. Admon. to the effects of James Hamlyn of Tawstock, granted 27th Jan., 1726, to Jane his wife.

Edward Lancey of Heanton and John Paddon join the bond.

1733. The last Will of Lewis Gregory of Barnstaple, Devon, Gentleman, 17th Jan., 1732-33.

Desires to be privately buried in the chancel of Barnstaple church.

He leaves his son George Gregory the advowson of the Rectory of Combmartin. Mentions daughter Anne and niece Mary Gregory. Residue to dear wife Joan, who is Sole Executrix.

Proved 2nd July, 1733.

NOTE.—Testator was the son of the Rev. George Gregory, son of Rev. Samuel Gregory, son of Rev. Anthony Gregory. The last was rector of Charles, 1654, and the first was instituted to same rectory 20th March, 1664. Testator's daughter Anne was the wife of John Drake, Town Clerk of Barnstaple, and the grandmother of the late Sir Wm. Drake, Kt.

The parish now known as "Charles," near South Molton, was anciently called Charneys. The Rectory was for some years in the patronage of the Gregory family.

1734. Roger Sanger of Mariansleigh, Yeoman, Feb. 13th, 1730.

To wife Elizabeth an annuity of £10, charged upon Higher Upcott. He also bequeaths her certain furniture, together with three rooms in his house, and liberty of ingress and egress for herself and friends "through the hall." To daughter Elizabeth, £120. To granddaughters Ann Sanger and Elizabeth, daughter of John Hill of Withypool, Somerset, £5 each at 21.

To the poor of Marleigh, 20s.

Residue to son John Sanger, who is Sole Exor.

Witnesses, Henry Bowden and John Rocke.

Proved 26th April, 1734.

1739. The last Will of Ann Drake, Widow, of Barnstaple, 10th Nov., 1718.

Mentions "brothers" William Yeo and Richard Evans of Cullompton; sister Amy Stephens of the parish of Denbury; daughter Christian Standish and grandson Henry Drake. Cousins Robert Daw of Exeter and John Pearce. Grandchildren Henry and John Drake are both under age.

Mentions Richard, George, William, and Elizabeth, children of said "brother" Richard Evans; Elizabeth and Amy, daughters of said William Yeo.

Desires a private funeral, no funeral sermon, orders "hatt bands and gloves," and appoints her "bearers," viz., Messrs. Bowchair (Bouchier?) and Spark, Nicholas Glass, Samuel Berry, John Richards, and Walter Tucker.

Said John Pearce Executor in trust during minority of said grandson.

Proved 17th Nov., 1739.

NOTE.—This will was proved twenty years after the death of testatrix, who was buried at Barnstaple, October 26th, 1719. She was widow of Henry Drake, sometime Mayor of Barnstaple, who died 1688, and at the date of her marriage with him the widow of William Noyse of Exeter.

Her "daughter" Christian Standish was the younger daughter and co-heir of Robert Hatch of Satterleigh, and after the death of her first husband John Drake, son of testatrix, she married Charles Standish of Barnstaple. The grandchild of testatrix, John Drake, mentioned in the will as "under age" in 1718, had been baptized 27th September, 1710. He died in 1770, and was succeeded by his son Henry Drake, born 1745, subsequently Town Clerk of Barnstaple, who died in 1806.

The latter was the grandfather, through his second son, of the late Sir William Drake, knighted 1st October, 1869, and, through his eldest son, he was the great grandfather of General John M. C. Drake, C.B., Royal Engineers, born 1833. who has issue.

1753. Nicholas Sanger of Marleigh, dated 10th May, 1711. He gives to the poor of the parish the interest of a sum of £10. To John, son of John "Sangor," "my great brasse pot." Residue to Jonathan Sanger and unto Johane, daughter of Roger Sanger, "my brother, my kinsfolk"; they are joint Exors.

Witnesses, John Adams and Roger Packer.

Proved Dec. 7th, 1753.

NOTE.—The above legacy to the poor of Mariansleigh was stated in a return made to Parliament in 1786 to have been given by deed of Nicholas Sanger in 1707. The "£10" was then vested in John Adams, and produced 10s. per annum. The principal sum was subsequently in the hands of William Adams, who paid 8s. a year in respect thereof; the parishioners had no security for the principal, and the Parliamentary Commissioners suggested that it should be placed in a bank. According to "White's Devonshire," edition 1878, the bequest is now lost.

1775. John Torsall of Lapford, 21st April, 1774. To daughter Mary Richards certain household goods. Mentions son-in-law John Richards.

Residue to "John Torsall," no relationship expressed, who is Sole Exor.

Witnesses—Peter and Susanna Richards, Wm. Cook.

Proved Nov. 4th, 1775.

1779. Susannah Tossell of Ashreigney, 26th May, 1777. To son-in-law Edmond Foss and to his wife Susannah, and to their five children, one guinea each.

To son James Babbage's six children one guinea each.

Legacy to Betty Pridham Babbage, and mentions "Jane Babbage."

Residue to the four children of son John Babbage, viz., Elizabeth, John, William, and Richard, who are joint Exors.

Proved by John Babbage and Elizabeth, wife of Samuel Alford, two of the Exors.

March 5th, 1779.

1780. "John Tossel," 4th June, 1779. To Humphry, son of George Tossel of Kingsnympton, one guinea. To Thomas Tow 1s.

Residue to John, son of George Tossel, who is Sole Exor.

Proved July 1st, 1780.

NOTE.—No parish is mentioned, but testator is described in the Calendar as of Kingsnympton.

Admon. granted to George Tossel in the minority of his son John, the Exor. named in the will.

1781. Admon. to the effects of John Sanger of Maryansleigh, Yeoman, granted 5th May, 1781, to Mary his widow.

1787. Elizabeth Tossel of Marwood, Widow, 11th June, 1787. Legacies to Elizabeth, wife of John Berry of Marwood ; to Elizabeth their daughter ; to John their son ; to Thomas Sharland of Marwood ; to Elizabeth, wife of Wm. Gammon of Marwood ; to Ann Scott of Fremington; to Jane, wife of John Manley of Marwood ; to John Radford of Marwood ; to Elizabeth, wife of Wm. Thorne of Martinho; to Mary Berry ; to George and Wm. Radford his son ; to Jane Paltryman of Tawstock ; to Mary Cross, George Radford, and Johanna, daughter of Hannah Stanbury, all of Marwood ; and to Thomas, son of John Berry.

Residue to John Berry, sen., of Marwood, who is Sole Exor.

Proved 2nd July, 1787.

1794. The last Will of John Mortimore of Torrington, Surgeon, 4th June, 1793. Wife Ursula universal legatee and Sole Executrix.

Proved 15th Dec. 1794.

PART II.

ARCHDEACONRY OF TOTNES.

1601. The last Will of Johane Tooker of East Allington, Widow, 13th Dec., 1600. Legacies to the poor; to son Zachary, and to his eldest son William; his daughter Rabyn Dodd and to her three children; to daughter Mary, wife of Nicholas Wakeham; to daughter Johan, and to son John Tooker.

Residue to said children John and Johane, who are joint Exors.

Proved 23rd Jan., 1600.

1601. The undated Will of Peter Tucker of Blackauton. "To the poor men's box, 2s.; to brother Thomas Tucker's two children, John and Samson, a lamb to each."

Residue to wife Margaret, who is Sole Executrix.

Proved 12th Oct., 1601.

1603. Dorothy Fry of Hatherleigh. Mentions son Henry Fry, daughters Mary and Avline.

Witness, Richard Fry and others.

Proved at Okehampton 6th Feb., 1603.

1605. The last Will of Joane Mortymore of Stokingham. Legacy to the poor of the parish. To daughter Ebbot, wife of Robert "Mortemor," £10. To Mychell, Thomas, and Elizabeth, children of John Mortymore, small legacies. To Julian Mortymore, "my great longe leged crocke, & my great pan."

Similar bequests of goods, &c., to Wilmot and Christian Mortymore, to Joan Stisson, to Elizabeth, daughter of John Hawkins, to William Knight, and William Pascow.

Residue to son Robert Mortymore, who is Sole Exor.

Proved 7th Feb., 1605.

1605. Admon. to the effects of John Mortimer, of Inwardleigh, granted 13th March, 1605, to Margery his relict.

1607. John Toker the younger of the parish of Blackawton, 8th Sept., 1607.

To the poor, 6s. 8d., to be distributed by brother Stephen Toker. Legacies at 21 to daughters Sylphine, Richorde, and Alice. To sons Richard and Christopher. To wife Jane the custody of his son John during minority, and to pay the sum of £100, due on bond, to his, testator's, father John Toker. To godson Stephen Toker, a lamb, and another to god-daughter Marie.

Residue to eldest son John Toker, who is Sole Exor.

Proved 22nd Feb., 1607-8.

Admon. granted to said wife Jane Toker in minority of Exor.

1607. The undated Will of Walter Tucker of the parish of Blackawton.

To be buried in parish church.

Legacies to eldest son John and to other sons Robert, William, and Richard.

To daughter Margaret and to her children Nicholas and Anna Clarke. To daughter Honor Elliot and to John Elliot her son. To daughter Thomsin. To Mary and Elizabeth, children of son John. Residue to wife Joan, who is Sole Executrix.

Proved 28th May, 1607.

1611. The last Will of Thomazin Tuke of the parish of Beaworthy, Widow, 9th July, 8th James I., 1610.

Bequests to all godchildren and to the parish poor and church.

Mentions sons John and William and daughter Thomazin Northam of Halwill.

To daughter Margaret Peerse, "my best coffer and all my apparel, my sylver hookes gilted, with my sylver ringe, and also a brazen crocke."

Legacies to John Northam's children; to Roger and John, sons of son William. To Grace, daughter of Richard Peerse. Residue to grandson David, son of said Richard Peerse, who is Sole Exor.

Proved 1st Aug., 1611.

1616. The last Will, nuncupative, of William Mortymer of Bovey Tracy. Legacies to daughter Joan and to the child now expected by his wife.

Residue to wife Joan, who is Sole Executrix.
Dated 29th Aug., 1616.
Proved 9th Nov., 1616.

1616.   "Soli deo laus."

The last Will of Nicholas "Tucker" of Blackawton, Yeoman, 6th Dec., 1616.

To the poor of Blackawton, 5s.

"A lamb a peece" to son Lewis Tucker, and to his children Nicholas, James, Roger, Agnes, Suse, and Jane Tucker.

To son Roger Tucker's first child a lamb; to daughter Jane Pook, two lambs; to William Dowell, a lamb.

To son Chrispine Tucker, £30. His wife Suse to have the use of certain farm implements, *inter aliis*, of "the plough, scuffle, wheels, and harrows."

Bequests to John Comyn, John Vynsent, Isabel Coome, and Margaret Wetyne, and kinsman Henry Tucker.

Residue to said wife, Suse "Tucker," who is Sole Executrix.
Proved Feb. 14th, 1616.

1616. Inventory of the effects of Nicholas Tucker of Blackawton, deceased, made 13th Jan., 1616.

Item, one yoke of oxen	... ...	£7
„ 2 milch kine ...	... ...	£5
„ 3 yonge bullocks	... ...	£4
„ 3 labor beastes	... ...	£6
„ 50 sheepe young & old	... ...	£14
„ 5 swyne hogges	... ...	30/-
„ A chattell lease of certain ground in Burlieton, in parish of Blackawton ...		£36
„ One ox that hath been sicke	... ...	30/-
„ His Armore ...	... ...	15/-
„ Eight silver spoons ..	... ...	20/-

Total of personal effects, £170 0s. 8d.

1618. The last Will of Joane Tooker, otherwise Webb, of "Edford" (Ideford), Widow. To the poor there, ten groats. To Mary Manninge, " my best gowne, one little milke panne, my best hat, best wastcoate, best saveguard, best cloake, and to every one of her four children a sheepe apeece, together with one down coverlet, one blanket, one canvas sheet, one pillow, and one pilloty." To servant Elizabeth Tottell, 40s. and a heifer of two years old. " Item, I give to 'Kathron' twelve pens." To goddaughter Sissy Swetland, twenty nobles at her marriage. To Edward, Thomas, and James, children of William Swetland, one sheep each. To goddaughter Joane Swetland, ten groats. Residue to son-in-law William Swetland, who is Sole Exor.

Proved 23rd May, 1618.

1618. The nuncupative Will of Margaret Tucker, otherwise Michelmore, wife of John Tucker of Totnes, dated 2nd April, 1618. She desires to be buried in Totnes yard. She leaves her servants sixpence each, and the residue of her separate estate to her husband the said John Tucker, who is Sole Exor.

Proved 10th July, 1618.

From the Inventory of said testatrix—" Item, a legasie of

£300 given unto the said Margaret by the last will and testament of Richard Michelmore, her father, deceased, payable six years after his death, £300."

1622. The last Will of John Towker of Whitecombe, in the parish of East Allington, 10th May, 1619.
To be buried in parish churchyard. To poor, 3s. 4d.
Legacies to son Nicholas Towker; to daughter Jone Michelmore; and to daughter Edith Bryan.
Residue to wife Anne, who is Sole Executrix.
Proved 17th Jan., 1622.

1625. Admon. to the effects of Roger Tucker of Slapton, Yeoman, granted 8th July, 1625, to Susie, his mother.
Inventory made by Lewis Tucker, Richard Tokerman, and Crispin Tucker.

" Item,	5 silver spoons	15/-
„	7 acres of wheat in ground	£12
„	6¼ „ of barley	£10
„	1½ „ rye	£2 15s.
„	20 „ oats	£20
„	3 milch kine	£8
„	64 sheep & 8 kine...	£21
„	40 lambs	£6

Total sum of personality, £100 6s."

NOTE.—Is is shown by his will, as recited by his mother, that he had paid "Crispin Tooker" the sum of £65, and Richard Pooke a like amount, for which they were respectively to free his mother's executors; but the will referred to is not in the bundle.
See *post*, March, 1633.

1625-6. Admon. to the effects of John Chapple of Modbury, intestate, granted 17th Jan., 1625-26, to Marie his relict. Osmond Pullablanke of Modbury joins the bond.
Inventory made by William Pullablanke.
Sum, £66 10s.

1633. The last Will, nuncupative, of Joan Mortymore of Stokingham, 16th May, 1633. To the poor of the parish, 1s. Bequests to Robert and Helene, children of Elizabeth Hingston; to Elizabeth, daughter of John Hingston; to kinsman Thomas Mortymore and to his children John and Joan; to John and Elizabeth, children of Nicholas Colle; to kinsman John Gould; to Ebbott, wife of Nicholas Garland; to the three children of Edward Milton; to William, Marie, Nicholas, and Agnes, children of Christopher Jilleard; to god-daughter Margery Edwards; to Rachell and Robert, children of Wilmot Eweine; and to daughter Julyan Mortymore.

Residue to daughter Wilmot Eweine, who is Sole Executrix.

Proved 8th June, 1633.

NOTE.—Refer to will of Joane Mortymore of same parish, February, 1605.

1633. The last Will of Suse "Tooker" of Blackawton, Widow, 2nd Dec., 1633. Legacies to the poor of Blackawton and Brixham; to daughter Jane, wife of Richard Pooke; to son Crispin and his children; to John, Lewis, and Elizabeth, children of son Roger; to Johan, daughter of son Lewis; to Jane, daughter of William Partridge of Chivelstone; to grandchildren by son Christopher. She recites that she administered to the goods of her son Roger.

Residue to son Lewis, who is Sole Exor.

Proved 21st March, 1633.

NOTE.—This will was disputed upon the affidavits of Nicholas and Jane Tooker; it appears to have been made by one "Henry Sharpham."

Refer to Feb., 1616, and to July, 1625, *ante*.

1635. The last Will of Julian Mortymer of Stokingham, Maiden, 1st April, 1635. Bequests to Marianne, Mary, Nicholas, and Robert "Gillord"; to Robert and Rachell "Ewen"; to William Cook, John Lowe, Robert and John Gould.

Residue to sister Wilmot "Ewen," who is Sole Executrix.

Proved 22nd Jan., 1635.

1636. Admon. to the effects of Elinora Tucker of Hatherleigh, granted 13th Sept., 1636, to John Wadland, cousin.

1637. The last Will, nuncupative, of Katherine Tucker of Okehampton, Spinster, 9th Nov., 13th Charles I. She gives 10s. "to the poor of Spreyton, to be employed and to remain to the use of the said poor for ever."

To Anne Arscott, her sister-in-law, "one oring coloured petticoat, one silver coloured waistcoat, one kupp band, my worst hatt, & greene apron."

To Katherine Luke, " two old petticotes & one old waistcoate, a saveguard, & a small laced band."

Residue to sister Johan Tucker, who is Sole Executrix.

Admon. granted, in minority of executrix, to Humphry Tracy of East Worlington.

NOTE.—The bequest to the poor of Spreyton is not noticed in the report of the Charity Commissioners. The Spreyton poor long had the benefit of 20s. per annum issuant out of West Bigbear, by virtue of the will of Thomas Hore, dated 14th May, 1746 ; for although this gift was void by the Mortmain Act of 9th George II, it was sometime paid by the owners of Little Bigbear.

They also had the interest of £50 left by John Cann for their use for the fifty years following his death, by will dated 13th March, 1798, and proved in the Principal Registry of the Bishop of Exeter in 1807 ; the term expired in 1857.

The testatrix, Katherine Tucker, left personality £58 10s. 4d., and the 10s. to the poor may have been absorbed in the £45 raised and paid to Arthur Kelly in 1760 for the property now known as " Poorlands," the said sum having been partly furnished by " pecuniary donations to the poor of this parish, some of which had been lost, and the residue laid out in this purchase " as far as they sufficed, the balance having been made up by the trustees of the said newly acquired poor lands.

1641-2. The last Will of Mary Chappell of Modbury, Widow, dated 9th Jan., 1640-41.

She makes her sons Samuel and John Chappell universal legatees and Sole Exors.

Inventory by William Cotley and Ralph Webber, who witness the will.

Proved 3rd Jan., 1641-42.

1644. Admon. to effects of Julyan Frye of Black Torrington, granted ——, 1644, to Lewis and Leonard Frye.
Inventory attested by Howard (Henry?) Frye.

1645. The last Will of John Tucker of Okehampton, 3rd March, 1644. He makes his daughters Elizabeth and Sara universal legatees and Joint Exors. Three trustees—Richard Heayne and Thomas Carter of Okehampton, and brother Philip Tucker of Rattery.
Proved 23rd April, 1645.

1646. Admon. to the effects of Michael Mortimer of Stokingham, to Joanna Mortimer of the same parish, Widow.
Hercules Giles joins the bond.
Granted 21st July, 1646.

1664. "The account of Nathaniel Tucker of Northlew, who bought the administration of the goods of John Tucker, deceased, at the Archdeacon's Court at Okehampton, 21st Feb., 1664.
" Paid for tithes that was due to the parson, £1 7s.
" Paid for a mortuary to the parson, 10s.
" To Michael Tucker for wages due to him, 7s.
" To John Tucker, due to him on bond, £2 13s.
" Due to myself from the said John Tucker, deceased, £6."
With other payments, total sum, £51 1s. 6d.
" So it appears from the account that the accountant has payd more than the inventory comes to, the sum of £11 4s. 2d."

1665. The last Will of Abraham Mortymer of Bovey Tracy, 14th June, 1664. To the poor there, 5s. Legacies to Edward, Nathaniel, and Gilbert Mortymer; to sister Thomasine Conant; to godson Abraham Conant; to mother Elizabeth Casely.
Residue to Jane Heath, who is Sole Executrix.
Witnesses, Christopher Tynes, William Heath.
Proved 3rd June, 1665.

1665. The last Will of John Tooker, the elder, of the parish of Milton Abbot, 6th June, 1665.

Legacies to Dorothy Drewe, grandchild, and to Daniel Drewe's four sons. To grandchild Dorothy Bragge, and to grandchildren Elizabeth and John Tooker; to Katherine and Elizabeth Horwill and to daughter Katherine Bragge.

Residue to son John Tooker, who is Sole Exor.

No act of proof. Inventory exhibited 17th Jan., 1665.

Sum, £19 7s. 8d.

1666. The last Will of Nicholas Tucker of Totnes, Merchant, 20th July, 1666.

To son Nicholas, dwelling-house and herb garden, "without the north gate," and the house called the "Vineyard," to him and his heirs male for ever. There is remainder to son Richard, to daughter Joan, to brother Richard, and to the heirs male of Grace Weekes, deceased, late wife of Thomas Weekes, and finally to sister Amy Tucker and her heirs. To said son Richard, £100, issuant from property at Alphington. Mentions property at Dartington; to daughter Joan, £140; to wife Edith, the best feather bed.

Mentions grandfather Richard Tucker, deceased, in connection with a legacy of £80 left to testator's brother Richard. To Mr. John Ford, minister of Totnes, 20s. for funeral sermon. For the poor of Totnes, Dartington, and St. David's, Exeter, 20s. to each parish. Residue to said son Nicholas, who is Sole Exor., but a minor.

Exors. in trust, "Brother Richard," Peter Windball of Exeter, distiller, and William Venning of Tor-Brian, clothier.

Proved by trustees, 23rd Oct., 1666.

Personality, £1,026 17s. 4d.

NOTE.—Refer to Edith Tucker, Jan., 1705, *post.*

1667.—The last Will of Margaret Tucker of Kingswear, Widow, 16th March, 1667. To Susannah, wife of William Rawlings, £5; to Edward Knight of Brixham, 20s.; to Agnes Knight of Yealmpton, 20s., and "my old red coat and waistcoat." "Item, I give to two children of John Crute of Woodis,

10s. a pece, and to thare mother, Elizabeth Ball of Cockington, a red coat and a cullered waistcoat." To Elizabeth Thomas, 20s. "and a red petticoat bound with a green lase." To the younger son of Mr. George Renoles, a "signight ringe," and in money 40s. ; to his children Elizabeth and George, 40s. each. To Susanna, wife of Richard Parker, £5. To poor of Kingswear, 10s. Mentions the "children of Cheston Collings, Suse Glover, Jone Sallis, Elizabeth Smith," and "Mr. Briyat of Plumleigh, William Parker, Susan Rawlings the younger, and daughter-in-law Christian Toker.

Residue to Richard Parker of Dartmouth, who is Sole Exor.

Proved 14th June, 1667.

NOTE.—This will is sealed probably with the "signight ringe" referred to; it is a poor impression, but evidently not armorial. Apparently a text T, surrounded with an ornamental border.

1668. Administration to the effects of John Hamlyn of Widecombe-in-the-Moor, granted 22nd April, 1668, to William Hamlyn his son.

1669. The last Will of Walter Hamlyn of Withicombe-in-the-Moor, 3rd Oct., 1668.

To wife Margaret leasehold interest in property at Buckfast, charged with support of daughter Margery.

To son Peter leasehold interest in Dunston, terminable on lives.

Mentions children Johane, Mary, and Richard, "sisters and brother of said Peter."

Residue to wife Margaret aforesaid.

Proved 15th Feb., 1669.

NOTE.—Testator was brother of Richard Hamlyn of Buckfastleigh. Will proved April, 1690, *post.*

1669. The last Will of John Hamlyn, sen., of Dean Prior, Yeoman, 2nd June, 1665. Mentions daughters Elizabeth, Grace, Agnes, Mary, and Barbara.

To sons, John and Henry Hamlyn, 16d. each. To John, son of said son John Hamlyn, 5s. To grandchild Mary, daughter of said Henry, 5s.
To the rest of son John's children, 1s. each.
Residue to wife Mary, who is Sole Executrix.
Proved 17th Sept., 1669.

1670. Admon. to effects of Phillip Fry of Ashwater, granted 19th July, 1670, to Margaret Fry.
Arthur Bassett joins the bond.

1670. Admon. to effects, &c., of Alexander Fry of Milton Damarell, granted 17th Nov., 1670, to Alexander his son.
Inventory by John Fry, Humphry Dene, and Walter Williams, 6th Nov., *ibid.*
Sum, £85 4s. 8d.

1672. Walter Mortimere of North Bovy, 16th April, 1672. Legacies to sons John, Thomas, and Walter, and to daughters Richord Mortimere and Thomasine Langdon. Residue to wife Richord, who is Sole Executrix.
Proved 3rd April, 1672.

1673. The last Will of Richard Hamlyn of Plymouth, Merchant, 14th Nov., 1672.
He leaves wife Prudence a messuage and tenement in parish of St. Andrew, and to poor of said parish, 15s.
Mentions son Timothy Hamlyn and daughter Elizabeth.
Overseer, cousin George Ceely.
Residue to said wife, who is Sole Executrix.
Proved 27th Nov., 1673.
His silver plate was valued at £13.

1674. The last Will of William Bartlett, the elder, of Marldon.

Desires to be buried in church or churchyard of Marldon.

He gives his "wife" "half the butter and chees in the house;" and likewise the "victuals"; 20s. each to grandchildren Alis and Katherine Bartlett.

Residue to grandson William Bartlett, who is Sole Exor.

Probate granted 14th Sept., 1674.

Inventory exhibited 28th May, 1675, in which deceased is described as a "yeoman."

1678. The last Will of John Tucker of Woodland (prope Ashburton, not "Woodleigh," as entered in the Kalendar), 20th Sept., 1662. The tenement called "Millcliff" to wife Mary, together with a house, &c., in St. Lawrence's lane, Ashburton, held of Hugh Woodley, and now in occupation of Gregory Holkmore, Esq. To sister Thomasine, 40s. Mentions daughter Mary, granddaughter Jane Tucker, and "Cozen" Francis Tucker.

Residue to wife Mary, who is Sole Executrix.

Admon. granted to Mary Tucker, daughter of deceased, 28th Feb., 1678.

1679. Admon. to the effects of John Mortimore of North Bovey, granted 26th July, 1679, to Isot, his widow.

1679. The last Will of Richord Mortimere of North Bovey, Widow, 5th Nov., 1678. To daughter Thomasine Langdon, "all my clouse woolling & lening except my best geompt." To granddaughter Thomasine Langdon, "my best goumpt towrn, and one pudyer dish."

Similar legacies to grandchild John, son of Thomas Mortimere; to grandchild John, son of John Mortimere; to son John Mortimere; to son Walter Mortimere; to grandchild William Mortimere; to daughter Richord White, "my meidle coat &

wascout." Residue to son Thomas Mortimore, who is Sole Exor.

Witnesses, Wm. Paulle, jun. ; John Knowling, John Brocke.

Proved 26th July, 1679.

1690. The last Will of Richard Hamlyn of Buckfastleigh. To son Richard my right in "Old Walls," situate at Buckfast, together with "Latherhole Park" in Widecombe. To son Giles Hamlyn land situated at Lana Water in Ashburton. To son Francis 1s. ; to daughter Mary, 5s. Said son Richard, his lease in Hembury during the life of Ann Gould the younger. He has also residue, and is Sole Exor.

Proved 25th April, 1690.

NOTE.—Testator was of the Southcombe branch of the family. His son Francis, who is "cut off with a shilling," was born 1660, and was the father of Peter Hamlyn of Southcombe, Widecombe-in-the-Moor, born 1690. Peter Hamlyn, great-grandfather of testator, had paid the subsidy on Southcombe in 1621. The latter was grandson of Richard, brother of Robert Hamlyn, ancestor of the Hamlyns now of Buckfastleigh.

1692. The last Will of Achilles Frye of Ashwater, dated 22nd Oct., 1692. Bequests to the poor of the parish; to sister-in-law Margaret Frye; to Anstis and Jone, children of Sidrach Frye; to kinsfolk Charity and Elizabeth Frye and Richard Bounde; to brother William and to kinsman William Frye.

Residue to John, son of Richard Martyn, and kinsman aforesaid Sidrach Frye; they are joint Exors.

Witnesses, Elizabeth Frye, Jeremiah Cross, and William Cruse.

Proved 25th Nov., 1692.

1692. Admon. to the effects of Thomas Mortimore of Hennock, granted to Joane his widow, 6th Dec., 1692.

1696. Admon. to the effects of Thomas Mortimore of Slapton, granted 11th Jan., 1696, to Rebecca Mortimore his sister.

1701. Admon. to the effects of Walter Fry of Tavistock, granted 31st Jan., 1701, to Henry Manaton "of Harwood, in County of Cornwall," Esq., the principal creditor, Honor Fry, the widow, having renounced.

NOTE.—Harewood (pronounced Harwood) forest, about ten miles west of Tavistock, and on the further side of the Tamar, the scene, according to Mason, the dramatist, and others, of the murder of Ethelwold by Edgar, the Saxon king, in 965, to enable him to marry his victim's wife, Elfritha, who, in her turn, murdered her step-son, Edward, hence called "the martyr," to make way for the succession of her own offspring, known in history as Ethelred "the unready." The Manatons, who inherited Kilworthy, near Tavistock, by virtue of the marriage of Ambrose Manaton with the daughter and heir of William Kelly, great granddaughter, maternally, of Sir John Glanville of Kilworthy, had also a house in Tavistock, rendered conspicuous by its heraldic decoration. They were remarkable for their kindness towards their poorer neighbours, and hence possibly Henry Manaton's connection with the private affairs of the above deceased intestate.

There are Manaton inscriptions in the church of Tavistock— Robert, 1740; Robert, 1769. The daughter of the last of them brought Kilworthy and other property to her husband, a clergyman called Butcher, who sold it to the Duke of Bedford. The Manatons, described "as of Southill, in the County of Cornwall," bore for arms:

Arg., on a bend, *sable*, 3 mullets, pierced, of the field.
Crest—A demi-unicorn rampant, *sable*.

1703. Robert Granger of Plymouth, H.M.S. "Pendennis," makes his friend John Little of the same ship universal legatee and Sole Exor., dated 30th Sept.

Proved 4th Nov., 1703.

1705. The last Will of Edith Tucker of Totnes, Widow, 10th April, 1703.

She leaves to Mr. Robert Burscough, Vicar of Totnes, or to the Vicar at the time of her death, as "a free gift," "one guinea of gold" to buy a mourning ring. To Thomasin Sanders, widow, of Totnes, 10s. To nephew Samuel Wimball, £5. To son Nicholas Tucker of Totnes, mercer, "my wedding ring and the picture of my late son Richard Tucker. Mentions Susanna, Isabella, Richard, and Nicholas, children of said son Nicholas.

"And whereas I formerly by an accident hurted my skull, and by the advice and management of my phisitians, some little part, or piece thereof, being broken, was taken out, which I now have by me, my desire is that the same may after my decease be putt att or soe neare the place in my head from whence it was taken, as possible may be without opening my head, and that the same may be buried with mee."

Residue to daughter Joane Tucker, who is Sole Executrix.

Proved 16th January, 1705.

NOTE.—See my "History of the Borough of Totnes," "Ashburton and its Neighbourhood," p. 115.

Mr. Burscough inherited the "guinea of gold." He was Vicar from March 2nd, 1681, and placed his library at the disposal of John Prince, his predecessor. and the author of the "Worthies of Devon." He died in 1709; his successor Arthur D'Anvers was instituted 7th Nov. that year.

1705. Administration to the effects of Abednego Fry of Inwardleigh.

Granted 9th July, 1706, to Joseph Vosper his nephew.

1706-7. The last will, nuncupative, of Mary Ford, of Berry Pomeroy, Widow, dated 1st Jan., 1706-7.

She leaves all her effects to eldest son Roger Ford of said parish.

Inventory by George Campion and Walter Mitchell.

Proved Jan., 1706-7.

1707. The last Will of Joseph Fry of Plymouth, Mariner. He makes his wife Elizabeth universal legatee and Sole Executrix.

Proved 25th July, 1707.

1708. Admon. to the effects of Edward Tossell, late of Plymouth, H.M. ship "Rupert," granted 12th Nov., 1708, to Elizabeth his widow.

1711. Administration to the effects of William Hamlyn of Rattery, deceased, granted 22nd Dec., 1711, to John Hamlyn of Dean Prior, and Samuel Cowling of Rattery, the son William Hamlyn having renounced.

1716. The last Will of Mary Hamlyn of Dean Prior, Widow, 2nd Feb., 1715. Mentions children Mary Tucker, Barbara Pearse, Rachell Hamlyn, Elinour Parsons, Henry, Richard, and Thomas Hamlyn, grandchildren Abraham Maine, William and John Hamlyn, Sarah, Susan, and Peter Hamlyn.

Residue to son John Hamlyn, who is Sole Exor.

Proved 7th July, 1716.

NOTE.—See 17th Sept., 1669, *ante*

1719. Administration to the effects of John Fry of Plymouth, granted ——, 1719, to Margaret Fry.

NOTE.—The admon. appears to have been lost; the wrapper only in the bundle.

1721. The last Will of Honor Fry of Tavistock, Widow, 21st April, 1721.

She divides her property between her children Walter Fry, eldest son, Nicholas, Peter, and Priscilla.

Mentions grandchildren Honor Condy, Walter, Katherine, and Mary Fry, and daughter-in-law Elizabeth, wife of son Peter.

Residue to said daughter Priscilla Fry, who is Sole Executrix.

Proved 1st June, 1721.

1724. The last Will of Andrew Mortymore of Kingsteignton, Husbandman, 10th March, 1723. To kinsman Samuel Holman's three children by Mary Lange, his first wife, 1s. each. To brother-in-law, John Lange, 1s. To the two children of John Skeen, deceased, 1s. each. To Humphry Milton's two children, 2s. 6d. each, and to his wife Mary, " half my linen clothes." To Richard Prowse's four children, 2s. 6d. each ; to brother William Mortymore, 3s. To Mary Colman, widow, 3s. Residue to John Mortimore and Joan Redstone, who are joint Exors.

Proved 19th June, 1724.

NOTE.—Refer to Joan Mortymore, of Stokingham, 8th June, 1633.
The executor, John Mortimore, was probably identical with "John Mortimore the elder, of Shaldon," who had leasehold property in Kingsteignton. His will was proved Archdeaconry Exon., Aug. 22nd, 1764 (*ante*). He left, with other issue, a son, Joseph Mortimer, of Shaldon, whose granddaughter, Charlotte, married Granville. The mention of " Humphry Milton's children " points to a connection with the " Mortymores " of Stokingham.

1741. The last Will of Edward Sinegar of Plymouth, H.M. ship "Grafton," 28th Feb., 1739. Makes his brother, John Sinegar of Mortlake, universal legatee and Sole Executrix.

Proved 17th April, 1741.

1741. The last Will of Edward Fry, His Majesty's ship "Orford," makes his beloved friend Joan Pasco, spinster, universal legatee and Sole Executrix, dated 13th July, 1740.

Witnessed by Edward Deeble, Mayor of Plymouth.

Proved Oct. 20th, 1741, by Joan Fry, widow, formerly Pasco, the Executrix, mentioned therein.

1743. Admon. to the effects of Walter Fry of Tavistock, granted 16th Nov., 1743, to Rebecca his widow.

1745. Admon. to the effects of Thomas Sing of Halwill, granted 17th Dec., 1745, to " Mary, wife of Moses Ham, his niece through his sister."

1751. Admon. to the effects of John Fry of Holsworthy, deceased, granted 7th May, 1751, to Jane, his widow.

1754. The last Will of Frederick Fry of the town of Plymouth, 4th July, 1746.

He leaves his gold ring and silver watch to his son Frederick.

To his "disobedient and undutiful" son and daughters George, Catherine, and Grace Fry, 1/- each.

Residue to brother-in-law Bampfylde Collins of Fowey, in trust for testator's four daughters Mary, Elizabeth, Amelia, and Sarah Fry.

Executor, in trust, said brother-in-law. Said daughter Mary to be Overseer.

Proved 6th July, 1754, by said daughter Mary, described as a "minor" in the will.

1760. The last Will of Walter Hamlyn of Widecombe-in-the-Moor, 21st May, 1756.

To son Walter Hamlyn he leaves the "Southaway" property during the lives of said Walter and daughter Jane, wife of William Medland.

To grandchildren, sons of deceased son Elias, John, Walter, and Thomas, an annuity of 40s. each in charge of their mother Mary Hamlyn; 20s. per annum each to daughters Mary Hamlyn, Jane Medland, and Margaret, wife of James Cornish.

Residue to wife Mary, who is Sole Executrix.

Seal of Hamlyn arms.

Proved 2nd Feb., 1760.

1760. Admon. to the effects of Frederick Fry of Plymouth, sailor H.M.S. "Iris," granted May 8th, 1760, to Mary his sister. Under £20.

1760. Admon. to the effects of John Tooker of Stoke Damarell, granted 23rd May, 1760, to Anne his widow.

1760. Thomas Mortimore of Plymouth, 13th April, 1760. He leaves all his houses in Plymouth, situate in Lower Lane and elsewhere, to sister-in-law Judith Mortimer and her heirs for ever.

Residue to said Judith, who is Sole Executrix.

Proved 9th June, 1760.

1760. The last Will of John Tucker of Buckfastleigh, 18th June, 1760.

To Daniel Bury of Moreton, £37 in trust for testator's daughter Mary at the age of 20 years.

To son John Tucker, gold watch. To father-in-law Samuel Chaffe, the £30 in trust for said son John, and £30 for daughter Elizabeth.

To brother William Tucker, "my best coat, two waistcoats, and my best breeches."

Residue to wife Philippa, who is Sole Executrix.

Proved July 16th, 1760.

1760. Thomas Tucker of Handsknoll, in the parish of Slapton, 16th Dec., 1758, desires to be "buried in a decent, handsome, Christian-like manner, and when I am so interred it is my will and desire that a tomb be erected or built upon my body." To the poor of Slapton, 30s. To wife Mary, the best bed and crocks. To son Thomas, £40; and to daughter Mary, £150. To nephew John Tucker, tenement at Burleston, in parish of Blackawton "for two years succeeding my death."

Residue to said nephew John Tucker, Nicholas Helmer of Charleton, and George Jellard the younger, for benefit of sons Thomas and Henry Tucker at 21.

Residue includes freehold lands in Blackawton, which are to revert, failing issue, male or female, to brother John Tucker's children.

The Trustees are joint Exors.

Proved 20th Sept., 1760.

1765. The last Will of Hannah Hamlyn of Widecombe-in-the-Moor, Spinster, 1st Dec., 1760.

She mentions her brothers Hugh and Edward, her "cousins" Joan, daughter of Edward Hamlyn, and Hannah, wife of George Wycott.

Residue, including "lands, hereditaments, messuages, &c," to "cousin" William, son of brother William Hamlyn, to "cousin" Hannah, and to Hannah, daughter of George Wycott, in equal shares. They are joint Exors.

Proved 15th May, 1765.

NOTE.—Testatrix was a sister of William Hamlyn of Dunstone, who had died 1736. "Cousin," really nephew. William, was a posthumous son and heir, who ultimately sold this ancestral manor, and died in 1782.

1767. The last Will of Mary Tucker of Blackawton, Widow, 29th Dec., 1755.

She leaves to Crispin Tucker of Harbertonford her leasehold interest in an estate called Clovelly, in Slapton, charged with annuities of 40s. to Thomazine, wife of William Mitchell of Halberton, and Rosa Pike of Stokefleming, widow.

She bequeaths to the overseers of the poor of the parish of Blackawton, and their successors, for ever, the annual sum of 40s. at Christmas in trust, to distribute it amongst such poor persons of the said parish as are not in receipt of monthly or other relief. The said annuity to issue out of land situated at Lupridge, in County of Devon, which she had recently purchased of Richard Hingston, thatcher, of Blackawton ; and subject to this annuity, and not otherwise, she devised the said estate in fee simple to Walter Square of Brixham, his heirs and assigns.

Proved Aug. 27th, 1757.

NOTE.—This gift was void by the Mortmain Act of 9th George II., c. 36, and is unnoticed by the Charity Commissioners. It should have been made by deed dated twelve months before the date of donor's death, and enrolled in Court of Chancery.

1774. Admon. to the estate of William Hamlyn of Widecombe-in-the-Moor, granted 6th Dec., 1774, to Francis his son, Agnes, the widow, having renounced.

1776. Admon. to the effects of Ann Hamlyn of Widecombe, granted 26th Aug., 1776, to her mother Ann, wife of Hugh Hamlyn of Blackslade.

NOTE.—Hugh Hamlyn, son and heir of Hugh Hamlyn and Mary Leaman, was the eldest brother of the John Hamlyn who settled at Brent.

1778. Admon. to the estate of Edward Hamlyn of Scobbetor, in the parish of Widecombe, deceased, intestate, granted 14th Feb., 1778, to Ann his widow.

NOTE.—The maiden name of the widow may have been Wakeham, as Elizabeth Wakeham of Totnes, spinster, probably her sister, joins the bond of obligation.

Deceased had a leasehold interest in the Scobbetor estate, terminable on the life of his eldest brother William Hamlyn of Dunstone. They were the uncles of John Hamlyn, who, having sold his inheritance in Widecombe, removed to Brent, and died there. See will, *post*, June, 1806.

1783. The last Will of Walter Hamlyn of Widecombe-in-the-Moor, 8th April, 1783. He leaves his wife Ann an annuity of £8 to issue out of "Wooder"; to second and fourth sons, John and James, £100 each. To daughter Mary, wife of Digory Hill, of the county of Cornwall, £100.

Mentions an illegitimate son, the child of one Margaret Steer, who is entitled to "a legal settlement" at Bovey Tracy.

He leaves the Wooder estate to son Thomas and his heirs in fee-simple. To son Richard, East Southway, in Widecombe. His "little mare" to John, son of said son John Hamlyn. Residue to wife Ann, who is Sole Executrix.

Sealed with the Hamlyn arms (see *post* June, 1806).

Proved 16th April, 1783.

NOTE.—Testator was the descendant of the third son of Robert Hamlyn of Dunstone, etc., who died 1556.

1787. The last Will of George Mortimore of North Bovey, 13th May, 1786.

He leaves the "Cumbe" estate in said parish to his four daughters Anne, Mary, Joan, and Elizabeth, in fee simple.

Legacies to "three children of daughter Ann; to John German and George Mortimore German, sons of daughter Mary; to granddaughters Elizabeth and Grace Richards; to be paid them by daughter Joan."

"The lands in Ashburton belonging to daughter Elizabeth to go after her death to her two daughters, Grace and Elizabeth Richards."

Trustee, son-in-law Richard Eastabrook.

To grandson John French, son of daughter Elizabeth.

Residue to daughters Mary and Joan, who are joint Exors.

Proved 19th Nov., 1787.

1806   The last Will of John Hamlyn of South Brent, dated 6th June, 1805, with codicil dated 3rd Jan., 1806.

Exor. and residuary legatee, son Joseph Hamlyn. Proved 6th June, 1806.

NOTE.—Testator was the second son of Hugh Hamlyn of Blackslade, in the parish of Widecombe, and younger brother of Hugh Hamlyn, also of Blackslade, who died without issue male. The executor, Joseph Hamlyn, was the grandfather of the Hamlyns now settled at Buckfastleigh. They are the direct descendants of Robert Hamlyn of Blackslade, lord of the manor of Dunstone, etc., who died 6th April, 1556. See their pedigree, "Visitations of the County of Devon," edited by Vivian. Their ancestor, referred to in the Domesday Record as "Hamelinus," held much property in Devon and Cornwall at the period of the survey, and his posterity became settled at Widecombe-in-the-Moor between the years 1187-1200. See Hamlyn Wills in Part I.

See also my "Suburbs of Exeter," pp. 187-202, for the history of this ancient stock in its several branches, and further notice of the family in part iii *post*.

Arms—*Gules*, a lion rampant, *ermine*, crowned, *or*.

1825. George Hamlyn the elder of Widecombe, 29th March, 1823.

Mentions son George, grandsons Elias and John, daughters, the wives of William Norris of Buckland and John Hodge of Christow. Residue to wife Mary, who is Sole Executrix.

Proved 29th Aug., 1825.

PART II.

CONSISTORIAL COURT.

1556. The last Will of Nycholas Mortymore of "Sampford Swythene" (Sandford, nigh Crediton), 12th Dec., 1556. Bequeaths his "soul to Almighty God and our Lady the Virgin, and to all the Holy Company of Heaven." To the "High Cross," 20d. To son John, six silver spoons; son Davye, a littell crocke, and a four gallon panne, and three silver spoons; to daughter Agnes, a white panne of five gallons; to Margaret Parkhouse, a five gallon panne. Like bequests to Edward and Joane Mortymore. Residue to wife Joan, who is Sole Executrix.

Witnesses, "Sir William Tristamb, John Vilvayne, James Mortymore.

"To Christey Hop, I owe 12s.; to John Mortymer, 40s."
Proved 19th Feb., 1556.

1558. The last Will of James Mortymer of Sandford, 19th Oct., 1558. To be buried in parish church, and leaves to the maintenance thereof two sheep.

He disperses the residue of his flock between his "godchildren" John Mortymer the younger and Ebbot Rowe. To John Hokeridge, £3 6s. 8d.; to Nicholas Tree, 33s. 4d.

Residue to son John Mortymer, "he to dispose of part of my goods for the wealth of my soul, and the rest for the preservation of his bodye."

Witnesses, Sir Thomas Lobone, clerk, and Thomas Mortymer.
Proved 15th Nov., 1558.

" Robert Gye, Gentleman," is a trustee.

1576. The last Will of John Mortemere of Brydgend, in the parish of St. Wynnowe, 4th May, 1575. To the poor men's box, one sheep. To eldest son John, a table board, the best I have, and six silver spoons.

Mentions other sons Nicholas and Richard, and grandsons Thomas and John, children of said John.

Residue to wife Johane, who is Sole Executrix.

Witnesses, Edward Battyn, curate of "Lostwythell," with others.

Proved 30th May, 1576.

1594. The last Will of Christian Bremridge, Widow, of Kerton, in County of Devon, dated 7th April, 1564. She provides for daughters Thomasine and Mary.

Mentions "brothers" John Ware and Nicholas Leache.

Proved —, 1594.

NOTE.—Testatrix was widow of John Bremridge of Bremridge in Sandford, nigh Kerton, otherwise Crediton. Her son and heir, John Bremridge of Bremridge, had pre-deceased her about 1581. Her great grandson, William Bremridge of Bremridge aforesaid, was aged 21 in 1598, as shown by Inq. P.M. on death of his father John.

See note on Bremridge family, p. 189, *ante*; and part iii. *post*.

1637. Administration to the effects of James Peter of Marldon, granted April 20th, 1637, to Alice Peter, Widow.

Gilbert Peter and Abraham Langdon join the bond.

1660. The last Will of Joane Grinfeld of West Teignmouth, 11th April, 1659.

She desires to be buried as near her husband as convenient.

Legacies to grandson William Smith; daughter Joane Bearne; son Richard Grinfeld; daughter Mary Grinfeld. She also mentions Wilmot and Ellen Cocke; daughter Ellin Smyth; and there are legacies to Thomas and John Stephen and to Mary Martin.

Residue to son William Grinfeld, who is Sole Exor.

Proved 29th Jan., 1660.

1660. Administration to the effects of Roger and Richard Grenfield, late of West Teignmouth, granted 25th Jan., 1660, to Mary, wife of Henry Martin of the same parish.

1663. The last Will of William Adams, the elder, of Paignton, 20th June, 1650.
Legacies to wife Joane; sons Michael, William, and John; granddaughter Agnes Adams.
Proved 6th Oct., 1663.

1663. The last Will of William Greenfeild of West Teignmouth, son and Exor. of Joane Grinfeld (whose will was proved 29th Jan., 1660, *ante*), dated 6th October, 1663.

He leaves his property in said town, and at Holcombe, to the child his wife may possibly bear after his death, and, failing such issue, to the children of his sisters Ellin Smith, Joane Bearne, and Mary Martin.
Residue to wife Elizabeth, who is Sole Executrix.
Proved 30th Oct., 1663.

1670. The last Will of William Adam of Stoke Gabriel, 6th July, 1669.
Legacies to Penelope Adam, to son John and to daughter Mary Adam.
Proved 7th April, 1670.

1674. Admon. to the effects of John Tossell of Morchard Bishop, granted 20th Nov., 1674, to grandson John Beare, daughter Elizabeth Comyns having renounced.
Account exhibited by said John Beare, 18th May, 1675, after debts paid, &c., &c. Balance of personality, £24 9s. 2d.

1677. Admon. to the effects of William Adams of Stoke Gabriel, granted Jan. 20th, 1687-88, to Eleanor Adams, Widow.
Henry Adams joins the bond.

1677-78. The last Will of William Adam, the elder, of Stoke Gabriel, 19th June, 1677.

Mentions "wife." Legacies to son George and to daughters Joan Bartlett and Ellenor Churchward.

Residue to son-in-law Thomas Bartlett, who is Sole Exor.

Proved 5th Feb., 1677-78.

1688. Admon. to the effects of William Adam of Paignton, granted 10th May, 1688, to Margaret his widow. William Penny, yeoman, joins the bond. Inventory by Nicholas Bound, yeoman, and Toby Belfield, clothier, both of Paignton.

NOTE.—The Belfields subsequently acquired property at Paignton, known as "Primley," by marriage with Finney, and also the manor, or reputed manor, of Leworth, in the parish of Hatherleigh. In Paignton Church are memorial inscriptions for Matthew and Protodorus Finney, 1731 and 1734, and for Allan Belfield, A.D. 1800. The latter endowed a school at Paignton with the sum of £1,000. Mr. John Finney Belfield, son of the Rev. Finney Belfield, succeeded to Primley and other property at Paignton in 1858. Query, whether the above deceased "William Adam," was identical with the William Adams buried at Paignton 1687, whose extraordinary escape from the Algerine pirates in an open boat has been recorded by Nathaniel Wanley, M.A , in his "Wonders of the Little World " (London, folio, 1678).

1689. The last Will of Tristram Fry of Bishop's Tawton, 17th Sept., 1688.

Legacies to Joane, daughter of Francis Vighill (?), widow.

To daughter Margaret and son John; to kinswoman Penelope Langdon.

Residue to Francis Uphill, who is Sole Executrix.

Proved 4th Jan., 1689.

1708-9. The last Will of John Ford of Stoke Gabriel, dated 3rd Dec., 1707.

Legacies to sister Agnis Doust, to John Doust, to sister Margaret Ford, and to mother Jane Ford.

Witnesses, Francis, Nicholas, and Richard Shepherd.

Proved Feb. 6th, 1708-9.

1716. The last Will of Martin Grenfield, otherwise Granville, of Northill, in the County of Cornwall, Feb. 18th, 1713.
He leaves Mary Nott and her three children £10 each. William, Sarah, Mary, John, and Edward Nevill £20 each.
Mentions wife.
Residue to Robert Nevill, who is Sole Exor.
Administration granted to Mary Nott, 22nd June, 1716, vice Robert Nevill, who renounced.

1729. The last Will of Simon Worth, 14th April, 1726.
To brother John Worth, Esq., £20, and a like sum to said brother's wife.
To Rev. Thomas Worth, £20, and to his present wife, £30.
To Gartrude and Thomasine Worth, daughters of the latter, £80 each.
To sister Gartrude Adams, £40, and to nephew John Worth, £20.
To sons and daughters of John Worth, Esq., £150.
Residue to niece Margaret, daughter of said Rev. Thomas Worth, who is Sole Executrix.
Proved 20th March, 1729.
Seal—The Worth arms, crest, and mantling.

NOTE.—Testator, who resided at Falmouth, was a younger son of John Worth, of Worth in Washfield, and of his wife, Thomasine Calmady of Wembury, whose mother was a daughter of Sir Richard Buller. His brother John's wife, a beneficiare under the will, was the daughter and heir of John Furse of Morshead, in the parish of Dean Prior. See her will, p. 45, *ante*
The "Rev. Thomas Worth" was testator's brother-in-law, and first cousin, he was a canon residentiary of Exeter Cathedral and Rector of Washfield and of High Bickington; he died 1737.

1729. The last Will of John Grenfeild of Falmouth, Yeoman, 4th Jan., 1728.
To son-in-law William Pearce of Falmouth, baker, and Jane his wife, 1s. each.
To grandson George Doubt the younger, son of George Doubt of Falmouth, mason, £5. Mentions grandchildren William, John, Andrew, Richard, Jane, and Dorothy Pearse.
To wife Phillippa Grenfeild, an annuity of £6.

Residue to son John Grenfeild, then under age, who is Sole Exor.
Proved at Penryn in Cons. Ct. of the Bp., Exon., 25th April, 1729.

1731. The last Will of John Sanger of Bishop's Nympton, 28th April, 1731.
To five poor people of said parish, and to a like number in Mariansleigh, 20s., *i.e.*, 2s. each.
He leaves his lands, etc., in Rose Ash and North Molton to son John and his heirs. Legacies to wife Mary; to daughter-in-law Mary Sanger; to brother Roger Sanger; to cousin Joan, daughter of John Galland of Rose Ash. To daughter-in-law Susannah Sanger "my hackney horse." To granddaughter Susannah Sanger, and to Mary, daughter of son Jonathan.
Residue to said younger son Jonathan Sanger, who is Sole Exor.
Proved 2nd March, 1731.

1731. The last Will of Richard Phillips of Marldon, Yeoman, 7th May, 1730. Legacies to grandsons Thomas and William Bartlet and to granddaughter Elizabeth Bulley. He leaves wife Margery "ye whome tenement of Compton Poole." He leaves son-in-law Thomas Bartlet 1s., and other landed property to daughter Elizabeth Bartlet and to son Richard Phillips.
Residue to said son Richard, who is Sole Exor. Proved March 31st, 1731.

NOTE.—Compton Pole, in Marldon, anciently the property of the Comptons, passed by the marriage of Alice, daughter and heir of Angier Fitz-Martin de Compton, to Sir Maurice de Pole, Kt. Their granddaughter and heir, Alice Pole, married Hugh Peverell of Leigh, and left two daughters co-heirs; the one, Johane, married Ralph de Doddescombe, the other Peter or Petre. The latter was maternal ancestor of the Gilberts of Compton Castle. Compton Pole, and Leigh, afterwards known as Doddescombleigh, belonged to Sir John Doddescomb in 1347. One of his daughters and co-heirs, Cicely, married Richard Worthe of Worth, and Compton Pole descended with the Washfield property until the time of Thomas Worthe of Worth, who left it to his younger grandson, Roger Worthe, Mayor of Exeter, 1482, but who was of Compton Pole and Doddescombleigh before 1464. From the latter date Compton Pole continued to be the principal residence of the second house of Worth down to the middle of the seventeenth century, when it was sold by John Worthe of Compton, about 1650. In consequence of a marriage with Bodley, cousin of the founder of the Bodleian library, Mr. Worthe's immediate predecessors had then sometime removed to Crediton and Exeter. See *ante*, p. 21.

Roger Worthe was *uncle*, not "brother," of Anthony Worth of Worth, as by a slip appears in the text note, *ante*, p. 103.

1741-42. Nicholas Adams of Marldon, Mariner, dated 8th Nov., 1778. Legacies to brother John Adams; to Susannah Bartlet, spinster; to Nicholas, son of Henry Braddon of Harberton; and Mary his wife. Residue to Mary, wife of said Henry Braddon, who is Sole Executrix.

"Rawleigh Gilbert," a witness.

Proved March 12th, 1741-2.

1760. Richard Fry of Sandford, nigh Crediton, 14th April, 1760. Mentions wife Margaret, and son John Fry.

Trustees, John Law and Robert Snow.

Witnesses, Susannah Greenslade and John Bragg.

Proved 9th Dec., 1760.

1763. Mary Sanger of Bishop's Nympton, 1st March, 1731.

Legacies to son Jonathan Sanger of Romansleigh; to Mary, daughter of son John; to Susannah and Mary, children of said Jonathan; to kinswoman Mary, daughter of Elias Bray of Rose Ash; to Mary, daughter of Lewis Pollard of "Marleigh"; to John Adams, sen., and Mary his daughter, both of Maryansleigh aforesaid.

Residue to son John, who is Sole Exor.

Proved 13th May, 1763.

1764. Admon. to the effects of Joyce Fry of Penryn, and County of Cornwall, granted 29th Nov., 1764, to John Tom, her kinsman.

1768. The last Will of John Sanger of Bishop's Nympton, 4th April, 1761. To wife Mary an annuity of £30. Mentions sons John and Edward, and daughters Mary, wife of James Loosemore; Ann, wife of Henry Smyth; and Jane Sanger. Proved 13th July, 1763.

1837. The last Will of Roger Densham of Middlecot, in Morchard Bishop, 4th Dec., 1836. He leaves his son Roger Densham all his lands, inclusive of "Hodges Middlecot and Wreford's Middlecot," both in said parish. Mentions wife Ann Densham, sons Richard and William, daughters Mary and Agnes; grandsons, children of said William, William, Roger, John, and Henry Densham.
Proved Jan. 18th, 1837.

PART II.

PRINCIPAL REGISTRY.

1413-14. The last Will of William Langeton, made at the Bishop's House, Manor of Clyst, 29th of January, 1413.

He desires to be buried on the right or left side of the tomb of Edmund, then Bishop of Exeter, in Exeter Cathedral, and leaves to the library of the said church five books, entitled "A Body of Civil Law," to remain in said library for ever. He bequeaths to the parish church of "Wellys," nigh "Walsyngham," in diocese of Norwich, one missal, one ordinal, and one book known as "The Apple of the Eye," as well as a set of vestments for priest, deacon, and sub-deacon, to be purchased by Exors. at a cost of £10. A set of vestments for priests, value 40s., to the parish church of "Rokeby," diocese of Coventry and Lichfield. The same to church of "Warbytton," and to Collegiate Church of Boseham, to the parish church of "Wysbergh" (Wisborough, near Billingshurst), all in diocese of Chichester. To Collegiate Church of Ottery St. Mary, diocese of Exon.

He leaves all the profits of his prebend of "Prustecomb," due at the time of his death, to the fabric of the nave of the Collegiate Church of the Holy Cross at Crediton, now ruinous (*jam fere ad terram prostrate*). A set of vestments to the church of Southpole, diocese of Exeter.

To the poor of the parish of "Wellys" (Wells next-the-sea) £3 6s. 8d., and to those of the parish of "Wysbergh," of my prebends of "Westbrok and Appeldurham," of the parish of "Warbytton," and of "my church" of Southpole, 20s. each. To William Pole, one silver cup, with its cover, standing on three feet in form of lions; to chaplain, John Wylle, "*ad orandum*," etc.; to the chaplains, clerks, and boys of the Episcopal Chapel at Exeter, £5; to the Bishop of Exeter's domestic servants, £5; to Margaret, wife of John Arderne, a scarlet jupon, trimmed with fur.

Residue to Exors. John Schute, vicar of Paignton ("Peyngton") and John Arderne, Esq., to be applied for two or three years to the education of "William Portour, my little son," and afterward "for the health of my soul and of those of all the faithful departed."

(The collated will is in Latin throughout).

Proved 7th Feb. 1413-14.

Under £212.

NOTE.—The "tomb" in which "Edmund, Bishop of Exeter" lies buried was evidently prepared some years before that prelate's death, which occurred 3rd September, 1419.

This prelate was Edmund, son and heir of Sir Richard Stafford, Lord Stafford of Clifton-Camville, near Tamworth, and was a relative, either uncle or cousin, of the reverend testator, who died on the same day his will was executed.

The Bishop had a brother, Sir Thomas Stafford, who left a daughter, the wife of Sir John Arderne of Elford; their son, John Arderne, was evidently the Exor. named in the Canon's will, and also his kinsman.

From between the hands of Canon Langeton's counterfeit presentment on his beautiful brass at Exeter, proceeds a precatory scroll, "Lord Jesu, do not judge me according to my act." That deceased possibly did not believe in the presumed celibacy of the clergy, is sufficiently evident by the mention of his "little son," for whose education he made due provision, although the expression "*filiolus*" as used by the clergy, has been held to bear a more spiritual signification. The cope on the figure of the deceased churchman is profusely ornamented with the Stafford knot.

1445-46. The last Will of John Carnell, Clerk, arch-priest of Haccombe, 11th September, 1445. Desires to be buried in the chancel of Haccombe Church.

He bequeaths 20s. and his "cow in calf" "to find a light for the image of St. Blase." Small benefactions for pious uses to the altar of St. Nicholas in Ringmore Chapel; to the fraternity of St. George in Stokeintinhead; and of the "Blessed Mary" at Combeintinhead; St. Michael, of Newton Abbot; St. Piran in Zabulo; the Trinity of St. Sithney;

St. Mary, of Camborne; St. Winnery; St. Michael; all in Cornwall.

For similar uses, he leaves his own "portiphory" (processional banner) and that of "Mr. Richard Olyver," to pray for his soul.

"Ivory white gown, trimmed with beaver fur," to George Doune.

Bequests to servant Henry Router, Mary, his wife, and to John Router, "*filiolo meo*" (see note to Canon Langeton's will, A.D. 1413, *ante*), to servant "Michael" and to Richard Doune.

An ivory white gown, trimmed with otter, and a cap of the same, to Sir John Lorde, chaplain. A blood colour gown and cap to Canon Sir John Byllyck, a gown of crimson to Canon John Stephens, of Holywell. To Richard, Canon of Coffinswell; John Jule, Vicar of St. Mary Church; Emma, mother of George Doune; Juliana, wife of John Vele of Kingsbridge; Alice, wife of Nicholas Stephyn of Exeter; Isabella, wife of Thomas Skinner of Dartmouth, small bequests.

George Doune to have eight marks per annum and a pipe of cider to celebrate for his soul continually in Haccombe Church.

Residue to said George Doune, Nicholas Stephyn, Robert Seaward, and Henry Router, who are joint Exors.

Proved 12th Feb., 1445-46.

NOTE.—The Arch-presbytery of Haccombe, one of the smallest parishes in England, with a population of seven or eight inhabitants, was founded in 1341 by Sir John L'Ercedekne, Kt., as an establishment for an arch-priest and five canons, who were, in fact, Chantry priests. The above Testator was admitted as "Arch-priest" upon the nomination of Sir Nicholas Carew (an account of whose family will be found in part iii., *post*), 31st July, 1434.

1594. The last will of Joan Fry, of High Bickington, 10th July, 1594.

Makes sister, Emma Fry, universal legatee and sole Exor.

Proved by Executrix, 20th July, 1594.

1601. (Memorandum). Administration to the goods of Matthew Fry, late of the city of Exeter, was granted in the Principal Registry, 20th June, 1601.

Admon. to the goods of Christopher Fry, of the City of Exon, was granted in the same registry, in 1703, but the bond is now missing.

1601. (May). The last Will, nuncupative, of George Mortimer, *alias* Tanner, of Pillaven, in the parish of Witheridge, Yeoman, 18th of May, 1601. His effects to be sold and debts paid, and the surplus over and above to be given to his "daughter" Margaret.

His sons, Lewis and Methuselah, to be joint Exors.

Proved 28th May, 1601.

1603. Inventory of the effects of John Mortimer, of Totnes, exhibited 10th September, 1603.

Extracts:—

"Item owing from Roger Mortimer	40s.
"One Cloke	£3.
" „ Doublett	5s.
" „ pair of hose	5s.
"Two hatts and hatt bands	20s.
"One rapier and ponyarde	6s. 8d.
"A girdle and paire of hangers	2s.
"A paire of busgyns	2s.
"Item in Allin Bartlett's hands, one golde ringe of three gymmes	15s.
"Item, five yardes of stripe stuff	12s."

NOTE.—"Busgyns."—From the reign of Henry V., Buskins, or short boots, called by the French *bottines*, may be traced. In the seventeenth century these wide-topped boots were generally used for riding, and they usually had a very curious clog or false sole, and were excessively high heeled, and must have been most uncomfortable for pedestrian purposes.

1608. The last Will, nuncupative, of Margaret Mortimer, *alias* Tanner, of Witheridge, Spinster, dated 29th March, 1608. She leaves her money to sisters Susan and Anne Mortimer, *alias* Tanner, and to sister, Frances Harwood.
Residue to brother Lewis, who is sole Exor.
Proved 4th April, 1608.
Refer to May, 1601, *ante*.

1617. The last Will of Andrew Mortymer of Sandford, 20th February, 16th James. He leaves "my wife" rent charge on land in Crediton and Cheriton Fitz Pain, terminable on the life of Thomas Mortymore, charged with an annuity of £5 to son, John Mortymer.

Trustees, in minority of said son, William Bremridge and Wm. Esworthy. Residue to wife (name not given) who is Sole Executrix.
Proved 20th March, 1617.

NOTE.—This Will was proved again, thirty-two years later, by "my wife's" second husband. (See *ante*, p. 189.)

1623. The last Will of Thomas Rattenbury of North Tamerton, in the county of Cornwall, Gentleman, June 24th, 1605.

All lands and tenements, situated in parish of St. Breage, to wife Marjory and to her heirs. To poor of North Tamerton, 20s., and to the churchwardens of the parish of Bridgrule in county of Devon, the sum of 20s., to be lent from time to time to some "poor man or maid" of the east side of said parish, born or married in it, for one, two, or three years, at the discretion of said churchwardens, etc., and so to be continued from time to time.

Bequests to godchildren Thomas Hooper and Francis Rattenbury, to daughter-in-law Mary Worther, and to sister Joan Bounde's children; to brother Edward Rattenbury, 20s.

Residue to said wife, who is Sole Executrix.

Overseers, brothers-in-law, John and Wm. Hooper. To be described on tomb-stone as "Captain Thomas Rattenbury.
Proved Nov. 11th, 1623.

NOTE.—The bequest of 20s. for the benefit of certain parishioners of Bridgerule is not noticed in the report of the Charity Commissioners.

1627. Memorandum that on St. James's day last past (25th July, 1627), John Mortymer of Exbourne made his last Will, nuncupative, in maner and forme followinge:—To daughter Mary he left one great crocke and one brass panne, and 40s. a year during the life of James Mortymer; her brother and the said James to be Sole Exors.

Witnesses, William Weekes, George Bond, Dorothy Baker.
Proved, 10th August, 1627.
Sum, £138 16s. 4d.

1631. The last Will of Nickolle Sanner of Buckfastleigh, Widow (no date). Legacies to Elizabeth, daughter of Peter Putteven and to Grace Putteven, inclusive of "one brason krocke and one limbricke thereto belonginge."

Residue to sons, Peter and Robert Putteven, who are Sole Exors.

No Act. Endorsed 1631.

NOTE.—The "Limbricke," properly Limbeck, derived from "alembicus"; *i.e.*, alembic was the distillatory appliance which fitted the crock, and was used for the manufacture of what was, and is, locally termed "still liqours," that is spirit from the dregs of cider.

1634. The last Will of John Mortymore of Faringdon, 15th May, 1634. Legacies to grandchild Abigail Trewant; to Mary, Edward, and Joan Streat; to Mary, daughter of son George Mortymer; to son Robert Mortymer; to daughter Grace Trewant; to son-in-law, Edward Streat, and Christian, his wife.

Residue to wife, Christian Mortymore, who is Sole Executrix.
Proved 11th June, 1634.
Witnesses, John Force and Richard Presforde.

1640. The last Will of Richard Grenvile of Norcott, in the parish of Poughill and county of Cornwall, Gentleman, 6th March, 1637.

Mentions wife "Garthered," daughter Grace Grenvile, and brother-in-law Lewis Enckledon of Braunton.

Residue to son, Chamond Grenvile, who is Sole Exor.

Proved 22nd May, 1640.

NOTE.—"Enckledon"—The Incledons of Inceldon, in parish of Braunton, were settled there as early as the year 1160.

Testator married Gertrude, one of the daughters of Lewis Incledon of Braunton, by his second wife, Wilmot, daughter of Andrew Pomeroy of Colyton. Her brother, Lewis Incledon, was of Buckland, in Braunton, an estate purchased by his ancestor "Godfrey Incledon, from Adam de Wickloe, in 1319." Testator was the second son of George, a brother of Sir George Grenvile, Kt., grandson of Digory Grenvile of Penheale, by his wife, Philippa Gough. Said Digory was third son of Roger Grenvile of Stowe and Bideford, known as "the great housekeeper," the direct descendant of Richard de Grenvile, Earl of Corbeil and Granville, in Normandy, son of "Hamon of the teeth." and the follower of William the Conqueror. (See my "Bideford" (Notes Genealogical and Historical), p. 21.)

1648. The last Will of Agnes Fry of Bratton Fleming, Widow, 14th May, 1648. She leaves the interest of her money, during their minority, to the two children of Thomas Reed; the principal, as soon as they have attained their majority, to be given to the poor of Bratton Fleming, unless said Thomas Reed undertakes the responsibilities of the estate.

Said Thomas Reed is appointed Sole Exor.

Proved 9th June, 1648.

NOTE.—There is no reference to such a bequest in the report of the Charity Commission.

1649. Admon. to the effects of Nicholas Sanger of Mariansleigh, granted 6th May, 1649, to Amy, his widow.

Sum £199 7s. 1d.

1672. The last Will of Robert Tanner, *alias* Mortimere, of Cruse Morchard, Yeoman, 7th November, 1672.

To the poor of Cruse Morchard, 20s. Legacies to Jesse Parker, to Sarah and her sister Jane (T. *alias* M.) of Crecombe; to Agnes Kelland, the elder; to John Handford's wife. To Robert Tanner of Crecombe, and to Jane Shapcot, a silver spoon each. To Grace Agnes (the younger), Mary and Jone Kelland, 20s. each. To Alice Webber, servant to John Bradford, the elder, of Poughill. To John Bradford, the younger, "one silver beare bowle." To John Tanner, *alias* Mortimere, of Cruse Morchard, £20. Residue to servant, Alice Thomas, who is Sole Executrix.

The gift of a silver spoon to Jane Shapcote is revoked by Codicil dated 5th January, 1672-73.

Witnesses, John Melhuish and John Bradford.

No act of Proof. Inventory exhibited 7th February, 1672.

NOTE—The witness, "John Melhuish" of Stockleigh, was brother of Thomas Melhuish, Esq., of Hill, in Cruse Morchard, who married Jane Courtenay; said Thomas was great-grandfather of that Richard Melhuish of Poughill Barton who married the heiress of Bremridge in 1775. (See *ante*, note p. 189.)

1674. The last Will of Henry Grenfeilde of Truro, Gentleman, 7th July, 1674.

He leaves his leasehold property in Kenwyn, held under Richard, Lord Arundell, and Hugh Boscawen, to his son Henry. Residue to wife Barsheba, who is Sole Executrix.

Proved 10th September, 1674.

1677. Administration to the effects of Philip Fry of Hatherleigh, granted 4th July, 1668, to Anthony Fry of Crediton, his son.

1697. The last Will of James Fry of Milton Damarell, 18th July, 1605. Mentions sons, James, Thomas, Henry, and William Fry; daughters, Barbara, Anstice, Mary, and Sarah. Residue to wife, Sarah Fry, who is sole Executrix.

Proved 23rd November, 1697.

1699. Admon. to the effects of Elias Sanger, of Mariansleigh, granted 22nd August, 1699, to Roger, his son. John Sanger, of the same, yeoman, joins the Bond.

1726. The last Will of Chamond "Granville," Rector of Kilkhampton, 29th Sept., 1720.

He leaves his brothers, Richard and John, 5s. each. Mentions his "Cosins" Gartrude and Catherine Granville.

He leaves Poughill Mills to kinsman, Robert Granville, after death of Executrix. Residue to wife Rebecca, who is sole Executrix.

Proved 11th Nov., 1726.

Seal—Three organ rests.

NOTE.—Arms of Granville, *gu.*, three rests, *or*. These arms are found on the seal of Richard Grenvile of Kilkhampton and Bideford, erroneously called "Thomas" in the Visit Ped., who died in 1204.

It will be noticed that Testator was rector of Kilkhampton (the right of presentation to which church had been established by Sir Richard Grenvile in 1242); he was grandson of Richard Grenvile (Will proved 1640, *ante*), and married Rebecca, daughter of Rev. A. Sleeman, *s. p.* "Kinsman Robert" of "Poughill Mills" was his nephew, son of brother Richard, a beneficiare under the Will, but who died some months before testator, April, 1725. "Gartrude and Catherine" were Testator's nieces, and sisters of said Robert.

1754. The last Will of Southcomb Sanger of Marleigh, 7th January, 1754. He leaves certain houses in Landkey to brother John Sanger, and his brothers-in-law John Hill and John Kemp, in trust for his daughter Ann, wife of William Mogford. Legacies to Elizabeth Zeal, and to Dorothy, Mary, and Joan Hill, and to John Hill, children of John Hill of Withypoole. 20s. each parish to the poor of Landkey and Marley.

Residue to brother John Sanger, who is Sole Exor.

Proved 1st November, 1754.

"Admon. *de bonis non*" of above, by John Sanger, the Exor., deceased, granted to John Sanger, 2nd June, 1788.

1788. Admon. to the effects of John Sanger of Mariansleigh, deceased, granted 2nd June, 1788, to John, his son. Under £300.

1794. The last Will of Diana Mortimer of Ringmore, St. Nicholas, Widow, 25th May, 1792. To brother Nicholas Watts, and brother-in-law John Mortimore, leasehold dwelling house, interest to pay the rents to daughters, Diana, wife of John Hugo of Newton, and Mary Mortimer. To said daughters and to daughter-in-law Elizabeth Mortimer, six guineas each for mourning. To sister Elizabeth Fox, £2 2s. Residue to son William Mortimer, and his heirs. Witnesses, Henry Bulley, James Crockwell, and Mary Owens.
Proved 10th April, 1794.

NOTE.—" Henry Bulley."—For note as to the Bulley family of St. Nicholas, &c., a branch of "Bolhay," of Blackborough Bolhay, see my "Devonshire Parishes," vol. ii., p. 267.
Testatrix was the second wife of William, brother of Joseph Mortimer, and of John Mortimer, named in the will.

1799. The last Will of Joseph Mortimer of St. Nicholas (Ringmore), Mariner, May 14th, 1768. He leaves his house with furniture and stock-in-trade, viz., "ships, boats, lighters, and craft" to wife for life, with reversion to daughter Mary, with a moiety of the "clay trade." To daughter Charlotte, his share in the new clay house at Hackney in Kingsteignton, and another third part to daughter Elizabeth. Remainder of all rights in above, with certain property in Kingsteignton, to son Joseph, and his heirs for ever.
Residue to said wife, Elizabeth Mortimer, who is Sole Executrix.
Proved 24th June, 1779.

NOTE.—Testator's daughter Charlotte married William Branscombe of Newton Abbot, and her daughter, Charlotte Branscombe, was the wife of Edward Granville. (Refer to Note, p. 285, and to p. 229 for the *Branch*. Son Hugh Mortimer is there *misprinted* "Sir.")
Testator died at Ringmore (Shaldon), March 7th, 1777.—Æ. 46.

DEVONSHIRE WILLS.

PART III.

SOME GENTLE HOUSES OF THE WEST.

INTRODUCTORY.

WE are told by an old writer that "by the custom of England, nobility is either major or minor. The first comprehends all titles and degrees from knighthood upwards, and the latter all from barons downwards." But, although families that can trace themselves to some forefather who *commenced* a pedigree at one or other of the Herald's Visitations have undoubtedly gentle position in right of "ancestry," such is scarcely superior to the status of those who have been made "gentle" by the operation of a modern grant of arms, and our "county gentry," as it is the fashion now to term, somewhat indiscriminately, all who happen to be provincial landowners, are by no means universally of real "gentle" extraction, or even position, at all, and, in the majority of instances, have certainly no claim to rank themselves amongst the "minor nobility," for such distinction can only be fairly claimed by those who are able to show their descent from such personages as, under the feudal system, held their lands directly from the Crown or under some great lord paramount—a stringent qualification which, it is to be feared, is too much overlooked at the present day, when it has come to be rather generally considered that anyone who can live without manual labour, even a tradesman apart from his business and in the seclusion of his suburban villa, is entitled to write himself "gentleman." But there are many, it is satisfactory to say, who are quite aware of the absurdity of this contention, and who are therefore increasingly anxious to ascertain their real claims to hereditary distinction or the reverse, hence it is that modern genealogical compilations are received with interest, and have their uses to searchers after truth, on account of the valuable information they convey from the necessarily unerring evidence of contemporary records.

However much people may be in possession of historic houses, or of ancient manors, by purchase from their original owners, the social position of the latter has by no means passed with their acres, besides which very many miscalled "county residences" of the present day are of importance only on the score of antiquity, their original owners having never had the least pretension to style themselves "gentlemen," and it may safely be added, any wish to do so either.

The advent of the House of Tudor was a death blow to the prestige of our ancient county gentry as a whole. A few families survived for ages, comparatively very few indeed have retained their ancient position and importance to the present time, hence it is that the genealogies of the "minor nobility" are not to be found, to any appreciable extent, in modern compilations upon "Landed Gentry" or "County Families." If for "gentry," the word "proprietors" were substituted, the first title would be much less misleading than the second. It is therefore in extension of my original plan that I have been induced to offer in the following pages a limited number of West Country genealogies. Some of the families I have selected in illustration of my contention, have perhaps not the same stake in the country that their ancestors enjoyed formerly; but, although their ancient local importance, like their lands, may have diminished in the course of centuries, they still have their long line of ancestry to rely upon, and can mostly claim the proud distinction of an inheritance of English minor nobility—a truly valuable privilege at the present day.

The feudal tenures ceased to convey much of their ancient importance upon their owners, primarily, in consequence of deliberate efforts of the Kings Henry VII. and VIII. to depress the great families and to create a new body of so-called "gentry," principally out of the higher orders of merchants; and the latter, as the late Professor Froude has observed, were thus "able to root themselves in the land by the side of the Norman nobility, first to rival, and then slowly to displace them." (See also my "Ashburton and its Neighbourhood," p. 150.)

These merchants recorded their pedigrees at the visitation courts, and thus founded what I may term modern gentle houses. Although the first "visitation" to ascertain the descent of families is said, upon the authority of a note to M S. Harleian, 1196, to have been held in 1412, many years before the actual incorporation of the Kings of Arms and Heralds, yet such courts were practically commenced by commission dated 20th Henry VIII. (1528-9); Cornwall, by Benolte, Clarencieux King of Arms, 1530, is one of the earliest. They are said to have been persevered in as a result of the dissolution of monasteries, which commenced in 1535, and which had hitherto been the repositories of genealogical records. Afterward they were continued at intervals of about a quarter of a century, in some cases as late as 1686. The Devonshire "Visitations" are dated 1531, 1564, 1572, and 1620 respectively. The *original*, of the several copies, of the last is preserved amongst the M.S. Harleian (British Museum), Nos. 1163-4.

Although these "visitations" are taken as legal evidence of descent, some of the pedigrees will not bear comparison with ancient family records, and, whilst the dates are often exceedingly unreliable, there are many positive anachronisms. Thus, in one pedigree, already sufficiently referred to in the notes to the foregoing wills (Worthe of Worth), Robert W., who is mentioned in a family deed of 1167, is made the *father* of his descendant in the *ninth* generation, Thomas W., who flourished in 1410, and there are dozens of similar instances that have fallen under my own observation from time to time.

All the gentry of the several counties were duly summoned to these courts by a circular letter from the Earl Marshal, addressed to the Lords Lieutenants after 1549, and were required to "register their arms, pedigrees, marriages, and issue," and the Kings of Arms and Heralds who presided were required "to reprove, confronte, and make infamous by proclamation all such as unlawfully and without just authority doe usurp or take upon them any name or title of honour or dignity as esquire or gentleman." There was, moreover, a special summons from the Heraldic Commissioners themselves directed to the bailiff of each hundred, commanding them "on sight thereof to require all knights, esquires, and gentlemen to appear before them personally, and to bring with them such arms and crests as they use or bear with their pedigree and descent, and such other evidence as will justify the same."

Doubtless, many families of incontestably social status regarded the whole system not only as a very great nuisance, but as a method of involving them in unnecessary expense, and therefore, as long as their general descent was sufficiently clear to satisfy the heralds, they did not trouble themselves much about detail, and hence both the omissions and anachronisms to which I have referred; at all events the officers of arms, who presided at these courts, do not appear to have taken the trouble to enforce absolute accuracy, and may well be considered, save in their refusals of *palpably flagrant misstatements*, to have looked chiefly to their fees.

Anyone who neglected to appear in response to an heraldic summons was liable to prosecution in the Earl Marshal's court, and to fine or imprisonment for contempt of its orders or decisions. Thus, down to the end of the reign of Charles II., the precise position of everyone was thoroughly understood, and anyone *who merely presumed upon a few generations of affluence* to assert "gentility" at a visitation court was not only registered as "ignoble," but had to pay the customary court fees for such a very unsatisfactory result, as is sufficiently evident by the lists of such "disclaimers," as they are called, which are found annexed to the "visitation" records. The "Feudal Services" were finally abolished by Act of Parliament of 12th Charles II., and English society has constantly become more and more "mixed" ever since the accession of William of Orange.

With respect to Devonshire, which is only exceeded in area by York and Lincoln, there are one or two families still resident upon their ancient properties for whom Saxon origin has been claimed, notably Kelly of Kelly (See *post*) and Coffin of Portledge; but the latter, although, as in numerous similar instances, their name has been preserved by royal license, has been long extinct, in *elder* male line at all events. The Chafes, formerly of Chafecombe and Exeter, undoubtedly held their lands from Saxon times, but were nevertheless of Norman origin; but their descent will be found on a subsequent page. The condition of the county towards the end of the eleventh century will be better understood by reference to my "Analysis of the Exeter Domesday," which I prepared originally for the 1878 edition of "White's Devonshire," and which has been subsequently included in fresh issues of that work. From this it will be seen that the Conqueror, who first arrived in Devonshire in the spring of 1068 and reduced the city of Exeter, then partitioned the land amongst his Norman followers, save in a very few instances, of which the manor of Kelly was, *to a certain extent merely*, an example. It was actually *given* to the King's half-brother, the Earl of Mortain, but it was held under the latter by a Saxon called Erchenbold.

Amongst the present landowners of the county, the name of Bastard only is identical with that of one of the Conqueror's grantees, "Robert le Bastard," but there is no actual evidence in existence that the owner of Kitley and Buckland Court is in reality his descendant. For a few generations Robert's posterity resided at Efford, one of the nine manors assigned to him by the Domesday record; but there is an hiatus of about a century and a half between the last Bastard of Efford and the "Thomas Bastard" who was registered as the *ancestor* of the family at the visitation of 1620. In the earlier visitations of the county the Bastards claimed but *three* descents from the *grandson* of this Thomas, and it is probable that the two generations in the later pedigree were a mere addition to the original visitation of 1564.

The Fulfords, still of Great Fulford, are, with the utmost probability, the descendants of the Norman sub-tenant of Folefort under Baldwin, Baron of Okehampton, and it is possible that the said "sub-tenant" was a brother of "Richard," who similarly held Belston under the same Baldwin, and that both were the natural offspring of the latter powerful noble. William Fulford was certainly of Fulford in the reign of King Stephen. His grandson married the great granddaughter of Richard of Belston, and the name of "Baldwin" has been constantly preserved in successive generations of this ancient family. (See *post.*)

The Fortescues and the Courtenays have been settled in Devonshire since the twelfth century, and a long chapter upon the Courtenay lineage and descent will be found in my "Suburbs of Exeter." By marriage they represent the lords of the two Norman baronies of Okehampton and Plympton, and, by maternal descent from the latter, still hold the Earldom of Devon.

Amongst those families which date their residence in the county from the thirteenth century, the names of Chichester, Carew, Cary, Fursdon, and Acland may be included, whilst the Cliffords, Calmadys, Woolcombes, and several others were not known in Devonshire before the sixteenth. Such names as Ashford, Arscot, Bury, Ball, Bidlake, Bruton, Cockram, Cooke, Giles, Haydon, Hele, Hunt, Herniman, Horton, Hulse, Melhuish, and, I may safely say, hundreds of others have long ceased to figure in modern works of "County" reference, but are by no means extinct nevertheless.

Amongst the "County Families of the United Kingdom," in a well-known and popular work, some four hundred names are set down in the portion assigned to Devon. For the term "county families," some other description might at the present day be more consistently substituted, or it should be properly extended to include all of ordinary position who may happen to reside in Devonshire. As it is, the list is necessarily full of invidious distinctions, although doubtless the whole of the families so described not only claim to be "county people," but are frequently disposed to assert superiority over such of their neighbours as may have escaped notice in the volume I refer to, but whose ancestors, nevertheless, were in many cases the landlords, and not unfrequently the absolute masters, of many of the pseudo "county families" of to-day. Out of the whole four hundred in the list referred to, the number that can truly claim the respectable antiquity of, let us say, three centuries, inclusive of those true " fathers of Devon " I have incidentally mentioned above, is considerably under forty ; and it is an unhappy fact that of the two hundred and odd families and their several branches who were of county rank in Devon three centuries ago, less than two dozen names are to be found amongst the present county magistrates. The majority of the ancient houses and manors have fallen, and are still constantly falling, into stranger hands. The descendants of their old owners are fighting the battle of life in the cities and in the colonies of this great empire, but are by no means either regardless or ignorant of their origin, and are ever increasingly careful to preserve it.

With these preliminary remarks upon the present social condition of the most popular of our English counties, for there are few that are not proud to claim connection with the land that produced " Drake, Hawkins, Frobisher, and Raleigh," with the land that, as an old writer says, "is inferior to few for worth, and only second (now third) for largeness to any in this island—extending from sea to sea, with Somersetshire and Dorsetshire for her friendly neighbours," I will proceed to offer my readers some particulars of a few of the most ancient houses of the west.

THE CHAFYS OF EXETER, CHAFECOMBE, AND ST. GILES IN THE HEATH.

The Chafys derive their name from their ancient heritage, "Chafecombe," now Chaffcombe, near Chard, which is the "ceaf cumbe" (in English, the light or breezy valley) of the Saxon period, and which was held by their ancestor, Hugo the

Thegn, or Thane, in the days of Ethelred "the Unready," and by his son, Raynald Fitz-Hugh, in those of Edward "the Confessor."

But although the Chafys can thus trace back with unerring certainty to a period long anterior to the Conquest, and so justify the assertion inscribed on the ancient tomb of one of them in Devonshire, as to his own identity with the "per-antiqua" race of the Chafes of Chafecombe (see *Post*, p. 326), yet they are not, paternally at least, of Saxon origin, which at once accounts for their continued possession of Chafecombe under Norman rule, for though their representative then nominally became sub-tenant under the Bishop of Coutance, he practically remained the owner of the land of his ancestors under the newly-devised feudal system. This was "Ralph Fitz-Reginald," the grandson of Hugo or Hugh, whose own names and those of his immediate posterity and their adoption of the Norman "Fitz" as expressive of their parentage, sufficiently prove that the long prevalent idea as to the "Saxon origin of the Chafecombe family" is as erroneous as the position of its earliest ascertained members in Saxon England is unique and interesting.

"Hugo," who is said by many of his English detractors to have been of "mean origin, and the son of a French churl," was the confidential adviser of Emma of Normandy, second wife of King Ethelred, and came to England in her train in the year 1002. It is a well-known historical fact that the constant incursions of the Danes, which marked that period, were secretly encouraged by the Queen, who detested the English and despised her husband, whom she had married purely from political motives. That her Norman follower was faithful to her, to her second husband, King Knut the Dane, and to her children, is shown by his retention of his property at Chafecombe under Saxons, Danes, and Normans, and although King Edward the Confessor had suffered for some quarter of a century by the interpolation of the Danish dynasty, he evidently recognised the fidelity Hugo had evinced towards his royal mother.

With the title of Ealdorman, or Earl, Hugo was sent into the West very soon after the arrival of Queen Emma. He had secret instructions, which he seems to have followed implicitly, and which resulted in the siege of Exeter by Sweyn, to whom the garrison, under the command of Earl Hugo, capitulated 19th August, 1003. The fortifications were demolished, the people were put to the sword, and the memory of the "Norman governor," who left with the besiegers, was long held in execration. Exeter was betrayed, says Hovenden, who wrote in the reign of Henry II., through "*perjurium, et proditionem, Normanici comitis, Quem Emma Domnaniæ præficerat.*"

The term "Ealdorman" was subsequently supplanted by "Thegn," and we next hear of Hugo as "Thegn of Chaffcombe" during the reign of Ethelred, which continued until April, A.D. 1016. His son, Reginald "Fitz-Hugo" is shown by the Domesday record to have been joint-owner of the "vill of Chaffecumbe on the day King Edward was alive and dead," that is to say on 5th January, 1065-66. He had also a separate manor in that parish, and other lands, quite independently of his joint holding. At the Norman conquest King William gave the whole of the Chafecombe property to his Chief Justiciary and powerful favourite, Jeffery, Bishop of Coutance, in Normandy, who, however, permitted "Ralph Fitz-Reginald" to succeed his father in the "whole township" as "sub-tenant." The latter's son, Robert Fitz-Ralph, succeeded to the lands held by his ancestor, Reginald Fitz-Hugh, and is described as "Lord of Chaffecumbe," and as holding lands of the King-in-Chief to the value of one knight's fee, in the reign of Henry I.

From the "Black Book of the Exchequer," we learn that his son and successor, "Ranulph Fitz-Robert," owned the manor lands together with the town of Chafecombe and the perpetual advowson and right of presentation to the parish church in the following reign, and that the Lord of Chafecombe in the time of Henry II. was Robert Fitz-Ranulph, who had a younger brother known as "Ranulph Fitz-Ranulph."

Robert, Lord of Chafecombe, had an only child, Agnes, who was "Lady of Chaffecumbe" in her own right. By her first husband, who bore the well-known Devonshire name of Avenel, she had two daughters, co-heirs, Emma and Margery. She married secondly one of the Justices in Eyre, John de Aure, and had by him a third daughter, Margaret, and a son, John de Aure, who died in his mother's lifetime and without issue.

The line of Emma of Chafecombe, the eldest co-heir, terminated with Idonea de Insula, her great-granddaughter, in the reign of Edward I. Margery had issue only by her second husband, Philip de Cantilupe, a family now maternally represented by Lord de la Warr, and well known in this county in connection with Broadhempston. Her son and heir, Balderic de Cantilupe, is mentioned in legal proceedings connected with the advowson of Chafecombe in 1275, being then in his minority. Margaret de Aure, the third co-heir, had two sons, John and Odo. They are also mentioned in law proceedings as late as the years 1294 and 1295.

Between these co-heirs and their representatives the lordship of Chafecombe seems to have become divided, although there was a certain amount of interpleading on the part of "Robert Fitz-Ranulph." The latter is the ancestor of the present race of Chafy and Chaffe; he was the son and heir of "Ranulph Fitz-Ranulph," already mentioned as younger brother of the Lord of Chafecombe and uncle of Agnes, the inheritrix of the property. His father had received, for his younger son's portion, "one carrucate of land in Chaffecumbe," as shown by existing documents. The son of Robert Fitz-Ranulph is especially noteworthy as being the first of the family who assumed a regular surname, which was, of course, derived from his property. As "Thomas Chafe" of Chafecombe, he was seized of land "of the inheritance of Robert, his father." He married Matilda, daughter of Andrew de Bosco (Anglice, Boys) of Knolle, Co. Somerset, and died in 1281. His widow recovered the custody of his son and heir, Thomas Chafe, against a certain cleric known as William de St. Esprit, in 1284.

This Thomas Chafe of Chafecombe married Christina, daughter and heir of Robert de Mandevill, youngest son of Geoffry de Magna Villa (Steward of Normandy in right of his mother, Margaret, daughter of Eudo Dapifer), by his wife Rohesia, daughter of the Chief Justice of England Alberic de Vere. Geoffry de Magna Villa was the first Earl of Essex so created by King Stephen and confirmed by the Empress Maud. He was afterwards in rebellion against the King and plundered the abbeys of St. Albans and Ramsey; ultimately, during a raid on a Kentish castle, he was shot through the head with an arrow, having discarded his helmet in consequence of the heat of the sun. His granddaughter, Christina Chafe, seems to have been dowered with lands in Somerset since known as Kingston Mandevill, and which were sold by her husband in or about the year 1310. She had two sons, the youngest being called Andrew.

The eldest brother of the last named left three daughters co-heirs, who divided the lands their father had held in Chafecombe about the middle of the fourteenth century. Their uncle, Andrew Chafe, who was seized of lands in Chafecumbe, seems to have died at Bridgewater subsequently to 1375, and his son, Thomas Chafe, is the last of the family who is described as of Chafecombe. He was living at Bridgewater in 1405, and his son, John Chafe, who succeeded him there, had also land in Devonshire, on which he is shown to have paid subsidy. He was alive at Bridgewater in 1413. His son, John "Chafie," who fought at the battle of Agincourt, left the property at Bridgewater to his son, also called John, who seems to have resided at Ilminster, and was the father of Richard "Chafy" of Sherborne, Dorset, who was also seized of the Somersetshire property in 1522, in which year he died.

This Richard "Chafy" had three sons, viz., John "Chafy" of Sherborne and of Holwell, Co. Somerset — the direct ancestor of the Rev. Dr. Chafy, now of Rous Lench Court, Co. Worcester; Richard "Chaffie" of Holwell, whose male line is extinct; and William "Chaffe" of Wellington, who also inherited property at Sherborne, and was the ancestor of the Devonshire branch of this ancient family. He had two sons, Robert and Nicholas. The latter's two younger sons, Peter and William Chaffe, acquired lands at Buckfastleigh, in this county, and were seized of them in the year 1660, and their name and race still flourish in that and neighbouring parishes.

The uncle of the said Peter and William, Robert Chaffe, resided in the parish of St. Petrock, Exeter, of which city he was mayor in 1568, 1575, and 1576, and he was also governor of the "Guild of Merchant Adventurers"—an important federation which was incorporated by Queen Elizabeth. His will, in which he mentions his birthplace at Wellington, was proved 13th August, 1580. He had been buried in the nave of Exeter Cathedral on 26th July. By his wife, Elizabeth Biggleston, he had five sons and two daughters. Of these Robert and George were both of Exeter, and were living there in 1605 and 1611; Richard, another son, was seized of land also in Exeter at his death, 12th May, 1596; and Thomas, the second son, resided in the Parish of St. Olave, in the same city. He married Dorothy, second daughter of John Shorte, of the parish of St. Petrock. His will was dated 24th May, 1604, and at his death he owned the parsonage of Constantine and the tithes of St. Winnow, both in Cornwall. His eldest son, William, died without issue in 1604. John, the second son, married Anne Mayho (and was father of Thomas "Chafe" of Sherborne; admitted of the Middle Temple, June 25th, 1631, to whom I shall have again to refer). Thomas, the third son, was of Doddescot, in the parish of St. Giles on the Heath. Besides these sons there were four daughters—Pascha, of whom presently; Elizabeth, who married John Mules; Dorothy, wife of Robert Biggleston; and Richarda (marriage license dated February 1st, 1611, "to be married at Penhoe,") whose husband, Humphrey Curzon, then of London, merchant, afterwards resided in South Street, Exeter, in a house recently removed, and which was situated on the right hand side of the entrance to College Hall, and in which was a shield of the arms of Curzon : *Arg.* on a bend between 3 wyverns' heads *sa.* 3 martlets? Imp. Chafe, *az.* 5 fusils in fesse *arg.*

Between Thomas Chafe and his third sister, Pascha, there appears to have been a very strong affection; and it was, perhaps, on this account that he took up his residence at Doddescote, a property with which he had no apparent family connection.

Pascha Chafe was the wife of Tristram Risdon of Winscot, the celebrated local antiquary, who, at the time of his marriage, 1608, had left Oxford, and had been at work upon his "Devonshire History" for three years. He does not appear at this time to have been particularly steady, or at all events during the few subsequent years, and did not succeed in acquiring the esteem of his mother-in-law, old Mrs. Chafe.

That lady made her will 23rd March, 1611, and was buried with her husband in St. Olave Church, 3rd October, 1612.

She describes herself as Dorothie " Chafe," widdowe, and leaves £5 to the poor of Exeter, and 5s. to the prisoners in the gaol of the Castle. She states that her late husband, Thomas Chafe, by his will gave all his silver plate amongst his children, to be allotted and divided between them at her discretion; and this plate, which must have been particularly handsome and valuable, she proceeds to apportion as follows :—

She gives to her daughter, Elizabeth Mules, a tankard of silver double gilt, with cover belonging to the same, and a double gilt silver goblet. To her daughter, Dorothy Bigleston, a tankard of silver with its cover " pcell guilted," a goblet of silver double gilt, and six silver spoons.

The next bequest to her daughter, Pascoe Risdon, must have afterwards formed a portion of the family plate at Winscot, and is therefore specially interesting. She gives her a white silver tankard with its cover, a "goblet of silver pcell guilted, a little trencher salt of silver double guilted, and half a dozen of silver spoons, with apostles' heads."

To her daughter, Richarda " Cursane," who, as I have previously mentioned, seems to have resided in South Street, Exeter, she gives her second-best silver salt, double guilted, with its cover, an ale cup of silver, double guilt, a "little silver bowle," and half a dozen apostle spoons. To her son *Thomas "Chafe,"* "a beere bowle of silver, a little ale cup of silver, and a little goblet of silver."

To her son John Chafe, she says, " I give during his natural life the use and occupation of my best salte of silver, double guilted, with the cover, a sack cup of silver, double guilt, and one white bowle of silver," with remainder to the son and heir of the said John, and in default to his eldest daughter.

Her son Thomas appears to have been the intimate friend of Tristram Risdon, and to have occasioned her no small amount of anxiety. He must have been much younger than Risdon, as the inscription on his tomb shows that he was born in 1585. He appears to have been educated for the law, and is described in the pedigree as a barrister; he took his degree at Exeter College, Oxford, but seems to have been both careless and extravagant, judging from the next paragraph in his mother's will.

After leaving him, in addition to the plate mentioned above, his father's gold signet ring and all his father's books, she adds: "Alsoe whereas the said Thomas my Sonne heretofore to my great greife and dislikinge, *in Ryston's manner*, hath most vainely wasted and consumed a farr greater porcion of my goods than my abilitie was or now is able to afforde him for his mayntenance, but now hath faithfully promised unto me reformacon and amendment of the same, therefore my will mynde and intent is, that if my said sonne doe nowe give over those his ill courses and practises wch he hath need with all other such lyke misdemeanors, and doth henceforth apply himself to learninge as he ought to doe, so as by reason thereof at the tyme of my death, by the opinion and judgment of my overseers hereafter named he shall be by them adjudged and thought worthie, uppon his amendment, and not otherwise, then I bequeath him £100 to be paid three months after my death." To this will her elder son, John, is executor, and administration was granted P.C.C., 3rd October, 1612.

The overseers were Philip Biglestone, her uncle, and Robert Chafe, her brother-in-law.

Whether Thomas Chafe reformed sufficiently to entitle him to the £100 I cannot say. He lived for many years subsequently at peace with his relatives, as shown by his own curious will, which bears date September 24th, 1648, and was proved P.C.C., 18th February, 164$\frac{8}{9}$.

He desires to be buried in decent and silent manner "some few hours before the candle doth inheritt the Suns office." He gives to the poor of St Giles 20s., and to his wife a mourning gown, and "his bedsted with the greene curtains while she lives."

To his niece, Mrs. Catherine Brookin, £20, and to her husband, Thomas Brookin, £5. He adds, "I would heartily acknowledge another niece, but her impious deserts deserve nothing for present but teares and prayers that she may prove second Mary."

He mentions his "dearly beloved" sisters, Mrs. Dorothy Biglestone and Mrs. Richard Curson. His nephews, Philip, John, and Thomas Biglestone, his cousin Peter, and his "gratious" cousin James Biglestone.

He also refers to his niece, Mrs. Dorothy Biglestone, and to his nephews, Thomas, John, and George Curzon. He gives his niece, Mrs. Mary Serrell, £6 for a "momento," to his "virtuous" niece Mrs. Margaret Yeo 20s., and to her good husband 10s., and desires "their noble goodness to accept of my myte." There are bequests to his loving niece, Mrs. Joane Serrell, to his nephew, William Ryledon, and to his friends, Arthur Rolle and Thomas Baylis, "a little piece of plate with my arms thereon," for the purchase of which money is devised to his executor. He leaves his nephew's wife, Catherine, £1 2s. for a ring with a death's head thereon, and he gives £40 to, and settles his plate upon, "my hopefull Godson and young nephew Thomas Chafe." He further requires his Exor. to inter his body "as neere as he can by my Sister Risedon, and I doe ordain appointe and require £30 rather more than lesse to be bestowed in a monument of my Effigies by my Executor, of whose love herein I am not diffident, who have reaped so many gratuities formerly from mee, and now in present burthening his conscience for effecting it as he shall answer Coram Deo. I desire him to inscript in my monument some memory of his good Aunt Rysedon, and of the family deceased there interred, also of my wife and her two children, no great onus to an ingenious, generous, and gratefull minde."

The executor and residuary legatee is his nephew, Thomas Chafe, Esq., councillor-at-law; and the will concludes with the following quaint words:

"This my last will and Testament written with mine own hande and soe well known that I do not greatly repute the subscription of Witnesses to strengthen it. And this my last will and Testament to corroborate and to make it legall I doe impresse my seale and subscribe my name the day and yeare above written.

"Vale T. Chafe, Scripsi."
"Item vale T. C. Laws deo pax Hominibus. T. Chafe de Doddescott."

In accordance with his uncle's injunctions, Thomas Chafe erected in the chancel of St Giles, and within the altar-rails, a high tomb to the memory of deceased, with his effigy thereon. The figure, with moustache and peaked beard, is lying upon the right side, the face supported by the hand, the elbow resting upon a cushion. The costume consists of a coif or skull-cap which entirely conceals the hair, a short cloak with tight sleeves, and which being open in front shows that the body is protected by a cuirass, frequently worn in those troublous times, fastened down the front with studs; breeches and long stockings gartered below the knee with roses or knots, and on the feet are low shoes similarly decorated. There *were* also two female figures, who probably represented the two children referred to in the will. Over the figure are three coats of arms. In the centre the ancient, but questionable, arms of Chafe, already blazoned, with mantling and crest: A demi lion ramp. *or*, holding between its paws a fusil, *az*.

On the dexter side; Chafe impaling Burgoyne: *As*. a talbot pass. *arg*. in chief a mullet.

And on the sinister side Risdon: *Arg*. 3 bird bolts *sa*., impaling Chafe.

During the "restoration" of St. Giles' Church, to which I have already alluded, this monument was taken down and removed from its original position to another part of the building. The two female figures then disappeared; and I understand that "they fell to pieces, and could not be put together again."

The inscription upon the front of the monument is as follows :

IN
PIAM
THOMÆ CHAFE
GENEROSI MEMORIAM

EX PER ANTIQUA CHAFORUM DE CHAFE COMBE FAMILIA IN COMITATU
SOMERSET
ORIUNDI EQ: COLLEGIO EXON. IN ACADEMIA OXON. ARTIUM MAGISTER VIRI
PROBITATE VIRTUTE AC INGENIO INSIGNIS QUI IN APOSTOLICA FIDE
CONSTANTER VERSATUS IN BEATA JUSTORUM RESURRECTIONIS SPE
ANIMAM EXSPIRAVIT XXV^{TO} DIE NOVEM^R ANNO SALUTIS 1648
AETATIS QUE SUÆ CLIMACERIO MAGNO
EXUVIAS SVAS EXUIT MEDICVS. UXOREM RELIQUIT MARGERIAM
FILIAM PHILIPPI BURGOYNE E CLARISSIMA BURGOYNORUM
PROSAPIA ORTI MATRONAM RELIGIOSISSIMAM BONORUM Q OPERUM
PLENISSIMAM
QUÆ ET OBDORMIVIT IN DOMINO —— DIE —— ANNO
A CHR^O. NATO 16— AETATIS VERO SUÆ ——

ABSTULIT A NOBIS MISERE QUEM FLEMUS ADEMPTUM
ABSTULIT E VIVIS MORTIS INIQUA MANUS
NEC CECIDIT SOLUS NAM Q ET PRUDENTIA VIRTUS
CANDOR AMOR PIETS INTERIERE SIMUL
TESTE VEL INVIDIA VITA LETHO QUE BEATUS
VIVUS ERAT DOMINI MORTUUS IN DOMINO.

The spaces left blank for Margery Chafe's death have never been filled in. She was buried with her husband 30th March, 1655.

Thomas Chafe must have passed his sixty-second birthday, since he died in the year of his "grand climacteric" (which was 7 × 9), and therefore in his sixty-third year. The inscription actually gives the age as 47, which is obviously owing to a mistake of the stone-cutter, who failed to enlarge the letters "u" in "medicus" and "x" in "uxorem," had this been done, the age would have appeared correctly—62. I have made the necessary alterations above, in view of the fact that the inscription has become very faint, and unless the words are recut, they will speedily become almost entirely obliterated. Chafe's sister, Pascha, had pre-deceased him, although she survived her husband, Tristram Risdon, for about six years. Her will was proved in the Prerogative Court of Canterbury, 10th September, 1647. It is dated April 21st, 1646, and in it she is described as "Pascoe" Risdon, of "Winscott," in the parish of St. Giles, and county of Devon, widow. She gives her son, William Risdon, "her heir and sole Executor," "the Manor of Winscott and the Barton farm & demesne thereof and all her other lands in Devon for ever." This bequest upsets the assertion of the authors of the additions to Risdon (p. 422, edit. 1811), who state that Giles Risdon (her eldest son, who had then been dead about two years) "inherited the estate after his father, and was succeeded by his brother William."

She gives her daughter-in-law, Mrs. Margery Risdon, two stocks of bees and her still. To "my daughter, Mrs. Joane Hearle, all my best woollen and lynnen apparel and my wedding-ring." To my grandchild, Margaret Rattenbury, £5 at sixteen years of age. Her daughter, Margaret, had died 26th of August, 1636, and her memorial inscription is given by Prince in the *Worthies of Devon*. She likewise leaves to her grandchild, Joane Hearle, "a bearing blanket and all my child bed linnen." There are also bequests to several of her god-children, and to John Maddcote, "godson of my husband, Mr. Tristram Risdon, deceased." The overseers are her nephew, Thomas Chafe, already mentioned, and her son-in-law, Mr. James Hearle.

William Risdon, of Winscot, the second son of the antiquary, proved his mother's will, and succeeded to the property at her death. He died in 1701, and was buried in St. Giles' Church with his family. He had one daughter, Mary, who by her first husband, John Prust, had one child, a daughter, who died in infancy. She was subsequently married three times—viz, to Amos Rolle, to John Holland, and to John Stafford—but had no issue by either of them, therefore Winscot ultimately descended to Joane, daughter of James Hearle and Joane his wife, the daughter of Tristram Risdon. This Joane, who by her grandmother's will is to receive "two bearing blankets," and other equally useful articles, became the wife of Edward Lovatt, of Corfe, in the parish of Tawstock, who was the sixth son of Sir Robert Lovatt, of Liscombe, in Buckinghamshire. Her husband gave a large silver flagon to the church of Tawstock. They had three children—Robert, who died without issue; Joan, who married Hatch; and Penelope, who was the wife of Sir Henry Northcote, M.D., the fourth baronet, and the present Lord Iddesleigh is now the representative of Tristram Risdon. Winscote, which descended in the Northcote family, has of late years become the property of the Hon. Mark Rolle.

Thomas Chafe, the Executor of his uncle's will, was, as I have stated already, the son of John Chafe, and of his wife, Anne Mayho. He survived until 1662, married Katherine, daughter of Sir Thomas Malet, and left a son and six daughters. The son, also called Thomas, acquired property near Sherborne, with his wife, Susanna Molyns, and went to reside at Folke. He was patron of the Rectory of Constantine, in Cornwall. The death of his only son, Molyns Chafe, S.P., in 1685, terminated the male line of this branch of the family.

Their ancestor, as I have already said, was William "Chaffe," of Wellington, who was the younger brother of John Chafy, of Sherbourne, who was buried at Stoke under Hamdon, 26th Sept., 1558. He was the father of Thomas "Chafye," of Sherbourne, whose grandson, "Robert Chaffie, of the same place, married Elizabeth, daughter and heir of William Hambridge, of East Coker, County Somerset, and niece and heir to Joseph Compton, of Yeovil. This William Hambridge was the second son of John Hambridge, of East Coker (who was twelfth in direct descent from Stephen de Hambrigge, Lord of Hambrigge, in Somerset, in the reign of Henry II.), by his first wife, Joan, daughter and co-heir of William Hemenford. (He married, secondly, Katherine, daughter of Sir John Sydenham.) Mrs. "Chaffie's" mother, Elizabeth Compton, ultimate heir to her brother Joseph, was sixteenth in descent from Walter of Compton, Co. Somerset, who held that property under the Bishop of Salisbury, at the time of the Domesday Survey, and whose younger great grandson, Martin de Compton, gave name to an estate in Marldon, Co. Devon, and there founded Compton Castle, which, with the heiress of Compton, passed to the Poles, and thence to Doddescombe, and ultimately became divided between Worthe and Gilbert. Through this marriage, the Chafys, who already quartered the arms of Boys and Mandeville, obtained the right to add those of Hambrigge,

Micheldever, Compton, de Alva, Newton, and Helpeston. Walter Chafe, of Sherborne, baptized there 28th December, 1653, was the grandson of the Compton heiress. He acquired the additional armorials of Scott, of Child-Okford, by his marriage with Ann Scott, heir to her brothers George and John Scott, of Sherborne. His son, John " Chafy," Rector of Lillingham, and of Purse Caundle, Dorsetshire, married Elizabeth, daughter and co-heir of Capt. John Corbyn, of Hazlebury Brian, and the direct descendant of Sir Philip Corbyn, Kt., of Corbyn, Co. Stafford, in the reign of Henry I., and thus acquired the quarterings of Corbyn, Brian (of Hazlebury Brian, Co. Dorset, *temp*. Hy. III.), De Cancy, and Warren. The Heraldry of the House of Chafy became repeated by the marriage of the younger son of the last named, the Rev. William Chafy, Vicar of Faversham and Sturry, and Minor Canon of Canterbury, with his first cousin's daughter Mary, daughter of John " Chafie," of Sherbourne ; their eldest son, Dr. William Chafy (C.C. Coll., Cambridge, Master of "Sidney Sussex," and Vice-Chancellor of the University, Chaplain-in-Ordinary to her Majesty the Queen, and to her three royal predecessors), married, 4th Dec., 1813, Mary, daughter and co-heir of John Westwood, of Chatteris, in the Isle of Ely, and the descendant and representative of William de Westwode, who was seized of lands in Lek, County Stafford, *jure uxoris*, 37th Hy. III. His wife was the daughter and heir of Clement de Dysteley, by Matilda, daughter and heir of Robert Fitz-John, the owner of the said manor of Lek.

Dr. Chafy was buried in Sidney Sussex College Chapel in May, 1843. He died, universally respected and lamented, on the 16th of that month.

Dr. Chafy, of Rous-Lench Court, Worcestershire, is the eldest son by his first marriage with Annette, daughter of the Rt. Rev. Samuel Kyle, D.D., Lord Bishop of Cork, Cloyne, and Ross, of the only son of the Master of Sidney Sussex College, who died in 1873.

Dr. Chafy was baptized by the names of William Kyle Westwood, 17th July, 1841, and assumed the additional name of Chafy in pursuance of a too loosely worded claim in the will of his grandfather, from whom he inherited a small property at Haslebury Brian, some scattered fragments of Chafy property in Dorset and Somerset, and an estate at Sheriff's Lench, in Worcestershire.

He graduated at Ch. Ch., Oxford; was ordained deacon in 1869, and priest in 1870. He was subsequently for two years curate in sole charge of Lydford, in this County; for an account of the church of that parish, see my "Devonshire Parishes," vol. i., pp. 220-248. Dr. Chafy, who took his D.D. degree in 1891, married, 2nd May, 1872, Mary Clara, the second daughter of the late Evelyn Philip Shirley, of Ettington, Co. Warwick, and Lough Trea, Co. Monaghan, the well-known author of the "Noble and Gentle Families of England," of the "History of the County of Monaghan," etc., and who was the great grandson of the Hon. George Shirley, of Ettington, fifth son of the first Earl Ferrers, who terminated the abeyance of the ancient baronies of Ferrers of Chartley, Bourchier, and Louvaine, his grandmother, Lady Dorothy Devereux, having been daughter and co-heir of Robert, last Earl of Essex, of the house of Devereux, from whom Mr. Shirley inherited his Irish property in Co. Monaghan. These baronies are now again in abeyance, between the representatives of the daughters of the eighth Lord Ferrers.

Dr. Chafy's son and heir, Hugh Edmund Chafy-Chafy, was born at Lidford Rectory, May 17th, 1876. He has also a second son and four daughters.

The arms used for many centuries by this family, "*asure*, five fusils in fesse, *argent*, a canton of the last," and which surmount the tomb already referred to in the parish church of St. Giles in the Heath, have been superseded, since 1822, by Dr. Chafy's predecessors. In pursuance of an Earl Marshal's warrant in that year directed to the Kings of Arms, consequent upon the application of the Rev. W. Chafy, great-grandfather of the present owner of Rous-Lench, a coat, which satisfactorily marks the descent of the Chafy's from Hugo, Thegn of Chafecombe, and his connection with the Saxon Earldom of Devon, the badge of which was a gryphon then, and down to the commencement of the third century after the Conquest, was granted to him and his heirs, and may be thus blazoned:—
Per pale *gules* and *azure*, a gryphon segreant, *argent*; on

a chief, engrailed *erm.*, three lozenges in fess of the second. Crest, on a mount *vert*, a peacock in its pride, between two palm-branches, all ppr.

HORNIMAN OF BRADWORTHY.

It is evident, from the fact that a certain portion of our coast was known as the *littus Saxonicum* during the last years of the Roman occupation of Britain, that some time prior to the evacuation of our island in 418 there had been periodical settlements in it of predatory Teutons from the neighbourhood of the Rhine and Elbe. These invaders, having settled themselves permanently in the country at various but uncertain dates, were of course subject to the Roman dominion, and took part with the Britons in their several struggles to throw off the Latin yoke. Thus it came about that there was a very considerable Saxon settlement established in this and other parts of the kingdom long prior to the arrival of the great horde of German invaders, in the first year of the Emperor Marcianus, A.D. 450, which was nearly seventy years prior to the actual establishment of the Saxon kingdom of Wessex by King Cerdic. That one of these so-called Saxon incursions was undertaken by the "Hermanduri" seems probable from the existence of the great Roman road known as "Hermin Street," which runs from St. Davids to Southampton, and the latter port was the favourite landing place of the several tribes of Saxon adventurers down to the arrival of the future King Cerdic at the close of the fifth century.

Thus a very ancient tradition as to the German origin of the Hernimans, or Hornimans, may be plausibly accounted for, and its strong probability may be very freely admitted ; but not so the period at which their migration from the European Continent has been usually fixed, or the supposition that the founder of their family in England was "a follower of Peter of Provence, the uncle of Eleanor, queen of Henry III.," who in such case must have settled here during the first half of the thirteenth century.

It is a significant proof of the very great antiquity of this family in Britain that their connection with the Saxon Manor, to which they certainly gave name, but not with the county, which has remained unsevered, had ceased apparently in the reign of Edward the Confessor. It is shown by the Domesday record that one of them held manors, under Norman rule, both in north and south Devon, notably in the neighbourhood of Totnes, in which a branch of the family have continued until modern times, and in that of Chulmleigh, where the name is still extant.

Amongst the property granted by King William to the Norman Bishop of Coutance was the manor of Hermon's Sward, "Hermondesuorda," and now known as Hermonsworthy, in the parish of Broadworthy, commonly called Bradworthy.

The Saxon word "sweard," as applied to the soil, signified that it was covered with grass; the affix "worthy," also of Saxon origin, that it was an enclosed estate; hence the name of such parishes as Bradworthy, Pyworthy, Hexworthy, etc., but I need not multiply instances of similar nomenclature.

When King William seized upon "Hermon's Sward," it was the property of Alward, the King's Thegn, who paid tax there for a sufficient quantity of arable land to occupy "two ploughs," exclusive of twenty acres of meadow, and five furlongs of pasture, two furlongs wide. The Bishop of Coutance sublet this property to the ancestor of the Drewes of Broadhembury and elsewhere, and in subsequent ages it was held by an old family known as " De Bosco," or Boys, *Anglice*, *Wood*, a member of which built a chapel upon it by license from the Abbot of Tor, and his male line became extinct in the reign of Edward III.

But although the "Hermons"—the name is, I should remark, variously written, Herman, Hermer, Herniman, Horniman, and Harniman, the latter spelling being in exact accordance with its customary pronunciation—had no special interest in "Hermon's Sward" in 1086, yet one of their name, "Hernan," which, allowing for contraction, would read Herniman, had been settled close to the old "Hermin" road, and had held the bishopric of St. Davids from 1023-1039 during the reign of Canute, and that the members of the family accommodated themselves to circumstances is sufficiently clear from the fact that, under

Norman rule, the Saxon landowner of the same name, who was, I think, clearly the progenitor of the Hornimans of the middle and later ages, was permitted to hold the three Devonshire manors known as "Nymet," near Sampford Courtenay, Washbourne, nigh Totnes, and another property called "Esprewi," under Norman rule, and to transmit them to his posterity, although, being a Saxon, he did not hold them directly from the king in chief, but under Goscelmus Brito (see "House of Brito," *post*), and another great Lord paramount, Walter de Douay, Baron of Bampton.

Thus much for the great antiquity of the race of Horniman, which I may now claim reasonably to have established. It is improbable that the immediate descendants of the Domesday sub-tenant, who doubtless founded the north and south Devon branches of the family, ever moved far from their first settlements, for we find them mentioned in the early parish registers both of Totnes and Sampford Courtenay, and in those of Winkleigh, South Tawton, and elsewhere, always of importance and consideration in their respective neighbourhoods, whilst their seventeenth century residence at South Molton took name from them, and was known as "Hernimans." This house stands on rising ground near the confluence of the rivers Bray and Mole, and in the midst of about a hundred and fifty acres of fertile land. Although it has been of late years divided into tenements for farm labourers, it bears evident signs of its ancient importance in vestiges of old oak panelling and similar decoration. One of its former owners, Luke Herniman, who died childless in 1686, was the son of Mr. John Herniman of South Tawton.

His ancestor, John "Hernaman," of the latter parish, dead before 1539, had three children, John, Thomas, and Ann, the latter married "Richard Wikes," October 30th, 1565, and the marriage of her nephew William Hernaman with Arminell, daughter of William "Weekes" of Honichurch, is recorded in the Herald's Visitation of Devonshire of 1620.

Her brother John's son "Henri" was baptized at Sampford Courtenay in 1559; one of her elder nephews by her brother Thomas, of South Tawton and Sampford Courtenay, married the one Maria Oxenham of Oxenham ; whilst the other, James

Herniman, was the ancestor of the Hernimans of Woodterald, in the parish of Winkleigh, and of his successors also at South Tawton.

The Totnes branch of this family, descended most probably from the Domesday owner of Washbourne, in the neighbouring parish of Harberton, were always of repute in South Devon, and held positions of confidence and importance. Their immediate ancestor was George, brother of Thomas Herniman, baptized in 1661, and their present representative is the Rev. J. W. Duncombe Hernaman, clerk in holy orders, son of the late John Hernaman of Clealand Hall, Sunderland, who was born in 1794, and was the son of William Hernaman of Totnes by his wife Elizabeth Lapthorne. A branch of the Totnes Hernimans migrated to Appledore, and have of late years been resident at Truro in the adjoining county.

Robert "Hernaman" of Wood-terald, a fair estate in the parish of Winkleigh, baptized there 15th October, 1598, was the father of John Herniman of Hernimans above mentioned, and also of William Herniman, who was born in 1619. The latter's son, of the same name, seems to have succeeded his cousin Luke at Hernimans, whilst the elder son, Robert "Herniman," baptized at South Tawton 1656, was the father of George "Horniman," who migrated to the neighbouring county of Somerset, and settled at Lydeard St. Laurence. The latter's great grandson John Horniman was the father of another John, who was born at Reading in 1803, and was one of the most eminent philanthropists of the present age. During a long life of ninety years, by close attention to business, and by unswerving rectitude, he not only succeeded in founding the great house known as "Hornimans," but amassed a very considerable fortune, and in addition to the large sums he similarly disbursed in his life-time, he left, at his death in 1893, no less than £89,000 in various charities. His eldest son, Mr. W. H. Horniman, still resides in the county adopted, as I have shown above, by his ancestors nigh upon eighteen hundred years ago. His second son, Mr. Frederick John Horniman now M.P. for Penryn and Falmouth, is the well-known owner and founder of the Surrey House Museum at Dulwich—a magnificent collection of art treasures, which is freely open to the public, and which will probably in the future be entirely dedicated to their uses. Although for some generations his own branch of this ancient family have been truly worthy and beneficent members of the Society of Friends, Mr. F. J. Horniman is an attached follower of the tenets of the Established Church, and munificently contributed £4,000 towards the new church of St. Peter on Dulwich Common.

The Horniman Museum is so varied in its character, so unique in its possessions, that few towns in England have anything to compare with it; it is the outcome of the labour and outlay of thirty years, and is distributed over no less than twenty-three rooms of a very capacious residence, behind which Mr. Horniman proposes to build lecture halls and technical schools before it is finally handed over to some public body for the exclusive good of future generations. If merely in memory of his father's charities and of his own beneficence, his name and history, apart even from its great antiquity, would have deserved commemoration in these pages; as it is, it must be admitted that no account of our old West country families could be complete without a somewhat extended notice of the race of Horniman. Mr. J. F. Horniman married, in 1859, the youngest daughter of John Elmslie of Dalston, county Middlesex, by whom he has a son and heir, Elmslie J. Horniman, born 1860.

The arms used by the Hornimans, *vert*, a lion passant guardant, *or*, between three annulets, *arg.*; and the crest a lion couchant guardant, *or*, beneath a palm-tree proper, were confirmed by Garter and Clarencieux, kings of arms to the family of Herman of Middleton Stoney, County Oxford, 10th December, 1630.

NORTHMORE OF CLEVE.

The Northmores of Cleve, in the parish of St. Thomas, nigh Exeter, are said by Lysons and others "to have migrated from Somersetshire," a statement which does not appear to have the slightest foundation in fact, and probably originated in the bequest by one of their collateral relatives, whose will was proved in the Prerogative Court of Canterbury, in 1411, of a considerable quantity of gold plate to the Church of St. Mary at Taunton. That a branch of the family long flourished in much repute in the adjoining county is as unquestionable as that their name, anciently written "Nordmoor," is derived from the residence of their Saxon ancestors upon the northern border of Dartmoor, in the parish of South Tawton, within which royal manor, held at the Conquest by King William, and which had been a portion of the dowry of Githa, the mother of Harold, a noble Saxon, called Alfric or Aluric, one of the higher or baronial thanes, had another "in partage" ("quam tenuit Uluricus pariter" are the words of the Survey) at the death of Edward the Confessor, and which was known as "Aissa" or Ash.

That the Northmores are the veritable descendants of this Saxon Thegn is as probable as their long connection with the manor of East Ash is certain; their first recorded nominal residence in the parish of South Tawton, however, under the name of "Northmore," was at "Wille," or Well, a residence now occupied by a farmer, and apparently of sixteenth century date, and which still exhibits the initials of Edward Northmore, 1600, and of John Northmore, " anno 1641," in one of its windows. This property is shown by an extant deed to have been granted by " William Ythel " (at Wille) to John Northmore, in the sixth year of the reign of King Edward III., A.D. 1332. On the 29th June, 1377, this John Northmore, or his successor of the same name, attested a deed at Tiverton. He was succeeded by Richard Northmore, who flourished between the years 1453-81, who obtained from Richard Wyke of North Wyke* certain lands in the manor of East Ayshe, already referred to, by deed dated 4th Edward IV., A.D. 1464, and they eventually acquired the whole manor, which manor, Lysons complacently remarks, "had belonged to the Northmores, for *some* years, in 1711." As Samuel Lysons was long " Keeper of the Records,' it is somewhat surprising and irritating to find that in this as well as in numerous other instances he did not trouble himself to be more precise and accurate. William Northmore

---

* See Wyke of Northwyke, *post*.

succeeded his father Richard in 1481, and was himself the father of John Northmore who was buried at South Tawton in 1577, and pre-deceased his mother, Joan Northmore, by eight years.

The South Tawton registers commence in 1540, and amongst the earliest entries I find the baptism of this John Northmore's son Bartholomew on February 24th that year.

He appears, however, to have been succeeded at Welle by his son Richard Northmore, who married Joan Southwood, or Southmeade, in 1567, and who was the father of Edward Northmore of Well, whose son (by his marriage with Philote, daughter of Edward Haywoode of Haywoode, in the parish of Bundleigh), John Northmore, was also of Welle, and was buried at South Tawton in 1671. This last John Northmore, who adopted the legal profession, and acquired a large estate, which included an eighth part of the manor of Okehampton, married Joan, daughter of John Stronge of Tor-hill, in the same parish, and left five sons and two daughters, married to Battishill and Weeks, both members of houses with recorded pedigrees.[*] I should have stated that Richard Northmore had granted to his son Edward above mentioned the lands of East Ash by deed dated 1587.

John Northmore of Well and of East Ash was the eldest of the five sons of John Northmore and of Joan Stronge. He was a lawyer, like his father, and also a magistrate, and long filled the office of town clerk of Okehampton, and married into an old county family, that of the Chudleigh branch of the Woolcombes, and died without issue in 1713. His next brother Edward, who was Vicar of Newton St. Cyres and of Chudleigh, predeceased him in 1687, so that his heir-at-law was his brother William Northmore, born 1639, who married, first, Mary, daughter and heir of William Knapman of Wonson, in the parish of Throwleigh, by which marriage he acquired that interesting property, and was also Mayor of Okehampton. In a panel of one of the rooms in the old house at Wonson there is, carved on panel, the semblance of an ace of diamonds, by which card this William Northmore is said to have lost the very large sum, in those days, of £17,000. However, his son succeeded to Wonson, and subsequently, as I shall presently

---

[*] For the marriage of Elizabeth Northmore with Richard Weekes, see "Weekes of Honichurch," *post*.

show, to Cleve as well. By his second marriage with a Miss Hutton, daughter of the rector of Northlew, William Northmore the elder left a daughter Elizabeth, who was the direct ancestress of the late wife of the present owner of Cleve, a property originally acquired by the said William of Wonson's next younger brother Thomas.

The latter had succeeded to the moiety of the profits of an annual fair at Exeter as a younger son's portion, which had been originally granted to John Northmore of South Tawton, who died in 1577, by King Henry VIII., in whose household he had in his younger days been a page of honour, and with whom he seems to have been a great favourite. Thomas Northmore, however, who was a Master in Chancery and M.P. for Okehampton, appears to have accumulated a great deal of money in the practice of his profession, and about the year 1675 settled in St. Thomas, nigh Exeter, and in 1705 he purchased Cleve, since the principal seat of the Northmores, from the devisees of one Robert Gubbs; he also obtained two-thirds of the rental of Topsham Quay, then the port of Exeter, and much other property in the city. He died (*S.P.M.*) in 1713, when he divided his wealth between his nephew John, son of his fifth and last brother Jeffery, then the owner of Well in South Tawton, and his daughter and heir Anne, at that time married to her first cousin William Northmore the younger of Wonson, who thus inherited Cleve in right of his wife. This William Northmore, of Wonson and Cleve, had been born in 1690, and, like others of his ancient race, some time represented Okehampton in Parliament. In 1722 he was permitted to register his arms, and the simplicity of the coat is sufficient to show its extreme antiquity; his first wife and cousin Ann Northmore only survived her father three years, and he was afterwards twice married; his second wife being Florence, daughter of Sir Arthur Chichester of Ralegh, and his third an Oxenham of Oxenham, in the parish of South Tawton. His first wife's stepmother, by the way, who died in 1735, was a daughter of John St. Aubyn of Clowance, and sister of the first St. Aubyn Baronet, as well as of the wife of Nicholas Martin of Oxton and Netherexe.

William Northmore of Cleve died (*S.P.*) in 1734, when that

property passed to his cousin John Northmore, son of his already mentioned uncle Jeffery Northmore of Well, by Grace Risdon of Spreyton, of the house of Bableigh. This third Northmore, owner of Cleve, married Anne, daughter of John Collacot of Chagford, but only enjoyed that property a few months, as he was buried at South Tawton in December, 1735. He was succeeded by his son Thomas, then only a few months old, and who had therefore a long minority. He was Sheriff of Devon in 1769, and left by his wife, the only daughter and heir of Richard Osgood of Fulham, three sons, Thomas of Cleve; William, in holy orders; and Edward, an officer in the army. Thomas Northmore of Cleve,[*] son and heir, married, secondly, Emmeline, daughter of Sir John Eden, Baronet, by whom he had a son, Edmund Shafto, who died, issueless, at sea, and six daughters. His first wife was a daughter of Sir W. E. Welby, first Baronet of Denton, County Lincoln, by whom he had issue Thomas Welby Northmore, born in 1791, who commenced life with a commission in the Guards, retired as a captain, graduated, became a clergyman, and was long Vicar of Winterton, in Lincolnshire. He married his cousin Katherine, daughter of Sir W. E. Welby, second Baronet, and was buried in the family vault in the church of St. Thomas. He was the father of the Rev. Thomas Welby Northmore, Vicar of Weston, Co. York, who has two sons and a daughter, and also of John Northmore, the present owner of Cleve. Mr. Northmore was born in 1826, and is a justice of the peace for Devon, and was for some years of H.M. Ceylon Civil Service; he married, secondly, in 1873, his far-away kinswoman, Olympia, a daughter of Northmore Herle Pierce Lawrence, the descendant and representative of Elizabeth, only daughter, by his second marriage, of William Northmore the elder of Wonson, as I have previously mentioned. She died in

---

[*] Mr. Thomas Northmore of Cleve, a well-known geologist and antiquary, and Fellow of the Royal Society, married, firstly, Penelope, only daughter of Sir William Earle Welby, first Baronet (creation 27th June, 1801), by his wife, Penelope, third daughter of Sir John Glynne, Bart., of Hawarden, Flintshire; and, secondly, Emmeline, daughter of Sir John Eden, fourth Baronet of West Auckland, Co. Durham, and sister of Lady Aghrim, afterward Countess of Athlone. Her father's baronetcy became extinct in 1841, but her uncle Robert was created a Barone in 1776, and his brothers, William and Morton, were respectively raised to the peerage as Barons Auckland and Henley, 1789-1799.

1875, leaving issue a son and heir, John Northmore, born in 1874, and one daughter, of her own name.

Mr. Northmore had previously married the only daughter of the late Rev. William Hames, Rector of Chagford, but by that lady had no issue; she died in 1869.

The Northmore arms may be thus blazoned :—*Gules*, a lion rampant, *or*, crowned, *argent*. Crest—A lion's head erased, *gules*, crowned as in the arms, charged with a rose, *argent*, barbed and seeded, *vert*.

Motto—" Nec Elata, Nec Dejecta."

The rose was evidently intended to mark Cadency, but it is hard to see why it was employed in lieu of a mullet, the usual distinction, since the fourteenth century, of the third son, from whom William of Wonson, who sought the interference of the officers of arms in 1722, unquestionably derived.

WISE OF SYDENHAM, MOUNT WISE AND WONWELL, CO. DEVON, AND OF CLAYTON HALL, CO. STAFFORD.

The Saxon race of Wise, in the vernacular written "Wis," and by the Danes "Viis," have resided in the west of England literally from time immemorial, and, although the principal seat of the family in the first half of the present century was removed to Staffordshire, in consequence of a marriage with the heir of Booth and Lovatt of Clayton, in that county, the name still flourishes in Devonshire. Humfrey "Vis" or "Wis" of Lew, since known as Lew Trenchard, near Tavistock, was living there in the year 1080, when that manor, which had belonged to Brictric, the son of Algar, the first-love of Matilda, the Conqueror's consort, had passed into Norman hands. According to ancient heraldic records, this Humfrey le Wis was the father, but I consider him to have been more probably the brother, of Oliver le Wis, who was at about the same period settled upon the manor of Greston, in Cornwall, and the latter was the undoubted ancestor of Sir John Wise, Knight, of Greston late in the twelfth century, whose younger brother, Sir Andrew Wyse, accompanied Strongbow to Ireland in 1169, and obtained great possessions in Waterford, since held directly from the

Crown; his descendant and representative, whose predecessors had inherited the lands of the Priory of St. John in 1495, was the late Sir Thomas Wyse of St. John, county Waterford, who married the daughter of Prince Lucien Bonaparte, and was long member of Parliament for the county.

Sir John Wise of Greston had three sons, viz., Henry, son and heir, Serlo, and Osbert, who founded branches of their name in Kent and Oxfordshire. Roger Wise, younger son of Sir Henry Wise of Greston, was the ancestor of the Gloucestershire Wises. His eldest brother, Sir William Wise of Greston, held sixteen librates of land in Cornwall in the year 1255, and by his marriage with Ela de Vepont ("Veteri ponte;" in English, Oldbridge) acquired the Devonshire manor of Thrushelton, a chapelry dependent on Maristow, County Devon, in which latter parish his son Serlo obtained the Sydenham estate by his alliance with Albreda Trevage. Their son, Thomas Wise, Lord of Sydenham, Thrushelton, and Greston, and eighth in descent from the aforesaid Oliver le Wise, left the Cornish property to his son of the latter name, who had no male issue, but by his granddaughter Margaret Beaumont, who married John Chichester of Ralegh, he became the ancestor of subsequent members of that ancient Devonshire house, and also of the Marquesses of Donegal.

Oliver's brother, John Wise of Sydenham, was the father of Thomas Wise, whose wife, Margaret, daughter and heir of Robert Britt (see "House of Brito," *post*), brought him much additional property in various parts of Devonshire, notably that since known as "Mount Wise," which has long been the military headquarters at Devonport, otherwise Stoke Damarel.

The next John Wise of Sydenham married Thomazine, daughter of Sir Baldwin Fulford, of Great Fulford, near Exeter, Knight of the Sepulchre, and Sheriff of Devon 38th Henry VI. He had two children, a son and daughter; the latter was the mother of the first Lord Russell, and the ancestress of the Dukes of Bedford.

Lord Russell's uncle, Oliver Wise, by his wife Margaret Tremayne of Collacombe, in the parish of Lamerton, had issue John, who was thrice married; one of his younger sons is supposed to have founded the Warwickshire branch of the family; by his first wife, Maria Chudleigh, of Ashton-under-Haldon, of the race of the celebrated Duchess of Kingston, he had a son and heir, James Wise of Sydenham, who married Alice Dynham. Their younger son, Sir William Wise, was knighted at the "Battle of the Spurs" in 1513; their elder, John Wise of Sydenham, by Alice Harris of Hayne, was the father of James, Charles, Erkenbold, Thomas, and John. Of these Thomas succeeded to Sydenham, and built "the faire mansion house" at Stoke Damarel, since called Mount Wise, and there his posterity principally resided afterward; by his wife, Mary Buller of Shillingham, he was the father of Sir Thomas Wise, Knight of the Bath, who died in 1629, whose son and heir of the same name, Sheriff of Devon 1638, Knight of the Shire 1640, married the Honourable Mary Chichester, daughter of Edward, first Viscount Carrickfergus, and sister of the first Earl of Donegal; they had a son, Sir Edward Wise, Knight of the Bath, who married Arabella St. John, daughter of Oliver Lord St. John, son of the Earl of Bolingbroke.

The two sons of this marriage, St. John, and Thomas Wise, both died childless, when the great Sydenham property, which was unfortunately unentailed, passed by the marriage of their sister Arabella to the Tremaynes of Collacombe, and since then of Sydenham. I say "unfortunately," merely because the present owner of Sydenham, Mr. John Tremayne, has inherited the property from his grandfather, who came to it by bequest from a kinsman of his own name in 1808, and is not descended from Arabella Wise, whereas the male line of her family did not become extinct by the death of her brothers without issue.

At that time the male heir-at-law was John Wise of Totnes, great grandson of John Wise and of his wife Emmot Vavasour, second son of John Wise of Sydenham and of Alice Harris.

This John Wise of Totnes, born in 1640, was the grandfather of John Wise, who married Margaret, daughter and sole heir of John Ayshford of Wonwell Court, in the parish of Kingston, near Modbury.

The Ayshfords, descended from Stephen de Eisforde, a follower of the Conqueror, were long of Ashford, in the parish of Burlescombe; Robert, second son of William Ayshford of Ashford, towards the end of the fifteenth century married

Philippa, daughter and heir of Robert Hyndeston of Wonwell, and from this marriage Margaret, wife of John Wise, was sixth in descent. She died in 1780, leaving five sons and six daughters; from her second son, George Wise of Woolston, in Loddiswell, the present Colonel Dacres Wise of that parish is descended.

Her eldest son, John Wise, succeeded to Wonwell, and married Elizabeth Froude, aunt of the late James Antony Froude, Regius Professor of Modern History; their eldest son, Ayshford Wise, sold the property in 1820, and removed to Ford House, a place memorable for its siege and capitulation to the Parliamentary forces during the great rebellion, and which from the Reynells passed by marriage to the Courtenays. Mr. Ayshford Wise married Mary, daughter of the Rev. Thomas Whitby of Creswell Hall, Staffordshire, long represented that county in Parliament, and died in 1847. His third daughter, Julia, married, first, in 1837, R. F. De Barry-Barry, by whom she had a son, Robert, late Captain 60th Rifles, and, secondly, in 1845, the late J. T. Coward, by whom she is the mother of Blanchard R. T. Coward, Lieutenant R.N., who married, in 1884, Geraldine, daughter of Major H. W. Portman, and niece of the first Viscount. His son and heir, John Ayshford Wise, a Deputy Lieutenant for Devonshire, Sheriff of Staffordshire 1852, and M.P. for the borough of Stafford, married the daughter and heir of Hugh Booth, by Anne, daughter and heir of Thomas Lovatt of Clayton Hall, whose ancestors had resided there from the sixteenth century. At his death in 1870 he was succeeded by his only son, the present Major Lewis Lovatt Ayshford Wise, formerly of the 8th, "King's," Regiment, who also owns property in Somersetshire. Major Wise has two daughters; his only son and heir died in infancy, A.D. 1877.

The arms of Wise are, *sable*, three chevronels, ermine; quartering, first, Vepont; second, Trevage; third, Britt (see "House of Brito," *post*); fourth, Prestwood; fifth, Brooking; sixth, Ayshford; seventh, grand quarter; first and fourth, Booth; second and third, Lovatt of Clayton.

Crest—A demi-lion rampant, *gules*, holding a sceptre.

Motto—"Sapere Aude."

Sir Thomas Wise had a grant of supporters as a Knight of the Bath, viz., dexter, a lion, *gules*; sinister, an ape, ppr.

PYKE OF WIDWORTHY AND PARRACOMBE.

Although the connection of the Pykes of Parracombe, with Widworthy, was long since completely severed, it appears to me certain that the first settlement in Devonshire of their Norman ancestor was within the latter parish, upon the manor of Sutton, afterwards known as Sutton Lucy, which was held in 1087 by " Richard " as sub-tenant to William the king's doorkeeper (" Gulielmus Portitor," sometimes called " Hostiarius," or the Usher).

The manor of " Acha " (Hæg), Anglice Hayes, long subsequently known as Lucy Hayes, in the same parish, was also then held by a certain " Richard," under Baldwin the Sheriff; hence it has been generally assumed that the two "Richards" were identical, but it is practically certain that " Richard of Acha " was Baldwin's brother, Richard de Redvers, afterwards Earl of Devon, and the fact that both Sutton Lucy and Lucy Hayes, after an occupation of several centuries by the Lucies, eventually passed to the Courtenays, who had then succeeded to the property of the Redvers family, has not rendered the matter more explicable.

The sub-tenant of "Sutton," under the King's porter, was probably Richard de Lucie, a son of Richard, Lord of Disce, in Norfolk, and grandson of "Geoffry" of Loiset, in Normandy, an admiral in the service of William the Conqueror, who fought at Hastings, and was afterwards one of the forty-four knights who were quartered for five years upon the rebellious monks of Ely. Richard de Loiset, afterwards known as De Lucie, received the lordship of Disce from Henry I., was guardian of the kingdom during the transfretation of that monarch in 1112, and also Chief Justice of England.

He seems to have left two sons, Geoffry and Richard. The first of these predeceased him, but had sons, Richard and Herbert, whose line soon expired; and daughters, Maud, who is said to have been, as a widow, the second wife of Richard, Earl of Devon (which may account for the acquisition of Lucy Hayes by her uncle or his descendants), and Rohesia, to whom I shall presently return.

Geoffry's brother, Richard de Lucie, held lands both in Devon and Cornwall in the reign of King Stephen. He had two sons, viz., Maurice, who was of Sutton Lucy, in Widworthy, in the time of Henry II., and Reginald de Lucie, the ancestor of the Multons, who assumed the maternal name, and were Barons of Cockermouth from the 14th Edward II. until 1369, when the property devolved upon Maud de Lucie, alias Multon, wife of Henry Percy, first Earl of Northumberland. She died without issue, but by settlement, 8th Richard II., her lands were secured to her husband and his descendants, who have therefore since quartered the Lucie arms.

Through the marriage of his younger son, Osbert,* Maurice de Lucie was the grandfather of Maurice de Lucie, who was of Sutton Lucie, co. Devon, late in the thirteenth century, but his eldest son, Geoffrey de Lucie, was Baron of Newington, co. Kent, and in litigation with his cousin Rohesia, above mentioned, as to the lands in Cornwall, which he had inherited from his grandfather, the aforesaid second Richard de Lucie.

This Rohesia, wife of Fulbert de Dovor, had succeeded to the lordship of Disce, in Norfolk, upon the death of her nephew, Richard, son of her brother, Richard de Lucie, and had livery of the whole barony in 1208; she therefore claimed all the Cornish lands of her second cousin, Geoffrey, as "of the honour of Lucie," and King John handed them over to William de Briwere, as the said Rohesia's devisee, in 1215.

Geoffrey de Lucie, of Newington, survived until 1252. His son of the same name was summoned to Parliament in 40th Henry III., and died in 1283, when he was succeeded by another Geoffrey, aged 21, 1287, who received his summons in 1296, and was the last Parliamentary Baron of this branch of the family. His father, the Lord Geoffrey, had acquired the manor of Kings-Nympton, in Devonshire, by the gift of Roger Le Zouch, and his posterity there, down to the reign of Henry V., were known as "De Cornwall." The last of them, Sir "John de Cornwall," died between 1415-1422, and was the son of Sir Bryan, whose father, Geoffrey de Cornwall, was a minor, and in the guardianship of Ingelram de Courcy, at the death of his father, who was also called Geoffrey, c. 1367. The family bore

---

* He witnessed a deed for Richard de Grenvile of Stowe and Bideford, c. 1202.

the well-known "canting" armorials, *gules*, three pikes hauriant, *argent;* these fish were termed "lucies" in early heraldry, from the Græco-Latin word "lucius," a term applied to the pike or jack, because it was looked upon as the wolf of the river.

The Lucys of Charlecote, Co. Warwick, are the descendants of the Norman "Gilbert de Ghent," who, after six descents in various surnames, for some reason which has never been satisfactorily explained, suddenly assumed the name of "Lucy" in the reign of King John. Sir Thomas Lucy of Charlecote was satirised by Shakespeare in the character of "Justice Shallow."

During the end of the thirteenth and commencement of the fourteenth centuries the descendants of the great Norman houses began very commonly to Anglicise their continental patronymics, thus "De Calvo Monte" became Chammond, "De Campo Arnulphi" Champernowne, "De Bosco" Boyes, or Wood, "De Lupo" Wolf, and "De Lucie" Pyke, and as Pyke or Pike the name is still extant, and has been always frequent in the neighbourhood, both of Kings-Nympton and Widworthy. Henry Pike was Sub-Dean of Exeter, in 1350, and the Pyke's gave name to Pyke's Ham and Pyke's Ash in the adjoining county of Somerset.

There have been numerous branches of the family in the course of long ages ; one of these terminated with co-heirs at the time when Alice Luce married Simon Cole of Slade, who died in 1497.

The head of another branch married the fourth co-heir of the great house of Valletort of North Tawton, and there was a subsequent marriage with a co-heir of Crewys of Netherex in the persons of Richard Lucy and Nichola, eldest daughter of William, the descendant of Sir Richard Crewys, who resided there in 1233, and was the second son of Richard Crewys of Cruse Morchard. George Pyke, in 1687, married again into this very ancient family ; his wife was Anne, daughter of John Crewys, great-grandson of John Crewys, by Anne, daughter of Humphry Keynes.

Their son and heir Humphry Pyke, owner of Nethercott, in the parish of Braunton, and co-patron of the vicarage of Chew-Magna, Co. Somerset, married Elizabeth, daughter and heir of

Robert Isaac of Westdown, by his wife Elizabeth, daughter and heir of Arthur Ellis of Herne; she was buried at Tawstock 11th April, 1675.

The said Arthur Ellis was maternally the grandson of Ann, daughter of Dr. Sutcliffe, Dean of Exeter, wife of Richard Hals of Kenedon, who was descended, through Fortescue, Speccott, Grenvile, Gorges, and Hankford, from Thomasine, daughter and heir of Sir Richard Stapeldon, grand niece of Walter Stapeldon, Bishop of Exeter, Lord Treasurer of England, and the munificent founder of Exeter College, Oxford, who fell a victim to the fury of a London mob on Tuesday, 15th October, 1326. (See my *Stapeldon*, pp. 10, 11. See also *Stapeldon, a Tragedy*, J. N. Pyke-Nott, Act v., scene 6, pp. 87 *et seq.*)

Through this marriage the Pykes, whose pedigree is recorded at the College of Arms, have, through the Grenviles, a descent from the Dukes of Normandy. In right of Robert Isaac, whose grandmother was Grace, daughter and co-heir of Richard Roberts of Combmartin, they inherited a moiety of that manor, once, as already mentioned, famous for its silver mines, which were first worked in the reign of Edward I., and successfully in that of Elizabeth, at which latter period a large cup was made by order of Sir Beavis Bulmer, who then had a lease of the property, and was presented with a suitable inscription to the Corporation of London.

Humphry Pyke of Nethercott and his wife, Elizabeth Isaac, were the great-grandparents of the Rev. John Pyke, who was born in 1798, and was lord of the Manor of Parracombe, six miles distant from Combmartin, and patron of his own rectory. He married Elizabeth, daughter of John Nott of Bydown, in the parish of Swimbridge, and co-heir to her brother John Nott of Bydown, who died in 1858. They were the parents of the present owner of Bydown and Parracombe, John Nott Pyke-Nott, who assumed the latter name, in addition to that of Pyke, by Royal license 1st September, 1863, and married, in 1867, Caroline Isabella, daughter of Frederick Ward of Gilhead, Co. Westmorland, by whom he has, with other issue, John Moels Pyke-Nott, first son and heir, who was born 3rd February, 1868.

The Pykes at one time owned the manor of Bowrings-Leigh, in the parish of West Alvington, acquired by marriage with Bowring about the year 1463, but they sold it in the seventeenth century, and it has been of late years the property of the Ilberts.

Arms of Pyke of Parracombe.—Quarterly *or* and *gules*, on a chevron, barry wavy of four *arg.* and *azure*, between two trefoils in chief and another in base, counterchanged, a lucy naiant ppr.

Crest.—On a mount *vert*, a demi lucy hauriant ppr. between two wings, *gules*, each charged with a trefoil, *or*.

NOTT OF BYDOWN AND PARRACOMBE.

The Notts derive their name from their early settlement upon the Saxon Manor of "Noteswrde" (the neat or compact enclosure), now known as Notsworthy, or more commonly, and incorrectly, as Natsworthy, in the parish of Widecombe-in-the-Moor.

This property, which in the Confessor's reign belonged to "Edward," was given by Norman William to his uterine brother, the powerful Earl of Cornwall, described in Domesday as "Robert, Earl of Mortain," and who was, with Odo Earl of Kent, one of the two sons of Harlowen de Conteville, or De Burge, by his marriage with Harlotta.

Under Earl Robert, Notsworthy was held, in 1086, by Richard Fitz-Turolf, and was then taxed for "a ferling of land," sufficient for two ploughs, in addition to five acres of pasture and six of coppice wood. Resident upon it were two villeins or farmers, as many cottagers, and one serf.

There is the strongest probability that the descendants of Fitz-Turolf took name from their residence, and that one of them, William of Notsworthy, was identical with the "William Notte" mentioned in Camden's list as one of the thirty-six principal officers who served in the Irish expedition of the year 1169 under Richard Earl of Pembroke, as all these adventurers belonged to the noblest Norman houses, and many of them, such as the Fitz-Stephens, Cogans, and Bohuns, were also Devonshire landowners.

The descendants of William de Notsworthy subsequently migrated to other parts of the county of Devon, one of them, John "Node," was a Fellow of Stapeldon Hall, Oxford (now Exeter College), between 1382-1388, whilst others of his name and kindred were considerable landowners at East Budleigh, and were benefactors to that parish, as shown by the deed of Ralph Node and Margaret his wife, dated December 8th, 1441, and although their benefaction has become somewhat involved in obscurity, it very possibly originated the foundation of the "Church house" at Budleigh, as to the history of which the Charity Commissioners have been unable to recover the particulars.

There is a tradition at Budleigh that Ralph Node met his death by attempting to fly from the summit of the church tower with the assistance of an unsatisfactory mechanical contrivance of his own invention; he seems to have been buried under a flat coffin-shaped stone, the Latin inscription upon which, "Pray for the soul of Ralph Node," has been recorded by Risdon and his contemporary writers of the seventeenth century, but has now become obliterated.

The Notts of Bydown, in the parish of Swimbridge, have been settled there and in that neighbourhood for very many centuries; they had also property at Irishcombe, an outlying portion of the parish of Lapford, which, however, was sold, some years since, to the Lanes, and subsequently to Sir R. G. Keats. In 1524, John Nott of Swimbridge was a party, with his son John Nott the younger, to a fresh trust deed of the parish lands; a little earlier James, son of John Nott, had married Cicely, called "Syffrels" in the Visitation record, daughter of John Bonville (a natural son of Lord Bonville), by the eldest daughter and co-heir of John Denis of Comb-Ralegh, and the daughter and heir of St. Albyn. Cicely Bonville had been first the wife of Morys More of Morehayes, in the parish of Cullompton, by whom she had sons, Humphry and Christopher, and a daughter Elizabeth; she was left a widow in the year 1500, and then married Thomas Wyvell, so that James Nott was her third husband; she inherited property at Comb-Martin, once famed for its silver mines, a portion of which, by virtue of subsequent marriages, ultimately descended to the Pykes (see the preceding genealogy), and still belongs to Mr. John Nott Pyke-Nott of Bydown. John Nott, who appears to have been the great-great-grandson of James Nott and Cicely Bonville, was of Cobbaton, in the parish of Swimbridge, and added Uppacott to his ancestral acres in 1587; by his wife Joan Lewes he was the father of William Nott of Cobbaton, whose descent is duly recorded at the College of Arms, and who married Ellinor, daughter of John Berry of Chittlehampton, of the ancient house of Berrynarber. She was the sister of Dr John Berry, Canon of Exeter, and Vicar of Heavitree, and the aunt of Colonel John Berry, a celebrated Parliamentary officer in the West.

John, son and heir of William Nott and Eleanor Berry, married Mary Bellew of Yarnscombe, marriage settlement dated 1644, descended from Patrick Bellew of Alverdiscott and his wife Anne Dennis of Orleigh, tenth in direct descent from Roger Bellew of Bellewstone, in the parish of Devildike, Co. Meath, the common ancestor of the Lords Bellew, of the Bellew baronets of the sister kingdom, and of the Bellews of Stockleigh Court, Co. Devon, and descended, maternally, from Archibald Flemyng, Baron of Slane, whose arms the Bellews quarter.

The issue of this marriage was William Nott, son and heir of Cobbaton, whose wife Mary, eventual co-heir of James Harvey, brought him a son John Nott of Cobbaton, whose memorial inscription in Swymbridge Church gives the date of his death 9th May, 1756.

He had married, in 1711, Agnes, the only daughter and sole heir of John Hamond of Okewill, grandson of Hugh Hamond of East Downe, by his marriage with Jane, youngest of the six children, but, nevertheless, eventual heir of William, third son of Philip Wyatt, Steward and Town Clerk of Barnstaple, and brother of Hugh Wyatt, the husband of Lady Mary Bourchier, and of Thomas Wyatt, whose wife Margaret, widow of Richard Inglett, was an aunt, paternally, of Tristram Risdon, the Devonshire antiquary.

The son of this marriage, James Nott, who was buried in 1790, at Swymbridge, married at Tawstock, in 1762, Emma daughter of John Mules, the descendant of Roger Moels, of the

Ernsborough branch of the great baronial house of Moels or Mules, of which Nicholas Lord Mules was Governor of Gascony and Guienne, and captured the King of Navarre, for which service Henry III. gave him the west country manor of King's Carswell. (See my *Devonshire Parishes*, vol. ii., p. 372.)

James Nott and Emma Mules were the parents of John Nott of Bydown, in Swymbridge, who by his wife Susannah, only daughter and heir of Richard Norris of Southmolton, had a son James, who died childless, and a son John, who succeeded to Bydown, was a justice of the peace for the county of Devon, and died without issue in 1855, when his sisters Elizabeth and Marianne became his co-heirs. The former married, in 1838, the Rev. John Pyke, M.A. and J.P., of whose ancestry I have already treated, and whose eldest and only surviving son John Nott Pyke-Nott is the present owner of Bydown.

Mr. Pyke-Nott, who was born in 1841, and was educated at Winchester and Exeter College, Oxford, assumed the arms of Nott in preferential addition to those of Pyke (together with the name of Nott), by Royal license, at the date already mentioned, 1st Sept., 1863.

Arms of Nott.—*Gules*, on a bend engrailed, *or*, between four leopards' faces, *arg.*, an estoile of eight points between two martlets of the first.

Crest.—Two mascles interlaced, in fess, *or*, thereon a martlet, *gules*, ducally gorged of the first, in the beak a sprig of laurel, ppr.

THE HOUSE OF BRITO.

It is shown by the Devonshire "Domesday" that, at the completion of the Conqueror's survey in the year 1086, the land in Devonshire had become divided into one thousand one hundred and twelve manors of varied extent and importance. Seventy-eight of these, inclusive of the seats of the subsequent important baronies known as Plympton, Barnstaple, and Torrington, were then held by the king in demesne; the Baron of Totnes, who was probably a "Brito," together with the Lords of Dartington, Bradninch, Bampton, Harberton, and Berry, owned four hundred and thirty-three between them. (Valletort of " Herberneforde," by the way, is incorrectly said by Lysons, who has also wrongly identified the property, to have been "sub-tenant" there to the Earl of Mortain, and the Barony of Harberton was ultimately annexed to that of Berry.) The said Earl of Mortain, as William's half brother, naturally acquired a somewhat undue proportion of the soil here as elsewhere; he had eighty-two, the Norman warrior Bishop of Coutance ninety-one, and Hugh de Abrincis, "Lupus," Earl of Chester, four, of these Devonshire manors. The Barony of the Bishopric of Exeter, then held by Osbern Britt or Britolio, absorbed twenty-four more, that of Galfred, Abbot of Tavistock. fourteen.

The Church in Devonshire, as well as in several other counties, and in Normandy, had become possessed of twenty-seven, the king's clerks and his domestic chaplain, "Gerald," of five, and his majesty's servants had been "gratified" with sixteen.

As "a sop to Cerberus," a very few of the noblest and most influential Saxons had been permitted to share in the common plunder, or to retain possession of fifty-one of their ancient heritages, by their unscrupulous conqueror. Thus two hundred and eighty-seven valuable properties had been left open for distribution amongst others of the leading Normans, and three alone of these, alike described as "Brito," and between whom there was an evident and intimate connection, and, indeed, very probably a close relationship, divided no less than fifty-six "lordships," besides being the virtual owners of many more, as sub-tenants to the puissant Robert of Mortain.

The Britos doubtless derived their distinctive surname from their native province, and, under Alan Fitz-Hoel, 'Fergant," Earl of Bretagne and Richmond, flocked to the standard of Duke William, and assisted him in his invasion of England. Hence it is that there are many "Britons, Brutons, Le Bretons, Brutaynes, and Bruttons," to be found in different parts of the country, who may be possibly unrelated to their Devonshire namesakes, or to each other, yet are, nevertheless, of kindred origin. But there were only six "Britos," positively so styled, who were "tenants in chief" at the period to which I am referring, viz., "Oger," "Waldin," "Mannus" or "Morinus," Alured, Ansger, and Goscelmus or Jocelyn, and all, save the first, were then Devonshire landowners, and their common name is still intimately associated with this and the adjacent counties.

"Maigno," "Mannus," or "Morinus" Brito, whose lands here are entered as those of "a free knight," was tenant in capite of the manor of "Linor" (Lyneham in Yealmpton), of Stottiscombe, in the same hundred, to which I shall presently refer again, and of Culbeer and Wilmington, in the parish of Offwell, near Honiton. The last three were held by him as sub-tenant to Baldwin de Brion, the Conqueror's nephew by marriage, and nearly of kin to him by blood ; he also held land directly from the Crown in Hertford, Northampton, and Leicester.

Waldin Brito, who was a tenant in chief in county Lincoln, held the Devonshire manors of Cary and Medland under Juhel (Brito ?) Baron of Totnes.

Goscelmus, or Jocelyn, Brito had twenty-seven manors in Devonshire as tenant in capite, and held similarly from the Crown, in the counties of Gloucester, Bedford, and Bucks.

The chief seat of his Devonshire property was at Halwell, in the parish of Brixton; he had a son Richard, who styled himself "Richard de Halwell," and who conveyed to the monks of Plympton his manor of Wembury (one of the "twenty-seven" above mentioned), as shown by the confirmation charter of King Henry II. to that Priory. The grandson of this Richard was evidently "Sir Richard Brito, Knt.," whose name is found, amongst the Pole "evidences," as a considerable landowner in the county in the reign of Henry II. (1154-1189), and whose brother (Edmund ?) probably continued the male line, but from this period the name of Brito was abandoned for several generations, and the family most certainly assumed that of "Halwell." Soon afterward "Martin de Halwell" was seised of the manor of "Stottiscombe," which, according to the survey of 1086, was then held by "Morinus" Brito, under Baldwin de Brion, and which points, I think clearly, to a relationship between Morinus and Jocelyn, or else to a subsequent matrimonial alliance between the two families of Halwell and Stottiscombe.

The latter manor is on the border line, between the parishes of Wembury and Plymstock, and after several descents the "de Halwells" of Stottiscombe re-assumed the name of Brito or

Britt, and became also the owners of the manor of "Widefelle" (Walreddon), and also of "Brucheswrde" (Britsworthy), both in the parish of Whitchurch, near Tavistock, and which had been held under Mortain, the one by Alured, the other by Ansger Brito; so that certain land which had been owned here by four of these "Britos" respectively ultimately became centred in the family of Britt or Britun of Stottiscombe, six of whom were successively called "Guy de Britt," and bore for arms, *sable*, a fess, *arg.*, between three escallops, *or* (the tinctures are found occasionally varied).

Guy "Bretun" was dead before 1348, in which year his son "Ralph de Britt of Stottiscombe" was Sheriff of Devon. Robert "Britt" of Stottiscombe, "son," or more probably grandson, of the said Ralph, and who is said in the Wise pedigrees to have been "eleventh in descent from *Alured* Brito," had an only child, Margaret, who married Thomas Wise of Sydenham (see Wise of Sydenham *ante*) during the first quarter of the fifteenth century, and through her the Wises became the owners of Halwell and Stottiscombe, as also of much property at Stoke Damarell, where they built Mount Wise, and in other parts of Devonshire. Thus the elder male line of Britt of Stottiscombe became extinct some time prior to the year 1435.

"Richard Brito," hitherto presumed to have been a descendant of "Ansger," and a son of Simon Brito, is said to have been identical with the third of the four murderers of Thomas à Becket.

There has been always some doubt as to the exact connection of this "Richard" with the Britos of the West of England from the complete absence of any contemporary confirmation of his traditional origin.

It is shown, by the De Banco Rolls, that, as a descendant of "Ansger," through "Simon Brito," an ancestor of the Bretts of Sandford Brett, "Sir Richard" must have been great-grandson of Adam, younger brother of Walter Brito of Odecumbe, who was third in descent from the said Ansger; but, although there are several pedigrees of these Britos entered on the De Banco Rolls, on which there are to be found three "Simons" in succession, there is no mention of any "Richard." I find notice of an "Edmund," the name of Sir Richard Brito's brother, but this

"Edmund de Sandford" was the half-uncle of the first Simon in the pedigree by the second marriage of his grandmother, "Alice."

Yet, as I have shown above, there actually was a Sir Richard Brito, Kt., of Devon, in the reign of Henry II., and the facts—that the Britos of Holwell subsequently repudiated that name for several generations, and adopted coat armour, as already blazoned, of a very suggestive character, and perfectly different from the bearings of other branches of the family—point strongly to the identity of this Sir Richard with the actor in the Becket tragedy.[*] Sir Richard Brito was a favourite at Court, and one of the gentlemen-in-waiting on his Royal master.

I need not enter upon the details of the murder, with which most of my readers are conversant, and which I have already dealt with elsewhere, suffice it that Brito appears to have inflicted the final blow, which severed the scalp from the skull, and "his sword snapped in two on the marble pavement of the desecrated church," in which its fragments were afterward long preserved.

The Archbishop thus met his memorable death on December 29th, 1170. Brito was one of the three who fled to Rome to "receive the sentence of the Pope," and is said, after three adventurous years in the Holy Land, to have been buried outside the church of the holy sepulchre at Jerusalem.

The escallops in the arms of the Britts of Holwell, Stottiscombe, and Stoke Damarell, now quartered by Major Ayshford Wise of Clayton, point, conclusively I think, to Sir Richard's crime, and consequent pilgrimage, undertaken by Papal order in its expiation; it is said that, although the male line was continued by his brother Edmund, Sir Richard left a daughter, Maud, whose daughter Alice was a benefactress to Woodspring Priory, Somersetshire, which had been founded in memory of the murder by William de Courtenay in 1210.

Collinson, "History of Somerset," asserts the parentage of "Maud and Alice," apparently in reliance upon the "hope," expressed by the latter, "that the intercession of the glorious

---

[*] Jocelyn Brito of Holwell, Co. Devon, 1086, father of Richard, father of Simon, father of Sir Richard Brito, 1170.

martyr might never be wanting to her and her children;" it is, however, noteworthy that there happens to have been a contemporary "Alice Brito," daughter of Walter of Odecumbe, one of the three sons of Walter Fitz-Ansger, and an elder brother of Adam Brito. This Alice was the mother of Richard de Hestercumbe, whose descendants bore the maternal name, for "Stephen le Bret," as the descendant of the said Alice, was shown to be heir-at-law to the reversion of Odecumbe, etc., which had then been alienated to the Brewers, by an "*Inq. p m.*," 49th Henry III., 1266.

William Brito, the third brother of Walter Brito of Odecumbe, as a younger son, inherited some property in Dorsetshire known as "Sidling," and land under the same name in the latter county had been held by Ansger de Montacute under Mortain. William Brito of "Sidling" appears to have inherited that property as "son and heir of William" in 1166, and in that same year we find "Simon Brito" holding a half knight's fee in Somersetshire under William Mohun. All writers have agreed that Richard Brito was "son of a father called Simon," and the connection between the Dorsetshire branch and this latter Simon is proved by the fact that in 9th Richard I., 1198, Henry le Bret admitted a liability of £5 with respect to a knight's fee in Maperton against "Simon le Bret;" so that "Sir Richard Brito" must have been actually of the same generation as the said "Simon," his hitherto reputed father.

Alured Brito, who is described also as Alured "Pincerna," and also as Alured "de Montacute," held property in Devon, Cornwall, and Somerset, and was, presumably, the ancestor of the Cornish Britos, and of one or more of the Devonshire branches of the family as well, particularly of those long seated at Morthoe, Alwington, Parkham, and High Bickington; but the chief seat of his barony appears to have been fixed at Chiselborough, in Somerset, where his descendants, under the name of "Montacute," flourished until the thirteenth century. Richard "Pincerna," who was probably his eldest son, was one of the earliest benefactors to the monks of Plympton, like his kinsman, "Richard de Holwell," as shown by their confirmation charter already mentioned.

Alured Brito "de Montacute" appears to have been of the

household of Robert of Mortain, and to have there occupied the position of chief butler; he was the sub-tenant, under the Earl, of ten Devonshire and of seven Cornish manors, besides which he was tenant-in-chief of no less than twenty-two manors in this county. He may also have been identical with that "Bretellus" who was the practical owner of the large manor of Colebrook under Mortain, and he was certainly so with "Alvidus Brito," the sub-tenant, under Ruald Adobat, of the manor of Painston, which is situated in the same parish.

As I have said above, he owned the manor of "Widefelle," now Walreddon, which subsequently went to the Britts of Stottiscombe, and, after several changes of ownership, has now long been held by the Powderham branch of the Courtenays; and it is particularly noteworthy that he was the tenant-in-chief of the very important manor of Wolborough, which eventually passed by sale to the Brewers, and formed a portion of the endowment of Tor Abbey.

And in connection with Brewer it should also be noted that Alured Pincerna held, under Mortain, the manor of Dunkeswell, "Donewoldham," and another estate adjacent to it, known as "Wifleurde" (Walford), in demesne. Both these properties afterward went to a certain "William" (who may have been identical with the "William," ancestor of Wydo Brito, who was a sub-tenant of Iudhel de Totnes, see *post*), and whose descendant, Henry Fitz-William, alienated both Dunkeswell and Walford to William Brewer to pay off a mortgage in security for money borrowed from one "Amades," a Jew. Brewer, with the consent of King John, as shown by that Monarch's deed of confirmation, gave both the properties to the Abbey of Dunkeswell in 1201. Walford, now within Dunkeswell, was long a separate parish, and known as "Walford Church."

I now come to Ansger Brito, also called "de Montacute," and as frequently "de Senarpont," who was a very large landowner under Mortain, both in Somerset and Dorset. In this county, of which I treat more particularly, he held six principal manors in chief—four under the Earl of Mortain, and twelve more as sub-tenant to Baldwin de Brion, the "sheriff." One of his estates, Brittsworthy, as already stated, subsequently became the property of the Stottiscombe family, and passed with its sole heir to Wise. His son Fulk, "Fitz-Ansgerii," was, like "Richard Pincerna" and Richard de Holwell, one of the earliest donors to the Plympton community.

Ansger Brito was the founder of the family of Brito of Odecumbe, in Somerset, which was the seat of his titular "Barony" or honour. He had another son, Walter, who confirmed his father's gifts to the monks of Bermondsey, and the latter was the father of Walter, Roger, Adam, and also of William Brito, who held the paternal acres at Sidling, and founded the Dorsetshire branch of the family, as already mentioned.

In the 25th of Henry II., however, the honour of Odecumbe was in the hands of the Crown; and, although it was afterwards temporarily restored to the Britos, it ultimately passed to the Brewers, as did Wolborough, in Devonshire, to which I have just above drawn attention as having been originally land of *Alured* Brito.

It is shown by contemporary records that William Brewer's Devonshire estates, known as "Bocland (now Buckland Brewer), Puttsford, Buckeford, Sutton, and Uppecotte," were held as "of the honour of Odecumbe," in Somerset, and the latter, as the seat of Ansger Brito's Barony, was in like manner held as of the Earl of Mortain's "honour of Montacute," as was Alured Brito's "honour of Chiselborough," and thus the surname of "Montacute," as adopted by both Ansger and Alured Brito, is to be readily explained.

According to the Survey of 1086, Ansger then held Sustatone (Sutton) in demesne—Bocland under Baldwin de Brion, Bocheforde and Poteforde under the Earl of Mortain; whilst Uppecotte (in Shebbear hundred), although it belonged to Baldwin de Brion, was held under him by Motbert, and must have been subsequently acquired by Ansger, and, with the others, annexed to his honour of Odecumbe.

Collins and others have supposed Ansger Brito, *alias* de Montacute, to have been a brother of Drogo de Montacute, the ancestor of the Dukes of Montagu and other illustrious houses.

It is certain that Drogo de Montacute was also a very important unit in the retinue of Robert, Earl of Mortain, and his name has been assumed, I think hastily, to have been derived "from the town of Montagu, in Normandy"; it is certain, however, that he held lands similarly under Mortain as of the "honour of Montacute" in Somerset, and that he was identical with that "Drogo" who was the Earl's sub-tenant of several manors in Devonshire, one of which, viz., Feniton, continued in the hands of his descendants for many generations, as proved by contemporary records.

The history of this Somersetshire "Drogo" prior to his arrival in England has never, to the best of my knowledge, even been suggested, beyond the supposition that he was a native of Montagu, in Normandy, which does not, I think, follow his appellation, "de Montacute." The original name of the place, afterwards so called in Somerset, was "Lutegarsbury" (Lutegar's Castle); it stood within the manor of Bishopstone, which Mortain had acquired from the Church in exchange for another property called Caudel, and within this manor of Bishopstone, Drogo held a single hide of land as of the Castle of Montacute, so called by Mortain without any reference to the Norman "Montagu," but simply in allusion to its position on the top of a steep hill. This castle then formed the head of his honour, and from it, in accordance with feudal custom, his numerous sub-tenants were said to hold their lands; hence I should suppose the name of Montacute became common to Drogo, to Alured Brito the butler, and to his relative Ansger Brito, de Senarpont—a fact which, taken alone, would not necessarily make them related either to the said Drogo de Montacute or to each other.

There was a "Drogo" who held seventy-three manors in Devonshire under Jeffrey, Bishop of Coutance, who was the ancestor of the Cliffords, Drews, and Bremridges, and whose descent from the Dukes of Normandy has been ascertained. It is evident from the respective pedigrees that this Drogo "Fitz-Ponz," or "Fitz-Mauger," was not identical with "Drogo de Montacute"; the latter, however, held the manor of "Wiborde," like "Finitone," under Mortain; and within "Wiborde," since known as Oakford, was another manor called "Sprewe," also held by "Drogo," but under the Bishop of Coutance, and which gave name to the family of Spurway, the present owners of Oakford, which, however, was sold by the Montacutes, Earls of Salisbury, to the Pollards, and by the latter to the Spurways of Spurway, who are quite possibly descended from Drogo de Montacute.

It is noteworthy that the arms of the D'Aubenys and those of the earlier descendants in Somerset of Drogo de Montacute should have been the same save for tincture. I should have explained this as merely evidence of feudal alliance, which was, I think, clearly the case with respect to the coat armour of Brito of Odecumbe. The Montacutes bore, "*argent*, five fusils in fess, *gules*" (although in later times two of these fusils became hidden by a sable bordure, which probably was intended to mark their feudal dependence upon Mortain's Cornish Earldom), whilst D'Aubeny (De Albini) bore, "*gules*, five fusils in fess, *argent*." Brito of Odecumbe bore quarterly, per fess, indented *argent* and *sable*, in first quarter a mullet of the last, apparently derived from De Vere; Jordan le Bret held knights fees in Northampton under Hugh, Earl of Oxford, 1234-1263, as shown by the *Testa de Nevil*; whilst Fitzwarine's coat, now quartered by Wrey as co-heir to their barony, is quarterly per fess indented *argent* and *gules*. Walter, son of Ansger Brito, acknowledged the service of fifteen knights, whose names have been preserved, and one of them, who held two fees of the honour of Odecumbe, was Alexander Fitzwarine.

But in the case of Montagu I think that it permits the suggestion that there was an actual relationship between Drogo de Montacute and the Britos.

Robert de Todeni, the Norman lord of Belvoir, County Lincoln, had a son William, who fought at Tinchebray in 1106, and is said by the strength of his single arm to have determined the fate of that day, which led to the annexation of Normandy by Henry I. to the prejudice of his Royal brother Robert.

This William was certainly a very liberal benefactor to the monastery of St. Alban, and is said to have at last professed there as a monk, and to have been known as William de Albini. But there was another William de Albini, his contemporary, who was the King's "Pincerna," an office held by Alured Brito in the household of the King's half brother, and this William "Pincerna" was the ancestor of the pseudo de Albini, "Earl of Arundell."

De Todeni's son, William de Albini, has been supposed to have assumed the name of Brito in addition to "Albini," to distinguish himself from William Pincerna; but, however he may have come by the name, he was certainly known as William Brito, and his eldest son William, who died 14th Henry II., was called "William Meschines *alias* Brito," whilst Ralph de Albini Brito was the ancestor of the Lords Daubeny. It is therefore quite possible, I think, that Drogo de Montacute was actually Drogo Brito, and that all the Britos who held lands in Devonshire in the years that succeeded the Conquest were near relatives, either originally or by subsequent intermarriage.

Another very probable ancestor of the Devonshire Britos must not be overlooked, viz., "Tehelus or Tehellus Britto," who was a tenant in capite in Essex and Norfolk, and quite possibly identical with that powerful Baron of Totnes and Barnstaple, "Iuhel of Totnes," whose extraction and parentage have been always open to a considerable amount of question.

That "Iuhel," or "Iuhellus," as he is styled in the Devonshire Domesday, stood very high in the Conqueror's favour is sufficiently proved by the enormous amount of land he was possessed of in 1086, and the King ultimately gave him the whole Barony of Barnstaple. John Burhed of Totnes, who wrote in 1433, and whose manuscript is preserved at Exeter, calls him "Ludhellus." In his foundation charters of the priories of Totnes and Barnstaple he styles himself "Juhellus filius Aluredi;" and Risdon, the seventeenth century historian of the county tells us that he was the son of "Alured, Earl of Bretagne," but as the charters referred to are, it is to be feared, but monastic transcripts of the original documents, they form but little authority for the original spelling of the names either of the son or sire. Whoever he may really have been, it is certain that several of his Devonshire Manors were held under him by a certain "William," and it is shown by the *Testa de Nevil*, that a number of knights' fees, in respect of the said manors, were held of Roger de Valletort, *temp.* Henry II., and up to the 5th of King John, as of the honour of Totnes, by "Wydo le Brette," who is also styled "Wydo de Bretteville."

Juhellus of Totnes was in arms against William Rufus, and

was consequently proscribed ; he escaped to the continent and never returned to England, and, as I have noticed in my chapter on the "Borough of Totnes" (*Ashburton and its Neighbourhood*, p. 108), William de Braose, his great-grandson, was permitted to hold a moiety of that honour, and "made partition thereof with Roger de Valletort, heir to Henry, son of Roger de Novant," who, upon the disgrace of "Juhellus," had obtained from the Crown a very considerable portion of his property.

Finally, there was an individual called "Brettel" in the Survey, who was sub-tenant to the Earl of Mortain in the manors of Ferentone, Colebrook, and "Cherletone," or Charlton, and, unless it has become extinct there very recently, the name of Britton may still be reckoned amongst the villagers of Colebrook, distant a few miles from Crediton.

With regard to the later social position of the family in the West of England, I find Oliver Breton returned member for the borough of Truro as early as 1309. Sir Adam le Bret represented Somerset in 1329-30; John Briton, senior or junior, represented Bodmin from 1384 to 1397; John Breton, Lostwithiel, 1386. William Breton of Canonsleigh, co. Devon, was returned for Bossiney, in Cornwall, in 1746.

Thomas "Bruerton," who was Mayor of Exeter 1580, received a letter from "Lord Thomas Howarde," dated April 11th, 1581 (Thomas, first Earl of Suffolk), desiring him to examine a thief who had stolen property from his house, and to forward said thief to "Wareham," "for that I mean to make an example of so lewde a part in myn own house."

Contemporary with this Mayor of Exeter was William "Bruton," whose depositions concerning the rent of a house belonging to the Dean and Chapter, and dated "June, 1586," are still extant. Guy "Breton" of Stottiscombe was appointed an attorney for Thomas West from February 1st to the "Feast of St. Peter ad Vincula," August 1st, 1328, during the latter's absence at Santiago on a pilgrimage. This "Thomas West" was the ancestor of the Lords Delawarr and the first peer of his family by writ of summons in 1342, and of Broadhampston, Co. Devon, in right of his wife Alianore de Cantalupe.

In 1333. April 24th, "Robert Briton" of Exeter (Jocelyn

Brito had property in that city in 1086) was pardoned unconditionally.

He seems to have been outlawed for contempt of court, in that he did not appear to answer a plea of trespass alleged against him by John Perer of Crediton.

BRUTON, *ALIAS* BRETON, OF LANGLEY AND BOROUGH.

Amongst the Devonshire property held by Alured Brito in 1086, there were two manors on the north or north-western side of this county, then known respectively as " Bacetesberie " and " Lege."

The latter, since known as Langley, *i.e.*, long leigh, or the long pasture, is situated in the parish of High Bickington, the greater portion of which at that time belonged to Robert, Earl of Mortain, in whose household Alured was " Pincerna," or chief butler. I have already remarked that the chief seat of Alured's barony was at Chiselborough, in Somerset, and that his son Richard " Pincerna " was the probable ancestor of the Devonshire branch of his family; in any case, however, it is certain that Alured's descendants, collateral or otherwise, held the manor of Langley for many centuries under the name of "Britton," and although there were doubtless several younger branches, as the name has never become extinct in the district, the daughter and heir of Britton of Langley brought that property to her husband, Roger Pollard, about the middle of the fifteenth century.

This Roger is unfortunately omitted from the pedigree recorded at the Visitation of 1620, and signed " Richard Pollard," which, however, is deficient in the matter of several generations, and, indeed, only records four of them between " Roger Pollard," who lived in the reign of Richard II., and the said " Richard," whose will was proved 8th May, 1626. The name of " Richard," I may remark, was peculiar to this branch of the Pollards of Way, and may possibly have been derived from the Brittons, as it accords with that of their presumptive ancestor " Richard Pincerna."

As an old topographer remarks in 1638, "Roger Pollard," on marriage with "the daughter and heir of Britton of Langley, whose lands they were in times past, planted himself so firmly that his posterity have hitherto possessed the same." He was fourth in descent from the Roger of the "Visitation," whose mother was Emma, one of the daughters and co-heirs of Sir John Doddiscomb of Compton Pole, and a sister of Cicelye, wife of Sir John Worthe of Worth, who had Compton Pole and other property for her portion (see *ante*, p. 297, where Sir John Worthe is inadvertently called "Richard.") The Pollards remained at Langley until about the middle of the seventeenth century, when the property passed by sale to Barry. Richard Pollard, the last of this branch, was living in 1667.

The manor of "Bacetesberie," which was also held in demesne by Alured "Pincerna" in 1086, has been since known as "Burgh" or "Borough," and is situated in the parish of Morthoe, on the north coast of Devon. In the reign of Henry III. and Edward I., Thomas le Brethon held the eighth part of a knight's fee there, as shown by the *Testa de Nevil*, and it is interesting, as confirmatory of the evident connection between the several families of Brito, to find that by an undated deed of the end of the twelfth century "Julian le Croc, in her widowhood, grants land in Morthoe to Hugh Valletort and Lucy his wife." The Crocs derived from Walter Croc, son of Annora, one of the sisters and co-heirs of Walter Brito in 1196, and the latter was the great-grandson of Ansger Brito aforesaid.

Although King John gave the barony of Barnstaple to the Tracys, his predecessor, King Stephen, had transferred much of Iudhel Fitz-Alured's property to Henry Tracy, who was the only Devonshire gentleman who openly supported his interests against Maud the Empress; amongst these lands was the manor of Combe, where "William" aforesaid was sub-tenant to Iudhel in 1086, and it has since been known as Wollacombe (the valley of the Walla), and probably passed by marriage with Grace, Henry Tracy's daughter, to John de Sudeley, and thence to their youngest son William de Sudeley, *alias* de Tracy, the prime actor in the murder of Thomas à Becket. Sir William de Tracy appears to have resided upon his manor of Wollacombe, and to have retired there after his return from Normandy in

1176; he must therefore have been well acquainted with his neighbours the Britos, and hence possibly the subsequent unfortunate association of Sir Richard Brito with the crime which Tracy is understood to have conceived and arranged.

There is, I think, sufficient heraldic evidence to prove that the Britos of Morthoe and Brixton must have been, even at that time, intimately related to each other.

Sir William de Tracy is said to have been buried in Morthoe Church, but the tomb there, for many years exhibited as his, is that of a namesake, priest of the parish in 1322, and the mistake as to its identity may be referred to one of Camden's numerous errors.

A pedigree of "Bruton of Heavitree" (Arms, "Per pale, *gules* and *azure*, a fess between two chevrons, *arg.*; Crest, a demi-wolf, ducally crowned, holding a mullet, ppr.") appears to have been entered at Heralds' College in 1622, but merely records the descent of William, third son of "Thomas Bruton *alias* Breton of Borough, in the parish of Morthowe," who married Elizabeth, daughter of William Ryder. This William had five brothers, Thomas, George, Philip, Robert, and Adam, and to the eldest of them I shall refer later on.

It appears from the will of the said Elizabeth, who died 21st March, 1610-11, and was buried in Exeter Cathedral, that the family resided at Whipton Barton, a hamlet in Heavitree parish, and that her husband must have been a man of considerable property is shown by his own will likewise. He appears to have been lay impropriator of several rectories in the diocese, situated both in Devon and Cornwall; he was also buried in the Cathedral, 23rd April, 1608, as were his two sons William and John; the latter survived him but three years; the former was interred in February, 1661-62. William Bruton, *alias* Breton, the elder, had also five daughters, the first of whom was the wife of Arthur Periman, and her sisters all married into well-known county families, viz., Eveleigh, Fortescue, Stroud, and Peter.

Margaret, wife of "Will Peter," is mentioned with her husband in her mother's will, and the latter is to have furniture and goods in the house at Whipton to the amount of several hundred pounds. He resided there for the few months that he outlived his mother-in-law, and a full account of his murder in January, 1611-12, by Edward, son of Edward Drew of Killerton, serjeant-at-law, and one of Prince's "Worthies," will be found in my *Suburbs of Exeter*, under the head of "Heavitree." His widow married, secondly, Edward Cotton, Archdeacon of Totnes, second son of William Cotton, Bishop of Exeter, and died 10th August, 1643.

Margaret's eldest brother, "John Bruton *alias* Breton," died blind, as noted in the registers of Exeter Cathedral, where he was buried, 19th October, 1611 ; his two children, William and John, were then aged six and three years old, and the license for the second marriage of their affectionate mother, who had been a Miss Dorothy Leigh of Heavitree, with Lewis Hayman, gentleman, of Dunchideok (" to be married at Heavitree "), is dated the following 4th December. Her first husband's only brother, William, was then a minor, and only twelve years of age ; he subsequently married " Edith," a daughter of Sir George Smith, of Madford, in the parish of Heavitree, and sister of Lady Monk and of Lady Grenville (see my *Suburbs of Exeter*, p. 17), by whom he had a family of ten children, all baptized at the Cathedral, of whom " William," 7th April, 1629, was the eldest. His wife died in giving birth to her youngest son George, and was buried the day after his baptism, 7th October, 1740.

In 1622 her husband, " William Bruton," then " aged 23," appears to have recorded the family pedigree ; on the 20th February, 1639-40, he made further application to the College of Arms for a crest and motto, and, under that date, was granted by Sir John Borough, Garter King of Arms, " a hinde couchant under a hawthorn tree, all ppr.," with the legend, " Quæ delectant desiderantur." The preamble sets forth that " William Bruton, of the city and county of Exeter, Esquire," had requested that a crest and motto might be assigned to him to bear with his paternal coat of arms " without doing wrong or prejudice unto any other person," and the crest and motto, above mentioned, is therefore " assigned and appropriated unto the foresaid coat of arms," as " depicted in the margin," and which is similar to the coat appended to the recorded pedigree, and which I have already blazoned. The said "*crest and motto*," however, are limited to the "said William Bruton and the heirs of his body lawfully begotten."

In the "margin" of the grant there is the usual painting of arms, helmet mantling, crest and motto, and, on the right of the illuminated border, the new crest of the hind and hawthorn bush, in the centre the Bruton arms impaling those of the said William's wife, Edith Smith, viz., *Sable*, a fess cotised between three martlets, *or*, and on the left the crest of the wife's family, a greyhound sejant, *gules*, collared and lined, *or.*

The anomalous introduction of the crest of the wife's family into an instrument, vouched for by Garter's signature, would claim more serious comment were it not for the fact that the heraldry of that period had shared the fate of Gothic architecture, and had become about as equally debased; nevertheless, such and similar irregularities are responsible for modern errors, such as the absurd and too prevalent decoration of carriages, plate, and servants' buttons with "*ladies' crests*," as they are very improperly termed. As I have remarked in *Practical Heraldry*, "ladies could neither bear, inherit, or transmit crests," and, "John Borough principale Kynge of Armes of Englishmen" nevertheless, this rule is, and always has been, in force, and very properly so, when it is remembered that in their origin crests could only be acquired by knights who had seen actual service in the field. The arms, called by Sir John Borough "the paternal arms of William Bruton," and therefore the legally admitted arms of the family of Bruton *alias* Breton of Borough, in Morthoe, are practically the same, save for tincture, as those accredited to Robert Fitz-Walter ("*or*, a fess between two chevronels, *gules*"), the Baron who headed "the army of God and Holy Church," and extorted Magna Charta from King John. These arms, again, are those of Clare, Earl of Gloucester, differenced by the apparent elimination of a chevronel, and the substitution of a fess in lieu of it, and their acquisition by Breton evidently points to a feudal dependency on the house of Clare, much of whose "honour of Gloucester" was situated in Devonshire. (See my *Manor of Winkleigh*, pp. 1-24, etc.)

It happens, singularly enough, that there were manors, both of "Leigh" and "Bickington," which were held from this honour, but both were Royal demesne lands at the period of the Survey, and not identical either with Alured Brito's manor of Langley, or Robert of Mortaine's "Bickington" holding. But the chief seat of the property of Jocelyn Brito was situated, as already stated (*ante* p. 353), at Halwell, in the parish of Brixton, and Halwell was held from the Crown as of the "honour of Gloucester," which "honour" came to the Clares in 1217, and remained with their heirs male for ninety-seven years. "Fitz-Walter" was actually a Clare, being the grandson of Robert, youngest brother of Gilbert de Clare, therefore he simply differenced his paternal arms by surmounting them with a fess, and thus one of the chevronels of Clare became entirely obliterated; but as Brito evidently assumed them to mark his mere feudal connection with the Earldom of Gloucester, such difference would not have sufficed without an entire change of tincture—a course which was adopted by his kinsman of Odecumbe to mark his own feudal connection with the De Vére Earldom of Oxford (see *ante*, p. 360); and both these Brito shields may consequently be reckoned amongst the most ancient and interesting examples of arms, which were indisputably feudal in their origin.

John Prince, having blazoned the escallop coat of Britt of Stottiscombe, already dealt with above, proceeds to remark, very carelessly and inaccurately, as to Breton of Bacetesberie or Borough. "And Britt of Bathin or Bachins arms were, *argent*, 2 chevrons, paly of six, *or* and *azure*."

In his "Worthies of Devon," Prince includes the biography of "Walter Britte," supposed, by himself, and Risdon, "to have proceeded from the British race," but to have been born at Stottiscombe. This Walter Britte, who flourished in the reign of Richard II., was one of the early reformers, and an advocate of the *doctrine* that "neither king or secular lord could give anything in perpetuity to Churchmen."

BRUTON OF ALWINGTON.

The Brutons of Alwington, a few miles south of Morthoe, are descended from Thomas Bruton *alias* Breton first son of Thomas Breton of Borough, in the latter parish, and eldest brother of William Bruton *alias* Breton of Heavitree. This

Thomas Bruton had three sons, Thomas, William, and George—the latter baptized at Alwington 2nd January, 1596-97—and two daughters. Of the sons, William's daughter, Margaret, married Edward Cotton, Archdeacon of Totnes, and a son of Dr. William Cotton, Lord Bishop of Exeter 1598-1621.

John Bruton, son and heir of Thomas, had a son, William, born 1607, who, by his wife, Elizabeth Atken, was the father of another William, and also of John Bruton, who died in 1694, aged forty-four. This John Bruton, "in, or about," 1683, is said to have purchased of the Carys of Cockington the ancient property and residence of the Yeos of Alwington, known as "Yeo Vale"*—a statement which is doubted by his present representative, who considers that his family had then resided at Yeo for more than a century at least. He was succeeded by his son, William Bruton, born 30th August, 1683. His eldest surviving son, Thomas, inherited Yeo Vale, and was followed, in 1769, by his son and heir, William Bruton, at whose death, 17th February, 1779, the property was sold to the Morrisons; by his wife, Ann James, a sister-in-law of John Meddon of Winscot, in the same parish, he was the father of five sons and two daughters. His second son, Richard, born 21st April, 1765, was the grandfather of Mr. D. Yeo Bruton, who now lives in Sussex.

In 1812 William Bruton's two youngest sons, William and Charles, inherited part of the Meddon property by devise of Mr. John Meddon, their cousin, and the last heir male of that family, which had settled at Winscot through a marriage with the daughter and heir of the Burgoynes, in 1624. Col. William Bruton, who had a moiety of Winscot, for many years commanded the North Devon Militia; he married into a younger branch of the Worths of Worth, in Washfield, his wife having been Gertrude, daughter of the Rev. J. Worth, Rector of High Bickington, and died in 1846. His second son, William, sometime Vicar of Siddlesham, Sussex, died July 10th, 1881. Col. Bruton's brother Charles married Frances Cory Walter; he was a Deputy Lieutenant for Devonshire, and held a commission for thirty years in his brother's regiment of militia, and was

---

* Lyson's *Mag. Brit.*, Vol. II., p. 10.

adjutant of that corps. He died in 1850, aged seventy-one; his eldest son, the Rev. Walter Meddon Bruton, Rector of East and West Worlington, died in 1885, and his son and heir, John Meddon Burgoyne Bruton, was born at Woolfardisworthy, April 5th, 1847.

THE BRITTONS OF BITTON.

The honour of Bitton in Gloucestershire, distant a few miles from Bristol, originally comprised two hides of land, one of which, in 1086, belonged to the Church, was afterwards known as the "Rectorial Manor," and was appropriated as a prebend to the See of Worcester.

The other hide, with an appanage known as "Hanham," and which included nearly the whole remainder of the parish, was given by Henry II. to Robert Fitz-Hardinge, and was thenceforth nominally regarded as parcel of the Berkeley barony, as shown by an assise of 1287; yet "Bitton" was held by the D'Amnevilles and their descendants, not from the Berkeleys, but directly from the Crown, as appears from a confirmation charter of 11th Henry III., in favour of Robert D'Amneville. The latter had two daughters, co-heirs, who each had a moiety of Bitton, from that time known as Bitton and Oldland.

Oldland passed by marriage to Oxehaye, with one of the co heirs, and after failure of her issue was sold to Richard de la More, who died 1292. The other co-heir married William de Putot, her only daughter, Petronilla, Hugh de Vivon, or Vivian, and in her widowhood she became the wife of David le Blund; and Bitton, not without litigation, went to her younger son of the same name.

In 1515, John Lord Hussey, of Bitton, in right of his wife Margaret Blund or Blount, sold Bitton to Dormer, who re-sold it to Berkeley, and with the Berkeleys it remained until 1633, when the manor was dismembered and the estates separated.

Similarly the manor of Hanham was divided into moieties known as "East and West Hanham." I need not follow the descent of this property through its several alienations. In the

4th Edward III., William de la Grene and John Bagworth gave the manor of West Hanham to the abbot and convent of Keynsham, in Somerset, and with that community it remained until the dissolution ; it was surrendered to the Crown 30th Henry VIII., and was always known as Hanham Court, and since then it has passed through various hands, and is now the property of Mr. Philip William Poole Britton, hereinafter mentioned. The manor of East Hanham, or Barre's Court, anciently the residence of Sir John de Button, a younger son of Adam D'Amneville, acquired its later name by the marriage of Sir John Barre with the granddaughter of Sir John de Button or Bitton, who died in 1382.

This Lady Barre died 2nd Richard III., 1485, seised of the manor of East Hanham, held of John Blount, as lord of the manor of Bitton; by *Inq. p.m.* her ladyship's heirs were found to be the daughters, or their descendants, of Sir John de Bytton, her maternal great-great-grandfather. Sir John's second daughter, Elizabeth, married Philip Hampton, her great-great-granddaughter, Lucy Hampton, Sir Thomas Newton, and the Newtons afterward owned Barre's Court, otherwise East Hanham. The Newton baronetcy became extinct in 1743, and the last baronet, Sir Michael Newton, pulled down Barre's Court shortly before his death.

As to the family of Britton, of Bitton, there is the same uncertainty as to the exactitude of their earlier descent as exists in the cases of other members of the family. Jocelyn Brito was a tenant *in capite* in Gloucestershire in the year 1086. Later on, Richard le Bret held three parts of a knight's fee in Weston, near Tetbury, *temp.* Henry II., of the fee of Ansger de Kylpec. In 1384, Joan, widow of Philip Vynour, claimed a capital messuage in Tewkesbury by devise of Stephen de Bruton (" De Banco," Mich. Term, 8th Richard II.). After the first quarter of the fourteenth century the then lords of Bitton, the Blounts, appear to have chiefly resided at Filton or Mangotsfield, and Bitton Court and the surrounding property was usually let upon farming leases. Prior to the sixteenth century I cannot recover evidence of the presence there of the Brittons, who were, I am much disposed to consider, cadets of the house of Breton of Borough, several members of which settled in the parishes of Parkham and Alwington considerably before the time of Thomas Bruton, the ancestor of the Brutons of Yeo Vale.

With respect, however, to Gloucestershire, Thomas and John Breton paid subsidy in Oldland, the moiety of the Bitton manor already mentioned, as early as 1523; Thomas Brytayne was taxed for Bitton and Hanham in 1545; John Breten and Walter his son held land at Hanham Abbots in 1556; whilst *Lewse* and Thomas Brytton were subsidised on the same estates in 1557.

John Bryttan in his will, dated 1st March, 1560, and proved at Gloucester, 9th October, 1562, describes himself as of the parish of Bitton; his son Thomas, who died in 1574, was twice married; by his first wife, Agnes, daughter of William Horsington, he had six sons and three daughters; of the sons I need only treat of the first and fifth.

The latter, John Britten of Bitton, married Jane Burnell at Bitton Church 26th June, 1571; his will was proved 14th September, 1612. His eldest son, Thomas Britten, baptized at Bitton 11th January, 1573, was the father of John Britten, who purchased the fee simple of the property upon which several of his ancestors are known to have resided, and became the owner of Bitton Court about the year 1633.

I must now return to the eldest son of Thomas Britten and Agnes Horsington, Jasper Britten, who resided at Swinford, in Bitton parish, and desires, by his will, dated August 12th, 1590, to be buried at Bitton near his father; his son John was the father of John, whose son, of the same name, by his wife, Elizabeth Deane, had three sons, John, Thomas, and Morris Britten. The last named, Morris, was baptized at Oldland in 1642. By his second son, Stephen Britten, he was the great-grandfather of Simon Britton, of the parish of St. George, Bristol, who by his second wife, Mary, daughter of James Gage (married 1781, died 1788), had, with other issue, a son, Simon Gage Britton, born 5th November, 1782, and a second son, Daniel Britton of Bristol, born 1784, died 1871, and who lived to welcome his great-grandson, Philip William Poole Britton (son of Henry William Britton, by his marriage with the daughter and heir of Benjamin Poole, who was only son of William Simon Britton of Caer Brito, Bristol, by his wife Caroline Gell, son and heir of the said Daniel Britton).

Mr. Philip William Poole Britton, F.S.A., now of Bitton House, Enfield, in the county of Middlesex, and of Hanham Court, in that of Gloucester, was born 13th October, 1863, and married at Bristol, in 1886, Agnes Cassandra, daughter of Charles Alfred Carlyon, in right of her grandmother, Emily Carlyon, a double descendant of the ancient family of Carlyon of Tregrehan, co. Cornwall, and who derive their name from their original property, Carlyon, near Truro. Winstanley Britton, eldest son of Mr. Philip William Poole Britton, was baptized at St. Saviour's, Bristol, 9th October, 1887, and, maternally, is twenty-second in direct descent from King Edward III. (*Coll. Ar. Arundel*, 2, No. 155); he has also, through a maternal great-grandmother, Mary Stackhouse, a descent from King Edward I., through Bohun and Courtenay.*

Simon Gage Britton, M.D., R.N., Surgeon of the *Victory* at Trafalgar, eldest son of Simon Britton, by his wife Mary Gage, long resided at King's Close, Barnstaple, and was buried at Ilfracombe in 1856. By his wife Jane, only daughter and heir of Thomas Hopkins, B.A., Jesus Coll., Oxford, and rector of Donyatt, co. Somerset, by his wife Mary, daughter of Robert Ford of Bridgewater, he had issue (with two daughters), Thomas Hopkins Britton, born 1817, and Paul Ford Britton, born 25th January, 1819 (M.A., Exeter Coll., Oxford), and now rector of Cadeleigh, near Tiverton, and who, by his wife Helen, daughter of William Short Tyeth of Pillhead, Barnstaple, is the father of the Rev. Arthur Paul Britton, M.A., the present rector of Ubley, co. Somerset, who is married, and has issue.

Thomas Hopkins Britton was educated at Barnstaple School (M.A., Exeter Coll., Oxford, 1842), and afterwards Vicar of Newlyn East, co. Cornwall. He married, in 1846, Frances Hamilton, second daughter of Thomas Hoskins, Captain R.N., of Broxbourne, Hants., and died at Exeter, 8th May, 1880, and was buried at Cadeleigh. He had issue, one daughter, Emily Jane, and two sons, Alfred Hoskins Britton, and Herbert Britton, born 1849 (B.A., Balliol Coll., Oxford).

---

* The second son of Henry William Britton and of his wife, daughter and heir of Benjamin Poole, Arthur Henry Daniel Britton, is a Lieut. in the 3rd Battalion Royal Fusiliers, in the 1st Volunteer Battalion of which regiment his elder brother also holds a commission.

Mr. Alfred Hoskins Britton,[*] born at Hockworthy, co. Devon, and baptized 13th September, 1848, is a Barrister-at-Law of the Middle Temple, and Director, Audit Department, H.M. Exchequer. He married, 13th September, 1878, Florence Mary, second daughter of S. E. Martyn, of Thurloe Square, South Kensington, and has, with two daughters, an eldest surviving son and heir, John Alfred Hamilton Britton, born 22nd September, 1882.

The Arms of this branch of Brito, as now recorded and attached to their pedigree, at Heralds' College, are thus blazoned in the "grant":—"*Quarterly, or* and *gules*, two lions passant in chief, and as many mullets of six points in base, within a bordure engrailed, all counterchanged."

Crest.—"A lion's gamb erect and erased *az.*, guttée d'eau, between two mullets of six points, also *azure.*"

Motto.—" Salut à tous."

WYKES OF NORTHWYKE.

There is a popular, but erroneous, tradition in this county that the "Wykes of Northwyke," in the parish of South Tawton, are as old as the Conquest; and a much more absurd one, to the effect that a fine table tomb in the parish church there, evidently Elizabethan, bears the counterfeit presentment of "old warrior Wykes," who is roundly stated to have been master farrier to "Norman William," and a trusted and highly valued retainer of that monarch, whose charger he is said to have supplied with a new set of shoes on the eve of the battle of Senlac.

Although there can be no question as to the great antiquity of the race of Wykes as Devonshire landowners, these tales are as hypothetical as another which very misleadingly describes them as having been originally known as "Wray, but styled Wyke, or Wykes, since the reign of Richard the Second."

In 1086, the manors of South Tawton with Ash, Wray, in

---

[*] His uncle, the Rev. Paul Ford Britton, who has now been for fifty years rector of Cadeleigh, in this Diocese and County, was ordained priest in 1843.

Moreton Hampstead, and Cheverstone, in Kenton (I am adopting modern spelling), all of which save Ash, had belonged to the family of Harold, were alike held, in demesne, by King William. Wray and Cheverstone were subsequently owned by a family long known as de Cheverstone; whilst Northwyke, in South Tawton, said by Risdon, with an anachronism as to date, "to have been anciently the lande of William de Wigoren, *alias* Chamberlain," was for several generations, subsequently to 1242, held by the De Wrays of Northwyke, otherwise *North Wigorn*.

It appears to me as certain that this William de Wigornia, rather than "Wigoren," was not only the common ancestor of the Wrays, Cheverstones, and Wykes, but that he also gave name to the several properties in South Tawton, afterwards corrupted into West-wyke, Week-Town, or "Wiggaton," and Northwyke, neither of which seem to be identical with the Domesday manors known as "Wic," or "Wice," the Saxon equivalent for a hamlet, from the verb, *vichian*, which signifies to reside or dwell; hence we get Prancras-wick, Germans-wick, Wick Dabernon, Great Wick, and many other parishes, towns, and manors, in this and other parts of the country.

But in Devonshire there are only "Wykes," thus written, in the parishes of South Tawton and Axminster; and North Wyke, in the latter parish, is also not a Domesday manor, but takes name from an adjacent property, long known as Wigost.

There is every reason to assume that "William de Wigornia"[*] gave his name to North and West Wyke, and to Wiggaton, in the parish of South Tawton; he was certainly the ancestor of the Wykes, and was also the owner of Wray, in Moreton Hampstead, and of Cheverstone, in Kenton, and seems to have been one of the younger sons of Robert de Bellomonte, Earl of Mellent, and *de jure*, Earl of Worcester, by his marriage with Maud, daughter and co-heir of Reginald, Earl of Cornwall. Hence he was known as "de Wigornia"—in English, William of Worcester. The whole of the South Tawton property I have

---

[*] His brother, "Robert de Wigornia," *alias* "Chamberlain," married Jane, daughter and co-heir of Baldwin de Belston, and seems to have died, *s. p.*

mentioned came into the hands of Henry the First upon the death of his brother, William Rufus, in the year 1100. King Henry, by Elizabeth, daughter of Robert de Bellomonte, Earl of Leicester, had with other left-handed issue, the aforesaid Reginald, Earl of Cornwall, possibly,* and a daughter, Constance, certainly, to whom he gave the whole of the manor of South Tawton, upon her marriage with Rosceline, Viscount de Bellomonte, and it is shown, by the Pipe Rolls, that she received the rents, etc., etc., in 1157.

Therefore, Elizabeth de Bellomonte was, in such case, not only the mother of the lady of the manor of South Tawton, but she was also the aunt of Robert of Worcester, Earl of Mellent, the husband of her granddaughter, Maud of Cornwall, and both the great-grandmother and the great-aunt of "William de Wigornia," who doubtless obtained, primarily, the Royal manors of Wray and Cheverstone, through his frail relative's connection with royalty, and the Wyke estates, subsequently, by arrangement with his cousin, Richard de Bellomonte, who succeeded his mother at South Tawton after 1157. This Richard had no male issue; his daughter and heir, Constance de Bellomonte, married Roger de Toni, about the year 1162, and the ultimate heir of de Toni brought the Devonshire property to Guy Beauchamp, Earl of Warwick, who died in 1315. The latter was maternally descended from Henry de Bellomonte, *alias* de Newburgh, brother of the first Earl of Leicester, and therefore uncle of the first Earl of Mellent and Worcester, as well as of Elizabeth, King Henry's mistress; and it was in consequence of the minority of Thomas Beauchamp, Earl of Warwick, who was only two years old in 1315, that the manor of South Tawton was sometime in the hands of King Edward II.—a fact worth mentioning, because the county historians who have referred to the Warwicks, as owners of South Tawton, have never attempted to explain how the manor came into their possession.†

---

* It has been sometimes *asserted* that the mother of Reginald, Earl of Cornwall, was a daughter of Sir Robert Corbet.
† The Earls of Mellent were of kin to the Dukes of Normandy. Adeline, daughter of Waleran, and sister and heir of Hugh, Earls of Mellent, married Roger de

As both Robert and William de Wigornia, who were equally related to the early lords of South Tawton, both before and after the separation of that manor from the Royal demesne, are sometimes called "Camerarius" or Chamberlayn, they probably held office, successively, under King Henry II., their kinsman. I may add that they were likewise the brothers-in-law, through the marriage of their sister Mabel, of William de Vernon, Earl of Devon, who died a very old man, in 1217. Her daughter Mary married Robert Courtenay, and hence it may have been that William de Wigornia's descendant, Sir John Cheverstone, some generations afterward, devised the whole of his property to the Courtenays, failing his issue by Jane, his wife, sister of his kinsman, Sir Philip Courtenay of Powderham; thus Cheverstone has descended in the Courtenay family since the reign of Richard II.

William de Wray, who, according to Sir William Pole and others, was seised of Northwyke 27th Henry III., was a grandson of William de Wigorn, and son of William de Cheverstone, and the uncle of Sir John Cheverstone, who owned Wray, and married the heir of Bozun, through which match he obtained Ilton Castle and other property, which was also eventually devised to the Courtenays.* William de Wray of Northwyke, thus described in 1242, seems to have inherited that property, together with the other estates in South Tawton, now known as West Wyke, Middlewick, Gooseford, and the Manor of Ash, and Ash House was an occasional seat of the younger sons of the family down to the end of the sixteenth century, and was last held, as a residence, by John, fourth son of the *real* "Warrior Wykes," who was buried at South Tawton in 1597, aged forty-five. Ash Manor was an appanage of the Royal Manor of South Tawton, and was originally held, in partage with Queen Githa, by Alric the Theign, and taxed

---

Bellomonte, and had sons, Robert, Earl of Mellent and Leicester, and Henry of Newburgh, Earl of Warwick.

Robert commanded the right wing of the Conqueror's army at Hastings, and afterward "exceeded all the nobles of England in favour and riches." His son Robert succeeded to the Earldom of Leicester, whilst Waleran inherited the Earldom of Mellent, and became officiary Earl of Worcester in 1144, and was thence known as "Waleran de Wigornia." He was the father of Robert, father of "William de Wigornia" of South Tawton, and of Robert de Wigornia of Belston.

* See Cheverstone genealogy, *post*.

for a virgate and a half of land. In 1086 the king had six villeins and one serf upon Ash Manor, together with three ploughs. William de Wray was succeeded at South Tawton by Walter de Wray of Wyke, in 1278, whose son William, a younger son of "Walter of Wyke," granted to "William, son of Anthony" of Tavistock, a meadow called "Blakedhic mede," with metes and bounds, reserving a six-foot way to his (the grantor's) other meadow, called "Le Ham," by deed dated "morrow of the Circumcision, 14th Edward I." (2nd January, 1285-86). This property was situated at Wilmington, near Tavistock. Both the Wykes, and their connections the Beaumonts, had outlying property at Tavistock, and the former are frequently mentioned in official connection with the Devonshire Stannary. The son and heir of Walter de Wray of Wyke, Roger de Wray of Northwyke, appears to have left Walter de Wray of Northwyke, son and heir, and "John atte Wyke." The latter was the father of John Wykes, a benefactor to Stapeldon Hall, now Exeter College, Oxford, 8th November, 1358, and who was Recorder of Exeter from 1354-1379.

The Recorder's uncle, Walter de Wray of Northwyke, was succeeded by his son Roger de Wray of Northwyke in 1345.

The Wray estate appears to have been settled upon the first Walter's younger son, William of Tavistock, 1285, and his heirs of body, and to have passed with his daughter and heir to a certain Ralph Abbot (see Wray genealogy, *post*), and by the marriage of Joane, daughter of "Archinalds" Abbot to Norris. During the reign of Richard II. it again reverted to a descendant of its early owners by the marriage of Richard de Wraye, whose branch had settled at "Trussell," with Alice, sister and heir of John Norris, and afterward descended, with successive heiresses, to Ford, Corsett, and Southmeade. That the "Wrays" of "Trussell," now represented by Sir Henry B. T. Wray of Tawstock Court, are collateral kinsfolk of the Wykes, is proved by the similarity of the armorial bearings of the two families. Until they removed to Trebitch, in Cornwall, they resided at "Trussell," otherwise Thrushelton, near Maristow, upon some barton land, to which they had given the name of their ancient property at Moreton.

The children of "Roger de Wray" of Northwyke were

contemporary with the Abbots of Wray, and it was probably for this reason that they abandoned the surname of Wray, an estate with which they had become disassociated, in favour of Wyke, the property with which for some generations they had been more closely identified. John (Risdon calls him "Joseph") Wyke replaced John Herle, Sheriff of Devon, during the latter portion of the third year of Henry IV., and "William Wyke of Northwyke," alive in 1421, commences the pedigree entered at the earlier visitations of the Heralds of Arms, which were first held in Devonshire in 1531.

He married Katherine, daughter and heir of John Burnell of South Tawton, a family which had been settled for several generations at Great Cocktree in that parish, and is said to have made his wife's home the principal future residence of himself and his immediate successors. That the King's Royal Manor of Elintone, in South Tawton, which also belonged to the Wykes, should have been subsequently known as "Ilton," the name of the Castle in the parish of Marlborough, built by the Cheverstones, and subsequently left to the Courtenays, may be another slight, but quite unnecessary, proof of the identity of the latter name with that of Wykes. These two "Iltons" are the only places so called in Devonshire.

William Wykes and Katherine Burnell had four sons, viz., John, the eldest, who married into the Luttrell family—the marriage settlement is dated in 1421—and died childless; Richard Wykes of Cocktree and Northwyke, second son and heir to his brother; John, whom I suppose to have been the ancestor of Weekes of Honeychurch, and who will be referred to later on; and Roger Wykes of Bindon, in the parish of Axmouth.

This Roger Wykes, by grant of Nicholas Bach, dated 7th Henry IV., 1406, appears to have acquired Bindon, perhaps in marriage with the devisee's daughter; he resided there afterward, and abandoned his paternal for his maternal arms, and bore the coat of Burnell of Cocktree, *arg.*, three barnacles, *sab.*, differenced with a chevron, *erm.* By his marriage, as a widower, with Jane Bisset, he obtained a life interest in Radbours, County Dorset. He was buried in Trent St. Andrew's, near Sherborne. By his first wife he left a son, John, who married into the house of Camill of Shapwick, and had issue John, whose wife, Elizabeth Lyte, of Lytes-Cary, County Somerset, brought him two sons, John and Richard. The latter eventually succeeded as heir of entail to his nephew William Wykes, married a Somaster, and left four daughters, who married Giffard, Hays, Barry, and Erle, and amongst them and their descendants the property became divided. Mary Wykes, the youngest daughter, was the wife of Walter Erle, who purchased his brother-in-law Giffard's share, and made Bindon his residence. He was the grandfather of Sir Walter Erle, a distinguished Parliamentary general, whose grandson, General Erle, commanded the centre of the English army at the battle of Almanza, 1707. The latter's daughter, Frances, married Sir Edward Erle, Bart., of Maddington, Wiltshire, and their only child was the wife of Henry Drax, of Ellerton Abbey, Yorkshire, secretary to Frederick, Prince of Wales. Bindon was sold by her son Thomas Erle Drax, who married Mary, daughter of Lord St. John of Bletshoe. Two of the sisters of the last owner of Bindon were the Ladies Berkeley and Castlehaven, another was the wife of Sir William Hanham, Bart. The Charborough Park estate and other property, inherited from Wykes through Camill, descended to the late Mr. J. S. Sawbridge, M.P., who assumed the name of Drax by Royal licence, and his daughters and their issue still represent the family of Wykes of Bindon.

To return to Northwyke. Richard Wyke, of Northwyke and Cocktree, brother of Roger of Bindon, was dead in 1476, by his wife, to whom he had been married at least thirty-eight years, and who was a daughter of John Avenel, of Blackpool, one of the direct representatives of the ancient Earls of Devon, of the house of Redvers, as I have shown elsewhere,[*] he had three sons and a daughter, Margaret, who married one of the Whiddons of Chagford, and was the grandmother of the well-known Judge Whiddon, who died in 1575.

It is to be feared that this Richard Wykes alienated much of the family property. It was about his time that the Battishills became settled at Westwyke, and it is certain, from an extant conveyance, that he sold a considerable portion of the manor

---

[*] See my *Suburbs of Exeter*, sub. "Earldom of Devon," pp. 81-87, etc.

of East Ayshe to his neighbour, Richard Northmore of Well (see Northmore Pedigree, *ante*). The deed is dated 4th Edward IV., A.D. 1464. It was also about this period that the Milfords (evidently a place-name, *Mill-ford*) became settled at Wigginton, *alias* Wyke-Town; the first of them, described as of *Wiccanton* in the Heralds' Visitation of 1620, was buried at South Tawton, in 1588.

Richard Wykes' son, William, is described as of Northwyke, in 1476; it is shown by an Inquisition, 15th Henry VIII., that his son of the same name duly succeeded to Northwyke; the latter, by his wife Jane Prideaux of Thuborough, in the parish of Sutcombe (a baronetcy, recently extinct, was afterwards created in this family) had sons, John, Richard, William, and Thomas, and a daughter, Jane, the wife of John Baron.

The eldest son, John, commences the pedigree of the family entered at the Heralds' Visitation of 1620, and is duly described as "John Wykes, of Northwyke, in com. Devon, Esq." His first wife, and the mother of his family, was Elizabeth, a co-heir of the Pokeswells of Criston, co. Somerset; but he married, secondly, a kinswoman, Jane, daughter of Walter Wray, of Wray, in Thrushelton, and left her a widow, 10th August, 1545.

His son and heir, John Wykes, of Northwyke, was "aged 20 years and more in 1545." He married Mary, daughter of Sir Roger Gifford, Knight, of Brightleigh, a direct ancestor of the present Lord Chancellor, died at the end of October, 1591, and was buried in South Tawton church on the following first of November. He was evidently the "Warrior Wykes" of the local tradition already mentioned. His fine specimen of an Elizabethan tomb may be seen in the north, or "Wyke's aisle," of the parish church, and supports his full-length effigy clad in the half armour and enormous ruff of the period.

He left a large family—eight sons and three daughters—and of them it is only necessary to mention here the two eldest, Roger and *Mark*, and to the latter I shall presently refer again. The eldest son, Roger Wykes of Northwyke, whose will was proved at Exeter, in February, 1603-4, was the father of John "Wikes" of "Northwicke," alive in 1620. His wife, Grace, was of the good old county family of Arscott of Tetcott, and by her he had seven children; of these his eldest son, Roger, predeceased him, and is the last entered upon the Visitation Pedigree, in which he is described as "over 15 years of age" in 1620. He married Mary, daughter of Thomas Southcote of Mohuns Ottery, and a member of a well-known county family.

His second son, John Wikes, baptized 2nd May, 1611, married Priscilla Kingwell, and succeeded his nephew, John Wykes of Northwyke, as *heir male at law*, in 1661, and died in 1680, but was unjustly deprived of his heritage, under circumstances which may well be regarded as a romance of history. By his wife Priscilla Kingwell, widow of Richard Hole, he had two sons and three daughters; his eldest son died before him unmarried; the younger, Roger Wikes, was twice married, died at sea in 1694, and left an only daughter and heir, Grace, who was baptized at South Tawton, 23rd April, 1673.

John Wykes, son of Roger, and Mary Southcote, and who had a sister Katherine, the second wife of Edmund Parker of Boringdon, ancestor of Lord Morley, succeeded to Northwyke upon the death of his grandfather. He was of an exceedingly weak and vacillating disposition, and fell into the hands of designing men, who, after his early death, from phthisis, in 1661, at about the age of twenty-five, literally entered upon Northwyke at the point of the sword, as will be fully explained hereafter. I have now, however, to return to Mark Wykes, his great-great-uncle, and his great-grandfather's second brother.

This Mark, the favourite son of his mother, Mary Giffard, was settled at South Tawton upon an estate known as Collibear; he was twice married, and had issue by both alliances. His eldest son, John Wykes of Collibear, by his wife Joan Hole of Blackhall, in South Tawton, was the father of John Wykes of Collibear, whose son, Nathaniel Wykes of Swansea, claimed the Northwyke estates as *heir male at law*, upon the death, at sea, of his kinsman Roger Wykes, in 1694. His pedigree is duly set forth in the pleadings connected with this memorable Chancery suit, which extended over forty years, and was never satisfactorily settled. He had several children, and of them his son, Nathaniel, was the father of William Wykes, buried at

South Tawton, 9th November, 1800, whose only daughter and heir, Mary Wykes, was married to Charles, grandson of William Finch, who married Agnes Lambert of South Tawton, in 1719; he was of the Kentish family which claims a common origin with the Herberts, Earls of Pembroke, and which is now represented in the peerage by the Earls of Winchilsea. Mary Wykes had a son, Charles Finch, baptized at South Tawton, 18th February, 1798, who was the father of the Rev. William Finch, M.A., St. John's College, Cambridge, now of Northwyke in the parish of South Tawton, and of Chaddesley Corbett, co. Worcester.

Mr. Finch, of Northwyke, married a daughter and co-heir of Josiah Perrin, of Wharton, co. Chester, and maternally descended from John Dudley of Davenham, co. Chester.

WEEKES OF HONEYCHURCH.

The connection between this family, and that of which I have just previously treated, must doubtless be referred to a certain Robert Wyke, whose daughter Joan married John de Honeychurche late in the fifteenth century, who resided at Tavistock, but was the owner of land in Honeychurch, situated seven miles from Oakhampton, from about the reign of Henry III.

This Robert Wyke was contemporary with William Wykes of Northwyke, who I consider must have been his first cousin, and the nephew of his father, John Wykes, who was living in 1435. Otherwise the arms of Wyke of Northwyke would not have been admitted to "Weeks of Honeychurch," as they appear to have been at the Heralds' Visitation of 1620.

That the primary settlement of this branch at Honeychurch was due to the marriage of Joan Wykes with John de Honeychurch is tolerably certain, but there is a hiatus in their history for three generations, since the ancestor of Weekes of Honeychurch, as recorded at the Visitation referred to, was "Sir Richard Weekes, Knight, of Honeychurch" (contemporary with John Wykes of Northwyke, "aged 20 years and more, 1545"), and who is reputed to have married an unknown daughter of Cary of Clovelly. Sir Richard was the grandfather of Simon

Weekes, also of Honeychurch, whose son William married Arminell, daughter of John Yeo of Hatherley by his wife Anne, daughter of William Honeychurch of Honeychurch and Tavistock.

Their son Simon seems to have removed to Broadwood-Kelly, and his eldest son Francis Weekes, aged thirty in 1620, married Wilmot Coffin of Portledge, and had six sons and a daughter. Of these, Richard Weekes, the third son, resided at Hatherleigh, was a "gentleman pensioner," that is to say, a member of the body now known as "The Honourable Corps of Gentlemen at Arms," and died in the Fleet Prison in February, 1670.

Mr. Richard Weekes seems to have been little better than a common adventurer, and his history has been handed down to us, very clearly, through the medium of original documents filed in the Court of Chancery; he made the acquaintance of poor young John Wykes of Northwyke, persuaded him that he was a near relative, although the family at that time, or since, have had no clue even to the slight connection, which doubtless subsisted between them, as above explained, and persuaded him, to the prejudice of his immediate relatives, to execute a conveyance of the Northwyke estates in his favour.

John Wykes of Northwyke was, as I have already said, a victim to consumption. Shortly before his death, in 1661, his friend, and very remote kinsman, of the Royal bodyguard persuaded him, in opposition to the wishes of his widowed mother and of his only sister Katherine, afterwards Mrs. Parker of Boringdon, to undertake a journey to Plymouth on the pretence of some special medical advice. Ultimately John Wykes was induced to execute a deed of settlement, dated 29th August, 1661, of the whole of his property, inclusive of the ancient seat of the family, to this Richard, under great pressure by the latter, and two medical men, his near relatives, whom he had secured in his interests. But this conveyance was endorsed with a power of verbal revocation, and left in the custody of the young squire of Northwyke, who then insisted on returning forthwith to South Tawton. He died at Northwyke shortly afterward, but in his last moments expressed sorrow to his mother, sister, and other witnesses, for the action adverse to their interests, which he had been induced to take, and solemnly revoked the deed by word of mouth, but failed to cancel it in writing.

John Wykes was gathered to his ancestors on Saturday, 21st September, 1661, and on the following Sunday evening Mr. Richard Weekes made his appearance at Northwyke, s·ated that he was "come to perform the devil's part and his own," drew his sword, and held it at the breast of Katherine Wykes and her mother, and threatened to kill them both unless they forthwith left the house and gave him quiet possession.

Ultimately, as sworn in the "pleadings," he knocked down the sister, locked up the mother, then broke into the room where "all the deeds, evidences, and writings of the family" were preserved, and carried them away. He survived for nine years, and died a prisoner for debt in London, as I have already stated, in 1670. His son Richard, despite the protracted Chancery proceedings, entered into possession by virtue of the deed of settlement, which had been duly signed and sealed by John Wykes before he left Plymouth; married the daughter of Mr. John Northmore of Well (see Northmore history, *ante*), and left at his decease, 1696, three sons and three daughters.

The eldest son, John Weekes, succeeded to Northwyke, married Elizabeth, daughter of William Northmore, of Throwley, and was buried at Lezant in 1750. He had no family, and in consideration of an annuity he sold the Northwyke estates to his sisters during his lifetime.

The manor of Ilton was thus conveyed to Robert Hole of Zeal Monachorum, the husband of Martha Weekes, together with Great Cocktree and other lands. Northwyke became the property of George Hunt of North Bovey, the second husband of Elizabeth Weekes, who administered to her brother's effects, unadministered, in 1751.

There are said to have been more than a hundred different suits in respect of the Northwyke lands between the years 1661 and 1700. Of late years the old mansion has been divided into two farmhouses, but is rich in mullioned windows and fine oak panelling of the Elizabethan period. It was not, however, as recently stated in a newspaper, "the residence of a

Lord Chief Justice Hunt in the sixteenth century," and history, moreover, is silent as to any such individual of the race of Hunt.

It has recently been sold by the executors of a late owner, together with four hundred acres of the surrounding property, and has been promptly purchased for over £4,000 by the Rev. William Finch, who, as I have already shown, is the great grandson, twice removed, of Nathaniel Wykes of Swansea, who became the head of the family of Wykes of Northwyke and South Tawton in 1694.

The Arms of Wykes of Northwyke, allowed also to Weekes of Honeychurch in 1620, are, *ermine*, three battleaxes, *sable*. The Northwyke family quarter Burnell, Avenel, and Powkeswell.

The Honeychurch branch was entitled to quarter Kelly by the marriage of Richard, eldest grandson of Sir Richard Weekes, with Alice, daughter and heir of Henry Kelly, but the right passed with her daughter and heir to the Haydons of Ottery St. Mary.

South Tawton extends over 10,878 acres of land, five thousand of which were owned by the Wykes of Northwyke for many centuries.

CHEVERSTONE OF CHEVERSTONE, WRAY, EAST AYSHE, AND ILTON.

"William de Wigornia," son of Robert de Bellomonte, Earl of Mellent, son and heir of Walleran, officiary Earl of Worcester, and whose brother, Roger de Wigornia, or "de Wyrescestrin," also styled "Roger de Meuelent," was a churchman, and held the prebendal stall of Bromesbury in St. Paul's Cathedral in 1192 (Reg. Dec. and Cap., Lond., f. 57), obtained a grant of the above manors, with the exception of Ilton, during the reign of Henry II., as shown by the preceding history of the family of "Wykes of Northwyke."

He appears to have had a son, William, who certainly inherited the South Tawton manor of Ayshe, and is mentioned also as the owner of Wray, in Moreton-Hampstead. He seems to have assumed the name of his Kenton property and to have been known as "William de Cheverstone." He was the father of "William de Wray," who was found seised of Northwyke in 1242, and also of another son, "Sir John de Cheverstone," whose son, of the same knightly rank and name, acquired Ilton Castle, in the parish of Marlborough, near Kingsbridge, in marriage with a co-heir of Bozun, whose sister, the other co-heir, married Ferrers of Bere. His son, Ralph Cheverstone of Ilton, *temp*. Henry III., has been described as the "father," but was actually the grandfather of Sir John Cheverstone, whose wife was Joan, a daughter of Hugh, Earl of Devon, and sister of Sir Philip Courtenay of Powderham.

The last Sir John's father, John Cheverstone, had license, 9th Edward III., to castellate his residence at "Ydilton" (Ilton) as shown by the Patent Rolls of the year 1335, and the latter had also a daughter who married into the Halwell family, of Harberton, and left a son, Thomas de Halwell.

Sir John Cheverstone the younger, by deed of settlement, gave the reversion of the whole of his property to his brother-in-law, Sir Philip Courtenay, failing his own male issue. His wife, Joan Courtenay, is mentioned in her mother's will, dated 28th January, 1390, and, although the Courtenays duly succeeded to the Cheverstone estates by virtue of the conditional reversion, Thomas de Halwell, upon his uncle's death, became heir general at law.

The latter's descendant, Sir John Halwell, appears to have assumed the arms of Cheverstone, and immediately after the accession of Henry VII., 1485, he commenced an action against Sir William Courtenay of Powderham, for the recovery of the Cheverstone estates. After a tedious litigation, which extended over some years, it was ultimately decreed that the Courtenays should continue in the quiet possession of their land, as they have since done, but only after payment to the plaintiff of the sum of one thousand pounds, upon a day named " within the King's Tower of London."

Sir William Courtenay, who survived until 1512, was exceedingly indignant at this award, after the lapse of so many years of undisputed possession of the lands, and is said to have counted the money out to his antagonist in *groats*, which he maintained to be an ancient, and still strictly legal, tender.

These Halwells of Harberton must not be confounded with their namesakes of the "House of Brito" (*ante*, p. 353), there were, and are, several places in the county called Halwell, the word being a corruption of "Holy-well." (See my *Ashburton and its Neighbourhood*, p. 7.)

Sir John Halwell of Harberton had a son and heir, Richard, and is also asserted to have had another son, the father of Andrew "Holwell," to whom I shall presently refer. Richard Halwell, son and heir of Sir John, married Anne, daughter and heir of Sir John Norbury, by whom he had an only daughter, Jane, erroneously described (Lyson's, *Magna Britannia, Devon*, Vol. I., p. clxvi.) as the eldest of "six co-heiresses."

The five ladies thus cited, minus one, "Fridiswide," who has been omitted entirely, were the daughters of the said Jane Halwell, by her marriage with Sir Edmund Bray, Knt., who was summoned to Parliament as Lord Bray, 21st Henry VIII. Jane's only son, the second Lord Bray, died *s.p.* in 1557; her eldest daughter, Anne Bray, was the wife of George Brooke, Lord Cobham; her grandsons, Henry, Lord Cobham, and his younger brother, George Brooke, were both attainted, consequently the abeyance of the Bray barony was permitted in 1839, to the descendant and representative of Jane Halwell's second daughter, Elizabeth Bray, who married Sir Ralph Verney, the ancestor of Sir John Verney, created Baron Verney and Viscount Fermanagh by Queen Anne. The third daughter of Lord Fermanagh, Margaret Verney, married Sir Thomas Cave, and her great-granddaughter, Sarah Cave, became, with Royal permission, Lady Bray, in her own right, at the date above mentioned.

Lady Bray married Henry Otway of Castle Otway, and survived all her four sons. At her death, in 1862, the Bray barony again fell into abeyance between her four surviving daughters, and was terminated, in 1879, by the youngest of them, Henrietta, the wife of the Rev. E. Wyatt-Edgell, and the mother of the present Lord Braye,[*] whose eldest brother, as Adjutant of the 17th Lancers, was killed in action at Ulundi, 4th July, 1879.

---

[*] The name, now thus written, appears to have been originally spelt as above.

Jane Halwell's great-grandson by her eldest daughter Anne, was, with his brother, Lord Cobham, implicated in the plot known as " Ralegh's Conspiracy," for the asserted advancement of Arabella Stuart to the throne, in 1603, and (although the principal actors, inclusive of his brother, were reprieved, and the sentence upon Sir Walter Ralegh was not carried out until 1618), George Brooke was executed, his property was attached, and his attainder was never reversed; he married, however, Elizabeth, daughter of Thomas, last Lord Borough, and had an only son, Sir William Brooke, Knight of the Bath, whose wife was Penelope, daughter of Sir Moses Hill, by whom he had three daughters, the eldest of whom, by her second marriage with Sir William Boothby, had an eldest son, William Boothby, who inherited the baronetcy at the decease of his step-brother's son, Sir Henry Boothby, and a younger son, Brooke Boothby, whose son of the same name became the sixth baronet in 1787, and was the great-great-grandfather of Sir Brooke Boothby, the present baronet, of Broadlow Ash, co. Derby, who is, therefore, the direct representative and heir at law of the Cheverstones of Kenton and Ilton.

As I have previously remarked, however, Sir John Halwell, who recovered the large sum of one thousand pounds in his litigation with the Courtenays, in right of his descent from Ann, sister and heir general of Sir John Cheverstone of Ilton, the husband of Joan Courtenay, is said to have had a younger son, who was the father of a certain Andrew " Holwell," who died in 1624, and who was the ancestor of an Exeter physician, William Holwell, whose grandson, Edward Holwell, of Exeter, married Isabella Newte, of Tiverton, and was the father of the Rev. William Holwell, Fellow of Exeter College, Oxford, 1779-93, when he was presented to the vicarage of Menheniot. He afterwards married Lady Charlotte Hay, eldest daughter of the fourteenth Lord Erroll, whose son, the sixteenth Earl, assumed his mother's name of Carr, a course which was also adopted by Lady Charlotte's husband in 1798, as additional to his own name.

Mr. Holwell-Carr, who died in London in 1830, was a distinguished amateur artist and Fellow of the Royal Society. He painted a portrait of Sir William Petre, which he presented to Exeter College, and bequeathed his fine gallery of examples of the Italian School, including da Vinci's "Christ disputing with the Doctors," to the National Gallery.

The Cheverstones bore a "canting" coat, viz., "*or*, on a bend, *gules*, three goats passant, *arg*."

THE WREYS OF TAWSTOCK.

As I have shown in the preceding genealogies, William de Wigornia appears to have left the whole of his Devonshire property to his son William, who assumed the name of Cheverstone, from the Kenton manor of that name, which, from the time of Sir John Cheverstone, who died in the reign of Richard the second, has belonged, by devise of the latter, to the Powderham branch of the Courtenay family, whose right to the Earldom of Devon, dormant after 1556, was admitted to Sir William Courtenay, Viscount Courtenay of Powderham, in 1831.* But the manor of Wray, in Moreton-Hampstead, of which the said William de Cheverstone was seised in the reign of King John, was evidently given to his other son William, who is known as William de Wray, and whose principal residence, in 1242, was at Northwyke. This William de Wray of Northwyke, had a son, Walter de Wray, of Northwyke, in 1278, who, as I have already shown, p. 378, *ante*, was the father of Roger de Wray, who carried on the line of Northwyke, and also of "William, son of Walter of Wyke," 1285-86, and I can only conclude that this last "William" must have inherited Wray, and have left it to his daughter and heir, the wife of Ralph Abbot, as the latter was found seised of it early in the fourteenth century.

The family known as Le Abbé, or Abbot, were at an early date settled upon the manor of Loughtor, within the parish of Plympton St. Mary, and were also the owners of the manor and church of Washfield, near Tiverton. I believe Ralph Abbot of Wray to have been a son of William Abbot of Loughtor, another of whose sons, Walter Abbot, presented to Washfield Church in 1335, and had an only daughter and heir,

* See my *Earldom of Devon* (*Suburbs Exon.*, pp. 74-118 and 200-202).

Alice Abbot, who married Humphry, second son of Hugh Beauchamp of White Lackington, co. Somerset, and gave the manor and advowson of Washfield to her son, Hugh Beauchamp, whose eventual co-heir, Margery Beauchamp, brought them to her husband, Thomas Worthe of Worth, in the same parish; and "Great Beauchamp," then the old seat of the manor of Washfield, in distinction to that of Worth, was the only property reserved from the sale of the ancient Worth estates, which was effected in the years 1887 and 1888. (See *ante*, p. 52, and *Worth of Worth, post*.)

Ralph Abbot was the father of Walter Abbot of Wray, and grandfather of Arkonald Abbot, whose daughter and heir, Joane, was the wife of John Norris, and the latter's daughter, Alice Norris, eventually inherited Wray, upon the deaths of her grand-nephews Thomas and John Norris, successively of Wray, and who died without issue.

This Alice Norris married a certain "Richard de Wray," a match which has created a considerable amount of confusion as to the actual earlier habitation of the Wreys of Tawstock, whose pedigree, entered at the Heralds' Visitation of Devonshire, in 1564 (Colby, p. 213), commences with "William Wray of Wray," great-grandfather of "Walter Wraye of North Russell," whereas the said William Wray was actually of Wray, in North Thrushelton, otherwise "North Russell," and not, as might be inferred from this description, of Wray in Moreton Hampstead.

That the Wrays of North Thrushelton, near Tavistock, were cadets of the house of Wray of South Tawton, is sufficiently evident from their coat armour, which, but for tincture and for one of the due differences of the period, is identical with the arms borne by the Wrays, afterward Wykes, of South Tawton, and it is probable that "William Wray" of North Thrushelton, who gave his name to his residence within that manor, which had been held in the reign of Edward III. by the Talbots, and who seems to have become possessed of it during the latter half of the fourteenth century, was a younger son of Walter de Wray of Northwyke, whose son and heir, Roger de Wray, was seised of Northwyke in 1346.

It is quite possible that "Richard de Wraye," the husband

of Alice Norris of Wray, in Moreton Hampstead, was a descendant of William Wray of Wray in North Thrushelton, or he may have been quite unconnected with the old "de Wrays," and may have simply been known from his habitation, *jure uxoris*, upon his wife's property of that name. On the other hand, his wife, Alice, cannot have succeeded to that property until late in life, upon the decease, without issue, of John Norris of Wray, the last of her grand-nephews, yet as the somewhat peculiar name of "Erkenwald" (pronounced Arkonald) was perpetuated in the Wykes' family, who only abandoned the name of Wray in favour of Wykes during the reign of Richard II., the evidence, on the whole, appears to be in favour of the conclusion that "Richard de Wraye" was a cadet of the Wrays of Northwyke and Thrushelton, but he was certainly nothing more than a collateral relative of the Wreys of Tawstock, as his issue was confined to an only daughter and heir, Christian Wraye, upon whose marriage with Richard de la Ford, the name of Wray became extinct at Moreton Hampstead.

William Wray of Wray and Thrushelton, and, presumably, a younger son of Walter de Wray of Northwyke, had sons, Walter Wray of Wray, and Thomas Wray, second son.

Walter Wray was the father of Robert Wray, who, by his wife Constance, daughter of John Shilston, had four sons, and a daughter, Alice, the wife of John Glanville.

Of the sons, I think it quite probable that Robert Wray, the youngest of them, and uncle of Jane Wykes of Northwyke, may have been identical with the husband of Alice Norris, called "Richard" Wraye in the unsigned Southmeade pedigree, which is included in the original "Visitation of Devon," and which is certainly more or less unreliable; Robert Wray's eldest brother, Walter "Wraye," the first described in the pedigree of 1564 as of "North Russell," married Bridget, daughter of Robert Shilstone, and had a daughter, Jane, incidentally referred to above, who became the second wife of John Wykes of Northwyke, in 1540, and subsequently married Thomas Walcot, and afterwards Robert Fry of Exeter.

Her brother, John Wraye, Sheriff of Cornwall in 1585, by

his wife, Blanch, daughter and co-heir of Henry Killigrew of Woolston, co Cornwall, had six sons and two daughters.

His second son, Sir William "Wrey,"* Knt., succeeded to the Killigrew Manor of Trebitch, otherwise written "Trebigh," or "Trebeigh," in the said adjoining county, of which he was sheriff in 1598. He married Elizabeth, daughter of Sir William Courtenay of Powderham, survived until 1636, and thus lived to see his son, Sir William Wrey, created a Baronet on the 30th June, 1628 ; the latter's wife was Ann, daughter of Sir Edward Chichester of Eggesford, afterwards created Viscount Chichester of Carickfergus, and by her, he was the father of Sir Chichester Wrey, second Baronet, who married Ann, youngest daugher and co-heir of Edward Bourchier, Earl of Bath, and Baron Fitz-Warine, and relict of James Cranfield, Earl of Middlesex.

The Earldom of Bath had been created in 1536 in favour of John Bourchier, Baron Fitzwarine, grandson of William, summoned to Parliament in his wife's (Thomasine Hankford's) maternal barony in fee, as Lord Fitz-Warine, 27th Henry VI.; the said Sir William Bourchier having been the third son of William Bourchier, titular Earl of Ewe, in Normandy, by his wife Anne Plantagenet, daughter and eventual sole heir of Thomas of Woodstock, Duke of Gloucester, and sixth son of King Edward III.

The father of the Countess of Middlesex died without surviving male issue in 1636, and was succeeded by his kinsman, Sir Henry Bourchier, as fifth Earl, at whose death, in 1654, the Earldom of Bath became extinct. But the Barony of Fitz-Warine in fee had previously fallen into abeyance between the three daughters of the fourth Earl, and, of these, Lady Middlesex was the youngest. By her second husband, Sir Chichester Wray, she had a son, Bourchier. who succeeded as third Baronet, and who married Florence, daughter of Sir John Rolle of Stevenstone, and died in 1695.

Henry, last Earl of Bath, had married Lady Rachel Fane, daughter of Francis, Earl of Westmoreland, and she had a

---

* The name is still pronounced in accordance with the ancient spelling, which was either "Wray" or "Wraye." The Baronets, however, have always written themselves "Wrey," as above.

life interest in Tawstock Court, and resided there until her death in 1680, when Sir Bourchier Wray inherited that property and also the manor of Holne, near Ashburton. (See my account of the latter, *Ashburton and its Neighbourhood*, pp. 122-28.)

From that date Tawstock Court has been the principal residence of the Wreys. Sir Bourchier Wrey's great-grandson, Sir Bourchier Wrey, D.C.L., born in 1759, by his first marriage with Anne, daughter of Sir Robert Palk, Bart., of Haldon, had a son, Sir Henry Bourchier Wrey, born 1797, and who died without male issue in 1879, when he was succeeded by his half brother, the Rev. Sir Henry Bourchier Wrey, Rector of Tawstock, at whose decease, in 1882, the title came to his eldest son, Sir Henry Bourchier Toke Wrey, the ninth and present Baronet.

Sir Henry Wrey married, in 1854, The Honourable Marianna Sarah, only daughter and heir of Philip Castell, ninth Lord Sherard, of the kingdom of Ireland, a title some time merged with the Earldom of Harborough, and has an eldest son and heir to the title, Robert Bourchier Sherard Wrey, R.N., born 1855.

Arms of Wray of Wray, and of Wraye of North Thrushelton, as now borne by Sir H. B. T. Wrey, Bart., of Tawstock—*Sable*, a fess between three battle axes, *arg.*, helved *gules*.

Sir Henry Wrey quarters Bourchier together with the Royal Arms of Edward III., in right of descent from Thomas, Duke of Gloucester, and is also a co-heir to the Barony of Fitz-Warine in abeyance.

GIDLEY OF GIDLEY AND HOLCOMBE PARAMORE.

This ancient family derives its name from the parish of Gidley on the north-eastern escarpment of Dartmoor, which land was given by William the Conqueror to his half brother the Earl of Mortain, and held under him, in 1086, by a certain "Godwin," and in the Confessor's reign it had also belonged to "Godwin," described as the "Priest."

Westcote, in his seventeenth century *View of Devonshire*,

declares that he had seen a grant of this land, by "Martine," Earl of Cornwall, in favour of his "nephew, Giles de Gidleigh,'' the seal bearing the impress of a triple towered castle, and that the said grant was "exemplified, under the great seal of England, in the reign of Henry VIII."

The said "Giles de Gidleigh," to have been a "nephew" of the Earl of Mortain, whose brother Odo, Earl of Kent, and Bishop of Bayeux, had no issue, should have been a son of his sister Emma D'Abrincis, the mother of Hugh, Earl of Chester, and there is no record that she had such a son as "Giles." Robert of Mortain, Odo, and Emma were the children of Harlotta of Falaise by her marriage with Harlowen de Conteville. Their half-brother and sister, King William and Adeliza, were the offspring of an earlier, and less respectable, intimacy on the part of Harlotta, with Duke Robert of Normandy, and it is most probable that the several personages who have been handed down to us as "nephews" and "nieces" of the Conqueror, or of Mortain, such as "Albreda," wife of Baldwin de Brion of Okehampton, William "Warlewast," Bishop of Exeter, and this Giles de Gidleigh, were children of the king's whole sister, Adeliza de Falaise aforesaid, who was married thrice, and had issue by each marriage, *inter aliis*, Adeliza, Countess of Albemarle in her own right, 1081-1090 ; Stephen, who succeeded his half sister in that earldom ; and Judith, wife of Waltheof, Earl of Huntingdon. The daughter of Albreda of Okehampton was also called Adeliza, and doubtless so after her grandmother.

It is certain that this Dartmoor property descended in the name of Gidleigh for some generations, and down to the middle of the fourteenth century, when the daughter and heir of Giles de Gidley married William, son of Walter Prouz, by the daughter of the Lord Dinham. Her eldest son and heir succeeded to Gidleigh, and his only child, Alice, married, first, Sir Roger Moels, and, second, Sir John Damerell. The latter family inherited Gidley for several generations, until it passed by intermarriage with one of them to the Coades of Morvell, in the county of Cornwall. It was during their ownership that Gidley Castle probably fell to decay ; the remains of it appear to be of early fourteenth century date, and consist chiefly of the large square keep, the lower chamber of which is barrel vaulted, and has two newel staircases communicating with the upper portion of the building.

The name of Gidley, however, appears to have been preserved by a younger branch of the family which settled at Winkleigh, the Devonshire seat of the Honour of Gloucester, upon a property called Holecombe, which had been held under those Earls by William de Portu Mortuo in the reign of Henry III., and was afterward corruptly known as Holcombe Paramore. Richard Gidley was buried at Winkleigh, 26th March, 1574. (See my *Manor and Church of Winkleigh*, p. 18.) He was the father of Bartholomew Gidley, whose son of the same name re-purchased the ancient family property at Gidley from the Coades.

Bartholomew Gidley, the elder, had nine children, and of these Bartholomew, born in 1611, was the first. He matriculated at Exeter College, Oxford, 16th July, 1632; married, in 1637, Joan, daughter of Robert Northleigh of Peamore, Exminster, (a property which of late years has belonged to the Kekewich family, who purchased it of H. H. Coxe at the beginning of the present century), and is described as of Gidley Castle and of Holcombe Paramore. He was captain of the Stannary of Chagford, during the great rebellion espoused the Royal cause, and raised a troop of horse for the king's service, of which he took command.

In commemoration of his bravery and zeal, during the troubles that preceded, and followed, the execution of the king, a large silver medal, nearly three inches in diameter, was struck in his honour, and is still preserved by the family ; on the reverse are his Arms, granted by Edward Bysshe, Clarencieux, 24th November, 1666, and which may be thus blazoned :—*Or*, a castle, within a bordure, *sa.*, bezantcé ; Crest, a gryphon's head, couped, *or*, between two wings, tinctured as the bordure in the arms. It is expressly stated in the grant that these Arms and Crest were granted him for "his eminent services" before "Lyme, Plymouth, and elsewhere in the West," and they were limited to "him and his heirs of body, and to those of his brother, John Gidley." There is a plate of the medal in the

Medallic History of England (J. Pinkerton, London, 1790), and it bears the following inscription :—

"M. S. Mnemosynon et vel ære perennius
Bartholomæi Gidley Armigeri Comitatus Devoniæ.
Quem non avita magis illustrant insignia
Quam se sua virtus illustrior insignivit ;
Quem regi suo constantem agnovere res Anglorum versatiles,
Et extrema fidelitatis tentamina pax et bellum.
Pro exule Carolo in bello Præfectum,
Pro reduce ad pacem Justitiarum
utro que munere fidelissimum,
Annos agit 72, Salutis anno 1683.
Non ætate non munere gravatus
vel adhuc dici voluit emeritus."

He was also an active magistrate, and a strong Churchman, and was conspicuous for his opposition to the Conventicles after the passing of the Act of Uniformity in 1662. He died without issue, in January, 1686; his will, dated November 28th, 1683, was proved at Exeter on the 5th of the October following his demise. He settled his real estate upon his nephew, Bartholomew, son of his brother John, who inherited the manor, park, and farm of Gidley, and the advowson of, and right of presentation to, Gidley Church, together with the manor of Holcombe Paramore, and all other messuages, burgages, lands, and tenements in the parishes of Winkleigh and Roborough.

Although prior to the middle of the thirteenth century we have no certain knowledge as to the official arms of the Earls of Cornwall, yet, whether they simply mean "*all peas*," and *refer to the province of Poitou* (as suggested by the late J. R. Planché), or not, is quite beyond the question, for, doubtless, Robert of Mortain knew as little about them as did Edward the Confessor of the cross and martlets with which he has been since accredited by English heralds.

In the seventeenth century the bezants on a sable field had been identified with the Cornish Earldom from time immemorial, and it is unlikely that Sir Edward Bysshe would have granted permission to Bartholomew Gidley to bear a representation of Gidley Castle, *within the Cornish bordure*, in the absence of fair evidence, both of his descent from its original owners, and of his connection with the earldom, and the fact that such a coat was granted "by letters patent under the great seal of England," is strong confirmatory evidence of the descent of the Gidleys from a sister or half sister of the first Norman monarch and of his brother, Robert of Mortain. Certain "tin bounds" within the ducal forest of Dartmoor are still owned by the Gidleys.

Bartholomew, nephew and heir of Bartholomew Gidley, of Gidley and Holcombe, died, aged thirty-four, 2nd August, 1702, leaving, inclusive of a son and heir, Bartholomew, a family of eight children. This Bartholomew was born in 1689, was a godson of the king, William III., and a Royal letter is preserved by the family in which his Majesty favours him with much practical advice, which, it is to be feared, failed to profit him to any considerable extent; he cut the entail of the property, which has since become dispersed, lived to the age of eighty-seven, and was buried in the "Gidley Aisle" of Winkleigh Church, 21st March, 1776; his son, Gustavus, was the ancestor of the present head of the family, Mr. Gustavus Gidley of Plymouth.

His grandfather, John Gidley, had married Rebecca Dunning of Winkleigh, in which parish he had inherited an estate called Beuford ; he was a Court surgeon, and resided chiefly in London, but his will is dated at Winkleigh, 21st September, 1712. He left his eldest grandson the Beuford property, and his silver plate, hangings, and other furniture in his house in London to his second but eldest surviving son, John, and to his daughter, Rebecca, after their mother's death. His said grandson, Bartholomew, born 1689, had a younger brother, John Gidley, born 1690, who married Margaret, daughter and heir of Robert Ellicombe of Kenn, by Theodosia, daughter of the Rev. John Mauduit, Fellow of Exeter College, Oxford, and Senior Proctor. His grandson, the late Courtenay Gidley of Honiton, was the grandfather of John Gidley, formerly Town Clerk of Exeter, who married, in 1823, Elizabeth, daughter of Robert Cornish of Exeter, and aunt of John Robert Cornish, who assumed by Royal license the surname of Mowbray, 26th July,

1847, was created a baronet 3rd May, 1880, is a Privy Councillor, and now, 1895, the senior active member of the House of Commons. By this marriage Mr. John Gidley had a son, Bartholomew Gidley of Hoopern, near Exeter, who, like his father, was town clerk of Exeter, and died in 1888, and left, with other issue, a son, the present Mr. John Gidley of Hoopern House.

HAMLYN OF WIDECOMBE, COLEBROOK, AND CLOVELLY.

Like the House of Brito, the family of Hamlyn is coeval with all that is really authentic in the history of Devonshire. Its name is derived from the Saxon words "*ham*" and "*lynna*," which, in composition, signify the home by the spring or pool; and as the "Hamelins," from the town of that name in Lower Saxony, they helped to swell the ranks of the Conqueror's army, and soon became settled in various parts of England, notably in Devonshire, Cornwall, Leicestershire, Warwickshire, Worcestershire, Oxfordshire, Gloucestershire, and Rutland.

The two most important Hamlyns of the eleventh century were those whose names are found mentioned in the roll of Battle Abbey as "Hammeline" and "Hammeline de Balun." The "Sire de Balun" had probably migrated from Germany to France, sometime before the Conquest, to the French town of Ballun, in the diocese of Mons; after the victory at Senlac King William gave him the land of Ober Went, in Monmouthshire, and he was the subsequent founder of the Castle of Bergavenny.

He died childless in the reign of Rufus, and was succeeded by his nephew "Brian," son of his sister Lucy. This "Brian" had two afflicted sons, so he made his nephew, son of his sister Emma, his heir, and this nephew, or "cousin," as, in accordance with old custom, he is loosely described, was Constable of Gloucester, and afterward High Constable of England. The latter's son was created Earl of Hereford in succession to Roger de Bretteville, *alias* Fitz-Osbern, whose younger brother was Bishop of Exeter in 1072. Roger Brito, or Bretteville, was eventually proscribed for treason, but is said to have had a son, Reginald, who married "Emmeline de Balun," who may probably have been a sister of the aforesaid Emma of Gloucester.

With the other "Hamelin" of the Battle Abbey Roll we have more concern here. He may have been a brother, or at least a near kinsman, of the Sire de Balun; at all events, he was a very important personage in the eleventh century, and, like the Britos, he came to the west of England in the following of Robert, Earl of Mortain.

He is called "Hamelinus" in Domesday, and was tenant *in capite* of many important manors in Cornwall. Some of his posterity remained in the latter county, and one of them was Portreeve of Launceston in 1207, but many of them settled in Devonshire, where "Hamelinus," at the period of the Survey, held the broad lands of Broadhempston and Alwington as sub-tenant to the Earl.

The Hamlyns soon disappeared from both their original settlements in Devonshire: Broadhempston went to the Cantilupes, one of whom, William de Cantilupe, was the husband of Eva Braose, granddaughter of Emma de Balun of Gloucester, which may be merely a coincidence; whilst Alwington passed to the Coffins afterward of Portledge, a family which, although its name has been preserved by assumption, has been now sometime extinct in the male line.

But, probably by exchange, and simultaneously with their disappearance from Alwington, the Hamlyns acquired the manor of Natsworthy, another of Mortain's concessions, situate in the parish of Widecombe-in-the-Moor, and but a few miles distant from Broadhempston, and also of the manor of Bratton, in the immediate neighbourhood of Alwington. The fifth in descent from "Hamelinus" of Domesday, Richard Hamlyn, acquired an estate known as Larkbeare, in the parish of St. Leonard, adjacent to the city of Exeter. One of his sons remained at Larkbeare, and was the ancestor of Hamlyn of Colebrook, of which branch I shall treat hereafter; the other, known as "Hamlyn the Harper," was of Hill, in Holne, a neighbouring parish to Widecombe, as shown by the "Fine Rolls" of 3rd Henry III.

The Hill estate remained in the hands of his posterity until it was sold some few years since by James Hamlyn, to whom it had descended. Hamlyn, "the Harper," of Hill, was the father of William, father of Sir William Hamlyn of Deandon, in Widecombe, Kt., and of Bratton, near Alwington. Sir William was one of the knights who returned the great assize for Devon in the year 1250, but died without issue. His brother, Walter, carried on the line, and was the father of William Hamlyn of Dunstone, 34th Edward I., of John Hamlyn of Chittleford, three years earlier, of Hugh and of Roger Hamlyn, both of Corndon, all estates in the said parish of Widecombe, and also of Robert Hamlyn, who represented Totnes in Parliament in 1311.

The Hennock branch of the Hamlyns derive from another brother of Sir William. William Hamlyn, of Dunstone, 1306, a property which was purchased from the Pomeroys, left a son, John Hamlyn, whose descendant, of the same name, 1412, was grandfather of John Hamlyn of Dunstone, 1442, and the latter bore the same relationship to Richard Hamlyn of Dunstone, 1506, who died in 1522. He left four sons, viz., Robert, son and heir; 2nd, Richard, ancestor of the Hamlyns of an adjacent property called Southcombe; 3rd, Thomas of Spitchwick, in Widecombe, and of Hill and Littlecombe, in Holne, ancestor also of branches of the family settled at Ash and Lake, both in Widecombe; 4th, John, ancestor of the Hamlyns of Clovelly.

Robert Hamlyn, son and heir of Dunstone, had "seisin" of Dunstone on his father's death in 1522. It is shown by the Inquisition upon his own death that he was the owner of Scobetor, Venton, and Dunstone in Widecombe, of Dawnton in Buckfastleigh, and had also land at Doddiscombleigh, near Exeter; he died 1556.

Dawnton then passed to his third son, Richard. His son and heir, Robert Hamlyn, was the direct ancestor of William Hamlyn of Dunstone (see the Ped., Vivian's *Additions to Visitations of Devon*), who sold that property, and died in 1782.

The uncle of the last owner of Dunstone, Hugh Hamlyn of Blackslade Manor, Widecombe, had a second son, John, who settled at Brent; the latter's son, Joseph Hamlyn, purchased land in Buckfastleigh, and died in 1866.

It is due to his energy and perseverance that the woollen trade, the old staple business of this county, and which in the past has afforded both honourable occupation and livelihood to very many cadets of our ancient county houses, still flourishes in the valley of the Dart. Joseph Hamlyn founded the great manufactory at Buckfastleigh, and thus recommenced there an industry which had been long fostered by the Cistercian monks of the neighbouring abbey of Buckfast, and which was afterward continued profitably by his sons Joseph, John, and William, and is now the property of James, Joseph, and William Hamlyn, who are the sons of the late William Hamlyn by his marriage with his kinswoman, Mary, daughter of James Hamlyn of Hill and Littlecombe, already mentioned, and the latter estate is still the property of their mother.

I must now return to "Hamlyn of Larkbeare," the brother of "Hamlyn the Harper" of Hill. He was the father of Sir John Hamlyn, Kt., whose son, Sir Osbert Hamlyn, Kt., of Larkbeare, married the daughter and co-heir of Sir William Pipard of Blakedon, in Widecombe. He was attainted for high treason in 1370, on which account, possibly, his posterity, who long resided at Exeter, St. Thomas, and Alphington, and were benefactors to the latter parish in the early portion of the seventeenth century, prospered in mercantile pursuits, gave mayors to the "faithful city," and filled other municipal offices from time to time ; one of them settled at Paschoe, in the parish of Colebrook, in 1611, by marriage with a co-heir of that family.

Robert Paschoe Hamlyn, of Paschoe, was the father of Christopher Hamlyn of Paschoe, who married Elizabeth, daughter and eventual co-heir of Vincent Calmady of Langdon, by Elizabeth, daughter and heir of John Pollexfen, and by this marriage acquired Leawood, in the parish of Bridestowe. Both estates were inherited by their son, Calmady Pollexfen Hamlyn, of Paschoe and Leawood, born 1775, who married the only daughter of Richard Cross of Great Duryard, near Exeter, and had a son, Shilston Calmady Hamlyn, J.P. and D.L., of Paschoe and of Leawood, who by his wife, Sarah Carter, of Neston, Cheshire, was the father of the present owner of these estates, Mr. Vincent Pollexfen Calmady Hamlyn.

The Hamlyns of Paschoe and Bridestowe bear for arms : "*Sa.*, two swords in saltire, the points upward, hilted *or ;* but their ancestor, Sir John Hamlyn, bore the ancient arms of the family, hereinafter blazoned, as shown by the "Boroughbridge" Roll of Arms.

John Hamlyn, youngest son of Richard Hamlyn of Dunstone, who died in 1522, appears to have settled, probably through marriage, at Mershwell, in the parish of Woolfardisworthy, and his arms, as under, with the date 1540, were to be seen in one of the windows of his house. His son, William, born in that year, married, about 1558, Agnes Yeo of Stratton, whose son William, born 1559, was the father of William Hamlyn, baptized at Woolfardisworthy, 21st October, 1579, and whose grandfather survived until 1597, when he inherited Mershwell.

His son, William Hamlyn of Mershwell, married Gertrude Cary, and died in 1708, and was succeeded by Zachary Hamlyn, the eldest of fourteen children.

The latter purchased the Clovelly estate of the Carys in 1729, died without issue, and left his property by will to his grand nephew, James Hammett, grandson of Thomazine Hamlyn. He recorded his pedigree at Herald's College, but did not carry it behind the William Hamlyn of Mershwell who married Agnes Yeo. Mr. Hammett assumed the name of Hamlyn by Act of Parliament in 1760, and was created a baronet in 1795. His son and heir, the second baronet, assumed his mother's name, Williams. The third baronet, Sir James Hamlyn-Williams, married Lady Mary Fortescue, but had no male issue, so the baronetcy became extinct; his eldest daughter succeeded to the Clovelly property, married Lieut.-Col. Fane, who assumed the additional name of Hamlyn, and had, with other issue, the present Mrs. Hamlyn of Clovelly, whose husband has taken her name.

Arms of Hamlyn of Widecombe-in-the-Moor, now of Buckfastleigh: "*Gules*, a lion rampant, *ermine*, crowned *or*."

THE VENNS OF PEYHEMBURY, ETC.

William "Pictavensis," who was a sub-tenant in Devonshire under the Norman Ralph de Pomeroy, was the ancestor of "Robert de Peytevin," the owner of the manor and church of Feniton, otherwise Veniton, or "Peytevin's Town," in the year 1273, as proved by the "Hundred Roll," and which afterwards passed to his neighbours, the Malherbes, who had then been resident in the parish for several generations. The Domesday entry of the manor of "Feniton" probably refers to the manor now called "Venton," in Widecombe, nigh Ashburton, and which belonged to King William's half-brother Robert, Earl of Mortain, or else to "Fenton" in Rattery.

Robert de Peytevin probably also gave its prefix to the adjacent parish of Peyhembury, anciently "Petit Hembury," but the manor of Broad-Hembury, which, in 1087, belonged to "Odo," was afterwards parcel of the Duchy of Lancaster, and was long held, from that honour, by the Abbey of Dunkeswell, but it is not my present purpose to trace the descent of the manor of Broad-Hembury, which, prior to the creation of the Duchy of Lancaster, pertained to the Barony of Torrington.

Both Peyhambury and Broad-Hembury, however, have been long associated with the Venns, who may possibly derive their patronymic from the earlier residence of their ancestors in the neighbouring parish of Venton, *alias* Feniton. John Venn of Broad-Hembury, whose will was proved at Exeter in 1595, had four sons and two daughters; his contemporary, Richard Venn, was a benefactor to the poor of Peyhembury, in 3rd James I., 1605, and his descendants have resided there ever since, and are still numbered amongst its principal landowners, and are also lords of the manor of Upton Prudhome, in the same parish. The eldest son of John Venn of Broad-Hembury, William Venn, was baptized there, February 8th, 1568-9. He graduated at Exeter College, Oxford, in 1595, and four years later, on March 21st, he was instituted to the vicarage of Otterton, which preferment he held for twenty-one years. His patron was John May, by grant, for that turn, of Richard Duke, whose family had then obtained the advowson, which formerly belonged to the Abbess and Convent of Sion, in the county of

Middlesex, and, originally, to the alien priory of Otterton, which had been suppressed in 1414. William Venn was buried at Otterton in 1621, and was immediately succeeded by Isaiah Faringdon, who resigned, probably by arrangement, in 1625, upon which the Dukes conferred the vacant benefice upon the son of their old vicar, Richard Venn, then twenty-four years old, and a graduate, like his father, of Exeter College, Oxford. Richard Venn was twice married; by his first wife, Elizabeth Westcott, he had two sons and a daughter; by his second, Margaret Venn, he had a further family of eight children, and the eldest of them became vicar of Holbeton.

Richard Venn suffered many and grievous hardships at the hands of the Parliamentary Commissioners, was ejected from his living, and confined in prison at Exeter for eleven months from October, 1646, to September in the following year. At one time he was siezed by a party of Puritan soldiers and taken out for summary execution, but his life was saved by the opportune arrival of a detachment of the Royal forces.

He left a record of his troubles in manuscript, portions of which are considered to be identical with some fragmentary MSS. at the Bodleian Library, and his adventures are included in Walker's *Sufferings of the Clergy*, part ii., pp. 386-7. Hence it appears that during the years of his deprivation he officiated temporarily both at Black Aveton and at Liskeard, but was similarly driven out of each parish. At the Restoration he is said to have been the first clergyman to resume the use of the Book of Common Prayer, at a service which he conducted at the neighbouring church of Ottery St. Mary.

Immediately after the Restoration of Monarchy had happily become an accomplished fact, he was at once replaced in his vicarage, which had been held by a Nonconformist of the name of Conant, who had characteristically refused to pay him his "fifths" throughout the fourteen years of his intrusion; when compelled to disgorge by the law, in 1660, Conant is said to have thrown the money at him, and it consequently fell on the floor, but Mr. Venn merely smiled and remarked, "Well, well, I will take the pains to pick it up." He survived his return to Otterton but two years, and was buried there, 28th June, 1662.

His son, Dennis Venn, born in 1648, was probably named after Dennis Rolle of Bicton, whose early death, in 1638, had been much deplored by his many friends and neighbours. Dennis Venn also graduated at Exeter College, and, at the age of twenty-five, was instituted to the vicarage of Holbeton, and held it for twenty-two years, and was buried there, 12th February, 1695-6. By his first wife, Lucy Fortescue, to whom he was married in 1683, he had a daughter, of her mother's name, who died in infancy; by his second wife, Patience (married 1689), daughter of the Rev. John Gay of St. Anthony, he had two sons and three daughters.

His eldest son, Richard Venn, was baptized at Holbeton, January 7th, 1690-1, was educated at Blundel's School, Tiverton, where he obtained a Scholarship, and proceeded to Sidney College, Cambridge. He was afterwards rector of St. Antholin's, in the city of London, from 1725-39, and died of smallpox, February 16th, in the latter year. His wife was the only surviving child of John Ashton, who was keeper of the privy purse in the household of Queen Mary D'Este, consort of King James II., who was Mrs. Venn's godmother.

John Ashton unfortunately twice failed to escape from England after the abdication of his Royal patrons, and on Monday, the 19th of January, 1690-1, he was indicted, together with "Sir Richard Grahame, Bart." (Viscount Preston), and Edmund Elliot, "for conspiring the deaths" of the new King and Queen, "and adhering to their enemies." Mr. Ashton appears to have made a bargain for a vessel to take him with his friends across to France on the previous "New Year's Day," and actually deposited the sum of ninety-three guineas for his passage with Mr. Burdett; they got away safely from the "Surrey Stairs," but were arrested and brought back from Gravesend, with treasonable papers in their possession. They were all found guilty, and Ashton was executed at Tyburn, January 28th following. A full account of the proceedings will be found in *Tryals for High Treason*, London, 1720, Vol. 5, pp. 614-1636. One of the eight grandchildren of this unfortunate political victim, Henry Venn, was baptized at Barnes, March 15th, 1724-5, graduated at Jesus College, and was afterward a Fellow of Queens' College, Cambridge. He was the author of *The Complete Duty of Man, or a System of Doctrinal and Practical Christianity*, which was first published in 1764, and has gone through numerous editions. He also published a volume of sermons in 1759; and *Mistakes in Religion, Exposed in an Essay on the Prophecy of Zacharias*, in 1774. His "Life," with a selection from his letters, was published by one of his grandsons, the Rev. Henry Venn, Fellow of Queens' College, Cambridge, and Vicar of St. John's, Holloway, and this work went through six editions.

He married, firstly, a daughter of the Rev. Thomas Bishop, D.D., and secondly Catherine, daughter of the Rev. James Askew, and widow of a clergyman of the name of Smith. By his first wife he had four daughters, and a son, John. He held the Vicarages of Huddersfield and Yelling during his clerical career, and died at Clapham in 1797.

His son, John Venn, born at Clapham, March 9th, 1759, graduated at Sidney College, Cambridge, in 1781, and was instituted to the Rectory of Little Dunham, Norfolk, in 1783. He died Rector of Clapham, July 1st, 1813, and was a well-known divine and one of the founders of the Church Missionary Society; he was the author of *Sermons*, in three volumes, London, 1814-18. By his first wife, Katherine, daughter of William King of Hull, he became the father of five daughters (the eldest of whom was the wife of the Right Honourable Sir James Stephen, K.C.B., the father of Mr. Justice Stephen) and two sons, John Venn, Fellow of Queens' College, already referred to above, and Henry Venn, who was born at Clapham in 1796, graduated at Queens', Cambridge, in 1818, and of which College he was a Fellow. In 1826 he was preferred by Simeon's Trustees to the Vicarage of Drypool, Hull, and was Vicar of St. John's, Holloway, from 1834-48, and Prebendary of St. Paul's Cathedral. He was for many years secretary of the Church Missionary Society, and died at East Sheen, January 16th, 1873. By his wife Martha, daughter of Nicholas Sykes of Swanland, Yorkshire, he was the father of the Rev. Henry Venn, M.A., Caius College, Cambridge, Rector of Clare Portion, Tiverton, in this county, from 1870-1885, when he removed to the Vicarage of Sittingbourne; and also of Dr. John

Venn, his eldest son, born at Hull, August 4th, 1834, and now Senior Fellow of Caius College, Cambridge,

Dr. Venn, who was ordained in 1858, has held the curacies of Cheshunt and Mortlake, but resigned his orders, under the recent Act, in 1883. Since then he has resided chiefly in his University, is lecturer in Moral Sciences, and a University examiner, and was Hulsean lecturer in 1869. He is the author of *Logic of Chance, Empirical Logic, Symbolic Logic*, and of various papers in scientific and other periodicals. He was elected a Fellow of the Royal Society in 1883, and is also a Fellow of the Society of Antiquaries. He edited the Baptismal Register of St. Michael's, Cambridge, 1588-1837, in 1891, and is at present engaged in the preparation of the Caius College admissions, one volume of which has been published. (See also *Men of the Time*, Edit. 1895, p. 853.)

Dr. Venn married, June 21st, 1867, Susanna Carnegie, daughter of the Rev. Charles Edmonstone, Vicar of Christ Church, Hornsey, and has a son, John Archibald Venn, born November 10th, 1883.

The arms of Venn, as borne by the Broad-Hembury branch for at least five generations, are thus blazoned :—*Arg.*, on a fess within a bordure engrailed *as.*, 3 escallops of the field.

Crest—A dragon's head erased *arg.*, about its neck a collar *azure*, charged with 3 escallops of the first.

KELLY OF KELLY.

The Kellys derive their name from the parish of Kelly, near Tavistock, and have been Lords of the Manor there from time immemorial. It is the "Celodelie" of the Domesday record, and has been curiously confused with Calverleigh, near Tiverton, by Lysons, in the Devonshire volumes of the *Magna Britannia*.

As to its earlier history, the neighbouring Manor of "Tavelande" (that of West Tavy, which includes the church of St. Mary) was held in the reign of King Edward the Confessor by a Saxon Thegn called "Godric," who was a very considerable landowner prior to the Conquest, after which, although he seems to have been deprived of the whole of his original property in the county, he appears in Domesday as tenant in capite of the Manors of "Celodelie" (or Kelly), and of "Bolehorde," since known as "Balbury" or "Balbeny," and now as Babeny, in the parish of Lidford, and fifteen miles distant from the Parish Church there. (See my *Ashburton and its Neighbourhood*, p. 71.)

Both these Manors had hitherto belonged to another, but less distinguished, Saxon known as "Almar."

The primary settlement of the Kellys at Kelly can only be a matter of conjecture. It is not only possible, but probable, that they are the veritable descendants of Godric the Saxon, but how the late Sir Bernard Burke can have considered that *their authenticated pedigree enables them to derive themselves from the ancient Britons*, it is somewhat difficult to understand.

The most complete pedigree of Kelly, which can at all be regarded as authentic, is that entered on the original roll of the Visitation of Cornwall in 1620 (M. S. Harl., 1079), and which commences with "Nicholas de Kelly," *temp*. Henry II., 1154-1189. He was probably the son of "Martin de Kelly," who flourished in the same reign, as Risdon, writing in 1638, tells us that "Kelly, in King Henry the second's time had its inhabitor Martin de Kelly, whom divers knights of that name succeeded." It is shown by the Exeter Episcopal Registers that John de Kelly presented, as patron, to Kelly Church in 1275, and he appears to have been the first of the family who had the Manor of Heavitree, near Exeter, under John de Pycot, and the latter property remained with his descendants until it was sold to the Barings, by Arthur Kelly of Kelly, in 1773. (See my *Suburbs of Exeter*, p. 8.)

The Visitation of Devonshire, 1564 (Coll. Ar. D. 7) commences with "Thomas Kellye of Kellye," who married Elizabeth, daughter and co-heir of William Talbot of Spreyton. This Thomas, who married, secondly, Mary Penhallow, died 14th September, 1404, as shewn by an "*Inq. p.m.* 6th Hy. IV." He was the father of Richard Kelly of Kelly, whose great grandson, John Kelly of Kelly, was second son of Oliver Kelly by Joan Tremayne of Collacombe. (For Tremayne genealogy see my *Devonshire Parishes*, vol. 1, pp. 171, 212, *et seq.*)

This John was ... ...her and heir of Oliver Kelly of Kelly, and the first of the family who was entered at the Devonshire "Visitation" of 1620. From him the pedigree is continued to William Kelly of Kelly and his family, and is duly authenticated by his signature (M. S. Harl., 1163, fo. 92b.)

This William "Kelley" was born 10th September, 1589. He married Philippa, daughter of John Conocke of Treworgie, co. Cornwall, by whom he had four daughters and two sons; at his death, 9th November, 1627, his eldest son, Thomas, was a minor, and afterward died childless, when he was succeeded at Kelly by his younger brother, John, whose will was proved at Exeter, 17th June, 1689, and, failing his male issue, he devised his property to his first cousin, Francis, eldest son of his uncle, the Rev. Authur Kelly, rector of the parish, who died in 1662.

Francis Kelly of Kelly married Elizabeth Tucker of Holsworthy, and died within eighteen months of his accession to the estate; his son and heir, Arthur Kelly of Kelly, by his wife, Susannah Handcock, was the father of Arthur Kelly of Kelly who married Mary Tucker of Coryton, and died in 1762. Their eldest son, Arthur Kelly of Kelly, who long commanded the South Devon Regiment of Militia, died in 1823, at eighty-one years of age. His eldest surviving son, Arthur Kelly, was the father of another Arthur, born in 1804, who was Sheriff of Devon in 1836, and died in 1873.

The late Mr. Kelly's eldest son, Arthur Kelly, who was baptized 6th October, 1830, predeceased him in 1846; he was therefore succeeded at Kelly by its present owner, Reginald Kelly of Kelly, J.P. and D.L. for Devon, Sheriff of the county in 1880, and who was born in 1834. Mr. Kelly owns the whole of the parish, which includes 1,700 acres of land (with a population of over 200), and is also patron of the Rectory of Kelly, to which 73 acres of glebe are appropriated. Kelly House, which is a picturesque residence of late Tudor style, is situated near the church.

Arms of Kelly of Kelly—*Arg.*, a chevron between three billets *gules*.

Crest.— Out of a ducal coronet *gu.*, an ostrich's head, holding in the beak a horse-shoe *or*.

This family quarters Talbot of Spreyton, viz:—*Arg.*, a chevron between three talbots *sa*.

BREMRIDGE OF BREMRIDGE.

I have already referred, in notes on previous pages (189 and 293), to the ancient family of Bremridge, as to which, Westcote, the seventeenth century author of the *View of Devonshire*, has observed, in his quaint language, whilst treating of "the progress of the Creedy river;" "his next neighbour, Bremridge of Bremridge, or rather (as it may be supposed) Bremel-ridge, a place full of brambles and briars, hath had the like good fortune for antiquity ; that race having enjoyed this place the best part of four hundred years, with such a temperate moderation in every succession that greedy desire of riches hath neither much increased nor prodigality decreased it." (See also my *Manor of Winkleigh*, p. 41).

The Bremridges appear to have derived their name from the ancient Manor of "Bremerige," in Southmolton (which afterward passed to the Tracys, and, in more recent times, to the Dodderidges), and to have given it to their subsequent residence, "Bremridge," within the Manor of Posbury-Bradleigh, in the hundred of Crediton and parish of Sandford.

Sandford is an ancient Chapelry in Crediton parish, and here the Dodderidges, and Dowrishs, were likewise settled at an early date, and gave name also to their respective properties.

In the year 1087 the Manor of Sandford, to the extent of two hides and a half of land, belonged to the Barony of Okehampton, that of "Bremerige" and Bradleigh, to the latter of which the land afterward known as Bremridge, in Sandford, was appendant, had been given by the Norman Conqueror to his Chief Justice, Jeffery, the warrior Bishop of Coutance, under whom both these Manors were held by the King's relative, Drogo Fitz-Mauger. This "Drogo" was a son of Mauger le Ponz,[*] who was the third son of Richard "le Bon," second Duke of Normandy, the Conqueror's grandfather, and nephew of Mauger, the ancestor of the Granvilles of Stowe and Bideford, whose descent from Rollo the Dane will be found in my *Notes, Genealogical and Historical*, p. 12, *et seq*.

---

[*] Lysons, and others, call him son of "Walter *de* Ponz."

Another son of Mauger, Richard Fitz-Ponz, was the ancestor of the noble house of Clifford.

Drogo Fitz-Mauger, although he did not hold directly from the Crown, was, as a sub-tenant to Jeffery de Coutance of no less than seventy-three Manors, one of the largest landed proprietors in Devonshire. His Manor of Bremerige in Southmolton, which passed at an early date to the Tracys, and from them descended to the Martins, probably came to the former in marriage with a granddaughter, heir, or co-heir to one of his several sons, another of whom, "Drogo," appears to have been settled upon his Manor of "Hagintone," since known as Hayne, in the parish of Newton St. Cyres, and has been claimed as the forefather through "a younger branch" of the "Drewes" of Grange, sometime of Killerton, and of the "Drews" of Youghal, co. Cork. Hayne, however, passed to the Northcotes, 17th May, 1585, by the marriage of Mary, daughter and heir of Edmund Drewe of Hayne, with Walter Northcote of Crediton, who had an only child, Elizabeth, first the wife of George Yarde of Churston, by whom she had issue, and afterward of Dr. Barnabas Potter, the Calvinist, Lord Bishop of Carlisle. (See my *Ashburton and its Neighbourhood*, p. 135). Hayne, however, has descended in the issue of Walter Northcote's elder brother, John Northcote of Uton. (See Northcote genealogy, *post*).

The pedigree of Drewe of Sharpham, afterward of Killerton, and since of Grange, in the parish of Broad-Hembury, as entered at the Herald's Visitations of Devonshire, commences with William Drewe of Sharpham, whose third son died 22nd June, 1548. His descendant, Edward Drewe, purchased the Grange, which had belonged to the dissolved Abbey of Dunkeswell, of Henry Wriothesley, third Earl of Southampton, in or about the year 1601. The same Edward (who was a sergeant-at-law, Recorder of Exeter, 1592, and grandson of John Drewe of the parish of St. Leonard, Exeter, second in descent from William, third son of the William Drewe who commences the pedigree, and who acquired Sharpham by his marriage with Joan, daughter and co-heir of John Prideaux of Modbury) also purchased Killerton of the devisors of the last daughter and heir of that name and house, and his son, Sir Thomas Drewe, Kt., sold it to Sir Arthur Acland, father of the first Baronet and nephew of Sir John Acland, Kt., who purchased Columb John, in the same parish, the ancient residence of the Culmes, of William Rowswell, and died in 1620. (See Acland genealogy, *post*).

Sir Thomas Drewe, the first of the family who resided at the "Grange," which was built by him in his father's life-time, 1610, died there 15th July, 1651.

According to their pedigree in Burke's *Landed Gentry*, the Drews of Youghal, co. Cork, and of Drewsboro', co. Clare, claim to originate from "Drogo," through Drewe of Hayne, in right of descent from Francis, asserted to have been the "second son of John Drew of Hayne, etc., by Joan Williams of Ivesbridge."[*] I have neither space nor inclination to notice, at any length, the very obvious errors and assumptions in the earlier portion of the genealogy I now quote, according to which this Francis "went to Ireland, a captain in the army of Queen Elizabeth, about the year 1598, was afterward of Kilwinny, co. Waterford, &c., married twice, and was the father of John Drew of Kilwinny, and of Barry Drew of Ballyduff, the ancestors of these Irish branches."

It is sufficient to say that it was Joane, not "John Drew," who was the wife, not "husband," of John Williams of Trobridge, co. Devon, that the father of Francis, younger brother of Edward Drewe of Hayne, not "Richard," does not appear to have been the Francis, if he ever had any real existence, who settled in Ireland; at all events Francis Drew of Newton St. Cyres, and the nephew, not "son," of Joan Williams, was buried there, as shewn by the parish register, 20th June, 1605.

"Walter," another son of Drogo Fitz-Mauger, and therefore brother of "Drogo," the ancestor of Drewe of Hayne (which estate now belongs to Lord Iddesleigh), was known, probably from his birthplace, as "de Bremerige." That he was settled upon that portion of his father's property which was situated in Sandford, that he must have given his name to it, and that

---

[*] Ivy Bridge, in the parish of Harford, on the Erme. For "Williams," see my *Devonshire Parishes*, vol. ii., pp. 220, 221.

it was appendant to his father's Manor of Bradleigh, otherwise Posbury-Bradleigh, is sufficiently proved by existing contemporary records, together with the fact that he was the father and grandfather of Richard and Robert de Bremerige.

The latter "recovered" his land in Sandford in or about the year 1218, upon doing the customary homage and service to the chief lord of the fee, and upon surrender of "one ox and one horse" as an heriot, as "son of Richard, son of Walter de Bremelrig, whose land it was." The tenure was the annual render of "three little sieves of chimney soot, five sieves of oats, and a small money payment." Amongst the witnesses to this "recovery" I find the name of his neighbour, "Gilbert de Dodarig."

In the third year of Henry III., 1218, Jordan de Coketrewe, in the presence of Josceline, Bishop of Bath and Wells, Roger Cole, Canon of Exeter, and others, acknowledged the right of " Robert, son of Richard de Bremelrigg," to one ferling of land in "Bremelrigg." His descendants continued to possess this Sandford property from generation to generation, but when the Manor of Posbury-Bradleigh became alienated from the posterity of Drogo Fitz-Mauger, I am, at present, unable to say. It is shown by an indenture dated 20th April, 12th Henry VIII., 1521, that John Bremridge then held Bremridge as of the Manor of Bradleigh, whose then owner was a certain John Ford. This John Bremridge, who had sisters, Thomasine and Mary, was the son of John Bremridge of Bremridge, by his wife, Christian Ware, and died in 1581, and the latter was the son and heir of William Bremridge of Bremridge (twelfth in direct descent from Drogo Fitz-Mauger), who had release of all tenements, lands, reversions, rents, etc., etc., in "Bremerygge," 18th January, 9th Edward IV., 1469.

On the 5th April, 23rd Elizabeth, 1581, John Bremridge, son of the John of 1521 above mentioned, did homage and service to George Pollard, then the Lord of the Manor of Posbury-Bradleigh, and duly recovered seizin of Bremridge, his inheritance. By an *Inq. p.m.* taken at Okehampton, 16th June, 41st Elizabeth (1599), it appears that he died "seized of one capital messuage or tenement called Bremridge, with three orchards, two gardens, seventy acres of land, four of meadow, and half an acre of wood, within the parish and hundred of Crediton, all held of Richard Pollard and John Hele, serjeant-at-law, as parcel of the Manor of Posbury-Bradleigh, by the eighth part of a knight's fee and by the annual rent of seven shillings and five pence, that he held no other Manors in reversion, remainder, or in use, on the day he died, and that William Bremridge was his son and next heir and aged twenty-one years or more."

The grandson of the latter, John Bremridge, was the father of John, son and heir, of Bremridge, and also of a younger son who liekwise resided in Sandford, and had a son, also of Sandford, the father of Samuel Bremridge, of whom hereafter, and of two daughters, Sarah (Langworthy) and Mary Force.

John, son and heir of John Bremridge, married Mary Reed of Priors Town, Sandford, and was the father of John Bremridge, who, by his wife, Elizabeth, daughter of William Smale of Witheridge, had a son, John, who died unmarried, and a daughter, Anna Maria,* heir to her brother, and who brought Bremridge, in 1788, to her husband, Richard Melhuish of Poughill (a brother of John Melhuish of Hill in Cruse Morchard), whose daughter, Elizabeth, married Jonathan Worthy. (See *ante*, pp. 79, 80; and "Worthe of Worth," *post.*)

Thomas Melhuish of Poughill inherited Bremridge in right of his mother, and married his kinswoman, Elizabeth, daughter of the Rev. T. Melhuish of Clawton and Ashwater, by whom he had Thomas Bremridge Melhuish, son and heir, born 1812, of Bremridge and Poughill, and rector of the latter parish. Upon his death, October 7th, 1885, his son John, then a minor, succeeded to Bremridge and the rest of the property, which has all been recently sold—1894-1895.

Samuel Bremridge, above mentioned, of Sandford, and afterward of Barnstaple, acquired a lease of a house in the latter borough in 1806, and was a Coroner of the County. He married Ann, daughter of Thomas Scott of High Bickington in 1763, and was the father, *inter alios*, of John Bremridge, first son

---

* She was married 20th November, 1775, and was the first wife of Richard Melhuish, who afterward married Prideaux.

and heir, who married Anne Colley; * Samuel Bremridge, whose son, Richard, some time represented Barnstaple in Parliament; and also of Thomas Bremridge of the H.E.I.C.N.S., who was born in 1769, and married, in 1818, Elizabeth Hicks, daughter and co-heir of John, elder brother of Jonathan Worthy of Exeter, above mentioned, by whom he had issue—James Philip, Thomas Julius, and Maria Worthy.

The eldest son, James Philip Bremridge, born 7th February, 1820, of St. John's College, Oxford, was for some years Vicar of Winkleigh, and married, in 1847, Mary, daughter of Henry Melhuish Ford of Exeter, and died in 1887, leaving issue— Philip Bremridge, eldest son, born 14th July, 1848, who now resides at Winkleigh; Henry, late of Exeter College, Oxford, and who was instituted to the Vicarage of Winkleigh in succession to his father upon the presentation of the Dean and Chapter of Exeter, and has issue; and a daughter, Mary. He had also a second son, John, who predeceased him, 11th September, 1884, æt. 31.

The second son, Thomas Julius Bremridge, of the Vineyard (Exeter Castle), was born 7th March, 1824, has long held the offices of Registrar of the Archdeaconry of Exeter and Clerk

* John Bremridge had, with three daughters, a son and heir, James Bremridge, who died s.p., and a second son, John, who died unmarried in 1878, æt. 76. Their mother, Anne Colley, who was married in 1796, and died in 1845, after a widowhood of thirty-seven years, was the grand-daughter of the Rev. James Colley, Rector of Martinhoe, great-grandson of Sir Anthony Colley, Kt., by his wife, Anne, daughter and heir of Sir William Turpin, Kt., by Elizabeth, sister of Richard Fiennes, whose claim to the Barony of Say and Sele (writ 3rd March, 1447) was recognised by letters patent of 9th August, 1603. His lordship was the grandson of Edward, who, for family reasons, never assumed the title, grandson of Henry "Lord Saye," who was never summoned to Parliament," and died in 1476. The latter was son and heir of William, second Lord Saye, by Margaret, daughter and sole heir of William Wickham, son of Sir Thomas Perot, Kt., who assumed the name of Wickham in memory of his grandmother, Agnes Perot de Wickham, wife of William Champneis, and sister of William Perot, otherwise "William of Wickham," the celebrated Bishop of Winchester, the founder of Winchester College and of New College, Oxford, and the architect of that portion of the fabric of Windsor Castle which was erected in the reign of Edward III. The Bishop died at South Waltham, Satuiday, 27th September, 1404. His ancestors, the Perots of Wickham, co. Hants, were the descendants of Sir Stephen Perot by his marriage with Princess Helen, daughter and sole heir of Marchin, son of Howel Dhu, surnamed "the good," who died in 947, grandson of Roderick the Great, King of all Wales.

The Colleys settled in Devonshire upon the preferment of Thomas Colley, Clerk in Holy Orders (son of Dr. Thomas Colley, Registrar to the Bishop of London, son of the aforesaid Sir Anthony Colley) to the Rectories of Georgeham and Sherwill. He married Mary, daughter of Sir T. Stukeley, and died in 1698. He claimed a common origin with the family of Colley of Castle Carbery, the paternal ancestors of the Wellesleys, Earls of Mornington and Dukes of Wellington, whose original name was Colley.

of the Peace for that city. He married in 1857, Margaret, youngest daughter of the late Henry Melhuish Ford, of Exeter, and younger sister of the late Mrs. J. P. Bremridge of Winkleigh.

Arms of Bremridge—*Sa.*, a chevron between 3 crosslets *or*.

Crest—An arm embowed in armour, holding a dagger point upward in pale ppr. hilted *or*.

Motto—"Nil Desperandum."

The Bremridges quarter Worthy (*ut post*, Worth of Worth, but differenced with a crescent).

FULFORD OF GREAT FULFORD.

There are so many discrepancies, inaccuracies, and palpable genealogical errors, in the several notices of the ancient owners of Great Fulford, for whom a "Saxon origin" has been commonly, but hypothetically, claimed, that I have decided, without unnecessary reference to other writers, to confine myself to the facts I have been able to recover as to their descent, and to dwell but lightly upon those points in their history which have manifestly originated in mere tradition.

Although the several pedigrees of this family, as recorded by the Heralds at the sixteenth century Visitations of the county, differ considerably in the earlier generations, the long residence of the Fulfords at Great Fulford—possibly from the time of Richard the first, positively from that of Henry III.—may be freely admitted; but this property, which is situated in the parish of Dunsford and hundred of Wonford, and invariably described in old records as the "Vill" of Fulford, has been strangely confused with the only manor of similar name mentioned in the Exeter Domesday, and written "Folefort" in that record, and "Foleford" in the Exchequer Copy of the Survey.

"Folefort," however, was the property now merged with "Shobrooke Park," and known as Little Fulford, which, in 1086, consisted of about forty acres of land, inclusive of four of meadow and twenty of pasture. It was rated, in the Confessor's reign, at seven shillings *p. a.*, and passed at the Conquest to

Baldwin de Brion, under whom it was held by Motbert, who was the owner, under the same chief lord, of other neighbouring estates, such as Kennerleigh and Eggbeare, in Cheriton Bishop, and after descending through several families it was ultimately sold by the Mallets (who had acquired it in marriage with Hatch, of Wolleigh, in Beaford), to Sir William Perriam, Lord Chief Baron of the Exchequer, who built a house there, and died in 1605; his co-heirs again sold it to the Tuckfields, who erected the mansion now known as "Shobrooke Park," which, from them, has descended by devise, through Hippesley, to its present owner, Sir John Shelley, Bart. This property is situated partly in Shobrooke and partly in the parish of Crediton.

The Manor of Dunsford did not change hands at the Conquest, but was left in the quiet possession of a Saxon Thegn called "Saulf," together with a neighbouring property, in Tedburn St. Mary, known as Melhywis (Melhuish). Saulf, however, was deprived of other lands which he had held in the reign of Edward the Confessor, which were given to Robert of Mortain and to the latter's powerful henchman, Alured Brito, and it is improbable that this Saxon owner was left at ease in his curtailed estates during the troublous times that followed the death of William the First and the reigns of his sons, Rufus and Henry, and their nephew, Stephen. Risdon (A.D. 1638) remarks that "Dunsford by Teign side was in ancient times the lands of William Bacon the Norman," and the "William Bacon" thus referred to can only have been the younger of the great-grandsons of "Grimbald," the kinsman of Earl Warren, and the commonly asserted ancestor of our *premier* Baronet. This William and his brother, "Robert," are both said to have taken the name of "Bacon," and they must have been contemporaries of King Henry II.

But the parish of Dunsford extends over nearly six thousand acres, and there are several estates in it, which, like Great Fulford, have not descended with the manor, which was not owned by the Fulfords until the sixteenth century, nor has any proof at all been adduced as to their connection even with the parish until the reign of Richard I. at the earliest, and then it is that a certain "William *de Turpi Vado*," or William of the *foul ford*, a designation which appears to point plainly to some memorable episode in the Holy wars, possibly to the defeat of the Army of the Cross at Tiberias, in 1187, is described as "de Fulford." This William de Fulford, or "*de Turpi Vado*," is traditionally believed to have distinguished himself greatly in the third Crusade, and is the first recorded ancestor of the family. It must be remembered, however, that there are other places of the same name both in Staffordshire and Yorkshire, and it was at the "foul ford" (Fulford) near York that Edwin and Morcar were defeated by Harold Hardrada, King of Norway, just before the Battle of Hastings, September 20th, 1066. Whatsoever he may have done to deserve such a signal mark of Royal favour as the grant of these lands must suggest, or however he may have come by his surname, it seems to me clear that "William *de Turpi Vado*" gave it, in its English form, to the "Vill of Fulford," and that the latter had been originally a portion of Saxon Saulf's great Manor of Dunsford, which had become subdivided when taken in hand by the Crown, as chief lords of the fee, probably very soon after the completion of the Domesday Survey, and thus the lordship of Dunsford, after an interval of some years, was again resumed by King John, and given by him to the Sackvilles; whilst that part of it since known as Fulford, was doubtless acquired by "William," either in the latter part of the reign of Henry the Second, or perhaps upon the return to England of his son, King Richard the First, in 1194, and after the second coronation of that monarch.

The pedigree of Fulford, as recorded at the Devonshire Visitation of 1564 (MS. Harl., 5185), commences with this "William *de Turpi Vado*," therein described as "William de Fulford, *temp. R. I.*," whose son, Nicholas de Fulford, was the father of "William de Fulford," whose first wife was Mary, daughter and co-heir of Baldwin de Belston, who was also the owner of the Manor of Parkham, near Bideford.

Both these Manors had been held, in 1087, by "Richard," under Baldwin de Brion, and it is probable that the succeeding "de Belstons," most of whom were called Baldwin, were the natural grandchildren of "de Brion," whose eldest son, Richard, had no lawful issue, on which account the hereditary

Shrievalty of Devon passed to his sister, Adeliza, as I have fully explained elsewhere. (*Devonshire Parishes*, vol. 1, pp. 78, *et seq*. *Suburbs of Exeter*, pp. 144, *et seq.*)

Mary de Belstone inherited a third of the Manor of Belstone, situated about three miles distant from Okehampton Castle, the seat of "de Brion's" Barony, and also a third of Parkham. Her husband, "William de Fulford," as co-patron with her brother-in-law, "Richard de Speckot," jointly presented to the vacant Rectory of Belstone, 23rd April, 1260 (44th Henry III.), and this is the first time the Fulfords are referred to in the registers of the Diocese of Exeter. The advowson of Belstone and the third share* of the manor of the parish were sold by John Fulford of Great Fulford, who died, *s. p.*, 1780, to the Rev. Joshua Hole.

According to the Visitation pedigree of 1564, "William de Fulford and Mary de Belstone" had issue, "Henry," who had issue, "William," *temp.* "Edward III.," who was the father of "Henry de Fulford, *Justic. in lege eruditus*," his legal skill, and status, being a mere family tradition. This "Henry," moreover, is made the father of "Baldwin de Fulford, Kt.," who was Sheriff of Devon in 1460, by the omission of very many generations.

The Visitation pedigree of 1620 commences with "Edmondus Fulford de Fulford," from whom the said "Sir Baldwin" appears to be eighth in descent, "Edmondus" being the grandson of the "Henry skilled in the law," of the Herald's record of 1564. The pedigree of 1620 is vouched for by the signature of "Andrew Fulford," who was a cadet of the family, and resided at Littleham, where he was buried in January, 1626-27.

The editors of Westcote's *View of Devonshire*,† 1627-42, published in 1845, have substituted a descent of their own, "compiled," as they remark, "on better authority" than that supplied by their author, "and his continuator," John Prince. This genealogy entirely overlooks the descent vouched for, to SS. George and Lennard, by the signature of Andrew

---

* The third sister married *de Wigornia*, see *ante*, families of Wykes and Cheverstone.
† The Rev. Dr. Oliver and Pitman Jones.

Fulford in 1620, and has added considerably to the already sufficient genealogical confusion; they have also made "Sir Henry, *alias* Sir William, Fulford," whose knighthood is not asserted in the Herald's pedigree, but who flourished in the reign of Richard II., the father of the Sir Baldwin Fulford of 1460.

I shall now endeavour to reconcile and correct these several contradictory descents. William de Fulford, son of Nicholas, and grandson of William, the first of his family of Great Fulford, presented, as I have said, to the Rectory of Belstone in the year 1260; by his wife, Mary, youngest daughter and co-heir of Baldwin de Belston, he had Baldwin and Amias, who appear to have been amongst the several gentlemen of this county who accompanied Prince Edward, the heir to the throne, to the Holy Land in the year 1269, and another son, Henry, who succeeded him at Great Fulford.

Doubtless Baldwin was the hero of an adventure, which may perhaps be referred to, the capture of Acre by the infidels in 1291 (when, it will be remembered, the Christian recluses in that city disfigured their faces in order to escape the lust of their conquerors), and which the figures of two Saracens, borne, by prescriptive right, as supporters to the arms of this family, are said to commemorate. I will give the story in the words of Tristram Risdon:—"Sir Baldwin Fulford of deserved memory for worth and valour, records testify that for the honour and liberty of a royal lady in a castle besieged he fought a combat with a Saracen, for growth an unequal match, and obtained victory by the death of his opponent." With respect to the "bulk, and bigness," of this redoubtable Saracen, John Prince adds, "as the representation of him cut in the wainscot, in Fulford Hall, doth plainly show."

The old writers have evidently confused this Sir Baldwin with a collateral descendant who flourished many generations later; but how the late Sir Bernard Burke can have gravely perpetuated such an anachronism, by explaining, when repeating the tradition, that its hero was "Sheriff of Devon in 38th of Henry VI." (1459-60), it is indeed difficult to understand. Henry de Fulford, brother of Baldwin and Amias, succeeded to Great Fulford, and was the father of William, Visitation 1564, who probably died without issue, as his brother, "Edmund Fulford of Fulford," commences the pedigree entered by Andrew Fulford in 1620. This Edmund was the father of John Fulford of Fulford, who, by his wife, Alice, daughter and co-heir of Ralph, son and heir of Sir Reginald de Fitzurse, had issue, Henry de Fulford of Fulford, son and heir. This Henry de Fulford is said, but erroneously, to have been a Judge, and in the Visitation pedigree of 1564 he is described as "skilled in the law." Prince misquotes Sir William Pole, and has published the hypothetical history, founded upon a misprint in Godwin's *De Præsulibus Angliæ Eboracenses*, p. 59, of "Sir William Fulford, Kt.," whom he describes as "a younger brother of Henry Fulford," and relates that, as one of the Justices of the King's Bench, he presided at the trial of Richard Scroope (L'Escrope), Archbishop of York, who was beheaded for opposition to the usurpation of Henry IV., June 8th, 1405. John Prince blandly explains that he cannot discover any such "Justice," but presumes that the first portion of his name must have been omitted and that he was identical with the "William Ford" mentioned by Dugdale as a "Baron of the Exchequer," 12th Richard II. and 1st Henry IV. However, as he gives us particulars of his education, and asserts his connection with the Fulford family, the inclusion of his biography is alone sufficient to disparage the general value of *The Worthies of Devon*, which is full of similar inaccuracies. In this particular instance, in which he has been misled by Bishop Godwin, the latter author doubtless intended to refer to Sir William Fulthorp, who was certainly "skilled in the law of the kingdom," *legum regni perito*, as the Bishop says, although others who have pointed out Prince's error, and have referred to Fulthorp as a mistake for Fulford, have asserted that he was "a Knight, not a Judge." Nevertheless, Fulthorp happens to have been one of the five judges* from whom King Richard obtained an opinion at Nottingham, August 25th, 1387, that the council of eleven, with the Duke of Gloucester at their head, and which had deprived him of all power since the previous October, was

---

* The five judges were Tresilian, Belknap, Holt, Burgh, and Fulthorp.

illegal, and that those who acted under it were traitors. All the extant records of the Visitation of 1564 are merely accepted *copies* of the original notes of the Heralds, and, as there does not appear to have been any such person as "Sir William Fulford," at the period referred to, it is probable that Godwin's error was perpetuated, perhaps by Dugdale, by the subsequent insertion of the words "Justic. in lege eruditus" after the name of Sir Henry Fulford, who was certainly not a judge, in the copies of the Visitation pedigree. The first edition of Godwin's work appeared in 1601. Henry Fulford, who is made the father of Sir Baldwin in the pedigree of 1564, had by his wife and kinswoman, Wilhelmina, daughter and heir of John Langdon, by a co-heir of Ralph Fitz-Urse, a son, William, who was born, probably about 1355, and was the father of William, son and heir, who seems to have died without issue and to have been succeeded at Great Fulford by his *brother*, Thomas, who is set down as his son in the original MS. of the Visitation of 1620.

Thomas Fulford of Great Fulford, born about 1378, married a daughter and co-heir of William de Moreton of West Putford (the other co-heir married Cary), and was the father of John Fulford, son and heir, c. 1399, whose son and heir, Henry Fulford of Fulford, married the daughter and heir of Philip Bryan, third son of Guy Lord Bryan of Tor Bryan, in this county, who died in 1391. He had a daughter, Katherine, wife of Ralph Prye, and who afterward married John Glynn of *Morvell*, and two sons, William, a Canon of Exeter and Archdeacon of Barnstaple, 1462, and who died in 1475, and Sir Baldwin Fulford, son and heir, of Great Fulford.

Sir Baldwin, who, as I have previously remarked, has been confounded both in family tradition as well as by the Heralds and by the several county historians, with his namesake, the Crusader, who was brother of his ancestor, Henry Fulford, the son of that William Fulford who flourished in 1260, was Sheriff of Devon in 1455-56, and again filled the same office in 1460-61. He was a Knight of the Sepulchre and subordinate to Henry Holland, third Duke of Exeter, in the office of High Admiral of England. He fought at Towton on the side of his Royal patron, and appears to have escaped from that sanguinary engagement, but he was afterward taken prisoner at Hexham and beheaded, by order of the Lord Montacute, May 15th, 1465. By his wife, Jennet, daughter and heir of John Bosome, *alias* Bozun, of Bosome-Hele, in the parish of Dittisham (a younger branch of the Bozuns of Ilton, whose heiress brought that property to Cheverstone (see Cheverstone pedigree, *ante*), and great-granddaughter of Robert Bosome, by Joan, daughter and heir of Henry St. George) Sir Baldwin had a son and heir, Thomas ; a son John, who was Archdeacon of Totnes, Cornwall, and Exeter, successively, between the years 1499 and 1518, when he died and was buried in Exeter Cathedral ; and two daughters, the eldest of whom, Thomazine, married Sir Thomas Wise, and, through her daughter, Alice, was the ancestress of the present Dukes of Bedford (see Wise pedigree, *ante*), whilst the youngest, Anna, married Sir William Cary, her kinsman, who fell at Tewkesbury in 1471.

Sir Thomas Fulford, who has been confused by Lysons, *Mag. Brit.*, with his younger son of the same name, has been said, by several authors, to have been beheaded in or about the year 1471. He was, however, attainted with other malcontents by Richard III. in October, 1483, but survived the accession of Henry VII., and died 20th February, 1489 (6th Henry VII., *Inq., p.m.*). By his wife, Philippa, daughter of Sir Philip Courtenay of Powderham, he had a son, Sir Humphry Fulford, Kt. of the Bath ; a third son, Thomas, above mentioned, and who was the " Sir Thomas " cited by Lysons as having assisted at the relief of Exeter in the Perkin Warbeck siege of that city in September, 1497 ; a second son William, and a fourth son Philip. Sir Humphry married a daughter and co-heir of John Bonvile of Shute, but as he died childless he was succeeded by his next brother, William, as heir-at-law ; the latter married Joan, daughter of John Bonvile of Combe Ralegh,* and had five sons, the eldest of whom was a minor at his father's death in 1517, and was left to the guardianship of his uncle, Philip Fulford, the fourth son of Sir Thomas and Philippa Courtenay, who survived until 1532.

---

* See note as to the Fulford Armorials, *post.*

Philip's nephew, Sir John Fulford of Great Fulford, Kt., attained his majority in 1523, was Sheriff of Devon in 1534-35, and again in 1540-41. His will, dated 11th July, 1544, was proved in London, 31st May, 1546, sometime after his death, which had occurred on the 14th November, 1544.

As I have remarked above, up to this date the Fulfords had not acquired the lordship of the Manor of Dunsford, although they had been settled for so many generations upon that portion of its ancient lands, which, in accordance with the reflection of the Psalmist, they "had called after their own names." According to Risdon, the successor of Saulf, the Saxon Thegn, in the Manor of Dunsford, appears to have been "Bacon," who can only have been identical with Sir William Bacon, of Monks Bradfield, co. Suffolk, brother of Robert, great-grandson of "Grimbaldus," the Norman kinsman of Earl Warren, who was created Earl of Surrey by William Rufus. This William, who, with his brother "Robert," flourished in the reign of Henry II., assumed the name of Bacon, but did not long remain the owner of Dunsford, which is said to have been given by King John to Robert Sachville, or Sackville, whose family owned Clist Sachville, in the parish of Faringdon. I may here remark that the lordship of the Hundred of Wonford, in which Dunsford is situated, was restored by the same monarch to the Mandeville family, whose gift of it to them by Henry I. had been forfeited by a subsequent attainder.

The Manor of Dunsford seems to have descended from Robert Sachville to his nephew, Philip Causbeuf, whose daughter and heir, Amisia, brought it in marriage to her husband, Robert de Blackford. John, son of Robert de Blackford, sold the Manor of Dunsford, with the advowson of the parish church, which had been dedicated, as the church of St. Mary, by Bishop Broncecombe, 29th July, 1262, to Bishop Peter Quivil, or Quiril, of Exeter, as *agent* for Maud, daughter of John de Lacy, Earl of Lincoln, and widow of Richard de Clare, Earl of Gloucester, in or about the year 1284, in order that it might form a portion of the magnificent endowment of that charitable lady to the priory of Canonsleigh, in the parish of Burlescombe, and which, originally dependent on Plympton, was turned into an Abbey for Canonesses of the order of St. Augustine in that year through the Bishop's exertions and influence with the said Countess. By deed enrolled before the King's Justices at Exeter, 14th Edward I., 1285-6, John de Blakeford executed a quit claim of this property with the reservation of an annual rent of one penny, to himself and his heirs, at Michaelmas, and by a further deed he authorised the purchasers to exchange it with the Dean and Chapter of Exeter for the Manor of Clist Hynton if they wished. The sale was duly confirmed April 7th, 6th Edward II., 1313, by the Lords of the Hundred of Wonford, as Chief Lords, under the Crown, of the Manor of Dunsford, viz., by John de Mandeville and Sir Robert Fitz-Payne.

On 5th August, 1314, Bishop Stapeldon assigned for the support of the then Vicar of Dunsford, *Pagan de Excestria* (who had been previously allowed a hundred shillings a year out of the Episcopal Treasury), and his successors, a house and garden on the south side of the church, a close near said garden on the east, with the altarage, the tithe of hay and apples, and the *great tithes of the Vills of Folforde and Cliffort.*

At this period the value of the rectorial tithes was assessed at £9 14s. 0d., whilst the manor rents amounted to £10 8s. 10½d. per acre. Dunsford Manor and Church, with the rest of the Canonsleigh property, was surrendered to Henry VIII. on February 16th, 1538-9. The manor was then worth £26 8s. 3d., the rectorial tithes £9 13s. 4d., and the vicarage was valued at £19 10s. 0d. a year; the net value of the vicarage in 1835 was returned at £297 a year, for a population of 903.

On the 11th June, 1544, King Henry VIII. sold the Manor of Dunsford, together with the Rectory and right of patronage of the vicarage, together with Dunsford Wood and other properties to "Sir John Fulford, Kt., and Humphry Colles, Esq." The former only survived the acquisition of Dunsford, which, with the church, has since remained with his descendants, a little over four months, as I have already shown. Within a month of the purchase he made his will, which was not proved by his eldest son and executor for nearly two years, probably because at the time of his father's death he had not attained his majority. By his wife, Lady Dorothy Bourchier, second daughter of the first Earl of Bath (who was a great-grandson of William

Bourchier, Earl of Eu, by Anne Plantagenet, daughter of Thomas of Woodstock, youngest son of King Edward III.), Sir John Fulford had a family of two sons and four daughters. The eldest son, Sir John Fulford, Kt., of Great Fulford, was over twenty years of age in 1544, and was Sheriff of Devon in Queen Mary's reign, 1558, and again in that of Queen Elizabeth, 1574-75. He died in August, 1580. He was twice married, first to his neighbour, Anna, daughter of Sir Thomas Dennis of Holcombe Burnell, and afterward to Ellinor, daughter and heir of Bernard Smyth of Totnes, who was a widow, and had, moreover, been four times a wife, at her death, sometime after 1610, when she is mentioned in the will of her eldest step-son. The latter, Thomas Fulford, was the eldest of eleven children, the sixth of whom, Andrew Fulford of Littleham, signed the family pedigree in 1620.

Thomas Fulford of Great Fulford died in 1610, aged 58, and was buried at Dunsford. By his wife, Ursula Bamfeild of Poltimore, he had three sons and four daughters; the second son, who was a Barrister of the Middle Temple, was buried at Bovey Tracy, in 1639; the eldest son, Sir Francis Fulford, Kt., was baptized at St. Mary Majors Church, Exeter, 1st September, 1583. He distinguished himself in the " troublous times " in which he lived, and held a Colonel's commission in the Royal Army and garrisoned Great Fulford House, which had been rebuilt in the reign of Henry VII., probably by Sir Humphry Fulford, and was compelled to capitulate to Fairfax in 1645, two years after his eldest son, Thomas Fulford, had fallen fighting before Exeter. One side of the quadrangle, round which the house is built, was then rendered ruinous, and has been for many years disused and uninhabitable. After the restoration, King Charles sent the Fulfords a full length picture of his unfortunate father, which has since hung in the great entrance hall, which is wainscotted with Tudor carving, a portion of which was intended to illustrate the traditional combat between Sir Baldwin Fulford and the gigantic Saracen already referred to. Besides Thomas Fulford, killed at the siege of Exeter in 1643, and whose issue male expired with the death of Col. Francis Fulford, his grandson, in October, 1700, Col. Sir Francis Fulford, who died in 1664, had, *inter alios*, a fifth son,

George Fulford, born in 1599, who settled at Toller Fratrum, in Dorsetshire, and whose great-grandson, Francis Fulford, born in 1704, eventually succeeded to Great Fulford, and was buried at Dunsford, 10th January, 1749. By his wife, Ann, daughter of Sir Arthur Chichester of Goulston, he had a numerous family, and many of his children predeceased him. He was succeeded by his fourth son, John Fulford, who died without issue in 1780, when Great Fulford passed to the eighth and youngest son, Benjamin Swete Fulford, born 1743. and who married Joan, daughter of Thomas Galpine. His son and heir, Col. Baldwin Fulford of Great Fulford, who long commanded the 1st Devon Militia, and had previously held a commission in the 6th Dragoons, Inniskilling, married Anna Maria Adams, of Bowden, whose son and heir, Baldwin Fulford of Great Fulford, and an officer of the 1st Devon Yeomanry, died childless in 1871, when Great Fulford passed to its present owner, Francis Drummond Fulford, his nephew, who is the eldest son of the late Rt. Rev. Francis Fulford, Bishop of Montreal and Metropolitan of Canada, who predeceased his brother Baldwin in 1868. Mr. Francis Fulford, now of Great Fulford, was born 25th October, 1831, married, in 1856, a daughter of Mr. Philip Holland of Montreal, and has, with other issue, a son and heir, Francis Algernon Fulford, who was born at Montreal, 15th September, 1861.

The very simple Arms of the family of Fulford, "*gules*, a chevron *argent*,' mark the extreme antiquity of the family; their Crest, "a Bear's head, erased *sa.*, muzzled, *or*," is evidently derived from Fitz-Urse; the origin of their supporters, two Saracens, I have already explained. They have, moreover, fully exemplified their motto, "*Bear Up*," perhaps under comparatively adverse conditions of late years. Since the sale of the Worth estates at Tiverton, within the last decade, no family in Devonshire can pretend to show a longer possession of, and residence upon, one of the most important properties in Devonshire than the Fulfords, save, possibly, Kelly of Kelly (*ante*), and Edgcumbe of Edgcumbe, in the parish of Milton Abbot (see my *Devonshire Parishes*, vol. 1, p. 253). Acland Barton, in the parish of Landkey, has long ceased to have any claim to be regarded as a county residence and can certainly never have had any pretension to equal such estates as those I have mentioned. But it is nevertheless still the property of the representative of its original owners, Sir Thomas Dyke Acland, Bt., of Killerton, and has belonged to that family since the twelfth century. (See Acland of Killerton, *post.*)

In the published edition of the original Visitation of Devonshire, 1620, recently edited by Lt.-Col. J. L. Vivian, a blazon of the Fulford arms and quarterings is affixed to their pedigree, as follows :—

"1st. Fulford. *Gu.*, a chevron, *arg.*

"2nd. Fitz-Urse. *Arg.*, a bend between three bears' heads, erased, *sa.*

"3rd. Moreton. *Arg.*, a chevron between 3 moorcocks, *sa.*

"4th. Bilston. *Or*, on a bend *gu.*, 3 crosses formée, *arg.*"

5th. ?—

"6th. St. George. *Arg.*, a lion ramp. *gu.*, a chief *az.*

"7th. Cantilupe. *Az.*, 3 leopards' faces jessant de lis, *or.*

"8th. St. Albyn. *Erm.*, on a cross *gu.*, 5 bezants.

"9th. Challons. *Gu.*, two bars, and an orle of martlets, *arg.*"

I desire to draw attention,

1st, to the entire omission of number 5 in the above quarterings.

2nd, to the introduction of numbers 7, 8, and 9, which are not only incorrectly marshalled, but are coats which the Fulfords do not appear to be entitled to quarter at all.

They evidently refer to the marriage of William Fulford, who succeeded his brother Sir Humphry, and died in 1517, with Joan, daughter of John Bonvile, who, according to an imperfect descent attached to the Visitation record, was the daughter of the said John, by Alice, daughter and heir of William Dennis, by daughter and heir of Thomas Challons, son of Sir Robert Challons, Kt.

In such case the quarterings would be—

7th. Bonvile.

8th. Dennis, brought in by Bonvile.

9th. Challons, brought in by Dennis.

And Cantilupe and St. Albyns are unaccounted for.

As a matter of fact, Challons, then entitled to quarter the

Arms of Leigh, married a daughter and heir of Cantilupe; the daughter and heir of Challons married St. Albyn, who then quartered Ralegh; the daughter and heir of St. Albyn married William Dennis; the daughter and heir of Dennis married John Bonvile; and Joan Bonvile was the wife of William Fulford. (An heiress of Ralegh was the grandmother of Alice St. Albyn; and an heiress of Leigh, the ancestress of Challons who married Cantilupe.)

So that the quarterings, correctly marshalled, would follow thus :—

1st, Bonvile; 2nd, Dennis; 3rd, St. Albyn; 4th, Ralegh; 5th, Challons; 6th, Leigh; 7th, Cantilupe.

That is to say, Bonvile should replace Cantilupe as No. 7 in the blazon affixed to the printed copy of the Visitation, and then proceed as above.

But Joan, daughter of John Bonvile of Combe Ralegh, inherited from Ralegh, as above, was not entitled to transmit arms to her descendants, as she had a brother John, who married Edith Blewitt, and was the father of Humphry Bonvile, who, besides daughters, left no less than five sons; so that it is indeed hard to understand how any claim to the arms and quarterings of this branch of the Bonvile family can ever have been suggested for the Fulfords.*

John Bonvile, the husband of Alice Dennis, was an illegitimate son of William, Lord Bonvile of Chewton, co. Somerset.

The arms of Fulford, in accordance with their successive alliances with heirs or co-heirs should, I venture to consider, be thus marshalled :—

1st, Fulford; 2nd, Belston; 3rd, Fitzurse; 4th, Langdon (*arg.*, a chevron between 3 bears' heads erased *sa.*); 5th, Fitzurse (repeated by Langdon); 6th, Moreton; 7th, Bryan (*or.*, 3 piles, in point *az.*); 8th, Bozun (*gu.*, 3 bird bolts *arg.*); 9th, FitzGeorge (by Bozun); 10th, Samways (*sa.* on a fess between 3 crosses pattée *or.*, as many martlets of the field).

---

* The Fulfords certainly acquired property with Joan Bonvile, *e.g.*, the Manor of Godford, in the parish of Awlescombe, but this fact would not entitle them to quarter her arms, failing proof of the absolute extinction of the issue, male or female, of her five nephews, or of any lawful descendants of her brother.

THE HOUSE OF WORTH.

Just previously to the Christian Era, there was a very considerable exodus of Roman emigrants to Neustria, since known as Normandy, who declined, as far as possible, any intercourse with their new neighbours, the aboriginal Gauls, but confined themselves to the towns and villages which in the course of ages replaced their primary encampments, and which were known in their own language as " Pagi," and their inhabitants as " Pagani," hence the French " Payen " or peasant, and the words " Paynim " and " Pagan," the medieval equivalents for infidel and heathen.

And long after Rollo, the son of Rognwld, had laid the foundation of the future Dukedom of Normandy in the early years of the tenth century these " Pagani " or " Payens " clung to their ancient rites and superstitions, although, of course, they had to be subservient to the laws and customs of their adopted country, so that in process of time they found it more and more difficult to keep themselves apart from the general population of the country, and ultimately they became attached to the rule of Richard *Sans Peur*, and to that of his successor, Richard *Le Bon*, and from time to time were notably connected with the public service of the Norman Duchy in accordance with their duties as good citizens. Yet, under such successive and varied changes in their conditions, they appear never to have been forgetful, and were doubtless, not unreasonably, proud of their descent from the ancient fathers of Imperial Rome, although by the tenth and eleventh centuries their distinctive *cognomina* alone remained to denote their remote connection with the yellow Tiber, and hence it was that many of these Normanized Romans helped to swell the ranks of that miscellaneous collection of continental adventurers which effected the conquest of this island under the ducal son of Harlotta of Falaise. And one of the most important of the Norman Pagani appears to have been " Ralph Paganel," or " Paynel," who heads the family pedigree[*] of Worth of Worth, in the parish of Washfield, and whose extraction is sufficiently commemorated by the

---

[*] *Vide* " *Visitations of the co. of Devon* " (Vivian), pp. 805-809.

ancient prescriptive arms which have been borne by them, in successive generations, ever since, indeed, such family distinctions became hereditary in England—the Roman eagle, with the addition of a second neck, as adopted by Charlemagne to denote his completed conquest of Germany in the year 802.

Ralph Paganel, or Paynel, whose immediate descendants were known as "Fitz-Payne," appears in Domesday as Sheriff of Yorkshire, in which county he had fifteen manors in 1087, a like number in Lincolnshire, five in Somerset, and ten, inclusive of the Manor of Washfield, in this county, in which all his lands are entered as those of "a free Knight." His three younger sons, Ralph, Reginald, and Robert Fitz-Payne, settled in Devonshire, and are believed to have first come here with the Conqueror's army in its march westward in the year 1067. (See my *Suburbs of Exeter*, p. 83.) His eldest son, Fulk Fitz-Paynel, married Beatrix, daughter and heir of William Fitz-Asculph, and thus acquired the Staffordshire Manor of Dudley, and had a son, Ralph,* whose son, Gervase Fitz-Paynel, as "Baron of Dudley," attended the ceremony of the coronation of Richard "Cœur de Lion."

Of the three great uncles of this Baron of Dudley, Reginald Fitz-Payne, afterward known as "de Worth" from his residence on that Saxon Manor, and by which name he is entered in the original Visitation of Devon in 1620, and as a "Knight" in the prior record of 1564, was Lord of the Manor of Witheridge under Mortain, and of Radford in Plymstock. In the latter parish, his brother Robert owned an estate known as Gosewell; in the former, his brother Ralph possessed "Dart," which has since been known as Dart Ralph.

He had also acquired, under William de Pollei, the Worth estate in Washfield, which appears to have descended to his brother Reginald aforesaid, doubtless through failure of his own issue. This property was adjacent to that Manor of Washfield which was held in demesne by his father, Ralph Paganel, or Paynel, and which afterward seems to have become merged with it. There was, however, a second Manor, which is still known as that of Washfield, a portion of which

---

* Another son of this Ralph, "William Fitz-Payne," acquired the Devonshire Barony of Bampton by marriage with the daughter and heir of Robert de Douay.

the Worthes subsequently acquired by marriage, as will be shown hereafter. I may remark here, however, that at a later period the Manor of Worth, presumably with Washfield "Paganel," was assessed at more than double the amount charged upon the other Manor of Washfield, which at the period of the survey in 1086 belonged to Ralph de Pomeroy. Sir Reginald Fitz-Payne, having succeeded his brother Ralph at Worth, assumed the name of that property; his son, Robert, otherwise "de Worthe," left Witheridge to a son of the same name (who was the ancestor of Robert Fitz-Payne, Lord of Witheridge in 1245), but Worth descended to his son Alexander.

Alexander "Fitz-Robert," *alias* "de Worthe," was the father of Sir Richard Worthe, Kt., whose son, Sir Hugh Worthe, Kt., of Worth, married Avis, eldest daughter of Richard de Redvers, third Earl of Devon, by his wife, Avis, daughter of Reginald, Earl of Cornwall, and thus his descendants not only derive a descent, on the same terms as the "Conqueror," from the Dukes of Normandy, and thence through Edgina, granddaughter of King Alfred, from Cerdic King of the West Saxons, but also co-represent, with the Courtenays, the ancient house of Redvers.[*]

Lady Avis Worthe, and her son and heir, Robert, are mentioned in an existing deed by her nephew, William Redvers "de Vernon," sixth Earl of Devon, c. 1166, and this deed is sealed with the three torteaux, since borne as the arms of the Courtenays, Earls of Devon. I have already given the general descent of the Worthes of Worth, and of the several branches of the family, on previous pages, in the form of foot notes to such of their testamentary documents as have been included in this volume, and as their pedigree has been already printed at length elsewhere,[†] it only remains for me to add a few particulars as to their history, fortunes, and misfortunes. The elder line failed at the death of Alexander Worthe, sometime after 1366, when Worth and other property at Topsham and Tiverton, which had been acquired in marriage

---

[*] For a further descent from Redvers, through Courtenay, see *ante*, p. 69, note.
[†] Vivian, *ut ante*. See also Visitation, 1564, Colby, pp. 212, 213. Sir William Pole (pub. 1791) has included several authenticated generations, which are *omitted* in the Visitation Records (*ante*, p. 312). Westcote, 1627-1642 (pub. 1845), "Worth of Exeter, Compton Poole, and Barum," p. 561.

with Lady Avis Redvers, passed to his younger brother, Sir John Worthe, Kt. Their grandfather, Alexander Worthe, of Worthe, had been one of the claimants to the Earldom of Devon in 1293, the succession to which dignity, after the death of Isabella "de Fortibus," and until it was finally granted to the Courtenays by their Royal cousin, King Edward III., was a bone of contention amongst the kin of Redvers[*] for over forty years.

Sir John Worthe of Worth, married Cicelye, daughter and co-heir of Sir John Doddescombe of "Leigh" (since known as Doddiscombesleigh, six miles from Exeter), and of Compton Pole, in the parish of Marldon. "Here," writes Thomas Westcote in 1630, "the family of Worth set a younger scion which prospereth well," and the descendants of this "younger scion" have since written their name "Worthy,"[†] instead of Worthe, as indeed some members of the family did as far back as the fourteenth and fifteenth centuries,[‡] from which it may be inferred that the final letter was always pronounced, although the name has been altered to "Worth" by the elder line, of Washfield, since the sixteenth century, and was entered by them as "*Worth*" (but as "*Worthe*" by the second house and their branches) at the several Visitations of Devon and Somerset in the following century.

By the marriage with Cicelye, who was granddaughter of Ralph Doddescombe, by Johanne, daughter and co-heir of Hugh Peverell, by Alice, daughter of Ralph Pole, by Alice Dalditch, and granddaughter and eventual co-heir of Maurice de la Pole, by Dionisia, daughter and heir of Compton, the family became entitled to quarter the arms of Doddiscombe, Peverell, Pole, Dalditch, Compton, de Alva, and Marldon.

John Worthe § of Worth, son and heir of John and Cecilia

---

[*] This family had become extinct, in the male line, at the death of Baldwin, 8th Earl of Devon, in the year 1261.
[†] See *Ante*, p. 44, note.
[‡] *Ep. Reg. Brantyngham*, Vol. I, f. 31 (1372).
Exeter Mun. Rec. No. 1116 (1424).
Ibid, 1127 (1425-6), 1159-1436.
Alys "Worthie," pensioned as a "nun of Polsloe." 31st Henry VIII. She was daughter of Otho Worthe of Compton Pole, and died 1586. Her maternal aunt presided over the community and died in 1530.
§ Burke calls him "Sir John Wrothe" (sub. Willington), an error which may be due to a misprint in Lysons, *Mag. Brit.*, Devon, vol. 1, p. 172, but which is corrected in vol 2, p. 18, of the same work.

Doddescombe, married Margaret, second daughter and co-heir of Sir John Willington of Umberleigh, by Matilda, daughter of Sir Walter Carminow. The Willingtons were descended from John Willington of Willington St. Michael, co. Derby, whose great grandson married Joan, daughter and heir of William Champernowne, and by this marriage the Worthes acquired a large addition to their property in the form of lands in Barnstaple and the surrounding district. (See *ante*, pp. 260-1, *note*.) And thus also became entitled to quarter the arms of Willington, Franc, Champernowne, Soleigny, and Loman, of Uplowman and Gittisham, and became co-heirs to the ancient Barony of Willington of Keirkenny, in abeyance, created by writ of 11th Edward I. (1283).

The son and heir of this marriage, Thomas Worthe of Worth, was the father of a son and heir, of like name, who married Margery, daughter of Hugh and sister and co-heir of Humphry Beauchamp, Lord of the Manor of Washfield and patron of the church. This was the second Manor of Washfield to which I have already referred, and which, in 1086, belonged to Ralph de Pomeroy of Berry, and in or before the time of Henry III., when it was held by William le Abbé, had passed to the Abbots of Loughtor, in the parish of Plympton St. Mary, and was held, not under the Lords of Berry, but under the Lords of Totnes Castle, the transfer having probably taken place during some period of forfeiture by the Pomeroys.

The seat of the Pomeroy Manor of Washfield, now and for many ages known as Great Beauchamp, came to Humphry, younger brother of Hugh Beauchamp of White Luckington, the maternal ancestor of the Spekes, by his marriage with Alice, daughter and heir of Walter Abbot of Loughtor and Washfield, who afterward married John Strokesdon.

This branch of the great house of Beauchamp was descended from Milo Beauchamp of Eaton, co. Bedford, fourth son of Hugh de Bello-Campo, Baron of Bedford, and younger brother of Walter Beauchamp, who was himself a third son, the ancestor of the Earls of Warwick. The great-grandfather of Humphry Beauchamp (the first of his race at Washfield), John Beauchamp of Hache, co. Somerset, married Cecilia, daughter and heir of John "Vyvon," or Vivian, by Maud, third daughter of William

Ferrers, Earl of Derby, and co-heir to her mother, Sibyl, daughter and co-heir of William, *le Marshal*, Earl of Pembroke. The third Earl of Derby married Margaret, daughter and heir of William Peverell of Nottingham, whose arms were :—Quarterly *gu.* and *vair*, a lion ramp *arg.*, and the husband of Cecilia Vivian usually bore a plain shield "*vair*" in lieu of his paternal arms, quarterly *or.* and *gu.*, a bend of the last, and thus the "*vair* coat of Beauchamp" came to be adopted as the arms of the prior and convent of Frithelstock, which, however, had been founded by Robert Beauchamp, the father-in-law of the said Cecilia Vivian.

By this marriage the Worthes acquired one-third, with the lordship, of the Manor of Washfield Pomeroy, and the right of patronage to Washfield Rectory, and sixteen additional quarterings to their family arms, including those of the old Earls of Chester, the Clares, the Marshals, Earls of Pembroke, and other powerful families.

Margerie Beauchamp, the wife of Thomas Worthe of Worth, who presented to Washfield Rectory, 11th January, 1410, was the eldest of three co-heirs, her sisters, Muriel and Matilda, having married Simon Bernville and Richard Donington.

Alice Abbot, described as "now wife of John Strokysdone," granted the Manors of Washfield and Loughtor to her son, Hugh Beauchamp, with the advowson of Washfield Rectory, by deed dated 36th Edward III. (1362). By deed dated at Worth, Tuesday after the Conversion of St. Paul, 5th Edward IV., John, son and heir of Simon Bernville, and Muriel, his wife, daughter and one of the heirs of Hugh Beauchamp and sister of Humphry Beauchamp, released his lands and rights in Washfield and the advowson of the church to "Thomas, son and heir of Thomas Worthe, son and heir of Margerie Worthe, daughter and co-heir of Hugh Beauchamp, and sister of the said Humphry." In the year 1500 Robert and George Whityng were co-patrons of this rectory with Thomas Worth and others. In 1517 Anthony and John Worth presented to it, with the consent of Christina Leche, widow, and Alice Rasshelegh, and in the fifteenth year of Henry VIII. (1523) Anthony, son and heir of Thomas Worthe, was amerced in the sum of fourpence at Totnes Castle for "one third," the heirs of Alice Rayshlegh, threepence for a moiety, and Joana, daughter of Richard Leche and next of kin to said Alice, threepence for another moiety of "Wayshefyld Manor," held by them "under the Lord of Totnes Castle."

Hence it is that the Worthes, having only inherited a third of the Maror of Washfield Pomeroy, the other two-thirds were from time to time split up into smaller holdings and passed to several owners, but from the date of the marriage with Margery Beauchamp, and until the sale of the property, with the exception of Great Beauchamp, referred to on a previous page (*ante*, p. 52), her posterity owned the whole of the parish of Washfield (3,319 acres in all), with the exception of two-thirds of the lands of the Manor of Washfield Pomeroy.

The grandson of Thomas Worthe and Margery Beauchamp, also called Thomas, married Isabell, daughter and co-heir of Humphry Bevill of Wolston and Barkenden, in the parish of Staverton, by which they acquired much land on the south-eastern side of the county and four additional quarterings, including Avenel, a family which co-represented, with themselves and Courtenay, the ancient house of Redvers. (See my *Suburbs of Exeter*, p. 87).

Thomas Worthe and Isabell Bevill were the parents, *inter alios*, of Thomas "Worthe," son and heir of Worth, and of Roger Worthe, second son, who, by devise of his grandfather, who died in 1463, inherited Compton Pole; property in Doddiscombesleigh, and the co-patronage of the latter church; together with much Willington property at Pilton and Barnstaple. His grandson, Otho Worthe of Compton Pole, had a son and heir, John, and a second son, Roger Worthe, who had the Barnstaple and Pilton property, and represented that borough in Parliament in 1553; his grandson, Paul Worthe of Barnstaple, who died in 1615, was the ancestor of the Worths of Penryn, represented in the last century by Charles Worth of Penzance, who died in 1766, and also of the Worths of Timberscombe, co. Somerset, descended from John Worthe, who was baptized at Barnstaple in 1541 and who was the third brother of the aforesaid Paul.

The Manor of Sydenham, and much other Somerset property, was held by several younger branches of the family, who were considerable landowners in that county also, from the fourteenth century until within the last seventeen years. Their pedigrees will be found in the Visitations òf Somersetshire, 1623, *MS. Harl. (original)* 1141 *and* 1445.

The son and heir of Otho Worthe, John Worthe of Compton Pole (brother of Roger, M.P. for Barnstaple), married Agnes, daughter of John Bodley of Dunscombe, Crediton, first cousin of John, the father of Sir Thomas Bodley, M.A., of Merton College, Oxford, Esquire of the Body in the household of Queen Elizabeth, and the celebrated founder of the Bodleian Library. Their son, John, resided at Dunscombe, but left Compton Pole to his eldest son, who was seised of it in 1638. His second son, George, of the city of Exeter, was the father of John "Worthy," who was a Parliamentary Commissioner for Devon in 1643, and the great great-grandfather of John Dewdney Worthy, son and heir, born 1760, and whose daughter and co-heir married Bremridge (see the history of that family, *ante*); and of Jonathan Worthy, second son, born 1762,[*] Sheriff of Exeter, 1797 and 1803, and Mayor of Exeter, 1799, who married Elizabeth, daughter of John Melhuish of Hill, in Cruse Morchard, and died at Ide, 26th of June, 1815, and was buried with other members of his family at Stoke Canon. See notes pages 46 and 80, *ante*.

Having now traced the descent of the Worthes of Compton Pole, I must return to the brother of their immediate ancestor, Thomas Worthe of Worth. He seems, like very many others his contemporaries, to have attracted the attention of Richard Empson, one of the iniquitous agents of Henry VII., for we find from the Royal Household Accounts (*MS. Add.* 21480, *fol.* 35) that " Thomas Worthe of Devonshire hath enfeoffed Richard Empson, and others in his manor called Berkenden, for a yearly annuity of £20, to be given at the King's pleasure," and further, that the said Thomas Worthe "shall owe, by obligacion, at Mydsomer, £150 4s. od." Thus, as is well known, the existing laws of that period were perverted for the purposes of extortion by the King's shrewd lawyers, Messrs. Empson and Dudley, and quiet country gentlemen like poor Thomas

---

[*] The issue male of their younger brothers, Richard and Thomas, is extinct; their third brother, James, died unmarried in 1823, aged 60.

Worthe were compelled to pay similar enormous fines to avoid utter ruin. This Thomas Worthe was the father of Anthony "Worth" of Worth, who, as I have already mentioned, was amerced at Totnes Castle for his Manor of Washfield in 1517, and who married Katherine, daughter of Simon Digby of Coleshill, the ancestor of the Lords Digby.

Anthony's grandson, Arthur Worth, had the Bevill property, Barkenden, settled upon him and his heirs male, by deed dated 9th May, 1559, and there is a fine *prie Dieu* monument to the memory of this branch of the family in Staverton Church. The body of Simon Worth of Barkenden, who died in Italy in 1669, was brought home and buried beneath it in that year. In the *Philosophical Transactions*, vol. 47, p. 253, is an account of the exhumation of his body during some repairs to the church, pending which the coffin seems to have been placed in a dry ditch in the churchyard. Although it had been then buried for eighty-one years, the corpse, which had been doubtless embalmed in Italy, was found perfectly fresh and the features quite recognisable, but, unfortunately, before it was returned to the vault one of the workmen accidentally jumped upon the coffin whilst it was resting in the ditch, and thus broke in the cover and destroyed the face of the deceased.

The elder brother of Arthur Worth of Barkenden, Henry Worth of Worth, was the direct ancestor of his successors in that ancient property, who, in successive generations, intermarried with the Frys of Yarty, the Bampfyldes of Poltimore, the Calmadys of Langdon, the daughters and heirs of Furse of Morsehead, and of Furlong of Langford Budville. The said Henry Worth's mother was a Fortescue, and after him there were two other Henrys, followed by three Johns, the last of whom died without issue, when Worth went to his younger brother, Henry Worth of Worth, who died in 1777. He was the great-grandfather of the late John Francis Worth of Worth, who died in 1878, when he was succeeded by his only surviving son, Reginald.

Thus the senior line of Worth, of Worth, commenced and ended with Reginald, and thus an old family tradition was fulfilled, that whenever a second Reginald succeeded to the property the land "would fade away." Some, but not many, of the younger sons had been called Reginald, but no Reginald had ever succeeded to the property since the time of Reginald Fitz-Payne, Lord of Witheridge and Worth, and the second Reginald of Worth inherited the property quite accidentally by the early deaths of two elder brothers, John and Henry.

Reginald Worth, who was in Holy Orders, married Elizabeth Susannah, daughter of John Barbensom, but died without issue at Sharcott Manor, Wiltshire, 12th March, 1880.

His only sister, Henrica Duntze Worth, married the Rev. W. L. Jones, Rector of Washfield, who, in 1882, assumed the name of Worth by Royal license, and died 8th January, 1884, leaving issue. His wife resided at Worth for a few years prior to the dispersal of the property by sale in 1887-8, when it realized £55,000 (see *ante*, p. 52), and died at Great Beauchamp in Washfield, 2nd July, 1891.

The mere name, *Worth*, or *Worthy*, is, of course, by no means singular to Devonshire, as it is simply a place name derived from the Saxon "weord," an enclosed estate, or land near the head of a river. This particular Worth is watered by the river Exe.

The Arms of the family, as admitted at all the county Visitations are:—*Arg.*, an eagle displayed with two necks *sa.*, beaked and legged *gu.*

Crest—An arm erect, vested *erms.*, gloved *erm.*, tasselled *or*, holding an eagle's leg couped at the thigh of the last.

Motto—"*Nec imbellem feroces progeniant aquilæ columbam*"

The field is sometimes tinctured ermine, as on the book plate of the late Jonathan Worthy of Exeter, who died December, 1784, and, according to Robert Glover, Somerset Herald, 1571, the arms of "Sr. de Worthe, Deuon," were: *Erm.* an eagle double headed, dispd. *s.*, beaked and legged *gules*.

The same arms as admitted to Worthe (of Compton Pole, etc.) in 1564 had the field *arg.* According to Westcote, his ancestor, Roger Worthe, surmounted his eagle with a bar *gu.*, and charged the latter with a crescent to mark his cadency, but his descendants never adopted the said "bar *gu.*"

The arms of Richard Worthe of Timberscombe, co. Somerset, who was second son of Richard Worthe of Luckombe, in the same county, third son of John Worthe of Timberscombe, are those of his family above blazoned and duly differenced with a mullet, thereon a crescent. Said Richard Worthe died 17th August, 1637, and his arms are "tricked." (*Coll. Ar., I.,* 24, *fol.* 101.)

Finally, the arms of Peter Worthe of Braunton, near Barnstaple, fifth son of Thomas Worthe of Worth, and younger brother of the said Roger Worthe of Compton Pole, have also the field *arg.*, and are duly differenced with an annulet. (*Coll. Ar. C.* 22. *MS. Harl.,* 1445.)

NORTHCOTE, EARL OF IDDESLEIGH AND VISCOUNT ST. CYRES.

No attempt has been hitherto made to trace the family of Northcote beyond the year 1103, when a certain "Sir Geoffrey," called in records "Galfridus Miles," was the owner of the Manor of Northcote, in the parish of East Downe, and presumably of another estate of the same name in the parish of Inwardleigh, which long remained with his descendants, and is said by our old writers, Pole and Risdon, erroneously according to the pedigree which was laboriously compiled by Robert Cooke, Clarencieux (1566-1592), to have passed to "Lutterell" in marriage with "Joan, daughter and heir of John Northcot," in the reign of King Henry IV.

The Manor of Northcote, in East Downe, however, from which the family name is derived, remained with the Northcotes until the commencement of the last century, when the house, having been then recently destroyed by fire, the lands were sold, in parcels, by Sir Henry Northcote, Bt., who died in 1729-30. Both these Manors of Northcote were held in 1086 by "Drogo," under Geoffrey, Bishop of Coutance, and this "Drogo" was one of four brothers, said in the *Clifford Pedigree*, published at Paris in 1817, to have been the sons of "Wm. de Owe,"[*] who was really the ancestor of the

---

[*] William de Owe, "Comte D'Eu," was an illegitimate son of Richard "Sans Peur," Duke of Normandy.

Duttons, from whom Lord Sherborne is descended on the "spindle" side.

"Walter," "Osborne," "Drogo,"* and "Richard," the last being the Clifford ancestor, were the sons of "Mauger Le Ponz" (uncle of William the Conqueror), by his wife, Basilia, nephew of Mauger, the ancestor of the Granvilles, and youngest son of Richard "Le Bon," Duke of Normandy, and I have come to the conclusion that "Galfridus Miles," the owner of Northcote in 1103, was the nephew of Drogo, the sub-tenant of Northcote in 1086 (son of his brother Walter), and that he was named after Geoffrey of Coutance the chief lord of the fee.

He should, in such case, therefore, in accordance with the custom of the times in which he lived, be described as Sir Geoffrey Fitz-Walter. He was, in any case, however, the father of Sir John Fitz-Geoffrey, "Johannes filius Galfridi Miles," who owned Northcote after him and transmitted it to his son, Geoffrey of Northcote, in the year 1118. The latter held one knight's fee of the Abbot of Tavistock, and owned lands likewise in Witheridge hundred, and had two sons, William and Walter.

William Northcote, son and heir, of Northcote, married Margaret de Afeton, and had three sons, Walter, Andrew, and Edmund; the line was continued by the second of these, who married a daughter and co-heir of Faber of Bovey Tracy in the 7th year of Edward I., 1278, and their eldest son, William Northcote of Northcote, by his wife Matilda, daughter and heir of Robert Hillion, had two sons, John and Andrew.

The wife, "*Uxor Hervei de Helion*," appears as tenant *in capite* of two manors in Devonshire in 1086. Her son Robert was the father of Gelenus de Helion, father of Alan, great-grandfather of Robert, whose daughter, Matilda, married William Northcote. Their eldest son, John Northcote, Sheriff of Devon, 1354-55, became the husband, in 1343, of Joan de Moels. Her father, Roger de Moels, who died in 1325, was the second son of Nicholas, Lord Moels, by Margaret, sister of Hugh de Courtenay, first Earl of Devon of that line. Her

---

* "Drogo" was the ancestor of Bremridge and Drewe. (See "Bremridge," *ante*.)

mother was. Alice, daughter and heir of Sir William Prowse; she had sisters married to Damarel and Wibery, with whom she divided the inheritance of her parents, as shown by a writ of partition dated 14th Edward III., 1340.

Her son and heir, John Northcote of Northcote, married Margery de Bickington, widow of John de Graas; their great-grandson, John Northcote of Northcote (son of Walter, by a co-heir of Hawkworthy, son of John, by his wife, Isolda Sutton), was the father of another John, who married Joan, daughter of John Luttrell, and to the error which this marriage has occasioned, with respect to the descent of the Northcote property at Inwardleigh, I have already referred.

The husband of Joan Lutrell, however, was a third son, and possibly did not inherit the Northcote Manor of Inwardleigh, although Northcote in East Downe seems to have descended in his line. His son Walter, by Alice, daughter and co-heir of Baldwin de Mamhead, was the grandfather of John Northcote (son of Walter) of Yewton, Crediton, who married Alice, daughter and co-heir of John Dart, *alias* Walleis, of Barnstaple and Colebrook. Their son, Walter, who was buried at Crediton 5th May, 1572, married Elizabeth Hill of Shilston, co. Devon, and was the father of John Northcote of Crediton, who married Elizabeth, daughter of Thomas Dowrish of Dowrish, in Sandford, and was the father of John Northcote, second son, described as of "Uton" (Yewton) "Esq." in the "Visitation" of 1620, and who, as third in descent from John Northcote of Yewton, signs the pedigree which was then entered; the previous generations, from "Galfridus Miles," being also on record at the College of Arms. This John Northcote, who was baptized at Crediton 27th May, 1570, and was buried at Newton St. Cyres 22nd December, 1632, had, according to Risdon, the custody of the county committed to him the third year of Charles I. He appears to have acquired Hayne, the old seat of the Drewes, in Newton St. Cyres, although it was his elder brother, Walter Northcote, who married on the 17th May, 1585, Mary, daughter and heir of Edmund Drewe of Hayne, by whom he had issue, Elizabeth Northcote, who married, first, Edward Yarde of Churston, by whom she had issue, and secondly, Dr. Barnabas Potter,

Bishop of Carlisle. (See my *Devonshire Parishes*, vol. 2, pp. 69, 292; and also *Ashburton and its Neighbourhood*, p. 135.)

John Northcote of Yewton and Hayne (the latter property still belongs to Lord Iddesleigh) married firstly, Elizabeth, daughter of Sir Anthony Rouse of Halton, co. Cornwall, by whom he had a son, Anthony, who died without issue in 1619; and secondly, Susan, daughter of Sir Hugh Pollard of Nymet-Regis (Mar. Lic., 10th April, 1596), and by that lady he had a large family, twelve sons and six daughters. There is a memorial to him and his two wives in the little church of Newton St. Cyres, which bears a somewhat singular inscription. Under the figure of the first lady are the words, "My fruit was small, one son was all, that not at all"; and under the second, "My John had by me as many sons as he'd daughters, twice three." The word *plus* before twice would have made this statement more intelligible.*

Of this family, the eldest son, John, born 1599, who was, according to the Visitation pedigree, "the first son living, and aged twenty-one," 1620 (his younger brother, Benjamin, the eleventh son, was buried 27th June that year), succeeded to the family property. He was Sheriff of Devon in his father's lifetime, third of Charles I., 1627, and was created a Baronet 16th July, 1641. At the outbreak of the Civil War he declared for the Parliament, and joined Lord Bedford's army in the west in 1642. In 1643 he was one of the Commissioners for the County who were appointed in that year to make arrangements for sequestrating the estates of their

---

* *The issue* of John Northcote and Elizabeth Rouse—one son, Anthony Northcote, died *s. p.*, 1619.

The issue of the said John and Susan Pollard:—

1st.—Sir John Northcote, the first Baronet, b. 1599.	10th.—Pollard Northcote, b. 1618.	
2nd.—Lewis Northcote, b. 1601.	11th.—Benjamin ,, b. 1620.	
3rd.—Amias ,, b. 1603.	12th.—Robert ,, b. 1621-2.	
4th.—Edmund ,, b. 1605-6.		
5th.—Edmund ,, (twin) b. 1608.	1st.—Elizabeth Northcote, b. 1604.	
6th.—Amias ,, b. 1613.	2nd.—Susan ,, (twin) b. 1607-8.	
7th.—Franciscus ,, (twin) b. 1614.	3rd.—Dorothy ,, b. 1609.	
8th.—William ,, b. 1615.	4th.—Gertrude ,, b. 1611.	
9th.—Walter ,, b. 1617.	5th.—Francisca ,, (twin) b. 1614.	
	6th.—Anne ,, b. 1619.	

The *sequence* of the twelve sons, according to Vivian, *Visitation of Devon*, p. 582, is quite inaccurate.

opponents, and he sat as a representative of the Borough of Ashburton in the "Long Parliament," 1640-1653. No writ for Ashburton appears to have been issued for the Parliament of 1654, but Sir John Northcote, with ten others, was returned for the county, 12th of July, 1654, to the "Protector's Parliament," which met on September 4th that year ; and again to the Convention Parliament, March, 1660, which voted the return of the King. He died 29th June, 1676, and was buried at Newton St. Cyres. By his wife, Grace, daughter and heir of Hugh Halswell of Wells, he had seven sons and four daughters ; his eldest son, Sir Arthur Northcote, second Baronet, born 1627. By his second wife, Elizabeth, daughter of Sir Francis Godolphin, and sister of the Lord High Treasurer of that name, he had,* *inter alios*, two sons who succeeded to the title. The younger of these, Sir Henry Northcote, fourth Baronet, born 1655, married Penelope, daughter and co-heir of Robert Lovett of Liscombe, co. Bucks., and of Corfe, co. Devon, and was the father of Sir Henry Northcote, fifth Baronet, who married Bridget Maria, only daughter and heir of Hugh Stafford, by which alliance the Northcotes acquired the picturesque property known as Pynes, in the parish of Upton Pyne, which is the present seat of the family. Lady Northcote's mother, Bridget, was the daughter of John Kellond of Painsford, M.P. for Totnes, 1678, son of John Kellond,† by Susannah, daughter of Thomas Fownes, by his wife, Joan, daughter of Walter Hele of Gnaton, by Elizabeth, daughter of William Strode of Newenham, by Elizabeth, daughter and heir of Philip, second son of Sir Philip Courtenay of Molland, second son of Sir Philip, grandson of Sir Philip Courtenay of Powderham, who was the sixth son of Hugh, Earl of Devon, by Lady Margaret, his wife, youngest daughter of Humphry de Bohun, Earl of Hereford, by the Princess Elizabeth, fifth daughter of Edward I., King of England, by Eleanor, daughter of

---

* His second daughter, Penelope, married, at Newton St. Cyres, 2nd January, 1708-9, John Hesketh of Exeter, and his wife's family purchased for him the patent office of Lancaster Herald. There is a painting of him at the College of Arms. Lancaster resigned his Tabard in 1727 in favour of Stephen Martin Leake, who was afterwards advanced to the position of Garter King of Arms.

† Although "Lysons," *Magna Brit.*, and others write the name "Kelland," it is spelt as above, both in the Parliamentary returns and on the mem. to John Kellond, 1679. See my *Devonshire Parishes*, vol. 1, p. 324.

Ferdinand, King of Castile. Sir Henry Northcote was long M.P. for Exeter, died in 1743, and was buried at Newton St. Cyres on the 28th May that year, when he was succeeded by his eldest son, Sir Stafford Northcote, as sixth Baronet, whose only son, Sir Stafford, seventh Baronet, married Jaquetta, daughter of Charles Baring of Larkbeare, whose brother, Francis, was the ancestor of the Lords Northbrooke and Ashburton.

Their eldest son, Henry Stafford Northcote, died v.p., and the late Sir Stafford H. Northcote succeeded as eighth Baronet on the death of his grandfather, 17th March, 1851. I have already dwelt elsewhere, and at some length, upon the life of that illustrious statesman,* who was born on the 27th October, 1819, and died, Lord-Lieutenant of his native county, and to the great grief of the nation, 13th January, 1887. On the 3rd July, 1885, he had been deservedly elevated to the peerage as Viscount St. Cyres and Earl of Iddesleigh. His Lordship married, 5th August, 1843, Cecilia Frances, daughter of Thomas, and sister of Sir Thomas Farrer, Baronet, by whom he had a family of seven sons and three daughters. His second son, the Honourable Henry Stafford Northcote, C.B., born in 1846, was created a Baronet 23rd November, 1887, and has long represented Exeter in Parliament. He married, in 1873, Alice, daughter of Sir George Stephen, Bt., who was raised to the peerage as Lord Mt. Stephen, 1891.

Lord Iddesleigh was succeeded in his title and estates by his eldest son, Viscount St. Cyres, born 7th August, 1845, who married, 1868, Elizabeth Lucy, eldest daughter of Sir H. S. Meysey-Thompson, Bt., of Kirby Hall, Yorks., and has issue, with three daughters, Stafford Henry Northcote, Viscount St. Cyres, who was born 29th August, 1869.

Arms of Northcote as admitted at the Visitation of Devon, 1620—*Arg.*, 3 crosslets in bend *sa.*

Crest—On a chapeau *gules* turned up *erm.*, a stag trippant *argent.*

Supporters—Two stags *ppr.*, from the neck of each suspended

---

* *Life of the late Right Honourable the Earl of Iddesleigh*, G.C.B., second edition, London, 1887, pp. 11-53.

by a chain *or.*, an escutcheon *erm.* charged with a pine cone of the second.

Motto—"*Christi Crux Est Mea Lux.*"

NOTE.—The Northcotes have customarily borne their arms:—
Quarterly, 1st and 4th *arg.*, a fess between 3 crosses moline *sa.* 2nd and 3rd *arg.*, 3 crosslets in bend *sa.*

One and four are very similar to the arms of Faber of Bovey Tracey. The daughters and co-heirs of Peter Faber of that parish, 1289, married Northcote, as above stated, Beare, and Bampfylde; and I consider that the second and third quarterings of Northcote may have been also founded upon Faber, and adopted subsequently to the marriage of Andrew Northcote with Matilda Faber in the reign of Edward I. Faber, as quartered by Bampfylde, bore *arg.* on a fess *sa.* 3 crosslets *or*, a bordure *asure.*

The Northcotes should rightly quarter, 1st Faber, 2nd Hillion, 3rd Meols, 4th De Bickington, 5th Hawkworthy, 6th de Mamhead, 7th Dart of Barnstaple and Colebrook, 8th Halswell, 9th Lovett of Liscombe, 10th Stafford of Pynes.

Although the Newton St. Cyres property has descended to Lord Iddesleigh it must be remembered that its devolution was not due to the match with Drewe of Hayne in that parish; the Yardes of Churston quartered Northcote and Drewe of Hayne in right of the marriage of Elizabeth, sole daughter and heir of Walter Northcote, by his wife, Mary, daughter and heir of Edmund Drewe of Hayne. According to Lysons, *Mag. Brit.*, Vol. 1, p. cx. (Devon), "the heiress of Passmere" married a Northcote subsequently to the match with de Mamhead. The surname of Alice, wife of Walter, son of Walter Northcote, by Alice de Mamhead, is omitted from the pedigree anterior to the Visit, 1620, which is preserved at the College of Arms.

The arms of Dart of Barnstaple, &c. (miswritten "Durke" in the Northcote pedigree) were "*Gu.*, a fess and canton *erm.*"

THE WALRONDS OF BRADFIELD.

In the years immediately subsequent to the Norman Conquest, the King's great Barons commonly granted smaller manors within their own honours to be held under them by persons of somewhat lesser importance, and in process of time many of these sub-infeudations acquired most, if not all, of the privileges of the parent manors, although being non-existent at the period of the Survey, they are not to be found entered in the pages of "Domesday Book."

One of such, in respect of which the latter record is silent, is the Manor of Bradfield, within the parish of Uffculme, a few miles from Cullompton, now the seat of Sir W. H. Walrond, Bt., and which, for more than six centuries, was the residence of the Walronds in direct male line ; it was originally parcel of the Domesday Manor, then known as *Offacome*, which became included in Walscin de Douay's great Barony of Bampton. The property within Offacome, in early records written "Bradfelle," or the Broadfield, gave name to a family who tenanted it under the Barons of Bampton for four generations, from the time of Henry I. to that of King John, and although the late Sir Bernard Burke has ventured to set them down as the ancestors of the House of Walrond, existing evidence is quite adverse to his assertion, and that these "de Bradfelles" were removable at the lord's pleasure is sufficiently evident from the fact that the then Baron of Bampton, "Fulke Paynel," as shown, Sir Bernard Burke admits, by a deed "still in possession of the family," *transferred* Bradfield "to Walerande" in the reign of King John, 1199-1216 ; and there is abundant evidence that since the latter date, that is from the period of the accession of Henry III., Richard, or Robert, Walrond's posterity have been hereditary owners of this property.

This Fulk Paynel, as I have previously stated,* was the son of Julian, granddaughter of Walscin de Douay, and was dead before the 10th of King John (1209), in which year his son and heir paid two hundred marks for livery of his inheritance, and for the further consideration that his mother, Ada, should not be disturbed in her "pure widowhood," or, in plainer terms, that she should not be constrained by the crown to take a second husband, in accordance with the agreeable fashion of those times.

It is almost needless to remark that the de Bradfelles, who were known by the name of their residence, and as "Robert," or "Richard," from the time of Henry I. to that of Richard "Cœur de Lion," were not of baronial rank, which the Walronds were in the reign of Henry II., at which time Walter Waleran, the great-grandson of the Norman owner of Sutton-Walrond, in Dorset, married Isabel, the eldest daughter of

---

* House of Worth, *ante*.

William, Earl of Salisbury (William Longespee), and his barony was divided by his three daughters and co-heirs. (Their mother afterward married Wm. Fitz-Eustace, *alias* de Vesci.)

He was probably the uncle of Robert and of William Walrond, the former of whom married Isabel, daughter and co-heir of Hugh de Kylpec, and thus obtained that lordship in the county of Hereford.

This Robert disinherited his nephew Robert, son of his brother, William Walrond, and gave the honour of Kylpec to another nephew, Alan Plugenet, son of Alice Walrond, his sister, and who was summoned to Parliament in his Barony of Kylpec in 1295.

William Walrond flourished in the reign of King John. He was, as I have shown, a younger son, and I believe therefore that Fulk Paynel's grant of Bradfield was made to him or to his son Robert, who is called "Richard" in the Walrond pedigrees.

Whether "Richard" or Robert, he was the father of William Walrond of Bradfield, whose daughter, Alice, married John Ayshford of Ayshford, in the parish of Burlescombe, who died in 1265, and whose brother, John Walrond, was the father of another John, whose wife, Alice, daughter and heir of John Stowford of Stowford, in Colyton, brought him that property, which remained with the Walronds until the sixteenth century, when it was sold by Humphry Walrond of Bradfield to William Pole, who died in 1587, and was the father of Sir William Pole, the antiquary.

William, son and heir of John Walrond and Joan Stowford, commences the pedigree of the family which was entered at the Devonshire Visitation of 1564; by his wife, Julian, he had, with two daughters, a son and heir, John Walrond of Bradfield, who, as Tristram Risdon tells us, "well increased their inheritance by an heir of Uflet that had formerly married an heir of Martin Fishacre, Kt." His wife was Agnes, daughter and heir of John Ufflett, by Agnes, daughter and heir to Sir Martin Fishacre, by an heir of Spekes, and thus the ancient heritage of the latter in the parish of Little Hempston and elsewhere came to the Walronds, "in which name Combefishacre doth yet remain," says Risdon, writing in 1638.

The issue of this marriage, according to the Visitation pedigree, 1564, MS. Harl., 5185 (Colby, 204), was John Walrond, son and heir, of Bradfield, and, according to Westcote, Joan, wife of Robert Battin of Dunsland. It has been asserted that there was another son, "William Walrond,"* who, by his wife, "Joan, daughter of John Bret, and widow of Higgens," was the ancestor of "Walrond of Bovey," "whose eventual heiress," says Sir Bernard Burke, "was the wife of Lord Rolle," creation, 1796.

But this "William Walrond of Bovey," if he ever had any actual existence, must, to have been the "ancestor" of Lady Rolle, have flourished at a much later period, because there were as many as nine generations between the issue of John Walrond and Joan Ufflett, and the year 1638, at which period, Risdon tells us, the then proprietor of Bovey, "Edmond Walrond," was its *third* owner in that line, and that this branch had therefore then become "a distinct family," but that previously this "ancient inheritance of the Walronds had been usually given to a younger son."†

The "Bovey" referred to is not either of the parishes of that name in South Devon, but a property at Seaton, near Axminster. Its last male owner of this name was William Walrond, after whose death it came to Judith Maria, daughter of Henry Walrond, who married Mr. (afterward Lord) Rolle, in 1778, and died without issue in 1820.

John, son and heir of John Walrond and Alice Ufflett, married Margaret Moore of Moorhayes, in the parish of Cullompton, and had issue John and Humphry; the latter was the ancestor of the Walronds of Eveleigh, in the parish of Broadclist, which estate had been derived by the Ufflett marriage, having come to the latter through Valletort, Speke, and Fishacre.

John Walrond, son and heir, of Bradfield, was the father of Humphry, son and heir, and of Oliver‡ Walrond, who settled in Somersetshire (and to whom I shall refer later on

---

* Burke's *Landed Gentry*, sub. "Walrond of Dulford." Vivian, *Visit. of Devon*, p. 768.
† Risdon, *Survey of Devon*, pp. 31, 32, edit. 1811.
‡ He is called "Osmond" by Burke and also by Vivian, *Visitations of Devon*, p. 768. He is not mentioned at all in Westcote's pedigrees.

as the ancestor of the Walronds now of Broadhembury), and also of Ellen,* wife of Anthony, son of Robert Fortescue ; of Eleanor, who married Michael Keys, and secondly, Nicholas Dillon, and of Elizabeth, wife of Walter Reigny ; although, according to Westcote (*Pedigrees* 484) he had but an only daughter, Alice, married to Robert Yeo of Heanton Sachville.

Humphry Walrond, by his wife, Eleanor, daughter of Henry "Owgan" of Saltwinch, co. Somerset, had, with a second son, John (and daughters, Jane, wife of William Tyllye, see my *Suburbs of Exeter*, p. 9, and Elizabeth, wife of John "Hall" —according to Westcote, of "John Hake"), of Collompton, an eldest son and heir, Henry Walrond of Bradfield, who died in 1550, and left, with a daughter, Ellen, wife of Thomas Yorke, a son, Humphry, who commences the pedigree entered at the Visitation of 1620, and had, according to the record of 1564, three younger brothers, viz., Thomas, William, and Alexander, the second of whom was probably the real ancestor of Lady Rolle.†

According to both the Visitation records I have cited, Humphry Walrond, of Bradfield, by his wife Mary, daughter of Sir Thomas Willoughby, Justice of the Common Pleas, was the father of William Walrond, son and heir, Thomas, and Alexander, who both died issueless, and of two Humphrys, the first baptized in 1554, and the second in 1555. Both these Humphrys lived to maturity. The elder of them resided at Upham, in the parish of Farringdon, a property which had belonged to the Dukes. He married Mary Audley, of Holbury, co. Wilts., had "no issue" in 1620, and died in 1632. His brother, Humphry, *the younger*, settled at Ash, in the parish of Ottery St. Mary, an estate which had been granted to his father, the son-in-law of Justice Willoughby, after the attainder of the Duke of Suffolk in 1553. He married Elizabeth, daughter of Richard Duke, of Otterton, and had issue, Humphry Walrond, son and heir, "aged 6, 1620."

His eldest brother, William Walrond, of Bradfield, married

---

* She is made "daughter," of *Humphry Walrond*, by Westcote and Vivian, who do not mention her sisters Eleanor and Elizabeth.
† See above, Walrond of Bovey, in the parish of Seaton.

Mary, widow of John Warre, and daughter of Nicholas Sanford, and died in 1627, but the family pedigree as entered before the Heralds, is signed by " Humphry " and by " H. Walrond." The latter was probably his son and heir, then thirty-six years old, and the husband of Penelope Sidenham, of Dulverton, by whom he had thirteen children. The eldest of them, William Walrond, "aged 10," in 1620, duly succeeded to Bradfield in 1650, and had, by his wife, Ursula Speccot, of Launcells, co. Cornwall, besides three daughters, an eldest son, Sir William Walrond, the owner of Bradfield in 1667, and who was knighted by the king at Bedford in 1671. Sir William died unmarried in 1689, and was succeeded by his only brother, Henry Walrond, a Barrister of the Middle Temple, who survived until 1724. By his first wife, Elizabeth Maynard, a widow, and daughter of Sir William Strode, of Newnham, he had two sons and two daughters. The youngest of the latter, Hester, was the wife of the Rev. John Carwithen, Rector of Willand and Woolfardisworthy, and Vicar of Crediton, who died in 1742.

Mrs. Carwithen's eldest brother, William Walrond, married Anne, daughter of Francis Courtenay, and had a son, Courtenay, who died without issue in 1761, when he was succeeded by his next brother, the Rev. H. Walrond, Rector of Woolfardisworthy, who married Dorothy Milford, at Woolfardisworthy in 1759, and died in 1787, and had, with two daughters, an only son, William Henry Walrond, of Bradfield, who married Mary Alford, of Sandford, and left two daughters, co-heirs, the eldest of whom, Frances Walrond, became the wife of Benjamin, son of John Dickenson, by his wife, Harriet Bowden. Mr. Dickenson assumed the name of Walrond by Royal License 21st April, 1845, and was the father of the late owner of Bradfield, Sir John Walrond, D.L. and J.P., Sheriff of Devon, 1874, and M.P. for the Borough of Tiverton. Sir John, who was created a baronet 24th February, 1876, married The Honourable Frances Caroline Hood, daughter of the second Lord Bridport, and his eldest son, Sir William Hood Walrond, M.P. for Devonshire (Tiverton Division), and now of Bradfield, was born 26th February, 1848. Sir William Walrond was formerly a Captain in the Grenadier Guards, and subsequently commanded the 1st Devon R.V. for many years; he married in 1871 Elizabeth, daughter and heir of the late James Pitman, of Dunchideock, co. Devon, and has had, with other issue, John Neville Hood Walrond, son and heir, born 26th November, 1874.

WALROND OF DULFORD, IN THE PARISH OF BROADHEMBURY.

"Osmond," or Oliver, Walrond, as he is called in the Visitation Pedigree of 1564, appears, by that record, to have settled in Somerset, and to have been the uncle of Henry Walrond of Bradfield, and second son of John Walrond, son and heir of John and Margaret Moore. According to the pedigrees, as printed,* he married "Emlyn, daughter of Buckthought of Devonshire,"† and had three sons, the eldest of whom, Humphry Walrond, in right of his first wife, Elizabeth Brokehampton, settled at Sea, in the parish of Ilminster. He married, secondly, Katherine, daughter of Sir John Popham, chief justice of the King's Bench. By his first wife, he had issue, Henry Walrond, who succeeded to Sea, and is said to be "named in the will of his cousin, Humphry Walrond, of Bradfield."

Henry Walrond, of Sea, married Elizabeth, daughter and co-heir of William Devenish, of Hellingleigh, co. Sussex, the descendant of Sir John Devenish, whose wife was Elizabeth, widow of Thomas Massingberd, and third daughter and co-heir of Thomas, first and last Lord Hoo and Hastings (so created by Patent 2nd June, 26 Hy. VI.) by his wife, Alianore, eldest daughter and co-heir of Leo, seventh Lord Welles (writ 27th Ed. I.), and, in right of descent from this marriage, the late Mr. Walrond, of Broadhembury, established his claim to the co-heirship of the Welles Barony, and "petitioned the King, in 1832, to terminate its abeyance in his behalf,"‡ a

---

* Burke, *Landed Gentry*. Vivian, *Visitation Devon*, p. 770.
† The *Buckthoughts* were Somersetshire people; but it is worthy of note that there was a family connection with the "Buckyats," variously spelt, one of whom married Jane Walrond of Bovey, and who were of Buckyat in the parish of Little Hempston in this county. See my *Devonshire Parishes*, vol. 2., p. 69.
‡ *Sir Bernard Burke.*

concession which was not accorded.* Henry Walrond, of Sea, died in the year 1616. His son, Humphrey, also of Sea, by his wife, Elizabeth Colles, was the father of the brave Col. Humphry Walrond, of Sea, who suffered much for the King's sake, and was one of the six hostages surrendered to Fairfax at Bridgwater after the capitulation of that town in 1645; his companions in misfortune being Sir John Hale, Sir Hugh Wyndham, Mr. Warre, Mr. Sydenham, and Mr. Speke. He was also, I believe, one of the four lieut.-colonels taken at Dartmouth in the following January with Lord Newport, the King's Governor there, with more than forty other officers of various rank.† He subsequently emigrated to Barbadoes, and became President of that island, which was our first settlement in the West Indies, and the cradle of the English sugar trade.

On the 5th April, 1653, Philip IV. of Spain created him, by patent of that date, Count of Parma and Valderonda, Marquis of Vallado, and a Grandee of the first class; and his own Royal Master, to mark his fidelity, permitted him to bear the crest of his ancestors upon a mural crown. He married first, Elizabeth, daughter of Nathaniel Napier, of More Critchel, co. Dorset, who died in 1635; but his second wife, "Grace Walrond," was alive thirty years later. He left a large family, six sons and three daughters. Of the sons, the third, Henry Walrond, attained the rank of Lieut.-General and died in 1693. The fifth, Col. Thomas Walrond, was resident in the parish of Christ Church, Barbadoes, 22nd December, 1679, upon three hundred and forty acres of land, and maintained there eighteen white servants and one hundred and seventy slaves. He married Frances, daughter of Col. Sir Jonathan Atkins, and had an only child, who was the wife of William

---

* Lady Devenish was, as above intimated, a second wife. She had, moreover, two sisters, co-heirs with herself, Eleanor, ancestress of the Carews, of Beddington, and Jane, ancestress of the Moyle-Copleys. Their mother, Alianore de Welles, had three sisters, similarly co-heirs—Margaret, wife of Sir Thomas Dymoke, of Scrivelsby, Hereditary Champion of England, and father of Sir Robert, who executed that office at the coronations of Richard III. and Henry VII. and VIII; Cicely, wife of Sir Richard Willoughby; and Catherine, who married Sir Thomas Launde, and had issue; so it is not surprising to find that Mr. Walrond did not receive a summons in the Barony of Welles.

† See my *Devonshire Parishes*, vol. 1., p. 352. But, in the return from which I copied, the name is written *Wadland*.

Adams. The eldest son, George Walrond, was a captain of the Royal Horse, and also settled in Barbadoes, where he died in 1688, and married Frances, daughter of William Coryton, of Coryton, co. Devon, by Elizabeth, daughter of Sir John Chichester, of Ralegh, and had two sons, Theodore and George. The latter was of St. Philip's, Barbadoes, married, and had issue.

His elder brother, Theodore Walrond, settled in the island of Antigua, died in the summer of 1766, and left by his first wife, Elizabeth Wills, of Wiveliscombe, co. Somerset, a son, Maine Swete Walrond, also of Antigua, who died in 1764, at the age of thirty-nine. By his wife, Sarah Lyons, of Philadelphia, he had, with two younger sons, a son Theodore, who survived him three years, and died in his minority, when he was succeeded by his next brother, Joseph Lyons Walrond, of Antigua, born 1752, who married Caroline, daughter of Admiral Sir Edward Codrington, in 1797, and re-established himself in England. After the death of the last Earl of Montrath (Coote), who died in 1802, he purchased of that nobleman's executors a house which his lordship had built within the manor of Carswell-cum-Dulford, in the parish of Broadhembury, then known as "Montrath House," the necessary land having been acquired from the Drewes, of Grange, in the said parish, and this property has since been known as "Dulford House." He died 13th January, 1815. Failing the issue of his eldest son, Lyons Walrond, who never attained his majority, Bethell Walrond, the second son, born in 1801, succeeded to this property at his mother's death, was a deputy lieutenant for Devon, and M.P. for the Borough of Saltash. He married Lady Janet St. Clair, daughter of the second Lord Rosslyn, and died in 1876, leaving an only son, Henry Walrond, now of "Dulford House," and Lieut.-Col. of the 4th Battalion Devonshire Regiment (1st Devon Militia), who was born in 1841, is married, and has issue.

Arms of Walrond — *Arg.*, 3 bulls' heads cabossed *sa.* armed *or.*

Crest — An heraldic tiger sejant *sa., semée of plates.*

Crest of Walrond, of Dulford House, Broadhembury; out of a mural crown *or*, an heraldic tiger *sa., semée of plates*, maned, and tufted, *or.*

THE FORTESCUES.

The Fortescue family, of Norman origin, as its name implies, is commonly said to be descended from a certain *Sir Richard le Fort*, and to have been settled in England since the eleventh century, as a consequence of the victory at Hastings. According to tradition, this *Sir Richard le Fort*, so styled in reference to his prodigious strength, was a "cup bearer" in the household of Duke William, and thrice saved his master's life at Senlac, by protecting him, whilst unhorsed, from the blows of his assailants, and was therefore afterward known as "Richard *le Fort Escu* (Richard the strong shield), and was rewarded, in the person of his son, *Adam Fortescue*, with "grants of Wymondeston, or Winston, and other lands in the County of Devon.* Sir Richard himself is reputed to have returned to Normandy and to have founded there a second family, and thus to have become the progenitor of those Fortescues who, in many branches, long flourished on the French sea-board known as the Cotentin.

It is possible that *Sir Richard le Fort* may not be an entirely mythical personage, although the only authority that has been cited in proof of his existence is that very unsatisfactory and unreliable document known as the "Roll of Battle Abbey," in one of the several pretended "copies" of which there is mention of the *Sire de la Ferte*, and in another of the *Seigneur de la Ferte*, otherwise *Fort*, but who is nowhere called "Richard," or identified in any way with the ducal household. But, granting the presence at Hastings of the " Seigneur de la Ferte," he doubtless took name either from Ferte-Alais or Ferte-Milon, both towns in the Isle of France, and without any reference to his bodily strength at all. The name is not to be found in either of the three lists of the Norman invaders which Stowe has included in his *Annales*, nor is it to be discovered in Fox's catalogue of those Normans who received territorial grants in return for their services at Senlac,† whilst it is abundantly clear, from the Devonshire Domesday,

---

* Burke, *Landed Gentry, sub.* " Fortescue of Fallopit."
† *Acts and Mon.*, Vol. 1, p. 237.

that neither a *Fort*, nor a Fortescue, held lands, either as tenant *in capite* or even as sub-tenant, at the period of the Conqueror's Survey.

The compound word "Fortescue" is evidently of military origin, and I am inclined to attribute its assumption to the period of the first Crusade rather than to that of the Norman Conquest, and there can be but little question that the previous possession of the place-name "le Ferte," or "Fort," primarily suggested the happy combination of the two words to its original owner, or to his appreciative knightly contemporaries. But, as "Fortescue," this family has been indisputably known for nigh upon eight centuries, and hence originated its famous canting motto, *Forte Scutum Salus Ducum*, and the legend as to King William's cup bearer. Unfortunately, however, the history of the house of Fortescue has hitherto been made to accord with the ancient and popular tradition rather than with historical facts. The two Manors of Great Modbury and Wimpston were both given by the Conqueror to his half-brother, Robert, Earl of Mortain, and were held under him by Reginald de Valletort. Either Reginald, or his son and successor, founded, at Modbury, a cell of Black Monks, which consisted of a prior and two religious brothers, and made it dependent upon the great Benedictine Abbey of St. Pierre, Sur Dive, in the lower Normandy Diocese of Séez.

In many cases, but not in all, it has become somewhat difficult to identify the several "Ralphs," "Reginalds," "Richards," and others, described only by their christian names, who were sub-tenants in 1086, under the King's tenants *in capite;* but it is noteworthy that the Manor of Little Modbury was at that time held by a certain "Richard," under the aforesaid Robert of Mortain, and if this "Richard" was identical with *Sir Richard le Forte, alias Fortescue*, it upsets the traditional story as to his return to France, but establishes the connection of the Fortescues with Modbury more than a century before the Wimpston property was *granted*, or confirmed, to them by King John, A° 1208, and that they certainly were connected with Modbury at a period anterior to this concession is proved by an existing record.*

---

* Assize, 1 John, 1199.

"*Sir Richard le Forte's*" reputed son, Adam Fortescue, had, according to the pedigree, a son, Ralph Fortescue, who, it has been asserted, without reference to the authority,* "granted lands to Modbury Priory by deed dated 1135," and in such case he must have been one of the earliest benefactors to the community, which, according to the commonly accepted date of its foundation, did not exist prior to that year. This grant of Ralph Fortescue, said to have been duly "confirmed by his son, Richard Fortescue," is not referred to in the *Monasticon Dioc. Exon.*, or in Oliver's *Ecclesiastical Antiquities*, and Dr. Oliver attributes the foundation of the Priory to the Champernowne family, on the evidence of the *Registers of the See of Exeter;* yet, although the Champernownes may have in process of time become to be regarded as the founders, they were quite unconnected with Modbury until some time subsequently to the admission of the earliest Prior, noted by Dr. Oliver, 21st July, 1275, and the name of a still earlier one has been found amongst the Charters of Plympton Priory.†

Whoever the "Richard" may have been who held the Manor of Little Modbury under the Earl of Mortain, that estate, which consisted of a hide of land, was owned, in the reign of Henry III., by Ralph, son of William Rous.

Reginald de Valletort, as sub-tenant under the same lord, was followed by his son and grandson in the Manor of Great Modbury, which comprised four hides, and possibly also in that of "Winestona," which was taxed for half a hide. His great-grandson, Sir Roger Valletort, who was alive and of full age 8th King John‡ (1208), married, after 1240, Joan, daughter of Richard, Earl of Cornwall, and titular King of the Romans, and had issue an only daughter and heir, Joan, who, as widow of Sir Ralph Valletort, married, about 1270, Sir Alexander Okeston, Kt., and had issue two children, James and Joan. The latter became the wife of Richard Champernowne somewhere about the year 1290. At about the latter period a family had become associated with the Valletorts who gave their name to their residence, Lapflode, within the Valletort

---

* Vivian, *Visitations of Devon*, p. 352.
† Tanner, *Not. Monas.*, sub., *Modbury*.
‡ See my *Ashburton and its Neighbourhood*, p. 108.

Manor of Bridford, and which the aforesaid Sir Roger Valletort had obtained in partition with William de Braose in 1208.*

In the ninth year of the reign of Edward II. (1316), by deed of that date, Henry Lapflode granted the Manor of Great Modbury, by power of the King's Charter, to James de Okeston aforesaid, and to Ida, his wife, for life, with remainder to Richard de Champernowne,† whose wife, as I have shown above, was the granddaughter of the former owner of the property, Sir Roger Valletort, and thus the Champernownes became settled at Modbury, which remained with their descendants for many generations.

To return to the Fortescues, Richard Fortescue, who is said to have "confirmed his father's gift to Modbury Priory in 1135," was certainly resident in the County of Devon in 1199, when, with William Bastard, the undoubted descendant of a Domesday tenant *in capite*, he was attached for non-appearance at an *Assise de Morte d'Ancestre.*‡ This Richard, according to some of the pedigrees of Fortescue, left a son, William, who was the father of Sir John, Sir Richard, and Sir Nicholas Fortescue. The two latter were companions in arms of Richard "Cœur de Lion" in the Holy Land, and Knights of the Order of St. John of Jerusalem.

Their brother, "Sir John Fortescue," is generally supposed to have become settled upon the Manor of Wimpston in Modbury, in 1208, by virtue of a "grant" from the Crown, but which was doubtless a mere confirmation of a previous grant by the Valletorts to one of his ancestors, as his son, Richard Fortescue, held the same in 1252, as "one knight's fee of the barony of Reginald de Valletort, whose ancestor, Reginald de Valletort, had been sub-tenant of the said manor under Robert of Mortain, to whom it had been given by King William."

Adam, son and grandson of Fortescues, of the same name (and great-grandson of the said Richard Fortescue), by his wife, Anna, daughter of "William de la Port, of Old Port," in the same parish, had, with sons Richard and Nicholas, a son and heir, William Fortescue, of Wimpston, who paid

---

* See my *Ashburton and its Neighbourhood*, p. 108.
† See Abstract of the Conveyance. Risdon, *Survey of Devon*, p. 187.
‡ *Rot. Cur. Reg.*, Palgrave, 2, 201.

his "knight's fee in 1345, at the ceremony of the knighthood of the 'Black Prince'"; Wimpston being held by him as "of the honour of Trematon" in Cornwall, which had also belonged to Robert, Earl of Cornwall and Mortain, and was one of his two castles and the head of his honour in that county. This William Fortescue married Alice, daughter of Walter Strechleigh, of Strechleigh, in the parish of Ermington, and thus obtained lands in Tamerton; and, in 1360, by grant of his kinsman, Richard Maldett (Malduit), *alias* Somaster, whose mother had been a co-heir of De la Port, he had a further extension of property in the form of tenements at Old Port, in Modbury, and at *Painston*.* He was succeeded by his son, William Fortescue† (alive 1394), whose son of the same name, married, *vitâ patris*, Elizabeth Branscombe, widow, who was a daughter of Sir John Beauchamp, and sister and co-heir of Thomas Beauchamp, of Ryme, co. Somerset. Her assignment of dower, dated Tuesday after the feast of St. Martin, 1394, is sealed with the Fortescue Arms, differenced with a crescent, which is, I think, conclusive evidence that the Wimpston Fortescues were not the elder, but the second, line of the family, or else that the father of the said William (described as "William Fortescue the younger") was not the eldest of the three sons of Adam Fortescue and Anne de la Port, as stated in the pedigrees.

William Fortescue and Elizabeth, his wife (who had no issue by her first husband, Richard Branscombe), were the parents of William and John. (To the latter I shall refer presently.)

The eldest son, William Fortescue, of Wimpston, by his wife, Isabel Falwell, was the father of John Fortescue, of Wimpston, who married Jane Preston, and had three sons, John, William, and John.

The second of these, William Fortescue, was the ancestor of Sir Peter Fortescue, "aged half a yeare" in 1620, who was

---

* Probably Painsford, in the parish of Ashprington, not "Painstone," which is in Newton St. Cyres, and belonged to the D. and C. of Exeter. There is another Painstone in the parish of Colebrook. Painsford, however, has been supposed to have been *purchased* by the Somasters in the reign of Henry VII. See my *Devonshire Parishes*, vol. i., p. 307.
† Omitted in the Ped. *Visitation Devon* Vivian, p. 352.

created a baronet in 1667, and was buried at Ermington, in 1685, when, by failure of his male issue, the title became extinct.

John Fortescue, youngest son of John and Jane Preston, and mentioned in the will of his brother William, was the father of Lewis Fortescue, Baron of the Exchequer, who died in 1545, and who, by his wife, Elizabeth, daughter and heir of Lewis Fortescue, of Fallapit, in the parish of East Allington,* was the ancestor of Sir Edmund Fortescue, of Fallapit, who was the governor of Salcombe Castle, near Kingsbridge, and held it for four months after its investment by Col. Weldon, the Parliamentary Governor of Plymouth, in 1645.

Sir Edmund, at length forced to capitulate, was permitted to march out with the honours of war, and, with his small garrison, retired to Fallapit, distant about four miles, and he carried with him the key of the great gate of the fortress he had so stubbornly defended, and which has since been known as Fort Charles, and this key has since been handed down as a heirloom to his descendants. His son and heir, Sir Edmund Fortescue, in return for the father's loyalty, who had died an exile in Holland before the restoration, was created a baronet in 1664; but the title became extinct at the death of his son, Sir Sandys Fortescue, in 1683.

Fallapit, in 1752, came to Elizabeth Fortescue, the grand niece of Sir Edmund, of "Fort Charles." Her sister, Dorothy, married Sir Thomas Bury, whose daughter, Catherine Bury, became the wife of the Rev. Nathaniel Wells, whose son and heir, Edmund Wells, inherited Fallapit, by devise of his great-aunt, the said Elizabeth Fortescue, and assumed her name. Of this branch, there is elder issue, Walter George, born 1866, who has brothers, sons of Captain Edmond Fortescue, of the Rifle Brigade; but Fallapit was sold about twenty years ago to Mr. E. Cubitt.

I must now return to John Fortescue, the elder brother of John Fortescue, of Spridleston, the ancestor of the Fallapit branch.

---

* She was great-granddaughter of Sir Henry Fortescue, chief justice of the Common Pleas, by his second wife, the daughter and heir of "Fallapit."

He was the son and heir of John Fortescue, by Jane Preston, and inherited Wimpston, which descended to his son and grandson. The latter, Henry Fortescue, of Wimpston, is described as "of that property," but the right heir was Joane, only daughter of Thomas, his elder brother, who had died *v.p.* She was the wife of Edmund Babington, of Wyke, co. Worcester. About this time Wimpston seems to have been sold, but Henry Fortescue was the grandfather of Edward Fortescue, who died in 1631, and left, by his wife, Elizabeth, daughter of William Bruton, of Heavitree,* an only son and heir, John Fortescue. It has been suggested that his ancestor, Sir John Fortescue, the first certain owner of Wimpston, by virtue of King John's "grant," or confirmation, may have been the husband of Margerie, "second daughter, and one of the eventual five co-heirs of William Lord Briwere by his wife Beatrice, widow of Reginald, Earl of Cornwall"; because this "Margerie," who was merely of about the same generation as the said Sir John Fortescue, is said, by Dugdale, to have married *La Ferts.*

This assertion, however, appears to have been one of the numerous errors for which Dugdale's works are remarkable, and which have been perpetuated over and over again by those who have simply repeated his statements without any attempts at verification, and in mistaken reliance on his accuracy. Margery Briwere was the eldest of the five sisters and married, not "La Ferte," or "La Forte," as others have styled him, but *De Fernac,* as shown by an almost contemporary record;† she had issue a daughter, Gondreda de Fernac, who married Payen de Chawerth, whose son and heir, Payen de Chawerth, died without issue, when his inheritance descended to Patrick, his brother, who married a daughter of Earl Warrenne; she was probably one of the illegitimate daughters of John "Plantagenet," Earl of Warrenne, Surrey, and Sussex, by Maud de Hereford, who, although he obtained a divorce from his Countess, Joan, daughter of the Comte de Barre, on plea of "pre-contract" to Maud de Hereford, does not appear to have

---

* See Breton, *alias* Bruton, of Borough, *ante.*
† See my *Devonshire Parishes,* vol. ii., pp. 97, 98.

ever actually married the latter, and his sister, as heir-at-law, carried the Earldom of Surrey to her husband, Richard Fitz-Alan, son and heir of Edmund, Earl of Arundel.

John Fortescue, son of William and Elizabeth Branscombe (*née* Beauchamp), and younger brother of William Fortescue, of Wimpston, lived in the reign of Henry V., and was in that monarch's following at the battle of Agincourt, October 25th, 1415. Upon the capitulation of the French town of Meaux, in 1422, he was appointed its governor, and has since been known in the Fortescue family as "Captain of Meaux."* By his wife, Eleanor Norries, he was the father of Sir Henry Fortescue, son and heir, Chief Justice of the Irish Common Pleas, whose issue by a first marriage terminated, after four descents, in a daughter, who married John Fortescue, of Preston, and was the ancestress of the afore-mentioned Sir Peter Fortescue, Bart., of Wood. By his second marriage, Sir Henry was, similarly, through Elizabeth Fortescue, the ancestor of the Fallapit branch. He had a brother Richard, from whom descended the Fortescues of Hertfordshire, Essex, and Bucks.

Sir John Fortescue, who was raised to the Chief Justiceship of England 25th January, 1441-2, and held it until, in consequence of the dethronement of King Henry VI., he was superseded on the 14th May, 1461, is said to have been a third brother of Sir Henry Fortescue (who is declared by some writers to have been his father), and a younger son of "the Captain of Meaux." Sir John was the learned author of the *De Laudibus Legum Angliæ*, but has made no mention of his parentage or extraction in this or either of his other works, although he has dilated at some length upon his experiences as a student of the law. It is not my present purpose to dwell at any length upon his history or career. The proof as to his extraction is of the slightest conceivable character, and rests principally upon supposition, upon the period at which he flourished, and upon his possession of the family name. His birthplace is as unknown as the exact date of his birth, and he

---

* As an evidence of heraldic inaccuracy, I may mention that in the *Visitation of Devon*, 1564" (Colby, p. 100), this John Fortescue, "Captain of Meaulk," is made fifth in descent from his usually accepted *nephew*, John Fortescue, and " son of William F." by "Isabella" Beauchamp, son of William F. by Catherine " Welch." Admon. to the estate of said Catherine Walch was granted 6th February, 1580-81.

never had ostensible connection with this county, and the property he acquired, by success in his profession, was situated at Ebrington, in Gloucestershire, in the chancel of which church he was buried at an unknown date, and at the age of ninety, according to tradition; and the inscription over his remains was placed there by Colonel Fortescue, of Weare Gifford, in 1677. In proof of his parentage, "a deed of the 16th of Henry VI.," without reference to its whereabouts, has been *asserted*, by which "Henry, son of John Fortescue, grants, etc., to brother John and Isabella his wife," and there is also a statement by Dugdale, *Origines Judiciales*, which may be accepted, as evidence of paternity, for what it is worth, that, as "Governor of Lincoln's Inn," 1422-1425, he is described as "Fortescue junior."

In the *Visitation of Devonshire*, 1564 (Colby, p. 101), he is described as "John Fortescue *Capit. Justic. de Banco, et in fine regni H. 6 Cancell. Angliæ.*" He is, moreover, there set down as son of Henry Fortescue, "*Cap. Justic. in Hib.*," brother of Richard, of "Valowpit," and Henry, of Wood, and as great-great-grandson of "Catherine Welch," whose will, as I have stated above, was proved in 1581, more than a century *after* her thus strangely asserted *descendant* in the fourth degree was "Chancellor of England." The original record of the Devonshire Visitation of 1620 is of course somewhat more reliable, and there "Sir John Fortiscue, Justice of England," whose ancestry is *unrecorded*, commences the pedigree of Fortescue of Buckland, Filleigh, and Weare Gifford—estates which were acquired by his son, Martin Fortescue, in marriage with Elizabeth, daughter and heir of Richard Densell, in 1454.

They had two sons, John and William; upon the latter the Buckland Filleigh property was settled by his mother, and through him it descended to John Fortescue, who was buried at Weare Gifford, in April, 1604.

By his wife, Anne, daughter of Walter Porter, and widow of Digory Thorne, he had, with other issue, Roger, who continued the line at Buckland Filleigh, and was the direct ancestor of John Fortescue, of Bampton, who, at the death of his kinswoman, Mary Spooner, of Fallapit, and Buckland Filleigh (only daughter and heiress of Wm. Fortescue, of

Filleigh, by Mary, daughter and co-heiress of Edmond Fortescue, of Fallapit), inherited the Buckland property, which, upon his death in 1776, reverted to his daughter, Rebecca, wife of Caleb Inglett, of Dawlish, and her descendants assumed the name of Fortescue, and resided at Buckland until that property was sold by Col. Inglett-Fortescue, who died in 1841.

Sir Faithfull Fortescue was the half brother of the aforesaid Roger Fortescue, of Buckland Filleigh, by the second marriage of their father with Susanna, daughter of Sir John Chichester, of Goulston, 22nd September, 1584, and sister of Arthur, Lord Chichester of Belfast, Deputy of Ireland. To advantage himself of his uncle's powerful patronage, he migrated to Ireland, and was Governor of Knockfergus in 1620. He is vaguely said, in the Visit. Ped., to have married "*an Irishwoman*"; his wife was Anna, daughter of Garret, Viscount Moore, of Drogheda; he afterward returned to England, and was one of the gentlemen of the Privy Chamber subsequently to the Restoration of King Charles II. He was buried at Carrisbrook, 29th May, 1666, being then nearly eighty-one years of age, and left several children, the third of whom, Sir Thomas Fortescue, of Dromisken, co. Louth, had two sons; the youngest of them was the ancestor of William Henry Fortescue, Baron, Viscount, and Earl of Clermont, so created 1720 and 1777, with remainder, of the viscounty only, to his brother, who succeeded to it, and died without issue, when the title became extinct.

The eldest of Sir Thomas Fortescue's sons, Col. Chichester Fortescue, of Dromisken, was the great great-grandfather of Chichester Fortescue, of Dromisken, whose eldest son, Thomas, the late Lord Clermont, obtained the revival of that Irish Barony in his favour in 1852, and was also created a peer of the United Kingdom in 1866. By special limitation, his lordship's brother, Chichester S. P. Fortescue, who had been raised to the English Peerage as Baron Carlingford 28th February, 1874, has inherited the said Barony of Clermont of Dromisken, failing the issue of the first peer of the last creation.

John, son and heir of Martin Fortescue, by his wife, Elizabeth Densell, was born in 1461, and died in 1503. He inherited the property now known as Castle Hill, in the parish of Filleigh, and hundred of Braunton, near South Molton, and which must not be confused with his brother's property, Buckland Filleigh, which parish is in the Hundred of Shebbear.* His descendant, in the sixth generation, Hugh Fortescue, of Filleigh, who was born in 1592, had a third son, Arthur Fortescue, of Penwarne, co. Cornwall, and of Weare-Giffard, in this county, whose elder brothers died without male issue. This Arthur married Barbara, daughter of John Elford, of Sheepstor (for whose somewhat singular and romantic history I must refer my readers to the first volume of my *Devonshire Parishes*, pp. 37 *et seq.*), and had four sons, of whom the eldest, Hugh Fortescue, married, firstly, Bridget, daughter of Hugh Boscawen, in 1692, by whom he had Hugh, son and heir, and eight other children; and, secondly, Lucy, daughter of Matthew, first Lord Aylmer, who was the mother of Matthew, second Lord Fortescue, and of Lucy, Lady Lyttelton.

Bridget Boscawen's mother, Lady Margaret Clinton, was the youngest co-heir of Theophilus, Earl of Lincoln, and her son, Hugh Fortescue, was permitted to terminate the abeyance, since 1692, of the Clinton Barony, and was summoned to Parliament, as fourteenth Baron Clinton, 16th March, 1721. On the 5th July, 1746, his Lordship was created Baron Fortescue of Castle Hill, in the parish of Filleigh, and co. of Devon, with remainder to his half-brother, Matthew Fortescue, his five whole brothers having died without issue.

At his death, unmarried, in 1751, the Fortescue Barony passed according to the limitation in its patent, whilst that of Clinton once again went into abeyance between his only surviving sister, Margaret Fortescue, who died unmarried in 1760, and Margaret Rolle, Countess of Orford, granddaughter of Lady Arabella Rolle, Lady Margaret Boscawen's elder sister, and, in view of such seniority, it is somewhat singular that Hugh Fortescue should have been permitted to terminate the previous abeyance. From 1760 to 1791 the Clinton Barony was merged with the Earldom of Orford; the third Lord Orford and sixteenth Baron Clinton then died unmarried, and three years afterward Robert George William Trefusis, who was fifth

---

* Both Filleigh and Buckland Filleigh came to the Densells, through Trewen, by the heiress of Filleigh.

in descent from the said Lady Arabella Rolle, through her daughter, Bridget, wife of Francis Trefusis, was summoned as seventeenth Lord Clinton, and was the grandfather of the present and twentieth Baron Clinton, of Heanton Sachville, now Lord-Lieutenant of Devonshire.

Matthew Fortescue succeeded his half-brother as second Baron Fortescue 3rd May, 1751; in the following year he married Anne Campbell of Cawder, and died in December, 1785, and was succeeded by his eldest son, Hugh, as third Baron, who was advanced to the dignities of Viscount Ebrington, in allusion to his ancestor's residence, and Earl Fortescue, 1st September, 1789. He died in 1841. By his wife, Hester, sister of the first Marquess of Buckingham, he had, with other issue, the late Countesses of Devon and Portsmouth, and a son, Hugh, born in 1783, who succeeded as second Earl, and was the father, by his wife, Lady Susan Ryder, of the present Lord Fortescue of Castle Hill, who was summoned to the House of Lords, during his father's life-time, in the Barony of Fortescue.

The present Earl married, in 1847, the eldest daughter of Lieut.-Col. the Right Honourable Dawson-Damer, and his eldest son, Viscount Ebrington, was born 16th April, 1854.

Although the Fortescues have frequently married cousins, and the name has thus been preserved, in many cases without assumption, all the houses derived, with *absolute certainty*, from the Wimpston branch have been long extinct in the male line, and the connection, with Devonshire, of the Filleigh, and Buckland Filleigh, Fortescues can only be referred, authoritatively, to the date of the marriage settlement of Elizabeth Densell and Martin Fortescue, 10th September, 1454, four hundred and forty-one years ago, since which time Lord Fortescue's ancestors have resided at Filleigh, and upon the property now known as "Castle Hill," in reference to an artificial ruinous castle which crowns the summit of an acclivity near the house, and which was, I believe, erected by Hugh, Lord Clinton and Fortescue, who made many alterations to the home of his forefathers at Filleigh, about the middle of the last century. Although their descent, in some way, from King John's grantee of Wimpston has been commonly accepted, yet it must be admitted to be remarkable that no attempt was made to carry the pedigree behind Chief Justice Fortescue, of Ebrington, at the Visitation of 1620, whilst his descent, as set down in the copy of the Visitation of 1564, is so manifestly erroneous, if only on account of its anachronisms, that it is not even worthy of serious consideration. It cannot, therefore, be a matter of surprise that the actual ancestry of the learned judge has, from time to time, given birth to a considerable amount of controversy. Possibly, too, some of my own statements may differ considerably from those of the late Lord Clermont (*History of the Fortescues*), with the contents of which work I am unacquainted.

An early deed of Fortescue, 30th Edward I., is sealed with an *estoile*; and the crest of Fortescue appears, at first, to have been an uncharged escutcheon, *arg.*

Lord Carlingford bears the same crest as Lord Fortescue, but the tiger supports, with fore paw, an escutcheon *arg.*, and by some authorities the crest is thus blazoned for Fortescue of Castle Hill.

The present Arms of the Earls Fortescue may thus be blazoned :—

"*Az.* a bend engrailed *arg.*, cotised *or.*" (Visitation, 1564).

Crest—An heraldic tiger statant *arg.*

Supporters—Two greyhounds *arg.*, ducally collared and lined *gules.*

Motto—"Forte Scutum Salus Ducum."

THE ACLANDS OF KILLERTON.

The Aclands are supposed to derive their name from Acland, in the parish of Landkey, near Barnstaple, which small but ancient residence, long utilised as a farmhouse, is still their property, and was originally named after the "grove of oaks by which the house is seated," according to Thomas Westcote, the quaint author of *The View of Devonshire.*

The Key of Alwyn's land, called in Domesday *Alwynelanclavile* belonged in 1066 to "Letwyn," the Saxon, and twenty years later to Ralph de Pomeroy. As "Landkey," it afterward became the property, for several descents of the

Beauples, one of whom was Sheriff of Devon, 21st Edward II., and passed, in marriage with a daughter of that race, to Sir Nigel Loring, during the reign of Edward III. But the " Eccelins, Acalans, or Akelanes," as the name is indifferently written, had then been living at " Accellana," within the said parish, almost, if not quite, as long as the Beauples, and although, apparently, they were not at that period of precisely the same importance as their knightly neighbours, yet that they were, even then, an eminently respectable family is proved by their marriage with the daughter and heir of Hawkridge of Hawkridge, in Chittlehampton, as early as the reign of Richard II.; and, prior to the reign of Edward VI., they had formed alliances matrimonial with other well-known county families, such as Prideaux, Fortescue, and Hext, so that it is somewhat surprising to find that no pedigree of the Aclands was entered at either of the earlier Visitations of the County in 1531, 1564, or 1572.

In 1620 Sir John Acland of Columb-John, then "aged 29," and who was created a Baronet 24th June, 1644,[*] appeared before Henry St. George, Richmond Herald, and Sampson Lennard, Blue Mantle, Deputies for William Camden Clarenceux, who held the County Visitation at Exeter on the latter's behalf that year, and attested the pedigree of his family which was then entered, and which commences with " Baldwin Eccelin," who is believed to have been the son of Hugh, and is set down as the great-grandfather of " Baldwin " of " Akelane," in 1320, son of " William " of Acalan," by " Sara, daughter and heir of John de la Pile," or Pyll.

The grandson of Baldwin de Akelane, who was of the same generation as the " Black Prince," father of Richard II., married Alice, daughter and heiress of William Hawkridge, and, after an interval of six generations, Hawkridge, in the parish of Chittlehampton, was left to the second son of " John Akeland of Akeland," by his wife, " Elizabeth Cruwys of Cruwys Morchard."

Anthony Akeland of Hawkridge married Agnes, daughter of John Courtenay of Molland, and his descendants, in the first and second lines, were of Hawkridge and Goodleigh, for

---

[*] Foster, and Vivian. But according to Burke, and Stockdale, *Eng. Bar.*, 1806, the original patent was dated 1st March, 1644-5.

several generations. The second son of Baldwin "Ackland" of Hawkridge, John Ackland, settled in Exeter as a merchant, was Mayor of that city in 1627, and died in 1640. His eldest son, Baldwin, Fellow of Exeter College, Oxford, was subsequently Senior Proctor of that University, but ultimately retired to his native county and was presented to the Rectory of Tedburn St. Mary, and died, treasurer of Exeter Cathedral, in 1672.

The treasurer's next brother, John Acland, merchant, of Exeter, died, without surviving male issue, in 1674. His mother had been a daughter of Richard Duck of Heavitree.

"John Akeland of Akeland," the eldest brother of Anthony, aforesaid, of Hawkridge, was born about 1523, and married the daughter and co-heir of a rich London tradesman, Hugh Ratcliff of Stepney, an alliance which seems to have largely contributed to the future prosperity of the elder Aclands. The good lady left much of her money to her favourite but second son, "John Akeland." Her eldest son, Hugh, however, married Margaret Monk of Potheridge (grandaunt of "the greatest general of the age," George, Duke of Albemarle, whilst her mother was Frances, daughter and heir of Arthur Plantagenet, Viscount Lisle). He was sheriff of Devon in 1611, and, at the age of seventy, became "right heir" to all the accumulated property of his fortunate and truly charitable brother, John.

The latter was born in or about the year 1565, and was, as I have said, the second of the two sons of "John Akeland, of Akeland," by Margery Ratcliff of Stepney. He was knighted by King James in 1603, in the following year he was returned to Parliament as a Knight of the Shire, and became Sheriff of the County in 1608. His elder brother, and his uncle, Anthony, having inherited respectively the lands of the family at Landkey and Chittlehampton, Sir John Acland, as the name is now written, purchased of William Rowswell an ancient property known as Columb John, in the parish of Broadclist, an old Domesday Manor, which, after passing through several families, such as the Culmes, Cliffords, St. Aubyns, Beares, Prideauxs, and Courtenays, became forfeited to the Crown by the attainder of the Marquess of Exeter, Henry Courtenay, in 1539. Queen Mary had granted it to Sir George Basset, a cadet of the house of Umberleigh; and the latter's son, Philip Basset, sold it to Rowswell aforesaid. Sir John Acland built a fine residence here, upon a foundation said to have been laid "by one of the Earls of Devon," but more probably by Richard, second son of Thomas Bamfield of Poltimore, who died 15th March, 1429, and who had had a grant of the Manor of Columb John, "to him and his heirs male," from Hugh, Earl of Devon, between the years 1419-1422, and upon whose death it had reverted to the Earldom, failing issue of the said Richard Bamfield. Its propinquity to Poltimore would have made it a very desirable residence for a younger branch of that house.

Sir John also restored and endowed an ancient domestic chapel upon this property, which was consecrated as a Chapel of Ease to Broadclist Church on Sunday, September 11th, 1608, and he usually resided at Columb John until his death, 14th February, 1620. He was a considerable benefactor to Exeter College, Oxford, and gave the sum of £800 towards the building of the Hall, and beer cellar beneath it, and also founded two Scholarships there of the annual value of £8, for boys from Exeter School. Over thirty parishes in the county, inclusive of six of the Exeter churches, have since participated in his gift of bread to the poor, the expense of which, to the amount of £80 per annum, was charged upon the proceeds of "the rectory and church of Churchstowe and chapel of Kingsbridge.* His will, dated 9th February, was proved P.C.C., 4th July, 1620.† By his first wife, Elizabeth, daughter of George Rolle of Stevenstone, he had one daughter, Dorothy, who died in her infancy, and had no further issue by his second marriage with Margery Hawley, a widow and daughter of Sir Henry Portman, Kt., of Orchard Portman. He was buried between his two wives, under a fine, but undated, monument, in Broadclist church, upon which there is a recumbent figure of himself in armour, with a lady on either side.‡ By an *Inq. p.m.* dated 20th James I. (1622), his "right heir" was found to be his elder brother, "Sir Hugh

---

* By deeds dated 20th January and 20th August, 13th and 17th James I.
† (Soame 76.)
‡ The Lysons I *Mag. Brit.*, vol. ii., p. 116, "Devon," state that it "appears by the parish books that he was buried in 1613." Moore, *History of Devon*, vol. ii., p. 433, carelessly plagiarises the same fable, although a few lines further on he cites the deeds of the said Sir John of "13th and 17th James I.," 1616-1619.

Akeland "; the will was proved by the said Hugh's second son as executor, who left no surviving issue at his death in 1649-50 (3rd February), and Columb John had then passed to his nephew, Sir John "Aclande," who thus signed the pedigree of 1620, son and heir of Sir Arthur Aclande, Kt., who had died in 1610, *v.p.*

This Sir John "Aclande," "aged 29, 1620," was created a Baronet, as above stated. He garrisoned Columb John for the king in 1643; in 1646 it had become the headquarters of General Fairfax, and that Cromwell, in person, was there during the period of its occupation by the Parliamentary forces is proved by a letter dated "Colomb John, near Exeter, 23rd July, 1646," and addressed to him by Elizabeth, Lady Acland,* in which she writes :—" I received such ample testimony of your love when you were pleased to quarter at my house, as that I cannot express my thankfulness for the same, and hope for your interest in favour of my husband with the Commissioners at Goldsmith's Hall." That this poor lady's supplication was of little avail is proved by the fact that at her husband's death, at Stoke d'Abernon, in Surrey, thirteen months later (24th Aug., 1647), his creditors proved his will, and even the patent of his baronetcy was lost or destroyed during the troubles to which he had been subjected. Lady Acland only survived him until 1649, and "admon. *de bonis non*" to her effects was also granted to a creditor, William Brown, 6th July, 1671, her son, Hugh Acland, having renounced further trouble with respect to his parents' personality.

The latter, in the following year, became fifth Baronet in succession to his two elder brothers, Sir Francis and Sir John, and the latter's son, Sir Arthur, fourth Baronet, who died in his minority. The king granted him a fresh patent of the baronetcy to replace the one which had been destroyed during the recent wars on January 31st, 1677-78, which gives precedence to the Aclands over all Baronets created since the date of the original patent. He married Anne, daughter of Sir Thomas Daniel, Kt., of Beswick, co. York, and was of Columb John and Killerton, which latter estate, in the same parish, had given name to a

---

* She was the daughter of Sir Francis Vincent, first Baronet of Stoke d'Abernon, and step-daughter of her husband's mother.

family who possessed it for many generations, and whose daughter and heir had married Sir John de Vére, and, secondly, Sir W. Courtenay, Kt. It was subsequently purchased by the Drewes, who were residing there when Edward Drewe murdered Will Petre, a tragical episode to which I have already sufficiently referred in these pages and elsewhere (*Suburbs of Exeter*, pp. 12 *et seq.*)

But as this happened in 1611, and as the property was sold to the Aclands by Thomas Drewe, *who succeeded to it in* 1622, the purchaser cannot have been "Sir Arthur Acland, Kt.," Sir Hugh's grandfather, as stated by the several county historians, since Sir Arthur had died *v.p.* in 1610, 26th December, and Edward Drewe, father of the said Thomas, and owner of Killerton, was interred in the parish church of Broad-Clist in 1622, M.I. Sir Hugh Acland, of Columb John and Killerton, was buried at Broad-Clist 9th March, 1714, and was succeeded by his eldest son, Hugh, as sixth Baronet, the third of whose sons, Arthur Acland, was the father of Sir John Palmer Acland, created a Baronet 9th December, 1818, and whose only granddaughter and eventual heir married Sir A. B. P. Hood, Bt., in 1849.

On the death of Sir Hugh, sixth Baronet, 29th July, 1728, the title passed to his eldest son, Sir Thomas, seventh Baronet, who was followed by his grandson, Sir John, whose mother was a daughter of the first Lord Ilchester, as eighth baronet, in 1785. On the death of the latter, without issue, within two months of his succession, viz., 15th April that year, the title passed to his uncle, Sir Thomas Dyke Acland as ninth Baronet, the additional name of "Dyke" having been assumed in right of his mother, Elizabeth, daughter of Thomas Dyke, of Tetton.

The ninth Baronet's eldest son, by his wife Henrietta, daughter of Sir Richard Hoare, Bt., was the tenth Baronet, and died at Killerton 22nd July, 1871, at the age of eighty-four. He was the father of the present Right Honourable Sir Thomas Dyke Acland, of Acland, Columb John, and Killerton, who was born 25th May, 1809, was M.P. for North Devon and West Somersetshire, and is a Privy Councillor. (See *Men of the Time*, p. 8.) Sir Thomas married, firstly, in 1841, Mary, eldest daughter of Sir Charles Mordaunt, Bt., and secondly, in 1856, Mary, daughter of John Erskine, and niece of James, second Lord Rosslyn. By his first marriage he has had, with other issue, a son and heir, Charles Thomas Dyke Acland, M.P., born 1842, and who married, in 1879, Gertrude, daughter of the late Sir John W. Walrond, Bt. Arthur, second brother of the present Baronet, assumed the name of Troyte, by Royal licence, in 1852. His fourth brother, Henry Wentworth Dyke Acland, K.C.B., Regius Professor of Medicine at Oxford, born 1815, was created a Baronet in 1890, and has seven sons.

Killerton House, which is surrounded by an extensive deer park, was built as a temporary residence by the seventh baronet, who died in 1785; the tenth and late baronet was the first of the family who presented to the Vicarage of Broad-Clist, through his trustees, in his minority, 7th December, 1795. The old mansion house at Columb John was pulled down some years ago, and the family have since resided permanently at Killerton. The new chapel there was provided by the late Sir Thomas Dyke Acland, who obtained an Act of Parliament to transfer to it the endowments of the ancient structure at Columb John, already referred to, 12th July, 1837.

The arms of Acland may be thus blazoned—" Chequy *arg.* and *sable*, a fess *gules.*"

Crest.—A man's hand gloved, and couped at the wrist, thereon a falcon, all ppr.

Motto—" Inébranlable."

THE BAMPFYLDES OF POLTIMORE.

Poltimore Park, the Devonshire seat of Lord Poltimore, is situated about four miles from Exeter, and the property is not identical with either of those which in the Domesday record are described as " Pontimora " and " Pultimora " respectively. At the period of the Survey, it had no separate existence as a manor, and appears to have been parcel of the Royal manor of " Clistone," since known as '' Broad·Clist," or great Clist, and to have been originally known as " Clist Moins," or Clist the less, and ultimately its identity became entirely overlooked and lost, through its acquisition by a family who were its owners for several descents, and who were known by the name of their residence, "Pultimore," in the parish of Farway, and three miles distant from Honiton.*

From a note appended to one of the copies of the *Visitation of Devon*, 1564,† it appears that "Stephen of Poltymore, *temp.*

---

* The early acquisition of the manor of "Clist Moyns, or Moins" by the Poltimores of Farway, and its consequent change of name from "Clist Moins" to Poltimore, has been the occasion of endless topographical confusion. Sir William Pole, whose error has been repeated by his contemporary, Thomas Westcote, and later on by John Prince, has corrupted "Moins" into Moys, and has asserted that it had "formerly owners of the latter name who had lands also so called in Glamorganshire." Neither Risdon (*c.* 1638) or Westcote (*c.* 1642) have supplied any information at all as to the early owners of "Clist Moins," otherwise Poltimore ; the first author has merely stated that "Poltimore was long since the seat of the Poltimores' knights," the last that, "Clist Moys, now called Poltimore, Sir Richard de Poltimore held, and his predecessors, and posterity for a while after him."

The authors of the *Mag. Brit.*, Devon, vol. ii., p. 419, confound this estate with that Manor of Poltimore, which was, and is, in the parish of Farway, and which belonged, in 1086, to Haimer de Arcis, and afterward gave name to the "Poltimores," as in my text, but this property did not pass to the Bampfyldes, but to a family known as "le Jewe," which, after several descents, terminated in daughters and co-heirs. In their "Table of the Domesday division of property" (*Mag. Brit.*, Devon, vol. i.) these same authors mention two other manors, which they alike term "Poltimore," and describe as, anciently written, "Pontimore," one of which they state, as "an appendage of Clist," was held by "Odo," and afterward by "Baldwin the Sheriff" in demesne ; the other by "Olmer," and in 1086 by the "Canons of St. Mary" in demesne.

But the Domesday record, in fact, has mention but of a *single* manor of "Pontimore," which was the property *of Baldwin the Sheriff*, and held *under him* at the period of the Survey by the Canons of St. Mary of Rouèn, in Normandy. This manor of "Pontimore" descended with Aylesbeare to Baldwin's posterity, the Courtenay Earls of Devon, and is now known as "Newton Poppleford," a modern parochial district, but an ancient chapelry, with a market and fair of its own, within the said parish of Aylesbeare.

The hypothetical manor of "Pontimore, or Poltimore," which the brothers Lysons assign to "Odo" the Saxon, and to "Baldwin the Sheriff," under the Normans, is a pure invention on their part, which seems to be founded on a very obvious clerical inaccuracy on the part of the Domesday scribes, and the careless perpetuation of the error is the less inexcusable, because the authors of the *Magna Britannia* have noted that this "Pontimore" was "an appendage of Clist."

The facts are as follows :—

The said Canons of St. Mary held, as sub-tenants to Baldwin, two manors, written "Clist" and "Cliste." The first of these has been since known as "Clist St. Mary," the second as "Clist William," and the latter is situated within the parish of Plymtree, near Cullompton, which, as "Plumtree," was held by Odo Fitz-Gamelin at the period of the Survey, from which record it appears that "one farthing of land, valued at twelvepence per annum," had been taken "from the manor of Clist, held by the Canons of St. Mary under Baldwin, and added to "Odo's manor of Pontimore," according to the Exeter Domesday, and "Ponamore," according to the Exchequer copy of the Survey.

And as no such manor as "Pontimore, or Ponamore," was held by any such individual as Odo, who was a king's thegn in Saxon times, or by "Odo Fitz-Gamelin," under Norman rule, and as it is only mentioned in connection with a portion of "Cliste," which was situated in "Odo's manor" of "Plumtree," it is evident that there was no such manor of "Pontimore" as Lysons mentions, and that "Pontimore," instead of "Plumtree," was merely an accidental error of description.

Finally, neither of the manors respectively written "Pontimore," or "Pultimore," in Domesday, had anything in common with the property now known as Poltimore Park, but the second of them is identical with the estate, still called "Poltimore," in the parish of Farway.

† See Colby, *Visit.*, 1564, pp. 10, 11.

Henry III., had issue, Bartholomew of Poltymore, who had issue Richard of Poltymore, Kt., who had issue Richard of Poltymore, Kt., who 21 Edward I. gave the manor by deed to a certain Simon de Montacute, Kt., called his "lord" or "master," in the deed by which he gave all his lands in Poltymore, Wibridge, Bocombe, and South Tawton to the said Simon de Montacute in case he should die without issue. Simon de Montacute afterwards, by a deed dated 26th Edward I. (1298) gave the manor of Poltymore to William Pontington, canon of the Cathedral of Exeter, and to a certain John de Baunfield."

The above notes add much to the "confusion" to which I have already referred. The reversionary conveyance by "Richard of Poltymore, Kt.," dated 21 Edward I., and which is also applied by Lysons' *Mag. Brit.* to "Poltimore, near Exeter," had literally nothing whatever to do with the latter property, as proved by the mention of "Wibridge and Bocombe," which, like Poltimore, are, and were, situated in the parish of Farway.

"Wibridge" (Woodbridge) is now a hamlet, whilst "Bocombe" (Boycombe) and Poltimore have been long occupied as farms. From the expression "lord" or "master," it may be inferred that the "Poltymores" held land under the Barony of Shipton Montagu, in the adjoining county, of which the said "Simon" was "seized" in the 5th Edward I.*

That these Poltimores of Poltimore, in Farway, were also the owners of Clist Moins, since known also as Poltimore, is sufficiently evidenced by the fact that Richard, son of Bartholomew de Poltymore,† presented John Blundell to the parish church of Clist Moins, or Poltimore, in July, 1259, and from the fact that he was the patron instead of his father, I think it probable that he may have then recently become the owner of Clist Moins. It is certain that the parish has been ever since known as Poltimore, and it is thus named in the "Taxatio" of Pope Nicholas IV., 1288-1291, when the "firstfruits" amounted to £2 13s. 4d.

Bartholomew de Poltimore, father of Richard, presented "Sampson of Hocesham" (Huxham) to Poltimore Rectory

---

* See "House of Brito," *ante*.
† *Ep. Reg. Exon.*

16th August, 1263, and again exercised the right of patronage in favour of "Adam de Stratton," 28th February, 1265-66.

It is stated in the Cartulary of St. John's Priory, Exeter (*Exeter Mun. Archives*), that this " Bartholomew sold Poltymore Manor to *Nicholas* de Potyngdon, *and to* John Bampfeld" (*c.* 1291). John Prince tells us that the last " Sir Richard de Poltimore, having no issue of his own, granted the property to Simon Lord Montacute, who sold it unto William Pontington, Canon of the Church of Exeter, for £200, in the twenty-sixth year of King Edward I., A.D. 1298, and he gave it unto John Bampfield, whom he had the care and tuition of, for he is styled his *alumnus* or pupil."*

The Pointingtons were settled for eight descents at Pennicott, in the parish of Shobrooke, near Crediton, from the time of Edward III., and their pedigree was entered at the Heralds' visitation of the county in 1564, and again in 1620. The names " William " and " Nicholas " are to be found in the recorded generations of this family, who seem to have migrated to Devonshire from Somerset, and to have derived their name from the parish of Poyntington, near Sherborne. Possibly William de Pointington was the son of Nicholas, mentioned as the co-purchaser with John Bampfeld of the manor of Poltymore, nigh Exeter, from Bartholomew de Poltymore in 1291. " The Canon of Exeter," " William de Puntyngdon," succeeded Thomas de Charleton as Archdeacon of Totnes 28th September, 1303, and had been precentor of Exeter Cathedral in the previous year; he was succeeded in that office by Walter Stapeldon, afterward Bishop of the See, and died in 1307. " John de Bamfeld" first occurs as patron of the Rectory of Poltimore 5th March, 1340-41, but his father is described, in the *Nomina Villarum,* as " Lord of Poltimore" in the year 1316.

With regard to the constantly asserted "gift" of the property, either to " William Pontington," or to the latter *and* to " John de Bamfeld," by *Simon de Montacute* in 1238, this was, I feel assured, nothing more than a " quit claim " and " confirmation " of the actual sale of " Clist Moins," alias Poltimore,

---
* Prince's *Worthies of Devon, sub* Sir C. Bampfeild, Bt. The story is repeated by Lysons' *Mag. Brit.*, Devon, vol. ii., p. 419.

to Poyntington and Bampfeld, by Bartholomew de Poltymore, in 1291, and was merely granted by the said Simon, in 1298, by virtue of his rights over the hundred of Wonford, in which Poltimore Park is situated. He had obtained from the king, 18 Edward I., 1289, a confirmation of his honour of Shepton Montague, and, with like rights in other counties, *the Lordship of the whole hundred of Wonford*, and was therefore, under the Crown, chief lord of the fee of Poltimore, otherwise Clist Moins.

The Bampfyldes have been independently settled at Poltimore, near Exeter, with absolute certainty since 1316, and have as certainly presented to its rectory since 1340. By what means their ancestors may have become possessed of the Poyntington moiety of the manor, whether by gift or purchase, is immaterial, but if it is a fact that "John de Baunfield was seized of the manor of Poltymore 1 Edward II.," as noted against his name in the copy of the Visitation of 1564,* that date synchronises with the death of Archdeacon William Poyntington, or "de Puntyngdon," in 1307, and supports the story as to his having been a "favoured pupil" of that clerical dignitary, but, as he was the son of *John* de Baunfeld, by Joan Hastings, his father was doubtless the original purchaser of the Bampfylde moiety of the manor in 1291.

The name of Bampfylde, which was spelt "Bampfield" by the fifth baronet, who died in 1823, and Bamfield at the creation of that title in 1641, has been also variously written Bamfeild, Bamfeld, Baunfelde, and Baunfeld.

John de Baunfelde, the father of the first Baunfelde of Poltimore, by his wife Joan de Hastyngs, appears to have been settled in the parish of Weston Baunfell, or Baunville, now Bamfyld in Somersetshire, and was most probably a cadet of the house of Bonville, derived from Sir Nicholas Bonville, who was a landowner in that county as early as the first year of King John, and who took his surname either from "Bonneville" in Savoy, or else from the town of the same name in the fertile province of Beauce, on the confines of the Isle of France. The "son" (or grandson?) of Sir Nicholas, Sir William Bonville,

---

* The several copies of the Visitation of 1564 are not authoritative; and this statement is *not* repeated in the original Visitation of 1620.

recovered his lands in Somerset upon the customary homage and service, in 1265, and was the grandfather of Nicholas Bonville, who married Avis, daughter and co-heir of Sir Thomas Pyne of Shute,* and died in 1294, leaving issue, Sir Nicholas, father of Sir William Bonville of Shute (an estate long subsequently, and after attainder, acquired from Petre, by Pole), the ancestor of William, Lord Bonville of Chewton, who was summoned to Parliament, as a baron, 28 Henry VI., and also a second son, John Bonville, who is said† to have married Joan, daughter of Waryn Hampton, of Musbury, and to have died without issue.‡

"John Bamfielde of Poltimore," who commences the pedigree recorded by the Heralds at the Devonshire Visitation of 1620, married Ellinor, daughter of Sir Humphry Beauchamp, of Ryme, and is named as "Lord of Poltimore" in the year 1316.§ He had a son of the same name, who married Isabella, daughter of John Cobham, by his wife Anne Bollay, and who presented to Poltimore Rectory, 5th March, 1340-41. His son and heir, also called John, married Joan, daughter of Geoffrey Gilbert, and was dead, 13th November, 1360, when the said Joan, as "relict of John Bampfeld the elder," presented William Seger to the rectory of Poltimore. Consequently her son Thomas, who married a "daughter of Coplestone, must have been also dead at that date, but the latter's son and heir, "John Baunfeld, Esq.," was of full age, 7th November, 1361, when he gave the family living to a certain J. de Cobham, who was doubtless his kinsman. This "John Baunfeld, Esq.," married Joane, daughter of Sir

---

* Vivian calls her "widow of Sir Thomas Pyne," whose *daughters* and coheirs, however, married Bonville and Umfraville, and thus Shute descended in the Bonville family.

† Vivian "*Visit. Devon,*" p. 101, who cites "Pole, various Harl. MSS., and Maclean's *History of Trigg Minor,* with additions and corrections." The *only* pedigree of Bonville entered before the Heralds, appears in the *copies* of the 1564 "Visitation," and refers to the illegitimate descendants of Lord Bonville of Chewton.

‡ Although the ancestor of the Bampfyldes may have belonged to an earlier generation, it is just possible that this John Bonville of Weston was identical with John Baunfelde, father of John of Poltimore, by Joan de Hastyngs. Joan Hampton was doubtless a *second wife, and the wife of his old age,* as she is said to have married twice, subsequently to her first widowhood. The arms of Bonville of Chewton were, "*sa.,* six mullets *arg.,* pierced *gu.*;" but several branches of the family bore, "*or.,* on a bend *sa.,* three mullets *arg.,*" and these latter, but for slight variation of tincture, are precisely similar to the present arms of Bampfylde, who are said, however, to have originally borne the field, "paly of six *arg.* and *vert.*"

§ *Nomina villarum, ut ante.*

Richard Merton,* but died at a very early age, on which account his father-in-law, the said Sir Richard Merton, Kt., presented to Poltimore only sixteen months later, 24th March, 1362, as "Guardian of John Baunfeld, a minor, son and heir of John Baunfeld." This youthful heir also died young, but added much to the fortunes of the family by his marriage with Joan, daughter and heir of John de Hocesham, through which alliance his posterity acquired the adjacent manor of Huxham,† which is still the property of Lord Poltimore. His widow, Joan, presented to Poltimore Rectory, as "relict of John Baunfeld," and by right of her dowry, 4th January, 1372-73. Her eldest son, Thomas "Bampfeld," presented to Poltimore 24th September, 1404, and to Huxham, as "true patron," 3rd February in the same year.‡ He married Agnes, daughter and co-heir of John Faber of Bovey Tracy, and was the grandfather of John Bamfield of Poltimore, who by his wife Agnes, daughter and heir of John Pederton, by Cecilia, daughter and heir of John Turney, was the father of Sir William Bamfield, son and heir of Poltimore. This John and his wife rebuilt the Parish Church of Poltimore, as shown by an inscription on a gravestone which was, some years since, removed from the nave to the chancel, and which bears the following inscription :—

"MC.C.C.XC."
"Hic jacent Johes Baunfeld et Agnes uxor ejus, Pater et Mater Willi Baunfeld, qui hanc Ecclesiam et maximam Campanam fieri fecerunt."

Their son, Sir William Bamfield,§ was sheriff of Devon in 1426, and died in 1474. The Manor of Huxham appears to have been settled upon his second son William Bamfield,

---

* According to the Visitation Pedigrees, the inaccuracies and omissions in which I can only thus slightly notice, the *Son* of John B. and Ellinor Beauchamp, married "Joane, daughter of Sir Richard Martin, Kt." The 1620 pedigree is not vouched for by the signature of any member of the family. Said Joane Martin is made the *mother* of Thomas, who married Agnes Coplestone. Martin is, of course, an error for Merton.

† By deed dated 28th September, 1461, and which is, or was, preserved at Wardour Castle, "William Bamfeld, Esq." mortgaged the manor of Huxham, with other lands in "Pynho and Beare," to Jane, widow of Sir Jno. Dynham, to her son John D. and to Richard Levermore, as security for the payment of £80.

‡ John Baunfeld, probably by arrangement with "William de Hocesham," had presented to Huxham, 13th August, 1349.

§ Where the spelling of the name differs from Bampfylde, it is in all cases a quotation.

who may have acquired the Pinhoe property, mentioned in the mortgage above noted, by his second marriage with Margaret Kirkham, widow of John Cheyney, of Pinhoe; he succeeded his elder brother Walter "Bamfield," at Poltimore, 1st Sept., 1478, and was the father, by his first wife Margaret St. Maur, of Sir Edward Bamfield of Poltimore, who married Elizabeth Wadham, and died in 1528. His son and heir, Richard Bamfeild, who was an only child and but two years of age at his father's death, was, presumably, the hero of a sensational story which has been handed down to us by John Prince, the author of the "Worthies of Devon," published in 1701, and which he tells us is "a most memorable passage of undoubted credit," and to the effect that "one of the heirs of the house, not many generations back," being ward to "some very great person in the east country," was taken away in his infancy, and brought up in ignorance of his real position and prospects. He was trained to be a servant, and, when discovered by one of his late father's tenantry, was employed as huntsman in his said guardian's establishment. The Poltimore farmer is then said to have abducted him, to have taken him before the proper authorities, and to have duly established the right of his young landlord to his inheritance.

This Richard Bamfeild, at the age of fifty, became Sheriff of Devon in the eighteenth year of the reign of Queen Elizabeth. His mother, a widow, at the time of her second marriage, was a daughter of Nicholas Wadham, of Merrifield, co. Somerset, and his wife was a daughter of Sir John Sydenham of the same county; by her he had a family of twelve children, viz., nine daughters and three sons. The eldest of the latter, Giles, predeceased him, having been drowned during his passage to Ireland, so he was succeeded in 1594 by his second son, Amias, then over thirty years of age, who was Sheriff of the county in 1603, and was knighted that same year at Windsor.* He married Elizabeth, daughter of Sir John Clifton, of Barrington, Somerset, and had ten children; one of

---

* This Sir Amias Bampfeild built, in 1618, the very interesting house in "Doddehay," now Bampfylde Street, Exeter, long the city residence of the family, and now used as offices. It is rich in armorial bearings of the families allied to Bampfylde by marriage. See *post*.

his daughters married the nephew of the great Sir Francis Drake, who was created a baronet in 1622, and whose sister, Elizabeth, was the wife of his eldest son and successor, John Bamfeild, of Poltimore, who was born about 1590. The latter also had a large family, fifteen children; one of the daughters, Dorothy, was the wife of Henry Worth, of Worth. The sixth son, Francis, was a Nonconformist minister, and died in Newgate Gaol in the spring of 1604; the eighth son, Thomas Bampfield, was Recorder of Exeter during the Usurpation, and member for Exeter in 1656. The third son, John Bamfield, was created a baronet 14th July, 1641, and through the deaths of his two elder brothers, Amias and Arthur, succeeded to Poltimore at his father's death, and married Gertrude, sister and co-heir of John Coplestone, of Warleigh. During the great rebellion this first baronet was active on the side of the Parliament, and Poltimore House was garrisoned by Fairfax in 1645; its owner died in 1650, aged forty, when he was succeeded by his son, Sir Coplestone Bampfield, the eldest of a family of nineteen, and who was as zealous for the Restoration of monarchy as his sire had been for its overthrow, and who was duly "pricked" Sheriff of Devon as soon as the king "came home again." He was, however, equally zealous in his promotion of the Revolution, being actuated, as evidently as his father had been, by perfectly conscientious motives, and on his death-bed he called his family around him, and impressed upon them the necessity of an invariable adherence to the "religion of the Established Church of England, and of allegiance to the right heirs of the Crown." He experienced a great domestic bereavement shortly before his demise, through a melancholy and fatal accident of which his eldest and promising son was the victim. This son, Colonel Hugh Bampfield, who commanded the county militia, was returning from a wedding, when his horse tripped whilst descending a hill near Plymouth, and the young rider's neck was broken. He left a widow, Mary, daughter of James Clifford, of Ware, who administered to the will of her father-in-law in the minority of her eldest son, Coplestone Warwick Bampfield, who succeeded as third baronet in 1692, and also, by devise, to the estates of his far away kinsman, Warwick Bampfield, of Hardington, co. Somerset * (Sir Coplestone was M.P. for Exeter, and also for the county, and was buried at Poltimore with his ancestors, 14th Oct., 1727), he left issue a daughter, Mary (Lady Carew), and a son, Richard Warwick Bampfield, fourth baronet. The latter, who also represented Devonshire in Parliament, married Joan Codrington, of Wraxhall, Somerset, and died at the age of fifty-four, 24th July, 1776, when he was succeeded by his second but eldest surviving son, Charles Warwick Bampfield, as fifth baronet.

The latter, who was born and baptized in Bristol, 23rd January, 1753, represented the city of Exeter in Parliament from 1774 to 1807, and, at the age of seventy, came to an untimely end at the hands of his servant, Morland, who immediately afterward committed suicide. He died at his town residence, No. 1, Montague Square, and was buried 25th April, 1823, at Hardington, co. Somerset, which he evidently preferred to his Devonshire home, as he is described as of " Hardington Park," without any mention of Poltimore, in the *London Directory* of 1822. By his wife, Catherine, daughter of Admiral Sir John Moore, Bt., and K.C.B., he left a daughter, Louisa, wife of Edward W. Wells, Captain R.N.; a son, Charles, in holy orders; and a son and heir, Sir George Warwick " Bampfylde," who was born 23rd March, 1786, succeeded as sixth baronet, was a Deputy Lieutenant for Devon and Somerset, and colonel of the North Devon Militia. On the 10th Sept., 1831, Sir George was raised to the peerage as Baron Poltimore, of Poltimore, and was afterward a Lord-in-Waiting to Her Majesty the Queen, and died 18th December, 1858. His Lordship by his second wife, Caroline, eldest daughter of Lieut.-General Frederick Buller, of Pelynt, was the father of the second and present baron and seventh baronet, who was born in 1837, and married the second daughter of Richard Brinsley Sheridan, M.P., of Frampton, Dorset, by whom he has, with other issue, a son, the Honourable C. R. G. Warwick Bampfylde, born 1859, late of the 1st Life Guards, who is married, and has issue.

Arms of Bampfylde.—*Or*, on a bend *gu.*, 3 mullets *arg.*

---

* Warwick Bampfield was descended from Peter (whose will was proved 7th June, 1499, P.C.C.), second son of John Bamfield, of Poltimore, by Agnes, daughter and heir of John Pederton, of Hardington, by his wife, Cecilia, daughter and heir of John Turney.

Crest.—A lion's head erased *sa.*, ducally crowned *or.*

Supporters.—Two lions ramp. reg. *sa.*, crowned as crest, and gorged with a collar gemelle *or,* an escutcheon of the arms pendent therefrom.

Motto.—" Delectare in Domino."

In the old house in Bampfylde Street, Exeter, to which I have already referred as having been erected by Sir Amias Bamfielde, Kt., in 1618, are the following coats, illustrative of the matrimonial alliances of the family :—

On a shield over the fireplace in oak—

1st.—*Or,* on a bend *gu.,* 3 mullets *arg.*—Bampfylde.

2nd.—*Or,* a maunch *gules*—Hastings.

3rd.—*Arg.,* a lion ramp. *sa.*—Hocesham.

4th.—*Arg.,* on a fess *sa.,* 3 crosslets *or,* a bordure *az.*—Faber.

5th.—*Arg.,* a bend *gu.,* between three lions' heads erased *sa.,* crowned of second—Pederton of Hardington.

6th.—*Gu.,* semée of crosslets, and a lion pass. guardant *arg.*— Turney* *alias* Mallet, of Enmore, co. Somerset.

7th.—*Arg.,* 2 chevrons *gu.,* a label *az.*—St. Maur.

8th.—Turney as above.

Over a doorway is a shield of the family impaling Clifton. *Sa.,* semée of cinquefoils, a lion ramp. *arg.*

In the hall window are six shields in painted glass, but the tinctures have in some cases suffered by injudicious repairs.

1st Bampfylde.—(Andrew, son and heir of Walter Bamfield, aged 4 years, *anno* 1478, died, *S.P.*)

2nd Bampfylde.—Impaling Turney quartering St. Maur. 'Wm. Bampfylde and his first wife, Margaret St. Maur, heiress to her niece, Mary Drury.)

3rd Bampfylde.—Impaling *erm.,* 3 lions ramp. *gu.,* within a bordure engrailed *sa.*—Kirkham. (Wm. Bampfylde and his second wife.)

4th.—The same as No. 3.

5th Bampfylde.—Impaling *vert.,* a chevron between 3 mullets *or*—Pudsey. (Walter Bampfylde, *ob.* 1478, son and heir of Sir William, and his wife Grace.

6th.—As 2, but St. Maur *quarters Turney.*

---

* The ancient arms of this family were "paly of six *gu.* and *or,* a lion statant guardant *arg.*"

GIBBS OF FENTON AND OF CLIST ST. GEORGE

There was an ancient tradition as to " Gibbs, of Derry," that the first of them came to England in the retinue of King William, and their name has been considered, by some, to be equivalent to " Gilbert," by others to be deduced from " an Arabic root."

Sir Bernard Burke has cited an "ancient roll," originally in the possession of "Jenkin Gibbes (*temp.* Henry VII.)," as authority for the statement that the De Guibes, or Gibbes, existed in Normandy long prior to the Norman Conquest, and adds, that " the name is said to be still found in France," in the first form ; it appears certain, however, that families known as " Gibbe," or " Gibbes," became settled, during the fourteenth century, in the West of England, and were also found long since both in Warwickshire and Kent ; the latter stock are said to be derived from Devonshire, the first of whom, " John Gibbes," has been asserted to have been the brother of Gibbes, " of Honington, co. Warwick, in the reign of Richard II.," whilst the Gibbs of Derry, assumed to be of the Devonshire branch, together with those of Bedminster, co. Somerset, the ancestors of Sir E. O. Gibbes, Baronet, alike bear Arms which seem to be connected with this county, and which, but for tincture, are precisely identical with those of Dennis, of Holcombe Burnell, and Orleigh, and also with those of Wyke, of Northwyke, already blazoned on a previous page ; whilst, despite the oft plagiarised assertion as to the Danish origin of the race of Dennis,* I think that it is more than probable that Ralph " le Dan," " Dacus," or " Dennis," who was settled at St. Pancras, near Holsworthy, since known as " Pancraswick," in the reign of Henry II., was responsible for the very suggestive affix of that parish, and that he was, actually, a brother of William, Robert and Roger de Wigornia, of whose ancestry I have already sufficiently treated.†

Sir Ralf de Wick, otherwise Dennis, who may have acquired the latter appellative from his arms, anciently blazoned as " three Danish axes," was of Wick St. Pancras in the twelfth century. He had issue two sons, *Robert* and *William ;* Robert's

---

* See Risdon, *Survey,* pp. 120, 234. Prince, *Worthies, sub* Dennis, Sir Thomas.
† *Ante,* p. 375.

line terminated after several descents in two co-heirs, Margaret and Agatha, the wives respectively of Sir Reginald Ferrers, of Beer, and of Sir Nicholas Kirkham. But William had a son, "Sir Alan le Dennis," whose son, Robert, married Maude, daughter and heir of William de Manworthy, of Manworthy, in the parish of Holsworthy. John Dennis, of Manworthy, grandson of the last Robert and Maude, and son of William Dennys, of Gidicot, in the parish of Bradford, acquired the latter manor in marriage with Joan, daughter and heir of John Dabernon, and left it to his own descendants; but his younger brother, Walter Dennis, succeeded both to Manworthy and Gidicott, and, after several descents, his "heir-general," Thomasine Dennis, married Philip Boterford, of Botterford in South Huish, and his daughter and heir, Margery Botterford, brought the property to her husband, a certain William May, or Mey, between the years 1399-1413. In the meantime Fenton, a hamlet in the parishes of Rattery and Dartington, had been alienated by one of the barons of Dartington at an early date to a family who styled themselves "de Fenton." "John de Fenton" was its owner in 1242, and Risdon says (*Survey*, p. 165) that "the inheritance thereof came to William Gibbs about the reign of Henry the Fourth" (1399-1413), and this William was doubtless the son of the "John Gibbes," also of Fenton, who is reputed to have been the "brother of Gibbes, of Honington, co. Warwick." John, grandson of William Gibbs, appears to have married Agnes Mey, or May, of Botterford, Manworthy, and Giddicott, the last two estates having been derived from Dennis; and hence the connection, between the family of Gibbes, of Fenton, and Dennis, originally of Pancraswick, whose arms the former appear to me to have assumed, is sufficiently clear; not so, however, the basis upon which these Dennis arms were admitted to the family of "Gibbes, of Bedminster and Bristol," at the Herald's Visitation of Somersetshire in 1672, since their pedigree shows no connection whatever with Gibbes of Fenton, locally pronounced Venton.

Fenton, Botterford, Manworthy, and Giddicott, descended in the family of Gibbes from the reign of Edward IV. to that of Queen Elizabeth. The last of them, William Gibbes, of Fenton, is said to have sold Manworthy to Hurst, of Exeter, and Butterford to Prestwood. His arms,* attached to his "Funeral Certificate," are impaled with those of his wife, Dorothy Berkeley. He left two daughters, co-heirs, viz., Silvestra, the wife of Walter Wotton, and Elizabeth, who married the said Walter's elder brother, Edward Wotton, and secondly, Edward Drewe, of Hayne, and by their representatives Fenton and the residue of the property was sold. Administration to his estate was granted in 1580, to John Ayer, of Penegett, in the minority of William, son of Silvestra Wotton, a minor.† Peter Gybbes, M.A., Fellow of Exeter College, Oxford, Lent Term, 1387, was possibly of this family.

In 1672 the Gibbes family, of Bristol, then represented by William Gibbes, aged 42, of Southwark, and Henry Gibbes, aged 31, alderman of Bristol, and to whom arms, as borne by Gibbes, of Fenton, viz., *arg.*, 3 battle axes in pile *sa.*, were *then* somewhat unaccountably‡ admitted, referred their ancestry to a certain William Gibbes, of Bedminster, who, by his will dated 18th March, 1602, desired to be buried with "his father" in the Church of St. Thomas, Bristol.

Sir Philip Gibbes, of Barbadoes, created a Baronet 30th May, 1774, was the son of Philip, grandson of Philip, uncle of the aforesaid Alderman Henry Gibbes, and of his brother William Gibbes, of Southwark. The said Philip Gibbes, on 20th December, 1679, was living upon a hundred and seventy-four acres of land in the parish of St. James, Barbadoes, and had there seven white servants, and sixty-nine negroes.

The first baronet, Sir Philip Gibbes, who was so created 30th May, 1774, married Agnes, daughter and heir of Samuel Osborne, of Barbadoes, and it is worthy of note that early in the same century Sir Philip's namesakes, at Clist St. George, had been associated as neighbours with the Osbornes of that same parish, in the church of which there are, or were, memorial inscriptions for Julian Osborne, 1614, and for Richard Osborne, 1706. The Gibbes failed to enter their pedigree at

---

* *Arg.*, 3 battle axes *sa.* Dennis bore *erm.*, 3 battle axes *gu.*
† See *ante*, p. 149.
‡ Scarcely "unaccountably" perhaps, as they were "admitted" by that eccentric officer of arms Sir Edward Bysshe, "Clarenceux."

either of the Heralds' Visitations of this county, so there is some amount of uncertainty as to the precise connection between the Gibbes of Fenton and those of the same name who had become settled in Exeter and its suburban parishes during the fifteenth century, and who are said to have been "a junior branch of the Venton family."*

The late Dr. Oliver "imagines" that the Gibbes of Clist St. George† "came there from Dartington," and notes that Bishop Lacy, on 22nd June, 1437, licensed "Thomas Gybbe and Margaret his wife to have divine service performed within his mansion situated at Dartington."

On the 1st May, 1560, a certain "John Gybb" appears to have been sometime the tenant of a small property called "Peyett," since known as Pytt, in the parish of Clist St. George, and upon that date he purchased the fee simple of his holding, described as "a messuage and tenement and forty acres of land," from his landlord, Thomas, Lord Wentworth, of Nettlested, for £110.

Henry Gybbes of Woodbury, died in 1549; George Gybbe, of Clist St. George, in 1562; and John "Gibbe," of the same parish, and who was probably the purchaser of Pytt, in 1573.

Two years previously the Rectory of Clist St. George, the patronage of which was in the family of Prideaux, of Nutwell, Woodbury, had become vacant by the death of the Rev. William Gybbe, and it is again noteworthy that Margery, daughter of Humphrey Prideaux, of Theuborough, who died 8th May, 1550, was the wife of Robert Gibbes, of Honington, co. Warwick.

The Pytt property appears to have descended in the line of George Gybbes, of Clist St. George, who died in 1606, who by his first marriage had an eldest son, John "Gibbe," whose son, Philip, was of Fulford in the parish of Shobrooke, and whose eldest son, George, was the father of George Gibbs,‡ of Pytt, who died without surviving issue August 9th,

---

* Burke, *Landed Gentry* (Edit. 1858), *sub.* "Gibbs of Belmont."
† *Ecclesiastical Antiquities*, vol. i., p. 153, published 1840. Clist St. George is now commonly spelt Clyst. Fenton is over two miles west of Dartington village, and both Risdon and Westcote mention it as parcel of the adjacent parish of Rattery. Isabella, daughter of Thomas Gybbe, of Fenton, married John Fortescue, of Wimpston, who died in 1519.
‡ His elder brother, John, born 1637, died 1643.

1723; and also of Abraham Gibbs, fourth son, who settled at Topsham, and who was the father of another Abraham Gibbs, also of Topsham, born 1686, and who by his first wife Mary, daughter of Nehemiah Monke, of the same parish, had a second son, George Abraham Gibbs, who resided at Exeter, and who succeeded to Pytt, in Clist St. George, as heir-at-law to his great uncle, George Gibbs, in 1723.*

George Abraham Gibbs married Anne, daughter and co-heir of Anthony Vicary, of Exeter, and had a large family, viz., five sons and six daughters. Of the sons, it is only requisite to treat of the second, third, and fifth.

The second son, who was called Vicary, after his mother, was born, in 1751, at his father's house in the Cathedral Close, near Palace Gate, was privately baptized 12th November, 1751, and was educated at Eton and at King's College, Cambridge. He was eventually called to the Bar at the Middle Temple, and his abilities secured the favourable notice of John Dunning, afterward Lord Ashburton. He became the leading counsel on the Western circuit, and succeeded Richard Burke as Recorder of Bristol. He subsequently represented his University in Parliament, became Chief Justice of the County Palatine of Chester, and in turn filled the offices of Solicitor and Attorney-General, and received the honour of knighthood. He was raised to the Bench in 1813, and soon afterward attained the Chief Justiceship of the Common Pleas, but resigned in consequence of the increasing infirmities of age in 1818, and survived his retirement but two years. He died at his town house in Russell Square 8th February, 1820. To the patronage of Sir Vicary Gibbs, the first Lord Gifford, so created 1824, and who was also a native of Exeter, was chiefly indebted for his advancement and celebrity.

Sir Vicary married a daughter of Major William Mackenzie (whose brother, Francis Humberstone Mackenzie, succeeded to the Seaforth Barony), and left an only daughter, Maria Elizabeth, who married Lieut.-General Sir Andrew Pilkington, K.C.B., and had two daughters co-heirs.

George Gibbs, younger brother of the Chief Justice, was of

---

* His elder brother, George, had died at Topsham in 1713.

Bristol, and of Redland, co. Gloucester, and was born in 1753. He had three sons and two daughters, who all died unmarried save one, viz., George Gibbs, who was of Belmont, co. Somerset, and a justice of the peace for that county. He married, secondly, in 1814, his cousin, Harriett, daughter of his uncle, Antony Gibbs, but died childless.

The latter, Antony Gibbs, youngest brother of the Lord Chief Justice of the Common Pleas, was the founder of the great mercantile house of "Antony Gibbs and Son." He married Dorothea Barnetta, second daughter of William Hucks, and eventual heir to her cousins, the nieces and co-heirs of Robert Hucks, of Aldenham Park, Hertfordshire, and died in 1815.

Of his five sons, the third, William Gibbs, of Tyntesfield, by his marriage, in 1839, with a daughter of Sir T. Crawley Boevey, Bart., was the father of Mr. Antony Gibbs, of Tyntesfield, born 10th December, 1841.

The eldest son, George Henry Gibbs, of Aldenham Park, and of Clifton Hampden, co. Oxford, married, in 1817, Caroline, sixth daughter of the Rev. C. Crawley, by his wife, the third daughter of George Abraham Gibbs, of Exeter, aforesaid, and died in 1842.

He had issue eight sons and two daughters, and his sixth son, the Rev. John Lomax Gibbs, born 1832, is the present Rector of Clist St. George. The latter's eldest brother, Henry Hucks Gibbs, now of Aldenham Park, Herts., was born 31st August, 1819, and was educated at Rugby and at Exeter College, Oxford, where he graduated B.A. 1841, and M.A. 1844. He is a Commissioner of Lieutenancy for London, and a justice of the peace for Herts. and Middlesex, a director and past governor of the Bank of England, and sometime M.P. for the city. On the 3rd January, 1896, Mr. Hucks Gibbs was raised to the Peerage of the United Kingdom, and on the 4th of February his Lordship was duly gazetted as Baron Aldenham, of Aldenham, in the aforesaid county.

His lordship married, in 1845, the third daughter of the late William Adams, LL.D., of Thorpe, co. Surrey, by his wife, the Honourable Mary Anne Cokayne, niece and co-heir of the last Viscount Cullen, and has had, with other issue, a son and heir, the Honourable Alban George Henry Gibbs, now M.P. for the city of London, born 1846, who married, in 1873, the sixth daughter of the late Rt. Honble. A. J. B. Beresford-Hope, and of the Lady Mildred, his wife, a daughter of James, second Marquess of Salisbury, K.G. She died February 27th, 1896.

Arms of Gibbes:—

"*Arg.*, 3 battle axes *sa.*, two and one."

Crest.—" An arm embowed, in armour ppr., garnished, *or;* bearing in the gauntlet a battle axe as in the arms.

Lord Aldenham bears the same coat, with due authority, *within a bordure nebulée, sa.*

NOTE.—The arms of "Dennys of Orleigh" were "*azure*, three battleaxes *or.*"

Those of "Dennys" of Bradford, Gidicott, and Holcombe Burnell, "*Ermine*, three bills," (*i.e.*, battle axes) "*gules.*"

The first "Dennys," or Dennis, of Holcombe Burnell, was the direct descendant of Walter Dennis, of Giddicott.

After the time of Henry VII., Dennis of Holcombe is said to have borne his arms within a bordure engrailed *gules.*

"*Post temp. H.* 7, *Thomas Dennys de Holcombe portabat insignia dicta (erm.*, 3 *bills gu.*), *cum bordura ingra de rubro, quo tempore, idem Rex A° 5° fecit eum militem.*"

— *Vide Visit. Devon.*, 1564, Colby, p. 78.

BASTARD OF KITLEY.

The late Sir Bernard Burke commences his account of this family with the statement that "it has been settled in Devonshire ever since the Conquest," and adds that " Robert Bastard appears in Domesday book to have had large grants in that county." " His descendants," he says, " have intermarried with the heiresses of Crispin,* and of Killiowe, in the county of Cornwall, and with the families of Fitz-Stephen,* Bessilis,* Damarell,* Gilbert, Reynell, Hele, and Bampfylde, and have, at different periods, served as Sheriffs of the county. Their seat was for many generations at Garston, near Kingsbridge, until about the end of the seventeeth century."†

---

* The names thus marked are not to be found either in the recorded or printed pedigrees of Bastard, nor does the late Sir Bernard Burke give any further explanation as to their connection with that family.

† *Dictionary of the Landed Gentry*, edit. 1858, p. 58.

In several of the hypothetical copies of the *Roll of Battle Abbey*,* but not in all, the name of *Bastard* is found amongst those who are said to have assisted in the subjugation of England by the warlike son of the fair and frail Harlotta of Falaise ; but it is evident that that personage was unconnected with this county from the earlier chronicle of John de Brompton,† who only mentions " *William Bastard, de graunt vigoure*," as one of the Conqueror's followers, whilst the commonly supposed ancestor of the Devonshire family was a certain *Robert le Bastard*, whose name, save possibly as a sub-tenant, and minus the rather equivocal distinctive affix, is not to be found in the "Exeter Domesday," but who appears as the tenant *in capite* of nine manors, viz., Batson, Bickford, Blackworthy, Efford, Hazard, Meeth, and Stonehouse (I give their modern names), in the Exchequer copy of the same record.

Of these manors, Efford, in the parish of Egg-Buckland, about three miles from Plymouth, seems to have been made the chief seat of his "honour," and to have been the residence of the said Robert le Bastard and his elder descendants for about two centuries and a half; but, at a very early period, a younger branch of the family appears to have settled at Whitfield, in the parish of Marwood, although how " William Bastard" (the owner of that estate in the reign of King John, and which had belonged, in 1086, to Robert de Albemarle, under whom it was held by "two Knights") became possessed of it, is not apparent, but in view of the ultimate devolution of both " Efford " and " Hazard," it is noteworthy that the said Robert de Albemarle‡ was also the Norman owner of two out of four manors in this county, alike known as " Witleie."

William Bastard was succeeded at Whitfield by his son Richard, known as " Richard de Witefell," and as Witefell, or Whitfield, his posterity remained at Marwood until about the year 1460, when the property passed to John Garland, by marriage with a co-heir of Whitfield.§

There were originally, as there are still, two manors in

---

* *Holinshed* (1577), p. 3. *Stowe* (1598), p. 107.
† Brompton, *Abbot of Jervaux*, A.D. 1200-1284.
‡ This may account for Burke's assertion as to an "intermarriage with Damarell."
§ The other co-heir married Hensleigh.

Egg-Buckland known as "Efford," which, in Saxon times, belonged respectively to "Brismar" and to "Alwin." The one was held, in 1086, by "Robert," under Baldwin de Brion, as parcel of the barony of Okehampton, the other by "Robert le Bastard," as tenant-in-chief from the Crown, and it is both possible, and probable, that this "Robert" was a natural son of the said Baldwin de Brion, and was thus distinctively described in the Survey to prevent confusion between him and his half-brother, Robert Fitz-Baldwin, the governor of Brion in Normandy.

It is not therefore surprising to find that several of "Robert le Bastard's" manors soon ceased to be identified with him, probably by their settlement upon his junior descendants, who, as Richard Bastard evidently did in the reign of Henry III., preferred to be known, henceforward, by the name of their lands; thus "Stanhus" (West-Stonehouse) was, as Risdon says, "the lands of one sirnamed Stonehouse until the latter end of King Edward the third's reign," and "Joel de Stonehouse" gave his own name to "Hepeston," which since the reign of King Henry III. has been known as "East-Stonehouse."

The subsequent owners of Batson, in the parish of Malborough, another of Robert Bastard's manors, were known as "De Batson," Peter de Batson having been settled there in King John's reign. The co-heirs of Batson married Beare and Davelle, and eventually the daughter and heir of John Davelle brought the property to Harris, from which latter family it was *purchased* by the late Edmund Pollexfen Bastard, M.P., who died in 1838.

But the Manors of Efford and "Herwarsore," or "Haroldesore," since known as Hazard, with other property, remained in what was doubtless the elder line of Bastard, and belonged to Sir Nicholas Bastard, Kt., the fourth of his name at Efford, in the year 1242; to Sir Richard Bastard of Efford, presumably his son and heir, in 1265; and to Sir Baldwin Bastard, Kt., of Efford, as late as the eighth year of the reign of Edward II., 1314; and after him the name of Bastard for considerably more than a century and a half disappears entirely from our county records.

I have already mentioned that the Manors of *Whitfield* and *Whitleigh both* belonged to Robert de Albemarle in the eleventh century, that the former of them became the residence of William Bastard in the reign of King John, and that his posterity were afterward known as "de Whitfield"; I may therefore consistently venture to suggest that the "Roger de Whitleigh" who was the owner of Efford in 1345, and for whose presence there our county historians have hitherto been unable to account, had simply inherited Efford, as heir-at-law, upon the decease of Sir Baldwin Bastard.

This "Roger de Whitleigh" of Efford, who was also the owner of Hazard, or "Haroldsore" (and otherwise variously written), in Harberton parish, was probably the direct descendant, through William Bastard of Marwood, of Robert le Bastard, the Norman tenant *in capite* of both these manors. He married Margaret, daughter and heir of Robert Beauden, Lord of Egg-Buckland, by Joan, his wife, daughter and heir of Nicholas Halton, and his descendants, the Whitleighs, were Lords of the two Effords and of Egg-Buckland for seven generations afterward, when the daughters and heirs of Richard Whitleigh of Efford, Joan and Margaret, married respectively Richard Hals of Kenedon and John Grenville of Stowe. Efford descended in the Hals family for many generations, until, with one of the co-heirs of Matthew Hals, it passed in marriage to Trelawny, and was afterward sold to Mr. William Clark of Plymouth, in whose family it still remains.

The primary settlement of a family of the name of Bastard, in the neighbourhood of Kingsbridge, may possibly have been due to the marriage of a certain Thomas Bastard with the daughter and heir of Thomas Ley, *alias* "At-Ley," of Leigh, in the adjacent parish of Churchstow, whose son John, or grandson of the same name, appears to have resided at Wolston, a few miles distant, in the parish of West Allington. Westcote, and Risdon, his contemporary, evidently after very cursory investigations of facts, have given the Manor of Wolston to the Bastards through a marriage with Crispin, and Westcote carelessly affirms that the "co-heir of that tribe was espoused to Baldwin le Bastard," and thus the possession of the property by John Bastard (who was fourth in descent from Thomas Bastard, and the heiress of Leigh, and died in 1634), in Risdon's time, would seem to conclusively prove his descent from Sir Baldwin Bastard of Efford, who must have died about the year 1315, whereas Thomas Bastard, the first ascertained ancestor of the Bastards of West Allington, could not have been born prior to 1460.

Moreover, the "heiress of Crispin" did *not* marry into the Bastard family—an error casually suggested in the *Magna Britannia*,* on the authority of Sir Wiliam Pole, who is quite wrong, however, as to the ownership, of Wolston, by "Stretch," through the heiress of Crispin aforesaid, although the Stretchs certainly were the owners of Wolston in succession to Crispin, as I have fully explained elsewhere.†

Richard Crispin, the last of his name at Wolston, married Arondella, eldest daughter and co-heir of John Arundell of Little Hempston, and had two sons only, who both died in infancy. Consequently Wolston, with other property, passed, by devise of said Richard and Arondella, to the latter's younger sister, Joan, wife of Walter de Bradestone, who is shown by the " Fine Rolls " to have been living in 1324.

The daughter and heir of the latter was the mother of Sir John Stretch, Kt., of Little Hempston and Wolston, whose son, Thomas Stretch, of Pinhoe, Little Hempston, and Wolston, was succeeded, through failure of issue, by his sisters, Elizabeth, wife of Thomas Beauchamp, of Lillesdon, co. Somerset, who seems to have had the Wolston property ; and Cicely, whose son, John Cheney (the offspring of her second marriage), succeeded to Pinhoe and Little Hempston.

Westcote, under " East Allington," which he admits, in a final parenthesis, he has confused with "West Allington," says, "wherein John de Rake held some land, and also the family of Bastard, of whose original some will perchance imagine the worst : be it so; yet the Duke, with whom he came into England, disdained not the title, and of this family there have been divers worthy men, as Sir Nicholas le Bastard de Efford, in this county, Kt., and continueth in worshipful estate to this age ; and therefore I think this name to be given for some other cause, for Wisdom saith, ch. iv. 3, ' *Spuria vitulamina non agent radices altas*,' which you see this doth and flourisheth." The Bastard

---

* Vol. ii., p. 6.   † *Devonshire Parishes*, vol. ii., pp. 58, 59.

genealogy, however, is not included in this author's "Pedigrees of most of the Gentry" of the county, which were continued to the end of the seventeenth century, by John Prince. In a list of the "Gentry of Devonshire, with their residences, about the commencement of the seventeenth century," the names of Bastard, Clavill, Culme, and Urflet are inserted, but in these four cases only their "residences" are not mentioned.

The Bastards did not record their descent at either of the earlier Visitations of the county. A pedigree of four generations only, and which is unsigned, is to be found in the original Visitation of 1620, and runs thus :—" Thomas Basterd," married, and had issue " John Bastard, sonne and heir," father of " John Bastard, sonne and heir," who married " Thomazine, daughter of Geffry Gilbert," and had issue " John Bastard, sonne and heir; Richard Bastard, 2 sonne; William Bastard, 3 sonne of Gerston, Recorder of Totnes, and Reader of the Midle Temple, living 1620," and who, it may be presumed, entered this very short and unsatisfactory record of his descent and connections. We have, through it, however, direct evidence that this "William Bastard" was of Gerston, in the parish of West Allington, otherwise Alvington, and he was doubtless also of Wolston, in the same parish, which certainly belonged to the Bastards in the reign of James I., although there is no mention of any such property in their recorded pedigree, as shown above.[*] He represented Dartmouth in Parliament in 1601. He died, without issue, on the 10th March, 1639, and was buried two days later at West Allington.[†] He was succeeded by his grand nephew and namesake, William Bastard, then in his twenty-third year, having been born 10th November, 1616, and baptized the same day at West Allington. He was the second son of John Bastard, deceased, by his wife, Alice Reynell, of Malston, eldest son of Joseph Bastard, of Dulo, in Cornwall, younger brother of the "Recorder of Totnes," whose name is not included in the Visitation of 1620, but has been interpolated in a later hand upon one or more of the copies of that of 1564,[‡] and this addition

---

[*] Wolston was subsequently the property of the Dukes of Bolton, Ext., 1794. Gerston has remained in the family of Bastard.
[†] Will dated 4th March, 1638-9, proved 10th May, 1639, P.C.C.
[‡] Rawlinson MS., Bib. Bod., Oxon., Colby, *Visit.*, 1564, p. 13.

makes no mention whatever of his brothers, but, according to it, his wife was "Ann, daughter of John Kelly, of Westworth, in Cornwall." According to the original Visitation record (1620) of that county, she was "daughter and heir of John Killyow, of Dulo."

His aforesaid grandson, William Bastard, married, in 1635, Joan, daughter of Sampson Hele, and had, with other issue, a third son, Sampson Bastard, born 1643, who was afterward Fellow of Exeter College, Oxford, 1664-1670, and Rector of Southpool, in the chancel of which church he was buried in 1676; and a son and heir, William Bastard, who was knighted at Whitehall in or about the year 1676. William Bastard, the elder, appears to have been Sheriff of Devon in the 22nd of Charles I., 1646,* and to have been followed in that office by Edmund Parker, of Boringdon. He was buried at West Allington 25th February, 1664.

His said eldest son, Sir William Bastard, of Gerston, married Grace, daughter of Sir John Bamfield, first Baronet, by Gertrude, daughter of Amias Coplestone.† He represented the borough of Beer-Alston in Parliament in 1678, and died in 1690, when he was succeeded at Gerston by his third but eldest surviving son, William Bastard, born 1667, who married Anne, daughter and heir of Edmund Pollexfen, of Kitley, in the parish of Yealmpton, and was buried at West Allington in February, 1704. His son and heir, Pollexfen Bastard, of Gerston, succeeded his mother, (whose father had died in 1710), at Kitley, in 1724; he married Lady Bridget, daughter of John, first Earl Poulett, and was buried at Yealmpton in 1733. Lady Bridget Bastard continued to occupy Gerston until her own death in 1773, since which the house has been customarily occupied by the tenant of the

---

* This is the *first mention* of any Sheriff of the name of Bastard, and the only one, in the list from which I quote, down to 9th Geo. I. (1722). According to Risdon's list of the sheriffs, but one of the name of Bastard occurs from the Conqueror to 50th Geo. III., 1809, viz., "Sir William Bastard," who is there said to have *replaced Edmund Parker*, who replaced John Arscott in "28th Charles II." (1676), and to have been himself replaced by Thomas Reynell in 1677. The fact seems to have been that John Arscott died during his shrievalty, but on 22nd September, 1675, his duties were taken up by his nephew and executor, "John Arscott, Esq.," but possibly Sir William and Ed. Parker may have acted for said executor to the end of the year.

† According to Vivian, *Visitation* (additions), p. 5~ his wife was "Grace daughter of Copplestone."

surrounding estate. The sheltered garden was long famous for its orange trees.

Pollexfen Bastard, of Kitley, was succeeded by his eldest surviving son, William Bastard, who was born at Kitley in 1727. Upon the appearance of the combined French and Spanish fleets off Plymouth, 16th August, 1779, Mr. Bastard offered the Governor to raise five hundred volunteers, and was thus an actual originator of the volunteer forces of this country; his regiment was complete and officered by the 19th of the month, and on the 23rd Colonel Bastard, with his gallant following, set out from Plymouth in charge of thirteen hundred prisoners of war, and duly handed them over to the officer in command at Exeter on the 25th. For this very notable, and truly patriotic service, King George III., without consulting the colonel, signed a warrant for a baronetcy in his favour, which was duly gazetted on the following 24th Sept., but as no steps were ever taken for expediting the patent, the title has never been assumed by him or his descendants. By his wife, Anne, daughter of Thomas Worsley, of Hovingham, co. York, he left two sons, John Pollexfen, and Edmund. The latter married Jane, daughter and heir of Philemon Pownall, of Sharpham, and thus acquired that beautiful property on the river Dart.*

The eldest son, John Pollexfen Bastard, born 18th September, 1756, at Kitley, was also of Buckland Court,† near Ashburton, over seven hundred acres of which delightfully picturesque property he converted into its present magnificently timbered woods. He married Sarah Wymondesold,‡ a widow, of Lockinge, co. Berks. He was sometime M.P. for the county, and died, without issue, 4th April, 1816.

He was succeeded by his nephew, Edmund Pollexfen, eldest son of Edmund Bastard of Sharpham, who was born in 1784, and married, in 1824, the Honourable Anne Rodney, daughter of the second Lord Rodney, and had three sons; he also represented the county in Parliament, and died, at his house in Cavendish Square, 8th June, 1838. His eldest son, Edmund

---

* See my *Devonshire Parishes*, vol. i., p. 312.
† See my *Ashburton and its Neighbourhood*, pp. 49 *et seq.*
‡ Her maiden name, I believe, was Bruton, of the Yeo branch of that family. See *ante*, "Bruton, of Yeo."

Rodney Pollexfen Bastard, was then a minor, in his thirteenth year, and afterward married Florence Mary, daughter of Simon Scrope of Danby, but on his death, without issue, 12th June, 1856, he was succeeded by his next brother, Baldwin John Pollexfen Bastard, then a subaltern in the 9th Regiment, and who is the present owner of Kitley and of Buckland Court.

Mr. Bastard, who was born 11th March, 1830, was educated at Winchester and Balliol College, Oxford, is a Deputy Lieutenant for Devon, served the office of Sheriff of the county in 1865, and for some years commanded the 4th Battalion D.R.V. He married, in 1861, his cousin, Francis Jane, youngest daughter of the Honourable Mortimer Rodney, by whom he has no issue. His younger brother, William Pollexfen Bastard, Clerk in Holy Orders, married, in 1869, Caroline, second daughter of Rear-Admiral Woolcombe of Hemerdon, and has, with other issue, a son, William Edmund Pollexfen Bastard, born 12th April, 1864.

Arms of Bastard—*Or*, a chevron *azure*, differenced with a martlet of the 1st (to denote descent from Joseph Bastard of Dulo, younger brother of William Bastard of Gerston, Recorder of Totnes, " living 1620.")

Crest—A dexter arm embowed in armour, grasping a sword, in bend sinister, point downward, all ppr., pommel and hilt *or*.
Motto—" Pax Potion Bello."

NOTE —According to Burke, *Landed Gentry*, edit. 1858, the Bastards of Charlton Marshall, co. Dorset, descended from Thomas Bastard of Bellchalwell, in said county, by his wife, Bridget, sister of Thomas Creech, the poetical translator of Lucretius, etc., etc. and who committed suicide at Oxford in 1700, bear these very ancient Arms of Bastard, undifferenced. And for Crest, " a griffin's head, collared and armed *or*."

DISCLAIMERS.

A list of those whose Pedigrees, by reason of insufficient proof, or for other causes, were "*disclaimed, ignobiles*," by William Camden, Clarenceux King of Arms, through his deputies, Henry St. George, Richmond Herald, and Sampson Lennard, Bluemantle Pursuivant of Arms, at the Visitation of Devonshire, A.D. 1620.*

		DISCLAIMED AT
77.	Alford, John, Zeale Monachorum	Barnstaple.†
23.	Allerston *alias* Searle, John,' Kingsteignton	Exeter.
88.	Amy, Edward, Tiverton	Tiverton.
20.	Austin, Robert, Chudleigh	Exeter.
61.	Avent, Thomas,* Brixton	Tavistock.
76.	Avery, William, Downe St. Mary	Barnstaple.
52.	Axworthy, John,* Brent-Tor	Tavistock.
24.	Babb, Christopher, Teigngrace	Exeter.
6.	Babb, William, Doddiscombsleigh	,,
39.	Ball, Nicholas,' Townstall	Totnes.
46.	Barley, Thomas, Bigbury	,,
68.	Barnefield, John, Buckland Brewer	Barnstaple.
96.	Barton, Henry, Silverton	Tiverton.
95.	Berrie, John,' Kentisbeare	,,
90.	Blakedon, John, Loxbeare	,,
99.	Boremonte, James,* Hemyock	,,
28.	Bound, Jeffery, Hempston	Totnes.
29.	,, John, Ipplepen	,,
32.	,, Peter, Torbrian	,,
55.	Brewer, John,* Tavistock	Tavistock.
17.	Burgoine, Michael,' Tedburn St. Mary	Exeter.
86.	Catford, William,' Hockworthy	Tiverton.
100.	Chant, Francis,' Chumleigh	,,
66.	Chapman, Arthur, Buckland Brewer	Barnstaple.
67.	Chappell, Robert,' Langtree	,,
80.	Chollacombe, Thomas, Combe Martin	,,
69.	Cliff, Robert, Merton	,,

* Extracted from MS. Harl. 1080, fo. 342. The numbers refer to the sequence of the names, in that list, which are not alphabetically arranged.
† The Court was held at Exeter on August 12th; at Totnes, August 26th; at Tavistock, September 1st; at Barnstaple, September 9th; and at Tiverton, September 18th, 1620. See *ante*, p. 313.

DEVONSHIRE WILLS. 501

		DISCLAIMED AT
31. Coldich, William (? Cholwich), Paignton	- -	Totnes.
19. Couse, William, Ide	- - - - -	Exeter.
22. Cove, Nicholas, Tawton Bishop	- - -	,,
12. Dart, Henry, Gidleigh	- - - - - -	,,
43. Dotting, Nicholas, Thurleston	- - -	Totnes.
72. Downe, Anthony, Woolfardisworthy	- -	Barnstaple.
81. Elston, John, St. Giles-in-the-Heath	- - -	,,
58. Eustace, Stephen², St. Budeaux	- - - -	Tavistock.
41. Foxworthy, Philip, Churston	- - -	Totnes.
102. Furse, John,¹ Nymet Regis	- - -	Tiverton.
45. Gay, John,¹ Aveton Gifford	- - -	Totnes.
54. Gery, John, Tavistock	- - - - -	Tavistock.
15. Gidley, George, St. Thomas nigh Exon.	- - -	Exeter.
75. Gidley, Hannibal, North Lew	- - -	Barnstaple.
13. Glanville, John,¹ Heavitree	- - - - -	Exeter.
50. Glass, Gawin, Ugborough	- - - -	Totnes.
11. Gorwyn, William, Sandford	- - - -	Exeter.
18. Gough, Richard, Topsham	- - - -	,,
1. Gover, Richard, Cheriton Fitz-Pain	- - -	,,
16. Harniman, Wm., S. Tawton	- - - -	,,
40. Harvey, Anthony,¹ North Huish	- - -	Totnes.
38. Hodge, William, Slapton	- - - -	,,
5. Hollacombe, John,¹ Crediton	- - -	Exeter.
79. Hooper (see Shepard).		
71. ,, William, Hartland	- - - -	Barnstaple.
37. Huxham, William, Harberton	- - -	Totnes.
101. Kelland, John, Chulmleigh	- - - -	Tiverton.
33. Lackington, John, Ashburton	- - -	Totnes.
7. Lee, William,¹ Sandford	- - - - -	Exeter.
14. ,, ,, ' Pinhoe	- - - - -	,,
78. Ley, Jasper, Atherington	- - - -	Barnstaple.
65. ,, Stephen, Buckland Brewer	- - -	,,
70. ,, Valentine, Little Torrington	- - -	,,
27. Lide, Allen,² Berry Pomeroy	- - - -	Totnes.
42. Maddock, Richard, South Brent	- - -	,,
82. Milton, William, Bampton	- - - -	Tiverton.
9. Mogridge, Tristram, Brampford Speke	- -	Exeter.
4. Moon, Thomas, Washfield	- - - -	,,
84. Norman, John, Clayhanger²	- - - -	Tiverton.
21. Paddon, John, Tawton Bishop	- - -	Exeter.
62. Pierce, Richard, Brixton²	- - - -	Tavistock.
47. ,, Thomas, Bigbury²	- - - -	Totnes.
97. Potter. Richard,¹ Silverton	- - - -	Tiverton.
48. Rich, Nicholas, Modbury	- - - -	Totnes.
87. Richards, John, Uffculme	- - - -	Tiverton.
56. Robins, Thomas, Bratton Clovelly	- - -	Tavistock.
30. Salter, Edward, Ipplepen	- - - -	Totnes.
23. Searle¹ (see Allerston).		
10. Seward, James,¹ Combintinhead	- - -	Exeter.
35. Sharpham, Thomas, Chivelston	- - -	Totnes.
79. Shepard *alias* Hooper, Robert, Bratton Fleming	-	Barnstaple.
74. Shute, William, Ashreigny	- - - -	,,
89. Skinner, John,¹ Loxbeare	- - - -	Tiverton.

		DISCLAIMED AT
93.	Skinner, Richard,¹ Cullompton	Tiverton.
53.	Sleeman, John, Milton Abbot	Tavistock.
44.	Slowley, Hugh,¹ Aveton Gifford	Totnes.
83.	Snow, Robert, Burlescombe	Tiverton.
25.	Sotherne, John, Teigngrace	Exeter.
85.	Southill, John, Clayhanger	Tiverton.
51.	Spratt, William, Ugborough	Totnes.
8.	Spurway, William,¹ Colebrook	Exeter.
49.	Swete, Adrian, Modbury	Totnes.
103.	Timewell, Thomas,² Rackenford	Tiverton.
36.	Tippett, Nicholas,² Harberton	Totnes.
57.	Tolley, Henry,² Okehampton	Tavistock.
91.	Toogood, John, Loxbeare	Tiverton.
63.	Treby, Henry, Treby ("Plympton Hundred")	Tavistock.
64.	Tucker, John Baptist, Bideford	Barnstaple.
26.	Tuckfield, Thomas, Tedburn St. Mary	Exeter.
98.	Vacey, John, Silverton	Tiverton.
94.	Venman, Gawen, Bradninch	„
59.	Walter, Richard,¹ Manadon	Tavistock.
73.	Westlake, Nicholas, Inwardleigh	Barnstaple.
2.	White, George,¹ Sandford and Exeter	Exeter.
3.	Wilson, George, Shobrooke	„
92.	Wolcott, Hugh,² Halberton	Tiverton.
60.	Worth, Walter,¹ Brixton	Tavistock.
34.	Yeabsley, Robert,² Blackawton	Totnes.

¹ Families thus marked, *but with whom the "disclaimed" failed to show their connection*, duly recorded their pedigrees.

² These names do not occur in the Visitation record, even incidentally.

CORRIGENDA.

Page 26.—For "1870" read *1670*.
,, 52.—First line of last paragraph, for "ninth" read *tenth*.
,, 103.—Line 1, for "brother Roger" read *uncle*.
,, 109.—One line from bottom, delete comma after "Walter."
,, 145.—General Bennett died Aug. 3rd, 1893.
,, 297. - Last line but one, for "Richard" read *Sir John*.
,, 339.—NOTE.—The first Eden Baronetcy did *not* become "extinct" in 1844, not "1841," but went to a cousin of the fifth Baronet, who was also fourth Baronet of the creation of 1776, and the present Baronet, Sir W. Eden, of West Auckland, has therefore two patents of Baronetcy, the first of them being dated 13th Nov., 1672.
,, 366.—End of second paragraph, for "1740" read *1640*.
,, 369.—Line 17, for "1769" read *1763*.
,, 373.—Line 11 from bottom, for "Pillhead" read *Pillhand*.
,, 374.—Line 3, for "Director Audit Department," read *Director H.M. Exchequer and Audit Department*.
,, 388.—Line 13, for "*minus*" read *plus*.
,, 416.—Line 9, for "St. John's College" read *Exeter College*, and line 13, for "Exeter" read *St. John's*.
,, 420.—Bottom line, for "SS. George and Lennard" read *St. George and Lennard*.
,, 499.—Last line before note, for "Potion" read *l'otior*.

NOTE.
Page 315.—Lines 4, 5, for "utmost probability" read *possibly*.
,, 315.—Line 10, for "King Stephen" read *Richard I*.
See *post*, page 418.

INDEX.

Abbe, 435
Abbott, 52, 103-77, 378-90-91, 435-36
Abraham, 29, 88, 138-58
Abrincis, 352
Acland (Ackland), 49, 248, 315, 413-29
ACLAND (Akeland-Akelane), 468-69-70-71-72-73-74
ADAM (Adams), 294-95-98
Adam (Adams-Addams), 38, 91, 109-16-28, 256-58-59-66-96, 428-55-90
Addicot, 155
Adobat, 357
Afeton, 442
Aghrim, 339
Aisse, 176
Albemarle, 395, 470-92-93
Albini, 360-61
Aldenham, 490-91
Alder, 80
Alford, 261-67, 452
Alfred (King), 433
Alfric, 336
Algar, 340
Allen, 120
Almar, 409
Alric, 377
Alured, 354-61
Aluric, 336
Alva, 329, 434
Alward, 332
Alwin, 493
Amerie (Amory), 69, 221
Andrews (Andrewes), 219-48
Anne (Queen), 52, 388
Anstey, 75
Anthony, 32
Archer, 124
Arcis, 475
Arderne, 301
Arnell, 90
Arnold, 216
Arscott, 275, 315-81, 497
ARUNDELL, 81, 103-20-22-27-34

Arundell, 119, 307, 463-95
Ashburton, 446-89
Ashe (Ayshe), 56, 132
Ashford (Ayshford-Ayshforde), 37, 315-42, 449
Ashmole, 106
Ashton, 406
Askew, 407
Atherton, 48
Atken (Atkin-Atkins), 47, 85, 369, 454
At-Ley, 491
Audley, 451
Aure (Awre), 255, 319
Avenel, 380-86, 437
Avis, 261
Axe, 40
Ayer (Ayre), 66, 148-64, 487
Aylmer, 466

Babbage, 267
Babbington, 462
Bach, 379
Bacon, 418-25
Bagworth, 371
Bailey, 236
BAKER, 123
Baker, 20, 40, 57, 132, 305
Balderstone, 80
Baldwin, 315, 419-75
Ball, 278, 315
Ballamy, 234
Ballemont, 6
Balliman (Ballyman), 77, 140-52, 237
Balun, 399, 4.0
Bamfeld (Bamfeild, Bamfield), 427-71-77 81-82-97
Bampfield (Bampfylde), 29, 70, 202, 439-47-91
BAMPFYLDE (Bampfeld, Bampfield), 474-75-77-78-79-80-81-82-83-84
Hampton, 448
Banbury, 39
Bandram, 93

Barbenson, 440
Bare (Beare), 150, 252-94, 447-70-93
Baring, 446
Baron, 39, 261, 381
Barre, 371, 462
Barrow, 168
Barry (Barry-Barry), 343-80
Barter, 191
BARTLETT (Bartlet), 109-10-11-12-13-14-15 - 16-51-67, 280
Bartlett, 108, 295-97-98, 303
Barton, 25, 175, 239
Barwick (Barwicke), 229-54
Basset, 47, 102, 261-75, 470-71
Bastard, 175, 243 49, 314, 459
BASTARD, 491-92-93-94-95-96-97-98-99
Bath (Earl of), 119
Batson, 493
Battell, 151
Battersby, 29
Battishell, 337-80
Battisholl, 263
Battyn (Battin), 293, 450
Baunfield (Baunfeld), 476-78-80
Bawden (Bawdon), 69, 74, 75, 263
Bayle, 176
Baylis, 324
Bearne, 293-94
Beauchamp, 52, 103, 376-91, 435-36-37-60 - 63-79-80, 495
Beauden, 494
Beauford, 124
Beaumont, 261, 341
Beauple, 469
Bedford, 282, 444
Bedlake, 99
Beedell, 176
Belfield, 295
Belknap, 422
Bellew, 153, 350

INDEX.

Bello Campo, 435
Bellomonte, 375-76-86
Belston, 375, 419-20-21-30
Bendall, 73
Bennett, 33, 145-66-98
Benolte, 312
Benson, 49
Berresford-Hope, 491
Berkeley, 149, 370-80, 487
Berne, 249
Bernville, 436
BERRY, 212
Berry (Berrye, Berrie), 90, 176, 263-64-66-68, 350
Berringe, 108
Besly, 29
Besse, 104-48
Bessilis, 491
Best, 37
Bevill, 437
Bickford, 167
Bickington, 443-47
Bicklie (Bicklye), 18, 107
Bicknell, 208
Bidlake, 315
Bidwell, 138
Biggleston, 321-22-23-24
Bildo, 18
Bilston, 429
Binford, 143
Bishop (Bishoppe, Byshop), 13, 42, 248, 407
Bisset, 379
BLACHFORD, 97
Blackaller, 135, 207
Blackford, 425
Blackmore, 25, 32, 205-30-37-40
Blake, 106-99, 228
Blakeford, 426
Blanchard, 254
BLATCHFORD, 93, 97
Blatchford, 100
Blewitt, 430
Bligh, 121
Blount (Blunt, Blund), 130, 370-71
Blundell, 476
Blyton, 153
Bobhyn, 147
Bobishe, 180
Bocher, 6
Bodley, 68, 119, 438
Boevey, 490
Bohun, 69, 348, 445
Bolitho, 142
Bollay, 479
BOLT, 122
Bolton (Duke of), 496
Bon, 411-31-42
Bonaparte, 341
BOND, 122
Bond, 54, 305

Bonithon, 110
Bonvile (Bonville), 349-50, 424-29-30-78-79
Boone, 74, 98
Booth, 340-43
Boothby, 389
Borde, 58
BORLACE (Borlase), 130-33-37-42
Borne, 8
Borough, 366 67-89
Borrowe, 173
Boscawen, 307, 466
Bosco, 319-32
Bosgrave, 103
Bosome, 424
Boteler, 128
Boteeford, 486
Bouchier, 350-93, 426 27
Bound (Bounde), 281-95, 304
Bowchair, 266
BOWDEN (Bowdon), 66
Bowden (Bowdon), 62, 142, 207-22 62-65, 452
Bowring, 348
Boys, 328-32
Bozun, 424-30
Braddon, 298
Bradestone, 495
Bradfelle, 448
Bradford, 186, 307
Bragg (Bragge), 76, 85, 199, 263-77-98
Brailey (Brayley, Brayly), 48, 71, 78
Brand, 42
Branple, 54
Branscombe, 309, 460-63
Braose, 362, 400-59
Braund, 63
Bray (Braye), 65, 259 98, 388
Bremelridge, 189
Bremelrigg, 414
BREMRIDGE, 293, 411-14-15-16-17
Bremridge (Bremerige), 304-59, 413-38
Brendon, 111
Bretellus, 357
Breten (Breton, Bretun), 354-62-68-72
Brethon, 364
Brett (Bret), 354-56-60-61-62-67-71, 450
Brettel, 362
Bretteville, 361-99
Breward, 19
Brewer, 212, 356-57-58
Brewsey, 96
Brian (Brion, Bryan), 30, 40, 273, 329-53-95, 419-20-23-30-93
Brice, 247
Brictric, 340
Bridgman, 124

Bridport, 223, 452
Bright, 56, 59
Brimcliffe, 22
Brindley (Brinley), 43, 130-50-65
Brismar, 493
BRITO, 351-53-54-55-56-57-58-59-60-61-63-64-65 68-71
Brito, 399, 400-18
Britolio, 352
Britt (Britte), 341-43 52-54-55-68
BRITTON, 370-71-73-74
Britton (Briton, Britten, Britayne, Bryttan), 362-64-72
Briwere, 345, 462
Broadmead, 44
Brocke, 84, 281
Brodbeare, 7
Broncecombe, 425
Brooke, 62, 68, 84, 388-89
Brookin, 324
Brooking, 50, 145 57, 343
Brown (Browne), 4, 89, 102-8-16-88-90, 224-63, 472
Browning, 10, 225
Brownsford, 151
Browse, 167
Bruerton, 362
BRUTON, 362-65-66-67-68-69-70
Bruton (Brutton), 159, 247, 315-72, 462-98
Bryannd, 38
Bryant, 64, 126
Bryatt (Briyatt), 73, 278
Buard, 242
Buckingham, 75, 467
Buckland, 148
Buckthought, 453
Buckyats, 453
Budd, 257-63
Budgood, 68
Bulleid, 61, 64, 67
Buller, 146, 296, 342, 483
Bulley, 297, 309
Bulmer, 347
Burdett, 406
Burge, 348
Burgess, 78, 79
Burgh, 422
Burgoyne, 369
Burhed, 361
Burke, 489
BURLACE, 137
Burn, 168
Burnaberie, 53
Burnaford, 89, 135
Burnell, 99, 372-79-86
Burrage, 196
Burridge, 42

INDEX.

Burroughs (Burrows), 25, 186
Burscough, 282
Burston, 6
Burton, 193, 213
Bury, 37, 287, 315, 461
Bushill, 82
Bussell, 13, 214
Butcher, 226-82
Butford, 32
Butsan, 19
Butstone, 12
Butter, 248
Button, 371
Byllyck, 302
Bynford, 252
Bysshe, 396-97, 487
Bytton, 371

Call, 138
Callard, 76, 211
Calmady, 296, 315, 402-39
Calverleigh, 209
Calvo Monte, 346
Calwoodleigh, 209
Camden, 469
Camill, 380
Campbell, 467
Campion, 283
Campo Arnulphy, 346
Cancy, 329
Cane, 93
Canham, 127
Cann (Canne), 8, 275
Cannington, 37
Cantilupe, 319-62, 400-29-30
Canute (Knut), 317-32
Capel, 80
Capron, 18
CAREW, 56
Carew, 302-15, 454-83
CAREY (Cary, Carye), 122-25-27-34
Carey, &c., 116-30 51, 315-69-83, 403-23-24
Carlingford, 468
Carlyon, 373
Carminow, 435
Carnegie, 408
CARNELL, 301
Carpenter, 186
Carr, 389
Carrickfergus, 342
CARSLEGHE, 157
Carter, 276, 402
CARWITHEN, 47, 48, 51
Carwithen, 124, 452
CARWITHY, 124
Casely, 276
Castell, 394
Castlehaven, 380
Castlyn, 5
Caswyll, 5
Caundle, 3-9

Caunter, 94, 96
Causbeuf, 425
Cave, 18, 388
Ceely, 279
Cerdic, 331, 433
Cha, 174
Chafe (Chaffe), 287, 314-19-20-21-22-23-24 - 25-26-27-28-29
Chafecombe, 318
CHAFY (Chafie, Chaffie, Chafye), 316-20-28-29-30
Challons, 429-30
Chamberlain (Chamberlyn), 198, 375
Chammond, 346
Champernowne, 260. 346, 435-58-59
Champneys (Champneis), 136, 416
CHAPELL (Chapple), 273-75
Chapell, 39, 42, 183
Chapman, 25, 38, 148, 232
Chardon, 258
Charlemagne, 432
Charles I, 121-27, 497
Charles II., 70, 127, 252, 313, 427-97
Charleton, 477
Chase, 226
Chastor, 91
Chave, 222-33-46
Chawerth, 462
Chears, 145, 235
Cheeke, 152-53
Cheney, 495
Cherriton, 162
Chester (Earl of), 395, 436
CHEVERSTONE, 386-87-89-90
Cheverstone, 375-77-79, 424
Cheyney, 481
Chichester, 130-33, 315-38-41-42-93, 428 - 55, 465
Chilcote (Chilcott), 34, 196
Chollashe, 19
Cholwill, 111
Chudleigh, 342
Churchward, 108-38, 295
Churly, 13, 17
Cisard, 93
Clapp, 154-68
Clare, 46, 130, 367-68, 425-36
Clark (Clarke), 75, 108-19-67-96, 214 - 22 - 25, 29-47-70, 494
Clatworthy, 29
Clavill, 496
Clemens, 29

Cleverton, 97
Clieve, 107
CLIFFORD, 123
Clifford, 315-59, 442-70-82
Clift, 97
Clifton, 481-84
Clinton, 466-67
Clipit, 57
Clode, 146
Clokye, 176
Clotworthy, 62
Clutterbrook, 152
Coad (Coade, Coades, Code), 104 - 46-47-60-88, 395-96
Cobham (Cobbam), 389, 479
Coblye, 58
Cock (Cocke), 44, 99, 230-35-93
Cockram, 315
Codner, 41, 188, 241
Codrington, 455-83
Coffin, 314-84, 400
Cogan, 348
Cokayne, 490
Coke, 124
Coketrewe, 414
Cole (Coles), 1, 65, 69, 105-28, 237, 346, 414
Coll (Colle, Colles), 97, 274, 426-54
Collacot, 339
Collard, 83
Colley, 416
Collier, 115
Collihole, 11
Colling (Collings), 85, 219-78
Collins, 24, 28, 65, 114, 214-86
Culman, 62, 285
Combe, 54
Comer, 6, 54
Comin (Commin, Comyn) 56, 98, 105, 250-71
Commins (Comyns), 75, 79, 144, 294
Compton, 297, 328-29, 434
Conant (Connante), 9, 138, 231-36-76, 405
Condy, 137, 284
Conebee (Coneby), 39
CONETT, 7
Connett, 11, 243-45
CONNAUNTE, 6
CONNAUTE, 8
Conocke, 410
Conteville, 348-95
Cooban, 97
Coodeney, 16
Cook (Cooke), 24, 267-74, 315, 441
Coombe, 182
Coome, 271

Coote, 455
Copp, 184
Copplestone, 479-80-82-
  83-97
Corbyn, 329
Cornish, 65, 83, 120-39,
  255-86, 398
Cornwall, 345-95, 433-58-
  59-62
Cornworthy, 184
Corrain, 37
Corsett, 378
Coryton, 455
Cotley, 275
Cottihole, 69
Cottle, 126
Cotton, 366-69
Coulton, 90
Countenay, 111
Courey, 345
COURTENAY, 121
Courtenay (Courtney), 4,
  69, 110, 262, 307-43-
  44-55-77-79-87, 389 -
  90 - 93, 424-33-37-42-
  45-52, 469-70-73-75
Courthill, 88
Coutance (Bishop of),
  332-59, 411-41
Coutance, 412
Coward, 343
Cowlin (Cowlen), 228-
  32-34
Cowling, 284
Cowyll, 118
Cox (Coxx, Coxe), 181,
  243, 396
Crabb, 109-26
Craddick (Cradocke), 54,
  234
Cranfield, 393
Crawley, 490
Creech, 499
Crewys, 346
Crispin, 134, 494-95
Croc, 364
Crocker, 56, 59, 252
Crockwell, 309
Croke, 56
Croker, 40
Cromwell, 472
Crook (Crook), 18, 76
Croome, 132
Croote, 83
Cross (Crosse), 39, 138-
  69-74-90, 221-68-81-
  402
Cruse, 281
Crutchard, 20
Crutchett, 191
Crute, 277
Cruwys, 49, 469
Cubitt, 461
Cudlipe, 85
Cullen, 490
Culme, 413-70-96
Cumbe, 221

Cundett, 97
CUNDYE, 83
Cunniby, 226
Curell, 162-64
Cursane, 322
Curson, 324
Curton, 321-24
Cutcliff, 155
Cuttaford, 25
Cuttiford, 26

Dabernon, 486
D'Abrincis, 395
Dacus, 485
Dagworthy, 196, 206
Dalditch, 434
Daley, 35, 210-12
Dally, 69, 231-33
Dallynge, 57
Damarell (Damerell),
  191, 395, 443-91
D'Amneville, 370-71
Dan, 485
Daniel, 472
D'Anvers, 283
Dapifer, 319
Darcy, 180
Dare, 248
Darke, 20, 169
Dart, 443-47
Daubeny, 360-61
Davelle, 493
Davide (Davids), 26, 58
Davis (Davys, Davise,
  Davies), 38, 109, 217
Davy (Davey, Davie,
  Davye), 29, 58, 102-
  19, 207-11-27
Daw, 265
Dawley, 214
Dawson-Damer, 467
Dayment, 68
Deament, 259
Deane, 372
Decble, 285
Delawarr, 362
Delliff, 118
Denard, 67
Dene, 279
Denet, 162
Denford, 82
Dennaford, 139
Dennis (Denis, Denys,
  Dennys), 6, 61, 81,
  153, 213-37, 349-50,
  427-29-30-85-86-91
Denny, 121
Densell, 464-65-66-67
DENSHAM, 61, 72, 252-
  53-99
Densham, 186
D'Este (Queen Mary), 406
D'Eu, 441
Devenish, 453-54
Devereux, 330

Devon (Earl of), 261, 344-
  87, 445-71
Dewdney, 237-44
Dhu, 416
Dickenson, 452
Dicker, 222
Digby, 439
Dillon, 451
Dinham (Dinhame, Dyn-
  ham), 81, 342-95, 480
Dingle, 237
Dodarig, 414
Dodd, 105, 269
Doddescombe (Doddis-
  combe), 261-97, 328-64,
  434-35
Dodge, 29
Dodridge, 175
Doidge, 135
Dollinge, 185
Domett, 139
Donington, 436
Doorleyne, 120
Douay, 333, 432-48
Doubt, 296
Doune, 302
Doust, 295
Dovor, 345
Dowdney, 194-99
Dowell, 271
Downe, 32, 42, 61, 132-
  77-78, 302
Downing (Downinge), 58,
  88, 181
Dowrish, 443
DRAKE, 5, 129, 265
Drake, 18, 166, 249, 316,
  482
Drax, 380
Drew (Drewe), 54, 116-
  23-49, 220-41-77, 359-
  66, 412-13-43-47-55-73-
  87
Driscoll, 129
Drogo, 441-42
Dromant, 65
Drury, 484
Druscombe, 187
Duck, 470
Duckham, 16
Dudley, 383, 438
Duelly, 170
Duke, 404-51
Dummitt, 46
Dunn, 80, 168
Dunning, 398, 489
Durant, 139
Dutton, 442
Dyer, 150, 237
Dyke, 473
Dymoke, 454
Dysteley, 329

Eales, 94
Early, 71
Eastabrook, 290

INDEX. 507

Eastchurch, 125
Eastcot, 220
Easterbrook, 200
Eastridge, 150
Ebrington, 467
Eccelin, 469
Eden, 339
Edgar (King), 282
Edgina, 433
Edgcombe (Edgcumbe), 97, 237, 428
Edmonstone, 408
Edward, 147
Edward I., 46, 319-64-78, 401-26-45-68-76-77-78
Edward II., 106, 345, 426-69-78-93
Edward III., 332,420-27-34-36-69-77-93
Edward IV., 336, 414-86
Edward VI., 157, 469
Edward the Black Prince, 469
Edward the Confessor, 317-32-36-97, 417
Edward the Martyr, 282
Edwards, 84, 91, 148-70, 274
Edwin, 416-19
Eisforde, 342
Eleanor of Castile, 69, 331
ELFORD, 82
Elford, 466
Elfritha, 282
Elizabeth (Queen), 1, 4, 121, 321, 414-27-81-86
Ellat, 176
Ellicomb (Ellicombe), 84, 398
Elliot, 6, 137-48, 270, 406
Ellis, 248-60, 347
Elmslie, 335
Elworthy, 215-19
Emling, 167
Emma (Queen), 317
Emmett, 95
Empson, 438
Enckledon, 306
Endell, 12, 175
Enty, 44, 154, 231
Erchenbold, 314
Erkenwald, 392
Erle, 380
Erlye, 29
Eiroll, 389
Erskine, 474
Esserye, 17
Esworthy, 189, 304
Ethelred, 282, 317-18
Eton, 104-47-48
EVELEIGH, 8
Eveleigh (Evelleighe), 9-38

EVANS, 25, 29, 30, 32, 34, 45
Evans, 33, 51, 138-52, 227-39-65
Evens, 109
Eweine, 274

Ewen, 187, 274
Ewin (Ewins, Ewings), 44, 165
Exeter (Bishop of), 121
Faber, 447-80-84
Fabyan, 163
Face (fface), 119
Facie, 5
Fairfax, 427-72-82
Falaise, 395
Falwell, 460
Fane, 393, 403
Farechilde, 252
Faringdon, 405
Farrer, 446
Farthinge, 41
Fenton, 486
Ferdinand of Castile, 446
Fermanagh, 388
Fernac, 462
Ferrers, 330-87, 436-86
FERRIS, 157
Ferris (Ferries), 25, 241-42-43
Feseye, 83
Fewins, 78
ffaris, 85-89
Finney (ffiney), 71-72, 136, 295
ffole, 92
ffolette, 26
FFUGARS, 6
ffures, 64
Fiennes, 416
Fillmore, 25
Finch, 383-86
Finnimore, 229
Fishacre, 449
Fisher, 254
Fitz-Alan, 463
Fitz-Alured, 364
Fitz-Anger, 356
Fitz-Angerii, 358
Fitz-Asculph, 432
Fitz-Baldwin, 493
Fitz-Eustace, 449
Fitz-Gamelin, 475
Fitz-Geoffrey, 442
Fitz-George, 430
Fitz-Hardinge, 370
Fitz-Hoel, 352
Fitz-Hugh, 317
Fitz-Hugo, 318
Fitz-John, 329
Fitz-Mauger, 189, 359, 411-12-13-14
Fitz Osborne, 399
Fitz-Payne, 426-32-33-40

Fitz-Paynel, 432
Fitz-Ponz, 359, 412
Fitz-Ralph, 318
Fitz-Ranulph, 318
Fitz-Reginald, 317-18
Fitz-Robert, 318, 433
Fitz-Stephen, 348, 491
Fitz-Turolf, 348,
Fitz-Urse, 422-23-28-29-30
Fitz-Walter, 367-68, 442
Fitz-Warine, 360-93
Fitz-William, 357
Flaycross, 14
Fleming(Flemyng, Ffleming), 93, 169, 350
Flood, 192-94, 249
Floyd, 247
Floyer, 237
Folker, 58
Follett, 210
Force (fforce), 149-50, 305, 415
FORD, 283-95
Ford (fford), 77, 80, 110-16-75, 277, 373-78, 414-16-17
Fort (Forte), 456-58-62
Fortescue, 46, 315-47, 403-6-39-51-69-88
FORTESCUE, 456-58-59-60-61-62-63-64-65-66-67-68
Foss (Fosse), 59, 77, 227-67
Foswell, 151
Fowell, 255
Fownes, 445
Fox, 128
Fox, 40, 83, 138, 309
Framingham, 165
Franc, 435
Francis, 446
Francklinge, 82
Frankpitt, 35, 218
Fratrum, 428
Frec, 143
French, 11, 100-34, 206-90
Freville, 261
Friend, 254
Frobisher, 316
Frost (Ffrost), 43, 118, 242
Froude, 343
FRY (Frye), 177-78-79-81 - 97, 210-11-12-69-76-79-81-82-83-84-85-86-95-98, 302-6-7
Fry (Frye), 44, 392, 439
FULFORD, 417-19-20-21-21-22-23-24-25-26-27-30
Fulford, 341
Fulthorp, 422
Furlong, 56, 439
Furneaux, 116

Fursdon, 15, 315
Furse, 46, 49, 64, 90, 296, 439
Furser, 245
Fursman, 89, 164

Gage, 372-73
Galard (Galerd), 30, 38
Gale, 213
Galfred, 352
Galland, 297
Galpine, 428
Gammon, 268
GANDY, 152
Gandy, 132-40-51-54
Gardiner, 184
Garland, 274, 492
Garnfit, 107
Garnsey, 181
GATTEY, 50
Gaunicliffe, 22
Gay (Gaye), 84, 406
Geare, 7, 231
GEARING, 67
Gefford, 95
Gell, 372
Genney, 68
Gennys, 137
George I., 497
George II., 49
George III., 49, 497-98
German, 290
Gerrard, 226
Ghent, 346
Gibbens, 22
GIBBS (Gib, Gibb, Gibbe, Gibbes, Gybbe), 10, 14, 20, 22, 23, 24, 42, 43, 44, 50, 51, 103-4-23-30 - 38-40-46-47-48-49-50 - 51-52-53-54-55-59-60-65-69-70,85-86-87-88-89-90-91
Gibbs, &c., 80, 132-33-41
GIDLEY, 394-96-98-99
Gidley (Gidleigh), 395
Gifford (Giffard) 92, 380-81-82, 489
Gilbert, 298, 328, 479-91-96
Giles, 276, 315
Gill, 126-53-87, 230-36
Gillard (Gillord),150, 274
Githa, 336
Glanfield, 200
Glanville, 282, 392
Glass, 35, 212-66
Glenvile, 221
Gloucester (Duke of), 393
GLOVER, 203
Glover, 17, 178, 278, 440
Glynn (Glynne), 339, 423
Goche, 189
Godfrey, 23, 150, 201
Godolphin, 7, 445
Godrick, 408

Godsland, 72
Godwin, 394
Gold, 198-99
Goldsworthy, 14
Goodridge, 28, 113
Goolde, 173
Gorges, 121-27, 347
Goring, 121
Gough, 306
GOULD, 87, 114-61-63
Gould, 84, 126, 247-74-81
Goulsworthy, 130
Govett, 245
Graas, 443
Grahame, 406
GRANGER (Graunger), 19, 36,129-35-39-40-42-43-62-64-65-66-67-68, 282
GRANVILLE, 308
Granville, 285-96, 309, 411-12
Gray, 87
Greane, 18
Gred, 55
Green, 44, 154, 231-33-36
Greenfield (Greenfeilde), 294, 307
Greenslade, 298
GREGORY, 265
Gregory, 172
GREGSON, 141, 265
Gregson, 152
Grendon, 105
GRENFIELD (Grenfeild, Greenfeild), 294-96
GRENVILE, 306
Grenvile (Grenville), 81, 345-47-66, 494
Griffin (Griffen), 58, 162
Grigg, 96
Grimbaldus, 425
GRINFELD, 293
Gubb (Gubbs), 262, 338
Gye, 175, 292
GYLES, 122

HACCHE, 257
Haccombe, 147
Haddridge, 19
Hager, 64
Hake, 18, 24, 451
Hakworthy, 139
Haldon, 164
Hale, 120, 454
Halkwill, 205
Hall, 132-52-54, 226, 451
Hal'es, 9
Hallet, 236
Hals (Halse), 102, 347, 494
Halsey, 173
Halswell, 445-47
Halswothy, 67
Halton, 494

Halwell, 353-87-88-89
Ham, 285
Hambridge, 328
Hambrigge, 328
Hameline, 399
Hames, 340
Hamilton, 373
HAMLYN (Hamlyne, Hamlin, Hamline, Hameline, Hamling, Hambling, Hamblyn, Hamlinge), 6, 14, 18, 61, 63, 85, 86, 88, 89, 90, 91, 92, 93, 94, 95, 96, 98, 99, 100, 101, 102-58, 250-51-52-53-54-56-58-60 - 61-63-64-78-79-81-84 - 86-88-89-90-91, 399, 401-402-403
Hamlyn (Hamling), 22, 45
Hamlyn - Williams, 61, 403
HAMMETT, 253
Hammett (Hamett), 196, 207, 403
Hamon, 306
Hamond, 262, 350
Hampton, 371, 479
Hancock, 55, 193
Handcock, 410
Hander, 116
Handford, 307
Hanham, 380
Hankford, 347-93
Hanniford, 163
Hanver, 254
Hardinge, 197
Hardrada, 419
Hare, 136
Harford, 229
Harlotta, 395, 492
Harman, 106
Harness, 48
Harold (King), 336
Harrett, 62
Harries, 196
Harris, 43, 48, 55, 59, 73, 78, 79, 83, 136-43. 210-16-28 - 37 - 38-50, 342, 493
Harrison, 151
Harrowhy, 246
Harte, 6, 184
Hartnell, 131
HARTON, 67
Harvey, 126, 350
Harward, 229
Harwood, 304
Hastings (Hastyngs),453-78-84
HATCH, 254
Hatch, 327
Hatherleigh, 134, 252
Hatherley, 254
Hathewell, 58

INDEX.

Haubsland, 38
Haviland, 237
Hawkins, 132, 270, 316
Hawkridge, 469
Hawkworthy, 443
Hawley, 471
Hawton, 130
Hay, 389
Haydon, 147-70, 211, 386
Hayleighe, 15
Hayman, 165-66-89, 366
Hayne, 32
Hays (Hayes), 151, 344-80
Haywoode, 337
Hayzell, 162
Head, 144
Headen, 59
Heard, 209-45
Hearding (Herding), 141, 262
Hearl (Hearle, Herle), 108, 327-79
HEATH, 97
Heath, 100-41, 276
Heaward, 87
Heayne, 276
Heddon, 77
Hedgeland, 172
Hele, 167, 415-45-91-97
Helion, 442
Hellyar, 176
Helmer, 287
Helpeston, 329
Hemenford, 328
Henley (Henly), 130-68
Henry I., 318-29-44-60, 448
Henry II., 318-28-45-53-55-58-61, 419-25-85
Henry III., 329-45-51-56-64-87-96, 400-14-17-20-48-58-76-93
Henry IV., 255, 379, 409-22
Henry V., 303, 463
Henry VI., 341, 421-53-63-64-79
Henry VII., 312, 414-21-24-27-38-54-60-85
Henry VIII., 102, 312-38-87, 414-24-26-34-36
Hensleigh, 492
Herbert, 383
Hereford, 462
Herman, 335
Herne, 164
Herniman (Hernaman), 315-33-34
Heron, 41
Herrick, 121
Herring, 136
Hert, 141
Hesketh, 445
  estercumbe, 356

Hewish, 76
Hewitt, 249
Heycraft, 14
Hext, 94, 469
Hickeridge, 80
Hicks, 416
Hide, 151
Hidon, 6
Higgins, 450
Hildersham, 257
HILL, 1, 125
Hill (Hille), 6, 12, 13, 18, 35, 125, 205-12-41-42-43-52-65-73-89, 308-89, 443
Hillion, 442-47
Hingston, 25, 274-88
Hinnimore, 231
Hippesley, 418
Hitchcocke, 199
Hoare (Hore), 275, 473
Hocesham, 480-84
Hockin, 92
Hodge (Hodge-), 233-45-48-91
Hogg, 77
Hoker, 124
Hokeridge, 292
Holcombe, 110
Holditch, 94, 116, 231
HOLE, 126-34-37-39-40-43
Hole, 73, 148, 382-85, 420
Holkmore, 280
Holland, 78, 151, 327, 423-28
Holle, 39
Holman, 6, 92, 285
Holmes, 30, 38
Holsworthie, 250
Holt, 422
Holway, 230
Holwell, 358-88-89
Holwell-Car, 389
Honeychurch, 383-84
Honniwill, 98
Honny, 134
Hoo, 453
Hood, 452-73
HOOKER, 124
Hookins, 205
Hooper, 39, 74, 213-26, 304
Hoper, 58
Hopkins, 50, 200, 373
Hopper, 222-26
Horne, 21, 151
HORNIMAN (Hernaman, Herniman), 331-32-33-34-35
Horsington, 372
Horton, 315
Horwell (Horwill), 107, 277
Hoskins, 373
Houdg, 242

How (Howe), 63, 108-78
Howarde, 362
HOWELL, 100
Howill, 55, 124
Howse, 211
Hueks, 490
Hugh, 23
Hughes, 190
Hugo, 309-16-17-18-30
Huish, 200
Hull, 231
Hulse, 315
Humphrey, 43, 452
Hunt (Hunte), 20, 131-36-48, 315-85-86
Huntington, 132, 395
Hurfer, 62
Hurrell, 114
Hurst, 487
Husband, 138
Hussey, 41, 126, 223, 370
Hustote, 59
Hutchings, 64, 239
Hutchin (Hutchyn), 146-48
Hutton, 338
HUYSHE, 46
Hyndeston, 343

Iddesleigh, 2, 328-29, 413-44
Ilchester, 473
Incledon, 77, 306
Inglett, 350, 465
Inglett-Fortescue, 465
Insula, 319
Irish, 88, 161
Isabella, 347
Isaac (Izacke), 45, 149-50, 219, 347
Iuhellus, 361

Jackson, 145-67
James, 13, 130, 369
James I., 4, 470-71
James II., 406
Jarman, 252
Jealfry, 173
Jeffery, 318, 411
Jefford, 92
Jellard, 287
Jenkin, 36
Jerman, 86, 89, 164
Jewe, 475
Jeweil, 25
Jilleard, 274
Joanes, 252
John (King), 345-46-61, 424-48-57-58-62-67-92-94
Johnson, 78, 139
Johnston, 73

510 INDEX.

Jones, 52, 92, 103, 200, 420-40
Jordan, 109
Jordeyne, 6
Joy, 248
Joyce, 147
Judd, 134
Juhellus, 361
Jule, 302
Jutsum, 228-31

Keats, 349
Keckwiche, 81, 396
Keirkenny, 261
Kelland (Kellond), 150, 307, 445
KELLY (Kellye), 408-9-10
Kelly, 67, 275-82, 314-86, 428-97
Kember, 81
Kemmett, 165
Kemp, 259, 308
Kenrick, 51
Kensbye, 2
Kente, 250
Kentisbeere, 170
Kerby, 240
Keridge, 10
Kerslake, 198, 249
Kertais, 157
Keyner, 160
Keynes, 346
Keys, 451
Killand, 60
Killigrew, 393
Killiowe, 127
KILLOND, 60
Killstone, 108
Killyow, 497
Kine, 83
King (Kinge), 6, 53, 144, 407
Kingdon, 105
Kingwell, 192, 382
Kingwill, 163
Kirkham, 125, 481-84-86
Knapman, 337
Knight (Knyght), 147, 262-70-77
Knill, 168
Knistone, 69
Knolle, 22
Knowling, 281
Knyle, 59
KYLLAND, 8
Kyle, 329
Kylpec, 371, 449
Kynes, 83
Kyte, 222

Lacy, 425-85
LAKE, 124
Lake, 146-48, 203
Lakey, 189
Lambe, 191

Lambert, 383
Lamplugh, 203
Lancey, 260-64
Landeman, 158
Lane, 74, 214
Laneman, 56
Lang, 41, 198
Langdon, 242-79-80-93-95, 423-30
Lange, 65, 285
LANGRTON, 300
LANGLEY, 104
Langley, 248
Langworthy, 176, 415
Lapflode, 459
Lapthorne, 334
Laskey, 114-63, 224
Latimir (Ladimir), 198
Launde, 454
Lavercombe, 257
Lavington, 44, 47, 151, 231
LAW, 125
Law, 162-95, 298
Lawrence, 76, 339
Leach (Leache, Leche), 176-77, 293, 436-37
Leake, 445
Leaman, 289
Leap, 231
Leate, 170
Lee, 196, 226
Leigh, 144, 366, 430
Lendon, 7
Lenfee, 121
Lenfield, 121
Lennard, 469
L'Ercedekne, 106, 302
Lerwill, 262
L'Escrope, 422
Lethbridge, 229
Letwyn, 468
Levermore, 480
Lewes, 350
LEWIS, 33
Lewis, 51, 73
Ley, 68, 238, 494
Leyman, 95
Liddon, 211-48
Light, 32
Limbery, 262
Lincoln, 130
Lincoln (Earl of), 466
Lithiby, 258-59
Little, 282
Lobone, 292
Lock (Locke), 62, 222-31
Lockyer, 226
Loisett, 344
Loman (Lowman), 108, 214, 435
Longespee, 449
Lorde, 302
Loring, 469
Loosemoore, 299
Loudon, 45
Loughter (Abbot of), 435

Lovatt (Lovett), 327-40-43, 445-47
Lovering (Loveringe), 10, 123
Loveys, 108
Lowe, 274
Lowes, 107
Luce, 346
Lucke, 58
Luckham, 94
Lucy (Lucie), 344-45-46, 446
Lugg, 226
Luke, 64, 275
Lupo, 346
Luttrell (Lutterell), 132, 379, 441-43
Lyde, 116-70
LYLE, 42
Lyle, 44, 138-54-65
Lyons, 455
Lyte, 380

Mabell, 147
McBride, 155
Macclesfield, 38
Mackenzie, 489
Maddcote, 327
Maddicke, 263
Madge, 264
Magna Villa, 319-20
Maine (Mayne), 62, 226-54-84
Mais, 148
Maldett, 460
Malherbe, 404
Mallet, 155, 328, 418
Mamhead, 443-47
Manaton, 282
Mandeville, 319-28, 425-26
Manley, 76, 218-19-21-68
Mann (Manne), 87, 91, 93, 94, 97
Manninge, 272
Manworthy, 486
Mapowder, 50, 190
Marcianus, 331
Mardon, 51
Marldon, 434
Marsh, 38
Marshall (Marshalle), 18, 29, 33, 232, 436
Martin (Martyn), 193, 240-81-93-94, 338-74, 412-80
MARWOOD, 2
Marwood, 21, 57, 106
Mary (Queen), 203, 427-70
Massingberd, 453
Mattack, 263
MATTHEWE, 146-47
Matthew (Mathewe, Matthews), 78, 146-76, 237
Maud (Empress), 320-64

INDEX.

Mauditt (Mauduit, Maudyt), 132-49-51-73, 398
Mauger, 442
Maunder, 66, 75, 80
May (Maye, Mey), 16, 42, 47, 197, 232-34, 404-86
Mayho, 321-28
Maynard, 452
Mayor, 153
MEACHIN, 49
Meachin, 154-55
Meavyseale, 18
Meddicke, 171
Meddon, 369
Medland, 286
MELHUISH, 56, 68, 69, 75, 76, 79, 250
Melhuish, 39, 46, 125-89, 201, 307-15, 415-38
Mellent (Earl of), 376
Meols, 417
Mercer, 50, 132-40-52
Merson, 13
Merton, 480
Meschines, 361
Meshutt, 258
Meuelent, 386
Meysey-Thompson, 446
Micheldever, 329
Michelmore, 273
Middlesex, 393
Miles, 70, 441-42-43
Milford, 45, 264, 381, 452
Miller, 55, 181
MILLS, 205
Mills, 223
Milles, 106
Milton, 274-85
Minchin, 45
Minifer, 18
Mitchell, 283-88
Moels, 350-95, 442
Mogford, 308
Mogridge, 180
Mohun, 356
Molland, 64
Molton, 25, 26, 27
Molyns, 328
Monk (Monke), 138-54-98, 366, 470-89
Montacute, 356 - 58 - 59 - 60-61, 424-76-77
Montrath, 455
Moore, 41, 132-34, 226-37, 450-53-65-83
Moorecroughte, 53
Morcar, 419
Mordaunt, 473
More, 349-70
Moreton, 423-29-30
Morgan, 102, 249
Morland, 483
Morley, 382
Morris, 163
Morrish, 57, 199

Morrison, 369
Morse, 36, 40
Mortain, 314-48-52-54-57- 58- 59 - 63- 94 - 95 - 97-98, 400-4-18-32-57-58-60
MORTAMORE (Mortimoor, Mortimoore, Mortimore, Mortymore, Mortimor, Mortemor), 15, 51, 93, 175 - 80 - 85 - 89 - 90 - 94-96-97, 201-4-6-7-13-15 - 16 - 17 - 19 - 21 - 22 - 26 - 27 - 29 - 34 - 35-45 - 46 - 47 - 52 - 53 - 68 - 69 - 74 - 80 - 81-82-85-87-90-92, 305
Mortamore, &c., 98, 304-9
MORTIMER (Mortymer, Mortimere, Mortemere), 11, 12, 98, 172-75-76-81-83-85-86-194-99, 200 - 7 - 22 - 23 - 33-35-41-42 - 43 - 44 - 45 - 46-48-52-57 - 59-62-69-71-74-76-79 - 80 - 92 - 93, 303-4-5-9
Mortimer, &c., 249-87, 307
Mory, 90
Motbert, 358, 418
Mount-Joy, 7
MOUNTSTEPHEN, 7, 8
Mount-Stephen, 446
Mowbray, 398
Moxey (Moxhay), 76, 178, 248
Moyle-Copley, 454
Moysey, 65
Mudge, 202
Mugford, 68
Mules, 248, 321-22-50-51
Multon, 345
Munn, 233
Murch, 98, 224
Murdock, 225
Myddleton, 159
Mylleton, 21
Mynefee, 18

Napier, 454
Nation, 71
Netherton, 91
Netheway 58
Nevill, 296
Newherry, 211-14
Newburgh, 376
Newcoman, 234
Newcomb, 137
NEWCOMEN, 91
Newson, 100
Newte, 36, 389
Newton, 131, 329-71
Nicholas IV. (Pope), 476

Node, 349
Norbury, 388
Norcott, 7
Norman, 46, 58, 74
Normandy (Duke of), 441, 42
Norris (Norries), 184, 351-78-91-92, 463
Norrish, 32, 68, 160-76, 201-47
Northam, 271
Northbrooke, 446
Northcot (Northcote), 102, 205, 328, 412
NORTHCOTE, 441-42-43-44-45-46
Northleigh, 135, 396
NORTHMORE, 335-36-37-38-39-40
Northmore, 381-85
Norwich (Earl of), 121
Nosworthy, 99, 187, 92
Notsworthy, 349
NOTT, 348-49-50-51
Nott (Notte), 167, 257-96, 347
Novant, 362
Nycholl, 57

Oats, 244
Odo, 475
Oke, 207
Okeston, 458
Oliver (Olliver, Olyver), 28, 48, 50, 132, 302
Orchard, 57, 139, 255
Orford, 466
Osborne, 3, 11, 487
Osgood, 339
USMAN, 210
OSMON, 16
OSMOND (Osmonde, Osmunde), 12, 13, 16, 17, 18, 19, 20, 35, 36, 39, 41, 44, 126-36-44-62 - 80 - 93-94-96-98-99, 202-5-8-9-10-11-12-16-17 - 18 - 19-20-24-25-26-27-28-30-31-32 - 33-34-35-36-40-41-47-48-49
Osmond, 451
Otway, 388
Owe, 441
Owens, 309
Owgan, 451
Owsborne, 118
OWSMENT, 15
Oxenheare, 160
Oxenham, 222, 333-38
Oxford (Earl of), 360

Packer, 266
Paddon, 264
Paganel, 431-32

INDEX.

Paige, 98
PALKE (Palk), 163-64
Palk, 394
Palmer, 12, 166, 205-52
Paltryman, 268
Pamer, 252
Parker, 38, 107-21-24-68-74, 255-78, 307-82-84, 497
Parkhouse (Parkhowse), 172, 292
Parma, 454
Parrington, 181
Parsons, 46, 284
Partridge, 144, 274
Pasco (Pascowe), 105, 270-85
Passavant, 46
Passmore, 94, 176
Passord, 189
Pathericke, 176
Paul (Paule, Puwle), 49, 64, 254-81
PAYNE, 133
Payne (Payn), 53, 56,133-48-75-76-89, 207 - 49 - 57-59
Paynel, 431-48-49
PEARCE, 51
Pearce (Pearse, Pearsse), 25, 119-37-64 - 70 - 74, 265-84-96
Pears, 104
Pease, 42
Peat, 104
Peddericke, 207
Pedler, 144
Pederton, 480-83-84
Peers (Peerse), 148, 271
Pembroke (Earl of), 154, 348, 436
Pendarvis, 137
Penguin, 142
Penhallow, 409
Pennington, 40
Penny (Peny), 96, 98, 295
Pep, 57
Peploe, 77
Percy, 345
Perer, 363
Periman (Perryman), 16, 365
Perkins, 165
Perot, 416
Perriam, 418
Perrin, 383
Perrye, 16
PETER (Peeter, Petre, Petter), 9, 81, 105-8-21-29, 293
Peter (&c.), 6, 111-13, 297, 365-89, 473-75-79
Peternell, 161
Peters, 138-65
PETOR, 62
Petsvene, 83

Pett, 138-65
Peverell, 297, 434-36
Peytevin, 404
Phelp, 166
Philip IV., 454
Phillip, 114-48
PHILLIPS, 297
Phillips, 46, 111-52, 211-14
Philpe, 175
Pidsley, 141
PIERCE, 51, 152
Pierce, 48, 140-41-53-54
Pike, 288, 346
Pile (Pyll), 469
Pilkington, 489
Pimme, 184
Pincerna, 356-57-63-64
Pincombe, 28, 257
Pine, 225
Pipard. 94, 402
Pitfield, 136-55
Pitman, 453
Plantagenet, 46, 393, 427-62-70
Plimpton, 148
Plugenet, 449
Pocock, 135, 200-29
Podycomb, 118
Podyn, 146
Pokeswell, 381
Pole, 297, 300-28-77, 422-34-41-49-75-79
POLLARD, 73, 74, 75, 77, 131-35-36-42-43
Pollard (Pollarde), 106, 298, 360-63-64 414-15-44
Pollei, 52, 432
Pollexfen, 402-97
Poltimore, 474-75-76-77-78-80-83
Pomeroy, 4, 237, 306, 404-33-35-68
Ponsford, 14
Pontington (Pointington, Puntyngdon), 476-77-78
Ponz, 411-42
Pooke, 9, 18, 273-74
Poole, 153-98, 372
Pope, 56
Popham, 453
Port, 459
Porter, 52, 464
Portman, 343, 471
Portour, 301
Portu Mortuo, 396
Potter, 121-28-99, 412-43
Potyngdon, 477
Poules, 4
Poulett, 497
Pounce, 109
Pounsford, 72
Powe, 53
Powell, 108

Powkeswell, 386
Pownall, 498
Powning, 41
Poynter, 108
Pratt, 227
Praunce, 61
Presforde, 305
Presser, 32
Preston, 460-61-62
Prestwood, 343, 487
PRIDEAUX, 131
Prideaux, 50, 140, 381, 412-68-70-88
Pridham, 139-80
Prigg, 47
Primridge, 43
Prince, 283
Pring, 230
Prouse (Prowse, Prouz), 111-43, 285, 395, 443
Prust, 61, 63, 67, 327
Prye, 423
Prystod, 158
Prystone, 158
Puddington, 16, 18
Pudnor, 144
Pudsey, 484
Pugh, 249
Pullablanke, 273
Pullen (Pullin), 200-31-33
Purchase, 216
Putot, 370
Puttercumbe, 95
Putteven, 305
Pycot, 409
PYKE, 344-45-46-51
Pyke-Nott, 347-50-51
Pyle, 43, 136
Pyne, 153, 479

Quant, 249
Quick (Quicke), 66, 144-73, 226
QUICKE, 2
Quivil, 425

Radcliffe, 226
Radford, 249-68
Rake, 495
Raleigh (Ralegh), 316-89. 430
Ramsey, 246
Rasshelegh (Rayshlegh), 436
Ratcliff. 470
RATTENBURY, 67, 304
Rattenbury, 305-27
Rawle, 261
Rawling (Rawlings), 13, 277
Rayner, 135
Reade, 21
Redstone, 285
Redvers, 52, 261, 344, 433-34-37

INDEX.

REDWAY (Radway), 21, 24, 25, 26, 27
Reed, 252, 306, 415
Reigny, 451
Remfrey, 69
Remmett, 156
Rendall, 33
Renoles, 278
Reyd, 57
Reynell, 343, 491-96-97
Reynolds, 247
Richard I., 189, 356, 417-18-19-32-48
Richard II., 189, 344 63-68-92, 469-85
Richard III., 420-21-22-24-54
RICHARDS, 80
Richards. 25, 34, 61, 62, 64, 154, 266-67-90
Richmond, 77
Ridgeway, 108
Risdon (Risedon, Rysedon), 85, 217-53, 322-23-24-25-26-27-28-39-50
Rither, 43
Robert (Duke), 395
Roberts, 68, 166, 347
Robbins, 162
Rocke, 265
Rodney, 498-99
Roger (Rogers), 57, 205-37
ROLLE, 71
Rolle, 229, 324-27-28-93, 406-50-51-66-67-71
Rollo, 431
Rols, 229
Rolston, 150
Roslyn, 455-74
Ross, 170
Rous, 41, 44, 165, 458
Rouse, 444
Router, 302
Row (Rowe), 85, 89, 91
Row (Rowe), 88, 101-38-63-65, 216-27-47-49-92
Rowell, 85
Rowles, 129
Rowswell, 413-70-71
Rudge, 60
Rugg (Rugge), 104, 208
Russell, 341
Ryder, 246, 365, 467
Ryledon, 324

Sackville (Sachville), 419-25
Saffin, 47
St. Albyn, 349, 429-30
St. Aubyn, 338, 470
St. Clair, 455
St. Cyres, 2, 446
St. Esprit, 319

St. George, 424-69
St. John, 342-80
St. Maur, 481-84
Saiward, 196
Salisbury (Bishop of), 328
Salisbury (Marquis of), 491
Sallis, 278
Salter, 13, 197, 215-49
Sampson, 152
Samways, 430
Sanders, 282
Sandford, 98, 223-33-34, 355
Sanford, 34, 42, 232-44, 452
SANGER, 39, 60, 83, 251-56-58-59-65-66-67-97-98-99, 306-8-9
Sanger (Sangor), 58, 61
Sangwill, 84
SANNER, 305
Sans Peur, 431-41
Sargent, 109
Saulf, 418-19-25
SAUNDER (SAUNDERS), 66, 68, 71, 72, 76, 78, 79, 142
Saunder (Saunders), 13, 42, 45, 94, 106-22-50
Savage, 83
Savery (Savory), 47, 87
Sawnder, 1
Saye, 416
Scholond, 5
Schute, 301
Score, 67
Scott (Scotte), 147-48, 268, 329, 415
Scroope, 422
Scrope, 499
Seaman, 246
Searle, 84
SEAWARD, 144
Seaward, 5, 145-96, 221, 302
Seely, 210
Segar, 28
Seger, 479
Sellack (Sellick, Sellicke), 35, 212-32-36
Senarpont, 357-59
Sercombe, 81, 243
Sergun, 9
Serrill (Serrell), 258, 324
Seward, 148
Seyman, 200
SEYMOUR, 131
Seymour, 49
Shackle, 18
Shafto, 339
Shapcot (Shapcote), 56, 250, 307
Shaplonde, 250
Shaptor, 157-58
Sharbrooke, 66
Sharland, 176, 268

Sharlen, 203
Sharpham, 274
SHEERES, 122
Shelley, 418
Sheper, 62
Shepherd, 237-95
Sheppard (Shepperd), 136-38-80
Sherborne, 442
Sheridan, 483
Sheriff, 255
SHERLOND, 5
Sherme, 261-63
Sherwill, 90, 99
Shilston, 207, 392
Shirley, 330
Shobrooke, 28
Shorte, 65, 254, 321
Shower, 32
Sidenham (Sydenham), 328, 452-54-81
SINEGAR, 285
SING, 285
SINGER, 92
SINGNAR, 93
Skeen, 285
Skinner (Skynner), 16, 24, 37, 78, 79, 129-39, 255, 302
Slade, 38
Slader, 55, 78
Slape, 237
Slee, 39
Sleeman, 308
Sloane, 75
Slowley, 131
Smale, 54, 71, 251-61, 415
Smardon, 157
Smeath, 162
Smerdon, 99, 164
Smith, 21, 27, 55, 74, 133, 278-93-94, 366-67
Smorth, 76
Smyth (Smythe), 14, 58, 174, 293-99, 427
Snow (Snowe), 57, 58, 205-61-98
Soleigny, 260, 435
Solomon, 87
Somaster, 380, 460
Somerhayes, 200
Somers (Sommers), 19, 74
Soper, 13, 173, 239
Southard, 22, 74
Southcombe, 73
Southcote, 130, 382
Southerne, 61
Southmeade, 337-78
Southwood (Southwoode), 106-62, 230-39, 337
Sowden, 68, 205-6
Spark (Sparke), 200 - 54 - 66
Sparrow, 173, 239
Speare, 67
Spearman, 55

34

Speckot (Speccott), 347, 420-52
Speke (Spekes), 103, 435-50-54
Spence, 248
Spencer, 259
Splatt, 126
Spooner, 464
Sprague, 41
Sprey, 107
Spry, 249
Spurway, 359-60
Squabble, 37
Square, 86, 288
Squer, 105
Squier, 105-6
Stabbicke, 180
Stackhouse, 373
Stafford, 93, 301-27, 445-47
Stanbury, 268
Stanckombe, 95
Standish, 265
Stapeldon, 347, 426-77
Starkey, 224
Starr, 151
Steer, 289
Stennett, 233
Stephen (Stephens, Stephyns), 40, 59, 155, 265-93, 302, 407-46
Stephen (King), 315-20-45-64
Stevens, 61, 223
Stifyn, 61
Stisson, 270
Stogdon, 189
Stokes, 142
Stone, 89, 195, 218-20-41
Stonehouse, 493
Stoneman, 25, 26
Stoning, 219
Stuodly, 155
Stottiscombe, 353
Stowell, 162
Stowford, 449
Strange, 82, 83
Stratton, 477
Streat, 305
Strechleigh, 460
Street, 226
Stretch, 495
Stribling, 251
Strode (Strod), 29, 445-52
Strokesdon (Strokysdone), 435-36
Strongbow, 340
Stronge, 337
Stuart, 389
Stubinges, 19
Stucley, 78
Stukeley, 416
Styling, 190
Suchespyche, 147
Suckespiche, 148
Sudeley, 364

Suffolk (Duke of), 451
Surete, 119
Surry (Earl of), 425
Sutcliffe, 347
Sutton, 443
Suxpitch, 43
Swade, 65
SWANGER, 45
Sweete, 119
Swetland, 272
Sweyn, 318
Sykes, 50, 407
Symes, 14, 221-49
Symons, 13, 62, 243
Synone, 7

TACKER, 182
Talbot, 409-10
Tallamy, 98
Tamlyn, 107
TANNER, 307
Tanner, 58, 79, 124-44-76, 252-53, 303-4
Tapper, 163
Taprill, 161
Tarr, 96, 163
TASSELL, 53, 56
Tassell, 61
Tasle, 53
Taunton, 143
Taverner. 7
Tavistock (Abbot of), 442
Tawse, 5
Taylor, 141 - 52 - 59 - 81, 219-27-28-34
Temlett, 11
Templeman, 246
THASSELL, 53
Thomas, 35, 52, 91, 153-90, 278, 307
Thomas a Becket, 354
Thorbridge, 15
Thorne, 16, 55, 60, 67, 268, 464
THUELL, 84
TIDBALL, 161
Tidball, 125
Tidbolle, 195
Titherly, 32
Toake, 130
TOCKER (Toker), 5, 21, 55, 57, 58, 59, 64, 107-28-58 - 71 - 82 - 83 - 89. 250-70
Tocker (Toker), 120, 278
Todeni, 360
Tolchard (Tolyard), 83
Tom, 298
Tombe, 61
Toni, 376
Tokerman, 273
TOOKER (Toocker), 9 17, 57, 59, 65, 87, 97, 109-26-72-74-81-82 - 84-86-91, 209-69-72-74-77-86

Tooker (Toocker), 25, 55, 56, 58, 107, 123-89, 251-73
TORNER, 58
Torner, 22
Torroway, 89
TOKSALL, 267
TOSSELL (Tossle), 53, 62, 63, 67, 73, 74, 75, 76, 77, 259-67-68-84
Tossell (Tossle), 58, 61
Tothill, 24
Tottell, 272
Totnes, 357
TOUCKER (Towker), 17, 56, 57, 59, 273
Tow, 267
Townsend, 90, 163, 235
Townsente, 17
Tozer, 113
Tracy (Tracey), 178, 275, 364-65, 412-42
Trais, 97
Treble, 67, 259
Tree, 292
Trefusis, 466-67
Tregoe, 226
Trehawke (Trehawkes), 51-84
Trelawney, 494
Tremayne, 171, 341-42, 409
Tremlett, 11
Tremure, 109
Trenhale, 91
Trent (Trente), 13, 199
Tresilian, 422
Trevage, 341-43
Trewant, 305
Tristamb, 292
Troke, 200
Trosse, 131
Troute, 262
Trowbridge (Trobridge), 119, 169
Troyte, 38, 474
Truelake, 130
Tryslade, 237
TUCKER (Tuker), 12, 14, 15, 17, 26, 29, 30, 31, 32, 33, 34, 35, 36, 37, 40, 66, 70, 73, 75, 77, 85, 86, 88, 91, 94, 96, 98, 105-6-7 - 34 - 37-68-71-72-73-74-75 - 76-77-78-79-80-81-82 - 83-84-85-86-87-88-89 - 90-91-92-93-94-95-97 - 98-99, 200-1-2-3-4-5-6-7-8-9-10-11 - 12 - 13 - 14-15-16-17-18-19-20 - 21-22-23-24-25-26-27 - 28-29-30-31-32-35-36 - 37-38-39-40-41-42-43 - 44-45-48-69-70-71-72 - 73-75-76-77-80-82-87-88

INDEX.

Tucker (Tuker), 10, 22, 25, 39, 65, 121-22-23-26-33-38, 266-84, 410
Tuckfield, 418
Tuckheye, 1
TUKE, 271
Tupper, 89
Turner, 27, 199
Turney, 40, 480-83-84
Turpin, 234, 416
Turpi Vado, 418-19
Twigge, 11
Twydell, 151
Tyeth, 373
Tynes, 276

Ufflett, 449-50
Umfraville, 479
Underhny, 98
Upcott, 240
Uphill, 295
Upton, 159
Urflet, 496

Vacinover, 35
Valderonde (Count of), 454
Vallado (Marquis of), 454
Valletort, 346-61-62-64, 450-57-58-59
Vavasour, 342
Veale (Vele), 135, 302
Venicombe (Venycombe), 9, 14, 106
VENMAN, 1
VENN, 404-5-6-7-8
Venn (Venne), 8, 190-97
Venning, 277
Venton, 488
Vepont, 341-43
Vere, 320-60-68, 473
Verney, 388
Vernon, 377, 433
Vesci, 449
Veysey (Veysy), 15, 106
Vicary (Vicarie, Vicarye, Vickery), 53, 62, 144-54-55, 246-56, 489
Vickers, 74
Vigers (Vigors), 33, 74
Vighill, 295
VIGOR, 46
VIGURES, 74
Vigurs (Vigures), 74, 107
Vill, 135
Vilvayne, 292
Vincent, 472
Vine, 263
Vinicombe (Vynecombe), 136, 215
Vivian, 429-36
Vivon (Vyvon), 370, 435
Vosper, 283
Vowell, 124
Voysey (Voysie), 56, 150

Vynour, 371
Vynsent, 271

Waad (Wade), 42, 257
Wadham, 481
Wadland, 275
Waite, 250
Wakeham, 98, 269-89
Wakely, 263
Walcot, 392
Waldron, 229-39
Walker, 205
Wall, 147
Walleis, 443
Waller (Wallers), 4, 167
Walleran, 386
Walrond, 47, 48, 449-50-51-52-74
WALROND, 447-48-53-54-55
Walsh, 251
Walter, 369
Wandricke, 21
Ward, 97, 193-94, 240, 347
Ware (Weare), 38, 132-34-37-48-51, 227-93, 414
Warlewast, 395
Warr (Warre), 319, 452, 54
Warren (Warrene), 129-35-73-74-81, 329, 418-25-62
Watts, 10, 309
Way (Waye), 74, 170, 242
Waymouth (Weymouth), 51, 233
Waynworth, 168
Webb, 272
Webber (Weber), 22, 54, 73, 75, 168-84-98, 200-46-75, 307
Wedcot, 143
Weeks (Weekes), 199, 215-77, 305-33-37-79-86
WEEKES, 383-84-85-86
Welby, 339
Weldon, 461
Welland, 13
Wellesley, 416
Wellington, 260
Wells (Welles), 453-54-61-83
Welsh (Welch), 254, 463-64
Wentworth, 46, 488
WERE, 218
Were, 147, 234
West, 212, 14, 362
Westcote (Westcott), 42, 47, 164-67, 405
Westlake, 24
Weston, 140-41-54

Westron, 126
Westwode, 329
Westwood, 329
Wetyne, 271
Wheeler, 36
Whiddon, 380
Whipham, 51
Whitbere, 57
Whitby, 343
White, 99, 100-37, 280
Whitehead, 235
White-Lackington, 103
WHITEWAY, 123
Whiteway (Whytwaye), 157-59
Whitfield, 492-94
Whitleigh, 494
Whitlocke, 226
Whityng, 436
Wibery, 413
Wick, 485
Wickham, 416
Wickloe, 306
Wicote, 137
Widlake, 77
Wiet, 192
Wiggington, 233
Wigoren, 375
Wigorn, 377
Wigornia, 375-76-77-86-90, 420-85
Wilcocke (Wilcocks), 98, 197, 210-25
William the Conqueror, 306-18-32-36-44-52-61-94-99, 404-11-42-56-57-58-97
William Rufus, 36, 99, 425
William III., 145, 203, 398
Williams, 5, 49, 58, 279, 413
Willing, 25
Willington (Wellington), 260, 435
Willoughby, 451-54
Wills, 86, 234, 455
Wilmott, 63
Wilson, 92
Wimball, 282
Windball, 277
Windham (Wyndham), 251, 454
Winter, 43
Wis, 340
WISE (Wyse), 340-41-42-43-54
Wise, 424
Wislade, 214
Witefell, 492
Wither, 153
Witheridge, 262
Withers, 44, 231
Withiell, 116
Wolacot (Wollacot), 66, 83

Wonstone, 11
Wood, 251-55
Wood, 43, 49, 172-81, 245
Woodley, 143
Woodley (Woodly), 11, 12, 90, 175-83, 280
Woollcombe, 337, 499
Woollcott, 167
Woolmer, 50
Worcester (Earl of), 375
Worsley, 498
Worth (Worthe, Wourth), 21, 28, 45, 48, 52, 54, 102-19, 296, 431-33-34-35-36-37-38-39-40-41
Worth (Worthe), 5, 44, 70, 261-97, 312-28-64-69-91, 482
Worthen, 201
Worther, 304
Worthevail, 128
Worthy (Worthie), 21, 44
Worthy (Worthie), 79, 125-45, 415-16-34-38-40
Worthy-Bennett, 145
Wotton, 149-60, 487

Wray (Wraye, Wrey), 71, 360-75-77-78-81-87
Wrayford, 28, 30, 38, 47, 87, 89, 119-20-31
Wrayford, 25
Wreaford (Wreaforde, Wreford), 11, 25, 37, 82, 83, 86, 117-42-44-59-61
Wreaford (Wreford), 39, 66
Wrey (Wray), 390-91-92-93-94
Wreyford (Wreyforde, Wreyfford, Wreyyfford), 13, 31, 82, 84, 87, 112-18-26-30-60
Wright, 192
Wriothesley, 412
Wyatt (Wyett), 144-94, 350
Wyatt-Edgell, 388
Wycott, 288
Wyke (Wykes, Wikes), 333-36-81-82-84-85-86-91, 420-85
Wykes, 374-75-76-77-78-79-80-81-82-83
Wylle, 301

Wymondesold, 498
Wyndeatt, 158
Wynn, 33, 171
Wyrescestrin, 386
Wyvell, 349

Yard, 135
Yard (Yarde), 18, 412-43-47
Yealland, 264
Yeard, 59
Velmacole, 61
Yeo, 263-64-65, 324-69-84, 403-51
Yeoinge, 68
Yewman, 37
Voning, 68
York (Duke of), 203
Yorke, 451
Younge, 223
Youatt, 236
Ysshel, 158
Ythel, 336

Zeal, 308
Zouch, 345

Lightning Source UK Ltd.
Milton Keynes UK
UKOW051442190911

178913UK00001BA/5/P